W9-DAU-704

Chile

LATIN AMERICAN HISTORIES

THOMAS E. SKIDMORE, SERIES EDITOR

James R. Scobie
Argentina: A City and a Nation
SECOND EDITION

Franklin W. Knight
The Caribbean: The Genesis of a Fragmented Nationalism
SECOND EDITION

Herbert S. Klein
Bolivia: The Evolution of a Multi-Ethnic Society
SECOND EDITION

Louis A. Perez, Jr.
Cuba: Between Reform and Revolution
SECOND EDITION

Ralph Lee Woodward, Jr.
Central America: A Nation Divided
THIRD EDITION

Thomas E. Skidmore
Brazil: Five Centuries of Change

Peter Flindell Klarén
Peru: Society and Nationhood in the Andes

Brian Loveman
Chile: The Legacy of Hispanic Capitalism
THIRD EDITION

Chile ✍

THE LEGACY OF HISPANIC CAPITALISM

THIRD EDITION

Brian Loveman

New York • Oxford
OXFORD UNIVERSITY PRESS
2001

CABRINI COLLEGE LIBRARY
610 KING OF PRUSSIA RD.
RADNOR, PA 19087-3699

*F
3081
.L68
2001*

#43810997

Oxford University Press

Oxford   New York
Athens   Auckland   Bangkok   Bogotá   Buenos Aires   Calcutta
Cape Town   Chennai   Dar es Salaam   Delhi   Florence   Hong Kong   Istanbul
Karachi   Kuala Lumpur   Madrid   Melbourne   Mexico City   Mumbai
Nairobi   Paris   São Paulo   Shanghai   Singapore   Taipei   Tokyo   Toronto   Warsaw

and associated companies in
Berlin   Ibadan

Copyright © 1979, 1988, 2001 by Oxford University Press, Inc.

Published by Oxford University Press, Inc.
198 Madison Avenue, New York, New York 10016
http://www.oup-usa.org

Oxford is a registered trademark of Oxford University Press

All rights reserved. No part of this publication may be reproduced,
stored in a retrieval system, or transmitted, in any form or by any means,
electronic, mechanical, photocopying, recording, or otherwise,
without the prior permission of Oxford University Press.

Library of Congress Cataloging-in-Publication Data

Loveman, Brian.
    Chile : the legacy of Hispanic capitalism / Brian Loveman.—3rd ed.
        p. cm.—(Latin American histories)
    Includes bibliographical references and index.
    ISBN 0-19-512019-1—ISBN 0-19-512020-5 (pbk.)
    1. Chile—History. 2. Social conflict—Chile—History. 3. Political
participation—Chile—History. 4. Chile—Social conditions. 5. Chile—Economic
conditions. I. Title. II. Series.
    F3081. L68 2001
    983—dc21   00-039938

Printing (last digit): 9   8   7   6   5   4   3   2   1

Printed in the United States of America
on acid-free paper

Contents

List of Maps

List of Tables

Preface

When the second edition of this book appeared in 1988, Chileans still lived under a military dictatorship. In 2001, as the third edition comes off the press, Chileans have completed a decade of civilian rule. The third elected president since the transition from military rule took office in March, 2000: Ricardo Lagos, a socialist who had participated in the Unidad Popular government (1970–73) and vigorously opposed the dictatorship from exile. Lagos spearheaded the anti-Pinochet forces during the 1988 plebiscite that defeated the dictator. Nevertheless, more than ten years after restoration of civilian government, the military-imposed 1980 constitution remained in place, and the legacy of the military regime (1973–90) continued to influence everyday life in many ways.

In the preface to the second edition of this book, I indicated that the "proper conclusion of the last chapter," the end of the military government, had not yet occurred. As I was preparing the third edition, the ex-military dictator was detained in England, at the request of a Spanish judge who requested his extradition to Spain on charges of violating international law regarding human rights (October, 1998). In Chile his supporters claimed that international communism was taking its revenge on him for "defeating communism." They also claimed that his arrest violated Chilean sovereignty. In contrast, human rights organizations and his political opponents applauded the British and Spanish authorities who sought to bring the general to justice—a justice they believed could never be done in Chile.

General Pinochet's detention in England altered Chilean political history, and perhaps that of the international human rights movement. His eventual return to Chile in March 2000, when the British authorities decided that he was too ill to be deported and stand trial, provoked new controversies over his congressional immunity as a "senator for life" and his potential accountability before Chilean courts for human rights violations. By mid-July 2000, an infirm, eighty-four year old Pinochet potentially faced over 140 separate criminal cases. He lost his immunity from prosecution in a decision of the Santiago Court of Appeals in June 2000. His lawyers appealed the decision to the Chilean Supreme Court. As Chileans awaited the Supreme Court's decision, numerous other military officers were called as witnesses in outstanding criminal cases or were charged with crimes committed during the military dictatorship.

Despite the government's inability to repeal or annull the 1978 amnesty decree or to fundamentally reform the 1980 constitution, the officers who had carried out the 1973 coup and their successors witnessed a mounting attack on their impunity and even on their version of their salvational role in Chilean history. In early July 2000, inauguration of a monument to ex-president Salvador Allende (1970–73) in the Plaza de la Constitución—in front of the Ministry of Justice and the La Moneda Palace, where he died on September 11, 1973—testified symbolically to the shifting political conditions in the country, and to the mounting pressures for further political reform.

In July 2000, Pinochet was too ill to stand trial, whatever the ultimate decision of the Supreme Court regarding his congressional immunity. He would play no significant personal role in the ongoing history of the country. But the legacy of the military regime and the 1980 constitution continued to influence pervasively Chile's present and its future. The challenges confronted by the Lagos government, the third government of the Concertación coalition, and also by the political opposition, included most directly the ongoing demands for "truth and justice" regarding the human rights violations of the past and for democratization of the political regime imposed by the military government in 1980. What part of the Concertación coalition's program of 1988 would be possible to achieve still remained uncertain in 2001, as did how successfully Chile would respond to the overwhelming pressures exerted on its natural resources and environment by the model of economic growth chosen since the 1970s.

In preparing this third edition I have called upon the talent, insights, historical creativity, and friendship of numerous Chilean scholars. I cannot thank them all here, nor can I avoid repeating names mentioned in the preface to the first and second editions of this book. In different ways they have all helped me better understand Chile. I must especially express my gratitude, in some cases for special moments of illustration and in others for years of conversation and shared professional dedication to Chilean history, to Felipe Agüero, Gonzalo Arroyo, José Bengoa, Eduardo Cavieres, Joaquín Fermandois, Hugo Fhrüling, Cristián Gazmuri, Sergio Grez, Iván Jaksić, Alfredo Jocelyn-Holt, Elizabeth Lira, Mario Garcés, Luis Ortega, Julio Pinto, Francisco Rojas, Rafael Sagredo, Sol Serrano, Augusto Varas, and Sergio Villalobos. The third edition has especially benefitted from four years of collaborative research and joint publications on Chilean historical topics with Elizabeth Lira. Kimlisa Salazar Duchicela prepared the index for this edition. At Oxford University Press Linda Jarkesy has collaborated in preparation of this third edition from the start and Justin Collins has done more than any other production editor I have ever encountered to improve the quality of the final product—for which I am very grateful.

Thomas M. Davies, Jr., Paul Drake, Iván Jaksić, Mara Loveman, Thomas Skidmore, and Louis Terrell have read drafts of new material for the third edition and spared me errors of fact and interpretation. Whenever I write about Chile, I take into account the wisdom and humor of my friend and colleague Frederick Nunn. The book still benefits from the contributions to the first and second editions of Jacques Barbier, Harold Blakemore, Simon Collier, Henry Landsberger, William Sater, William Sherman, and John Whaley. Like anyone writing about Chilean history, I must acknowledge an intellectual debt to Diego Barros Arana. Also a thank-you is due to my favorite nineteenth-century storytellers, J. Joaquín Vallejo (Jotabeche) and Vicente Pérez Rosales.

Solana Beach, California   B. L.
August 2000

Preface to the Second Edition

I have completed the second edition of this book at a time when Chileans are in their fourteenth year under an authoritarian, military-dominated dictatorship. This dictatorship, led by General Augusto Pinochet, has effected radical changes in many aspects of Chilean life.

Unlike the military-dominated governments in Argentina, Uruguay, Brazil, and Peru during the 1970s and early 1980s, the Chilean government came to be identified ever more closely with the personalist control of one officer rather than the institutional control of the country by the armed forces. For this reason, an appropriate conclusion to the last chapter of this edition of the book would have been the departure of General Pinochet and the transition to another sort of political leadership. Unfortunately, while the passage of time and the many changes that have transpired in Chile made a second edition essential, the proper conclusion of the last chapter still has not occurred—though it is inevitable.

As in preparation of the first edition of this book I have had the advantage of relying upon the important research and historical analysis of a number of Chilean writers and intellectuals too numerous to identify individually. In addition, conversations and discussions with Alejandro Foxley, Manuel Antonio Garretón, Sol Serrano, Gonzalo Tapia, Francisco Tomic, Maria Elena Valenzuela, and Augusto Varas have assisted me greatly in understanding the last fourteen years. Luis Ortega's valuable published critique of parts of the first edition and suggestions offered by him for improvement have also proved useful in making revisions. Likewise, an extensive set of suggestions for revision by Michael Monteón assisted me in preparing the second edition.

Thomas M. Davies Jr., Paul Drake, Iván Jaksić, Sharon Loveman, Frederick Nunn, Michael Stanfield, and Augusto Varas have all struggled through drafts of new material for the second edition, and spared me errors of fact or interpretation. Naturally, the errors that remain are my responsibility.

I have also been fortunate to have the assistance of Iliana Sonntag in revising and updating the bibliography, Melinda Wedgewood in preparing new maps, Kirsten Mulvey and Cecilia Ubilla in copyediting, and Helen Kanavel in preparation of the new tables. Michael Arguello once again constructed the index.

San Diego   B. L.
July 1987

Preface to the First Edition

Chile is a nation where historians and social theorists have participated actively in public life as well as in scholarship. Presidents, ministers of state, legislators, and party leaders have contributed to Chile's historical tradition, to its literature, and to its art. No historian, Chilean or foreign, can undertake a new look at Chilean history without returning, first, to the great intellectual contributions of Chile's national writers. While this book departs in some important ways from conventional interpretations of Chile's past, it owes much to the insight and thorough research of generations of Chilean writers.

To the intellectual debt I owe to Chilean writers must be added the use I have made of the studies of hundreds of non-Chilean "Chileanists" who have dedicated their attention to Chilean history. As the format of this book generally precluded systematic footnote citations, I have attempted to note appropriately those works upon which I relied extensively in the selective bibliography at the end of this volume.

As I wrote this study, my friend, teacher, and general editor of Oxford University Press's Latin American Histories Series, James Scobie, offered his advice, encouragement, and critical reviews of the manuscript for which I am extremely grateful. The manuscript has also benefitted from the comments and suggestions made by Jacques Barbier, Harold Blakemore, Simon Collier, Thomas M. Davies, Jr., Philip Flemion, Henry Landsberger, Sharon Loveman, Vincent Padgett, William Sater, William Sherman, and John Whaley. Larry Stickell generously allowed me to read chapter drafts of his doctoral dissertation on the development of the nitrate industry in Chile and to use data from his research in the present volume. While the insights of these scholars have greatly improved the present book, I am, of course, responsible for any errors of fact or interpretation that remain in the volume.

I have been fortunate to have help from a number of people in the preparation of the manuscript. Special thanks go to Veva Link, Helen Triller, Jeri Haddon and Paula Forrester, and to Phoebe Hoss for her careful copy-editing. Nancy Ferris provided invaluable assistance in preparation of the bibliography as did Michael Arguello in construction of the index.

A final thank you must also go to my friends in Trovolhue who taught me the political meaning of life's daily struggle against the legacy of four centuries of Hispanic Capitalism.

San Diego   B. L.
August 1978

Chile

Asi nació la guerra patria.
Valdivia entró la lanza goteante
en las entrañas pedregosas
de Arauco, hundió la mano
en el latido, apretó los dedos
sobre el corazón araucano,
derramó las venas silvestres
de los labriegos
    exterminó
el amanecer pastoril,
    mandó martirio
la casa del dueño del bosque,
cortó las manos al cacique,
devolvió a los prisioneros
con narices y orejas cortadas,
empaló al Toqui, asesinó
a la muchacha guerrillera
y con su guante ensangrentado
marcó las piedras de la patria,
dejandola llena de muertos,
y soledad y cicatrices

Pablo Neruda
Canto General, Clandestine edition, 1950: 63–64
Illustration by José Venturelli, especially for the
1950 edition of Canto General.

And so the people's war began.
Valdivia drove his dripping spear
into Arauco's stony bowels,
he plunged his hand
into the pulse, squeezed his fingers
around the Araucanian heart,
emptied the tribe's
wild veins
    exterminated
the pastoral dawn
    sent martyrdom
to the kingdom of the forest, burned
the master of the forest's house,
chopped off the chieftain's hands,
returned the prisoners
with their noses and ears cut off,
impaled the Chief, murdered
the woman warrior,
and with his bloody glove
soiled the country's stones,
leaving it full corpses,
and solitude and scars.

Translation: Jack Schmitt
Canto General/Pablo Neruda
University of California Press, 1991

Introduction

In January 1520, almost thirty years after Christopher Columbus' first voyage to the Caribbean, Ferdinand Magellan sailed from Buenos Aires toward the southern tip of South America. According to Chilean historian Francisco Encina, ten months later as the Europeans sailed through what later became the "Strait of Magellan," the many bonfires they saw on land to the south inspired them to designate the territory as *Tierra del Fuego* (land of fire), "a name that posterity has preserved." Magellan's small fleet entered the deceivingly calm (therefore, *"pacífico"*) Pacific Ocean in late November, then continued to the Marianas and the Philippine Islands without further contact with the native peoples of Chile. In a second Spanish expedition to the region in 1526, one of the ships, the San Lesmes, separated by storms from the rest of the tiny fleet, accidentally discovered Cape Horn (*Cabo de Hornos*). With these two voyages, the webs of global exploration cast outward from Europe first touched the territory that would become the Republic of Chile.

Over the next three centuries conquest and colonization in the name of God, the Holy Catholic Faith, and the imperial authority of the monarchs on the Iberian peninsula enmeshed Chile and its peoples in a global economy and an international political system. The Iberian invaders altered fauna and flora, subjected Indian peoples to forced labor and slavery, and engendered through rape, promiscuity, and concubinage a new ethnic and cultural identity: *la raza chilena*.

As elsewhere in the Western Hemisphere, encounters with the Europeans afflicted Chile's native population with disease and decimation. Most of the Indian peoples of the Caribbean islands and those of Chilean Patagonia are now virtually extinct as a consequence of European colonialism. In most of Spain's American empire, however, including the rest of Chile, disease, labor exploitation, and miscegenation disrupted and transformed indigenous societies, rather than entirely eradicating them.

Almost from the outset of conquest some Spaniards, especially individual Catholic priests, opposed the brutality and the cultural-religious premises of conquest. On Advent Sunday 1511 in Hispaniola, the Dominican priest Father Antonio Montesinos condemned the Spaniards for their despicable treatment of Indian peoples: "Tell me, . . . by what right or justice do you hold these Indians in such cruel and horrible slavery? By what right do you wage such detestable wars on these people who lived idly and peacefully in their own land, where you have consumed infinite numbers of them with unheard-of murders and desolations?" Four decades later, in a letter written to the Council of the Indies from Lima in 1553 regarding the situation in Chile, the Dominican friar Francisco de Victoria reported: "[I]it is evident that Christian principles and charity are completely lacking in that colony, and the abominations that occur there cry out to heaven for vengeance."

In Chile, as elsewhere, history does *not* repeat itself. But many historical experiences, sociocultural practices, and evolved institutional patterns remain active influences in daily life. History, in that sense, is not "passed" nor the past, but an ongoing presence in the present.

Approximately four centuries after Victoria's letter to the Council of the Indies, Alberto Hurtado, a Chilean Jesuit priest beatified in 1994, founded an organization to help the homeless: the Hogar del Cristo. Hurtado also helped organize workers' unions based on Catholic social doctrine. In 1951 he introduced the first issue of the magazine, *Mensaje*. The new magazine (which in the late 1990s could be read on the Internet) was prefaced with the words of French Cardinal Jules-Gerard Saliege: "We are partially responsible for the destiny of humanity. We are called on to make history, rather than to be molded by it. Let us bring creative imagination to the task. The past lives in the present. The present carries within it the future. What will tomorrow's world be like? It will be what our faith, our hope, and our efforts to overcome human misery make it."* Father Hurtado's editorial called on Chileans to apply Christian principles to everyday life; to reject materialism, whether capitalist or Marxist; and to value human life and defend human rights. His message was a call for modern-day Chileans to apply Christian principles to life in their times, to a Chile inserted in a bipolar world, an international system framed by the Cold War.

Alberto Hurtado had written a book called *Is Chile a Catholic Country?* (*¿Es Chile un país católico?*) He concluded that most Chileans did not know or practice the social teachings of the Church, that the country's chronic social and economic problems imposed a continuous state of misery on the workers and peasants who made up the majority of the population. Hurtado's calls for social justice echoed the pleas of Father Francisco de Victoria in 1553 and of the Jesuit priests Luis de Valdivia and Diego de Rosales in sixteenth-century Chile for "peaceful conversion" of the territory's indigenous population—pleas ignored by Spanish colonial governors and soldiers who hunted, branded, and exported Indians to northern mines and Peru.

In 1620, more than eighty years after the first Spanish expedition to Chile, the king of Spain ordered an end to coerced labor and the payment of a minimum daily wage to agricultural laborers. Resistance by landowners and *encomenderos* and failure of government officials to enforce the decree made it a dead letter. More than three centuries later, in 1953, a Chilean national government enacted a minimum wage law for agricultural workers and sought to regulate labor conditions in the agricultural estates (*fundos, haciendas*). Landowners generally resisted successfully the Ministry of Labor's feeble and underfunded efforts to enforce the law.

In 1620 Indian and mestizo laborers living on the haciendas of Spaniards were required to work for the landlord 160 days a year. In 1953 Chilean rural tenants and laborers typically worked over 200 days a year and provided landowners not only their own labor but also that of family members or other hired hands. In 1620, with land more plentiful than labor, landowners attempted to attract tenants to work their estates. In 1953, with most good land concentrated into several thousand large rural estates (*fundos*), landowners punished labor indiscipline, the protest of working conditions, or union organizing by expulsion from the *fundo*. Expulsion meant loss of the small house with dirt floors, the garden plot, and perhaps pasture rights for some animals that were the rural tenant's only security.

---

*Archbishop of Toulouse, Jules-Gerard Saliege, led the moral resistance to the anti-Jewish measures in Vichy France. He declared in a Pastoral letter: "There is a Christian morality that imposes duties and recognizes rights. . . . Why does the right of sanctuary no longer exist in our churches? The Jews are real men and women. They are our brothers, like so many others." Father Hurtado's decision to invoke the voice of Archbishop Saliege in the inauguration of *Mensaje* presaged the magazine's role in the 1970s and 1980s as a voice against human rights violations during the military government that ruled the country from 1973 until 1990.

No matter. Chile had achieved a record of constitutional government that made it unique in Spanish America from the 1840s. Chileans were proud of their distinctive tradition, their institutional stability when compared with "tropical America." Foreign historians and political leaders also lauded Chile's "exceptionalism." Chileans "forgot" that their 1833 constitution was the first among the independent Spanish American republics to provide for state of siege and constitutional dictatorship; it would be emulated by constitution-writers in the Dominican Republic, the Provinces of Rio de la Plata (Argentina), Bolivia, El Salvador, and, later, other Latin American countries. Chile became a "model" of stability and progress in nineteenth-century Latin America; Chilean presidents and political leaders repeatedly reminded their compatriots, and other Latin Americans, of the country's "exceptionalism."

Addressing Congress in 1858, the year that South America's first animal-drawn tramway (*carros de sangre*) began operations in Santiago, President Manuel Montt declared that Chile's record of political stability and economic progress was "an example for all the Spanish American republics." Montt's government encouraged the first railroads in the country, connecting northern mines to Pacific ports and then to European and North American markets. Chile sent wheat, flour, wine, and adventurers to California, responding to gold fever and commercial opportunity. Public and private schools multiplied; telegraph wires began to connect the principal cities and towns. Andrés Bello, Venezuelan intellectual, advisor to the Chilean government, and author of Chile's *Civil Code* (1855), wrote in 1857: "[T]the progress made in the last five years can be called fabulous."

For some the progress *was* fabulous. But in 1858, the same year that President Montt acclaimed the country's economic progress and unique political stability, he twice declared states of siege to repress the political opposition and control elections for Congress. Civil war followed in 1859. Chile's "exceptional" political system had its own special authoritarian institutions and practices that, with small modifications, persisted to the end of the twentieth century. Modernization came to Chile from afar, as had the colonial regime; it was imposed top-down, by authoritarian governments, and excluded from many of its benefits the great majority of the country's peoples.

For its perpetuation in the twentieth century the Chilean political system also required recurrent declarations of states of siege, delegation of "extraordinary authority" (*facultades extraordinarias*) to presidents, and jurisdiction of military courts over civilians for "crimes against the internal security of the state." After 1930, laws to protect the "internal security of the state" (1932, 1937, 1958) and then a law "for the permanent defense of democracy" (1948) were added to the government's arsenal of legal repression to protect Chile's much-vaunted democracy against more militant labor movements and the rise of populist and Marxist political parties. This corpus of "protective" legislation, beginning with Decree Law 50 in 1932, melded Chile's modern political history to the colonial inquisition and the post-1833 autocratic republic. Article 1 of Decree Law 50 began: "Any person who propagates or foments, by word of mouth or in writing, doctrines that tend to destroy the social order or the political organization of the State through violence, shall be considered an enemy of the Republic." Law 6.026 (1937) reaffirmed this language and provided new sanctions for persons who threatened the "internal security of the state." Building on this legal foundation for repression of its "enemies," Chilean democracy contained the threats of destabilization and revolution until the early 1960s.

In 1964 Chilean president Eduardo Frei Montalva initiated a "revolution in liberty." Priority was given to increasing participation of workers, artisans, peasants, rural workers, women, and Indian peoples in national life; to promoting social and economic opportunities for the poor and lower-middle classes; and to stimulating the internal market and enhancing social justice. It soon became evident that agrarian reform, agricultural unionization, peasant cooperatives, activation of community organizations, increased labor militancy, and expansion of the electorate could not be reconciled with maintenance of the existing socioeconomic order. Mounting pressures for further and more drastic socioeconomic reforms induced counter pressures to detain and constrain what was perceived as runaway social mobilization.

By 1970 antagonistic dreams for the future had acutely polarized Chilean politics and society. Revolutionaries and reformers joined in an effort to destroy the institutions and values of the old order. Once again Chile was "a model," becoming the first Latin American country to elect as president, in free and fair elections, albeit by plurality rather than majority vote, an avowed Marxist, Salvador Allende Gossens. The coalition of parties and movements that supported the socialist president called itself Popular Unity (Unidad Popular). Leaders of the Popular Unity coalition also thought Chile was exceptional; it would be the only country ever to install a truly Socialist regime via elections, constitutional reform, and extensive legislative initiatives. Unlike any other country, Chile would find a "peaceful road to socialism."

Like Chile's rulers since colonial times, the Popular Unity coalition determined to transform Chile *from the top down:* by decree, by force, and by pragmatic evasion and subtle application of the law. Socialists, Communists, Catholic reformers, and revolutionaries allied in the Popular Unity coalition were as Chilean as their adversaries. They relied on a centralized bureaucracy augmented with party loyalists and hangers-on, a style of hierarchical, conspiratorial politics imbued with the prejudices and defects accumulated from the time of colonial governors and notaries. Unlike the governments of the past, however, the policies adopted by the Popular Unity government threatened to unleash *poder popular,* an ill-defined "power from below" that menaced the old order from the bottom up, including the authority of the Unidad Popular government itself.

Unfortunately for the Popular Unity coalition, it lacked control over the armed forces, the Congress, the Supreme Court, and other agencies of *El Estado.* It also lacked the support of a majority of the Chilean electorate and faced the challenge of paramilitary rightist opposition. Opponents counted also on the meddling and intervention of the U.S. government and its intelligence agencies. Overt and clandestine policies of the U.S. government and international corporations weakened and subverted the Popular Unity government. The attempt to take the country on the "Chilean road to socialism" did not prosper.

In 1973 a military coup cut short the Chilean road to socialism. Repression of heretics and adversaries, now labeled subversives and other less pleasant names like "Marxist cancer," imposed a new inquisition in the name of "western Christian civilization" and economic progress. Opponents of the new military government lived in an atmosphere of fear, much as had the liberal adversaries of the Conservative government minister, Diego Portales, before his assassination in 1837. Portales directed the installation of Chile's "autocratic republic" after a brief civil war in 1829–30 and the promulgation of the 1833 constitution. His methods would later be repeated: repression of political opposition, press censorship, courts-martial, summary executions, imprisonment, and exile for his adversaries. An aphorism attributed to Portales set the tone for the struggle between liberty and autocratic order that characterized Chile in the nineteenth and twentieth centuries: "The stick and the cake, justly and opportunely administered, are the remedies with which any nation can be cured, however inveterate its bad habits may be." As Portales observed, the social order in Chile was preserved by the "weight of the night. . . . [T]he masses near universal tendency to repose was the guarantee of public tranquility." In case the "weight of the night" should lighten, Portales and his successors never hesitated to use "the stick" to secure that tranquility. From 1833 until 1874 liberals battled without success to change the 1833 constitution. After forty years, Congress finally enacted reforms to limit presidential emergency powers and a decade later legislated a statute on civil liberties and rights that lightened the "weight of the night." More than a half-century had been necessary to dilute, but not eliminate, the institutions of the autocratic republic.

The military government that took power in 1973 proclaimed: "In every soldier there is a Chilean; in every Chilean a soldier." The junta ruled the country from an office building named after Diego Portales. The Diego Portales Building was located on Santiago's main boulevard, named after Captain-General, then "Supreme Director of the Nation" (1817–23), Bernardo O'Higgins. Now Captain-General Augusto Pinochet Ugarte would rule the country from this building as "Supreme Chief of the Nation" (*Jefe Surpremo de la Nación*) until the Junta Militar designated him President of the Republic in December 1974. Like Portales in the 1830s, the military junta that took power in 1973 decreed the death penalty for exiles who returned to Chile without government authorization.

In answer to this apparent return to the spirit of conquest and inquisition, Cardinal Raúl Silva Henríquez issued a plea for "Reconciliation" in April 1974 (*"La reconciliación en Chile"*), reminding his compatriots that "there are rights essential to human dignity; they are absolute and inviolable. The Church must be the voice of all, and especially the voice of those who have no voice of their own. We are convinced that it is not possible to build a lasting order on repression." Silva Henríquez became a symbol of resistance to repression for the next fifteen years, as the Vicariate of Solidarity he founded in 1976 struggled to protect thousands of Chileans against the repressive fury unleashed by the Junta de Gobierno Militar.

From 1973 until 1990 the military regime and its civilian advisers and ministers intensified the exploitation of natural resources and the conquest of internal frontiers. New roads penetrated virgin forests and the southern wilderness. Modern energy and communication networks crossed the deserts, the Andes, and the oceans, linking mines, forests, fisheries, and wineries to global markets. As in the nineteenth century, Chile was "the model" in the Western Hemisphere, a virtual "economic miracle." Once again the political and economic changes came top-down, imposed by force. The military government maintained the country under "state of siege" from September 1973 until March 1978, and under one or another regime of exception until 1988.

The costs of the miracle wrought by the military government were high for many Chileans: widespread human rights violations, evisceration of the labor organizations, a new constitution in 1980 that enshrined "protected democracy." As had occurred after adoption of the 1833 constitution, a small cadre of religious leaders and opponents of the military regime rejected the legitimacy of the 1980 constitution, urging political liberalization and more attention to social justice.

Writing in 1860, liberal politician and future president Federico Errázuriz had attacked the 1833 constitution as a regime of tyranny that "falsified all principles of democratic government." He wrote that "until civil liberties and rights are a reality, there will not be in Chile a solid and durable tranquility, founded in a sincere love by its citizens of its institutions." Eleven years later Errázuriz, elected president, swore an oath to uphold the constitution that he had denounced as tyrannical, although still proclaiming his desire to see it reformed. In 1874, more than four decades after its promulgation, Congress finally approved important reforms of the "autocratic republic's" constitution by limiting presidential authority under state of siege and restricting the scope of "extraordinary authority" that could be delegated by the legislature.

Similarly, in March 1990, Patricio Aylwin, a politician who six years earlier had de-

nounced the 1980 constitution as a "regime of permanent dictatorship," swore to uphold the 1980 constitution until it could be reformed. A plebiscite in 1988, carried out
under the terms of the 1980 constitution, had paved the way for restoration of civilian
government. Voters said "No" to another eight years of General Pinochet's presidency.
But the plebiscite also confirmed the "legitimacy" of the constitution imposed by the
military junta.

From 1990 to 2000 two elected presidents governed in Chile. They achieved virtually no change in the military-imposed political system. Economic growth continued at
an accelerated rate, at least until the 1997–99 recession partially caused by the so-called
"Asian crisis" (approximately one-third of Chilean exports went to Asia in the late
1990s). Inflation declined decidedly, as did the percentage of the population that qualified as "poor" and "indigent." Foreign investors poured billions of dollars into new
mining ventures, forestry, fishery, and agricultural industries. In 1998 the U.S. State Department "Country Report on Economic Policy and Trade Practices" for Chile reported
that "as of a result of legislation passed in December 1997, business opportunities for
foreign banks in Chile and Chilean banks abroad have been enhanced substantially.
Legislation is also now in place for privatizing Chile's ports, water and sewage companies." The next year, the Chilean government's official Internet Web site proclaimed:
"Chile: A Country Open to the World."

The political coalition that had replaced the military government in 1990, the Concertación of Parties for Democracy, had first enthused voters in 1988 with the slogan
"happy times are coming" ("la alegría ya viene"). After taking office, the Concertación
government quickly transformed the promised "happy times" into a call for moderation, prudence, and "justice, to the extent possible." Fear of military and business reaction to overly populist policies restrained government policymakers. Army general
Augusto Pinochet Ugarte, who headed the military junta and served as the country's
unelected constitutional president from 1981 to 1990, stayed on as Commander of the
Army and then, in 1998, became a "senator for life" as stipulated in the 1980 Constitution. For some he remained a hero who had saved the country from the abyss, for others a villain who had ordered death, torture, and exile for thousands of Chileans and
now enjoyed the impunity afforded the powerful in Chile since colonial times.

Surprisingly, in October 1998, General Augusto Pinochet Ugarte was arrested in
London at the request of a Spanish judge for extradition to that country for prosecution
for human rights abuses. The Chilean government, including a Foreign Minister exiled
during his dictatorship, and Pinochet's supporters denounced what they called a violation of Chilean sovereignty. Others applauded the General's detention, believing that
justice could never be done in Chile. During the next year Senator-for-life Pinochet remained in limbo in England while his supporters in Chile denounced his "kidnapping"
by the British government. Some political pundits quipped that the country was so
"open to the world" that it even depended on foreigners for justice. On October 8, 1999,
a British judge ruled that Pinochet should be extradited to Spain for crimes against humanity covered by international law regarding state terrorism and torture. The armed
forces' commanders and those who had supported the military regime squirmed, but
also threatened to "protect the constitutional order" if the need should arise. Pressure
for constitutional and political reforms mounted; perhaps it would not require four
decades to achieve fundamental reform as it had from 1833 to 1874?

As the December 1999 presidential elections approached, both candidates sought to
downplay the "Pinochet question," but the basic dilemmas persisted. How could liberty be enhanced in Chile while maintaining political order? How could economic
progress be achieved without exploiting the working classes and degrading even fur-

ther the natural environment? How could the country mediate international economic and political influences over national destiny? How could an end be brought to the impunity of the powerful and social justice be promoted? This was the historical legacy and current challenge of Chile as the nation entered the third millennium headed by recently elected president Ricardo Lagos—the victor in January, 2000 in the country's first-ever presidential run-off election, after failing to obtain the required fifty percent in the first round.

President Lagos promised that he would be the president of all Chileans. He told them that the past could not be forgotten, but that he intended to focus on the future. He called on the courts to administer justice with independence and respect for the rule of law, for the Congress to reform the constitution and the political system, and for the armed forces to cooperate in discovering the "truth" about the disappeared and in determining their final resting place. With most of the Concertación program of 1988 still unachieved, and the opposition initially suspicious of the country's "second socialist president," the road ahead looked difficult. Nevertheless, President Lagos pushed his agenda of promoting political tolerance, economic realism, and increased social justice—for democratic *convivencia* in the present even if full reconciliation of the conflicts of the past proved impossible.

1 Land and Society

The territory occupied by the Chilean nation is the prize of military conquest. From Copiapó south to the Biobío River, Spanish conquistadors took the land from a variety of indigenous peoples in the sixteenth century. From an undefined point somewhat north of Copiapó (lat. 27° 22' S), nineteenth-century Chilean armies extended the national domain by defeating Bolivian and Peruvian forces in the War of the Pacific (1879–83). The territory Chile acquired then has remained a source of friction and potential conflict among the three countries. South of the Biobío River the Araucanian Indians successfully impeded consolidation of Spanish and then Chilean rule until after 1880, when modern weaponry finally overcame the descendants of the Indian groups that had offered the most determined resistance to the Spanish conquistadors. Only at the end of the nineteenth century, therefore, did the political unit that is now Chile effectively achieve its present boundaries, extending some 2600 miles from the northernmost city of Arica (lat. 18° 28' S) past the Strait of Magellan and the world's southernmost town, Puerto Williams, to latitude 56° S. Chile also claims substantial portions of Antarctica (lat. 53° W-90° W) and, since 1888, Easter Island, located in the middle of the Pacific Ocean, 2700 kilometers from the Chilean coast and 4000 kilometers from Tahiti.

For most of its history Chile did not include the great northern desert containing the vast mineral wealth for which the country became known around the world. Nor did the territory south of the Biobío River form an integral part of European settlement. In colonial times (1535–1810) Chile meant a small number of semi-urban places, from La Serena through the central valley, in addition to the precarious frontier fort towns south of the Biobío River which Araucanian Indians periodically destroyed. Bounded on the east by the Andes Mountains, on the west by the coastal mountain range and the Pacific Ocean, and on the north by one of the world's driest deserts, the Chilean colony was little more than a backwater of the Spanish Empire.

Between Copiapó and the Biobío River the Andes chain occupies from one-third to one-half of the width of present-day Chile (though certain areas in what is now western Argentina—Tucumán in the early colonial period and Cuyo until the late eighteenth century—also pertained to the Chilean colony). Moving south from Copiapó, the Andes narrow and become a single dominant cordillera, with some of the highest peaks in South America. In Argentina at the headwaters of the Aconcagua River, Mt. Aconcagua, the loftiest peak in the western hemisphere, rises some 22,835 feet (7000 meters). In Chilean territory in the same Andean region, Mt. Salado reaches over 22,500 feet (6900 meters). The Andean passes as far south as the central valley town of Curicó (lat. 35° S) are typically found at more than 10,000 feet. Los Leones, Lagarto, and Casa de Piedra are located at more than 13,000 feet, and less than ideal weather makes passage extremely difficult. Near Aconcagua, the pass at Los Patos (4,720 meters) served as a conduit for the liberating army of the independence movement led by General San Martín in 1817. Through the gap at Juncal, almost due east of the city of Los Andes, lies the railroad between Chile and the Argentine city of Mendoza. In general, however, the Andes represent a significant barrier to transport and communication.

South of the Biobío River, the Andes lose height and passes are found at lower elevations southeast of Concepción, at Antuco (2000 meters); east of Valdivia at Hua Hum, at less than 1000 meters; and northeast of Puerto Montt at Paso Pérez Rosales, at almost 1100 meters. Permanent snow levels are also lower, so that inland from the city of Valdivia (lat. 40° S) snow persists above 5000 feet year round. In this area beautiful yet treacherously active snow-capped volcanoes edge magnificent lakes. Southern Chile is a region of pine and eucalyptus plantations, forest industries, natural fisheries and aquiculture, cereal production, diversified agriculture, livestock raising and dairies set within the spectacular forested cordilleras, fjords, channels, glaciers, and hundreds of islands and islets. At the southern extreme are the inhospitable Patagonian plains and Tierra del Fuego, where the Strait of Magellan affords a perilous transit around the tip of South America. Before the opening of the Panama Canal in 1914, this southern passage made Valparaíso a commercial competitor of Lima-Callao for the Pacific shipping trade.

In the late nineteenth century Chile incorporated much of the Atacama desert into the national domain and consolidated control over the provinces south of the Biobío River. This gave the country more territory with great natural resources, but these northern and southern territories remained sparsely inhabited. To this day some 70 percent of Chile's population resides between Aconcagua and the Biobío River. On a map, the nation that emerged in the twentieth century looks like a long, irregularly scalloped ribbon trimming south-western South America. Seen from the air the country is an indentation of varying depths between the Andes on the east and the coastal mountains to the west. Its territory of approximately 757,000 square kilometers (292,000 square miles) is more than double the size of Italy and stretches a distance approximately that of San Francisco to New York or from Madrid to Moscow. Chile's continental coastline extends some 6435 kilometers and is rich in sea life, in part due to the frigid Humboldt Current that runs its full length.

Chile's major urban centers—Santiago, Valparaíso-Viña del Mar, Concepción-Talcahuano—and the regional and provincial capitals from Arica in the north, through the central valley to the southern cities of Temuco, Valdivia, and Puerto Montt are situated in one of the world's most geologically active regions and over the centuries they have been repeatedly damaged or destroyed by earthquakes and tidal waves. Indeed Chileans assume that "every president will have his earthquake." Beyond earthquakes, floods and droughts make agriculture risky in the south as well as in the north and the central valley. Landslides, volcanic eruptions, and avalanches add to the natural violence that persistently threatens Chilean lives and property. According to one of the country's most important nineteenth century historians, Benjamín Vicuña Mackenna, as late as 1650 the Spanish authorities considered abandoning the Chilean colony due to the periodic droughts, floods, and earthquakes.

Nature provides Chile not only a continual challenge but also an incredible variety of landscapes, climates, and natural ecologies, ranging from the arid northern deserts to the Chilean antarctic in the south. Partly for this reason, Benjamín Subercaseaux titled his classic and unconventional geography *Chile, o una loca geografía (Chile, or A Crazy Geography)*. Subercaseaux began his story by referring to the explorer Magalhaes' (Magellan, in English) "heroic craziness *(locura heroica)*; he then told the reader that in the Aymara language *Chilli* means "where the world ends," and in Quechua, *Chiri* means cold—then confessed that no one really knows where the country, this "long and narrow sash" *(la larga y angosta faja)* got the name Chile. (Another version, Agustín

Edwards, *My Native Land,* claimed that Chile "comes from the Quichua word *Chili,* signifying "earth's best"; still another that it came from the word *Killing* or *Kildinghe,* the Flemish for cold). Subercaseaux then asks whether "it is worth straining our eyes to study a country so small." The answer? Chile "has the highest mountains in the world, excepting the Himalayas, its coasts are among the longest and most interesting that exist; its strange shape for the length of 4200 kilometers makes our country a small world of the most varied climes and territories that the world possesses." Unfortunately, says Subercaseaux, the existing geographies are economic, written for businessmen, but something of art is needed to understand the fatherland (*la patria*). And Chile is a vast, imposing country that is the pride of geographer, naturalist, and traveler. "A Country, in a word, that is the satisfaction of Man in his most legitimate sense, and with more reason still, the artist, that is Man at his maximum potential and sensibilities."

Elías Almeyda Arroyo, a somewhat less poetic Chilean geographer, whose *Jeografía de Chile* in its multiple editions was read by students from the early twentieth century into the 1940s told readers on the first page of his text: "our country is in an unfavorable location, besides being at the extremes of a continent and of the commercial world, it is so isolated from its neighbors that it developed only a small commerce with them. For this reason we live as if on an island, or better said, as if on various islands. **The entire history of Chile has developed as if our territory were an archipelago.** From the first voyages of discovery to our wars and revolutions; from our oldest commerce until today [1914, and also 1930 when the 9th edition was published and Jeografia had become Geografía], . . . everything reminds us that **to prosper Chile needs to control and actively exploit its beautiful Ocean.**" Agustín Edwards also emphasized Chile's isolation: "the Chilean people have grown up with their eyes set on the obstacles which separate them from other people. . . . [T]heir geographical situation gave them, on the one hand, a certain natural protection against aggression, and on the other it isolated them from enforced contact and left them open only to associations laboriously sought and dearly won."

Even when written, these ideas were a bit overstated. The oceans had connected Chile to much of the world since at least the sixteenth century. In the eighteenth and nineteenth centuries British and other merchants came without much "laborious seeking" by Chileans. Chilean ports and the sea's bounty increased even more in importance from the mid-twentieth century; the coastline was riveted with small and larger maritime openings to the world that collected the country's commodities and industrial production for embarkation and received sundry industrial, fuel, and foodstuff imports. The military government that ruled the country from 1973 to 1990 initiated programs of port modernization that forcefully overcame the resistance of dockworkers and stevedores, whose loss of control over working conditions reduced shipping costs. Chilean products became more competitive in international markets as Chilean workers' real income declined.

The country's internal "isolation" was also gradually overcome with railroads, highways, transverse road networks, and air travel. By the end of the twentieth century Chileans blithely spoke of bioceanic corridors (*corredores bioceánicos*) linking the country's ports to rail and road networks that extended across the Andes to Brazilian, Uruguayan, and Argentine ports and urban centers. Approximately forty permanent mountain passes connected the country to Argentina by land, with various other seasonal passes and cattle trails also operating legally and clandestinely as they had since colonial times.

From north to south the country is internally tied together by the Pan American Highway running through the middle of the country some two thousand miles from

TABLE 1–1. CHILEAN PORTS AND MAIN CARGO ACTIVITY, 1999

Major Ports: *North to South*	*General Description and Cargo Activity*
Arica	Northernmost city. Port serves city and transit cargoes to and from Bolivia. Bulk minerals, metals, timber, fishmeal. Imports: grains, fertilizers, flour, consumer goods.
Iquique	Port serves fishing industry, industrial and consumer goods for the Iquique free zone. Bulk and bagged fishmeal, copper, canned fish, and fish oil. Imports: consumer goods, industrial raw materials, wheat and other grains. Terminal Minero Patache, copper concentrates from Miñera Doña Inés de Collahuasi. Terminal Celta, off-loads coal for thermoelectric plant. Terminal accedes, receives liquids for processing copper.
Antofagasta	Largest port in north (until completion of Mejillones "megaport"), serving the major mines in region II: Chuquicamata, Radomiro Tomic, El Abra, Minera Escondida, Mantos Blancos, Zaldívar y El Lince. Also serves Bolivia and Argentina. Metallic copper, copper concentrates, copper mining subproducts and fishmeal; zinc lead, tin, and antimony from Bolivia; bagged beans from Argentina. Imports: grains, flour, general cargo for Bolivia, and consumer and industrial goods for Chile. Mejillones located 37.5 miles north, to become a "megaport" complex, for copper, containers, bulk solids and liquids, general cargoes; discharging of liquid ammonia by pipeline (1999); 120 miles north is the Carolina de Michilla mining company's terminal used for discharging sulphuric acid; 12.5 miles south is the Minera Escondida facility at Caleta Coloso, which handles copper concentrate.
Valparaíso	Chile's largest port, 100 kilometers west of Santiago. Road and rail links with rest of the country. Manufactured goods, metallic copper, fresh fruit, wine. Accounts for large share of country's imports of all sorts. Sometimes moves cargoes to and from Argentina. Major container port and naval base. Heavily damaged in 1985 earthquake, rebuilt and modernized after 1990.
San Antonio	Most imports and exports of bulk cargoes, including bulk liquids, other than petroleum products, for central Chile. Also general cargo and fresh fruits. Major container moving port (with Valparaíso accounts for over 70 percent of container movement).
Talcahuano	One of several ports in, or near, Concepción/San Vicente Bays. Forestry, seafood and fishmeal; imports: industrial products. Naval base and shipyards.
San Vicente	Bay of San Vicente, forest products, fishmeal, steel products; discharging coal and ore, fertilizer, general cargo.
Punta Arenas	Southernmost commercial port. Methanol, wool, mutton, and seafood. Imports: general cargo and industrial goods. In the Strait of Magellan there are several small ports/terminals used for loading natural gas and crude oil.

Smaller Ports: North to South

Caleta Patillos	Private terminal, 33 miles south of Iquique; loading rock salt.
Tocopilla	Nitrate, fishmeal. Codelco pier, built for the discharge of coal for the power plant supplying Chile's largest copper mine.
Chañaral	Metallic copper, copper concentrates, iron ore. Imports: supplies for copper industry. Petroleum terminal.
Caldera/ Calderilla	On opposite sides of peninsula separating two bays. Bulk and bagged fishmeal, fresh fruit. Imports: coal and fuel.
Huasco	Iron ore loading port, some general supplies for mining industry. Privately owned piers: Guacolda I, fully mechanized coal discharging pier; Guacolda II.
Coquimbo/ Guayacán	Copper ores and concentrates, fishmeal, minerals, early season fruit. Guayacán: iron ore loading terminal 1 mile south of Coquimbo.
Quintero Bay	20 miles north of Valparaíso, port of Ventanas is a liquid gas terminal; crude oil and petroleum products. Ventanas used by the thermoelectric generating plant for unloading coal and loading copper concentrates. Some general cargo.
Lirquén, Coronel, Lota	Privately owned ports in, or near, Concepción and San Vicente Bays. Forestry, including wood chips, paper, wood pulp, seafood, and fishery products. Before 1997 major coal exporting port. Some general cargoes.
Puerto Montt	Forestry, seafood and fishery products; imports of fertilizer.
Chacabuco	Lead and zinc concentrates, frozen fish; imports supplies for Puerto Aysén and Coihaique.

PRINCIPALES
PUERTOS DE
CHILE

- Capital regional
● Puertos

Escala Aproximada:
1/13.500.000

MAP 1: CHILEAN PORTS AND MAIN CITIES OF THE CENTRAL VALLEY

Arica to Puerto Montt. For most of the distance the highway runs parallel to the longitudinal railroad, much of which the national government built and has operated since the late nineteenth century. In the 1980s the military government carved a far southern road system (the *carretera austral*) from Puerto Montt into the almost-pristine splendor of the lake region to Coihaique and south to Cochrane. Airline service also connects most major cities, and the expanding network of ports provides an increasingly modern infrastructure. New shipping docks, giant cranes, and container facilities link Chile's computerized mines, industry, forest sector, and products of the countryside with domestic and international markets. In the late 1990s the government moved toward privatization of the major port facilities to encourage additional investment and competition; one project, at Mejillones, had an initial announced cost of $200 million dollars for its first phase, as an effort to better service the more than twenty major mining operations in Region II, involving over 2.5 million tons of copper cathodes and other mineral-related commodities. Chilean ports advertised their specialized capabilities and functions on the Internet. The Mejillones venture told Web users in 1998:

> The Port of Mejillones is an enterprise formed in equal shares by Ultramar and Belfi, who won the concession for unloading 600,000 tons of coal annually to supply the Edelnor thermoelectric plant in Mejillones. The Ultramar Group is a major maritime firm, with more than forty years experience, and with agencies from Africa to Puerto Williams. . . . [I]t is also the owner of container ships [and other specialized vessels]. Belfi has constructed infrastructure projects since its founding in 1955, among them the major portworks of Chile since that date. Puerto Mejillones is a commercial maritime terminal which, at the present time, principally moves sulphuric acid and coal.

This company advertising blurb is followed by the technical description of the port, its docks, cranes, storage tanks capacities, and storage yard.

In September 1997, ENAEX, S.A., the major Latin American producer of industrial grade ammonium nitrate and nitric acid, awarded a contract to Krupp Uhde GmbH of Dortmund (Germany) to construct in Mejillones the largest nitric acid plant in the world using the Krupp Uhde high-pressure process and an ammonium nitrate plant with capacity of 1060 tons a day. Similar descriptions appear for the other terminals at Antofagasta and Tocopilla and for new investments in mineral, chemical, and fishing industries. Thus while the northern desert, the Andes to the east, the Pacific Ocean, and the bleak Patagonian steppes historically somewhat isolated Chile, post-1980s investments in transport, ports, airports, pipelines, transandean power generation and transmission, and highways, in addition to state-of-the-art communication technology, including fiber optics (beginning in 1991) and a fully digitalized telephone system (after 1994), new submarine cables linking Chile to the west coast of the United States, Europe, and, via Unisur, Argentina, Brazil, and Uruguay, made Chile ever less "the end of the earth." Chilean multinational firms and their transnational subsidiaries invested around the globe; North Americans, Europeans, and Asians purchased stock in Chilean enterprises in New York, London, and Tokyo. The value of Chilean exports more than doubled between 1990 and 1997, then slightly declined due especially to recession in Asia. Imports likewise greatly increased; as in the past the northern and southern ports contributed considerably to the volume and value of exports, but well over 60 percent of the value of imports entered the main ports of the central valley, Valparaíso, and San Antonio.

The geopoetic Chile of Benjamín Subercaseaux, and its "crazy geography" at the "end of the world," were succumbing ever more to the economic geography of resource exploitation and transnational enterprise as the twenty-first century began. In-

TABLE 1–2. CHILEAN EXPORTS, 1990–98, BY COUNTRY OF DESTINATION
(IN MILLIONS OF U.S.$ FOB*)

	1990	1991	1992	1993	1994	1995	1996	1997	1998
United States	1469.2	1596.3	1649.4	1655.2	2012.1	2559.1	2710.5	2710.5	2609.7
Japan	1388.2	1644.0	1707.3	1502.3	1976.2	2906.4	2495.7	2675.8	1959.3
United Kingdom	558.7	408.4	571.5	554.4	523.0	1076.0	886.5	1061.6	1161.2
Brazil	487.4	447.6	450.9	407.1	604.7	1056.8	934.5	957.2	781.2
Argentina	113.5	257.4	461.6	588.9	637.1	585.6	700.9	780.9	735.1
Italy	406.2	344.8	388.2	330.3	359.3	608.8	475.3	499.5	668.5
Germany	941.3	709.4	603.7	486.5	582.4	837.4	742.3	747.0	538.4
Taiwan	279.8	395.3	490.9	407.7	538.5	703.2	629.1	785.6	525.0
Mexico	57.7	43.5	92.4	130.8	212.2	132.3	146.6	376.3	488.5
China and Hong Kong	70.1	137.5	443.3	260.2	217.5	374.8	467.2	598.1	459.7
France	402.3	389.9	395.6	373.7	404.0	508.2	392.8	458.0	443.5
Holland	314.8	362.9	333.7	260.3	345.5	437.6	393.6	423.2	432.6
South Korea	259.3	263.2	242.8	413.4	583.7	896.5	864.1	989.7	384.7
Peru	74.2	146.0	172.6	204.2	329.3	438.0	321.3	347.8	352.9
Belgium	233.3	234.7	186.5	129.7	203.8	391.5	247.6	272.4	345.1
Spain	268.3	345.5	366.5	240.7	219.1	319.5	281.8	345.2	271.1
Bolivia	73.3	112.5	151.4	161.9	171.5	196.9	207.9	228.5	249.6
Colombia	80.2	53.7	74.0	71.7	116.9	189.0	194.8	227.9	211.2
Ecuador	41.3	58.1	64.2	55.3	82.7	124.3	144.2	156.3	194.5
Venezuela	35.6	54.8	75.2	73.7	73.3	135.3	141.1	158.3	176.8
Canada	56.2	53.1	63.7	61.1	70.4	96.0	139.6	131.0	143.5
Sweden	65.2	60.9	74.8	64.5	67.0	90.1	73.6	104.5	103.6
Greece	–	29.1	35.8	41.5	40.4	51.8	39.2	57.6	71.6
Paraguay	24.0	37.8	42.7	48.6	57.6	76.0	66.5	64.4	60.7
Uruguay	–	27.1	35.3	44.6	52.9	56.3	57.9	60.6	56.7
Singapore	33.2	39.0	57.0	47.7	55.6	79.4	86.2	115.2	55.3
Indonesia	55.7	31.8	59.1	70.8	102.1	158.1	145.0	155.5	55.1
Norway	–	–	8.0	13.1	27.1	44.6	38.9	37.4	50.5
Thailand	33.3	31.7	35.0	65.1	112.7	149.6	117.9	133.5	45.8
Saudi Arabia	44.2	48.5	59.0	52.7	43.8	56.1	57.4	48.5	40.4
Finland	–	29.1	45.9	26.7	37.6	66.5	85.1	108.7	39.8
Phillipines	–	–	45.3	43.5	52.3	65.6	103.4	67.7	38.1
South Africa	68.6	79.0	59.8	30.4	84.0	91.0	62.8	62.0	33.4
Russia	–	–	–	–	–	113.8	119.9	42.2	21.0
Portugal	33.4	42.9	36.5	9.1	12.2	16.3	16.7	11.1	13.4
Poland	1.4	32.9	54.9	3.5	3.6	29.4	11.2	5.3	3.9
Subtotal			9048.4	8930.9	11,012.1	15,555.7	14,447.8	16,005.0	13,821.4
Others			491.0	484.1	631.3	911.0	948.4	1,019.8	935.7
Total	8580.3	9048.4	10,125.5	9415.0	11,643.4	16,444.7	15,396.2	17,024.8	14,757.1

Source: Dirección Nacional de Aduanas, Zofri, S.A. (www.chile-exporta.com/estadísticas/)
*Free on board (without charge to buyer for goods on board a carrier at the point of shipment).

deed, never before did entrepreneurs enjoy more prestige in a country where intellectuals, politicians, landowners, merchants, and bankers had historically predominated. Presidential candidate (1999) Joaquín Lavín's 1997 best-seller, *Chile, the Silent Revolution* (*Chile, la revolución silenciosa*), attributed much of the credit for this economic transformation to the atmosphere created by the military regime, "which favors individual ini-

TABLE 1–3. EXPORTS 1990–98, BY REGION (CUSTOMS) (IN MILLIONS OF U.S.$ FOB)

Region	1990	1991	1992	1993	1994	1995	1996	1997	1998
1: Tarapacá	256.83	369.90	437.28	379.49	498.72	708.39	751.96	887.78	819..
2: Antofagasta	2451.56	2509.82	2694.26	2369.69	2859.05	4374.27	4240.23	4982.64	3951.
3: Atacama	468.0	430.26	426.75	361.58	455.89	845.31	768.04	899.25	750..
4: Coquimbo	223.62	188.22	233.11	163.36	189.38	172.26	204.50	170.38	159..
5: Valparaíso	3289.61	3156.28	3486.36	3444.28	4023.75	5462.60	5402.64	5549.81	5423.
13: Metropolitan	642.99	876.44	800.74	829.81	978.59	1100.43	1322.45	1315.25	13122..
8: Talcahuano	1011.47	1089.64	1311.308	1272.21	1679.65	2508.56	2038.60	2031.96	1786..
10: Los Lagos	88.4	167.09	257.15	271.31	272.37	351.36	309.17	329.44	251.
11: Aisén	47.10	49.5	65.43	53.89	60.24	76.57	86.77	13.80	252..
12: Magallanes	141.52	153.30	162.53	179.81	351.04	302.12	282.47	402.60	302..
Total Chile	8522.13	8989.43	9920.89	9325.45	11,368.68	15,901.87	15,406.84	16,682.94	14,841..
Chile plus reexport	8915.23	9712.13	10,733.29	10,059.05	12,351.88	16,993.37	16,450.14	17,830.34	15,969..

Source: Dirección Nacional de Aduanas, Zofri, S.A. after COMEXI. (www.chile-exporta.com/estadísticas/)

TABLE 1–4. IMPORTS, BY REGION OF ENTRY, 1995–98 (IN U.S.$, MILLIONS, FOB)

Region	1995	1996	1997	1998
1: Tarapacá	712.90	667.92	713.49	592.91
2: Antofagasta	960.81	1078.80	1300.17	1042.28
3: Atacama	119.34	43.40	41.40	21.71
4: Coquimbo	50.84	38.36	43.28	31.47
5: Valparaíso	9740.44	11,028.45	11,869.83	11,145.75
13: Metropolitan	2037.20	2297.63	2666.43	2974.77
8: Bío Bío	1104.87	1352.36	1335.73	983.26
10: Los Lagos	35.73	60.32	70.97	44.57
11: Aisén	5.92	2.71	2.84	2.91
12: Magallanes	138.0	322.11	103.75	246.09
Total Chile	14,903.06	16,810.06	18,111.92	17,087.80
Chile plus Zofri	16,978.86	18,745.66	21,086.92	19,338.20

Source: Dirección Nacional de Aduanas, Zofri S.A., after COMEXI.

tiative, creativity, innovation, entrepreneurial audacity and capability." Agreeing with Lavín, in 1988 Manuel Feliú, president of the Confederation of Production and Commerce, wrote that in the past "cultural circles underestimated the central role of the entrepreneur in economic expansion . . . subordinating them to political decisions. . . . [E]conomic liberty makes possible the organization of production and distribution of wealth without need for the discretional intervention of [government] authority" (*The Enterprise of Liberty, La Empresa de la Libertad*). Now the entrepreneur was a hero, someone to be emulated. Books authored by, and about, the economists who helped invent the neoliberal program implemented in the 1970 multiplied: *"The Brick": Bases of the Chilean Military Government's Political Economy* (Sergio de Castro, 1992); *The Economists and President Pinochet* (Arturo Fontaine, 1988); *Privatization in Chile, an Economic Appraisal* (Dominique Hachette and Rolf Lüders, 1993).

As these economists and policymakers emphasized, Chile's increased insertion into the world economy changed its internal economic geography, but perhaps more importantly, the status given to business—instead of to government. Chile in 2000 was hardly the "island" depicted by Almeyda Arroyo for generations of Chilean students. In 1975 some 200 Chilean firms with overseas markets exported perhaps 500 products to 50 markets; in 1998 approximately 6000 firms with operations in Chile exported over 4000 products to some 170 different foreign markets. First the military government, then the two succeeding elected governments vigorously pursued expanded trade opportunities. Chile became a full member of the Asia-Pacific Economic Cooperation Forum (APEC) and the Pacific Economic Cooperation Council (PECC), an associate member of MERCOSUR, the common market of the southern cone, and signed free trade agreements with Canada, Mexico, and other Latin American countries. Chile also signed a Framework Cooperation Agreement with the European Union to liberalize trade. In 1997 the World Economic Forum's Global Competitiveness Report ranked Chile among the world's fifteen most competitive economies.

Politics and administrative reforms also conspired to further integrate the regions of Chile into national and international grids of control and commerce. The military government (1973–90) reorganized the country into twelve regions plus the Santiago metropolitan area. *Intendentes* now headed regions, and *gobernadores* administered the provinces into which the regions were divided. Municipalities (*municipalidades*) were charged with local administration of jurisdictions called communes (*comunas*) under the direction of mayors. The mayors were subordinate to the provincial *gobernador* and the regional *intendente*. The Organic Law of Municipalities (Decree Law 1289, 1976) specified three types of *comunas* (urban, rural-urban, and rural) along with the legal authority, functions, and administrative organization of each type of local entity. After 1990 local officials were once again elected and some effort made to decentralize regional administration; but the intendentes, governors, and lower level officials (except municipal councilors and most mayors) remained direct agents of the president and their appointments depended on the patronage system within the party coalitions that dominated the national government. Political and administrative centralization was a hard-to-overcome way of life in Chile. One of Chile's great storytellers, Vicente Pérez Rosales, wrote a satirical account in the *Revista Chilena* in 1877 called "Something about What We Call Here Centralization" ("*Algo sobre lo que por acá llamamos centralización*"). He described the efforts of a local government in a southern province to obtain budget approval for a latrine, made necessary, he explained, "because of the inevitable consequences of providing victuals to the prisoners in the town jail, their chewing and digesting them." According to Pérez Rosales it was no easy task to secure authorization to pay for the ceramic fixture (*bacín*) commissioned by the town council.

Centralized planning and administration still plagued the country in the 1990s. With almost 40 percent of the population in Santiago, even the military government's innovation of moving the national congress to Valparaíso for its reopening in 1990 (making the congressmen drive back and forth between the capital and the port with their cell phones glued to their ears) gave political cartoonists good material but failed to break the hold of Santiago on the rest of the nation. By mid-1999 serious political bargaining was underway to bring the congress back to Santiago near the ministries, Supreme Court, and executive office buildings from whence the country was governed.

From north to south the variety of Chilean landscapes may be illustrated by comparing Chile's several natural subdivisions with the strip of land running from the desert of Baja California to the Yukon and Alaska: the deserts of the Chilean "great north" or *norte grande* (regions I, II, and part of III as indicated in Map 6—see Map 3 for an enlargement of this area); the transitional steppes and transversal river valleys of the "little north" or *norte chico* (part of region III, region IV, and part of region V—Map 3); the fertile central valley (part of region V south, including part of region VIII—Map 4); the "frontier" region of cereal production and forests south of the major industrial center of Concepción

Long. 70° (map)	Lat.	Mean Annual Temperature (C.)	Rainfall in Millimeters	Major Economic Activities
Iquique Antofagasta	20°	18.3	25	Oasis cultivation, mining, nitrate, fishing and limited industry.
La Serena	30°	14.4	114	Early vegetables, fruit, nuts, limited vines and cereals, goats, sheep, limited cattle mining, fishing.
Viña del Mar Valparaíso Santiago Rancagua Talca Chillán		13.9	359	Central valley agriculture, fruits, vines, wheat, corn, hemp, tobacco, vegetable oils, diversified livestock –70% of all Chilean industry.
Concepción Temuco		13.5	1319	Coal, steel, petro-chemicals, forest products, cereals, potatoes, dairy and cattle, limited vegetables, orchards and vineyards, fishing aquaculture.
Puerto Montt	40°	11.8	2511	
Aisén		8.9	2865	Forest industries, livestock, subsistence agriculture, fishing, sheep.
	50°			
Punta Arenas		6.2	2754	Sheep and livestock, wool, coal, oil, and natural gas.

CHILE:
Climate and Major Economic Activities

MAP 2: CHILE: CLIMATE AND MAJOR ECONOMIC ACTIVITIES

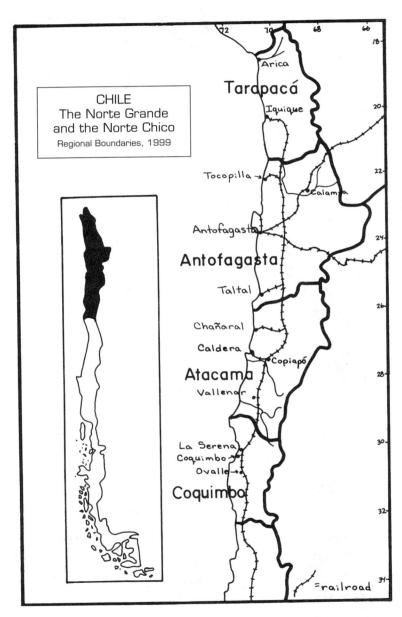

MAP 3: *The Norte Grande and the Norte Chico*

(most of region VIII and all of region IX—Map 4); the lake region (most of region X, excluding Chiloé—Map 5); and the sparsely settled region of southern continental Chile (Chiloé and regions XI, XII—Map 5).

The Chilean *norte grande* is part of South America's western coastal desert which extends northward through Peru and into Ecuador. In much of this region the coastal range amounts only to rounded hills which drop sharply to the Pacific. From the Loa River south, the first major surface water to reach the Pacific flows in the Copiapó. The major urban concentration and farming belt around Copiapó (almost 90 miles long) is often taken as the southern limit of the Atacama desert. At the time of the initial Spanish expedition of conquest from Peru into Chile (1535), Copiapó marked the northern boundary of the territory that became Chile.

This northern region is a vast desert. Scattered oases and river valleys provide slight relief from the barren landscape. Charles Darwin's description of a part of this region near Santa Rosa and Huantajaya as a "complete and utter desert," in which he saw only cacti and lichen, matches that of Preston James in the twentieth century: "No part of the west coast of South America is more forbidding, more utterly desert-like in aspect than the stretch of about 600 miles between Arica and Caldera." Despite the fact that weather stations in some parts of the *norte grande* have never recorded rainfall, there are noticeable differences in climate between the coastal and the interior regions. The coast experiences much greater relative humidity and often cloudiness, due to the cooling effects of the Humboldt Current. Inland, skies are cloudless and humidity much less. For example, humidity in the coastal city of Iquique averages about 81 percent, while in Calama, to the southeast, it averages about 48 percent.

For thousands of years small groups of people lived as fishermen along the coast or took advantage of the limited water resources in this region for oasis valley agriculture, especially in the fertile valleys of Azapa and Lluta. Available evidence suggests that the site of Chile's northernmost city, Arica, supported small population clusters many centuries before the Spanish conquistadors came south from Cuzco. To the present, lack of water and the ecological constraints of the desert environment severely limit agricultural activity in this region. The few irrigated valleys and oases such as Azapa and Belén, east of Arica, and Pica, southeast of Iquique in Region I, and Calama, southwest of the port of Tocopilla (near the copper mine at Chuquicamata), as well as San Pedro de Atacama and Toconao, northeast of Antofagasta in Region II, contribute olives, fruit, herbs, and a variety of food and specialty crops to the regional economy.

Many of the population centers in the *norte grande* owe their origins to the mining activity made possible by the great mineral wealth of the desert. The major ports—Iquique, Antofagasta, Tocopilla—as well as minor ports and interior cities arose, and prospered or declined with mineral finds (silver, gold, nitrates, copper, iron). Iquique owed its colonial significance to silver strikes at Huantajaya and its nineteenth-century boom to nitrates. In 1870 a silver strike at what came to be called Caracoles, 200 kilometers northeast of Antofagasta, attracted some 10,000 miners in its glory days and transformed Antofagasta into an urban and commercial center. Tocopilla and Antofagasta both prospered from copper mining, and then from nitrates in the nineteenth and twentieth centuries. Other settlements briefly flourished and then died when the mineral deposits to which they owed their existence were exhausted. The remains of mining camps and settlements that litter the desert are reminiscent of the ghost towns of the western United States in an even bleaker setting.

In the late nineteenth century the ports of the *norte grande* served as service centers and transshipment outlets for the nitrate works (*oficinas*) and copper mines. At the time these ports seemed more like overgrown villages than real cities, though in several, particularly Iquique and Antofagasta, luxurious mansions and new public services

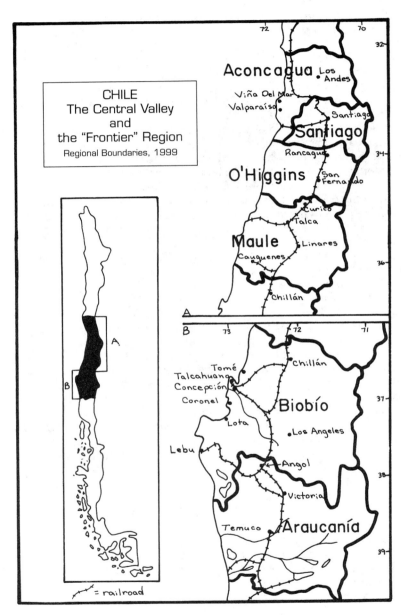

MAP 4: CENTRAL CHILE AND THE FRONTIER REGION

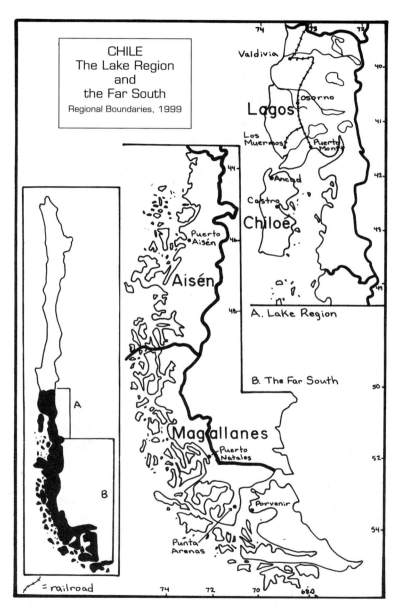

MAP 5: THE LAKE REGION AND THE FAR SOUTH

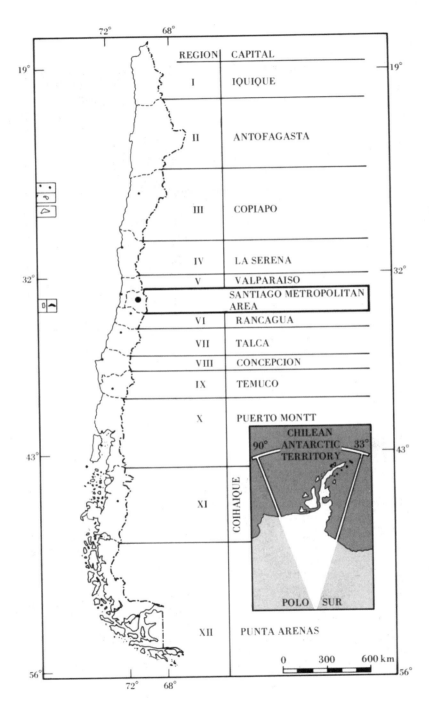

REGION	CAPITAL
I	IQUIQUE
II	ANTOFAGASTA
III	COPIAPO
IV	LA SERENA
V	VALPARAISO
	SANTIAGO METROPOLITAN AREA
VI	RANCAGUA
VII	TALCA
VIII	CONCEPCION
IX	TEMUCO
X	PUERTO MONTT
XI	COIHAIQUE
XII	PUNTA ARENAS

CHILEAN ANTARCTIC TERRITORY

90° 33°

POLO SUR

0   300   600 km

MAP 6: ADMINISTRATIVE SUBDIVISIONS AND REGIONAL CAPITALS, 1999

gave the wealthy a sense of living in modern comfort. This was made possible by importing fuel, food, and even topsoil for plazas while piping water over great distances. An early twentieth-century description of these mining ports tells us that they were sometimes "mere collections of tin shanties crowded at the base of cliffs . . . connected by little lines of railways with the mines in the interior."

Mining of *caliche* ore dates from the 1830s, when sodium nitrate was used in explosives and fertilizer. Not until after the War of the Pacific (1879–83) would nitrate become the most important Chilean export and source of foreign exchange. The nitrate deposits themselves occur at elevations between 3000 and 9000 feet above sea level, at distances varying from 10 to 80 miles from the Pacific coast. Layers of *caliche* or raw nitrate sometimes lie on the surface of the earth; at other times they are found 20 to 30 feet below the surface. In addition to the nitrate itself, important byproducts of processing include iodine, salt, sulphur, and sulphuric acid. In 1968 the Chilean government and private partners created the Chilean Chemical and Mining Company, SOQUIMICH (SQM) to stimulate the decaying nitrate industry. CORFO and the Anglo Lautaro Nitrate Company held shares in SQM. During the Popular Unity government (1970–73) the company was nationalized, only to be privatized again after 1983. In the early 1980s, important byproducts of the nitrate industry included iodine, salt, sulphur, and sulphuric acid. In 1986 SOQUIMICH entered into new contracts for nitrate sales to China, which, along with Japan, had become an important destination for Chilean mineral, seafood, and forest products. By 1988 the company had been fully transferred to private ownership. Significant investments followed in modern technology and new plants built at the Pedro de Valdivia, María Elena (south of the port of Tocopilla), Sierra Gorda (processing of mine tailings, southeast of Tocopilla), and the Coya Sur facilities. According to official publications, the company added new product lines such as potassium nitrate and iodine derivatives. SQM gradually became a multinational company with subsidiaries and manufacturing establishments in Latin America, North America, and Europe. It operated plants manufacturing products for agriculture and industry near Santiago and acquired a 49 percent interest in the U.S. company Ajay North America L.L.C., which produced inorganic and organic iodine derivatives. In addition, potassium chloride production began at Salar de Atacama in 1995.

SQM was only one example in the 1990s (albeit the most important) of the webs of international finance, technology, marketing, and mergers that thoroughly transformed the nitrate business in the northern deserts. New investors and industry specialization brought the Atacama Minerals Company to Aguas Blancas, near Antofagasta. From export sales of approximately $80 million a year (1980–85), the value of nitrate and related products such as iodine, sodium sulphate, and potassium nitrate exports reached $200–300 million in the 1990s.

Though the *norte grande* occupies about one-third of the national territory (Antofagasta is as large as the territory from Santiago to the Biobío River), it contains less than 8 percent of the country's population. Despite its sparse population, the region has played an extraordinary role in determining Chilean economic development since the nineteenth century. The extraction of silver, nitrates, nitrate byproducts, and copper allowed foreign investors and Chilean capitalists to accumulate incredible wealth. It also allowed Chilean politicians and governments to avoid fundamental political and institutional issues well into the twentieth century, as they could depend upon revenues from the desert to finance public service and projects instead of devising rational and equitable systems of internal taxation and public finance.

While the desert was yielding wealth to foreign investors and a Chilean elite in the nineteenth and the early twentieth century, its ports, rail lines, and mining camps were the principal battleground for Chile's emergent proletariat. Both the wealth of the

desert and the experience of working-class organization and struggle came south to influence the rest of Chile. Nitrate revenues and the earnings from copper financed the
public sector of the Chilean economy, providing funds for public works and government services. Peasant workers returning south with the new experience of class organization, strikes, blacklists, and sometimes massacres by police or military, brought
a new consciousness to the wheat fields of the frontier or the grape harvest of the central valley. Union organizers in the north became national leaders of the Chilean working classes and spread their message from the deserts to the centers of economic and
political power in the cities and countryside of the "real" Chile to the south. Our
geopoet Subercaseaux, partly for these reasons, told readers that "the North is an ulcer
(*llaga*) in the healthy body of Chile, it discharges pus and attracts the maggots of death.
Even politics was poisoned by contact with it."

Even with the decline of the nitrate industry after World War I, and the depression of
the 1930s, the minerals (especially copper), and byproducts such as molybdenum) of the
norte grande still constituted the principal source of foreign exchange for the Chilean
economy. Most of the country's copper came from the *norte grande*, though to the south
there are significant deposits in the coastal cordillera and the lower elevations of the
Andes. Chuquicamata began production in 1915 and was acquired by Anaconda Copper Mining Co. in 1923; in 1927 the Andes Copper Mining Co., a subsidiary of Anaconda,
began exploiting the mine at Potrerillos. The largest open-pit copper mine in the world,
Chuquicamata, is located inland almost due east from Tocopilla and slightly north of
Calama. Until the early 1970s, when the leftist coalition government of President Salvador Allende nationalized the largest copper operations, this mine, like most of Chile's
largest copper mines, was controlled by United States companies. Other important
mines in region III include Exótica (closed in 1975 and later reopened as Chuqui sur),
Mantos Blancos, El Abra, Tuina, Leonor, Lomas Bayas, Santa Catalina, Zaldívar, and the
Escondida mine, which accounted for 27.5 percent of Chilean copper production in
1997. Major copper firms and other large mining operations in region II accounted for
almost 30 percent of all Chilean exports in 1998, contributing over $4 billion. The cop-
per mines in region III (Candelaria and Manto Verde) and IV (El Indio/Tambo and Andacollo) also add thousands of tons to Chilean copper exports. In addition impressive
growth in gold and silver mining and investments in the iron sector added to the
1990–97 economic expansion in the northern provinces. CODELCO remained the most
important mining enterprise in the Region III as well as Region II, but other firms also
contributed significantly to exports from this area. Numerous small and medium-size
copper operations also contribute to the *norte grande's* copper output and provide full or
part-time employment for thousands of the region's inhabitants. Gold and silver are
among the important byproducts of the copper refining process. Copper in the 1960s
and 1970s accounted for 70 to 80 percent of the value of Chilean exports, making the
economy highly sensitive to small changes in the international price of this commodity.
In 1974–77 drastic declines in copper prices played a significant role in exacerbating the
substantial economic depression of 1974 to 1976 in the first years of the military government headed by General Augusto Pinochet.

Economic recovery from 1977 to 1980 brought expansion of copper production to
over one million tons in the early 1980s. At the same time, however, a new emphasis on
exports of fruit, fish products, wood and paper products, and other non-traditional
Chilean exports reduced the relative share of the value of copper exports ($1.6 billion
to $2 billion in the early and mid-1980s) to approximately 50 percent of the value of all
Chilean exports. The Chilean National Copper Corporation, CODELCO, the largest
copper company in the world in the 1980s, controlled most of the large copper mines,
called the *gran minería*, including Chuquicamata, El Salvador, and the Radomiro Tomic

TABLE 1–5. REGION OF ANTOFAGASTA: EXPORTS, BY FIRM
(1998, IN MILLIONS OF U.S.$)

Firm	U.S.$ FOB	Percentage
CODELCO Chile	1749.0	43.5%
Minera Escondida	966.7	24.1%
Minera El Abra	329.3	8.2%
Minera Zaldívar	200.2	5.0%
SQM Nitratos	155.9	3.9%
Minera Mantos Blancos	117.7	2.9%
Minera Michilla	97.9	2.4%
Fundación Refimet	90.5	2.3%
SQM Químicos S.A.	53.5	1.3%
SQM Salar S.A.	41.6	1.0%
Others	216.1	5.4%
Total	4018.4	100.0%

Source: Unidad Regional MINECON, after data provided by PROCHILE.

TABLE 1–6. REGION OF ATACAMA: MINING PRODUCTION (INDEX 1990 = 100)

Year	Copper (F. Tons)	Index 1990 = 100	Gold (Fine kg)	Index 1990 = 100	Silver (F. Tons)	Index 1990 = 100	Iron (M. Tons)	Index 1990 = 100
1990	154,966	100.0	8534.5	100.0	198.4	100.0	4679.6	100.0
1992	164,109	105.9	13,246.3	155.2	552.5	278.5	3594.9	76.8
1994	182,777	117.9	15,730.7	184.3	430.6	217.0	4273.1	91.3
1996	360,318	232.5	19,978.0	234.1	458.4	230.0	4955.5	105.9
1997	378,617	244.3	20,311.9	238.0	456.3	230.0	4834.1	103.3

Source: Unidad Regional de Minecon, from data provided by INE and SERNAGEMIN.

TABLE 1–7. REGION OF ATACAMA: EXPORTS, BY FIRM (1998, IN MILLIONS OF $U.S.)

Firm	Exports, U.S.$ FOB	Percentage
CODELCO Chile	248.9	26.1%
Compañía Contractual Minera Candelaria	246.0	25.8%
Compañía Minera Mantos de Oro	96.1	10.1%
Empresa Minera de Mantos Blancos S.A.	81.4	8.5%
Puerto Guacolda II	72.1	7.6%
N.D.	47.2	4.9%
Compañía Minera Maricunga	44.9	4.7%
Compañía Minera Can-Can S.A.	14.8	1.6%
Aguas de la Falda S.A.	13.9	1.5%
Sociedad Punta del Cobre S.A.	10.3	1.1%
Others	78.8	8.3%
Total	954.6	100.0%

Source: Unidad Regional MINECON, after data provided by PROCHILE.

facility that opened in 1995, at an elevation of 3000 meters in the Andes some 45 kilometers north of Calama. In the north, as well as El Teniente and Andina to the south, CODELCO counted for some 80 percent of the country's production. In the years after 1974, liberalized foreign investment legislation and new mining laws allowed millions of dollars of new foreign investment in the copper sector and in other mining operations. Large investments in exploration and opening new mines more than tripled Chilean copper output by 1997. The booming mining economy, not only in copper but also in gold, silver, molybdenum, boron, lithium, nitrate, and related products, such as iodine and fertilizers, broke all records in 1996. Chile became the number one supplier of copper concentrates to Japan and also sent copper to Korea, Hong Kong, the Philippines, Indonesia, Malaysia, China, Singapore, Thailand, and Taiwan. Mining expansion promoted large-scale energy production and transmission projects across the northern Andes from Salta to the desert and then to the port of Mejillones.

Northern Chile was being transformed by the "economic miracle." The "miracle" also brought increasing environmental degradation and, finally, a new environmental law (Law 19.300, 1994) requiring environmental impact studies before approval of major new economic projects—in mining and other sectors of the economy. It remains to be seen, however, whether environmental regulations will be rigorously enforced when they impede "progress." Early signs indicated that, at the least, the law would make companies and the public more aware of the consequences of resource-based economic growth and its industrial byproducts. The Ministry of Mining announced in March 1998 that the "Maritime Governor of Antofagasta ordered an investigation into the dumping of industrial wastes generated in the copper industry, from tanks located some 270 kilometers south of Antofagasta in the Punta Grande sector." A Navy helicopter had detected direct dumping of industrial wastes into the sea by the Santo Domingo Mining Company—a firm that was buying minerals from small mining firms whose operations had resulted in the "virtual extinction" of marine life, both flora and fauna, in the immediate area. For its part, CODELCO announced in 1996 a massive decontamination program involving treatment of gas emissions from its El Salvador (Potrerillos), El Teniente (Caletones), and Chuquicamata operations and water and energy conservation from the northern deserts to its El Teniente mine near Rancagua. This portended the evolution of the private *gran minería* alongside the state-controlled mining firms. By the late 1990s, CODELCO remained the largest copper producer and exporter, accounting for 36 percent of production, followed by the privately owned Escondida mine (27.5%) and other private mining firms.

The extensive coastline of the *norte grande* makes fishing and fish-related industries of great potential importance. In the early 1960s fishmeal production rapidly expanded, only to decline after 1965 as the *anchovetas,* the small fish whose processing induced large investments in plants at Iquique and Arica, seemed to disappear. Renewed emphasis on the fishing industry in the mid 1970s brought dramatic results. Between 1975 and 1983 the fish and shellfish catch more than tripled, reaching some 4 million tons. After 1980, Chile passed Peru as the world's leading producer of fishmeal and fish oil. More than 80 percent of this production came from the northern coast, with the port of Iquique concentrating some 60 percent of the catch. The Chilean government claimed that Iquique had become the largest fishing port in the world in terms of volume handled. Impressive expansion in fish product exports contributed significantly to the increasingly diversified composition of Chilean exports and, even with declines in prices for fishmeal, accounted for over 450 million dollars in export sales in 1985. In 1997 this figure had increased to over $1.6 billion, including large quantities of fishmeal (although Chile dropped to second place among world fishmeal producers) derived largely from anchovies and sardines (harvested out of Tocopilla and Iquique) and a substantial role for products of aquaculture, especially salmon from the Biobío region and further south. In 1984 Chile exported 100 tons of salmon; in 1996 salmon exports exceeded 130,000 tons. Diversification of markets also was impressive, with increasing quantities sent to Asia and Europe, although the United States remained an important customer.

To great extent, the continued expansion after 1990 resulted from the shift in economic policies adopted after 1973 by the military government's economic advisers. Emphasizing liberalization of the domestic economy, privatization of public enterprises and services, attraction of foreign investment, and export promotion, the government had gradually lowered tariffs, with a brief blip back up to 35 percent in 1984 then back down to 15 percent in 1985. It also eliminated most nontariff barriers and inserted Chile aggressively into the international economy. In 1974 Decree Law 740 established the Instituto de Promoción de Exportaciones (PROCHILE). Acting semiautonomously until 1979, PROCHILE became a part of the Ministry of Foreign Relations in 1979 and encouraged Chilean firms to enter new markets, diversify export products, and began actively promoting Chilean products in its overseas offices. PROCHILE maintained data banks accessible to Chilean firms and also active Internet Web sites promoting Chilean goods and services. Other government policies, from special tax credits to favorable commercial credit for "nontraditional" exports, transformed Chile's inward-looking nationalist trade and development policies of the 1950s and 1960s into policies among the most liberal in the world. Exports as a percentage of gross domestic product increased from 11 percent in 1970 to almost 30 percent in 1987 and almost 40 percent in 1997. Diversification cut the share of mining exports from over 80 percent to less than 50 percent, despite the boom in the mining sector.

In 1991 the Concertación government further reduced tariffs to 11 percent. Despite the political opposition's criticism of the military economic model during the 1988–89 electoral campaigns, government spokespersons later acknowledged the "positive legacy" of the economic transformation orchestrated after 1973, in contrast with the continuing battle to overturn the constitutional, political, and human rights legacies of the military regime.

The economic expansion accelerated in the 1990s, still based overwhelmingly, but not so completely, on the mining operations of the *norte grande*. Inequalities in distribution of wealth and income persisted, as did gender discrimination (women earned approximately 65 percent of male counterparts with similar education, and even less for university-educated women in 1995). Nevertheless, Chileans lived longer, obtained higher levels of formal education, earned more, and had access to more consumer choices than ever before in the country's history. More tourists and business travelers made Chile their destination; more Chileans had telephones, televisions, automobiles, and even access to the Internet. Use of cellular telephones expanded rapidly to almost 500,000 by 1998 (2.78/100 inhabitants compared with 12/100 in the United States). Modern shopping malls, located at first in upper-income *barrio alto* neighborhoods, sprang up by the late 1990s in lower- and middle-income neighborhoods in Santiago and could also be found in many regional capitals.

As in Europe, North America, and elsewhere, some Chileans lamented the hectic pace and "consumer-society values" that had transformed and "uglified" the Chile of the 1960s, substituting global fast-food chains and advertising for items to satisfy every imaginable whim. Other Chileans welcomed "modernity": Cable News Network; the next generation computer; air miles awarded for frequent flyers; and decent prices for goods put out of reach in the past by high tariffs and lower incomes. Whatever side of the modernity debate taken, most all Chileans lived in a dramatically different country

TABLE 1–8. INDICATORS OF CHILEAN ECONOMIC GROWTH, 1987–98

Year	1987	1988	1989	1990	1991
Population/1000	12.081	12.275	12.474	12.675	13.100
PIB/GDP, millions U.S.$	20,694	24,154	27,547	30,323	34,650
Exports, billions U.S.$	–	7.052	8.080	8.373	8.942
Industrial Exports, millions U.S.$	–	2,273	2,613	2,741	3,316
Exports of wine, millions U.S.$ (FOB)	–	–	–	52	84
Exports of salmon and trout, millions U.S.$ (FOB)	–	–	–	114	160
Exports of cellulose, millions U.S.$ (FOB)	–	–	–	314	305
Copper production 1000 metric tons	–	1,451	1,609	1,588	1,814
Exports of copper, billions U.S.$	–	–	–	3.820	3.603
Imports billions U.S.$ (FOB)	–	4.833	6.595	7.089	7.456
Tourists, millions	–	–	–	–	–
Tourist income, millions U.S.$	–	–	–	–	–
Investment, % of GDP	19.6	20.8	23.5	23.1	21.1
National savings, % of GDP	17.3	22.3	23.7	24.2	24.1
Unemployment	10.6	11.1	8.4	8.1	8.2
Real wages, index 1990 = 100	78.6	84.2	93.6	100	109.0
Inflation, %	21.5	12.7	21.4	27.3	18.7
Telephone lines/1000	–	629	691	864	997
Cellular phone subscribers/100	–	–	–	–	–

Sources: Banco Central; INE; Subtel; Infor; Sernatur, CNE; CoChilco; Sernageomin.

1992	1993	1994	1995	1996	1997	1998
13.300	13.514	14.095	14.289	14.495	14.712	14.987
41,882	44,474	50,919	65,216	68,568	75,777	72,949
10.007	9.199	11.604	16.024	15.405	16.923	14.895
4,033	4,056	5,115	6,608	6,487	6,923	6,713
119	129	143	182	293	412	501
267	297	354	475	534	668	715
527	444	716	1.229	725	679	692
1,933	2,055	2,220	2,488	3,116	3,436	3,707
3.910	3.266	4.485	6.392	5.839	6.851	–
9.285	10.189	10.872	14.655	16.500	18.218	17.391
–	1.413	1.634	1.540	1.450	1.693	1.8
–	744.4	845.6	900.4	905.3	1047.9	1,200
23.9	26.5	26.3	27.2	28.3	–	–
24.8	23.9	25.4	27.6	23.3	–	–
6.7	6.5	7.8	7.4	6.5	6.2	–
113.8	119.5	123.9	129.5	135.0	–	–
12.7	12.2	8.9	8.2	6.6	6.0	–
1.213	1.324	1.545	1.754	2.056	2.394	2.650
0.48	0.61	0.82	1.38	2.19	2.78	–

TABLE 1–9. SELECTED SOCIAL INDICATORS, 1920–98

Year	Deaths/ 1000	Deaths/ 1000 Infants	Male Life Expectancy	Female Life Expectancy	Illiteracy	Age 6–14 in School (%)	Age 15–18 in School (%)	In University and Professional Schools (%)	Average Number of School Years Completed	Social Security Coverage: Employed Covered (%)	With Access to Potable Water (%)	With Access to Sewer (%)
1920	30.5	250.0	31	32	36.7							
1930	24.1	200.0	40	42	25.3							
1940	21.3	170	41	43	27.1							
1950	13.0	129.0	53	57	19.8							
1960	12.5	120.0	54	60	16.4						44.8 (1963)	21.3 (1963)
1970	8.7	82.0	58	64	11.0	94.4	37.9	7.8	4.3		66.5	31.1
1974	7.7	65.2	63.9 (1975–80)	70.6 (1975–80)	10.2		51.2	12.8			69.2	38.2
1978	6.7	40.1			8.9	97.7	51.8	10.2	7.5 (1976)	76.9	86.0	56.3
1980	6.1	23.6	67	74	8.7	93.6	55.5	8.7	7.6	53.6	92.1	70.0
1986	5.9	19.1			6.2	92.9	68.2	10.4	8.2	57.6	97.0	77.2
1990	6.0	16.0	71	77	5.4	89.2	75.5	11.3	8.6	58.7	98.0 (1988)	80.9 (1988)
1995	5.5	11.1	71.5 (1990–95)	77.4 (1990–95)	4.9	87.1	68.5	18.0	9.6	62.6	95.0	NA*
1996	5.3	11.1	72.3	78.3	4.8	NA***	NA***	NA***	9.6	NA***	NA**	
1997	5.2	10.0	72.3 (1995–2000)	78.3 (1995–2000)	47 NA***	NA***	NA***	NA***	NA***	NA***		

Source: INE; Anuarios de Demografía; Banco Central, Indicadores Económicos y Sociales; Ministerio de Educación, Compendio de Información Estadística; Dagmar Raczynski, "Para combatir la pobreza en Chile: Esfuerzos del pasado y desafíos del presente" in Cortázar and Vial (1998).

*This category changes in official statistics after 1990, incorporating latrines, and other methods of disposing of human wastes.

**This category changes to "access to safe water" in official statistics after 1995.

***These data are not reported after last entry in each case by government agencies.

TABLE 1–10. EXPORTS AS PERCENTAGE OF
GROSS DOMESTIC PRODUCT

Year	Percentage of GDP
1960	12
1965	12
1970	11
1973	10
1974	14
1975	17
1976	20
1977	21
1980	24
1981	20
1982	25
1983	25
1984	25
1985	26
1986	27
1987	28
1990	32
1996	38

in 2000 than they had in 1970, a country ever more connected to the web of globalization. Other efforts to industrialize the *norte grande* included installation of vehicle assembly plants in Arica, expansion of copper refineries, smelters, and other mineral-related industries, and the processing of agricultural commodities. Above all, however, the *norte grande* remains a copper-mining region which, in the words of ex-President Salvador Allende, provides the "salary of Chile."

South of the *norte grande*, part of the province of Atacama, Coquimbo, and part of Aconcagua form a transition from desert to steppes and then to the fertile central valley. Here, in the *norte chico*, the desert gives way to scrub and brush vegetation which increases toward the south. The transitional character of this region is well illustrated by the average rainfall for selected stations from Arica in the *norte grande* to Quillota at the southern margin of the *norte chico*. Average annual rainfall increases from 1 to 2 millimeters (mm) in Arica or Iquique to 28 mm at Copiapó. It is 65 mm at Vallenar and 133 mm in La Serena. Copiapó and the surrounding region are a transition between the arid desert and the semi-arid *norte chico*. At the Aconcagua Valley around Quillota, where average annual rainfall exceeds 400 mm, there is another transition to the temperate climate of central Chile (see Map 3).

Once called the "region of ten thousand mines," the *norte chico*, like the desert to the north, contains great mineral wealth. In 1811 silver discovered near Vallenar, inland from Huasco, led to the opening of some 150 mines. From 1830 to 1850 mining activity in the region reached a peak with new silver strikes at Chañarcillo, south of Copiapó. Production continued here until the 1890s. In this region, in July 1851, Chile inaugurated one of the first three railroads in South America, to transfer ore from the inland mines to the port at Caldera.

While not as large as the Chuquicamata deposits, copper from Potrerillos and then El Salvador contributed significantly to Chilean copper production. The smelter at Paipote, just south of Copiapó, serves what is called the small and medium copper sector, which gives employment to thousands of Chileans. The smaller mines are usually less efficient and contain lower ore content, making them highly vulnerable to changes in world prices. Government policy toward this sector is often controversial since inability to compete in the world market as prices decline produces temporary shutdowns and mine closures, unemployment and demands for further subsidies through the Empresa Nacional de Minería (ENAMI), a government enterprise created in 1960. The economic recession in Asia (1997–99) produced just such a dilemma in the region, giving rise once again to pressures to end government intervention to support the small mine sector. Held up as a counterexample was the large-scale Phelps-Dodge owned La Candelaria mine (near Paipote), which produced almost 5 percent of Chile's copper in 1997.

ENAMI served the medium and small mine sector by purchasing, smelting, refining, marketing, and subsidizing ore produced by thousands of small operators. It maintained purchasing agents in various locations and processing plants in TalTal, Manuel Antonio Matta, Vallenar, and El Salado in addition to the smelter at Paipote and the smelter and refinery at Las Ventanas (region V). In the late 1990s ENAMI's copper sales amounted to some $800 million (less than 4% of the national total) and also contributed to gold and silver exports, which became increasingly important in the 1990s. Chile became a major gold producer after 1978 with the startup of the El Indio mine; in 1997 Chile was the third leading silver producer in Latin America, after Mexico and Peru.

Abrupt declines in copper and gold prices in 1997–98 and pressures for modernization of facilities to meet new environmental standards renewed debates regarding ENAMI's future. According to Sergio Bravo Yuraszeck, a company director, at the beginning of the 1980s ENAMI served 1500 small and medium-sized mining enterprises; rising mineral prices increased this number to almost 4000, which then dropped to only 410 in 1998. In June 1999, the National Mining Association's *Boletín Minero* featured a photo of protesting miners outside ENAMI headquarters in Santiago, demanding more resources and subsidies for the small mine sector. Meanwhile, government policymakers considered bringing private capital to the rescue or even total privatization of ENAMI.

In the *norte chico,* unlike the *norte grande,* a number of rivers cross the otherwise arid region, making possible important agricultural activities and the existence of a number of important interior urban concentrations. Still, this region contains only 3 percent of Chile's arable land. During the colonial period, tiny coastal settlements served as collection points for gold or silver brought down from the cordillera and the inland valleys for shipment to Lima and Spain. English, French, and Dutch buccaneers repeatedly menaced these towns and occasionally sacked them, terrorizing their inhabitants.

Initially agriculture in the *norte chico* met the needs of a limited local market and of the workers in nearby mines. Only later did agriculture expand to supply wheat, specialty crops, and fruits to southern and foreign markets. Always, however, the interdependence of agriculture and mining persisted and has dominated the economy of the *norte chico* to the present.

Like the *norte grande,* although to a lesser extent, the *norte chico* has played a disproportionate role in shaping the development of Chilean labor movement and working-class organizations while at the same time exporting its products to support the Chilean economy. Owing to the tendency of many rural laborers and peasants in this region to work alternately in agriculture and mining, depending upon weather conditions and access to cultivable land, the militancy of the mine workers spread to the rural regions. In the valley of Choapa, southeast of Illapel, and in much of Aconcagua, the natural ecology and political economy of the region forged a rural working-class militancy in the early twentieth century; it spread to the rest of rural Chile only after the 1930s.

Agriculture in the *norte chico* combines pastoral activities (goats and sheep espe-

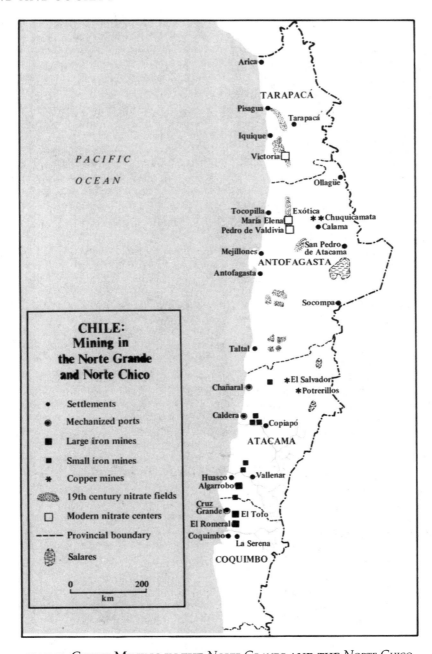

MAP 7: CHILE: MINING IN THE *NORTE GRANDE* AND THE *NORTE CHICO*

(*Source:* Harold Blakemore, "Chile" in *Latin America: Geographical Perspectives*, Metheun & Co. Ltd., London, 1971.)

cially) in the cordillera with intensive cultivation of vegetables and fruit, especially grapes, orchard crops, tomatoes, and melons. These products command excellent prices in urban centers, particularly Santiago, because they arrive before the harvests in the central valley. Cereal crops are also cultivated, but the region's susceptibility to periodic droughts makes all agriculture risky. Experiments with drought-resistant pastures have given good results in some areas for sheep and goat forage. After the mid-1960s expanded plantings of fruit orchards increased production of apricots, peaches, avocados, and walnuts in selected area of Coquimbo to complement chirimoya, papaya, and olive production.

Also in the *norte chico*, especially Coquimbo, there prevails a distinctive pattern of partially communal land tenure called *comunidades*. Many of the *comunidades* originated in colonial times with mining concessions. Depletion of minerals or failure to strike pay dirt turned the laborers' attention to agriculture and animal husbandry. Today the limited land of the *comunidades* forces young adults to migrate in search of better opportunities. Thus the *comunidades* have a disproportionate number of the very young and of older adults.

The *comunidades* typically contain large extensions of dry, hilly or cordillera land which the members, called *comuneros*, use as a common pasture. In addition, the *comuneros* have small amounts of permanently or seasonally irrigated land divided into parcels which they work individually. Wheat, barley, potatoes, corn, and beans are cultivated, and in the higher valleys (Limarí, Hurtado, Rio Grande, Rapel) fruits and vineyards play an important part in the *comunero* economy. Goats constitute the main animal resource, providing dairy products, hides, and meat to the *comuneros* along with some cash income. Intensified goat husbandry has produced significant erosion of soils in the common pasture lands.

The circumstances of the small and medium-size mining operations and of agriculture in the *norte chico* make stable employment a considerable problem for its population. In the dry years *comuneros* seek work in the nitrate fields, the gold, silver, copper, or iron mines in order to support their families who remain on the land. Despite their poverty, the desperate hope of striking it rich holds many peasant-prospectors in the region. From the exploitation of iron, however, the small miners are essentially excluded. Large foreign interests (Bethlehem Steel) have dominated ore production beginning in 1921 at El Tofo, 68 kilometers north of La Serena, and then, when the ore at El Tofo was practically depleted in the early 1960s, at El Romeral, also to the north of La Serena some 25 kilometers. From these sites the ore is sent south to the steel mill at Huachipato near Concepción for processing or is exported. Other centers of iron production include Cerro Imán, southeast of Caldera and Algarrobo, some 40 kilometers southwest of Vallenar (see map 7). The value and quality of iron exports increased significantly from the mid-1970s until 1981 when it reached over $160 million; international recession reduced this to around $100 million from 1984 to 1986.

In 1996 Minera Huasco, owned by the Compañía Minera del Pacífico (CMP), and M.C. Inversiones, a subsidiary of Mitsubishi, Japan, announced the opening of a new mine at Los Colorados to replace the practically exhausted Algarrobo mine. According to CMP company information, iron ore exports increased from 5.7 million long tons in 1986 to over 8.3 million in 1996 along with other products from the Algarrobo, Los Colorados, and El Romeral facilities. The company shipped ore on the privatized and internationalized railway (FERRONOR, majority interest acquired in 1997 by Rail America) and the line that connected El Romeral to the mechanized port at Guayacán. In the same immediate region in 1995–96, the Empresa Eléctrica Guacolda, S.A. (owned 50% by Chilgener), put a new mechanized port for unloading coal and two new thermoelectric plants into operation, connecting them to the central power grid (SIC). Financing and construction of the port was contracted out to Mitsibushi Corp. Thus the *norte chico* took part in the transnationalization and modernization of mining in post-1980s Chile much as it had from the 1830s to the 1870s: by importing capital, technology, fuel, water, and foodstuffs and exporting its minerals via expanding coastal ports.

Unlike the nineteenth-century experience, however, from the late 1970s, despite these major investments, the *norte chico* lost population. The long-term trend of net out-migration continued—over 3 percent from 1977 to 1982 and the same for 1987 to 1992. In a relative sense, almost all regions of the country saw their *share* of the population reduced from 1970 to 1992 as the Santiago metropolitan region went from 28 percent to almost 40 percent of the country's population. While the overall population growth rate of 1.6 percent/year in the late 1990s was down significantly from the 2.5 percent rate in the 1960s, the growth in the Santiago metropolitan region was many time higher because of internal migration. From 1952 to 1992 the city of Santiago grew from approximately 1.5 million to almost 5 million people, an average of over 3 percent/year for the forty-year period. Some other major urban areas also experienced over 3 percent/year average growth for this period: Arica (over 5 percent), Iquique, Antofagasta, Copiapó, La Serena-Coquimbo, Rancagua, Los Angeles, Temuco, and Puerto Montt.

Apart from processing of agricultural commodities, pisco* production, fruit drying and canning, fishing, and mining, the *norte chico* lacks significant industrial establishments. Periodic droughts and the limited agricultural resources of the region, notwithstanding some increase in irrigation and vineyard as well as fruit production near Copiapó in the 1980s, make rural poverty endemic. This leaves many inhabitants dependent for survival upon part-time mining endeavors, government make-work projects, and food distribution for survival. Extremely large investments in irrigation, crop development, and agricultural extension are necessary before the *norte chico* can overcome the obstacles to economic development imposed by nature.

At the southern extremity of Aconcagua province, the fertile region known as the "Vale of Chile" marks the northern boundary of Chile's heartland (Map 4). The central valley of Chile contains some 70 percent of Chile's population, provides more than 70 percent of industrial employment, and even accounts for 20 percent of copper production. Within a 100-mile radius of Santiago lives more than 50 percent of Chile's population. The central valley, like all of Chile, is dominated by the capital city, Santiago, and the surrounding metropolitan area. Santiago city has more than thirteen times the population of the country's next largest city, Concepción. The metropolitan area grew faster from 1970 to the 1990s than any region in Chile except sparsely populated Tarapacá, bordering on Peru. Despite policies intended to decentralize economic activity and public administration, Santiago's traditional overbearing influence on the rest of the country increased in the last decades of the twentieth century. Traffic snarls, air pollution, overtaxed public utilities and communication systems, problems with water quality—in short, all the travails of late twentieth-century cities—afflicted Santiago as the center of Chilean "modernization." Consuming agricultural land at its perimeters for suburban housing developments, the capital city spilled its traffic and other urban problems into the central valley south toward Rancagua, west toward the port at San Antonio, and into the Andes *cordillera*. More than ever, Santiago was a primate city, a megalopolis in a country without another city over 500,000 people, although the major

---

*A clear South American brandy made out of grapes.

TABLE 1–11. SPATIAL DISTRIBUTION OF POPULATION, 1952–92 (PERCENT OF TOTAL)

	1952	1960	1970	1982	1992
Population in cities over 100,000	33.7	37.9	46.0	56.0	60.3
Population in cities over 20,000	47.5	55.0	62.4	68.6	72.2
Total urban population	60.7	68.2	75.1	82.2	83.5
Population in localities with less than 2000	41.2	35.5	27.8	21.5	15.5
Total rural population	39.3	31.8	24.9	17.8	16.5

Source: CELADE, Proyecto DEPUALC, based on national census for each year.

ports and metropolitan areas of Valparaíso-Viña del Mar and Concepción-Talcahuano both were growing toward 1 million by the late 1990s.

At its widest the central valley measures some 45 miles between the Andes and the coastal mountains or the sea, and only along the Biobío River at its southernmost boundary does the flat valley floor extend all the way to the Pacific. Valparaíso, the major port in the region, is the primary doorway for imports to the Santiago market. To the south, Chile possesses only two other major ports—Talcahuano (Concepción) and Valdivia.

The Chilean central valley has a mediterranean climate with rainfall increasing gradually toward the south. The climate and the fertility of the soil, reminiscent of central California, are ideal for intensive truck farming, orchards, and vineyards in addition to cereal crops and livestock. With the advantage of a harvest season that occurs during Europe's and North America's winter months, the central valley offers Chile a source of foreign exchange through export of high-quality fruits, vegetables, wines, dairy products, and specialty crops.

Despite this potential, prior to the 1970s extensive wheat cultivation and cattle operations, along with vineyards located in a relatively small number of large estates, dominated the valley's agricultural history. Only a minority of these estates had moved to more modern agricultural practices, making the backwardness of Chilean agriculture a critical obstacle to economic development. After 1964 massive agrarian reform programs disrupted traditional agricultural and land tenure patterns by creating agrarian cooperatives operated by *campesinos* under the not always benevolent tutelage of government administrators. After the military coup of 1973, former owners recovered many of the large farms (perhaps 30 percent of those expropriated from 1964 to 1973), and the new government made efforts to break up the production cooperatives into individual family farms.

More than half of the residents of the farms in the reformed sector of agriculture failed to receive land allotments under the military government's scheme. As a result the policies created a group of over 35,000 landless rural workers who resorted to occasional, seasonal, and migratory labor in agriculture, artisanship, or movement to towns and cities in order to survive. Others sought shelter in small makeshift settlements (*villorrios*) which sprang up in the countryside. At the same time a new group of relatively prosperous small- and medium-size commercial farms emerged. Auctions of land from the reformed sector still controlled by the land reform agency, CORA (before its abolition in 1978), added additional units to the small and medium farm sector.

The policies of the military government emphasized creation of an active land market to encourage efficient utilization of farm land. These policies, accompanied by the overall focus on export promotion and on opening the Chilean economy to international trade, altered old patterns of production and discouraged reconstitution of the archaic *hacienda* system. Output of traditional agricultural crops such as wheat, sugar beets, potatoes, corn, oats, and barley grew slowly or declined, though production of some food crops, such as beans and rice, experienced notable increases. Fruits, vegetables, flowers (and lumber products from the south-central and southern regions), and other commodities previously of relatively little importance were responsible for huge increases in Chilean agricultural exports. In 1986 Chile satisfied 27.5 percent of total consumption of table grapes in the United States, and exports of grapes, apples, nectarines, plums, pears, and peaches, along with other assorted fruits and vegetables, amounted to over 58 million boxes.

In the decade that followed, fruit and wine exports dramatically increased. Chile became the Southern Hemisphere's leading exporter of fruit, with over 150 million cases shipped in the 1997–98 crop year compared to 12 million cases in the early 1970s. The FIB value of fruit exports in 1996/97 grew to U.S.$ 1.77 billion—almost equal to the value of copper exports a bit more than a decade before. In 1984 the entire agricultural sector had accounted for less than $350 million in exports. By the late 1990s over 12,000 growers from region III to region VIII (Chillán) produced fruit on some 18,000 hectares, with most of the fruit coming from region VI and the metropolitan area. As with minerals, seafood, and forest products, a growing assortment of Chilean fruits and wines went to increasingly diverse markets on every continent of the world. Table grapes, apples, kiwi fruit, pears, plums, and nectarines led the list of nearly thirty major fruit exports. As with the mining boom, the environmental costs of orchard and wine production was heavy: increasing residues from pesticides and herbicides, fertilizer run-off into streams, and chemical poisoning of agricultural laborers—whose union movement had been virtually destroyed in the 1980s. Like other sectors of the economy, the fruit export business came to be dominated by a small number of transnational firms (in the 1996/97 crop year four firms accounted for over 40 percent of fruit exports). After 1993 Dole Chile was the leading export firm, followed by David del Curto, U.T.C., and Unifrutti. Dole, and the other leading firms, also directly controlled many orchards, packing plants, and wood crate and carton factories. In 1999 agriculture employed approximately 15 percent of the active labor force; more and more these were seasonal and migrant workers in the fields and the packing sheds, in the vineyards "as needed," and in the forests as "subcontractors" with chainsaws logging native forests and commercial plantations to send logs, pulp, and chips to Asian (especially Japanese) markets.

The dynamism in speciality crop and timber exports to Europe, Japan, Korea, other Latin American countries, and the United States was accompanied by a trend toward importation of more and more of the basic foodstuffs consumed internally—including as much as 40 percent of the country's wheat requirements in the early 1980s. Justifying this trend and the government policies that encouraged it, an ex-Minister of Agriculture noted in 1983 that fruit production from only 34,000 hectares would produce enough foreign exchange to purchase more than one million tons of wheat. To produce this same wheat in Chile would have required more than 200,000 hectares of agricultural land. Nevertheless, under pressure of international recession, growing indebtedness, and declines in foreign exchange earnings, the military government reversed policy by strengthening price supports and introducing barely disguised import barriers to protect local agricultural producers. In the 1985–86 crop year, after five years of steep declines in production, wheat output again reached some 800,000 tons. According to government sources this covered 90 percent of domestic consumption. By 1989 wheat production more than doubled, then varied from 1,200,000 to 1,700,000 tons until 1998. Like most traditional crops (corn, barley, oats, rice, potatoes, sugar beets), wheat took a back seat to the dynamic fruit, vineyard, and forest sectors. Increased production came as a result of greater efficiency as acreage planted declined and indirect government subsidies ("price bands") somewhat insulated these crops from international competition.

With cropping patterns and land values highly responsive to international demand and radical shifts in domestic agricultural policies, the Chilean countryside experienced considerable economic and social instability in the years after 1973. Agro-industrial firms linked to urban capital and transnational firms and markets increased in importance at the same time that small- and medium-size farm units also played a more significant role in the rural sector. Seasonal labor requirements in the production of fruit, vegetables, and in the vineyards induced unprecedented levels of labor mobility and social dislocation. With the gradual disappearance of the old pattern of resident rural labor on the traditional haciendas and continuing rural-urban migration (over 80 percent of Chile's population was considered urban in 1999), it appeared that social, economic, and political domination of the central valley by the large traditional agricultural estates had finally ended.

The large rural estates in Chile's central valley historically influenced much more than agricultural production. They constituted the single most important political and social institution in Chile. Their owners belonged to a small social elite that has controlled most of Chile's best agricultural land as well as its political institutions. As late as 1930, from 60 to 75 percent of Chile's rural population resided on the haciendas. The tremendous power exercised by landowners or proprietors over the rural labor force made each rural estate a quasi-political unit. The landowner controlled access to land, housing, and employment. The resident rural laborer who disobeyed the landlord's orders risked being fined, whipped, dispossessed, or otherwise punished. Service-tenants, or *inquilinos,* worked the landlord's land in exchange for access to perhaps half an acre or an acre of land, a house and garden plot, and various in-kind payments or perquisites, such as food rations, firewood, or permission to graze a designated number of animals on the *fundo's* pasture.

After adoption of minimum wage legislation for agriculture in 1953, landowners theoretically paid these workers a minimum wage established by the government, provided minimally decent housing, and obeyed a number of labor laws intended to protect the workers. In practice, landowners successfully ignored or evaded the minimum wage legislation as they had previously evaded other labor laws; workers who complained or registered protests with the Labor Department faced reprisals or dismissals. In 1952 an inspector of the Chilean Labor Department reported:

> In the *fundo* Las Pataguas, owned by the Archbishop of Santiago but rented to Mr. Dario Pavez, the administrator Ramiro Ramírez, aided by the foreman [*mayordomo*], applied about 100 lashes to the worker [*voluntario*], Roberto González. The same administrator has also whipped other workers [four named] and for this has been nicknamed "The Lash" [*El Azotador*]. In fundo La Carlina, owned by Carlos Aspillaga Sotomayor, and administered by Vicente Salazar, if workers ask for their social security booklets so they can go to the health service, they are insulted and offered a kick in the ass.

Families who had lived for generations on a *fundo* could be fired and evicted at the landowner's whim, with no compensation for improvements they had made to their residence or to the land by way of fences, fruit trees, or outbuildings.

The dependence of the central valley's agriculture upon a rigidly stratified social system and the economically inefficient *fundos* permeated Chilean society and made relations between the upper classes and working classes authoritarian, patronizing, and exploitative. This situation prevailed after 1932 as the Chilean political system apparently developed into a functioning formal democracy. The inherent contradictions between a truly democratic political system, efficient agriculture, and maintenance of the centuries-old hacienda system generated intense political conflict in Chile in the years 1964–73.

It is difficult to understand the pervasive influence of the haciendas of the central valley on Chile's politics, economy, and social relations unless one has witnessed the ritual subservience of the campesino listening to his landlord's orders—the bowed head, eyes toward the ground, hat held over the genital area—all symbolic admissions of the huge gap separating the hacendado from "his" workers.

Lack of opportunities in the countryside, and the stifling hacienda system in the central valley in the mid-nineteenth century, pushed rural workers to northern mining camps, railroad construction gangs, and the cities in search of employment and a better life. The rural to urban trend has continued throughout the twentieth century. In 1999 the Santiago metropolitan region accounted for approximately 40 percent of Chile's population, while over 70 percent of all Chileans lived in cities with over 20,000 inhabitants—most of these in the central valley. As the twentieth century came to an end continued urbanization and suburbanization was gobbling up the last major vineyard located in the country's capital, the historic Viña Cousiño Macul, established by Matías Cousiño in 1856. A large sign at the corner of Quilín and Tobalaba announced a major subdivision project by Crillón Desarrollos Inmobiliarios offering high-end housing in Peñalolén.

Not only have agriculture and the hacienda system made the central valley the political, economic, and social heartland of Chile, but historically, industrial activities (other than the mines) have been concentrated in Santiago, Valparaíso, and Concep-

TABLE 1–12. ESTIMATED POPULATION OF MAJOR CITIES AND SANTIAGO METROPOLITAN AREA

	1992 *Census*	1999
Santiago (metropolitan area)	5,170,293	5,922,990 (1998)
Santiago (city)	4,048,282	4,739,946
Concepción	308,581	374,166
Viña del Mar	296,488	338,779
Valparaíso	240,611	284,679
Talcahuano	232,959	277,104
Antofagasta	219,976	248,968
Temuco	193,926	266,727
Rancagua	175,929	209,890
Arica	163,443	183,281
Talca	150,299	179,954
Iquique	133,102	166,647
Chillán	133,073	168,503
Calama	104,624	125,854
Punta Arenas	104,487	122,897
Osorno	101,730	130,014
Quilpué	99,608	118,629
La Serena	99,467	128,042
Los Angeles	92,272	114,398
Copiapó	94,249	119,861
Valdivia	88,937	124,740
Puerto Montt	86,683	135,125
Coronel	80,983	91,101
Coquimbo	72,143	132,754

Source: INE: 1992 census and estimate for 1999, courtesy INE and Fundación Terram.

TABLE 1–13. GROWTH OF POPULATION, BY REGION, 1970–99

Region	1970	1982 Census	1992 Census	Percent Increase, 1970–92	1999 ⋅ Population, INE Estimate
Tarapacá	184,180	275,144	341,112	85	386,226
Antofagasta	265,028	341,702	407,409	53	456,083
Atacama	162,081	183,407	230,786	42	264,464
Coquimbo	355,519	419,956	502,460	41	561,665
Valparaíso	1,016,099	1,210,077	1,373,967	35	1,525,494
Metropolitana (Santiago)	3,316,289	4,318,097	5,170,293	56	5,922,990
Libertador Gen. B. O'Higgins	510,869	586,672	688,385	34	768,663
Maule	649,161	730,587	834,053	28	898,418
Biobío	1,319,669	1,518,888	1,729,920	31	1,895,160
Araucanía	631,245	698,232	774,959	22	855,585
Los Lagos	782,734	848,699	953,330	22	1,039,478
Aisén	52,771	66,361	82,071	56	92,214
Magallanes and Chilean Antarctica	94,020	131,914	143,058	52	155,274
Total					14,821,714

Source: INE census, 1999 INE estimate, courtesy Fundación Terram.

ción. Modern industry in Chile resulted largely from import-substitution through World War II, but later expanded considerably into secondary products, heavy industrial products, and capital goods. In the mid 1950s over 70 percent of all manufacturing centered in Santiago (51%) and Valparaíso (20%). Since that time decentralization resulted in the emergence of a major steel and petrochemical complex in Concepción-Talcahuano, at the southern extreme of the central valley. Lumber industries, manufacturing based on processing of agricultural products, textile firms in southern Chile, and limited industrialization in the north, typically based on mineral processing, food production, seafood processing or canning, complement the core industrial establishments of the central region.

At the Biobío River the central valley gives way to the frontier region (see Map 4) (regions VIII and IX after 1974), marked by year-round rainfall. Instead of the central valley's irrigated fields on alluvial fans sloping toward the sea, the cereal and pasture lands of the frontier region still bear the scars of forest clearing, which makes cultivation possible. From Arauco to Cautín, the overgrazed, overutilized land of the Mapuche Indians and other smallholders present a red-brown image of eroded soil on the increasingly denuded coastal mountains and the valley floor. To the east the Andes continue to dominate but are not as high as they are north of the Biobío River. The climate in this region is comparable with the Pacific Northwest of the United States, with stormy wet winters and cool, less damp summers. The region takes its name from the historical role it played in the struggle between the Spanish invaders and the indigenous Indian population. Until late in the nineteenth century the Biobío River marked the limits of Spanish and then Chilean control (see Chapter 2). In a social and economic sense it also remained a frontier region with very limited urban population, agricultural production or industry into the late nineteenth century.

Concepción dominated the development of the frontier provinces from the time of the conquest, serving first as the main base of the frontier garrison and later as the Biobío region's commercial center. Livestock and cereal production, which supplied the raw materials for mills and other processing industries, paced economic development.

Talcahuano is the region's major port and features the country's most important naval shipyards owned by the Navy's ASMAR. Created as an autonomous government agency in 1960, ASMAR also operated smaller and less sophisticated facilities in Valparaíso and Punta Arenas. A joint venture with General Electric Company of England (GEC), SISDEF Ltda. founded in 1983 and located at Viña del Mar has developed various military systems, such as command and control, mission control, fire control systems, and simulators (many listed on the companies' Web site product page). The ASMAR Talcahuano facilities are the most important, offering repair, maintenance and modernization of naval and commercial vessels, specialized armaments, and electronic works. The naval presence in Talcahuano and ASMAR's new initiatives have contributed to the region's growth since the 1980s; it also makes the port city extremely important politically as the government considers control of the seas, economic growth, and civil-military relations.

Mining activities, principally coal, also played a role, and the mines around Lota remained economically important into the 1980s. A traditional bastion of coal mine unions and leftist political parties, Lota and environs suffered the political and economic consequences of the military regime's policies. In the 1997, the deepening of the neoliberal model and the losses accumulated by the government-owned National Coal Enterprise (ENACAR) resulted in the Lota mine's closing, despite strikes and violent protest marches in Santiago. The government announced a redevelopment plan for the region, based in part on a major upgrading of the port, sales of ENACAR properties as industrial condominiums, and public investment in roads, waterworks, and housing. Miners and ex-ENACAR employees received severance pay, pensions, and some retraining, but the immediate impacts of ENACAR's decisions were a combination of bitterness and nostalgia for a "way of life" that was being lost.

In political terms, the government's decision on the Lota mines seemed to ratify the decline of the old political left, the weakness of the labor movement, and the turn to private initiative as the engine of economic growth. The opportunity to modernize the port of Lota was offered to private international bidders and the Lota-ENACAR properties were also put on the auction block. An effort to promote tourism through the coal mines at Lota, under the Pacific Ocean, remained limited to an "adventure excursion" for those willing to be lowered in the iron cage some 120 feet below the surface to begin a claustrophobic, kilometer-long trek to a mine face. The tour, led by ex-miners through the empty shaft, bereft of light except for the battery-powered lamps on the borrowed miners' hats, reminded visitors of the hellacious conditions suffered from the 1840s to the 1990s by generations of coal miners—so vividly described in Baldomero Lillo's short stories, such as "The Devil's Pit" (1904): "Between starving and being crushed by a cave-in, the latter was definitely preferable. It had the advantage of being quick. . . . So they had to submit, to fill the vacancies that this Devil's Pit constantly opened in the files of the weak unfortunates who spent their lives in constant struggle against the adversities of fortune, abandoned by all and against whom any injustice and indignity was permitted."

Agriculture in the frontier region depends much less on irrigation than is the case in the central valley of Chile with its Mediterranean climate. Farms in the frontier provinces accounted for around 40 percent of Chile's wheat production in the mid-1980s—a relative increase since the 1970s—attributable in part to a 40 to 50 percent decline in national wheat output in the period 1976-77/1982-83. The region also contributed some 35 to 40 percent of the country's cattle output, while an often backward timber industry provided seasonal employment for numerous rural workers and raw material for Chile's expanding paper and cellulose manufacturers in the region around the Arauco, La Laja, Nacimiento triangle. Between 1975 and 1994 the forestry sector in Chile grew at an average rate of 6.7 percent/year, faster than agriculture, mining, and industry. Saw wood; pulp; wood chips (*astillas*); finished wood products such as furniture, windows, and doors; paper; particle board and plywood (by 1995 Chile was the largest medium density fiberboard producer in Latin America); and newsprint were the main exports. In 1997 approximately 45 percent of forest exports went to Asian markets, much of them from the port at San Vicente (Talcahuano). Though over 1500 sawmills were in operation, less than ten firms dominated the pulp industry, headed by major transnational companies: Copec, Shell, CMPC, and Attihholtz. The trend toward even further concentration of production and ownership was ongoing, making any snapshot of the industry almost immediately inaccurate. To illustrate, in late 1997: "The Royal Dutch/Shell Group of Companies (Shell) announced the acquisition of interests held by Empresas (CMPC, Companía Manufacturera de Papeles y Cartones, the major firm in the Matte group conglomerate, 19.95%) and Inversiones Citiminera Limitada, ICL (19.95%) in Forestal y Agrícola Monte Aguila S.A. (Monte Aguila), a company of the Santa Fe Group owning and managing Eucalyptus plantations in region VIII. As a result Shell would own 99.97 percent of Monte Aguila while .03 percent would remain with existing shareholders. At the same time, CMPC would acquire from Shell and ICL their respective shareholdings in Forestal e Industrial Santa Fe S.A. (Santa Fe), the Santa Fe Group company owning and managing a Eucalyptus pulp mill in Nacimiento, Chile. As a result, CMPC would become the 100 percent owner of Santa Fe." In addition, a long term wood supply agreement was signed between Monte Aguila and Santa Fe. Thus, like the Chilean national economy and the environmental resources upon which it depended, the Concepción area's regional history was more and more being determined and written amongst large transnational corporations and their local Chilean conglomerate associates (labeled *grupos económicos* in Chile, the major groups in 1997 were Angelini, Matte, Luksic, Yuraszeck, and Said). Expanded hydroelectric capacity installed in the *cordillera* near Lake La Laja to the east of Los Angeles, including plants at El Toro, El Abanico, and the newer facility slightly to the west at Antuco, supported the agroindustrial complex of the region and exported power to the central valley.

In 1989 the Chilean government approved plans for the hydroelectric development of the Biobío River by ENDESA, the privatized electric and resource development company. The river runs through the ancestral lands of the Pehuenche Indians, and the proposed project had massive environmental impacts. ENDESA, relying on the 1982 Electrical Services' Decree Law promulgated by the military government, intended to exercise the right of eminent domain to take the Pehuenche lands. Before 1994 no law existed that required environmental impact statements for even such large-scale projects. ENDESA asked the World Bank Group for financing for six dams, though it argued that the first project, the Pangue dam, was "stand alone" in the event the others were not built. The Chilean government and ENDESA built a road in 1990 from the Pan American highway into the upper Biobío escarpment. Passage of environmental legislation and the Indigenous Peoples Law (1993) gave environmentalists, the Indian peoples, and international human rights activists a new basis for resisting the massive hydroelectric scheme, involving at least six major dams and displacement of hundreds of Indian people.

ENDESA claimed that the 1982 Electrical Services Law took precedence and insisted on the need, first, to build the Ralco dam (upstream from Pangue) and then continue with the rest of the project. In 1996 the National Indigenous Development Commission (CONADI), the agency created by the Indigenous Peoples Law, charged that the EN-

DESA projects violated the law; the Chilean president and his cabinet seemed to support "development," forcing the resignation of CONADI's director. The Pangue dam was completed in 1996, but the World Bank admitted it had erred in supporting the project and that ENDESA had violated the environmental conditions stipulated in the financing agreement. Controversy continued into 1999, with all sides maintaining active international and domestic public relations campaigns.

Environmentalists and some of the affected Pehuenches, with political support from leftist groups and students, engaged in protests, some violent, in efforts to stop the Ralco project. Like many of the massive projects in the desert north, the expansion of the hydroelectric system in the frontier provinces raised numerous political, legal, and environmental issues. In a special report (1998), the Committee for Human Rights of the American Anthropological Association summed up these issues as follows: "[T]he damage to the environment, society, and human rights inflicted by the Pangue-Ralco project has many precedents in World Bank-financed, grand-scale development projects requiring the removal and resettlement of local populations. . . . [The chronic institutional problems] result from the recently intensified emphasis on privatization in development financing associated with economic globalization, and accompanying pressures for the abolition of public control over economic activity." But the rapidly expanding forest, mining, chemical, and fishery industries of the region and the country required more power; almost 75 percent of Chile's electricity was from hydroelectric plants in the late 1990s. Meanwhile, the United States Energy Information Administration lauded Chile in 1997 as "a shining example of how free trade policies and privatization efforts can fuel economic growth."

Fishing and related industries, especially fishmeal, also contribute significantly to the regional economy in the Biobío region, but much less so to the south in Araucanía. In the mid-1990s Talcahuano, Tomé, San Vicente, and Coronel along with other smaller embarkation points shipped over 50 percent of Chile's expanding fishery exports, and lesser shares of shellfish (5–10%) and algaes (10–15%). As in the case of mineral and agricultural products, Chilean seafood and fishmeal exports increasingly went to Asian markets, but shipments also increased to the United States and Europe. Control over exports of the fishery sector, from fishmeal to frozen seafood, also became more and more concentrated in a small number of firms, dominated by the major economic groups and foreign investors.

Also found in the frontier provinces are the remaining communal landholdings (*reducciones*) of the Araucanian (Mapuche) Indians. Deprived of much of their land by the Spanish conquest, and further despoiled by speculators and politicians in the nineteenth century, many Mapuche continue to eke out a livelihood through pastoral, agricultural, and artisan activities. Estimates of the number of Mapuche in the reducciones vary considerably, but there are probably between 300,000 and 500,000. Some reducciones are located in Valdivia, but most are in the provinces of Biobío, Arauco, Malleco, and Cautín—the last alone accounts for almost 200,000 Mapuche. In Cautín the *reducciones* contain some 343,000 hectares, accounting for 22 percent of the agricultural land in the province, and 86 percent of all agricultural units.

The Mapuche on the *reducciones*—or sometimes "ex-reducciones," or *comunidades* without legal title—are family groups that exploit the land, both in common and on individual parcels. Data from an investigation carried out in 1966 by the Dirección de Asuntos Indígenas on 493 *reducciones* indicated that the average reducción amounted to 290 hectares with a population of 83 persons. Economic activity in the reducciones includes fishing and seaweed collection along the coast, lumbering, charcoal making, and extensive production of pigs, sheep, chickens, and cattle, as well as crops. Household manufactures include basketmaking, weaving, and metal working.

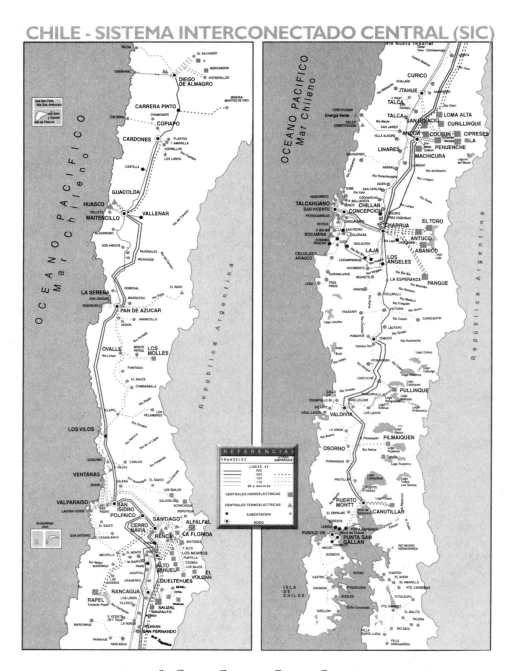

MAP 8: CHILE: CENTRAL POWER GRID, 1997

(*Source*: CDEC-SIC Estadísticas de Operaciones, 1988–1997.)

The Mapuche are a poor people subjugated by outsiders after a four-century struggle to maintain their independence. The bravery of the Mapuche, celebrated in Alonso de Ercilla's epic poem *La Araucana,* may afford a source of national pride for educated Chileans, but the persisting poverty of these Indians seems to have little effect on the national conscience. Chileans adore Indian heroes such as Lautaro and Caupolicán who defeated the conquistadors but, like their North American counterparts, ignore the present-day plight of the Mapuche. One study of the Mapuche in the 1970s concluded: "The Mapuche works his depleted lands and waits. For a long time he has lived . . . in a world not under his control. He has lost his land. . . . He lives exploited, submerged in poverty." From 1965 to 1973 agrarian reform programs mobilized many Mapuche for land occupations or "recuperations." After 1973 the return of land to former owners and repression of organized rural militancy have restored "calm" to the region, but at the cost of the assassinations of Mapuche leaders and the deaths of Indian farmers.

As part of its program to modernize Chilean agriculture and create a national land market, the military government implemented a new law in 1979 promoting subdivision of the Mapuche reservations. At the time this decree-law took effect the government estimated that some 58,000 Indian families controlled 2066 "properties" consisting of a total of 375,500 hectares. To encourage subdivision the government offered property tax exemptions of up to twenty years; by the end of 1982 the government reported that more than 42,000 Mapuches had requested "regularization" of their land titles, and that more than 30,000 had already received title to individual parcels. Systematic studies of the impact of this legislation on the Indian communities remain to be completed, but initial indications suggest that intracommunity conflict and social dislocation have resulted, along with intensified outmigration to towns and urban centers. Many of the Indians work as day laborers on neighboring farms or seasonal hands during peak agricultural periods. Beyond the economic consequences of the subdivision law, however, parcelization of the Indian *reducciones* threatened the cultural foundations of the Mapuche community, based as it was on kinship relations and communal land-tenure patterns. Indicative of the plight of these Indian peoples was the title of a revealing study of the Mapuche published in 1983: "Poverty and Subsistence in Contemporary Mapuche Society." The previously mentioned report by the American Anthropological Association regarding the Pehuenche people in 1998 in the upper Biobío region is illustrative:

> [T]he Pehuenche struggle for economic survival under harsh climatic and economic conditions, maintaining a close attachment to ancestral territories and nature. . . . Access to forest products protects those below the poverty line from becoming indigent and those below the indigence line from starvation. Wood cutting provides the principal source of income for at least 30% of the households. Taking advantage of summer pastures, Pehuenche collect *piñón* (Araucaria pine nuts) which are their primary source of nourishment.

Often little better off than the Mapuche, thousands of campesinos work their small parcels throughout the frontier provinces, barely scratching out a subsistence from depleted soil. During the winter rains long periods of relative idleness are spent around wood-burning stoves in small houses built from the native trees of the region. Larger farms also exist, but they lack the large resident populations previously characteristic of the central valley.

While most of the frontier region is rural and agricultural, more than 70 percent of the population lives in urban places (almost 80% in the Biobío region and more than 60% in the region of Araucanía). Significant industrial activities include Chile's steel industry at Huachipato, textiles, forest industries, including cellulose, paper, and furniture, petrochemicals, seafood, and processing of agricultural products, such as flour, beet sugar, matches, cooking oil, cheese, and butter. Southeast of Concepción, Temuco, the historical capital of "Indian territory," experienced extraordinary growth from the mid-1980s and a construction boom changed the face and the character of a formerly tranquil provincial center. Remodeling of the old rustic central market greatly improved sanitary conditions at the cost of a certain authenticity. The ubiquitous ox and horse carts of the 1960s and 1970s were a much rarer sight in the 1990s. Urban traffic snarls, pedestrian jams on the narrow streets, and industrial and automobile pollution of the air and water made Temuco and environs a part of the Chilean "miracle." Paved roads from Temuco to the coast at Puerto Saavedra replaced the rutted gravel and dirt kidney tortures of the past. Nostalgia aside, this was a great improvement for the entire region's commerce and tourism that also facilitated exploitation of its remaining forests and suburbanization of the countryside in an expanding radius from the regional capital. Although many of the region's indigenous peoples still remained outside the socioeconomic "mainstream" and discrimination against them persisted, the Biobío River no longer separated a "frontier region" (except in name) from the rest of the country. Significant industrial activities of the region include Chile's steel industry at Huachipato, paper and cellulose manufacture, textiles, petrochemicals, and processing of lumber, flour, beet sugar, matches, cooking oil, cheese, and butter.

The lake region—the provinces of Valdivia, Osorno, and Llanquihue—begins south of the Toltén River and is an extension of the frontier provinces (Map 5). Storminess increases as one moves south and is greater, latitude for latitude, in Chile than in North America. Valdivia (lat. 39° 48' S) receives almost three times the annual rainfall of Tacoma, Washington. Founded by Pedro de Valdivia in 1552, the city of Valdivia witnessed one of the most memorable amphibious military operations in South American history when, in 1820, Lord Cochrane led a seemingly suicidal assault against Spanish fortifications to capture the port for the independence movement.

Renowned for its natural beauty, the lake region contains numerous snow-capped volcanoes; the tourists it draws supplement agricultural activities. Valuable natural hardwood forests as well as plantations of pines are the basis for an expanding timber industry. Depletion of the natural forests, however, meant that more of all lumber came from the pine plantations. Dairy farms, beef cattle, and other livestock dominate the agrarian economy, though cereals and diversified small-scale farming also contribute. The lake region supplies much of the country's potatoes, oats, and barley.

Valdivia, Osorno, and Puerto Montt are the most important urban centers in this region, where almost 40 percent of the population still lives in the rural sector. Most of the industries, like that in the frontier provinces, depend upon agrarian production—lumber, wood products, flour mills, textiles, canneries, beer, beet sugar, leather products—or else upon the harvest of the sea. From the remaining native forests and pine plantations of the region comes high quality lumber, while the sea yields a variety of fish and shellfish, thereby supporting a number of canneries and processing plants in Puerto Montt, Chiloe, and Valdivia. In the 1990s the Lake region accounted for almost 50 percent of shellfish exports.

Many industries owe their existence to the influence of German immigrants enticed to Chile in the mid-nineteenth century. When the newly formed Society for Industrial Development (Sociedad de Fomento Fabril, 1883) published a preliminary list of industries in Valdivia and Osorno in 1884, all the breweries, tanneries, brick factories, bakeries, machine shops, furniture manufacturers, and mills (except one) belonged to persons with non-Spanish (mostly German) surnames. While this was the principal region of Chile in which the national government actively intervened to promote colonization in the nineteenth century, the relatively small number of immigrants (perhaps 3000) heavily influenced the economic and cultural development of the provinces from Cautín south, and especially Osorno, Valdivia, and Llanquihue. For example, in 1902 a list of the rural estates in the commune of Valdivia valued at over 40,000 pesos contained not a single Spanish surname. The descendants of these immigrants who cleared dense forest land and prospered through their toil and intellect are still a dominant force in the economy of the lake region.

The territory south from the Gulf of Reloncaví, comprising almost a third of continental Chile, contains no more than 3 percent of the nation's population. This is a region of cold driving winds, great storminess and rainfall, and rough seas. In places rainfall exceeds 200 inches a year. Between Puerto Montt and about latitude 44° S the main structural features of central Chile continue—though the coastal mountain range now runs partly beneath the sea or becomes a chain of forested islands. The snowfall in the eastern cordillera descends to only 2300 feet above sea level at Tierra del Fuego.

The island of Chiloé (lat. 42° S), in a geographical position similar to Vancouver Island in North America, is a forested territory where smallholders and a small number of indigenous peoples engage in subsistence agriculture, sheep raising, lumbering, fishing, and potato cultivation. Chiloé makes no great economic contribution to the national economy, although shellfish and salmon aquaculture took off in the 1990s. Its main towns are Ancud and Castro.

Aisén province is made up of canals, lakes, islands, and mountains, though grasslands and plains support thousands of sheep. Aysén, along with Magallanes, is Chile's last frontier. Punta Arenas, located on the Strait of Magellan, is Chile's most southerly city (pop. 107,000 [1985]). It supports a number of industries based on the thousands of sheep raised on the Patagonian plains. Oil wells and natural gas exploration have increased the economic importance of Magallanes in recent years. Most of the petroleum is shipped to Concón, near Valparaíso, or to Concepción for refining, though a topping plant at Manantiales, where the first wells were exploited in 1945, supplies Magallanes with gasoline, kerosene, and diesel fuel.

In the early 1980s oil wells in the Strait of Magellan accounted for over 70 percent of total output. New oil production in the years after 1980, combined with expanded coal production, made possible by exploration and investment by foreign firms, allowed Chile to cover approximately 50 percent of its hydrocarbon requirements. Development of new coal mines in the Peckett deposits, 36 miles northeast of Punta Arenas, promised to alleviate to some degree Chile's deficit of fossil fuels, with output destined to a great extent for the thermoelectric plant at Tocopilla. After 1992 the Compañía de Carbones de Magallanes, S.A., an affiliate of COCAR, S.A., which had begun production in 1987, exploited the Peckett coal deposit with open-pit technology and produced around 1 million tons a year. In 1997 underground methods were introduced in hopes of improving output to satisfy the country's thermoelectric appetite at Tocopilla, Mejillones, Patache, and elsewhere. Increased production and exports of natural gas along with large-scale foreign investment in the Cape Horn Methanol plant near Punta Arenas also gave increasing importance to Magallanes in the national economy. Nevertheless, Chile still imported annually between $500 million and $980 million worth of fuel—the equivalent in value to 25 to 40 percent of the value of copper exports (1980–85). In the next decade Chile's oil demand more than doubled, and crude oil production declined by two-thirds. Oil imports increased significantly, from Argentina, Nigeria, Ecuador, Venezuela, and Angola. Sipetrol, S.A., an affiliate of the National Petroleum Company (ENAP) operating in the Argentine Patagonia, provided much of the Argentine crude; the other major Argentine contribution came from the Transandean Oil Pipeline running from Neuquén, Argentina, to Talcahuano. The country's major refineries, operated by ENAP at ConCon (RPC), Talcahuano (Petrox), and Magallanes imported over 90 percent of their crude oil, a major item in the country's international trade and balance of payments, ranging from 800 million to 1.2 billion dollars annually from 1990 to 1999. Offshore exploration continued, both in the Magallanes region and in the far north; additional Methanol plants were planned near Punta Arenas.

The vast majority of Chileans descend from the European invaders of the sixteenth and seventeenth centuries and the Indian peoples resident in Chile at the time of Spanish conquest. Africans and non-Iberian Europeans contributed much less to the formation of the Chilean nationality. As elsewhere in Spanish America, Spanish racism and social prejudices have generally reserved the highest social and political positions for those who claimed "purity of blood" (*limpieza de sangre*), thereby creating caste-class stratifications that distinguished Spaniards from "white" mestizos, "Indian" mestizos, Indians, blacks, mulattoes, and *zambos* (offspring of Indian and black). From generation to generation stratification could become quite complex within the *castas* (racially mixed peoples), but customs and legal practices sought to ensure the "integrity" of the ruling class, especially after the massive miscegenation of the sixteenth and seventeenth centuries.

Legal suits filed in the late eighteenth century by family members who feared that a proposed marriage might put a stain on the family honor reveal the fundamental racial and social biases of colonial society. Royal officials were asked to prohibit marriages on the legal grounds of "inequality of castes." An irate mother could "charge" a would-be son-in-law with being the grandson and great-grandson of blacks, "mulatto-colored," or "a pure mulatto" with "obviously Negro hair." While official Spanish policy declared that "being an Indian is not a rational or just motive for denial of parental consent," Chilean colonists looked with disfavor upon "staining the family honor" with marriage to Indians or "Indian mestizos." But these attitudes no more prevented widespread concubinage and miscegenation in the later colonial period than they had in the formation of Chilean nationality in the *mestizaje* of the first century and a half of conquest.

While Chilean national mythology claims descendancy from Spaniards and Araucanians, the Indian component of Chilean racial stock was somewhat more varied than this simple union of the heroic Araucanian Indians with their European enemies. About the indigenous population in Chile at the time of the conquest much less is known than about the Indians of Mexico, Central America, and Peru. Some investigators believe all originated in a single racial stock, differentiated in customs, language, and organization over time in response to local conditions. Other researchers affirm the diversity of the indigenous groups in Chile, noting differences in language, culture, farming implements, weapons, and political organization. The nomenclature adopted to describe Indian groups often referred merely to their location—for example, *puelches* (people of the east, eastern *cordillera* down to Mendoza); *picunches* (people of the north—though those south of the *puelches* called them *picunches*). Less gradually the Spaniards came to refer to *los pencos, los quillotanos, los mapochos,* and so on, but again these names simply denote Indians of Penco, Quillota, and Mapocho.

As there are neither important archaeological sites south of Copiapó, nor a written language, nor any large territorial political units, we are unlikely to have any great clarification of the evolution of pre-Hispanic Indian cultures in Chile except in the north, where the desert has preserved artifacts and cemeteries thousands of years old. Conventional designations of major Indian groups in Chile at the time of the conquest depend upon the work of a limited number of scholars, most notably Ricardo Latcham. Latcham adopted the generic terms *Diaguitas* (valley of Copiapó to the Choapa River), Mapuche or Araucanian (Itata River to Toltén River), and *Huilliches* (south of Toltén River). In reality no such clear-cut divisions are possible since Araucanian is an independent linguistic family, and each region or tribal group in Chile apparently had only small differences of dialect. The authoritative *Handbook of South American Indians* divides the Araucanians into the following main groups: Picunche, Mapuche, Huilliche, and Cunco (west of the Andes), Pehuenche (Andean Highlands), Argentine Araucanians (east of the Andes). New research by Guillaume Boccara (1999) and others on the response of native Indian peoples in Chile to the Spanish conquest suggests that the term *mapuche* only came to be commonly used after the mid-eighteenth century and that before that time it was more appropriate to use the term *reche* (*hombre auténtico o verdadero*, the "authentic or true man") to refer to the native peoples between the Itata and Toltén rivers. Use of "Araucanians" refers indiscriminately to the native peoples living in the territory of Arauco and does not include other native peoples. Present-day usage in Chile refers to the major Indian groups south of the River Itata as Araucanos or, more frequently, simply Mapuche. Estimates of the Araucanian population at the time of the Spanish conquest range from 500,000 to 1,500,000. According to the 1992 census, "Araucanians" or "Mapuches" numbered over 900,000, making them by far the largest ethnic minority in the country (although many people identified as Mapuche in the census were, biologically, mestizos), followed by main Indian groups in the far north: Aymaras, Quechuas, Atacameños, and Kollas. The National Indigenous Development Commission (CONADI), created in 1993 by the government of President Patricio Aylwin, estimated that these groups together numbered perhaps 100,000 people in the late 1990s. Handfuls of other native peoples, such as the Kawashkar (less than one hundred) and the Yaganes (less than fifty), still "survived" in the Canal zone to the south and around the Strait of Magellan. The other major ethnic group recognized by the CONADI is the native people of Rapa Nui, Chile's Pacific Island territory.

Prior to the arrival of the Spanish, Inca influence and tribute collection extended as far south as the Itata River or perhaps the Biobío River, but gradually diminished toward the south. Despite initial resistance and occasional revolts, by the mid-seventeenth century the Spaniards had pacified, enslaved, or exploited most of the Indian groups north of the Maule River, exacting tribute and recruiting military auxiliaries, as had the Incas. From the River Maule south and into what became the frontier provinces (south of the Biobío River), the Araucanians effectively resisted Spanish domination, as they had that of the Incas. By 1568 the Araucanians were making significant use of cavalry in battle against the Spaniards, and well before the end of the sixteenth century they had adopted Spanish firearms, swords, armor, and any other armaments they could capture. By 1600 the Indian stock of horses, estimated at over 10,000, greatly exceeded the horses available to the Spanish settlers and frontier garrisons. Though a simple people with limited handicrafts, a subsistence agriculture, and highly dispersed settlement patterns with no centralized political authority, the Araucanians developed a complex system for organizing large-scale military forces to defend their territory. Indeed, their very dispersion and lack of centralized political structure made virtually impossible either a definitive "victory" or the administration of a Spanish conquest on a scale like that of Peru.

Though they attained no definitive military victory, the Spanish did subjugate thousands of Indians to work in mines, fields, or households. In addition, many Spaniards transferred "their" Indians (Huarpes) from Cuyo (including the towns of present-day Mendoza, San Juan, and San Luis in Argentina) to Santiago or La Serena. Miscegenation and the gradual reduction in the number of "pacified" Indians meant that by the mid-seventeenth century *mestizos* constituted a majority of the rural population. Population data on Chile in the colonial period must be viewed with great caution since contemporary writers provided widely disparate estimates. Chilean historian Francisco Encina estimated that at the end of the seventeenth century the population of Chile, north of the Biobío River, consisted of 110,000 Spanish and "mestizos classified as such," 20,000 Indians and "Indian" mestizos, 15,000 blacks, mulattoes and *zambos*, and 7000 pacified Indians in Chiloé. Most Chileans lived in rural districts on the vast haciendas or encomiendas. According to the educated estimate of Chilean researcher Rolando Mellafe, as early as 1620 "white" mestizos already outnumbered European and *criollo* settlers by a ratio of some four to one.

As in the rest of Spanish America, the total population of Chile was substantially reduced due to the effects of the conquest on the native peoples. Mortality among the Spaniards was also high; at the close of the sixteenth century 20 to 25 percent of the Spanish population were killed in the Indian uprising which liquidated eight of the twelve "cities" then in existence. Disease and natural disasters, including earthquakes and floods, also contributed to the losses. Only in the mid-nineteenth century (1843) did the population of Chile (including the unconquered Indians south of the Biobío River) approximate what it had been in 1540—about one million! Of these, historian Luis Galdames has estimated that no more than 40 percent were of European descent and the remainder were Indian and *castas*, including several thousand Negro slaves.

From the outset the towns were the centers of European civilization in Chile, but none could really be called cities until the eighteenth century. Near the end of the colonial period (1810), Chile contained thirty or more so-called cities; Santiago had some 40,000 inhabitants, and the next largest town, Concepción, some 5000 to 6000. Increasingly, however, the population of Chile moved to towns and cities, so that by 1875 over 25 percent of the population could be found in "urban" places; by 1907 this had increased to 43 percent. According to official estimates in the mid-1990s, approximately 85 percent of all Chileans lived in urban areas.

Unlike Argentina and Brazil, Chilean population growth in the nineteenth and twentieth centuries depended little upon the waves of European immigration that also greatly changed the composition of the United States's population during these years. In 1895 only 2.9 percent of Chile's 2,687,985 inhabitants were foreign born, and in 1907 this had increased but to 4 percent of a total population of 3,114,755. While by the early 1900s hundreds of thousands of Italians had become agricultural laborers or tenant farmers or had settled in urban areas in Argentina, from 1889 until 1914 total net immigration to Chile reached only about 55,000. The largest foreign contingents arrived from Peru, Bolivia, and Spain. Despite their small numbers, however, European immigrants owned nearly one-third of Chile's commercial companies (1907), 20 percent of the 554 most valuable rural estates (1908), and, by 1914, 49 percent of all industrial establishments. European, Syrian, and Lebanese immigrants to Chile rarely became rural laborers or urban workers, as in Argentina, but instead formed an upper-middle-class commercial element which often intermarried with Chilean social elites.

The role of the immigrants was most apparent in the mining districts of the north, in the major cities of Antofagasta, Santiago, Valparaíso, Concepción, and Valdivia, and in the farming regions of the south, heavily influenced by Germans. The immigrants' role in Chilean urban society continued into the 1960s, when estimates indicated that three-fourths of Santiago's major industrial establishments were owned by immigrants or their offspring. Emigration to Chile, consequently, little affected the race and class stratifications that grew out of the miscegenation and politics of conquest, and only served to insert a small, heterogeneous, non-Hispanic, upper- and upper-middle-class group

A *huaso* on horseback, 1953.
(Courtesy of Archivo
Universidad de Chile.)

Campesino and ox-team,
Central Valley, 1952.
(Courtesy of Archivo
Universidad de Chile.)

TABLE 1–14. ESTIMATED POPULATION OF CHILE, JUNE 30, 1998
(RURAL AND URBAN DISTRIBUTION AND DISTRIBUTION BY SEX AND REGION)

Region	Male			Female		
	Total	Urban	Rural	Total	Urban	Rural
Total	7,336,118	6,153,975	1,182,143	7,485,596	6,469,084	1,016,512
Tarapacá	196,806	184,698	12,108	189,420	181,247	8173
Antofagasta	231,500	221,198	10,302	224,583	221,005	3578
Atacama	136,058	120,731	15,327	128,406	119,774	8632
Coquimbo	279,244	199,229	80,015	282,421	211,306	71,115
Valparaíso	746,221	676,124	70,097	779,273	717,411	61,862
Libertador General B. O'Higgins	390,564	255,357	135,207	378,099	259,445	118,654
Maule	453,546	273,805	179,741	444,872	288,158	156,714
Biobío	944,228	741,473	202,755	950,932	772,898	178,034
Araucanía	429,233	270,489	158,744	426,352	286,765	139,587
Los Lagos	524,910	329,742	195,168	514,568	343,360	171,208
Aisén	48,361	34,091	14,270	43,853	34,370	9,483
Magallanes and Antarctic	82,050	73,388	8,662	73,224	69,658	3566
Santiago metropolitan region	2,873,397	2,773,650	99,747	3,049,593	2,963,687	85,906

Source: INE, Compendio Estadístico, 1998: 85.

between the upper castes of Hispanic society and the mass of Indian, mestizo, and *casta* laborers in the fields, mines, docks, and factories.

Class and caste stratifications have also produced certain Chilean stereotypes which serve both as national symbols and pejorative epithets, particularly the *roto* and the *huaso*. The huaso is the Chilean cowboy but connotes much more. The flesh and blood huaso is a campesino on horseback or in the fields, who, before the 1970s, worked from sunup to sundown, frequently barefoot or in crude sandals called *ojotas,* and wearing an apron or a flour sack around his waist. When not at work he sported a jacket inherited from his father or older brother and a well-worn hat. There is also the tourist's huaso, dressed for the rodeo in a three-colored *manta* and a sash around his waist (red, white, and blue like the Chilean flag). He rides a strong, well-kept horse which he prods with silver spurs. This was the hacendado, or his hireling, dressed in his best huaso outfit to visit the countryside at the harvest or to make sure the campesinos attend to their labors. The first huaso, the rural worker, bears the brunt of hundreds of country bumpkin jokes. The latter, the postcard huaso, typifies the historic rural basis of the wealth and power of many of Chile's leading families. Together they are the story of Chile—a national symbol which denotes hard work, sacrifice, and struggle to the campesino, and power, leisure, and privilege to the hacendado.

The *roto* is the urban counterpart of the huaso. The roto is the Chilean worker, courageous, strong, persistent, quick to take advantage of a favorable opportunity (*Vivo!*). But *roto* also means "broken one." The command ¡No sea roto! lets one know that he is lacking in social graces, that his behavior is out of line. Perhaps only the typically southern Chilean insult ¡No sea indio! ("don't act like an Indian") is as denigrating a way to put someone "in his place" as to call him roto. Yet used among family and friends, with the right tone of voice, with the appropriate adjective—*roto choro*—roto becomes a compliment, even a sign of affection.

El roto chileno, Central Market, circa 1960. (Courtesy of Archivo Universidad de Chile.)

Chilean Congress, 1961. (Courtesy of Archivo Universidad de Chile.)

Joaquín Edwards Bello, a leading twentieth-century Chilean novelist, published *El Roto Chileno* just after World War I. It depicts the underworld of Santiago society—the brothel, the gambling den, the police station . . . the Senate. There was a bit of the roto at all levels of Chilean society, but while the working-class roto languished in prison or died in the streets, the upper-class roto, the Senator and his collaborators at the police station, lived the good life. Edwards Bello's *El Roto* makes clear that the good life of these latter depended upon the exploitation and suffering of the former. Like the huaso then, the roto is a complex symbol of *chilenidad* ("Chilean nationality") which signifies both the misery of the poverty-stricken worker and the *viveza* ("opportunism") of those who benefit from the sweat of his toil.

Since the conquest this tension between the powerful minority and the vast majority of the territory's population has been at the core of Chilean history. The most recent chapters of this story saw the breakdown of the country's much-celebrated "democracy," almost seventeen years of military dictatorship, and return to civilian government in 1990. At the beginning of the third millennium, Chile sought to find finally a balance between its authoritarian legacy and its urge for social justice and political democracy, to reconcile not only the antagonists of the recent past, but also almost five centuries of exploitation of land, resources, and peoples for the benefit of the ruling minorities.

2 The Politics of Conquest

In the sixteenth century Spanish soldiers, ecclesiastics, and administrators created a vast colonial empire in North and South America. Moving from their initial bases in the Caribbean—Haiti, Santo Domingo, Cuba—the Spanish and their Indian allies conquered and despoiled the major indigenous civilizations of Mexico, Central America, and the west coast of South America. In the name of the monarchy and the Church they sought to Christianize the native peoples of America while exploiting their labor in the mines and on the land of the "new world" they called *las indias*. Shiploads of treasure came back to the Iberian peninsula as the Spanish exacted tribute from the new subjects of the king of Spain. After each new conquest, groups of Spaniards who failed to make their fortunes, or who lost the booty acquired, or who dreamed of obtaining even greater wealth and power in new expeditions, sought to extend the empire still farther to as yet unknown lands. From Cuba to Mexico, to Central America, and then to Peru, the Spanish conquistadors reaped the spoils of the conquest as rewards for their daring and their brutality.

As a political and economic venture the Spanish conquest initially combined national-imperial aggrandizement with a semi-feudal form of private enterprise. Individual conquistadors raised armies and financed their own expeditions by authority of the Spanish monarch. In exchange for authorization to collect tribute from the subjugated natives, to operate mines, to use the land for crops or livestock, or to engage in commerce, the king claimed for the royal coffers a share of all the spoils of conquest and of the production of colonial enterprises. In Mexico, Peru, and parts of Central America booty from the accumulated wealth of sophisticated indigenous civilizations constituted a source of quick fortunes for the first Spanish expeditions. Afterward, however, the accumulation of wealth and capital depended upon large-scale exploitation of labor in mining, agriculture, and commercial enterprises.

Social attitudes of fifteenth- and sixteenth-century Spain reserved manual labor and even craftsmanship to the "lower orders." As the Spanish invaders had no intention of working either the mines or the land themselves, this made control over or access to Indian laborers critical for any productive endeavor. The Indians had no tradition of daily work obligations and, still less, of contractual or wage labor. But the success of conquest as an economic enterprise turned upon somehow mobilizing Indian labor or importing African slaves to work the mines, tend livestock, and cultivate the land. Consequently, despite the flow of bullion and commodities from the colonies into intercolonial and international markets, and the predominance of "private" enterprise in the conquest economy, the earliest modes of production in Spanish America, including Chile, were less capitalistic (in the sense of relying upon wage labor) than they were bastardized or transitional forms of feudal labor dues, fixed-term labor contracts for "indentured" servants (*asientos de trabajo*), forced labor, or slavery.

Over time Spain created an elaborate administrative apparatus to direct the conquest and the government of *las indias*. All authority emanated from the Spanish monarch who claimed a divine right to rule. From 1524 the crown governed the new territories through the Supreme Council of the Indies, which began as a handful of officials and expanded to about twenty under the Hapsburg monarchs. The Council of the Indies legislated for the colonies and supervised administration. The royal *patronato* extended by the Pope granted the Spanish kings the right to name religious functionaries in the New World, thereby extending the authority of the Council of the Indies to matters of religious concern.

In practice the great distances between Spain and the New World left daily or, more accurately, yearly governance of the colonies in the hands of appointed officials. To govern the largest administrative units, the viceroyalties, the king named viceroys, and to lesser territories, captains-general or governors. In addition, a royal judicial council or *audiencia*, composed of judges called *oidores*, and ecclesiastical authorities shared and to some extent checked the power of viceroy or governor. Local officers responsible to the viceroy or governor—or, in their absence, to the *audiencia*—governed smaller jurisdictions or Indian districts. In the towns and cities, municipal councils called *cabildos* legislated and administered regulations of local concern, including fixing prices of commodities, granting licenses to engage in business, and regulating the activity of artisans. Wealthy colonial-born Spaniards (*criollos*) tended to dominate the *cabildos*, while the higher administrative posts usually were reserved for native-born Spaniards or *peninsulares*. Some peninsular officials, however, established local roots, founded prominent *criollo* families, and acquired interests that conflicted with their bureaucratic duties. From the late seventeenth century onward, sale of offices to *criollos* accentuated tensions between royal policies and their implementation in the colonies. Moreover, in some cases the cabildos sought to extend their authority and frequently found themselves in conflict with royal officials. Eventually the cabildos would become a rallying point for independence movements in the nineteenth century.

On paper the government of the empire resembled a strictly hierarchical, neatly arranged chain of command. In reality overlapping authority and conflict between the Council of the Indies, viceroys, governors, ecclesiastical officials, and the cabildos made for continual bureaucratic maneuvering, evasion of royal decrees, and corruption. Though justified by the "donation" to the Spanish monarchy of most of the so-called New World by Pope Alexander VI—in his role as Vicar of Christ—in order to expand the realm of Christendom, the Spanish conquest gave rise to numerous doctrinal and theological conflicts over appropriate treatment of the indigenous peoples. Did the Indians have souls? Could they achieve salvation? If so, could they be forced to accept Christianity, or should conversion be accomplished only through persuasion? Could the Indians be enslaved? Could they be forced to pay tribute? If so, could tribute take the form of forced labor? Everywhere in Spanish America, Church officials and theoreticians debated these questions. In every colony and administrative sub-unit the conquistadors and those who came after them resisted efforts by royal officials and certain churchmen to regulate the exploitation of the conquered peoples. Nowhere did the idealism of the reformers effectively prevent the abuse and eventual decimation of the Native American peoples, as economic realities won out over spiritual and humanitarian objections to the exploitation of Indian labor.

By the time Pedro de Valdivia undertook the conquest of Chile (1540) the formal resolution of numerous doctrinal questions had already resulted in official policies prohibiting many of the early abuses of the Indian peoples. For example, a decree signed by Charles V in 1528 prohibited enslavement of the Indians as well as the widespread practice of using the Indians as pack animals or for other "personal services." It also required that the conquerors provide Indians laboring in the mines with religious instruction, including Mass on Sundays and feast days. Later ordinances outlawed the removal of Indians from cold climates to work in hot climates, and vice versa, as well as the "renting out" of Indians by those commended to supervise their care and religious instruction. But the Spanish colonials evaded or violated these restrictions and the hundreds of others adopted in the protolabor codes contained in the royal decrees and ordinances that regulated taxation or tribute paid by the Indians to Spanish officials. Thus, the history of the Spanish conquest in Chile and elsewhere must be seen on three levels: Church doctrine and official policy, administrative implementation or non-implementation, and the reality of everyday life—or death—for the native population.

As a primary institution of conquest and colonial economy in Chile as throughout the Spanish empire, the *encomienda,* with all its variations, illustrates the tremendous gap between Church doctrine or official policy and its implementation upon the subjugated peoples of America. As a reward for military service, and with the obligation to provide for Christianization of the Indians, the crown or its representative "commended" the care of groups of Indians for a specified time—for example, two or three generations—to selected Spaniards and their heirs. The crown insisted that the Indians were free peoples, not to be enslaved except as punishment for rebellion or for resisting Spanish authority. As free vassals, however, the Indians were subject to tribute or taxation. This gave rise to the questions of the form of the tribute and how it could be collected. Concessionary, rather than proprietary, rights to Indian tribute or labor provided incentives to exact *quickly* whatever profits could be made from Indian labor. A new governor might give the encomienda to someone else; a court proceeding could alter the terms of the grant; a new decree might effectively limit the tribute or restrict forced labor. Quick profits through intensive exploitation of the labor force became the main endeavor of individual conquistadors.

A year after the foundation of Chile's first settlement at Santiago in 1541, the New Laws, issued by the Spanish king to control the ambitions of the encomenderos in the American dominions, prohibited enslavement of Indians even as punishment. They also forbade the granting of new encomiendas and ordered ecclesiastics and royal officials to give up any encomiendas they held. Existing encomiendas could be retained but not passed on to heirs; tribute was to be strictly fixed and regulated by crown officials to avoid abuses by the encomenderos. The encomenderos rebelled against these laws in Peru and other parts of the empire, defending the spoils of conquest. Although the crown partially repealed these laws, it subsequently enacted a succession of legal codes and ordinances that specifically defined the obligations of encomenderos and limited demands upon the Indians.

The history of Chile for its first two centuries as a Spanish colony centered upon the implacable resistance of the encomenderos to regulation of their exploitation of the native Chilean peoples and the never-ending struggle of these peoples to maintain their freedom against the Spanish invaders. This struggle shaped the social and economic structure of colonial Chile and its development within the Spanish Empire. Formation of the Chilean ethnic stock, race relations, social stratification, and economic development depended upon the ebb and flow of warfare. No other Amerindian peoples resisted Spanish conquest as did the Araucanians, although many groups partially submitted to mestization, evangelization, and acculturation. No other Spanish colony drained the royal treasury and expended the lives of thousands of Spanish and mestizo troops for more than two centuries after initial contact with indigenous peoples. Nowhere else in the Spanish Empire did warfare or the threat of warfare so significantly shape the development of the colonial economy or influence the fate of Spanish towns. Only in Chile did pillage and slave raids, or *malocas,* constitute an important source of wealth for colonial administrators and military personnel into the mid-seventeenth century. In Chile alone among the South American colonies did provisioning a standing army become a principal stimulus to colonial production and internal commerce, buttressed continually by a military subsidy, the *situado*, from Peru and Spain.

Recurrent warfare and the periodic destruction of Spanish settlements gave a unique character to the Chilean colony. Plunder, illegal trade with the Indians, slave raids, and profiteering from the military budget provided unique opportunities for social and economic mobility, at the same time that the risks of an uprising or reprisal raid made economic enterprises in the southern regions insecure. The insecurity of the southern territory encouraged concentration of the Spanish population in the central valley, thereby promoting the development of a relatively homogeneous, geographically integrated society to the north of the Maule River.

Episodic warfare also perpetuated Indian slave labor and the encomiendas in Chile long after these institutions had declined in most of Spanish America. In contrast to the more established colonies, Chilean military leaders and soldiers in the seventeenth and eighteenth centuries could still obtain booty, privileges, and rewards from the king for their efforts to subjugate the indigenous population. In a sense, the prolonged resort to violence as a means of acquiring fame, position, and wealth made physical brutality and coercion an integral part of daily life on the Chilean frontier among Spaniards, mestizos, Indian allies, and enemies. This coercion, or threat of coercion, carried over into the encomiendas and haciendas and became the principal mechanism governing relations between the workers and their masters. The inability to enforce the royal decrees regulating these relationships merely added disrespect for law, evasion, and cynicism to the other legacies of the Chilean colonial experience.

Spanish religious and government authorities periodically negotiated peace treaties with Indian leaders in what became a ritualized system of conferences (*parlamentos*) and peace accords (*paces*), followed by breaches of the agreements and renewed conflict. From the peace agreements promoted by the Marquis de Baides and the treaty at Quillín (1641) that recognized Mapuche sovereignty beyond the Biobío River, Spanish and Indian leaders repeatedly warred and reached truces, but never resolved the underlying antagonisms. The Spanish desired to enforce the Indians' subjugation to royal authority, to concentrate the Indian population in villages, to end polygamy, to convert the Indians to Catholicism, to have access to Indian labor, to secure Indian collaboration against other European invaders and pirates, and to obtain the return of Spanish prisoners and hostages, especially women, whom the Indians incorporated into the system of polygamy, and "Christian" Indians (thus taking women and children from the Indian communities). They also attempted to force the Indians to recognize Spanish jurisdiction over "wrongdoers."

The Indians, for their part, wanted to maintain their land, freedom, and cultural autonomy and to end slavery and forced labor, in exchange for allowing the Spanish priests to evangelize. They offered to end raids against Spanish farms and towns and permit a loose system of frontier commerce. From 1641 the provisions (*capitulaciones*) of the peace agreements detailed the reciprocal obligations of Spaniards and Indians. Intermittent conflicts and occasional major insurrections (1655, 1723) resulted in important *parlamentos* and *paces* in 1647, 1651, 1738, 1756, 1760, 1764, and 1767. In 1767 the Spanish agreed that the Indians were "not obligated to live in villages and would be left in the tranquil possession of their lands." Renewed conflict led to another major *parlamento* in 1794.

The conquest of Chile was an extension of the Spanish victory, led by Francisco Pizarro and Diego de Almagro, over the Inca empire in Peru. In 1534 the Spanish crown divided the land south of Ecuador into four political units (*gobernaciones*): Nueva Castilla, assigned to Pizarro; Nueva Toledo, 200 leagues from Ica to latitude 25° 31' S, assigned to Almagro; and two others assigned to Pedro de Mendoza and Simón de Alcazaba. Mendoza sold his claim to Almagro, and Alcazaba led a disastrous expedition, which was to go by sea to the Strait of Magellan and from there overland to the north but only reached Puerto de los Leones on the east coast. Almagro contested Pizarro's control of Cuzco but agreed to lead an expedition south to explore the rest of Nueva Toledo while awaiting the king's resolution of the conflicting claims.

The Peruvian Indians, who were plotting a rebellion against the conquering Spaniards, had told exaggerated tales of the wealth of the land to the south. These tales, along with Pizarro's prodding, had persuaded Almagro. In organizing the expedition to Chile, he rapidly depleted the fortune he had acquired in the Peruvian conquest. He assembled a force of more than five hundred Spaniards (almost half cavalry)—a larger army than Cortés had led into Mexico or Pizarro into Peru. Many of these Spaniards had participated in earlier expeditions to Mexico, Guatemala, and, of course, Peru. According to various estimates, 10,000 to 15,000 Indian auxiliaries and a small number of Negro slaves accompanied the Spaniards on the first expedition to Chile.

After sending out advance parties—including Inca emissaries to collect tribute from the Indian subjects to the south—as well as some forces by sea, Almagro left Cuzco in July 1535. The main expeditionary force, more than two hundred Spaniards and thousands of Indian auxiliaries, crossed the Bolivian plateau through the Andes range bordering Lake Titicaca. After much privation the expedition reached Tupiza, where it rested for about two months. Here Almagro received a message informing him of the arrival in Cuzco of an emissary from Spain authorized to settle the dispute with Pizarro. The message urged Almagro to return to Cuzco to defend his interests, but he decided to go on to Chile. He led his forces on to Chicoana, near the present Argentine city of Salta; there they encountered hostile Indians while reprovisioning themselves and preparing for the Andes crossing.

Upon leaving Chicoana, many of the Indian bearers fled. Rivers flooded from the melting snow, and summer rains drowned numerous llamas, used as pack animals, and destroyed provisions, so food had to be rationed. Almagro's force crossed the Campo del Arenal desert and pushed into the cordillera at the San Francisco pass. In this part of the cordillera the Andes average more than 13,000 feet. There was no pasture for the animals, and often no firewood could be found. *Soroche* or *puna*—a condition of nausea, headaches, and sometimes convulsions produced by the altitude—and frostbite added to the misery of the expedition. Many of the scantily clad Indians froze to death, as did horses—to be "defrosted" and eaten five months later by other Spaniards coming to join Almagro in Chile.

Almagro's forces stayed in Chile until the end of 1536, exploring as far south as the Maule River or perhaps the Itata. Periodic skirmishes with hostile Indians, as well as the Indians' strategy of hiding food and possessions, hindered Almagro's efforts to establish control. Exploratory expeditions found no gold, no silver, no cities. Failure to find a new Peru, combined with news that Cuzco apparently fell into the jurisdiction of Nueva Toledo, persuaded Almagro and his lieutenants to return to Peru. At the end of 1536 they joined forces at Copiapó, and then crossed the desert in small groups, from water hole to water hole, as a ship followed them up the coast.

Upon arrival in Peru, Almagro found the Indians in rebellion and Cuzco under control of Pizarro's brothers. Almagro liberated the city but proved unable to resolve the conflict with the Pizarros. Civil war ensued. At the battle of Las Salinas in 1538, Almagro was taken prisoner and executed by the Pizarros.

The tales of Almagro's men discouraged further expeditions to Chile for nearly five

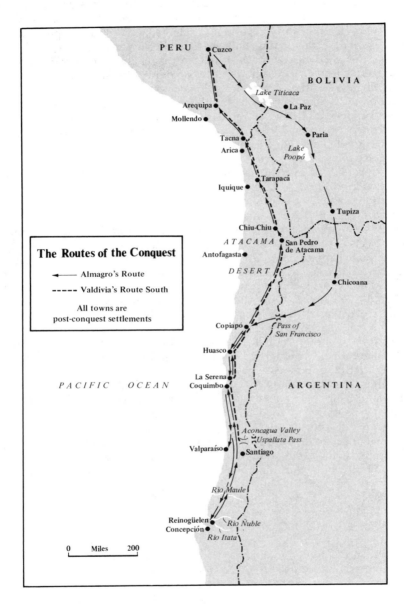

MAP 9: THE ROUTES OF THE CONQUEST

(*Source:* H. R. S. Pocock, *The Conquest of Chile,* Stein and Day, New York, 1967.)

years. As Chilean historian Diego Barros Arana wrote, "After the return of Almagro this country [Chile] was the most discredited of the Indies in the minds of the conquistadors . . . a cursed land without gold . . . inhabited by savages of the worst kind and incapable of repaying the costs occasioned by the conquest." The failure of Almagro's expedition also meant that Chile's Indians could not again be surprised or intimidated. They now knew that the Spanish were human, not gods, that they could be barbaric and treacherous, and that their horses could be killed or captured.

It therefore came as somewhat of a surprise to the Spanish elite in Peru when the commander of Pizarro's forces at the battle of Las Salinas, Pedro de Valdivia, gave up his valuable encomienda and a silver mine at Porco in exchange for permission to explore and conquer Chile. Valdivia's motivation cannot be known with certainty, but it seems clear that it went beyond mere wealth, as he sacrificed an immense fortune to organize his Chilean expedition.

In 1540 Valdivia left Cuzco with a few Spanish soldiers (from 5 to 20 according to various estimates), his mistress, Inés de Suárez, and perhaps a thousand Indian auxiliaries. Along the way from Cuzco to Arequipa other Spaniards joined him, among them some former members of the Almagro expedition. At Tarapacá, Valdivia waited for reinforcements, but when the army set out across the Atacama desert, it numbered fewer than 110 Spaniards including two priests. After eleven months of hardship, skirmishes with Indians, and internal conflicts Valdivia's forces arrived in the valley of the Mapocho. Almost immediately they were attacked by an Indian army led by the local chief Michimalonco. The Spaniards eventually drove off the Indian warriors and soon thereafter convinced the local Indians to aid in the construction of Chile's first "city"— Santiago—founded in February 1541. Less than a month later Valdivia created a cabildo, which, in turn, called upon Valdivia to make himself governor of Chile in the name of the king of Spain rather than as Pizarro's lieutenant. After appropriate objections Valdivia acquiesced. Seven months later (September 11, 1541) the Indians of the region attacked Santiago, burned the straw-roofed houses to the ground, and left the Spaniards little more than grain for seed and some livestock. The battle for Chile had begun in earnest.

From 1541 until 1553, Valdivia's forces pushed south from Santiago, warring against the Indians and establishing a number of fort towns. These included Concepción, La Imperial (at the site of present-day Carahue), Valdivia, and Villarrica. In addition, on the other side of the Andes, Francisco de Aguirre governed Santiago del Estero. With the foundation of each "city," Valdivia handed out encomiendas to selected conquistadors, thereby granting them authority to collect tribute from the Indians in their jurisdiction and take charge of the Indians' Christianization. Since the Chilean Indians had little accumulated wealth, tribute typically took the form of forced labor in the mines or gold washings that the Spaniards "discovered." Of course, if the Indians were to be forced to work, they had first to be subjugated; and south of the Maule River this proved no easy task. Instead of a unified Spanish army, each encomendero had to pacify the Indians in his own grant, and his fortunes depended upon his success at this, not upon a salary from a government treasury.

On Christmas day 1553, the Araucanians, led by the cacique Lautaro—who, in his earlier service as Valdivia's groom, had acquired knowlege of Spanish tactics and limitations—lured the Spanish leader into a trap and obliterated his force of about fifty men at the still smoldering ruins of Tucapel. There were no survivors. Although a legend has the Indians capturing Valdivia and pouring molten gold—the metal so sought after by the Spaniards—down his throat, it is more likely that his decapitated head ended up on the point of an Araucanian lance, the Indians' customary treatment of conquered enemies. Following up the victory at Tucapel, the Indians defeated an army led by Francisco de Villagra at Marigüeñu, despite Villagra's use of six small cannon and thirty harquebuses.* The defeated survivors abandoned Concepción. After twelve years of "conquest," a fearful group of Spanish at Santiago welcomed the refugees from the southern towns fleeing the Araucanian armies.

The Spanish, under Pedro de Villagra, maintained a presence in the south only at Valdivia. Between 1555 and 1557 efforts to resettle the other southern towns met with further defeats at the hands of the Indians, and were complicated by a struggle for power among Valdivia's lieutenants. At first the *audiencia* at Lima left matters in the hands of the local cabildos, but the ensuing chaos led to the appointment of Francisco de Villagra as the ranking officer in Chile. As Lautaro marched toward Santiago, Villagra's forces and Indian auxiliaries surprised the Araucanians at Peteroa, killed Lautaro, and after a gruesome battle, emerged triumphant. This victory avoided total liquidation of the Chilean colony, just as a new governor, García Hurtado de Mendoza, the twenty-one-year-old son of the Peruvian viceroy, arrived at La Serena with 500 soldiers. This was only the first installment in the continuing and costly flow to Chile of reinforcements and war materiel from Peru and Spain.

By authorizing the expenditure of funds from the royal treasury at Lima, the viceroy also recognized the inadequacy of the private seigniorial model of conquest in Chile. Despite the crown's general policy of relying upon private financing of the conquest, by the mid-1560s Chilean governors expended small sums from the royal treasury to help feed and equip soldiers on the Indian frontier. And while Philip II continued to insist upon the traditional policy of avoiding crown expenditures for the conquest of new territories, by 1572 he had authorized the viceroy at Lima to spend moderate sums from the royal coffers to support the war effort in Chile. Until 1600 most financing for the Chilean venture came from the private fortunes of royal officials, encomenderos, and merchants; but the crown gradually moved toward assuming financial responsibility as it became clear that private resources could not pay for the armaments and soldiers necessary to maintain Chile and Peru secure against the threat of Spain's European rivals and the Araucanians.

Shortly after his arrival, Hurtado de Mendoza arrested Aguirre and Francisco de Villagra in order to assert his own control, and then continued the war against the Araucanians. Numerous brutalities followed, including the torture of the *cacique* Galvarino, immortalized in Alonso de Ercilla's epic *La Araucana*. In 1558 Mendoza ordered the resettlement of Concepción, for the third time. Ensuing military engagements reestablished a line of southern forts. Just as Mendoza believed he had pacified Araucania, the king decreed his dismissal at the same time his father was removed as viceroy of Peru. Powerful conquistadors had complained that Mendoza was rewarding his own followers and, more important, was enforcing measures devised by his legal adviser to regulate forced Indian labor.

Replaced by Francisco de Villagra, García Hurtado de Mendoza would return to the colonies as viceroy of Peru some twenty years later. But his hope that the Araucanians had been pacified proved illusory, though a terrible smallpox epidemic from 1561 to 1563 certainly reduced their war-making capability. The best estimates available suggest that 20 to 25 percent of the Indian population perished, though reliable data do not exist. Renewed warfare and persistent conflict among the conquistadors and royal of-

---

*A harquebus was an early type of fuse-fired gun.

ficials led the king to decree the establishment of a royal *audiencia* in Chile in August 1565. The *audiencia* failed to resolve either the internal political or the military problems of the colony. While the encomenderos resisted any restriction on their exploitation of the Indians, and refused to subordinate private interests to public necessities, the Araucanians renewed their struggle against the European invaders.

The Araucanians' relative success against the invaders resulted largely from their adaptability and ingenuity in warfare. When the Spaniards arrived, Araucanian armaments consisted of bows and stone-tipped arrows, hardened wooden spears or lances, clubs, and slings. For protection they wore helmets and coats of sealskin or whalebone and carried thick skin shields. Like other Amerindians their initial encounters with horses and the Spaniards' killer dogs provoked panic and dismay. The Araucanians, however, quickly modified their weapons and their tactics. They constructed new weapons to fight the Spanish cavalry, including lances tipped with pieces of Spanish swords and nooses to yank the Spanish from their mounts. By the late 1560s the Indians frequently used horses and were improving as cavalrymen. A system of double-mounting allowed a lancer and an archer to ride a single horse. Near the end of the sixteenth century the Araucanians even occasionally utilized captured harquebuses, though having learned the limitations of the fuse-fired weapons they attempted to confront the Spaniards when rain or surprise prevented the lighting of fuses.

To avoid the Spaniards' scorched earth tactics, the Indians began to sow hidden fields and to retaliate in kind—waiting until the harvests of the fort towns reached maturity and then trampling the fields at night in cavalry raids. By the end of the sixteenth century the Araucanians had become accomplished guerrilla fighters, effectively harassing the cumbersome Spanish armies, in which each soldier traveled with several Indian servants to do his cooking and bear his weapons. Lack of mobility combined with scarcity of munitions and artillery to assist Indian resistance. At the time of the general uprising at the end of the sixteenth century, Chilean historian Crescente Errázuriz claimed that in Chillán, Concepción, Angol, Arauco, and Santa Cruz the Spaniards had only 282 harquebuses, 44 muskets, and 26 cannon and lacked sufficient powder and fuses for even these. But above all, the Indians' determination, inventiveness, and courage stifled the enterprise of conquest.

Half a century after Pedro de Valdivia's forces entered Chile, the colony remained a frontier, governed by military officers who repeatedly took to the field against the Araucanians. The population resided in dispersed fort towns that increased or decreased in number according to the vicissitudes of warfare. Initially, the only significant source of wealth for the conquerors other than crafts in the towns, consisted of limited placer gold mines and the exploitation of Indian labor. Control of the mines and Indians or permission to engage in industry or commerce stemmed from rights vested in the conquistadors by the governor or the cabildos as the reward for military service or simply as personal patronage. Whether in the form of an encomienda grant or a concession for a flour mill, economic opportunity and wealth originated in the manipulation and control of the law and of political authorities. If Indian labor made possible agricultural production, manufacturing, and mining activities, only "politics" determined the distribution of the booty—including the Indian workers themselves. Valdivia granted encomiendas to his followers shortly after founding Santiago and rewarded other conquistadors as well as religious orders with encomienda grants of Indians surrounding all the towns and forts founded between 1541 and his death in 1553. In contrast to the more established colonies such as Mexico or Peru, his successors continued to grant encomiendas until almost the end of the eighteenth century—

though by that time their importance had greatly diminished in relation to the large rural estates employing tenant labor.

The perpetual state of war in Chile led the crown to put the Chilean Indians in a "special" category which, through contorted legal and doctrinal reasoning, made them subject after 1608 to legal enslavement as well as to the usual abuses of the conquistadors. This eventually made war not only a fact of life in Chile but a great business venture—based on raids of pillage or "slave hunts" called *campeadas* or *malocas*. Before such slave hunts became legal, however, over half a century of warfare had led the Spanish monarch to establish a permanent Chilean garrison and a yearly budget to sustain the war against the Araucanians. The Chilean encomenderos, the royal officials stationed in Chile and Peru, and the small merchant class would soon owe a portion of their wealth and power to the Araucanian war and the budget associated with maintenance of the Chilean garrison. Thus the war that periodically devastated the Concepción-southern region, made livestock and agricultural enterprise insecure, and deprived the colony of its richest gold mines, enriched royal officials and merchants in Santiago, La Serena, and Lima.

Following continued defeats at the hands of the Araucanians, despite more reinforcements from Peru, and an earthquake that destroyed Concepción in 1570, King Philip II abolished the *audiencia* in Chile in 1573 and named a veteran conquistador, Rodrigo de Quiroga, as governor of the territory. Quiroga, a lieutenant for both Valdivia and García Hurtado de Mendoza, actually assumed office in late January 1575. Two months later another earthquake destroyed La Imperial, Villarrica, Osorno, Castro, and Valdivia and also affected Santiago and Valparaíso. Nevertheless, Quiroga pressed forward with a brutal campaign of terror against the Indians in order to end the war. Supported by the viceroy of Peru, Quiroga executed captured caciques and deported prisoners to the north to work the mines in Coquimbo. In order to prevent their escape, Quiroga ordered that their feet be mutilated with a machete or a chisel; to avoid loss of blood and subsequent death, each stump was thrust into a pot of boiling tallow. The governor's concern with the lawfulness of this policy is enlightening. Legal proceedings against the Indians, in their absence, had condemned them to death for rebellion against the empire—and then Quiroga generously reduced the sentence to mutilation and forced labor. The king also instructed Quiroga to ship rebellious Indians to Peru, but the latter replied, on behalf of Chile's encomenderos, that the Indians would survive neither the trip nor the change in climate. The king reconsidered his decree and thus saved most of the human booty for the Chilean conquerors. In the meantime the English corsair Francis Drake sacked Valparaíso and attacked La Serena, thus increasing the military pressure upon the colony.

Between 1580, when Quiroga died, and 1598 three more governors sought to combine warfare and conciliation in order to pacify Araucanía. The last of these three, García Oñez de Loyola, was a nephew of the Peruvian viceroy and also a relative of Ignatius de Loyola, founder of the Jesuit order. When Oñez de Loyola arrived in Chile, a major economic activity of the southern-based army garrisons consisted of hunting down Indians for personal use or for sale. Since the soldiers found it easier to capture Indians from pacified tribes, many more of them were seized and sold into slavery than rebel Indians captured in war. Despite the new governor's decrees outlawing such practices, Chilean historian Domingo Amunátegui Solar wrote that the whole territory of the Bishopric of Imperial "had been converted into an immense human 'meat market,'" where the soldiers enriched themselves through the sale of Araucanians, and where the encomenderos and wealthy residents of Santiago and Serena found their domestic servants or replaced the personnel of their *encomiendas* as the local natives died off from overwork or disease. In January 1598, Oñez de Loyola wrote to the king that throughout the country one saw multitudes of lame or mutilated Indians, Indians without hands, noses, or ears, and blind Indians whose tragic condition "incites the others to die rather than surrender."

Ironically, García Oñez de Loyola attempted to end deportation of Indian prisoners beyond the Maule River and otherwise to moderate the abuses of the encomenderos, yet he ended up like Pedro de Valdivia, decapitated after the massacre of his soldiers at the battle of Curalaba in 1598. The defeat at Curalaba marked the beginning of a general uprising by the Araucanians. All major Spanish settlements south of the Biobío River were destroyed or abandoned: Santa Cruz and Valdivia in 1599; La Imperial and Angol in 1600: Villarrica in 1602; Osorno and Arauco in 1604. At about the same time Dutch pirates attacked Valparaíso and Chiloé. Four governors succeeded one another in rapid succession, and the efforts to subdue the Araucanians continued to no avail.

In 1600 the king of Spain established a permanent military subsidy, or *situado*, for Chile, and war in Chile became a permanent, institutionalized business of the Lima merchants and shippers until almost the end of the seventeenth century. The *situado*, a symbol of the poverty of the Chilean colony, also freed the encomenderos from most financial and military obligations of the war. Conquest and pacification thus became largely a public venture instead of a private semi-feudal imitation of the Spanish reconquest of their homeland from the Moors.

Exasperated by the loss of all the towns and mines of southern Chile after 1598 and the continued fighting, including the loss of more than a hundred Spanish soldiers at Boroa in 1606, the Council of the Indies proposed the *legal* enslavement of all captured Indian males over ten and one-half years old and females older than nine and one-half years; captured children would be commended to "virtuous" Spaniards to serve them and to be instructed in the Faith until the age of twenty. On May 26, 1608, the Spanish king signed a royal decree that legalized, indeed encouraged, the enslavement of "rebellious" Indians in Chile. Though in practice, enslavement of Indian captives was common from 1570 onward, this royal decree legitimated slave raids and pillage by the Chilean garrisons. Interim governor and *audiencia* judge, Luis Merlo de la Fuente, promulgated the decree in Santiago in August 1610, and then led a force to the south which took nearly a thousand Indian prisoners.

By 1610, seventy years after Valdivia's entry into the country, Chile boasted five "cities": La Serena, with 46 adobe houses, 11 with tile roofs and the rest of straw; Santiago, 200 houses; Chillán, 52, eight with tile roofs, 39 with straw, and five *ranchos* of wood and thatch roofs; Concepción, 76 houses, 36 wooden with straw roofs; and Castro, on Chiloé, with 12 straw-covered houses. The rest of the Chilean population resided in the countryside on the immense territories of the encomiendas* where subjugated Indians panned gold, tended flocks of sheep and cattle, and cultivated the land. With the loss of the encomiendas south of the Biobío River, gold mining near La Serena, Santiago, and Concepción took second place to agriculture and livestock as the major source of occupation for the Chilean work force.

Accustomed by the Inca conquest to the idea of tribute long before the arrival of the Spanish, many of the Indians of northern Chile (Copiapó to Maule) gradually submit-

---

*Strictly speaking, the encomienda grant did not involve title to land; it merely conveyed the right to exact tribute from the Indians. Nevertheless, encomenderos in Chile often exercised a patrimonial authority within the territory of a grant.

ted to Spanish domination. They provided the labor that produced gold, food, hides, and tallow—the major exports to Peru—to enrich the encomenderos. As forced labor, mistreatment, and disease (especially smallpox) decimated the encomienda Indians, their periodic replacement was necessary in order to maintain the conquest economy. The war against the Araucanians, as well as the capture of the Huarpe peoples in the eastern cordillera, provided the main source of this replenishment and of concubines for Spanish males; it also supplied Indian labor to Peru. The cruel treatment of captured Indians, in "peacetime" or in war, reinforced their will to resist. The Spaniards used the struggle of the Indians to justify their enslavement, mutilation, "commendation," or "deposit" for use by the encomenderos. Even as the war persisted, so did the never-ending succession of decrees, taxes, and ordinances, which the colonizers applied, appealed, or ignored as suited their convenience.

From 1558 until the general uprising after 1598, the crown's major representatives enacted numerous tribute regulations aimed at controlling the encomenderos and protecting the Indian laborers. In each case Catholic clerics influenced adoption of these codes. But in each case Chilean encomenderos subverted or prevented their implementation.

In 1557, Hernando de Santillán, an adviser to Governor García Hurtado de Mendoza, promulgated in Chile the royal decrees that prohibited using Indians as pack animals, forbade the encomenderos to employ more than one-fifth of "their" Indians in the gold washings or mines, and ordered them to pay the Indians one-sixth of the gold they mined. In addition, they were to free pacified Indian servants and, if these Indians voluntarily worked the mines, to give them one-fourth of the ore extracted as well as adequate food and tools. Further decrees sought to regulate the conditions of the Indians laboring in the fields, the vineyards, the artisan industries, and even in households. A similar tribute was promulgated in mid-1558 for the region of Concepción and the south.

Taking account of the recent rebellions in Peru, Santillán did not seek to abolish the encomiendas themselves. Nevertheless, the Spanish settlers had no intention of ameliorating the lot of the subjugated Indians and thereby decreasing their own income. In a communication to the Council of the Indies after his departure from Chile in 1560, Santillán described the brutality of conquest from the first entry of the Spanish: "[They] killed, maimed and set dogs upon the Indians, cut off feet, hands, noses and teats, stole their lands, raped their women and daughters, chained them up and used them as beasts of burden, burned their houses and settlements and layed waste their fields." In La Serena in 1557, Santillán had reported that the encomenderos sent the Indians to the mines as pack animals, as well as employing them in other personal services, leaving them not an hour to rest.

In the tradition of Bartolomé de Las Casas, the best-known clerical defender of the New World Indians against the abuses of conquest, another Dominican, Fray Gil de San Nicolás, provided more ammunition for the growing "black legend" of Spanish barbarism:

They take the Indian men and women prisoners in chains and use them for "dog bait," watching the dogs tear them apart for sport.

They destroy the crops, burn the houses and villages full of Indians, shutting the doorways [of the houses] so none can escape.

Describing the mines, he wrote that at first the Indians were to receive a sixth part of the gold they extracted and then an eighth part, but they often received nothing at all.

In any case, the regulations obligated the Indians to pay the salary of their "protector" from their "earnings." Either purchased in Spain or acquired from a royal official, the post of "protector" allowed venturesome Spaniards to make their fortunes in the New World by mediating between the encomendero and the native peoples. From limited evidence it appears that the gold earned by the Indians was often actually a source of risk capital for Spanish pastoral and commercial enterprises as the "protectors" and encomenderos colluded in defrauding the Indians.

In 1563 Pedro de Villagra promulgated a dozen new tribute ordinances, including provisions that limited the work period in the placer mines to six months, reaffirmed payment of one-sixth of the gold mined to the Indians, prohibited use of Negro taskmasters, and required the "protectors" of the Indians to buy sheep for them with their gold. The new ordinances also split the obligation of the *protector's* salary between the Indians and the encomendero and increased the number of "protectors." Once again, the encomenderos largely evaded the new regulations. However, the recently created posts did provide a source of income for the new "protectors" authorized to defend the Indians' rights.

Another major reform of the tribute system in 1580 was the *tasa* of Gamboa, which also failed to halt the encomendero's abuse of Indian labor. The *tasa* of Gamboa sought to substitute a fixed money or commodity tax for forced labor. The encomenderos and even some churchmen opposed the new tax as "prejudicial to the colony and the Indians." Its principal innovation consisted of a commutation of labor tribute for a money or commodity tribute. This innovation in no way benefited the encomenderos since it fixed the tribute at seven to nine pesos a year—one-fourth to one-twelfth the value that an Indian could produce in a normal work cycle of eight to twelve months.

Despite the resistance of the encomenderos, the *tasa* of Gamboa merely appeared benign in contrast to previous policies. Illustrative is the tribute owed by the Indians to Luis Jufré, who inherited from his father the encomiendas of Macul near Santiago, Peteroa and Mataquito in Curicó, and Pocoa north of the Maule River. The Macul grant contained 22 tributary Indians; Mataquito, 142; and Pocoa, 57. These Indians owed collectively to their encomendero the following monies and commodities each year.

Macul: 110 gold pesos plus two gold pesos to pay the priest, corregidor,* and the administrator of the encomienda; 30 *fanegas*† of wheat, 20 fanegas of barley, and 20 fanegas of maize delivered to the house of the encomendero; sufficient fish, chickens, or sheep necessary to equal 44 pesos. In addition, the Indians of Macul were to supply nine household servants who would receive a salary and not pay tribute.

Peteroa: In addition to two gold pesos for administrative costs, 985 gold pesos; 394 pesos worth of fish and agricultural commodities, including 200 fanegas of wheat, 100 of barley, 120 of corn, and six of beans; 11 household servants to the encomendero.

Mataquito: two pesos each for administrative costs; 710 gold pesos; 284 pesos in foodstuffs: 150 fanegas of wheat, 80 of barley, five of maize, four of beans, and sufficient quantity of fish, tools, sheep, vegetables, or other commodities to complete the tribute; 10 servants for the encomendero's household.

Pocoa: In addition to two gold pesos for administrative costs, 285 gold pesos; four

---

*The corregidors were representatives of royal authority in towns and rural districts. *Corregidores de Indios* were responsible in particular for Indian settlements or areas of Indian population.

†A fanega is approximately equivalent to 1½ bushels.

domestic servants; 114 pesos in commodities, including 80 fanegas of wheat, 40 of barley, and 50 of maize.

Ruiz de Gamboa prohibited any tribute beyond that specified, but allowed the encomenderos to purchase, at a "just price," commodities to eat and drink or other necessities. In order to avoid abuses, copies of the tribute regulations were given to the encomenderos and the Indian caciques; and to ensure compliance, Gamboa appointed new officials to inspect the mines of Coquimbo and Quillota. The Indians could, of course, choose "personal service" instead of paying the tribute. Around La Imperial continual war made enforcement of tribute largely academic, but north of Maule initial implementation of the tribute aroused the animosity of the encomenderos.

The encomenderos emerged again victorious when the king sent a new military expedition and a new governor, Alonso de Sotomayor, with the charge to defend the colony and the wealth of Peru against the attacks of English pirates and to pacify the Araucanians. Sotomayor reinstated forced labor, thereby gaining the encomenderos' cooperation for a new campaign to the south. In this campaign he ordered that the hands and noses of Indian prisoners be cut off before they were released, in order to terrorize their fellows. Terror again failed to intimidate the Araucanians, who fought back with vigor. According to García Oñez de Loyola some years later, Sotomayor's policies forced the Indians to produce more than 100 pesos in goods and services in exchange for garments worth at most three to four pesos. Sotomayor also appointed to the Indian districts new corregidores whose salaries consisted of one-fourth of the grain and livestock raised by the natives, and approved a work cycle or *demora* of eight months instead of the six established by Pedro de Villagra. To "benefit" the Indians, the governor named clerics to the rural districts; their salaries also came out of the Indians' sweat and blood in the fields and the mines.

Although encomenderos continued to evade the regulations intended to improve the conditions of the Indians, the periodic rebellions, and then the disaster following the defeat of the Spaniards at Curalaba in 1598, gave increased credibility to the voices of those few clerics who sought "justice" for the Indian peoples. The best known of these, the Jesuit Luis de Valdivia, finally persuaded the Spanish monarch to introduce a policy of "defensive warfare," which had been suggested earlier by officials in Lima. After 1612 official policy forbade sorties or settlements across the Biobío River—except by Jesuit missionaries. Luis de Valdivia returned to Chile with a new military governor, Alonso de Ribera, and with comprehensive authority to impose the policy of defensive warfare. This included pardons for rebellious Indians, suspension of the decree permitting slavery of captured Indians, prohibitions on selling outside of Chile those previously captured, dismantling the forts of Angol and Paicaiví, and a recommendation to the *audiencia* to suspend the labor obligations of the Indians and replace them with money and commodity tribute.

Frontier garrisons resisted defensive warfare for both professional and economic reasons. Encomenderos and most other colonials also sought to reverse governmental policy. Governor Ribera openly violated his charge, while other Spanish violations made a mockery of the defensive warfare policy. New instructions from the king, at the insistence of Luis de Valdivia, reaffirmed this policy, but Alonso de Ribera had died by the time these arrived in Chile (1617).

His interim successor received explicit instructions to comply in all respects with the defensive warfare policy; but when the next governor arrived in Concepción, he wrote to the king that forced Indian labor still had not been eliminated from Chile. At the instruction of the viceroy of Peru, still another tribute regulation, the *tasa* of Esquilache, attempted to limit the encomenderos' abuse of the Indians, while officials also suggested that the importation of one thousand black slaves to be sold "at cost" would help to liberate the Indians from *their* slavery. The *tasa* of Esquilache prohibited *any Indian*, whether peaceful or not, from providing "personal service"; it specified a new formula for taxation or tribute; it limited the percentage of encomienda Indians obligated to work to one-third each year; and it freed the others to sell their labor if they desired. If the encomendero did not need all his laborers, he could rent them to other encomenderos or deserving Spaniards.

The encomenderos, nevertheless, resisted all prohibitions against Indian slavery or forced labor in the mines, and any limit on the number of days that Indians could be forced to work. Luis de Valdivia's departure for Spain in 1619, along with the deaths of the Chilean governor and King Philip III, soon eliminated even the pretense of defensive warfare. Chile's governor from 1625 to 1629, Luis Fernández de Córdoba y Arce, boasted to King Philip IV that he had captured more than 250 Indians in fighting near Imperial in 1627 and had killed or captured more than 2500 in Yumbel and Arauco. According to this governor:

> I entered in the province of Imperial and thereabouts, where Spanish have not trod since the uprising twenty-eight years ago, with such good results that I burned many houses and more than 14 or 15 thousand fanegas of food of all sorts, and destroyed 4 or 5 thousand head of livestock. . . . Despite the obstinate resistance of the enemy we have only lost thirty Spanish dead and some hundred Indian allies.

Still, the governor attempted to ameliorate somewhat the condition of non-hostile Indians—by prohibiting the branding of Indians who were not, within three months of their capture in war, registered in the appropriate government office! Araucanian counteroffensives, led by the cacique Lientur, inflicted important defeats on the Spanish in the La Imperial region, including a total rout of Spanish forces at Las Cangrejeras. The Indians killed 70 Spaniards or mestizos and took 36 Spanish prisoners, including Francisco Nuñez de Pineda y Bascuñan, who later described the battle and his long captivity in a diary of his life with the Indians called *Cautiverio Feliz* ("Happy Captivity").

The long history of war, brutality, pillage, and unenforced decrees "protecting" the Indians continued as Governor Laso de la Vega (1629–39) persisted in the offensive in Araucania. An initial Spanish victory at Albarrada in 1633 ended with butchery or enslavement of the routed Indians—812 dead and some 600 prisoners—and halted the Indian advance into the central valley, blunting yet another threat to Concepción and Santiago. The new governor also faced a new royal order abolishing "personal service" or forced labor "wherever and in whatever form." Despite the determined resistance of the cabildos of Santiago and Concepción, this reform and others emerged in yet another decree—the *tasa* of Laso de la Vega in 1635.

The new *tasa* consisted of sixteen regulations, including the elimination of "personal service," although the Indians still were to pay tribute to the encomenderos in money or commodities each year in the presence of the "protector" and the priest in the encomiendas, or of the administrator and priest in the Indian villages. In general, this new legislation was meant to complement, not replace, the *tasa* of Esquilache by giving the Indians a choice of paying tribute with either labor or commodities and by adding more paternalistic supervision and enforcement. The Indians could pay tribute in labor if they so informed the corregidor, who would also evaluate the commodities delivered by the Indians to the encomendero. In addition, the Indians were authorized to "rent" themselves, with preference to their own encomendero during the time necessary to pay the tribute, and after that to anyone whose property was located within four leagues of the town or hacienda where they resided.

The new restrictions on the encomenderos met with resistance and were little enforced. In 1639 a judge of the *audiencia* of Chile reported to the crown that while some of the poorer Spaniards observed the *tasa,* the rich and powerful continued as always "using the natives as if they were slaves, treating them harshly, without paying them the small wage of their sweat and labor . . . bringing them from as far as Tucumán and Río de la Plata . . . and working them day and night in the copper mines at La Serena or . . . to mine gold at Andacollo." The judge also noted that due to the brutality of the soldiers and the venality of the corregidors and priests, as well as to the exploitation of the encomenderos, most of the Indian villages had been depopulated and the lands gradually appropriated by Spaniards. In a classic understatement concerning the judge's report, Chilean historian Amunátegui Solar suggested:

> From this exposition, it can be deduced that the *tasa* of Laso de la Vega was as inefficacious as those of Santillán, Ruiz de Gamboa, Sotomayor, Ribera and Esquilache; and that at the end of his [Laso de la Vega's] government the Chilean natives were subjugated to forced labor with the same harshness as in the times of Pedro de Valdivia. The orders of the king and the ordinances signed by viceroys and governors came to nothing.

In 1639 another professional soldier—Francisco López de Zúñiga, who had fifteen years' experience in Flanders and Germany—replaced Laso de la Vega as governor. Faced with continued Indian resistance, the new governor attempted to carry out a modified policy of defensive warfare by arranging the Pact of Quillín, in which Spaniards and Mapuche celebrated a "peace treaty." The Spanish formally recognized Indian sovereignty south of the Biobío River with the exception of the fort at Arauco and the region thereabouts. In all the enterprise of conquest since 1492, Spain had never before recognized the sovereignty of an Indian people. The Spanish also agreed to discontinue the slave hunts and forced labor. In exchange the Indians agreed to return Spanish captives, to allow missionaries to preach in Indian territory, and to ally themselves with the Spanish against English and Dutch corsairs. King Philip IV approved the pact in 1643. But despite the governor's half-hearted efforts, the frontier garrisons as well as other royal officials and encomendero-commercial interests refused both to observe the *tasas* and to comply with the terms of the Pact of Quillín. Indian labor was too valuable to give up merely because of a peace treaty or official policies.

The soldiers on the frontier continued slave hunts and pillage as their principal source of enrichment. Events slowly led to still another general uprising on the scale of the butchery between 1598 and 1606, as Araucanian resistance to "Christianization," especially to the ban on polygamy, frustrated clerics and governors alike.

Despite reaffirmation of the Pact of Quillín in March 1651, Indians in the region of Cunco killed the shipwrecked survivors of the Spanish vessel bringing the military subsidy to Chile. A punitive expedition slaughtered a number of Indians and sent many women and children north as slaves. Then a series of raids led by the governor's two brothers-in-law provoked increasing Indian retaliation.

The governor and his brothers-in-law took over provisioning of the troops, stole supplies, and launched a large-scale commerce in Indian slaves, with the Boroa fort town serving as a clearing house. The 1608 decree allowing enslavement of rebellious

Indians provided the basis for a lucrative "certification" business, in which frontier officials certified that the Indians were captured in battles with rebellious tribes.

In February 1655, a mestizo called Alejo, an ex-soldier in the Spanish garrison, led an Indian uprising and at the same time inspired rebellion by the prisoner-slaves still in the frontier region. The Indians again destroyed the towns and forts south of the Biobío River and forced the abandonment of towns as far north as Chillán. According to the historian Carvallo y Goyeneche in the years following the uprising, the Indians captured 1300 Spaniards, sacked 396 estates, took over 400,000 head of cattle, horses, and sheep, and caused property damage estimated at 8 million pesos. The Spanish lost Arauco, San Pedro, Colcura, Buena Esperanza, Nacimiento, Talcamávida, San Rosendo, Boroa, and Chillán, along with over half the armaments in the region. An angry mob in Concepción—shouting, "Long live the king! Death to the bad governor!"—temporarily deposed the corrupt governor, and he was officially replaced in 1656. By then the Spanish held only the town of Concepción in all the Bishopric of Imperial, and communication with Santiago was possible only by military patrols. For all practical purposes Chile consisted of the towns of La Serena, Santiago, and Concepción, along with the encomiendas, mines, and rural estates from the valley of Coquimbo to the Maule River.

From 1657 to 1662 Spanish and Indian soldiers battled each other without resolution, until a Spanish army of 600 soldiers surprised and defeated 1500 Indians led by the cacique Misqui near Curanilahue. Soon thereafter the interim governor ordered the resettlement of Chillán and requested still more troop reinforcements to press the war against the Araucanians. In the meantime the king named a new royal governor and, in order to secure another force of 1000 soldiers in Spain, promised the recruits for Chile the same benefits enjoyed by soldiers who served in Flanders.

Governor Francisco de Meneses came to Chile in 1664 and ruled it as a Hispanic robber baron until 1668. Taking full advantage of the warfare economy, the governor demanded heavy bribes for renewal of encomienda grants, sold military and civilian government posts, and made those he promoted pay him in gold; he taxed ships carrying on commerce between Valparaíso and Callao before they left port—unless they carried his merchandise; and he appropriated for sale in his own retail outlet a large part of the goods arriving as part of the military subsidy. Supported by the Peruvian viceroy's desire to increase the flow of Indian slaves to the mines and fields of Peru, Meneses renewed expeditions to the south, especially against the pacified tribes, where it was easier to obtain human merchandise. In a single raid around Paicaví, Cayucupal, and Tucapel, the Spaniards obtained 400 *piezas* (a weighted equivalent of four hundred Indians, allowing for the lesser value of the labor of children or the old) and assassinated twenty chiefs who spoke out against these "military" operations. Meneses's arbitrary, corrupt rule also adversely affected the interests of important Chilean colonists. Eventually he was replaced owing to their letters of protest and after an unsuccessful attempt on his life.

With a permanent force of some 2500 soldiers, Meneses's successor Juan Henríquez vigorously carried the war into Araucanian territory and also withstood attacks by English Corsairs, including Bartholomew Sharp's sack and burning of La Serena in 1680. He also accumulated vast wealth from slaving, despite the royal decree of 1674 prohibiting Indian slavery. Chilean historian Luis Galdames claims that during his tenure Governor Henríquez took prisoner some 800 Indians and sold them as slaves. The governor set the price at 500 fanegas of wheat for each Indian, with the fanega valued at 50 centavos (in the mid-seventeenth century a first-class Indian, *pieza de lei*, sold for 200 to 300 pesos and lesser valued Indians, *piezas de servidumbre*, for 150 to 200 pesos). When he had accumulated 400,000 fanegas of wheat, he sold the grain to the contractors of his own army at two pesos a fanega and was paid from the royal treasury. War was good business! Henríquez left office after almost twelve years (1682) with a fortune estimated at close to one million pesos.

In 1674 and 1679, during Governor Henríquez's tenure, new decrees abolishing Indian slavery challenged the ingenuity of Chilean encomendero and business interests. In response the Chileans adopted a legal device called the *depósito*, which placed captured Indians in the custody of encomenderos or landowners who agreed to supervise them in exchange for the right to use their labor. An Indian under the *depósito* did not legally "belong to" a particular Spaniard as did a slave, but in practice he might as well have. The Chilean economy continued to depend upon warfare, slave hunts, pillage, and exploitation of the rural labor force.

At the end of the seventeenth century, not only the Indians but also the Spanish-mestizo troops manning the frontier outposts suffered the consequences of government corruption. As Chilean historian and liberal political leader Benjamín Vicuña Mackenna noted, the military subsidy became "an open bag of money into which everybody dug with both hands, except those [the soldiers] for whom the subsidy had originally been established." The war budget profited Lima merchants, royal officials, and Chilean colonials, while the human booty of the continual raids "stocked" the mines, farms, and *obrajes*. Until 1685 the *situado* consisted largely of commodities, many of which were of no use at all to frontier garrisons which lacked shoes, clothing, and munitions. Moreover, the purchase of oil, salt, and soap in Lima for shipment to Chile benefited only the Lima military contractors, since these commodities were generally available in Chile. The shipwreck of the *San Juan de Díos*, which was bringing the *situado* to Chile, provided the pretext for a request by Chile's governor that the subsidy be sent overland from Potosí—in coin of the realm—thereby avoiding the risks of loss at sea and attack by pirates. The approval of this request in 1685 meant that the soldiers were to be paid in cash and buy their supplies at lower costs in Chile. Unfortunately, however, from the mid-1680s onward the subsidy often arrived late if at all.

An earthquake which shattered Lima-Callao and led to the loss of the Peruvian wheat crop in 1687 induced a temporary boom in Chilean wheat exports and also a considerable increase in prices (see Chapter 3). This made it difficult to buy the needed provisions for the Chilean garrison within the constraints of the military budget. By the time the last seventeenth-century governor of Chile (1692–1700) took over, the Chilean frontier army could not depend upon the annual subsidy as a sure source of support. From 1692 to 1697 the export boom allowed the governor to maintain the army with loans from colonial merchants. But with the military subsidy almost seven years in arrears, Chile's governor wrote the king in August 1697 that the soldiers were not only unclothed, but in debt for what they had purchased or borrowed in recent years; and "what never before has occurred, now is happening, the captains and the corporals of the army leave their posts, as they find themselves in the same misery as the soldiers . . . going to the rural estates to feed and clothe themselves . . . [destroying] order and military discipline."

In the first years of the eighteenth century, the Wars of the Spanish Succession in Europe intensified difficulties in the Spanish-American colonies. When in 1702 the new Chilean governor, Francisco Ibáñez de Peralta, received a payment of 292,000 pesos—against a debt of over 2 million pesos, he made sure that his own salary and certain other obligations were paid in full, leaving little for the garrison. (Ibáñez had already opened a butcher shop, sold a number of official positions, and collected payments for renewal of the encomiendas.) This situation provoked a military uprising that led to serious internal disorders. The governor ordered rebellious soldiers tried by military tribunals, and executed a number of the revolt's leaders, despite an earlier promise of pardon if they surrendered. In 1704 the military subsidy was eight years in arrears, and the army lacked armaments and munitions. In these conditions official policy sought to avoid provocation of the Araucanians by soldiers or missionaries.

By the last two decades of the seventeenth century, the effects of the 1655 uprising had been largely overcome north of the Biobío River. To the south the Araucanians remained in control. The degeneration of Spanish military capabilities from the Homeric exploits of the sixteenth century to the professional rabble-garrisons sent from Lima in the seventeenth left the conquest incomplete. Corruption, war-profiteering, and insufficient troops combined with the fierce resistance of the Araucanian and allied Indian armies to prevent Spanish control of the regions most coveted by Pedro de Valdivia and his followers.

In the first decades of the eighteenth century, tentative initiatives to renew the conquest and establish settlements in Araucania met with another general uprising (1723). In response, Governor Gabriel Cano y Aponte (1717–33) ordered the dismantling of the forts of Colcura, Arauco, and Tucapel and the erection in their stead of forts with similar names north of the Biobío River. Apparently the Indians did not share Francisco Encina's judgment that "contrary to the fantasies and neurotic mysticism of the Jesuits and the nineteenth century historians, the Indians' condition when left to themselves was much worse than the harshest servitude imposed by the Spanish." A new agreement, celebrated at Negrete in 1726, established the usual obligations of the Indians to receive Christian missions and to ally themselves against enemies of the king; it restored "peace" temporarily, until the next major conflict later in the century (1766).

In 1700 some 100,000 to 150,000 Spanish, mestizos, Indians, mulattoes, and Negroes lived in Spanish Chile. From 1541 until 1664, 20,000 to 30,000 Chilean soldiers and settlers had died fighting the Mapuche at an official cost of 17 million pesos—though the Jesuit Diego de Rosales estimates the toll from 1545 to 1674 at 42,000 Spaniards, including deaths from accidents and epidemics, and a military subsidy of 40 million pesos from the Peruvian and Spanish treasuries. This does not include the vast personal fortunes expended in sixteenth-century enterprises of conquest. Estimates of Indian losses are too varied to be relied upon, but there can be no doubt they amounted to many times those of the European invaders, especially taking into account death through epidemic diseases. The material losses of the indigenous peoples of Chile likewise cannot be accurately measured—for they had no great stores of wealth but rather lost their autonomy, their land, and ultimately their cultural integrity.

The uncompleted military conquest would be resolved only late in the nineteenth century, but the authoritarian politics of conquest had already created in Chile the foundations of a highly stratified class society in which labor was denigrated and laborers were exploited. The politics of conquest also institutionalized political corruption, arbitrary use of government authority, disrespect for and evasion of law—in short, impunity for the powerful—and consolidation of the institutions of Hispanic capitalism that would condition the development of a more complex social and economic system in Chile in the nineteenth and twentieth centuries.

These latter characteristics Chile shared with most of the Spanish colonies. Unlike the principal colonial centers, however, relative geographical isolation, poverty, and lack of significant gold and silver mines contributed to the development of an agrarian-based economy in Chile. Relative ease of communication and concentration of population in the central valley, along with the constant threat and challenge of the Indian frontier, forged a colonial elite with strong localistic orientations, a fortress mentality, and a significant military tradition. An impressive ability to coopt royal officials through business or marital ties and to absorb new wealth and successful immigrants created an integrated political, economic, and social elite with interests in agriculture, commerce, and mining. Intermarriage, shared social values, and dependence for economic well-being upon the exploitation of the rural labor force unified the Chilean upper classes and helped forge a unique variant of Hispanic capitalism on the periphery of the Spanish Empire. Chilean "exceptionalism" thus began in the colonial era; it would persist in a number of ways into the twenty-first century.

3 Hispanic Capitalism

The colonial experience in Chile drastically reduced the indigenous population of the territory between Copiapó and the Strait of Magellan and resulted in a deterioration in the quality of life for the overwhelming majority of the territory's population. Disease, warfare, and exploitation destroyed the fabric of Indian life. At the same time miscegenation gave rise to a new people descended from the conquistadors and their Indian or Negro slaves and servants, or from Indians and their Spanish captives. Accustomed to polygamy, Indian women adapted to Iberian promiscuity if they were not forcefully subjected to it, and bore increasing numbers of "Spanish" children. To a lesser extent Spanish women gave birth to the children of their Indian captors or lovers. Though by 1810 the entire population of Chile had probably not reached the size of the indigenous population at the time of conquest, its character testified to the profound ethnic transformation that accompanied the social and economic evolution of colonial Chile.

If, in retrospect, the most important product of colonialism in Chile is the mestizo, the Spanish had not come to Chile with that intention. They came to take mineral wealth and the booty from Indian empires—as they had done previously in Mexico, Central America, and Peru. Shortly after the founding of Santiago in 1541, gold from the mines at Marga Marga and other gold washings in the northern and southern districts seemed to justify the prospect of a profitable extractive economy based upon the forced labor of subjugated indigenous peoples. But by 1600 the relative poverty of easily worked gold mines in Chile became evident, and when the Spanish lost all the southern settlements (1598–1604), the products of the countryside came to dominate the colonial economy. Rapid proliferation of livestock soon made tallow and hides Chile's most important exports.

Both in the export of gold and tallow, Chile's Spanish settlers operated from the outset in the intercolonial and international market. The essentially commercial motivation of the Chilean conquest and the distinctly export orientation of the colony's leaders contradict the common characterization of the early colonial economy as feudal, autarkic, or merely subsistence. Yet caution must be exercised in labeling this colonial economy capitalist merely because of its participation in international commerce. The colonial economy functioned within a Hispanic, absolutist juridical order that had more in common with a bastardized Iberian feudalism than with nineteenth-century capitalism. Spanish imperial theory, property institutions, and commercial policy, as well as the economic enterprises of the religious orders and the Araucanian war, combined to give a distinctive character to colonial economy and society. If it was capitalist, then it was a special sort of capitalism, modified by the unique milieu of colonial Chile—a miserably poor backwater of the Spanish Empire. The colonial economy of Chile produced a surplus for export, but it did not do so under the fundamental conditions of capitalist production—the sale by free workers of their labor to the possessors of money and the means of production. Private enterprise and private profit depended upon coerced labor and the protection of royal authority for commercial

TABLE 3–1. ESTIMATED POPULATION OF CHILE, 1540–1620

	Spanish and European Creoles	"White" Mestizos	Negros and "Nonwhite" Mestizos	Encomienda and Peaceful Indians	Unpacified Indians	Total
1540	154	–	10	–	1,000,000	1,000,164
1570	7000	10,000	7000	450,000	150,000	624,000
1590	9000	17,000	16,000	420,000	120,000	582,000
1600	10,000	20,000	19,000	230,000	270,000	549,000
1620	15,000	40,000	22,000	230,000	250,000	557,000

After Rolando Mellafe, *La introducción de la esclavitud negra en Chile*, 1959, p. 226.

monopolies, price-fixing, and severe limitations upon economic competition. Thus, while Hispanic capitalism in Chile certainly entailed commodity production for local, regional, and international markets, it did not depend upon a significant wage-labor force until the nineteenth century.

In principle, every economic enterprise in colonial Chile operated only with the permission of the royal authorities or the cabildo, which fixed by decree the price for commodities, labor, and services. Spanish imperial policy sought to limit trade among the colonies to approved channels and to direct the economic surplus to Spain. In turn the colonies were expected to import goods carried from Spain in Spanish vessels. The high cost of transport made many colonial agricultural products noncompetitive when moved great distances from the point of production, but the necessities of frontier life often led local artisans and landlords to ignore prohibitions on local industries or limitations on the cultivation of particular crops such as grapes. Almost from the outset smuggling played an important role in commerce both among the colonies and between the colonies and non-Spanish merchants. Chile could trade legally with Spain only via the merchant fleet that came to Panama once a year or, sometimes, less often. After sailing to Panama via Peru, Chilean merchants had to cross the isthmus on mules to obtain merchandise from the annual fairs where Spanish merchants dictated the prices. The Spanish merchants greatly overvalued their own merchandise. While they sought profit margins that often reached over 500 percent, they paid poorly for colonial commodities. The rigors of travel, the rigged markets, and the capital required severely limited the access of Chileans to this commerce, and left most legal Chilean commerce in Peruvian hands.

Resource allocation within the colonial economy did not occur as a result of the functioning of a capitalist market. Official policy discouraged economic competition, established publicly authorized monopolies, and, by the seventeenth century, created a number of publicly owned haciendas and industries intended to supply food, clothing, shoes, and materiel to the Chilean frontier garrison. For all these economic activities, the labor force consisted largely of slaves, subjugated or tributary Indians, fixed-term "indentured" laborers (*asientos de trabajo*), and agricultural tenants until well into the eighteenth century. Even then the development of a wage proletariat came slowly as class relations in the countryside moved toward tenant labor.

Three primary bases of wealth initially underlay the colonial economy: land, Indian or Negro labor, and the authority to exploit them. To these were added commerce and artisanship and, after 1600, the military *situado*. Always, however, the most important "commodity" remained political authority: from government concessions, licenses, grants, or official positions stemmed all economic opportunity, including land grants (*mercedes*), mining concessions, and the right to exact tribute or exploit Indian labor.

In the early years of the colony, gold mining took first place in the incipient economy. The most fortunate of the conquistadors appropriated the mines and washings worked by the Indians prior to the arrival of the Spanish, and obtained respectable quantities of the yellow metal. At Marga Marga, near Valparaíso, mines that had supplied the natives with the tribute for the Incas now passed into the hands of Pedro de Valdivia and several of his companions. With the relatively simple techniques employed, gold production required large numbers of laborers. Estimates of the number of Indians forced to work in the mines and gold washings are neither systematic nor reliable, but the contemporary chronicler Pedro Mariño de Lobera claimed that in 1553 more than 20,000 Indians worked the mines of Quilacoya alone. While this figure is probably exaggerated, there can be no doubt that thousands of Indians were forced to extract gold for the Spanish from La Serena in the north to the southern mines in Osorno and Valdivia.

Work in the mines was strenuous. The Indian labor force detested their virtual enslavement, the separation from their families, and the harsh working conditions. As disease and overwork killed off Indian laborers, the Spaniards sought to replenish the labor supply from the encomienda Indians (Huarpes) transported across the Andes and with the captives from the war to the south.

In the mining process itself, groups of Indians dug the earth and put the excavated material into tubs, or *bateas*. Other Indians then carried the dirt-filled tubs to the water's edge. Still other laborers, usually Indian women or Negro slaves, spent almost entire days in water up to their knees washing the dirt in a procession of *bateas* until only gold remained at the bottom. Along the streams and rivers the laborers also employed techniques similar to the gold-panning methods of the later California gold rush (1849). Thanks to Indian and Negro labor, a few of the earliest conquistadors managed to turn the dream of gold into reality in the Chilean colony.

Owing to the frontier conditions on the Chilean periphery of the Spanish Empire, it is impossible to make accurate estimates of the quantity or the value of the gold extracted in the sixteenth century. As 20 percent of all gold mined (the *quinto*) belonged legally to the royal treasury, there was, of course, no incentive for precise accounting by the conquistadors. During the first few months following the settlement of Santiago, the Spanish obtained some 7000 pesos' worth of gold at Marga Marga, and in 1547 Pedro de Valdivia sent a large gold shipment to Peru. Royal officials estimated that to that time the *quintos* equaled approximately 40,000 gold pesos. Taking into account the inevitable losses to corruption and unreported gold, the Indians produced well over 200,000 gold pesos for the Spaniards at the mines from 1541 to 1547. While this was not an inconsiderable sum, the Chilean mines could not compare with the incredible wealth of the silver mines at Potosí in what is now Bolivia or with the mines of Mexico later in the sixteenth and seventeenth centuries.

In 1552 the most important mines were located at Quilacoya near the Biobío River. The defeat at Tucapel (1553), where Valdivia died, took these riches from the Spaniards, but new mines were discovered shortly thereafter at Osorno and Valdivia. The Jesuit chronicler Diego de Rosales tells us, with obvious exaggeration, that in 1561 the Indians' labor produced some 1.2 million pesos at the Madre de Dios mines near Valdivia and in the mines at Choapa in Coquimbo. About Osorno, Father Rosales reported that "the land has gold and silver mines, and it is taken in such abundance that with one or two days' work the Indians mine enough to fill their quota for the week; mining stones so large that they break them into pieces and give them to the encomenderos [to pay off their obligations]." A less poetic account by Juan López de Velasco suggests that from 1542 to 1560 gold output in Chile reached more than 7 million pesos.

As the sixteenth century progressed, gold production dramatically declined. The royal *quintos* went from 35,000–40,000 pesos in 1568 to 32,000 pesos in 1571 and 22,000 in 1583. By way of contrast, Potosí produced 170,000 pesos in *quintos* in 1570. Chronic warfare in the southern territories limited output, and at the height of the Indian uprising in 1600 total royal income from Chile, including the *quintos*, amounted to only 3000 pesos. A royal official reported that "this is all the royal income there is here for now, because the whole territory is so afflicted with war that the pacified Indians cannot mine gold, because they are all employed in making supplies for the war." Even before the uprising another report to the king (1594) had noted that "the Indians serving in the cities of La Serena, Santiago, Concepción, and the others have so diminished in number that gold is hardly mined in all the kingdom and their number [the Indians'] is barely sufficient to sustain the cultivation of the haciendas and tend to the cattle of the encomenderos." Thus, with the possible exception of the mines at Andacollo, gold mining had dropped off sharply by the last decade of the sixteenth century.

Despite this decline, the location of the mines had influenced substantially the sites the Spaniards chose for the towns that were to become the cradles of European culture in Chile. Though all of the first settlements were destroyed at least once by Indian attack or by pirates and several times by earthquakes, tidal waves, or floods, each was refounded. Their names can be found on modern maps of Chile: La Serena, Santiago, Concepción, Imperial (now Carahue, to the west of Nueva Imperial), Villarrica, and Valdivia. In each town the settlers looked to the municipal council, or cabildo, to order urban economic activity and also, initially, to establish regulations governing exploitation of the mines, agricultural lands, and the cottage industries created in the towns and encomiendas. These towns, however, remained little more than struggling villages with one-story adobe or wooden houses roofed with tiles or straw. Only an occasional two-story building or the larger constructions of the religious orders even hinted at the skyscrapers of later years. In Santiago most of the houses were built around patios—many planted in gardens or fruit trees. Through the middle of the cobbled or dirt streets of the town ran open sewers. The other towns were much smaller and even less prosperous.

In these towns soldiers with seigniorial aspirations formed households with Indian women and servants. As the colony grew, the number of domestic servants increased; the more held by a household, the higher its social status. As few skilled artisans came to Chile in the early years, these households developed a sort of pioneer self-sufficiency, until increased population permitted more economic specialization. For those artisans who did set up shop in Santiago, the cabildo attempted, with little success, to replicate the guild system of Spain. The cabildo regulated the quality and price of almost all manufacturing services, and commodities, including such items as bread, tools, clothing, and fish. As soon as brickmaking took on a commercial character, the cabildo decreed official prices and established a fine of ten pesos in addition to forfeiture of goods sold in excess of these prices. To establish a brickyard required an official permit, and at times a permit was denied if the proposed location posed environmental hazards to the town. As early as 1548 the cabildo approved official prices for different types of clothing made by tailors and for the products of armorers, smiths, and carpenters. Adjustments took place as business interests or consumers pressured the municipal officers. Public policy in colonial Chile left no room for the "free competitive marketplace," and the tradition of government responsibility for regulating industry and ensuring availability of basic commodities at reasonable prices survived even the superficial imposition of liberal capitalist ideology in the nineteenth century. In at least one case the cabildo even prevented a settler from leaving town lest Santiago lose its only blacksmith.

The earliest colonial manufacturers met demands for food, shelter, clothing, and armaments. The first recorded flour mills were established at the foot of Santa Lucía by Rodrigo de Araya and Bartolomé Flores (Blumenthal). Other early enterprises included shoemakers, smiths, armorers, tanners, and saddle makers. Pottery, textiles, and cordage became important cottage industries. In the manufacture of textiles the Spanish took advantage of the developed Indian traditions in weaving. Boatbuilding also gained importance around Valdivia, Osorno, Concepción, and Valparaíso-Concón.

Some of the early manufactures testify to the entrepreneurial skill of the conquistadors. For example, Antonio Nuñez arrived in Chile shortly after Pedro de Valdivia and acquired large rural estates near Santiago and Valparaíso. Nuñez built the first warehouses at Valparaíso, engaged in commerce between Peru and Santiago in his own ships captained by his sons-in-law, established the boatbuilding works at Concón, and negotiated a fishing concession with the cabildo at Santiago (1579). In a business transaction that could be understood by any modern Chilean capitalist, Nuñez offered to bring fish to Santiago *if the cabildo would fix a convenient price for a period of three years.* The cabildo agreed, but Nuñez recalculated his costs and, before delivering a single fish, petitioned for an increase in price "due to the high costs of boats and nets, which will be at least 500 pesos, and since seven or eight workers will be required to cast the nets, in addition to three or four Indians." Colonial entrepreneurs, like their modern counterparts, sought monopoly market positions, guaranteed prices, captive markets, and cheap labor in collusion with government officials. This tradition of Hispanic capitalist enterprise carried over from the conquest to become the prevailing spirit of the colonial economy.

Whereas Spanish colonial towns were the centers of political authority and the beginnings of urban culture and industry, most of the population lived in the countryside, and the agricultural encomiendas, mines, and rural industries produced the bulk of colonial commodities. The encomenderos and hacendados created textile sweatshops, oil presses, wineries, tanneries, mills, rope and tool manufacturers and even, briefly, sugar mills in Copiapó and Aconcagua, to process the produce of the land. At the end of the sixteenth century Chile paid for its imports of European and Peruvian merchandise with exports of tallow, hides and leather goods, sheepskins, wine, wood, apples, hemp, salted meat, olives and olive oil, and copper. Despite recurrent warfare, the Chilean economy produced a considerable surplus of food and agrarian products. Excellent yields in the territory's virgin soil converted the river valleys into gardens, while the proliferation of livestock made meat available to all classes. In 1565 shippers charged 46 gold pesos a head to transport cattle from Callao to Valparaíso. The success of the Chilean livestock industry meant that thirty years later 300 head of cattle sold for 450 pesos (1.50 pesos per head) in Santiago. Due to the unending Araucanian war, however, the encomenderos preferred to raise mules for trans-Andean transport, which the royal governors would not requisition as they would horses. At the end of the century a horse brought 150 pesos or more as compared with 1.50 pesos for a cow. A shortage of horses led Governor García Ramón to prohibit further mule breeding (1607); and when this measure failed, Governor Jaraquemada (1611) ordered the gelding of all jackasses within twenty days, subject to a fine of 100 gold pesos per animal for noncompliance. The extensiveness of the Chilean countryside and the value of mules for transport and as export commodities to Potosí made this measure as unsuccessful as the one decreed by García Ramón.

With the loss of all the southern towns and mines at the end of the sixteenth century, the Chilean economy was reduced to several regional economies centered upon the small towns of La Serena (46 houses), Santiago (200 houses), Concepción (66 houses), and Chillán (52 houses). Gradually the trans-Andean settlements of Cuyo were incorporated de facto into the economy of Río de la Plata, though Santiago continued to import Huarpe Indian laborers from the encomiendas across the Andes. Though the foundation of wealth and power throughout the colony remained control of land, labor and commercial opportunities subject to the discretion of government decision makers, the varied natural ecologies of these regions, and their location with respect to the battlefields contested by Spanish and Araucanians, led to distinctive patterns of social and economic development. Thus an accurate portrayal of socio-economic evolution in colonial Chile requires focusing some attention on the diversity of regional development from the northern provinces to the central valley and then to the southern frontier.

In 1544 Pedro de Valdivia ordered Juan Bohon to found a city somewhere in the valley of Elqui or Coquimbo as a way station between Peru and Santiago. After four years as little more than an encampment, an Indian attack destroyed the settlement entirely. With the arrival of reinforcements at Santiago from Peru, Valdivia sent Francisco de Aguirre to refound La Serena. Aguirre chose the modern site some 2000 meters from the sea. Valdivia gave all the land and Indians from the valley of Choapa to the valley of Copiapó to only eight *vecinos*.* Unlike the rapid turnover among most of the Chilean encomiendas and land grants in the early years, the northern encomienda grants often remained in the same family for many generations. No better example of this could be found than the Aguirre family whose descendants retained the encomiendas of Copiapó and Coquimbo until the abolition of all encomiendas in Chile in the late eighteenth century (1791), and remained important landowners in the region into the twentieth century.

The town of La Serena grew slowly. By 1610 nine square blocks contained a church, Augustinian and Franciscan convents, and government buildings, surrounded by fields and orchards. No more than one hundred Spaniards and mestizos and some eight hundred tributary Indians resided in or about the town. Growth continued slowly until 1680 when pirates led by Bartholomew Sharp sacked and burned the settlement. Many of the principal *vecinos* abandoned the town and fled to their rural estates. After another pirate attack in 1686 the cabildo attempted to prevent total abandonment of the city by decreeing heavy fines for those leaving without permission. Increased wheat exports and mining activity in the last decade of the seventeenth century brought renewed vitality to La Serena, while its port at Coquimbo became an important point of transshipment of copper to Peru. Copper smelters near Coquimbo sent the elaborated red metal to Callao, and artisans sent their copper wares south to Santiago as well as north to Lima. Nonetheless, in the first decades of the eighteenth century the French engineer M. Frezier still remarked on the "scarcity of population, the rudeness of the streets without pavement, the poverty of the houses built of mud and roofed with straw, which gives La Serena the aspect of a country village [*campo*]."

In the first decades of the seventeenth century the major export commodities from the *norte chico* included, along with copper, tallow, hides, lard, and sheepskins. Small amounts of wheat also went from the northern valleys to Peru or Potosí. Although data on agricultural production and exports for the seventeenth century are incomplete, re-

*A *vecino* was a principal citizen in an urban center, a tax-paying property owner with a "voice" in the cabildo; he was also often an encomendero.

cent studies suggest that between 1620 and 1690 agriculture gained in importance relative to livestock, and the *norte chico* became an important source of hemp, cordage, aguardiente, pisco, wine, and wheat for the Peruvian market. By the beginning of the eighteenth century the present-day agriculture-livestock-mining triad had already emerged, along with the accompanying cycles of mining booms and depressions.

The regional economies of the *norte chico* between Copiapó and Quillota, furthest removed from the Araucanian wars and closest to Peru, developed within a far more stable environment than did the regions south of Santiago. Indians imported from across the cordillera along with Araucanian captives worked the gold mines, planted, tended, and harvested crops, and labored in the limited number of artisan industries, or *obrajes*, and mills. But the limited grain exports to Peru belied the delicate balance between population, agricultural potential, and food supply throughout the region. As population increased in the late seventeenth century, hints of future regional grain deficits were evident. In 1695, in response to expanded Chilean wheat exports to Peru and the accompanying rise in local prices, the cabildo in La Serena ordered producers to sell one-tenth of their output at a fixed price to the town's bakers in order to ensure availability of flour and bread below market prices. By 1724 more drastic measures prohibited export of grain or flour outside the region, even to Copiapó or Illapel. These measures, adopted also in modified form in central Chile, sought to guarantee local consumption at reasonable prices. The need for those measures and others like them from 1692 to 1750 pointed to a basic conflict between participation in the international economy and the provisioning of local markets at regulated prices. This conflict, which reappeared frequently in the history of Chilean agriculture, inspired the age-old responses of smuggling, black market trading, and hoarding of commodities until more favorable prices could be obtained. Thus, in 1747 the cabildo in Copiapó authorized the corregidor to regulate producers in order to assure adequate supplies. Later it noted that a number of *vecinos* had violated the decree, which established a maximum price for wheat and flour, and had hidden away the wheat. As late as 1798 the cabildo complained about "manipulation of grain prices by a small number of persons in times of scarcity."

In the middle of the eighteenth century the region around Copiapó still was essentially a mining district, producing silver, gold, and copper. The region imported foodstuffs, such as wheat, jerked beef, lard, and livestock products, to support the mining population, though it exported wine to Peru. This situation changed little in the rest of the century. La Serena also experienced a renaissance of mining after 1735–40 but barely produced enough wheat to supply its own needs. Like Copiapó, the La Serena district imported tallow, lard, flour, and livestock, in contrast to its relative self-sufficiency in these products earlier in the century.

These economic changes in the *norte chico* were accompanied by an alteration in the composition of the population and the work force. The decline of encomienda Indians throughout the seventeenth century coincided with an increase in mestizos, mulattoes, and other ethnic mixtures, or *castas*, as the offspring of conquistadors, Indians, and Negroes made the population more heterogeneous. Miscegenation and the urban population increased more in the *norte chico* than further south—in large part because the north avoided the costs and scars of the Araucanian wars which devastated the Concepción-Biobío region. By the mid-eighteenth century the attraction of work in the mines contributed to the growth of urban centers in the *norte chico*; between 1755 and 1778 Copiapó expanded from a settlement of 2900 to a small town of 5300, with a rate of increase in excess of 3.5 percent per year.

Both natural increase and migration to the mineral districts added population to the *norte chico*. Still, the encomenderos resisted employing mestizo, Indian, or *casta* free laborers, preferring to rely on traditional labor arrangements with "their" encomienda Indians. The mestizos, free Indians, and *castas* thus became a sort of underclass, prohibited from occupying official posts, joining the priesthood, or obtaining the status of master artisan. As the encomienda system declined, this underclass found its way into the mines and haciendas as labor-rent tenants, renters, sharecroppers, or peons. Others took up the life of vagabonds or criminals. Cattle rustling was so serious by the middle of the eighteenth century that the hacendados received judicial authority within their estates, which often covered entire regions; and punishments for robbery increased in severity from floggings or banishment to prison sentences or, when a theft involved more than five cows, death. In addition, the authorities attempted to force transients into productive work. Local registers kept track of all those living within a district and required "all *vecinos* to report vagabonds and all those entering or leaving the district to present themselves to the corregidor." Those who could not prove they had jobs were assigned to public works.

The existence of a growing and mobile proletariat did not suit the needs and expectations of colonial elites and threatened to "corrupt" the sedentary labor force. The concentration of agricultural lands into vast estates along with the political limitations on creation of private enterprises prevented absorption of this underclass into the economy as small farmers, artisans, or merchants. Many could find no employment or could do so only seasonally in the mines or at harvest time. In a report on the state of Chilean agriculture, industry, and commerce at the end of the eighteenth century, a royal official commented that "this lack of employment makes common the lamentable use of certain modes of forgetting their plight, of removing the weight of such a sad, languid existence; of those beverages with which the unfortunate, with the pretext of enjoying their afflictions, seek a cure for living." In the same report Manuel de Salas noted the tendency of these vagabonds to remain single, to be promiscuous, and to avoid the responsibilities of a family, thereby "becoming the fathers of a new generation of the underclass [*miserables*], vagabonds like their fathers, without homes and with little more possessions than those sufficient to cover their bodies." By the end of the colonial period, the conditions leading to intergenerational "inheritance" of misery had already taken shape in the *norte chico*.

From these transients or drifters sprang also in the period 1690–1750 an incipient wage-labor force of peons, or *gañanes*, in the mines of the northern district. Often, however, an advance loan of food, clothing, or tools reduced the peon to a sort of debt-servitude, even though decrees at the end of the century prohibited advance payment of more than one month's salary to single workers or two months' to married workers. To obtain employment in the mines, workers had to have a document, or *boleta*, in which the last employer confirmed that the worker owed no further debt. This system of internal passports served to monitor the movements of thieves or other "undesirables" as well as of indebted laborers who sought entry into a new mining camp. If an Indian, a mulatto, or a Negro fled from the mines while he owed money, he could be punished by a fine and by flogging "to serve as an example to the others." Even the worker with a *boleta* could not legally leave the mine without giving notice to his employer. In this manner debt-peonage and mining on shares replaced the encomienda. In both cases Hispanic capitalism depended still upon an exploited but essentially pre-proletarian labor force, though by the middle of the eighteenth century a true wage proletariat was beginning to emerge in the mining districts of the north. Gradually this mestizo and *casta* labor force replaced the dwindling numbers of encomienda Indians.

The miner worked from sunup to sundown with a noonday meal and rest period of two hours. He received jerked beef and bread as food rations. With his earnings and perhaps some minerals "stolen" from the mine owners, the miner could enjoy Sundays or holidays at the combination store-saloons, or *pulperías* and *bodegones,* of the nearby camps or villages. These *pulperías* served as social centers, gambling dens, dance halls, and houses of prostitution. In 1781 fifty-two such *pulperías* could be found in Copiapó and ten at the small settlement at Huasco.

Despite the increase in population in the *norte chico,* until the end of the seventeenth century not a single new major city was founded—only a large number of mining camps, trading centers, and small settlements. Indeed, at the end of the colonial period La Serena with 5000 to 6000 residents still ranked as the largest urban center in the north. Throughout the region the population was concentrated in the river valleys— Elqui, Sotaqui, Salsipuedes, Andacollo, Limarí, Quillota, Aconcagua—and the mining camps, as it is to this day. At the end of the colonial period the *norte chico* remained a sparsely settled, agro-mining region which sent copper, silver, gold, and livestock products, especially goatskins, to international and intercolonial markets.

In the early years Santiago and the central region served as a base camp for the enterprise of conquest. Rebuilt after an Indian attack that left the town in ashes a mere seven months after its foundation, Santiago grew slowly during the first half-century of its existence. It suffered, nevertheless, from some problems common to most urban places. In 1551, taking note of the frequent disorders and robberies at night, Lieutenant Governor Rodrigo de Quiroga and the cabildo decreed that no one could go out of his house at night after curfew under penalty—for Spaniards, of losing their weapons and being arrested, and for the Indians or Negroes, of 100 lashes.

In addition to dealing with law and order, the cabildo had to provide essential public works. The Mapocho River periodically inundated the town. Residents needed a safe supply of potable water. Lack of bridges across the river impeded communications and commerce. Dusty or muddy streets required cobbling. During the sixteenth century the cabildo began to deal with the physical needs of the city. In 1578 water was brought from the cordillera to the central plaza, but the service could not be maintained, and in 1588 Santiago residents again turned to water from the Mapocho. In 1578 the cabildo also cobbled a number of streets. By the first decade of the seventeenth century, after a flood had destroyed the Hermitage of Saturnino and part of the lower sections of the town, construction began on the flood-control works. Notwithstanding these improvements, the town continued to have a rural flavor: the cabildo prohibited pigs from slogging around the water in the plaza and, while the public waterworks underwent rehabilitation (1613), prohibited washing of clothes at certain points on the river bank, under penalty of 200 lashes.

At the turn of the century 500 to 700 Spanish and mestizos and several thousand Indians resided in this village capital. Despite the frontier simplicity of the physical environment, the wealthiest residents imported luxury goods from Europe and China via Peru. Merchants brought velvet, silk, and damask to a colony that often lacked munitions, horses, and military supplies and whose very existence remained in jeopardy. In the midst of frontier warfare a would-be aristocracy clung to its pretensions. According to one chronicler, "every Spanish woman wanted thirty Indian servants to do her washing and sewing as if she were a princess." Even in the face of the loss of the most prosperous colonial towns (those south of the Biobío River) after 1598 and the threat to Santiago itself, the conquistadors and their successors maintained the superficial forms of a European nobility they wished to emulate.

The elite of the new-society-in-formation consisted of encomenderos, public officials, including religious functionaries, and merchants. After Pedro de Valdivia's initial generosity, the relative scarcity of sedentary Indians in Chile forced the first governor to reduce the number of encomiendas granted to the *vecinos* of Santiago from sixty to approximately thirty between Copiapó and Maule. When Valdivia died in 1553, a very small number of encomenderos, including his mistress, Inés de Suarez, had been granted the natives in most of the territory of Chile. These grants served as the basis of wealth and power over generations for certain of Chile's colonial elite.

The abbreviated case history of the encomienda of the German-born conquistador Bartolomé Flores is illustrative. To Flores, Valdivia commended "all the caciques and principals, with their Indians, named below, to wit, Talagante, Mavellangai, Codamolcalebi, Upiro, Lebalo, Guarcamilla, Acai, Nabalquivi, Conquemangui and Namarongo, with all their Indians and subjects in the valley of Mapocho." Flores consolidated these grants into the two estates of Talagante and Putugán (Linares), where he raised horses, chickens, and pigs and cultivated wheat, barley, beans, and corn. On these estates Flores built the first oxcarts in Chile and taught the Indians certain manual skills. Flores married the daughter of the cacique Talagante, and his heir from this union, Doña Argueda, married another German-born conquistador, Pedro de Lisperguer, who had arrived in Chile with Governor García Hurtado de Mendoza (1557). Two other children born in Peru also came to Chile and obtained encomienda grants through marriage. These lands, and others conceded throughout the seventeenth century, remained in the hands of Flores' descendants until 1721–24. Many of the Indians from the southern grant were transferred to the Santiago region, but as was typical of the encomiendas during this period, decimation or flight reduced radically the number of tributary peoples. In 1721 the Talagante grant had a mere fourteen tributary Indians. Nevertheless, these estates and those of the other encomenderos played a significant role in the economic development of the central region during the colonial period. At least twenty of the original grants persisted intact until the final abolition of the encomienda in Chile in 1791.

In Santiago and central Chile there was a rapid growth of livestock and agricultural production, centered in the vast estates of the encomenderos and the hacendados. By 1571–74, according to a nineteenth-century historian, the Santiago regional economy produced "a great quantity of wheat and barley, much wine, and all the other commodities, fruits, and livestock of Spain; there are also many orchards and gardens within and without the city." Commerce with Peru developed immediately, with the arrival in 1543 of reinforcements for Valdivia and goods sent in exchange for the gold dust collected by the settlers. The extent of this trade can be judged by the loot taken by Sir Francis Drake when he sacked Valparaíso in 1578: 2500 to 3000 jugs of wine, salted meat, flour, agricultural and livestock products ready for shipment to Lima and Potosí.

In the first years a sea trip from Callao to Chile could take over a month. Maritime communication was irregular; only 24 ships arrived from Peru between 1543 and 1556, and seventeen sailed from Valparaíso to Callao-Lima, a trip that took three to four months due to the southerly winds and the Humboldt Current. Six others were lost at sea. A trip from Santiago to Madrid could easily take a year. Despite the difficulties and perils of communication, the export economy developed steadily, and Valparaíso, with only a handful of residents, began to serve as a port of commerce.

While the countryside produced most of the colony's wealth, the principal beneficiaries were colonial administrators and merchants in the towns. The colonial merchants, who took great risks to bring goods to Chile and to send them from Chile to Lima or Spain, charged prices that yielded enormous profits. A study of the wealthy residents in Santiago and La Serena from 1567 to 1577 shows that only 15 to 25 years after the conquest, merchants paid almost as much into the royal treasury on the gold registered for payment of the *quintos* as did the encomenderos. The amount of smuggled or unregistered gold acquired by merchants in urban shops or through trade with the Indians cannot be estimated. Some encomenderos also invested the gold "their" Indians mined in commodities or merchant ventures; from the outset, merchant capital and encomendero interests formed an interrelated elite, rather than two distinct social groups. Thus, trade and commerce took their place as integral elements in the colonial economy even under the harsh conditions of sixteenth-century conquest.

Unlike the La Serena region, however, the *vecinos* of Santiago bore a heavy burden in the Araucanian war. The military disasters of the sixteenth century threatened the very existence of the regional economy as well as the maintenance of the Chilean colony itself. The development and character of the economy of the central region at that time depended substantially, therefore, upon the vicissitudes of warfare.

The monarchy's response to the colony's distress after the fiasco at Curalaba at the turn of the century created a new source of wealth, which relieved the colonials of much of the economic burden of warfare and also allowed them to pay greater attention to their economic enterprises. By decree of March 21, 1600, the Spanish monarch authorized a yearly subsidy, or *situado*, of 60,000 ducats, or 82,500 pesos, from the royal treasury in Peru for three years to assist the Chilean colony in its struggle to survive. The new Chilean governor, Alonso de Ribera, received most of this subsidy in the form of clothing and supplies for the troops en route to Chile. Ribera's reports to the king on the desperate conditions of the Chilean garrisons—"so poorly disciplined that their style of warfare seems more like confusion and barbarism than like Spanish militia"— persuaded the crown to create a permanent military establishment of 1500 soldiers whose salary would be paid by the viceroy of Peru. Later this number was increased to 2000. In 1603 the crown raised the military budget to 140,000 ducats; and in 1606, to 212,000 ducats, or 293,000 pesos.

Thus to secure its Chilean outpost, the Spanish state took over the administration and the financing of conquest, for which it utilized the wealth of the mines at Potosí and the income of Peru. Ribera added to this subsidy the revenues obtained through taxes on the sale of captive Indians, and also organized royal estates to provision the troops with grain, beef, and livestock products. At Melipilla the governor established royal textile workshops to supply clothing, blankets, and other goods to the garrisons. These estates—Loyola, between Chillán and Concepción; Catentoa, between Maule and Chillán; and Quillota—harvested 7410 fanegas of wheat, 500 of barley, and 200 of potatoes in 1604. Large herds of sheep and cattle as well as hemp plantations at Quillota provided part of the basic necessities for the army. In 1607 the Loyola estate earned slightly more than 53,000 pesos, and the Catentoa estate, some 75,000 pesos. Ribera also created a tannery in Santiago and a number of artisan industries in Concepción. Following Ribera's example, his successor established a cordage industry at Quillota and constructed a large number of oxcarts as baggage wagons for the military.

The military subsidy stimulated the colonial economy by increasing demand for supplies and by largely freeing the settlers from the obligations of annual military campaigns. It also brought a continual flow of Spaniards and mestizos as troops, especially to the Concepción region. But the purchase of many supplies for the army in Lima limited the beneficial effects on the Chilean economy; and owing to the institutionalized corruption at Lima, the Chilean army received silk stockings, damask, and honey as well as a number of commodities available in Chile such as soap and oil. The luxury items profited Chilean officials and merchants but did little to help the war effort. The Peruvian viceroys insisted that the major share of the subsidy be spent in Peru, which benefited Peruvian producers and merchants much more than the Chileans. Not until 1685 did Governor José de Garro get authorization to have the subsidy sent in money from Potosí. But, as noted in Chapter 2, at the end of the seventeenth century the subsidy arrived late or not at all.

Throughout this century the royal *situado* and warfare against the Indians reinforced the agro-commercial economy of the Santiago-central region. Loss of the agricultural and livestock output between the Itata and Maule rivers after the uprising of 1655 forced the central district to supply most of the needs of the entire colony; and as the century progressed, it had to respond to demands for grain from Peru, though the quantities of grain sent to Lima remained paltry (9000 to 12,000 fanegas per year) until late in the seventeenth century.

The Santiago-central region provided most of the wheat needed by the colony until the 1680s without pushing prices over three pesos per fanega. Except under the extreme conditions of warfare or siege, even the poorest Chilean produced enough to eat or could purchase food at reasonably low prices, while animal products in particular were available in abundance. Existing external markets did not permit a significant expansion of commercial agricultural production. In contrast, livestock products, such as tallow, salted beef, lard, hides, and sheepskins, as well as wine could compete favorably in the Lima-Potosí markets. At midcentury (1647) Martín de Mugica wrote to the king that Chile exported 20,000 quintals of tallow to Peru (and internal consumption amounted to about the same).

The livestock economy fit nicely with the social attitudes of the encomenderos and hacendados who preferred the prestige of horses, cattle, or sheep to the plebeian tasks of farming. As the livestock economy also required considerably less labor than cereal production, there was also less need for Indian laborers whose numbers were declining in the encomiendas.

The perilous state of the Chilean colony at the end of the sixteenth century had induced the viceroy to exempt Chilean products from the traditional import duties, or *almojarifazgo*. From this time the number of land grants, or *mercedes de tierra*, around Santiago greatly increased in number; by 1604 most of the territory of modern Valparaíso and Santiago provinces had been legally granted to Spanish owners. Important factors in the rush for *land*, in contrast to the earlier desire for grants of Indians, included the Peruvian demand for Chilean livestock products, the need for sheepskins used to transport quicksilver from Huancavelica to Potosí, and the needs of the army to the south.

Land grants varied considerably in size, but some exceeded 5000 hectares. Sometimes grantees sold portions of the land in order to obtain capital to purchase livestock and initiate an agrarian enterprise; or the land grants emerged indirectly from previous encomienda grants. In either case the land became valuable as the livestock-export economy opened up business opportunities. Most of the large landowners or encomenderos were *vecinos* of Santiago, even when they held rural estates located in Cuyo, La Serena, or Chillán. According to the *audiencia* in 1647, Santiago had 516 established households with a total of almost 5000 residents. At least one-third of the *vecinos* held encomiendas. Of a list of 164 encomenderos called upon by the governor for aid in putting down the Indian rebellion of 1655, over one-third (59) were royal officials or descendants of sixteenth-century encomenderos. The remaining two-thirds (105) came from families that arrived in Chile in the seventeenth century or that had not earlier obtained encomiendas. Increased land values, participation in commerce, and the casualties of war made entry into the small Chilean elite relatively open for the able or for those with "good" family connections.

In 1604, to safeguard their investments, and supposedly to protect the remaining Indian villages, the cabildo of Santiago commissioned a land survey and boundary markings by Ginés de Lillo. Lillo's survey became the basis for the boundaries of many of the Santiago region's most important estates in the following centuries. From 1604 to 1620 *merced* holders attempted to acquire unclaimed lands near their properties through grants of *demasía* which added "leftover" land to existing estates. By the middle of the seventeenth century the legal basis for the Santiago region's vast haciendas was firmly established. Concentration of landownership peaked in the period from 1670 to 1680. The extensive seigniorial estates precluded formation of a large class of small independent farmers.

An earthquake at Lima in 1687 produced a crisis in the agricultural valleys that supplied wheat to the Lima market. Destruction of irrigation systems left the lands "infertile" for a number of years. Prices for wheat soared as high as 25 to 30 pesos per fanega, ten times the normal price. Chilean and Peruvian merchants took advantage of the catastrophe and Chilean wheat was shipped to Lima. In the *norte chico* the Peruvian crisis intensified already existing patterns of trade; for the Santiago region the opening of the Lima market offered the chance for a radical transformation of its pastoral economy. At first, the limited grain surplus produced in the region permitted only a weak response. Soon thereafter the valleys of Aconcagua, Mapocho, and regions to the south were planted in wheat, and 150,000 to 200,000 fanegas were exported annually. In 1712, though prices had returned to 2 to 3 pesos per fanega, the Santiago-central region sent some 180,000 fanegas of wheat to the Peruvian market.

Land values increased with the expanding demand for wheat. Wheat cultivation also required greater labor input than the livestock enterprise. In order to attract tenants, the landowners offered rentals, or *préstamos*—land "loaned" with only a token rent. As the encomienda Indians died off or fled, mestizo, *casta,* or even poor Spanish workers replaced them as peons or tenants. Indians, slaves, indentured labor, "free" laborers, and tenants all played a role in the expanding agrarian economy. Even the indentured or "free" laborer rarely obtained a money wage but rather received the equivalent of 5 to 7 pesos a month (1685–1707) in food, clothing, and other payments in kind. As these arrangements excluded from the money economy the great mass of Chileans who worked in the countryside, the internal markets for manufactures were exceedingly small.

As the eighteenth century progressed, the role of the encomienda Indians drastically declined, while tenancies and the system of *inquilinaje* became more important. The origin of the *inquilino* laborer, who became the backbone of the rural labor force in Chile, still stirs controversy among Chilean historians. A traditional interpretation has the encomienda Indian as the forerunner of the *inquilino.* More recent studies of several regions in the central valley point to the *arrendatario* and the worker receiving *préstamos de tierra* from the early eighteenth century onward. Of course, as wheat cultivation expanded, many of the remaining encomienda Indians fled to other farms and/or took on mestizo culture and were incorporated as peons or *arrendatarios* in the rural economy. Thus, the institutions of tenancy, as they evolved, allowed for absorption of the Indian laborer, as well as the rural *casta* and mestizo, as *inquilinos,* while encomenderos continued to exploit tributary Indians as long as possible.

In the large estates more tenants could be absorbed without seriously disrupting the livestock economy, and the tenants produced an increasingly larger share of the wheat of the central region. The *préstamos de tierra,* or rentals, consisted of variously sized parcels, but as land increased in value, the token rental fees and commodity rents often became labor rents, or the landlords required labor services in addition to commodity rents. As land became scarcer and its value increased, the hacendados required more service from the tenants. Soon the landlords required individual *inquilinos* to provide a worker year round for the agricultural labors of the *estancia* or hacienda. They also demanded additional labor at peak agricultural periods, such as planting, round up, or harvest. In the later years of the eighteenth century, the term *arrendatario* was less used and thereafter replaced by *inquilino*—the service tenant who predominated until the mid-1960s in Chilean agriculture.

Lack of land outside the large estates made possible establishment of a service tenantry, and labor-rent obligations multiplied as internal and external demand for wheat increased. However, if *inquilinaje* in Chile bore some resemblance to *colono* or service-tenant labor systems in other Latin American nations, its origins and the predominantly mestizo composition of its work force distinguished it from the harsher arrangements involving Indian labor in Peru, Bolivia, and Ecuador. Even when economic conditions worsened, Chilean *inquilinos* as a class did not experience systematic cultural and ethnic repression on the scale of the rural labor force in the Andes, nor did debt-peonage typically restrict their mobility.

Neither external nor internal markets placed great demands on the Chilean landlords in relation to the territory's agricultural potential. By mid-eighteenth century Chile produced perhaps 400,000 quintals* of wheat on less than 50,000 hectares. Even the largest rural estates rarely cultivated more than 100 hectares of wheat. Commercial expansion of agriculture enriched a number of landowners and provided considerable opportunities for improvement to a relatively small portion of the rural labor force who succeeded at crop farming or stock raising as tenants. But even the "boom" after 1687 and continued expansion in the eighteenth century did not absorb the growing numbers of floating population which squatted on "vacant" land, took up banditry, or served the landlords as a pool of seasonal laborers. Labor surpluses made debt-peonage unnecessary and, therefore, relatively rare.

The sharp increase in demand and massive exports of wheat to Peru (1687–1700) not only influenced rural land-tenure and labor systems but also created serious problems for local consumers. The Santiago cabildo first attempted to monitor the harvests and retain a fixed proportion in the region in order to avoid scarcity or excessive increases in price. Landowners registered only a fraction of the harvested grain to circumvent the cabildo's regulations. In response the cabildo in 1695 urged the governor to prohibit wheat exports. With the *audiencia*'s approval the governor revoked all licenses for export of wheat. Opposition from landowners and merchants included the clever request by the Jesuits—who owned many of the most important rural estates in Chile—for permission to "transfer" 1000 fanegas of wheat from their storehouses in Chile to their college in Lima. The governor rejected this request and even forced a merchant ship at Valparaíso to unload wheat already in the ship's hold.

In the following years the tension continued between the need to provision the local market at reasonable prices and the economic opportunities of the Peruvian market. Dual pricing schemes attempted to limit the price of wheat sold locally, but the rapid expansion of commerce made effective regulation practically impossible. Increased production, however, lowered prices substantially. In 1713 over 140,000 fanegas of wheat left Chile for Peru in thirty ships; two-thirds of these embarked from Valparaíso with wheat from the central region, seven from Penco-Concepción, and two or three from Coquimbo.

The wheat trade also promoted the commercial and physical growth of Valparaíso.

---

*One metric quintal equals 100 kilograms.

A small group of merchants and warehouse owners soon controlled the wheat market in the port. Despite the efforts of the cabildo to limit commercial corruption, this group often defrauded producers with discounts for spoilage. As the years went by, the Lima shippers also conspired to depress the price paid to Chilean wheat producers. The wheat trade epitomized commerce in the context of Hispanic capitalism: a monopoly or a small clique of suppliers colluded with government officials to fix prices and restrict supplies of basic commodities in order to guarantee "reasonable" profits. In the context of Hispanic capitalism, doing business most always meant "doing politics." The most valuable commodities in this colonial system were government authority, favors, patronage, and concessions.

The end of the seventeenth century saw not only the transformation of agriculture in the Santiago-central region but also a significant increase in contraband trade with European powers. The succession to the Spanish throne of the French Duke of Anjou, who governed Spain as Philip V, placed Spain alongside France in a long war against England, Austria, Portugal, Savoy, and Holland. Unable to defend or supply its overseas empire, Spain authorized French vessels to maintain communications with its colonies. Contraband trade mushroomed, and Chilean governors profited enormously from new commercial ventures. When the French engineer Frezier arrived in Valparaíso in 1713, he commented on "the abundance of merchandise in the country when we arrived and the low prices." The limited market for European goods in Chile ruined many merchants in Lima who could not compete with French manufacturers. The contraband trade also brought a reversal in trade patterns as merchandise arrived in Concepción and Valparaíso from Europe and then was shipped to Lima. On a lesser scale, merchandise also arrived via Buenos Aires and the base for contraband at the Portuguese settlement of Colônia do Sacramento. In 1712 the Spanish crown worked out an arrangement with the French King, Louis XIV, to halt the contraband trade. However, it had become so excessive that the Spanish waited seven years to re-establish the fleets bringing merchandise to the "annual" fairs at Portobello (Panama) in order to allow the surpluses from contraband merchandise to be absorbed. In 1724 the French expeditions temporarily ended, but British merchants had by then replaced them.

The Treaty of Utrecht (1713), ending the War of the Spanish Succession, gave the English a thirty-year monopoly on the slave trade with the Spanish American colonies; during this time the English were to bring 144,000 Negroes to the Atlantic ports. Of these, 400 could come yearly to Peru and Chile. Queen Anne of England granted the slave monopoly to the South Seas Company, which established itself in Buenos Aires. From 1715 to 1739, sixty-one ships brought over to Buenos Aires 18,000 Negroes, nearly 4000 of whom were shipped on to Chile and Peru. Since they were not as successful at slaving as they had anticipated, the English turned to smuggling. On the pretext of transporting necessities for the Negroes, all sorts of merchandise came into Buenos Aires and from there via Mendoza to Chile. In return, the English took silver or gold in payment. Traders loaded merchandise into oxcarts for the trip across the pampas and in Mendoza transferred their goods to mules for the Andes crossing. Mendoza's merchants and cabildo identified so closely with the contraband trade that they banished the new corregidor who had been sent from Santiago to stifle it.

By 1722 commercial reform allowed greater shipping activity through the so-called "registered ships," or navíos de registro. Direct trade between Europe and Buenos Aires was extended overland to Chile. Protesting Lima merchants urged an end to this link, but the Spanish fleets could no longer compete with the French and the English. In 1735 the merchants of Cádiz and Peru requested that no further fleets come to Panama until they could dispose of the merchandise on hand. Nevertheless, a fleet arrived in 1739, only to be re-routed to Cartagena due to the destruction of Portobello by an English squadron under Edward Vernon. This marked the end of the fleet system and forced the crown to open a new Pacific route for the *navíos de registro*.

After two hundred years as a colony Chile could finally trade with Spain by sea, although Callao remained an intermediary port of call. Due to the war with England, however, French vessels contracted by merchants at Cádiz, carried out the first legal trade between Chile and Spain. In the following three decades the Chilean market never lacked for European manufactures; indeed the market was so glutted that prices declined considerably for most imported merchandise, and many merchants, unable to sell their goods, went bankrupt.

In the last quarter of the eighteenth century, new reforms further reduced commercial restrictions. Prohibitions on much intercolonial trade disappeared in 1774; and with the creation in 1776 of a new viceroyalty centered in Buenos Aires, trade restrictions were eliminated between Chile and Río de la Plata. Despite protests regarding the coincident separation of the western Argentine province of Cuyo from Chile, the creation of the Río de la Plata viceroyalty benefited the Chilean economy. The initial measures of the viceroy encouraged Chilean commerce by opening the ports to European goods destined for Cuyo. Lastly, the crown also removed Callao as a mandatory stop. Between them these measures eroded Peruvian domination of Chile's commerce.

Yet with all the commercial restrictions of the colonial period, it is difficult to point to any that fundamentally impeded development of Chile's agrarian economy. Inconveniences for merchants or small groups of elite consumers resulted from prohibitions on bringing sugar from Mexico or trading directly with Buenos Aires and Potosí. But Lima was the logical market for most Chilean products. In 1650, and even by 1800, there was little European or North American demand for the commodities of Chile's agrarian economy, as there came to be in the middle of the nineteenth century. In 1788 the value of all (official) Chilean exports (676,222.50 pesos) did not pay for Chilean imports of sugar and yerba mate (684,617.04 pesos); total imports exceeded 2 million pesos.

Efforts by Captain General Ambrosio O'Higgins (1788–96) to stimulate expansion of production, in part through import substitution, and to open new markets for Chilean commodities met with little success. Sugar, cotton, and other tropical products, even when the crops survived in Chile, could not compete with Peru or Mexico. Likewise, Chilean industries could not compete with European or North American manufactures. Imports of luxury goods—fine textiles, furniture, jewels—could only be paid for by minting coins from the gold, silver, and copper taken from the earth and exporting money to maintain the pretensions of the colonial aristocracy. European merchants brought manufactured goods to the Chilean market and took gold, silver, or livestock products in return, but offered no great prospect, at the time, of absorbing significant amounts of rural Chile's products. Chile's economic development, given its agro-mineral output, depended upon fluctuations in the international economy's demand for a range of primary or semi-elaborated products. This remained the case long after the end of Spanish colonial domination. Mining booms in the *norte chico* in the eighteenth century increased import capacity, but the concentration of wealth and the inability to compete with imported manufactures stifled internal industrial development.

European manufactures entered Chilean markets throughout the late seventeenth and the eighteenth centuries. At the end of the eighteenth century import duties amounted to one-third those charged by the first national government after 1810. The textile "factories" in Chile declined after 1650, as did the sugar mills. The only surviving industries were shipbuilding, cordage, foundries, and those processing products of the agrarian economy such as tanneries, wineries, and flour mills. Perhaps more extensive commerce in mineral products with British and French merchants might have

allowed even greater imports of European manufactures, but this could not have benefited colonial industrial development or altered the institutional structure of the agrarian economy. Unlike the Spanish prohibitions on direct trade with Buenos Aires prior
to 1778 and the demands for "free trade" which inspired Argentine independence, freer
trade offered little benefit to overall Chilean economic development in the seventeenth
and eighteenth centuries.

If Spanish commercial policy did less to shape Chilean development than is often
supposed, the internal dynamics and customs of Hispanic capitalism left an indelible
mark on Chilean society. It molded economic and social practices and expectations so
as to create numerous institutional obstacles to political and economic advancement
for the colony and the future Chilean nation. Much more important than the often-
evaded commercial regulations, the factors that impeded social and economic development were the authoritarian, arbitrary processes of policy making, the bureaucratic
modes of implementation or circumvention, the use of public resources for private
profit, the mingling of public and "private" enterprise, the denigration of labor, and the
exploitation of the labor force. More important than any Spanish mercantile restrictions
as impediments to Chilean development were the institutions of enterprise which condemned the vast majority of laborers to a subsistence existence outside the money
economy. The encomienda system in Chile practically made slaves of the Indians. Extreme concentration of land in the large estates condemned the mestizo rural laborers
to generations of exploitation. State-supported monopolies on commerce and the artisan trades limited opportunities for the evolution of a prosperous middle class. The
royal bureaucracy's comprehensive regulation of prices and economic activity ensured
that private enterprise was never really a private matter—that public policy inhibited
operation of anything like a market economy. The combination of Spanish seigniorial
institutions, neofeudal labor systems, and monopolistic commercial enterprises created a highly stratified society in the Santiago–central region, and the lack of effective
internal demand inhibited the development of domestic industry. Chilean elites maintained much of this legacy of colonialism long after they had rejected Spanish imperial
rule.

At the end of the eighteenth century the Santiago–central region was still an essentially rural society. Only Santiago, of all the urban places, looked like a city. With a population of 25,000 in 1780, Santiago grew to an urban center of 34,000 to 40,000 in the first
decade of the nineteenth century. In a territory with between 500,000 and 750,000 inhabitants outside of Indian territory, the urban centers contained barely 10 percent of
the population. While this was similar to general trends of urbanization in the Western
world, it meant that the daily existence of most Chileans consisted of toil from sunup
to sundown in the countryside or mines.

Between 1740 and 1754 governors Manso de Velasco and Ortiz de Rozas organized
and partially financed the foundation of new towns in the central region: San Felipe,
Los Angeles, Cauquenes, Talca, San Fernando, Melipilla, Rancagua, Curicó, Copiapó,
Florida, Casablanca, Petorca, Ligua. These towns, which would later become important
urban centers in the region, were still, in the words of Amunátegui Solar, "miserable
villages" at the end of the eighteenth century. Valparaíso, despite its importance as the
major port for the commerce of the central region, had a population of only 4500 as late
as 1808.

The relative smallness of the urban population belied the overriding concentration
of political and economic power in Santiago and Valparaíso. In the capital the cabildo
and royal officials determined the regulations that would affect the economic interests
of the colonial elites and granted the concessions, monopolies, and privileges that were

the source of economic opportunity. Hispanic capitalism linked urban elites to the landowners, miners, and merchants when they were not one and the same. Despite the rural base of economic production, family connections, business partnerships, and the politics of colonial society knit together the economic life of the colony in the major urban centers. Unlike the dispersion of economic power and decision making characteristic of European feudalism, Hispanic capitalism in Chile concentrated wealth and decision making in urban centers even while feudal-like production generated the economic surplus.

In the last quarter of the eighteenth century important public works enhanced the city of Santiago. Under direction of the architect Joaquín Toesca, the city rebuilt the dikes destroyed by the floods of 1783, and work on the new mint, La Moneda, was intensified. In 1795 George Vancouver admiringly called the Santiago mint the "best building in all the Spanish colonies." Roads between Santiago and Valparaíso also received attention made necessary by the expansion of commerce. Sidewalks on major streets and beautification projects testified to the fact that the town had become a city. Here lived the colonial aristocracy, a mixture of landowners, merchants, and the growing number of royal officials brought to the colony as a result of administrative and commercial reforms implemented by the Bourbons in the late eighteenth century. A number of elite *criollo* families intermarried with the colonial administrators and the new arrivals from Spain. Between 1701 and 1810 some 24,000 immigrants came to Chile from Spain, including numerous Basques. Arrival of these Basques at a time of commercial expansion altered the composition of the Chilean elite. The Basques succeeded in commerce, bought rural estates (including some of the estates confiscated from the Jesuits expelled from Chile in 1767), and soon occupied official positions in the colonial administration.

Marriage of royal officials with the daughters of *criollo* elites, a violation of royal policy, created significant conflicts of interest. These led frequently to complaints by those negatively affected as well as to injury to the public interest: "By their [the *oidores*] marriages here, infinite [numbers of] relatives, the connections and haciendas that they have, and by their maximum opposition to that which is . . . advantageous to royal finances, all is reduced to becoming a [victim] of their passions." Not only intermarriage but also expanding opportunity for *criollos* in the royal service created problems for the crown. In 1759 six of the eight members of the *audiencia* were *criollos* and in 1776 all the *oidores* had been born in the colonies. This contrasted with general patterns of peninsular dominance of high administrative and judicial offices throughout the Spanish Empire. Though decrees in 1776 purged *criollos* and their peninsular relations from the *audiencia* to overcome their supposed opposition to fiscal reforms, in the last decade of the eighteenth century *criollos* and *peninsulares* related to Chileans reassumed influence in the *audiencia* and in other official positions. Jacques Barbier's study of colonial elites in Chile confirms that from 1796 to 1810 there were always at least two Chilean *oidores* in the audiencia. Still, tension existed between the aspirations of the colonial aristocracy for control of the local society and the efforts of the crown to limit the corrupting influence of family ties and local loyalties. Above all, however, the efforts by the Chilean elites to influence or control royal officials merely point again to their own awareness that in the context of Hispanic capitalism wealth, economic opportunity, and status were ultimately linked to politics.

By the beginning of the nineteenth century the institutions of Hispanic capitalism had shaped the Santiago–central region into a highly stratified socio-economic system. A small elite lived well—if not as splendidly as the upper classes in Peru or Mexico—from the returns on colonial commerce, the salaries of official position, and the corruption linking politics and business. Landowners reaped profits from agriculture and livestock. Rural workers and tenants lived in misery. The economy grew, and the living conditions of much of the rural population and the emergent proletariat *worsened*. Economic growth within the context of Hispanic capitalism led to the development of a society in which, as one royal official said, "nothing was more common in the countryside, where harvests had recently been taken in and sold for the lowest of prices, than to see the hands that had recently harvested the crops extended for alms." In Santiago the same official reported that he continually saw "similar conditions in regard to the public works of the capital, where numbers of the unfortunate present themselves seeking jobs, begging for admittance to work."

The internal contradictions of Hispanic capitalism already constrained Chilean development. In the words of Manuel de Salas, "the decadence of this kingdom was a necessary result of its economic structure."

Of all the Chilean territory, the Concepción–southern region offered the brightest prospects to the conquistadors with Valdivia in the first years of conquest. Here could be found gold mines, good land for livestock and agriculture, and large numbers of Indians for a potential work force. Some of the conquistadors gave up encomiendas in the Santiago region in exchange for grants south of the Biobío River. But the defeat at Tucapel (1553) marked the first of many military disasters that thwarted Spanish dreams of enrichment in what appeared to be the most attractive region of Chile. For the entire colonial period this southern region was an open wound—an insecure frontier where Spanish economic enterprise and urban culture barely managed to survive against the Indians and the calamities of nature.

Valdivia's forces first established the city of Concepción in 1550 near the site of present-day Penco. The town was destroyed in 1554, symbolically refounded in 1555 and abandoned then re-established again in 1558 when Hurtado de Mendoza arrived with reinforcements from Peru. In recognition of the town's role as the principal fort on the Indian frontier, the crown created Chile's first *audiencia* at Concepción in 1565. But in the words of Carvallo y Goyeneche, "This had no purpose: all were military men and a *consejo de guerra* would have been more appropriate than a legislature; pens were as useless then as swords were necessary." When an earthquake and tidal wave destroyed the town again in 1570, a chronicler tells us that the residents "didn't know what to do, believing that the world was coming to an end, because they saw black water gush up from the cracks in the earth, and a smell of sulphur that seemed like the inferno. . . ." To the end of the sixteenth century Concepción remained a small military camp; only after 1603 did it begin to take shape as a permanent town with the stationing there of the large permanent military garrison.

The other settlements founded south of the Biobío River in the sixteenth century constituted no more than small fortified encampments. Mining activity around Imperial (present-day Carahue), Osorno, and Valdivia made them relatively prosperous, though they were always menaced by the threat of Indian attack. In 1575 an earthquake damaged the southern settlements, but the settlers rebuilt them; and in 1580 Governor Martin Ruiz de Gamboa founded the city of Chillán during the annual military campaign. These southern settlements developed around the prosperous livestock and agricultural estates of the encomenderos as well as around gold mines.

The dispersion of the Spanish forces among so many small settlements left each town extremely vulnerable to any large-scale Indian attack. Had enmity not existed among various Indian groups, these southern outposts could not have survived at all. For most of the last decade of the sixteenth century the Spanish lived as prisoners in their own forts.

Despite its insecurity, the southern territory developed important agrarian enterprises and sent large quantities of gold north to Santiago and Peru. The rural estates produced wheat, barley, oats, vegetables, and great quantities of apples, which in later years became a major Chilean export. Abundance kept prices low. Livestock multiplied rapidly among the Spanish and also the Indians, who soon had large herds of sheep and horses as well as lesser amounts of cattle. Southern industries included the well-known textile workshops, or *obrajes*, at Osorno as well as mills, tanneries, crafts, and the mines. The Osorno *obrajes*, utilizing local Indian labor, produced cloth that the chronicler Mariño de Lobera compared favorably with the textiles of Flanders. Much of this production found its way to Santiago, Lima, and even Europe. Indeed, Osorno, Valdivia, and Imperial were the most prosperous settlements in Chile—until the military disasters after 1598. In 1598 the town of Valdivia had 600 Spanish and mestizo residents, and over 60 percent of all Spanish and mestizo settlers in Chile lived south of the Biobío River. By 1600, 90 percent of all Chilean Indians also lived south of the Biobío, as disease, enslavement, and warfare radically reduced their population in the north.

In the years 1598 to 1604 the Araucanians erased all Spanish settlements south of the Biobío River. Chile thus lost all the wealth of its southern economy. Unsuccessful military campaigns (1603–12) followed by a policy of "defensive warfare" (1612–26) left this territory in the hands of the Indians. After 1626 the crown ordered a return to active efforts to reconquer the lands south of Concepción, but these efforts degenerated into periodic pillage and slave hunts and proved ineffective. The only "products" harvested by the Spanish in these years were Indian slaves and concubines. Though able to send military expeditions through Indian territory, the Spanish could not guarantee the safety of permanent settlements. After years of raids, pillage, and occasional battles the Chilean governor ordered resettlement of Angol in 1637. A fire reduced the fort to ashes in 1638, and in the peace of Quillín (1641) the Spanish agreed to abandon Angol and to establish the Biobío River as a frontier between the sovereign Indian people and the Chilean colony.

In order to defend the Chilean colony against Indian and European adversaries, the viceroy of Peru committed a large expeditionary force (12 ships, 1800 men, 188 artillery pieces, as well as artisans) to the resettlement of Valdivia in 1645–46. For some years to come Valdivia depended directly upon the viceroyalty instead of on the Chilean authorities. It served as an isolated outpost in Indian territory, strongly defended and communicating only by sea with Peru or Santiago.

North of the Biobío River, between the Maule and Itata rivers, the Spanish maintained ongoing rural enterprises even after the loss of the southern towns. This district became the granary for the limited Concepción region; its wheat and livestock products fed the frontier garrisons and even provided a surplus for export. But the Spanish slave raids and pillaging finally provoked the Indians into another large-scale uprising in 1655 in which the Spanish lost the forts and fort-towns of Arauco, San Pedro, Colcura, Buena Esperanza, Nacimiento, Talcamávida, San Rosendo, Boroa, and Chillán. As a measure of the impressive economic growth that had occurred in this region, Carvallo y Goyeneche estimated that in sacking 396 rural estates, the Indians took 400,000 head of livestock and occasioned losses amounting to over 8 million pesos—in addition to capturing some 1300 Spaniards and over half the colony's armaments. Also destroyed were the entire farm infrastructure and small manufacturing enterprises such as mills and tanneries, which had been established between 1603 and 1654, along with crops in the cultivated fields and vineyards. The Spanish army lost some 900 men—over half its effective strength—and the surviving settlers retreated to Concepción or dispersed across the Maule River.

Two years later (March 15, 1657), with the Indian rebellion uncontained, an earthquake and tidal wave again utterly destroyed Concepción, the only remaining town in the southern region. Casualties amounted to forty dead; the survivors faced a winter without supplies or shelter. This tragedy, combined with the Indian threat, prompted an official of the *audiencia* at Santiago to propose moving the frontier north to the Maule River. Instead, the new governor, Pórter Casanate, led a successful campaign against the advancing Indians, pushing them back across the Biobío. Slowly the Spanish rebuilt Concepción, and by the 1670s the Maule-Concepción triangle regained self-sufficiency in basic foodstuffs. By the end of the century both wheat and wine production had recovered to pre-1655 levels, and the region again sent livestock products, wine, and wheat to Lima. The opening of the Lima market to Chilean wheat in the 1680s stimulated the rural economy of the Concepción region as it had the central valley, but the direct export trade remained relatively small; an average of only two to three ships a year trafficked between Concepción and Callao during the last two decades of the seventeenth century.

Delays in the arrival of the military subsidy between 1700 and 1717 seriously injured the southern economy and debilitated the frontier garrisons. The crown reduced the annual *situado* to 100,000 pesos after 1705; it actually arrived only in 1706 and 1717. By the early 1720s the effective garrison consisted of about 700 soldiers instead of the authorized 1500 to 2000. The reduced garrison found itself dispersed in a number of small forts, including some south of the Biobío River. These served as centers of trade with the Indians, but the abuses of soldiers and traders also provoked the Indians' anger.

The Indians took advantage of the decline in colonial military capabilities and in a general uprising in 1723 besieged and forced abandonment of the southern forts at Tucapel, Arauco, Colcura, and Purén. Raiding the haciendas between Laja and Chillán the Araucanians took thousands of cattle (40,000 according to one estimate) and again disrupted the rural economy. In a midcentury report to the king, a Jesuit urged a new frontier policy. He also conveyed an idea of the character of the forts destroyed in the 1723–26 uprisings: "If the forts don't defend us nor scare the enemy, what good are they? They serve merely to conserve a few 'ranchos' covered with straw, for—with the exception of Arauco, that is all they amounted to, in an area with few Spanish families. . . . To defend so little did not justify provoking the Indians' hostility." An indication of the economic effects of this uprising was that the tithes, or *diezmos*, collected by the Bishopric of Concepción declined from 18,000 pesos in 1717 to 7000 pesos in 1724. The same report tells us "in the year of 1738, the *diezmos* did not exceed 11,000 [pesos] because the Indians took over 100,000 head of cattle and again as much of smaller livestock from 1724."

Despite the intermittent warfare, cattle rustling, and minor incidents, the pastoral-agricultural economy in the Maule-Concepción region survived. Some settlers, called *conchabistas*, even carried out a good amount of trade with the Indians, exchanging wine, hardware, and trinkets for Indian ponchos, textiles, and livestock.

Just as Concepción was recovering from military disasters and natural calamities, still another earthquake and tidal wave (July 8, 1730) leveled most of the city. The bishop wrote to the king that two-thirds of the principal buildings and houses of the city, along with granaries, storehouses, and shops, had been destroyed. Emergency relief and military supplies arrived from Santiago to avoid a military disaster while the city recovered from the earthquake. The viceroy at Lima advanced 50 percent of the next year's subsidy, and the governor in Santiago contributed over 10,000 pesos to the churches and residents. Twenty-one years later (1751) an even worse earthquake entirely destroyed the settlement again; after struggles between the bishop and those wishing to relocate the town, Concepción was officially refounded in 1764 in the valley of Mocha, between the Andalién and Biobío rivers.

Apart from Concepción, a city of perhaps 6000 residents by 1800, few significant urban centers grew up in the southern district. At the end of the eighteenth century Carvallo y Goyeneche reported 449 families at Chillán (also destroyed by the earthquake of 1751) living in small adobe houses. The plaza "which is 150 *varas* square lacks the adornment of impressive buildings, with the exception of the house of the priest . . . built in the style of the capital." Other towns of the region, founded in the 1740s and 1750s by administrative order of the governor, included Quirihue (1741) which "merits not even the name of village with its five families"; Gaulqui, in the district of Puchacai, where 14 families resided; San Luis Gonzaga (1766), in the district of Rere, with 40 *vecinos* and a total population of 201; Los Angeles (1741), the most important town in Rere with 159 *vecinos* (less than 800 residents). In a number of small forts handfuls of soldiers also formed "urban" nuclei on the frontier. Farther south the colonial authorities in Lima and Santiago financed the refounding of Osorno, in the last decade of the century, with expenditures of over 30,000 pesos; in 1796 some 1,012 settlers (170 families) had established themselves in a region lost to the Spanish for many years. In all, however, if we accept the estimates of Marcello Carmagnani, fewer than 8 percent of the population in the southern region lived in "urban" situations near the end of the eighteenth century, and most of these resided in Concepción.

Social structure and land-tenure patterns in this region differed from those in the central valley and to the north of Santiago. Lack of security made maintenance of large estates extremely difficult. Most of the Spanish and mestizos who wanted to farm had access to parcels and could provide for their own sustenance. With a population composed largely of soldiers, ex-soldiers, and the families of soldiers, racial and social stratification was much less rigid than in other parts of the Chilean colony. Most of the inhabitants led a life of subsistence scratched from the soil, or from the low military pay, small mines, trade with the Indians, livestock and related manufactures, or pillage. In the last decade of the eighteenth century Carvallo y Goyeneche described the region's pathetic state:

> Almost all of its inhabitants are laborers, the only work available. With this they do not want for food but they live a miserable life. Those who do not want to believe this need merely enter the houses (or I should say, huts) and observe the rustic clothing, food, and manners of the men, the weariness of the women and the nudity of the children. . . . It is a cause for tears that a region so potentially rich, does not produce for itself or for the peninsula Spain the immense wealth [which it could].

In the last half of the eighteenth century the rural economy of the region grew—but not dramatically. From 1750 to 1778 no more than seven ships a year departed from Concepción harbor with the tallow, hides, sheepskins, fruits, and wine from the rural estates. In the last decades of that century and the first decade of the nineteenth, commerce and contraband increased with the appearance of whaling ships and smugglers from the United States, Great Britain, and elsewhere. Nevertheless, the southern region remained a real frontier, with the unconquered Indians south of the Biobío still outside effective jurisdiction of colonial political authorities. Not until the 1880s did an independent Chilean nation definitively incorporate this southern zone.

With regional variations Hispanic capitalism shaped colonial Chile. The sparsely settled northern agro-mining district, the dominant Santiago–central region, and the Concepción frontier territory had impressed upon them a common juridical mold, altered in practice by local conditions, but uniform in its formalism and its flexibility of application—at the discretion of government officials. Overt deference to authority combined with systematic evasion of the law became the norm. Intermingling of private and public business blurred the distinctions between corruption, "conflict of interest," and routine public administration. The war against the Araucanians conditioned economic development while offering royal officials, soldiers, and merchants enormous opportunities for profit, promotions, and patronage. Centralized, authoritarian, and often arbitrary policymaking became the expected, accepted pattern of government. Concentration of wealth, status, and real estate in the hands of a privileged few, denigration of work, and exploitation of labor were all essential ingredients in the socioeconomic structure of the colony.

As long as the legitimating symbol of empire—the monarchy—remained intact, there was only minor resistance to the institutions and processes of Hispanic capitalism in Chile. Colonial elites made no significant attack on the legitimacy or fundamental character of Spanish rule prior to 1810. And even when events in Europe precipitated independence movements in Spanish America, Chilean leaders ultimately re-established political order by reaffirming the basic assumptions and institutions of the colonial era, with the exception of submission to Spain and European monarchism. The Spanish crown might lose its dominions in America, but Chile would retain the indelible markings of Hispanic capitalism.

4 Independence and the Autocratic Republic

In the last decades of the eighteenth century administrative reorganization of the Spanish Empire left Chile an autonomous captaincy-general, no longer subject directly to the viceroy of Peru. Until 1808 the colony was governed by a succession of capable, professional administrators; its gradual material progress and the public sentiment of the leading *criollos* gave little premonition of the violent movement for political independence that occurred after 1810. Perhaps overstating the case, Manuel de Salas, the well-known colonial administrator and intellectual precursor of independence, claimed that Chileans "desired only to be good Catholics and good Spaniards, which they regarded as the two inseparable conditions of their happiness."

The last royal governors administered Chile with vigor and correctness. Ambrosio O'Higgins—whose illegitimate son, Bernardo O'Higgins, would become the George Washington of Chile—began his term of office (1788–96) with an extended tour on horseback of the northern regions, visiting the towns and mining districts. Intent on stimulating the Chilean economy and reducing its dependence upon imported commodities, O'Higgins attempted to introduce new crops and to reestablish colonial plantations such as sugar, cotton, and rice as well as to encourage increased exports of mineral products, hides, and wool to Spain. He also sought to establish direct trade between Chile, Guayaquil, Central America, and Mexico. To revive old trade patterns between Chile and Charcas, O'Higgins helped form a commercial enterprise with an eight-year monopoly to promote exports of copper, aguardiente, wine, and other products of the northern districts.

Though well-intentioned, this economic program (which anticipated to some extent the policy of import-substitution by Chilean governments after 1930) brought very limited results. The tropical and plantation crops failed to survive in the difficult conditions of northern Chile; the colony continued to import large amounts of sugar, cotton, and rice from Peru or elsewhere in the empire. Exports expanded slowly, and local industry did not develop to provision local markets with substitutes for the luxury goods imported from Europe, Lima, and Buenos Aires. Many of the structural constraints on economic development that plagued Chile in the twentieth century were already evident in the obstacles facing Ambrosio O'Higgins' economic program during the last decade of the eighteenth century.

In the last days of O'Higgins' administration the crown established a *tribunal de consulado* in Chile. This was both a commercial court and an agency to promote economic development. The royal decree creating the *consulado* assigned it responsibility for "protection and stimulation of commerce . . . the advancement of agriculture, improvement in crops and commercialization of the fruits of the land, introduction of beneficial machinery and implements." Whatever the limitations imposed by colonial status, the establishment of the *consulado* indicated that Spain was not entirely ignoring the problems or the needs of the Chilean economy.

O'Higgins' achievements and his rectitude as governor of Chile earned him promotion to the Viceroyalty at Lima. His successor, Gabriel de Aviles y del Fierro, had lengthy experience in the colonial bureaucracy and military establishment. Aviles continued in the footsteps of O'Higgins and supported public projects such as dikes, cobbling of streets, and beautification of Santiago. In cooperation with Manuel de Salas, the syndic of the *consulado*, Aviles provided competent administration of the Chilean colony during his short tenure (in 1799 he was promoted to the Viceroyalty at Buenos Aires).

As the eighteenth century ended, Chile received a new governor with all the pomp and ceremony that it could marshal, including bullfights, feasts, theatrical presentations, and other public festivities. Far from hinting at any desire for independence from Spain, Santiago society welcomed the new governor with subservient splendor.

When the last of the royal governors assumed office in 1802, the colony remained loyal to Spanish authority. A long-standing dream came to fruition with initiation of work on the canal from the Maipo River to irrigate the land in the valley and augment the water in the Mapocho. Public works in Santiago continued with the completion of dikes and, also, after fifteen years, of the future presidential palace, La Moneda. When the governor died at the age of seventy-three in February 1808, few Chileans could have anticipated the juntas that would soon spring up throughout Spanish America to cut the bonds linking it to Spain. Notwithstanding Bourbon efforts to implement administrative reforms, no great change in internal administration or unusual abuses occurred to anger the colonials; there was in Chile nothing like the Stamp Act or the tea tax that incited the North American colonies to rebellion.

Though the colonials remained loyal to Spain, certain persistent complaints or dissatisfactions did exist. The *criollos* resented the preference given to native-born Spaniards in royal appointments and also the condescending treatment they themselves frequently received from Spanish officials or merchants. They also disliked certain of the commercial regulations and taxes that burdened Chilean commerce, and the lack of educational opportunities in Chile which necessitated travel to Lima or Spain for professional training. A belief of many Chileans that Peru maintained a privileged position vis-à-vis Chile—despite the favorable impact on Chile of certain of the Bourbon reforms—contributed to a resentment of royal policy. Geographical isolation and the evolution of a distinctive Chilean culture had also eroded the allegiance of some colonial elites to Spain. Finally, a very small minority of intellectuals, attracted by liberal, republican ideology and propaganda, had come to blame Chile's backwardness on Spanish imperial rule.

Even taken all together, however, these criticisms of the imperial system proved mild in comparison with those in Buenos Aires, Guayaquil, Caracas, and Mexico City. In the words of Chile's well-known nineteenth-century historian, Barros Arana, "the most advanced men were persuaded that the reform of a few laws, the growth of population, and the diffusion of useful knowledge would make Chile a region privileged by her products and by the virile and enterprising character of her people." Most elites opposed Protestant or liberal doctrines imported from Europe, Britain, and the United States in the increasing number of foreign ships in Chilean ports after 1790 (when the Convention of San Lorenzo opened the South Pacific to European and North American shipping). Deliberate ideological subversion of Spanish rule was clearly the goal of a small number of North American merchants and seamen. Some of the 257 North American ships that plied Chilean coastal waters between 1788 and 1810 carried copies of the Declaration of Independence and the Federal Constitution. Nevertheless, while most Latin American republics can point to at least one or two pre-revolutionary conspiracies of some import, no serious anti-Spanish conspiracies occurred in Chile prior to 1810.

Just as the conquest of Chile was an extension of the Pizarro-Almagro venture in Peru, so the Chilean independence movement depended on events in Europe and other parts of Spanish America. The movement for Chilean independence, like that of most other Spanish American republics, originated in European politics and warfare. Napoleon Bonaparte, in an effort to impose French hegemony in Europe, took his armies into Portugal and Spain in 1807. Charles IV and his son, Ferdinard VII, yielded the Spanish throne to Joseph Bonaparte. Spanish insurgents resisted his usurpation of the Spanish crown. In the name of Ferdinand VII, a junta at Seville directed the struggle against the Napoleonic armies; and in the Spanish American colonies, local juntas organized to defend the legitimate king of Spain.

News of Napoleon's invasion of Spain arrived in Santiago via Buenos Aires in mid-1808. The French usurpation of the Spanish crown raised the issue of how best to administer the colony on behalf of the legitimate monarch and what to do if the French occupation should become permanent. For a small minority of Chilean leaders this political dilemma provided an ideal context for pursuing complete independence from colonial rule. The majority of Chileans, however, saw the events in Europe as a temporary interruption of legitimate Spanish domination. Nevertheless, confrontations occurred between those professing to favor the temporary "nationalization" of authority in a local junta and those favoring continued submissiveness to French authorities in Spain. The former group found its principal leadership in the cabildo of Santiago, and the latter in the governor, Francisco Antonio García Carrasco, and the *audiencia.*

Unlike the seasoned colonial administrators who had governed Chile ably in the late eighteenth and early nineteenth centuries, García Carrasco lacked administrative experience and political skills. He had assumed the governorship due to a reform that left the office in the hands of the highest military official above the rank of colonel in the case of the incumbent's death. With the continual arrival of disturbing news from Buenos Aires—especially reports of the revolt of May 22–25, 1810—the governor decided to take repressive measures. His inept actions, including the arrest and deportation to Lima of three prominent *criollos* on charges of subversion, increased the tensions in Santiago. The *audiencia* attempted to restore calm by announcing García Carrasco's resignation and his replacement by the aged Conde de la Conquista, Mateo de Toro Zambrano, whose rank as brigadier of the royal armies gave him rightful claim to the office. But this desperate effort to maintain legitimacy failed. On September 18, 1810, a *cabildo abierto,* or "town meeting," convened in the *tribunal de consulado* in Santiago, accepted the resignation of the governor, and proclaimed the creation of a national junta.

For the next two decades a dizzy succession of juntas, assemblies, congresses, military dictatorships, and supreme directors sought to impose their authority in Chile—with a three-year interlude (1814–17) when Spanish royal authority reasserted itself. At first the contending factions all proclaimed their loyalty to King Ferdinand VII or to Spain. The national junta set up September 18, 1810, swore "to govern and to protect the rights of the king during his captivity." A leader of the Chilean independence movement, José Miguel Infante, even justified establishment of the junta by citing Spanish legislation in the principal preconquest codification of Spanish law, the venerable *Siete Partidas*. If, as was probably the case, a minority of Chileans who were bent upon independence from the outset hid their motives behind the mask of loyalty to the king, this mask was enough to gain recognition for the junta from the council of the regency in Spain, making the Chilean junta the only one in Spanish America ever recognized by that body.

The political history of these two decades (1810–30) is conveniently divided into four main periods: (1) four years of civil war and uncertain advance toward independence, 1810–14 (called the *patria vieja*, or "old fatherland"); (2) reimposition of Spanish authority by the viceroy at Lima through force of arms, 1814–17 (called the *reconquista*, or "reconquest"); (3) dictatorship of Bernardo O'Higgins, 1817–23; (4) a chaotic succession of governments proclaiming liberalism, federalism, and republicanism, 1823–30.

After 1830 the internal strife was stifled by a coalition of conservative business interests, the clergy, and the landowner class—led by a businessman named Diego Portales—which installed a unique political regime. Republican in form and authoritarian in practice (thus the epithet "autocratic republic" some Chilean historians have given to this regime), the new political order reconsolidated the Hispanic ideal of a strong, centralized executive who imposed order through decrees and the necessary coercion to ensure their implementation. A man who openly claimed he would have shot his father if it were necessary for public order, Portales wrote bluntly: "Democracy, which self-deceived men proclaim so much, is an absurdity in countries like those of America." Agreeing with the *criollo* intellectual Mariano Egaña that liberal principles were "the greatest enemies of America and would eventually bring her down to total ruin," Portales and his colleagues brooked no opposition to their programs and spared no effort to save Chile from the perils of imported liberal ideology. A great irony of Chilean independence was that the political order devised by Portales, Egaña, and the three presidents who served from 1831 to 1861 exhibited more than a passing similarity to the autocratic tradition of colonial rule.

Even so, this authoritarian republic was only consolidated after three civil wars (1829–30, 1851, 1859) and with the institutionalization of modes of political repression that became routine Chilean practices: concession of emergency powers (*facultades extraordinarias*) to the presidents; periodic declaration of states of siege and suspension of civil liberties and rights; subjecting civilians to courts-martial, military law, and summary execution; preventive detention, physical abuse, and exile of political opponents; and censorship and closing of the opposition press. Congressional and presidential elections, managed by the incumbent government through patronage and fraud, brought political violence and the civil wars of the 1850s mentioned earlier. Chile's exceptionalism, that is, its vaunted institutional stability, would have its price in political liberty. For much of the nineteenth century liberal factions struggled to overturn this "autocratic republic."

Parallel to this struggle between conservative and liberal factions to control the government and its patronage, there developed a formalistic constitutionalism premised on pragmatic repression and iterated amnesties and pardons that enshrined impunity for rebels and government leaders alike after each major political rupture. Chilean political culture integrated the ritual of repetitive conflicts followed by amnesties that almost emulated the *parlamentos* and *paces* between Spaniards and Mapuches under the colonial regime (see Chapter 2).

Independence liberated elite *criollos* from the restraints of Spanish authority and left them free to exploit rural labor, miners, and urban shanty dwellers. It also opened Chile to British, North American, and European merchants along with a few European set-

TABLE 4–1. POLITICAL CRISES, PARDONS, AND AMNESTIES, 1814–1925

Major Political Crises and Civil Wars	Political Pardons (indultos) and Amnesties*
1814 Reconquista, reimposition of Spanish authority	1814
1817 Patria Nueva	1822 (new constitution)
1823 End of O'Higgins government	1826 pardon of army deserters (conditional pardons)
1827 Constituent Congress dissolved (elections for provincial assemblies)	1827 (*indulto general*) 1828 (new constitution and political amnesty)
1829–30 Civil War	
1836–39 War with Peru-Bolivia Confederation Freire invasion from Peru to oust Prieto; country ruled under state of siege	1836 Freire sentenced to death; commuted from death to exile; President Prieto seeks reconciliation with political opponents after Portales' assassination; selective pardons and return of exiles 1838, 1839
1839 End of war; return to constitutional "normalcy"	Pardons for military deserters; 1/4 reduction in sentences for all prisoners to celebrate the victory at Yungay
1841 Manuel Bulnes presidency	1841, 1842 pardons and amnesty
1845–46 Electoral violence; coup threats	1846 (minister orders prisoner release, allows exiles to return after elections)
1850–51 Civil war	1851–56 (selective pardons) 1857; conditional amnesty
1858–59 Civil war	1861 general amnesty
1861–71 President J. Pérez ("government of all, for all")	
1865 War with Spain	1865 "Talca" amnesty for national guard officers convicted of offending judges (officers fighting against Spanish at the time)
1879–84 War of the Pacific (Peru, Bolivia)	
1891 Civil war	1891–94 limited amnesties
1893–94 Failed rebellions; state of siege	1894 general amnesty; 1895 amnesty for crimes under military jurisdiction during War of the Pacific
1924 Military coup; 1925, second coup	1925 new constitution and general amnesty

*General amnesties for electoral law violations or for violations of obligatory military service not included.

tlers. It did not mean political, social, or economic improvement for the vast majority of Chileans.

In the process of establishing the postcolonial order, political and constitutional conflicts developed which would recur often during the nineteenth and twentieth centuries. These included disputes over the basic character of the constitution, especially the balance of power between executive and legislature; over the relationship between Church and State; over the inclusiveness of citizenship and civic participation, at first limited to a small minority of wealthy Chileans; and over the scope of the state's authority to confiscate or expropriate private property in the public interest. This latter issue emerged with particular intensity in political maneuvering over abolition of slavery (1811–24) and elimination of titles of nobility and entailed estates (*mayorazgos*).

In the social and economic realm, the chaos of the years 1810–30 also raised critical policy issues that would endure in Chilean national life. Domination of mining output and commerce by foreign (mostly British) merchants and the Chilean government's dependence upon foreign loans, ships, armaments, and technicians to pursue the internal war of liberation against the royalists and carry out the naval expedition to Peru, made clear that shedding the colonialism of Spain would bring a more subtle informal economic colonialism by Britain, the stronger European nations, and North Americans. Lack of efficient internal taxing mechanisms and reliance upon revenues from foreign trade, particularly import-export duties, made public finance highly vulnerable to fluctuations in international trade and to the extensive smuggling and corruption at the ports. Attempts to raise revenues through authorizations of exclusive commercial monopolies and special concessions continued colonial practices and set precedents for policies that later surrendered Chile's most important economic resources, especially mineral wealth, to foreigners. Opening the ports to international shipping—but with significant import duties—generated debates between free trade advocates and early proponents of protection for Chilean industries. These debates set the tone for a persistent conflict over this issue which carried over into the twentieth century—and dramatically re-emerged in the 1970s.

The independence decades also saw an initial statement by a handful of Chilean elites of the need to attract immigrants from Europe in order to populate the country with peoples they considered racially superior to the predominantly mestizo and *casta* work force in the mines, countryside, and towns. The tendency for the most radical *criollo* leaders to blame Spain for Chile's backwardness added to the desire for Europeanization (especially immigrants from England, Ireland, and northern Europe) of the Chilean ethnic stock as well as for the Anglicization of Chilean institutions. This propensity to disparage the mental and technical capabilities of the working classes endured into the twentieth century; it reached its maximum expression in Francisco Encina's twenty-volume *History of Chile to 1891*. Over and over again Encina bemoaned the debilitating effects of miscegenation. Critical of the economic effects of free trade, Encina nevertheless emphasized the "precious gift of European blood" which the resident foreign merchants contributed to the "Chilean race."

The independence movement used Negro and *casta* troops to expel the Spanish, and decreed emancipation of the *offspring* of the approximately four thousand remaining slaves as a wartime expedient; but it ended by reinforcing the tremendous social gap between Chilean elites and the common folk. These class divisions would be the basis for bitter confrontations later in the nineteenth century, even as the newly formed Sociedad de Fomento Fabril (Society for Industrial Development, 1883) repeatedly called for European immigrants to replace the "lazy, shiftless, mongrel" Chilean laborers.

Independence brought a change in political form but not in social structure. While the English and French displacement of Spanish or Peruvian merchants in Valparaíso and Santiago after 1817 influenced furniture and architectural styles in the homes of the wealthy, the dwellings of the rural tenant laborers typically remained little more than straw-covered huts or, at best, small adobe *ranchos*. In the towns and cities, lower-class residents could spend their leisure hours in the *chinganas* (these were a combination of bar, dance hall, and brothel), which were increasing in number, or at horse races, but they continued to live in "suburban" huts ringing the solid homes and commercial centers spreading out from the central plazas. As the towns and cities grew and became more affluent in the later part of the nineteenth century, the fusion of liberal political ideology with social Darwinism would both recall the racist sentiments of the early proponents of European immigration in the independence decades and "justify" the misery that modernization and "progress" brought to a growing proletariat after 1850.

From 1810 to 1814—a period labeled *patria vieja,* or "old fatherland"—by Chilean historians, the personalities and ambitions of those later enshrined in the pantheon of the independence movement's heroes determined the politics of Santiago and Concepción. The national junta formed on September 18, 1810, largely dominated by Juan Martínez de Rozas, was followed by experiments with a national congress and then gave way to the dictatorship of José Miguel Carrera and his two brothers. Feuds between Carrera, the prominent Larraín family, and Bernardo O'Higgins created an environment of intrigue and uncertainty. Jealousies between Santiago and the provincial junta at Concepción further confused and debilitated political authority. In the meantime the United States consul, Joel Poinsett, allied himself with the Carreras and promoted Chilean independence.

Mindful that, despite protestations of loyalty, the Chilean situation was developing into a full-blown separatist movement (as had already occurred in Venezuela in 1811 and in New Granada and Mexico shortly thereafter), the viceroy of Peru sent a military expedition to restore order in Chile. The military force disembarked at the island of Chiloé, which was still directly dependent upon the viceroyalty, and, after gathering new recruits, proceeded to Valdivia, where royalists had already gained control. From there the expedition went by sea to Talcahuano and captured Concepción, where a great part of the garrison also took up the royalist cause. These events induced the major southern cities to swear again their allegiance to Ferdinand VII.

Early in 1814 a second royalist expedition commanded by General Gabino Gainza entered Chile. After a number of encounters with the military forces led by Carrera, O'Higgins, and Juan Mackenna, the royalist armies captured Chillán and Talca in the southern part of the central valley. Thereafter a stalemate occurred between the opposing movements. In 1814 British commodore James Hillyar mediated a treaty agreement (Treaty of Lircay) that ended hostilities with Chile's recognition of Ferdinand VII, an exchange of prisoners, suppression of the Chilean national flag introduced in 1812, and a promise by the Spanish-Peruvian forces to leave Chile within a month.

This treaty proved unacceptable to both the viceroy and prominent *criollo* leaders in Chile. Carrera carried out still another coup in Santiago, banished his personal enemies, and determined to carry on the war against the royalists. O'Higgins refused to recognize Carrera's authority. To complicate matters, the Peruvian viceroy sent a new military expedition to Chile commanded by General Mariano Osorio. Osorio's advance from Talcahuano to Chillán brought Carrera and O'Higgins together again to meet the royalist threat. At the battle of Rancagua (October 1–2, 1814), Carrera failed to reinforce the besieged patriot army, and Osorio defeated O'Higgins. This ended the *patria vieja.* The remnants of O'Higgins' army as well as Carrera's forces fled to Mendoza, accompanied by a mass exodus of prominent *criollos* from Santiago. In Mendoza, José de San Martín, leader of the Argentine independence movement, welcomed O'Higgins. Plotting began for the campaign that would liberate Chile and Peru from Spanish rule (1817–25).

For three years Spanish officials sought to purge Chilean society of separatist sentiments. Secret police, courts-martial, and imprisonment of leading citizens alienated even moderate *criollos* previously uncommitted to independence. Instead of ameliorating *criollo* resentment, the Spanish "reconquest" (1814–17) greatly intensified discrimination against native-born Chileans. Spanish army personnel received salaries up to five times larger than those of *criollos* of the same rank; Chileans were denied government appointments and were refused the economic concessions that stemmed from official largesse. When Chileans complained of these conditions, the governor was reputed to have told his entourage: "I shall not leave to the Chileans even tears with which to weep."

Polarization of sentiment in Chile coincided with San Martín's planning of an expedition to oust the Spanish from all of the southern cone of South America and Peru. While San Martín's agents collected intelligence, and the general prepared his forces in Cuyo, Manuel Rodríguez, former secretary to Carrera, carried out the guerrilla activities against the royalists which made him the hero of the independence movement most acclaimed by leftists and revolutionaries in Chile in the 1960s and 1970s. In the mid-1980s, the most prominent guerrilla opposition to General Augusto Pinochet would call itself the Manuel Rodríguez Patriotic Front.

Crossing the Andes in early 1817, San Martín defeated the royalist army at Chacabuco to the north of Santiago. Mobs in Santiago ransacked the houses and property of royal officials and wealthy royalists; they also destroyed the portraits of royal governors (back to Pedro de Valdivia) hanging in the government place. No longer did those bent on independence mask their intentions. On February 14, 1817, San Martín and O'Higgins entered Santiago at the head of the victorious army. After San Martín declined the cabildo's offer to become dictator of Chile, O'Higgins accepted the "supreme directorship" of the colony.

During the ensuing year Spanish victories in the central valley again threatened Santiago until San Martín won the decisive battle on the plains of Maipo (April 5, 1818). By mid-1818, therefore, despite continued royalist resistance in the south, Chilean territory from Copiapó to Concepción was free of Spanish authority. In 1820 the British Lord Cochrane, lending his services to the rebels' cause, returned from an unsuccessful strike at Callao and captured Valdivia in a daring amphibious assault. Attention then turned to the liberation of Peru—though not until 1826 did Chilean soldiers commanded by Ramón Freire wrest control of the island of Chiloé from the Spaniards.

Notwithstanding these military victories, the political chaos and economic costs of more than a decade of civil war, together with continued instability, made political independence cause for less than unconditional jubilation even to the separatists. And like many revolutions, the personal and ideological struggle within the circle of separatist leadership took its toll among most of those later included in the pantheon of revolutionary heroes: José Miguel Carrera, like his brothers earlier, executed in Mendoza; Manuel Rodríguez, assassinated, seemingly with O'Higgins' knowledge; O'Higgins, exiled to Peru (1823), from whence he would never return to his native land.

Bernardo O'Higgins, though born in Chile, spent much of his youth in England and Europe. Despite a number of efforts to gain the approval of his father, the former governor of Chile and viceroy of Peru, the latter seems never to have responded to the desire of his illegitimate offspring for formal recognition. In Europe, O'Higgins met Francisco de Miranda, the leading Venezuelan proponent of Latin American independence, and was influenced by Miranda's zeal for liberation of the colonies from Spain. O'Higgin's returned to Chile as one of a small minority of *criollos* committed to independence even prior to the Napoleonic invasion of Spain.

After leading separatist troops from 1813 to 1814 and fleeing to Mendoza when defeated by the royalists at Rancagua (1814), O'Higgins returned to Chile as a subordinate of General San Martín in an army aspiring to liberate Chile and Peru from Spanish rule. O'Higgins also belonged to the secret revolutionary group called *logia lautarina*. This lodge, dedicated to independence for the Spanish American colonies, swore its members to secrecy on pain of death and required that members who gained high position in any of the liberated colonies submit for prior approval the names of those they would appoint to military, government, or other positions in the new regimes. The lodge also sought to control government policy. Critics of the lodge saw it as a group of anticlerical, masonic subversives bent on destruction of the old order.

A modern biographer of O'Higgins even suggested, with obvious hyperbole, that "the lodge controlled the new Chilean administration as completely as the Party controls the government in a Communist state." Due to his association with the lodge, a segment of Chilean opinion came to see O'Higgins as somewhat less than a truly national leader and blamed him and the lodge for the executions of the three Carrera brothers as well as for the assassination of Manuel Rodríguez.

O'Higgins believed that it was necessary, with a people like the Chileans, "to confer good upon them by force" when other means failed. He promulgated a new constitution in 1818. The document called for a five-man senate with members elected from the provinces. O'Higgins essentially handpicked the membership, as he also did later the delegates to the constitutional convention of 1822.

Despite manipulation of government appointments, the O'Higgins government lacked firm institutional supports. Conflicts with Church leaders over a variety of issues—expulsion of a priest who asked the wife of an O'Higgins supporter to leave a church because she was wearing an inappropriate low-cut dress; establishment of Protestant cemeteries; and introduction of Protestant teachers to develop an anticlerical educational system—weakened O'Higgins' position. Confrontations with certain aristocrats over elimination of titles of nobility, and efforts to abolish the entailed estates, as well as strife with his "own" senate also created problems for O'Higgins. Finally, the implacable resistance of friends and supporters of the Carrera brothers, who never forgave O'Higgins for the Carreras' death, undermined his administration.

Financial difficulties associated with the war effort and corruption also contributed to O'Higgins' failure. Describing the situation in Chile in 1820, a sea captain wrote in his journal:

> No permanent System of Finance had yet been established whereby the Expenses of the Government & of the War might be defrayed and on every emergency Recourse was had to temporary loans and forced contributions. Nothing like a regular appraisement of Land & other Permanent Property had yet been attempted, or any one Species of Regular Taxation resorted to, and when arbitrary contributions were levied the quotas were evidently determined by favoritism or Caprice.

In attempting to raise revenues, O'Higgins re-established the colonial tobacco monopoly, or *estanco*, only to suspend it for two years after protests by foreign merchants. At the same time the Supreme Director's confidant and finance minister and a prominent merchant were apparently speculating in tobacco and other commodities. Furthermore the finance minister, although a Chilean by birth, had sided with the royalists and even accompanied one of the early Spanish expeditions from Peru which sought to reconquer Chile. These circumstances—in addition to the general amnesty for most former royalists who had sworn loyalty to Chile, and the government's attempts to return to the royalists some property confiscated from them—provided effective ammunition for those who wished to discredit O'Higgins. Resistance by merchants to new commercial regulations, political intrigues surrounding a new constitution (1822), a debate concerning a loan secured in London, failure to pay the fleet in Valparaíso, and a threat to replace Ramón Freire, commander of the army at Concepción, all contributed to O'Higgins' downfall.

In 1822 two of the country's five senators left on diplomatic missions. Another expressed a desire to leave public office. O'Higgins then suggested that the senate temporarily suspend its sessions and transfer legislative authority to himself as Supreme Director. The senators met this breach of the principles of liberalism with categorical opposition. Ramón Freire led his forces at Concepción against Talca and threatened to march northward. The city of La Serena followed Concepción's lead, and O'Higgins' opponents in Santiago adhered to the movement to oust him from office. With an emotional farewell speech, O'Higgins surrendered the presidential sash and left for Peruvian exile, never to return to Chile. O'Higgins thus experienced what Chileans ironically call "*el pago de chile,*" that is, *ingratitude,* for his leadership and sacrifices during the independence wars.

Political uncertainty followed O'Higgins' abdication. A barrage of political slogans, ideologies, and personalities accompanied a confusing succession of congresses, assemblies, interim supreme directors, presidents, and military rebellions. Ramón Freire, who had led the Concepción forces, attempted to govern the country from 1823 to 1826 and returned to office several times between 1826 and 1829. Freire later attempted an invasion of Chile from Peru (1836), after being forcibly exiled to the former viceroyalty.

Freire's term in office and his interventions between 1826 and 1830 were associated with superficial experiments with liberalism and federalism. Exponents of European or North American liberalism sought to impose republican institutions and practices on Chile's traditional administrative, economic, and social structure. To many, liberalism also meant religious toleration or anticlericalism. Implementation of liberal principles implied confrontation with perhaps the most significant social institution and symbol of Hispanic society: the Catholic Church. This alone assured bitter resistance to liberalism by some prominent *criollo* families.

A small number of influential intellectuals and political leaders also proposed a federalist regime, with considerable regional autonomy. The schemes for decentralizing political authority or copying North American federalism appealed to certain regional interests seeking to cast off the economic and political domination of Santiago and Valparaíso as well as to those intellectuals who equated progress and freedom with emulating the institutions of the United States. But neither liberalism, nor liberal principles and a federalist constitution, corresponded to the socio-economic reality of Hispanic capitalism in Chile after independence.

In 1824 the Freire government confiscated the possessions of the regular clergy. This ruptured Church-State relations, including dismissal of the ex-royalist bishop, Rodríguez Zorilla, whom O'Higgins had re-established in his office in an effort to negotiate diplomatic relations with the Pope. Regional uprisings and Freire's inability to organize effectively the national public administration resulted in continued intrigues, polarization of sentiments by opposing forces, and ruin of the public finances. By 1825, in the words of Chilean author Agustín Edwards, "Freire . . . distracted and impotent, saw his authority being set at naught. Santiago alone recognized the Governing Junta. . . . Meanwhile neither Concepción nor Coquimbo recognized either Freire or the junta. The anarchy into which the country had fallen was reaching a climax; it was under the rule of four governments." Totally frustrated, Freire resigned from office. Personal ambitions combined with rabid commitments to misunderstood slogans threatened to dismember the new nation.

After an enthusiastic speech by federalism's most avid supporter, José Miguel Infante, in July of 1826, Congress formally approved a federal system for Chile. The legislature then embarked upon a piecemeal program designed to define the nature of Chilean federalism. Congress divided Chile into eight provinces, each of which would have a provincial assembly and its own constitution. In addition, local government would continue to exercise a broad range of authority in the *municipios*. In a country lacking provincial political and administrative machinery, let alone provincial constitutions, federalist ideology did not correspond to political reality, but it did intensify regional conflicts that made effective national government illusory.

Meanwhile the army went unpaid, the public treasury remained empty, and president succeeded president. Civil strife reached such a level that Congress requested

Freire to reassume the presidency and impose order. After winning several battles against opposing forces, Freire again resigned, to be followed in office by the vice-president, Francisco Antonio Pinto. In August 1827 the country reverted to a unitary form of government, ending its brief flirtation with federalism.

Pinto's administration adopted a new constitution in 1828 that pleased neither ardent federalists nor important liberal factions. Conservatives viewed the constitution as an unrealistic document inspired by imported utopian ideology. By abolishing the *mayorazgos*, the constitution generated opposition in the old aristocracy, while President Pinto's anticlericalism disturbed a broader segment of "public opinion." Conflict and disputed elections after adoption of a new constitution in 1828 degenerated into civil war (1829–30).

Led by the personalities who would dominate Chilean politics for the next two decades—Diego Portales, Manuel Rengifo, Joaquín Prieto, and Manuel Bulnes—conservative forces defeated the remnants of the liberal army, commanded by Ramón Freire, at the battle of Lircay in April 1830. The new government banished Freire to Peru—just as Freire had earlier done to Bernardo O'Higgins.

Political activity in the post-independence decades took place within very restricted social circles. Intellectuals wrote constitutions and liberal legislation for a country unfamiliar with the practical meaning of federalism, inalienable rights, or effective limits on government authority. Chileans understood the idea of benevolent despotism and the practice of pragmatic despotism. Royal officials had implemented well-intentioned decrees as their consciences, local interests, "reality," or corruption determined. Involvement of "the people" in legislation or administration conformed neither to the theory nor to the practice of Hispanic politics. It proved no surprise, therefore, that after independence the emergence within elite circles of overlapping ideological factions and personalist movements, such as those of O'Higgins, the Carreras, and Freire, anticipated the multiparty politics of later years without involving the masses except as cannon fodder. Those who supported liberal and/or federalist principles were known as *pipiolos* ("upstarts" or "novices"), and those defending more traditional principles, including the existing privileges of the Church, as *pelucones* ("bigwigs"). But within these two camps, factional disputes and personal loyalties prevented the development of unified political movements, let alone political parties in the modern sense. The highly partisan tabloid newspapers slandered the opposition at will. Political factions and various governments stretched freedom of the press to its limits. No end seemed in sight to the quick succession of presidents and constitutions which accompanied the movement of armies, rebellions, and bandits across the country.

In these conditions public finance fell into a dreadful state. Tax farming on the colonial model continued with respect to the tithes (*diezmos*) and the tolls paid by muleteers and carters on the principal roads. Lack of respect for shifting government authorities and knowledge that the tax farmers retained 30 to 40 percent of the taxes levied increased still further the propensity to evade payment. This held true especially in the case of the *diezmos* paid in kind by the peasantry. Corrupt administration of the customs houses also kept needed revenues from the government. The observations of John Miers, an English businessman more than disenchanted with Chile, summarize the deplorable state of affairs:

> I have elsewhere alluded to the mode in which the duties upon the custom-house were paid, and to the great extent of the contraband introduction of foreign goods. It now remains to say a few words upon the mode of levying the customs. The duties are always, after the Spanish system, estimated and levied at so much percent upon a

valuation, not determined by the market price of the articles, but by the arbitrary valuation of the vistas, or custom-house searchers: it is, therefore, impossible for a merchant to calculate upon the actual cost of introduction of foreign goods; but, as the government of Chile does not allow their officers a sufficient salary, they are obliged to connive with the merchants, both in smuggling and in fixing undervaluations, receiving from the latter a proportionate bribe. Similar parcels of goods may at one time be valued in the custom-house at 1000 dollars, at another 100 dollars, and the usual tariff duties paid thereon accordingly; the difference is a robbery to the state, no advantage whatever results to the foreign manufactures, but goes entirely into the pockets of the custom-house officers, merchants, and agents.

Miers concluded that "the foreign trade of Chile, like all matters in state, justice and police, is maintained by empino [sic] influence, intrigue and bribery."

Ironically, however, it was the chaos of public finance that brought to the fore the businessmen and military leaders who ended two decades of near anarchy with a conservative restoration. Led by Diego Portales, a merchant who had remained aloof from the independence struggle, an alliance of the Concepción military elite, merchants, prominent *pelucón* families, and the Church hierarchy established—at bayonet point—a unique political regime in Chile. This regime set it apart from its sister republics as a model of political stability and economic growth in the nineteenth century. So would be born the cult of Chilean "exceptionalism."

Diego Portales was born in 1793 in Santiago, the son of an influential royal official who served as superintendent of the mint. Distantly related to two colonial governors, his ancestry linked him to Chile's Basque-Castilian aristocracy. After giving up his own position at the mint, Portales formed a commercial partnership with Manuel Cea in the export-import trade, and moved to Lima. Failure of the joint enterprise brought both partners back to Chile where in mid-1824 they contracted with the Freire government to take over the state monopoly (*estanco*) on tobacco and certain other commodities in exchange for servicing the loan contracted by Chilean agents in London in 1822.

The Portales-Cea Company obtained the *estanco* contract amidst rumors of improprieties in the bidding process, including an allegation that a rival firm lost the contract despite its higher bid. If these allegations were true, it proved fortunate for those who lost the contract. Contraband imports of goods subject to the *estanco*, illegal tobacco plantations, and the high price paid for the contract contributed to the enterprise's commercial failure. Portales and his partner attempted to enforce their monopoly rights by destroying illegal tobacco plantations and seeking stronger intervention by government authorities to stop the contraband trade. While personal enemies of the partners and opponents of the government accused the firm of fraud and bribery, it struggled unsuccessfully to meet its obligations on the British loan. In September 1826 Congress voted to liquidate the *estanco* concession and return the monopoly to the government. Though Portales bitterly resented the government's failure to negotiate new terms or even to allow his firm to administer the government monopoly on a fee basis, the equitable manner in which Manuel Rengifo liquidated the *estanco* contract formed the basis for the future cooperation between those two hard-headed businessmen who would dominate Chilean political economy after 1830.

Many people believed Portales' participation in politics stemmed from a desire for revenge against those who had deprived him of the *estanco* contract. Others saw Portales' motivation in his distaste for liberalism and the continual disorder following independence. Whatever the motivation, Portales' solution for political disorder, imposed in cooperation with conservative interests, the higher clergy, and the military forces of Prieto and Bulnes, emphasized *restoration* of legitimacy, law and order, and fiscal integrity. Implementation of this program required a strong, centralized government which did not tolerate opposition or even criticism. Acting as President Prieto's chief minister and then as "informal" adviser, Portales cashiered the liberal officers of the army, many of them "heroes" of the independence period, persecuted the opposition press, and controlled elections to ensure the victory of government candidates. This was the beginning of the "autocratic republic" which one Chilean historian described as "the last and most beautiful chapter of Spanish colonial history." Less romantically, an English historian suggests that "the atmosphere in Chile after 1830 was one of fear and trembling."

Portales' style and beliefs left little room for constitutions or formal principles. He favored decisive, pragmatic action unconstrained by legal obstacles or constitutional limits. While Portales concerned himself with action, however, other conservative leaders and intellectuals felt the need for a constitution to define the nature of the new regime, to formalize its structure, and to legitimize its practices. Portales played almost no official role in elaborating the Constitution of 1833 which institutionalized what historians have called the "Portalian state." Nevertheless, the centralized, authoritarian character of the constitution owed as much to Portales as to its principal author, Mariano Egaña.

Both Portales and Egaña sought restoration of legitimacy, law and order, and public morality. They recognized the critical need to build viable national political institutions as instruments through which to govern effectively and stimulate economic recovery. Above all, they sought to provide political stability. Both Portales and Egaña disdained democracy, popular suffrage, and liberalism. Egaña called for establishment of an authoritative centralized regime that did not allow "anarchy in the shadow or name of popular rule, liberal principles, republican government." Portales urged creation of a "strong, centralizing government," in order to set the citizens on the straight path of order and virtue." The Constitution of 1833 formalized these authoritarian principles. The new constitution created a strong executive with authority to declare a state of siege in any part of the country when Congress was in recess. Declaration of a state of siege entailed suspension of all constitutional guarantees in the affected territory. In each province and administrative subdivision the president appointed intendants and governors as his direct agents. All pretense of provincial initiative, let alone federalism, disappeared. The power of Congress to approve annually the budget, taxes, and the size of the military provided the basis, later in the century, for bitter executive-legislative confrontations and even civil war (1891). But from 1831 to 1861 three strong presidents each served two constitutional five-year terms, rigged congressional and presidential elections, and efficiently suppressed opposition forces.

The 1833 constitution also maintained the Roman Catholic apostolic religion as the state faith and excluded from "public exercise" all other religious doctrines. The founders of the autocratic republic thus sought to transfer the privilege of appointing Church officials, or *patronato*, from the Spanish crown to the new national regime—though the Church did not concede that the republican government had inherited the *patronato* from the empire. Summarizing the intent of the constitution, General Prieto called it "a means of putting an end to the revolutions and disturbances which arose from the confusion in which the triumph of independence left us. For this reason the system of government to which the republic was subjected . . . may be called autocratic in view of the great authority or power . . . concentrated in the hands of the citizen elected as president."

Executive control over distribution of certificates qualifying citizens to vote made effective challenges to the incumbent nearly impossible. This system of executive dominance of elections was adroitly described by Chilean historian Luis Galdames:

> The constitution permitted the re-election of the president to succeed himself for a second period of five years, and while this provision remained in force all the presidents availed themselves of it to have themselves re-elected. This meant, then, ten-year presidential terms. Re-election was achieved without difficulty, owing to the irresistible power placed by the constitution itself in the hands of the chief of state, who named the mayors and members of the municipal councils, the governors, intendants, and judges. . . .
>
> In practice, the intendants and governors controlled the elections of senators and representatives within their own jurisdiction. The chief of state and his ministers made lists of the people who were to make up each chamber for a constitutional period, and the elections were carried out according to these lists. It was rare that more than three or five opposition candidates succeeded in defeating the government candidates in the different departments. The orders of the minister of the interior to the agents of the executive were expressed more or less in these terms: "His Excellency instructs me to make known to you that Señor or Señores [here the names] should be chosen in your department for the post of [here the name of a senator or deputy]." If any candidate of the opposition attempted to electioneer at any point whatever in the country, the respective government agent would receive from the minister of the interior a communication like this: "Manage to prevent Don [name] from coming to your department by advising him to refrain from presenting himself in it. If he insists you can have him arrested as a disturber of the public peace.

Suffrage limitations restricted the vote through property or income qualifications and literacy requirements. But lax enforcement and deliberate delays in implementing the literacy requirement allowed land-owners to enroll their tenants as voters and commanders of the militia to do likewise with their troops. After 1840 the Congress allowed those already registered to continue to vote despite efforts to impose the literacy requirement on *new* voters. In this way the votes of the rural work force became a valuable asset of the owners of large rural estates and artisans serving in the militia served as voting cattle for the incumbent government.

Along with electoral manipulation, the alliance of merchants, land-owners, clergy, and military officers which restored law and order did not lose sight of Portales' admonition: "The stick and the cake, justly and opportunely administered, are the specifics with which any nation can be cured, however inveterate its bad habits may be." Thus, Chile would largely avoid the chaos and instability of the rest of Latin America, despite the brief civil wars in 1851 and 1859, by imposing a modified version of "benevolent" despotism. Only later would incipient industrial groups and renewed anticlericalism among prominent elite families upset the mutuality of interests shared by members of the relatively small ruling class. The Constitution of 1833 provided a viable instrument for maintaining existing class relations, including restoration of the *mayorazgos* and consolidating the political position of prominent *criollo* families. It also helped create a business climate attractive to foreign capitalists and Chilean merchants alike.

At Portales' urging, Manuel Rengifo served as Minister of the Treasury from 1830 to 1835. Rengifo reorganized the system of public finance, transferred the customs houses to the ports, rationalized regulations and duties on the coastwise trade, and took a number of measures intended to increase fiscal revenues. Though some of Rengifo's tax policies drew criticism, the overall effect of his program was to establish a sound basis for Chilean public finance and to inspire the confidence of domestic and foreign capital. Unfortunately Rengifo's successes made him a likely presidential candidate for an alliance of dissatisfied conservative elements and certain liberal fractions. Rengifo also favored conciliatory policies and an amnesty for the liberal officers cashiered and exiled after the Battle of Lircay in 1830.

In September 1835, Portales returned from his self-imposed "absence" from politics and assumed the ministries of War and the Interior. Joaquín Tocornal, President Prieto's firm supporter and perhaps the most proclerical member of the government coalition, replaced Rengifo as Minister of the Treasury. Despite Rengifo's successful economic policies, his spirit of political conciliation and his moderation on the politico-religious issues of the times lost out to the expediencies of the presidential election of 1835 and Portales' intolerance of any drift toward liberalism. Under Portales' leadership Prieto was re-elected—after the agitation and propaganda of the electoral campaign had led to reimposition of government through "state of siege." Notwithstanding the considerable economic progress and improvement in public finance, when Prieto began his second presidential term (1836–41), institutionalization of the political system detailed in the Constitution of 1833 seemed far from certain.

A new constitution has nowhere guaranteed political stability. This is especially the case in Latin America. It is important therefore to attempt to understand how the repressive policies of the Prieto administration, a fortunate stroke of international politics—that is, a successful war against the Peru-Bolivia confederation—the "martyrdom" of Portales, and the character of Prieto's successor, Manuel Bulnes, solidified the "autocratic republic."

In the wake of civil wars and clashes of personalist factions from 1810, numerous Chilean émigrés found themselves in Peru, while Peruvian exiles went to Chile. Shortly after Prieto's re-election (1836) General Freire sailed from Peru with a military force, landed in Chiloé, and moved to the mainland. Internal dissidents also threatened rebellion. Freire was captured and eventually exiled to Australia. But in response the Prieto government broke relations with Peru.

Relations between Chile and Peru had been tense in any case, due to Peru's failure to repay the loan extended for the San Martín expedition (1820–22) and to disputes over import duties that discriminated against Chilean merchandise as well as over goods deposited in the warehouses at Valparaíso or ships landing in Chilean ports. General Andrés Santa Cruz's efforts to unify Peru and Bolivia and the Peruvian government's support for Freire exacerbated this tension.

Portales saw Santa Cruz's policies and armies as a direct threat to Chile. He sent two ships to Callao, which took the Peruvian navy, such as it was, by surprise. Santa Cruz negotiated a settlement that left the Peruvian ships in Chilean hands, but Portales remained unsatisfied because Santa Cruz refused to apologize for the imprisonment of the Chilean chargé d'affaires. Bent upon war, Portales believed the judgments of the numerous Peruvian exiles in Chile that large-scale rebellion against Santa Cruz would result if a Chilean army merely appeared in Peru.

The Chilean Congress declared war and sent Mariano Egaña to Peru at the head of a small squadron. The Chileans demanded (1) satisfaction for the injuries done to their chargé d'affaires, (2) dissolution of the Peru-Bolivia confederation, (3) an indemnity for the Freire expedition, (4) recognition of liability for the loan extended for the San

Martín liberation expedition, and (5) limitations on Peruvian naval forces. When Santa Cruz rejected these humiliating conditions, the Prieto government prepared for war by declaring a state of siege in all of Chile. With Portales exercising extensive emergency powers, those who "disturbed public order" or were "disrespectful toward the government" faced banishment or execution at the hands of military tribunals.

Portales' regime of terror incited rebellion. In June 1837 mutinous troops, led by Colonel José Antonio Vidaurre, assassinated Portales. Government defeat of the rebellious troops was followed by the execution of the assassins. Vidaurre's head was exhibited on a pike in Valparaíso. Now Portales became a martyr as the government tried to link his assassins and the rebellion to General Santa Cruz's agents in Chile.

During 1837 Chilean forces under Admiral Blanco Encalada faced defeat in Peru from Santa Cruz's armies. Surrounded and in despair, Blanco Encalada recognized the Peru-Bolivia confederation and returned the ships earlier seized at Callao. The Chilean government rejected these concessions, blockaded Peruvian ports, and dispatched a new force commanded by General Manuel Bulnes, the victor at Lircay and Prieto's nephew. Accompanying this expedition were a number of Peruvian exiles, including ex-President Agustín Gamarra and the future Peruvian caudillo Ramón Castilla. Troop movements by both sides in and out of Lima and the interior culminated in early 1839 at Yungay, where Bulnes decisively defeated Santa Cruz and dissolved the Peru-Bolivia confederation. He returned to Santiago a military hero.

The war against the Peru-Bolivia confederation united Chilean political elites. While defeat, in Encina's words, might have sent "leaders, government and order tumbling to earth," victory contributed to a new national pride. According to Barros Arana, when Bulnes made his triumphal entrance into Santiago, "he was greeted by a fanfare unknown until then in the celebration of public festivities." For months after the victory, Chile celebrated its new-found "greatness" with public festivities and theater productions that re-enacted the military glories of the Chilean armies.

Bulnes' victory made him the perfect successor to Prieto and at precisely the right time in the five-year electoral cycle. In control of the army, and enjoying popular acclaim, Bulnes then married the daughter of ex-President Francisco Antonio Pinto, his principal opponent in the presidential race. For the first time in Chilean history a peaceful transition to the presidency took place with Bulnes' inauguration in 1841. During the next decade Bulnes' great popularity, his support for the development of legislative and judicial institutions, and his refusal to become a *caudillo* on the model of contemporary Latin American rulers, all served to solidify the "Portalian state." Thus the fortuitous outcome of Chilean bellicosity provided the basis of solidarity and legitimacy, as well as the leadership that spared Chile the political disorder and *caudillismo* common to Latin America in much of the nineteenth century. It also institutionalized a centralized autocratic regime that discouraged liberalization of Chilean politics.

Consolidation of the autocratic republic also depended upon the improved state of public finance and of the economy in Chile after 1830. From 1810 to 1830 loss of perhaps 15 percent of the male population in the 20-to-40 age group, in the military campaigns in Chile, Río de la Plata, and Peru, caused a temporary scarcity of labor in the northern mines and in the countryside. Marauding soldiers and bandits in the rural areas discouraged agricultural production. In addition, Peru's internal strife and financial crisis disrupted Chile's normal export trade in wheat, livestock products, and other agrarian commodities.

Estimates for the value of agricultural and livestock production, by region, illustrate

TABLE 4–2. AVERAGE ANNUAL VALUE OF AGRICULTURAL
AND LIVESTOCK PRODUCTION (IN PESOS)

Years	La Serena	Santiago	Concepción
1750–59	44,377	427,084	181,615
1760–69	41,409	461,086	189,530
1770–79	40,055	621,086	262,961
1780–89	33,543	551,441	270,669
1790–99	45,198	556,046	244,242
1800–09	84,296	885,292	425,376
1810–19	80,766	623,877	271,357
1820–29	76,156	824,439	187,740

Source: M. Carmagnani, Les mecanismes de la vie économique dans une société coloniale, Le Chili, pp. 213, 235, 249.

the decline in output that accompanied the independence struggle.* Declines in the northern region and even in Santiago were relatively moderate, with recovery beginning after 1820. In the Concepción-southern region continued warfare and Indian problems contributed to a persistent decline in output until 1830; the absolute value of production in 1830 failed to regain the level attained in the decade 1760–69.

The most serious decline in economic activity occurred south of the Maule River where, in any case, Chilean agriculture was least secure due to the Indian frontier. Short-term local food shortages resulted from the seemingly unending civil wars. In 1822 the cabildo at Concepción reported that "eleven years of a ferocious, devastating struggle have reduced the province to the most extreme calamity in its history. Its residents . . . have consumed whatever work animals or beasts of burden, not taken by their enemies or their defenders, to keep themselves alive."

In the La Serena–northern region the independence movements little affected agricultural production. Free trade meant expanded demand for minerals and stimulation of the northern economy. But migration to the north, due to the war and to the hope for opportunities in the mines, placed increased pressure on the region's limited food-producing capabilities. In 1826 the provincial assembly of Coquimbo lamented that this city "must buy everything, for it produces little but metals. Smaller animals are brought from Chillán, more than six thousand animals come each year from the environs of Santiago; . . . tallow from Maule; flour and grain from Aconcagua, wood from Chiloé, Valdivia, and Concepción."

With the achievement of independence, the northern region's mines provided the primary source of the copper and silver that financed imports of European goods, paid for military supplies, and attracted foreign investment. In the 1820s, however, many foreigners who invested in mining enterprises lost their capital, as the cost of food, fuel, and supplies and the lack of adequate transport undermined these speculative ventures. Indeed, the prospectuses of some of these "mining" ventures seem to have deliberately misled British investors. For example, the Chilean Mining Association declared that "few countries are so well watered as Chile, affording means of conveyance by water to the ports of the Pacific." This was true, of course, but the prospectus failed

*Naturally, given the internal situation, these estimates are more suggestive than definitive—and the price inflation at the time probably leads to an underestimate of the decline in output.

to mention that there were no navigable rivers in the northern region, no coal, no lumber, and that provisions had to be brought over a considerable distance from the south. Despite the disappointments suffered by many speculative investments, new discoveries of copper and silver augured well for the development of mining in the northern region. Gold production declined, but the mint in Santiago maintained the level of silver coinage achieved in the period 1790–1809, despite increased contraband and the dislocation of war. In 1832 a silver strike at Chañarcillo created boom conditions in the northern territory and brought also some of the earliest significant labor conflicts in Chilean national history. Even at this early date the harsh conditions experienced by the peons spawned an incipient militancy among the growing mining proletariat. A rebellion at Chañarcillo in 1834 foreshadowed hundreds of future confrontations between miners and mine operators in the nineteenth and twentieth centuries.

Though the northern mining districts afforded the most glamorous economic potential and paid for the bulk of imports, agriculture and livestock remained the foundations of the economy. Based in the Santiago–central region—especially with the war time dislocations in the south—agriculture continued to be extensive and backward. Wooden plows pulled by teams of oxen broke the ground for sowing the traditional colonial crops. Productivity declined with the spread of agricultural pests and the reduced fertility of the land. Threshing still depended on horses and was carried on during extended fiestas and accompanied by considerable consumption of wine, *chicha,** or *aguardiente*. As in the rest of Latin America at this time, winnowing with wooden pitchforks evoked images of biblical harvests.

Livestock production also remained primitive. No new breeds were introduced before 1830; animals took five or six years to "fatten" on natural pastures before slaughter. Even then they yielded only 60 to 70 percent of what cattle provided in Europe. Nevertheless, hides and tallow contributed substantially to Chilean exports, as they had since early colonial days. But while the Chilean countryside was admirably suited to dairy production, the output of milk, cheese, and butter was quite low; to 1820, at least, butter cost more in the Concepción region than in the United States. Although the contesting armies of the independence decades provided markets for foodstuffs and drove up prices, they also created conditions of uncertainty or devastation in which Chilean agriculture barely held its own (in the central region) or retrogressed (in the Concepción–southern territory).

Through all the strife, however, the large rural estates continued to dominate in the countryside. Ironically, by 1827 the independent nations of Chile and Peru had reestablished the basic structure of colonial trade. Chile exported over 500,000 pesos of wheat, flour, salted meat, tallow, barley, wood, and other agricultural commodities and minerals to Peru. In exchange, Peru sent back almost 350,000 pesos of goods to Chile— approximately half in sugar. The blood spilled to win political independence consecrated the reconfirmation of colonial patterns of commerce as well as colonial economic institutions in the rural areas.

While internal productive activity stagnated, the arms trade, whaling and contraband of all sorts made Valparaíso an important Pacific way station to North America as well as to western Spanish America and to British colonies in Asia. The port's strategic location brought increasing numbers of British, North American, and other foreign merchants to Valparaíso, Santiago, and other principal towns. Some of these merchants settled permanently in Chile, founding businesses and families which became fixtures

---

Chicha is a hard cider made from grapes or apples.

of Chilean high finance and Chilean society—including Waddington, Sewell, Walker, Chadwick, Davies, Bunster, Clark, Gibbs, Lynch, and Eastman. Two future Chilean presidents would descend from an Italian immigrant-merchant, Pedro Alessandri, who arrived in Valparaíso in 1820.

Provisioning the army of liberation provided economic opportunities for colonial merchants and public officials, much as had the royal *situado* in the past. In contrast to Santiago, which changed little from 1810 to 1830, Valparaíso grew rapidly from a town of 5500 to a city of almost 20,000. A floating population of several thousand from the ships in the bay frequented the increasing number of shops, cafés, billiard parlors, bars, and brothels. An underworld of muggers, thieves, and murderers preyed upon drunken sailors and began to make Valparaíso the rough-and-tumble, bawdy Pacific port for which it became famous.

By 1822 foreigners represented nearly one-quarter of the residents of the port and virtually dominated commerce. Establishment of warehouses in which shippers could deposit merchandise for a set fee helped increase mercantile activity. Chile's merchant marine grew from three ships, owned by Spaniards, in 1810 to well over seventy by 1830. Foreigners owned many of these, but native Chileans and naturalized citizens also took part in the shipping trade. The dramatic growth of international trade also reinvigorated the shipbuilding industry. Despite the great increase in shipping, however, port facilities remained exceedingly inadequate. No docks existed. Peons, up to their waists in water, carried ashore heavy bundles on their backs from small boats sent from the anchored wooden sailing vessels. From Valparaíso merchandise went overland on mules to Santiago or to the northern towns and mining districts. Not until several decades later would railroads and steamships dramatically alter colonial modes of transport and communication.

Expansion of commerce confronted Chile's leaders with numerous political issues related to domestic industrial development, public finance, and, in the short run, successful completion of the war against Spain and achievement of diplomatic recognition by England, the United States, the Holy See, and other European powers. Diplomatic efforts by the Chileans to maintain the neutrality of England and, more important of the British Pacific squadron, during the years of war against Spain made Chilean governments cautious in dealing with powerful English merchants. The need to pay for military supplies and to meet salaries of public personnel, along with the ascendancy of English, French, and North American "free trade" doctrines, pushed Chile away from protective tariffs and toward a commercial policy that emphasized revenue-producing export and import duties.*

Chile had opened its major ports to trade with all friendly or neutral nations in 1811. The decree authorized introduction of all commodities except rum, beer, wine, aguardiente, hats, and items subject to the government *estanco* (especially tobacco). Foreign merchants could engage legally only in the wholesale trade; retail trade and coastal navigation were supposedly reserved for Chilean citizens, but violations of these provisions were common. From 1810 to 1830 import duties averaged 35 percent or more *ad valorem*, but contraband or corruption in assessing the value of imported goods significantly reduced government revenues. Export duties varied considerably from product to product, ranging from 6 to nearly 20 percent.

Government policies allowed low-priced imports to eliminate almost entirely the re-

---

*"Free trade" in this context meant opening ports to international commerce—not the elimination of import duties.

maining Chilean manufactures save for some household production, food processing, mining and livestock-related artisan activities such as soap- and candle-making and tanneries. These developments conflicted directly with the commitment of elites like Manuel de Salas or José Antonio Rodríguez Aldea to stimulate industrial growth through some form of protection for Chilean enterprises. Efforts to combine limited protective tariffs with revenue-producing duties, and the repression of contraband, which probably accounted for over half of Chile's imports, displeased the merchant community and contributed to O'Higgins' ouster.

The penetration of the economy by foreign interests in the period between 1810 and 1830 paved the way for a much more serious domination of Chile's economic development by British and North American enterprises later in the nineteenth century. By 1849 some fifty British firms controlled most Chilean exports: nearly 50 percent of the value of these exports went to England, and English goods accounted for 30 to 40 percent of the value of Chilean imports. Reacting to these trends more than a century later, historian Francisco Encina declared:

> What resulted in these years was not, as usually suggested, an intensification of international trade. Rather what occurred was an exploitation of the Chilean economy by foreign interests. They traded 60 percent of their goods, at least, for silver, gold, or copper . . . avoiding the customs house. . . . Luxury goods went down in price while the price of articles of primary necessity which the country did not produce went up. . . . Between 1823 and 1830 some three or four thousand foreigners . . . sucked the blood from the Chilean economy . . . while 95 percent of the Chilean people had retrogressed to the life style of the last third of the seventeenth century.

This view perhaps exaggerates the effects on Chile of the replacement of Spanish influence by that of England and North America. Chilean miners, landowners, small manufacturers and merchants, sometimes in partnership with foreign investors, also participated in the import-export trade. Likewise, Chilean policymakers and minor officials exerted their influence over (or exacted their price from) foreign businessmen and merchant houses. However, lacking the basic financial infrastructure and economic clout to compete in international markets, the Chilean economic elites, practically of necessity, allowed themselves to be incorporated into the web of international commerce which the British spun throughout Latin America and elsewhere in the nineteenth century.

When installation of the "Portalian state" brought an end to the political chaos of the independence movements, the Prieto government faced the enormous tasks of reorganizing public finance, rationalizing commercial policy, and determining the direction of economic development. The government fulfilled these tasks by adopting strict internal economies and by accepting Chile's role as a supplier of raw materials to the more developed capitalist economies and importers of manufactured goods. Public personnel were dismissed, government expenditures on frills were reduced, and a good climate was created for business. Emphasis was placed on honesty and efficiency. This meant two things. First, law and order were re-established, and harsh penalties were meted out to common criminals. Second, government sought to encourage private enterprise. As Minister Rengifo put it in his report to Congress in 1835:

> The measures which favorably affect the economy of a State may be reduced to two types: First, . . . laws that remove obstacles to industry, that protect property and its use, that reduce the costs of production, and that open free channels for the export

[*salida*] of national products; second, . . . laws which regulate taxes with moderation and discernment . . . and prevent expenditures from the public treasury for purposes other than those of strict administrative necessity.

To attract foreign trade and shipping, a decree of 1832 established warehouses of deposit (*almacenes francos de depósito*) in Valparaíso; by 1835 the government was operating sixteen such warehouses and renting out another twenty-seven. Administrative reforms put the public treasury in order and established confidence in public credit. Gradually the government attempted to pay off the public debt.

More than anything else, government policy aimed at stimulating production of traditional colonial commodities and incorporating Chile into the world capitalist economy. Summarizing this strategy, Chilean author Miguel Cruchaga tells us that "They believed the country was not ready . . . for the development of manufactures, and desiring to give it easy access to articles of consumption and easy export opportunities for what was produced, they sought to facilitate commerce with the foreign countries who could provision us at least cost." This strategy suited the interests of the major economic groups in Chile, landowners, mine owners, exporters-importers, and domestic as well as foreign merchants. It allowed the upper classes to import luxury goods from Europe, live the good life, modernize the cities, and maintain traditional social relationships and property institutions in the countryside. But it also contained serious internal contradictions which would become ever more evident as modernization of transport and communication, along with economic growth in the nineteenth century, created industrial and working class-interests for whom liberal political economy meant ruin or deprivation. In the short run, however, the autocratic republic proved a highly pragmatic reconciliation of the economic interests of the upper classes with both the demands of foreign capitalists and the need for internal order. It restored centralized political authority, and maintained the social stratification of the colony, while allowing "free trade" to cater to the tastes of the upper classes. This was the fruit of Chilean independence in the 1830s.

5 Modernization and Misery

Consolidation of authoritarian government after 1839 gave Chile a truly national political system with administrative capabilities that paved the way for impressive economic growth during the next three decades. Attracted by the relative political stability, foreign investors brought the wonders of modern technology to Chile. The first railroad, built between 1849 and 1851; connected the mining regions of Copiapó to the port of Caldera; by 1863 another line linked Valparaíso to Santiago and was extended south to San Fernando. The American entrepreneur William Wheelwright, who had introduced steam navigation to Chile in the 1840s, directed construction of the telegraph line between the capital and Valparaíso in 1851–52; twenty-five years later the telegraph provided communication to forty-eight Chilean towns as well as connections to Peru and Argentina. Steamships and railroads permitted increased movement of products from the northern mines and the agricultural hinterlands of the central valley and the Concepción region to the port cities and the exterior. From Talcahuano, Valparaíso, La Serena, Caldera, and other legal and illegal points of departure, Chilean commodities left for North America, Australia, Asia, and Europe. An apparent economic miracle quadrupled the value of Chilean exports between 1845 and 1875, while the number of ships entering Chilean ports more than doubled in the decade of the 1860s alone.

Beginning with the discovery of silver at Chañarcillo in 1832, followed by strikes at Tres Puntas to the north of Copiapó and at other mines in the mid-1840s, silver production increased dramatically. After reaching an official level of 100,000 to 200,000 kilos annually between 1851 and 1856, recorded output hovered in the neighborhood of 10,000 kilos a year until the 1870s, when the Caracoles mine came into production. Copper production likewise expanded from a level of 8,000 to 10,000 metric tons a year in the period 1844–50 to almost 35,000 metric tons in 1860. In that year the value of copper exports exceeded 14 million pesos—double the national budget and approximately 56 percent by value of all Chilean exports. During the next decade annual average copper production more than doubled again, with the principal center of production remaining at José Tomás de Urmeneta's mine at Tamaya (see Map 10). To the south, in the Concepción region, coal production also dramatically expanded from some 7800 metric tons in 1852 to more than 186,000 metric tons in 1876.

From the outset mining and modernization took its environmental toll, especially on the forests, streams, and desert soils. Charles Darwin wrote in his *Journal during the Voyage of H.M.S 'Beagle' Round the World* that the shortage of firewood and primitive smelting techniques made it more economical to ship copper to Swansea for refining than for local processing. Claudio Gay, a French scientist working for the Chilean government, delivered a report in 1838 lamenting deforestation in the *norte chico*. He recommended establishing copper smelters in the southern provinces, where firewood was abundant. By 1839 the government of president Joaquín Prieto ordered a study regarding the feasibility of using coal to fuel mining operations as the mines in the north consumed the region's limited timber. According to Chilean historian Luis Valenzuela (*Tres estudios sobre el comercio y fundición de Cobre en Chile y en el mercado mundial 1830–1880*), fuel represented approximately 45 percent of the costs of smelting copper; deforestation raised prices of firewood inordinately. In 1845 the Chilean congress eliminated tariff duties on imported coal disembarked from Papudo to the north, encouraging conversion of the copper smelters to coal from firewood.

Steam navigation encouraged the first important coal shipments from the Concepción region (Lirquén and Coronel) in the 1840s. Matías Cousiño Jorquera, a miner from the north, married into the fabulously wealthy Gallo family and initiated more extensive coal mining operations at Lota and Coronel in 1852. This gave origin to the Compañia Carbonífera de Lota—an enterprise whose history would be intimately connected to the socioeconomic and political development of the country—and to its literature, through Baldomero Lillo's collection of short stories (*Subterra*)—until its closure in 1997. Bringing machinery and technicians from Europe and the United States, Cousiño made a fortune in the coal industry, created hundreds of jobs, and incubated a new working-class mining subculture. His enterprises in the region extended to copper smelters, lumber, sawmills, agriculture, flour mills, glass, and porcelain, complementing his mining and railroad investments in the north. By the late 1870s the local coal mines finally overtook English coal imports as the major suppliers to the northern mining districts.

The coal mines in the Concepción region, like the copper and silver mines of the north, left their marks: deforestation, slag heaps, coal dust, water pollution, mine accidents, and lung diseases among the workers. As in Europe and North America, modernization, incipient industrialization, economic internationalization, and growth had their costs. Chile shared these costs with the rest of independent Spanish America in the global economy of the nineteenth century. As Chilean historian Eduardo Cavieres puts it (*Comercio chileno y comerciantes ingleses 1820–1880*),

> Chile came into the world economy as a producer of primary products, being integrated into the growing British copper industry. For decades copper was its main export and for decades copper exports balanced the value of imports and contributed to internal growth. . . . Chile could not control the copper business and international copper prices became a negative factor. . . . Chileans did not adopt policies to encourage economic diversification or to stimulate internal markets.

Agricultural production also grew significantly in the middle years of the nineteenth century. Cereal, livestock, and vineyard output increased to meet the demands of the transitory foreign markets opened with the discovery of gold in California and Australia. The growth of the northern mining economy, and the commercial expansion of the principal towns and cities, further encouraged the agricultural economy. Between 1844 and 1860 the value of agricultural exports—led by wheat, flour, and barley—quintupled; between 1871 and 1876 the value of agricultural exports exceeded by fifteenfold the levels attained in the mid-1840s. In the 1850s, complementing expanded cereal cultivation, North American and British entrepreneurs sparked development of a new flour-milling industry, which soon took second place only to copper as the major industry in the Chilean economy. But as Cavieres indicates, agricultural cycles were different from those in mining, especially after the mid-1850s, as more efficient producers such as Argentina, Australia, and the United States not only replaced Chilean wheat exports with local production but also entered international markets as competitors. England, which accounted for over 50 percent of Chilean exports, continued to import Chilean wheat, corn, barley, flour, and livestock products, such as hides and wool. Other significant markets for Chilean agriculture were the United States, Peru, France, and Germany; only 6 percent of exports went elsewhere in the mid-1850s.

Shortly thereafter the first Chilean joint stock companies, banks, and credit institutions took shape, and the *Caja de Crédito Hipotecario,* established in 1855, soon became the most important mortgage bank in South America. The first joint stock companies in commercial banking, which emerged in the early 1850s, allied Chilean, British, and North American capital in insurance and railroad enterprises. Landowners, merchants, and mining interests came together to capitalize new economic activities through the modern financial institutions of Western capitalism—the corporation, or *sociedad anónima.* Significantly, the Chilean government also participated in the financing of railroads, setting an important precedent for "mixed" public-private economic ventures linking an ever more integrated economic elite to the apparatus of the state.

Accompanying these trends came diversification of retail trade and an incredible rise in imports of tropical commodities and manufactured goods by the wealthy residents of Valparaíso, Santiago, Tomé-Concepción, and the northern mining districts. In a study published in 1874, entitled *Our Enemy, Luxury!,* a Chilean author captured both the glitter of a superficial prosperity and the dangers of the preference by national elites and foreigners for imported luxury goods.

Economic expansion created new economic interests, made social stratification somewhat more complex, and exacerbated regional animosities as both the southern and northern provinces sought to keep pace with the progress of Santiago, Valparaíso, and the central valley. With some 115,000 residents, Santiago no longer seemed merely a colonial administrative center. Connected by rail in 1863 to the port of Valparaíso, which was itself a bustling commercial center of over 60,000 people, Santiago was becoming more and more a real urban capital in a growing new nation.

As the towns became cities, there developed an impressive liberal intellectual movement. Made possible, in part, by the policies of President Bulnes and his minister, Manuel Montt, favoring intellectual activities and expansion of the educational system, the movement gave rise to the "Generation of 1842" led by Victorino Lastarria and to the creation of the University of Chile. The new university began to function in 1843 under the direction of Andrés Bello, eminent Venezuelan philosopher, jurist, and statesman, who wrote the Chilean Civil Code (1855), steeped in the Roman legal tradition, and dedicated his life to public service in Chile until his death in 1865. Soon after a normal school was established, and in subsequent decades, the system of primary instruction expanded: the 1850s witnessed the creation of more than 500 public schools. The Montt government (1851–61) also stimulated construction of libraries, technical schools, and even special institutions for the deaf. By 1861 some 45,000 children attended public and private institutions of learning, and several thousand were enrolled in secondary schools. Nevertheless, the vast majority of the population—especially those living in the countryside—still could not obtain even a minimal education for their children. Like the superficial prosperity of the nation, the educational system remained accessible primarily to the privileged few in the principal urban centers.

The intellectual movement of the 1840s combined the talents of Chileans with those of expatriates from Argentina, Venezuela, and Colombia, who found refuge from *caudillismo* and tyranny in an orderly Chile, whose authoritarian regime spared it from the widespread anarchy characteristic of Latin America at the time. Although the movement was made possible by Chile's stability, it soon proved subversive to the incumbent regime. Typifying the anti-Hispanic spirit of this movement was an article by Francisco Bilbao that appeared in 1844 in a periodical called *El Crepúsculo ("The Twilight")*. This article, entitled "Chilean Society," harshly criticized the colonial past, the

Church, and most of the country's political institutions. The government ordered the burning of all copies of the periodical in which the article appeared. In September of the same year José Victorino Lastarria delivered the first annual paper on Chilean history at the national university. Lastarría's paper, called "Investigation into the Social Influence of the Conquest and the Spanish Colonial System upon Chile," blamed the Hispanic heritage and the Church for most of the nation's problems. The government that funded the National Institute at which Bilbao studied and created the University that gave Lastarría a public forum could not tolerate a direct confrontation with the Church or so bombastic a challenge to the social order. Government leaders viewed the University as a training ground for political and professional elites; the emergence of political opposition and challenges to the foundations of the Chilean society within the University community set the stage for an ongoing drama of intellectual and political ferment in Chile's institutions of higher education. For the next two decades the intellectuals of the "Generation of 1842" could be found at the forefront of social and political movements that opposed the leadership and policies of the autocratic regime.

Despite criticisms by liberal intellectuals, Chile's apparently impressive economic growth and political stability temporarily overshadowed both the vulnerability of its economic system and political frailties. Because it depended upon duties from international trade for most of its revenues, the government tended to centralize power and resources at Santiago and Valparaíso. Even though the northern mining districts and the southern cereal-flour complex produced a disproportionate share of the nation's exports, Chile's political leaders made only marginal budgetary allocations to the northern and southern provinces. As a result, considerable regional opposition arose against the autocratic regime. Reflecting this provincial resentment, an editorial in *El Curicano* in December 1858 decried the fact that

> while the capital absorbs all the income, receives all the material improvements, concentrates all the benefits, the provinces . . . languish in misery and backwardness. . . . Under the Spanish regime the provinces were exploited and paid heavy taxes to support the Spanish court. Now, there is little difference. We pay heavy taxes and are exploited in a thousand ways to beautify the court of Santiago. In our jurisdiction [department] the government does not invest a tenth of the funds we contribute to the national treasury.

The growing ideological, political, and regional fragmentation of the Chilean elite would lead to civil wars in 1851 and 1859 and to a gradual, but fundamental, transformation of the autocratic republic and its authoritarian underpinnings by the 1870s. In 1891 another civil war reaffirmed the victory of the oligarchic transformation of the 1833 constitution against a resurgent presidentialism.

Just as the apparent stability of the political system masked its gradual transformation, so, too, did favorable international economic trends disguise the fragility of the Chilean economy. Temporary markets in California and Australia had stimulated agricultural production, processing industries, and shipping from 1849 until almost 1860. Soon, however, California wheat and flour competed favorably with the Chilean products even at Valparaíso.

Foreign and immigrant-owned commercial firms in Valparaíso controlled much of the country's credit system. Operating under a flexible option-buying scheme, these merchant lenders loaned capital to mining and agricultural interests against future production. They reserved the option to pay for agricultural commodities or minerals at the market price current when credit was extended or at the market price at the time of delivery. Under this system producers bore the risks of price changes, while lenders benefited from either a decline or a rise in market prices. Foreign investors also gained control over much of Chile's flour-milling industry, mining, shipping, and commerce. Fluctuations in demand and prices for Chilean minerals and agricultural commodities in the international marketplace produced periodic economic crises with serious political implications.

Above all else, the mid-nineteenth-century Chilean economy continued to depend upon mineral exports. Periodic discoveries in Chile's northern provinces stimulated the rise of mining towns and their accompanying ports throughout the *norte chico* from 1832 until the late 1870s. Export duties from the mineral sector provided the national government with over 50 percent of public revenues during the entire period. Continuing essentially colonial politico-economic relations, the central government siphoned off most of the tax revenues from the mines without investing substantial resources in the northern provinces.

The independence period commenced in 1811 with the opening of the Agua Amarga silver mine south of Vallenar (see Map 10). This and other mines helped pay the costs of the war for independence. Establishing a pattern later followed by other northern regions, the area around Vallenar experienced rapid growth in population along with increased cultivation of nearby agricultural land. Then, with exhaustion of the silver veins, population in the zone decreased to perhaps 3500 by the early 1850s. Following the Agua Amarga strike in 1825, the rich Arqueros discovery located inland from Coquimbo seemed so important that the Chilean government established a new mint at La Serena. After Arqueros the next big silver strike occurred at Chañarcillo in 1832. Chañarcillo reportedly yielded more than 12 million pesos' worth of silver in less than a decade, and the surrounding region, especially Copiapó, enjoyed boom conditions. New discoveries in the late 1840s, in particular at Tres Puntas between Copiapó and the "port" of Flamenco to the northwest, prolonged the silver fever. In 1843 the government officially proclaimed Copiapó a city. Graced by this blessing, population in the department of Copiapó mushroomed from 11,300 in 1843 to almost 65,000 in 1865.

Tres Puntas exemplified the difficulties facing the mining industry in Chile's northern provinces: poor roads, lack of water, and scarcity of almost all basic necessities including food, fuel, and implements. Yet within five years a settlement of some 4000 residents had sprung up around the mines. Despite the high cost of everything needed for survival, Tres Puntas, like the other mining towns, grew and prospered as long as the ore held out. As late as the mid-1860s mining activity persisted at Tres Puntas, and miners still sent ore by mule and wagon to Flamenco over what a contemporary writer called a "tolerable road."

Other less significant silver discoveries kept the miners' hopes alive until the next big strike in 1870 at Caracoles (legally in Bolivia), located on the road between Antofagasta and San Pedro de Atacama. Again the pattern of rapid urbanization occurred; by 1873 Caracoles had become a growing, prosperous town with more than 2500 residents. Commercial houses from the coast established branches, hotels opened, and the usual proliferation of cantinas, houses of prostitution, billiard parlors, and retail shops proclaimed the importance of the new northern mining district. This development took place despite the total lack of nearby water sources, fuel, and local agriculture. Everything had to be brought in from the coast or across the Andes. Carters and muleteers charged twice as much to carry goods between Antofagasta and Caracoles than did shipping companies to bring freight to Antofagasta from Europe. Nonetheless, miners dug out the ore; more than 1200 carters and thousands of mules carried it to Antofagasta—now, due to Caracoles, a growing Bolivian port city.

Located in a region disputed by Chile and Bolivia, the Caracoles minerals renewed a conflict only partially resolved in a treaty of 1866 in which the two nations set Chile's northern boundary at latitude 24° South and specified that the two countries would divide equally revenues from guano and mineral deposits within the territory located between latitudes 23° and 25° South. Bolivia agreed to finance construction of a port at Mejillones and to maintain a customs house with a monopoly for exacting export duties on the minerals of the region. The 1866 treaty also promised Chile one-half the revenue collected at Mejillones from export taxes on guano or minerals. This stipulation gave Chilean agents the right to audit the accounts of the customs house, a provision the Bolivians bitterly resented as insulting to national sovereignty. In time Bolivia ignored the terms of the treaty by exporting minerals extracted from the shared territory through the more northerly port of Cobija, and refused to pay Chile its share of the custom receipts. In 1871, shortly after the Caracoles silver strike, a new Bolivian government disavowed all international agreements made by the previous administration. Subsequent negotiations and a new treaty in 1874 failed to resolve the fundamental issues. Less than a decade later Bolivia would lose all the territory and riches under dispute, along with its access to the Pacific, when it was defeated by Chile in the War of the Pacific (see Chapter 6).

Despite the great importance of silver to Chile's northern provinces, copper mining proved even more significant. Since colonial times Chilean copper had found its way to Europe, Asia, and North America. In the 1830s British vessels carried the red metal from Chile to India. British capitalists made significant investments in Chilean copper mining from the mid-1830s and early 1840s when Joshua Waddington exploited mines at Chañaral Alto in the department of Combarbalá. By the mid-1860s British interests had invested more than 4.5 million pesos in the Caldera area alone, almost all of which involved copper.

Although British and other foreign interests made substantial investments in the copper industry, a small number of daring, persistent Chilean capitalists and adventurers played a key role in the northern copper business. Suggestive, if untypical, was the eighteen-year quest of José Tomás de Urmeneta at Tamaya, northwest of Ovalle (see Map 10): in 1852 he finally hit an incredibly rich vein. During the next eleven years the Tamaya mine reportedly produced copper valued at 5 million pesos. Urmeneta subsequently established foundries at Guayacán and Tongoy on the coast and also contracted with Henry Meiggs to build a rail line from the port at Tongoy to the mines. Urmeneta expanded his investments to coal and railroads in the southern region, a fleet of steamships purchased in Europe and public works in Santiago. He also acquired the important Hacienda Limache near Valparaíso. An unsuccessful candidate for president in 1871, Urmeneta was an extreme example of how the mineral wealth of the northern regions filtered south to Santiago, Valparaíso, and beyond, incorporating a new commercial and mining element into the Chilean agrarian elite. His career epitomized the opportunities available to a favored few in the years from 1835 until the outbreak of the War of the Pacific in 1879.

Copper mines also provided the rationale for the first railroads in Chile, built by William Wheelwright between the copper-rich Copiapó littoral and the port of Caldera to the northwest. Arrival of the railroad converted Caldera from a small settlement of perhaps fifty residents in 1850 into a port town of 2,000 by 1853. The number of ships putting in at the port increased from 160 a year in 1850 to more than 600 five years later. In contrast, the previously favored point for copper shipment at Puerto Viejo, to the southwest, was practically abandoned. Writing in the late 1850s, Vicente Pérez Rosales

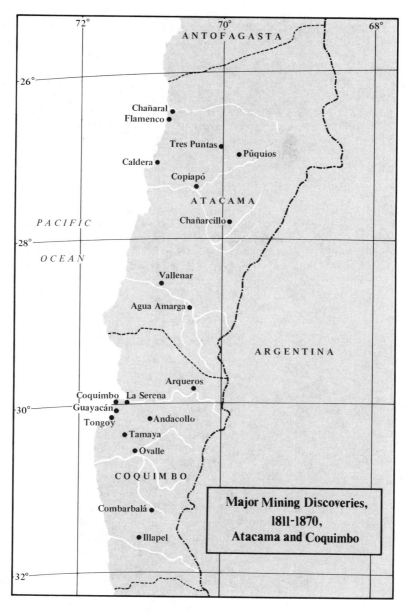

MAP 10: MAJOR MINING DISCOVERIES 1811–70, ATACAMA AND COQUIMBO

noted that "the railroad to Copiapó brought gas, beautiful buildings, theater, conveniences, luxury, abundance of fuel and food, along with a spirit of enterprise, attracting thereby numerous foreigners and Chileans to the city and the surrounding regions." Extension of the line to the mines near Púquios and around an irregular semicircle to the northern Bay of Chañaral stimulated economic activity throughout the departments of both Chañaral and Copiapó. The region's physical and economic subsistence soon came to depend more upon steamships, steel rails, and locomotives than upon mules, wagons, and the precarious river-valley agriculture of southern Coquimbo.

While copper deposits encouraged investments in modern transportation, the copper mines themselves generally remained technologically backward. As in the case of silver, the Chilean copper industry relied upon technology essentially unchanged from colonial times until the introduction of the reverberatory furnace at mid-century. Miners extracted only the richest ore and sold the slag to traders for delivery to more modern refineries in Germany, France, and England.

Technological modernization in copper mining took hold gradually from the 1840s as the major foundries and smelters converted from firewood to coal. By the 1860s the most important enterprises, like those of Carlos Lambert, Joaquín Edwards, and José Urmeneta and Maximiano Errázuriz, had installed more modern reverberatory furnaces and used the updated "Napier methods" imported from England. Production and exports were gradually concentrated in several major companies. According to Luis Valenzuela, in the decade of the 1860s the firm of Urmeneta and Errázuriz, which operated the country's most important smelter at Guayacán, accounted for 25–50 percent of copper bars and ingot exports. In 1859 Urmeneta and Errázuriz also acquired the Tongoy smelter established by the British "Mexican and South American Smelting Company" ten years earlier. In the words of Chilean historians Luis Ortega and Julio Pinto, the Urmeneta and Errázuriz smelters and related mining industries were "truly an industrial vanguard for their era." Until the end of the 1870s Chile was the world's leading copper exporter.

As the copper industry expanded, it utilized British coal along with domestic supplies shipped from the Concepción region. Higher-quality British coal made the Chilean coal industry around Lota, Coronel, and Lebu in southern Chile vulnerable to British oversupply of the copper districts. As late as 1862 a large importation of British coal resulted in serious production cutbacks at Lota and Coronel. Fortunately for Chilean producers, a combination of British and Chilean coal proved technically most desirable; and consequently the foundries at Caldera tended to use a 50-50 mixture of Swansea and Chilean coal. The overall share of the coal market in the copper districts going to the British varied year to year from 25 to 50 percent.

In addition to silver and copper, a number of less significant mining activities, along with extraction of guano and nitrates, hinted at Chile's economic future by the end of the 1870s. Like the silver mines and copper discoveries, exploitation of other mineral resources encouraged related agricultural and commercial ventures. In the favored river valleys of Coquimbo and Atacama provinces, crop cultivation and livestock husbandry increased production to meet a part of the growing demand for food and animal products. Towns rose, stagnated, or declined with the fate of the mineral discoveries that had created them.

The sequence of mineral discoveries from the 1830s to the early 1870s brought waves of fortune hunters to the provinces of Atacama and Coquimbo. The former province tripled its population between 1843 and 1875, while the population of Coquimbo province doubled. This contrasted markedly with the relatively stable population of the predominantly rural departments of the middle central valley. By the mid-1870s most of the population of the northern provinces lived in "urban" settlements of more than 2000 people, though overall population density of these provinces was much sparser than those of the less urbanized middle central valley. The overwhelming influence of mining and the lack of large areas of cultivable land concentrated the population of the north into ports, administrative centers, and mining districts.

The obvious physical and economic contrasts between the northern provinces and the central valley lent a distinctive character to life in the north. Higher salaries, higher costs of living, and the concentration of wage workers in isolated production centers gradually forged a militant proletarian labor force. The great power of the mine owners in association with government officials, also often on the payroll of the mining enterprises, and the dramatic ups and downs of the mining ventures encouraged the evolution of a volatile political culture among northern workers. The agricultural export boom of the 1850s, which so greatly benefited Valparaíso merchants and Chilean landowners, meant higher food prices for the northern miners. Demands for higher wages led to strikes, violence, and looting by miners during the civil war of 1851. Miners, artisans, dockworkers, and muleteers in the *norte chico*, especially the region around Copiapó, played an even more significant role in the subsequent civil war of 1859. In the railroad machine shops and foundries of Caldera, workers cast cannon to use against government forces; in Chañarcillo, Copiapó, and other mining centers workers formed battalions that helped make the *norte chico* a temporarily "liberated zone." If the motivation of the mining entrepreneurs for rebellion could be detected in the decrees promulgated during this temporary "liberation"—for example, reduction by 50 percent of export duties on minerals—the experience of armed revolt by thousands of northern workers made the northern labor force more aware that government authority and the interests of the propertied classes conflicted with their own. With the War of the Pacific (1879–83) and the Chileanization of the nitrate fields, the northern work force would expand even more dramatically, class consciousness would become more acute, and class struggle would intensify. Soon thereafter the reality of the "social question" and industrial conflict would sweep southward from the northern provinces into Chile's heartland.

Modernization and material progress in the middle decades of the nineteenth century brought hard times to many of Chile's people in the central valley. While acreage under grain cultivation and production more than tripled between 1850 and 1875, thousands of rural families migrated to Santiago, Valparaíso, or the northern mining districts or looked for work in railway construction and public works projects. Whereas the population for the entire country increased from about 1,000,000 in 1835 to 2,100,000 (outside of Indian territory) in 1875 and to over 2,700,000 in 1895, that of rural central Chile had by 1895 barely changed from its 1865 level of 950,000.

Santiago, Valparaíso, and provincial capitals drew substantial population from the rural areas (see Table 5–1). Between 1865 and 1875 alone, Santiago's population increased from 115,000 to more than 150,000, while Valparaíso grew from 70,000 to almost 100,000 (42%). Favored central valley towns such as Curicó also experienced dramatic growth in the decade 1865–75; this provincial town almost doubled its population, growing from 5900 to 10,000, while the population of Curicó province remained almost stable at 90,000.

Although immigrants played a relatively minor numerical role in the urbanization process, at Valparaíso and in the northern mining towns a foreign presence was ever more apparent. For the country as a whole, immigrants composed less than 2 percent of the population in 1875; but in the province of Atacama they accounted for 11 percent,

A horsedrawn street car (*carro de sangre*), the first tramway at Santiago Central Station, 1858. (Courtesy of Archivo Universidad de Chile.)

Santiago Central Station, 1886. (Courtesy of Archivo Universidad de Chile.)

TABLE 5–1. COMPARISON OF URBAN AND RURAL POPULATION IN
SELECTED NORTHERN AND CENTRAL VALLEY DEPARTMENTS, 1875

Department, Northern Provinces	Total Population	"Urban" Population as % of Total
Copiapó	31,877	68
Caldera	10,511	78
Vallenar	13,569	51
Freirina	15,541	53
Serena	29,057	67
Coquimbo	12,650	73
Elqui	12,147	52
Ovalle	39,567	32
Combarbalá	14,002	17
Illapel	32,011	41

Department, Middle Central Valley Provinces	Total Population	"Urban" Population as % of Total
Melipilla	32,253	23
Rancagua	98,092	13
Caupolicán	75,186	15
San Fernando	72,668	15
Curicó	57,312	24
Vichuquen	35,546	8
Lontué	19,791	16
Talca	90,597	30
Loncomilla	31,689	21
Linares	53,420	14
Parral	33,652	16

and in the department of Copiapó, approximately 20 percent. More important than their numbers was the financial and commercial power wielded by these groups.

The prosperity of foreign merchants at Valparaíso or in the mining districts contrasted sharply with the plight of the mass of rural laborers in the central valley. After 1860 wages in the countryside fell further and further behind the rising cost of food and basic necessities. The conditions of the *inquilinos* worsened as landlords required the service tenants to work more days, provide more family labor, or pay additional peons to fulfill the family's labor obligations. The tenants received ever smaller land allotments and faced restrictions on pasture rights for their animals. By 1858 a Chilean writer told his countrymen to "open your eyes and every day you see families leaving their homes. . . . Their single purpose is to leave the place where they cannot earn a living. . . . Travel our roads and you will see numerous families with all their belongings on their backs moving toward the capital to increase the existing pauperism." Rural banditry and cattle rustling, a problem from colonial times, persisted from the 1820s to the 1890s as the backside of agricultural commercialization and rural poverty. Landowners, vigilantes, and police failed to curtail the banditry despite whippings, beatings, and occasional executions. Repressive legislation against rustlers and horse thieves in the 1870s and the creation of a new Rural Police force in 1882 were symptoms of the continuing affliction.

Between 1849 and 1855 Chileans went in search of gold in California or to work on the railway under construction in Panama. The California census of 1852, which probably underestimates the Chilean presence, enumerates over 5500 in California at that date. Railroad gangs constructing the Santiago-Valparaíso line occupied a work force of 9000 to 10,000 a year; railroad projects in Peru (1868–72), directed by American entrepreneur Henry Meiggs, recruited 25,000 to 30,000 Chilean workers. Extension of the Chilean line to San Fernando (1862), Curicó (1868), and Talca (1874) employed thousands more. The Chillán-Talcahuano line (1869–74) provided jobs for over 9000 peons—and yet the army of rural unemployed increased.

Despite complaints by hacendados that construction projects and Meiggs' Peruvian venture created a shortage of hands, Chilean agriculture in the central valley experienced peak performance between 1868 and 1872. More important, except in critical periods of the agricultural cycle such as harvest, wages for rural labor failed to climb above the typical 10 to 25 centavos a day plus meager food rations. Upset at the inconvenience of competing for harvest labor with railroad crews, landowners filled the country's newspapers with exaggerated reports of the awful conditions and epidemics suffered by Chileans in Peru. Meanwhile the tide of migration carried thousands out of the rural districts as the rural poor sought better opportunities elsewhere.

The fact that a promise of a wage of 62 centavos a day plus food rations could move 30,000 Chileans to Peru indicates the plight of the Chilean rural lower classes. Thousands of families endured precarious lives in squatters' huts on marginal land along the coast; thousands more lived an ambulatory existence following the crops from Aconcagua south. Still others turned to banditry and cattle rustling, making some of the rural districts unsafe for travel. Official reports of the 1840s and 1850s contain many references to the large "vagrant" population of the central valley. Under these conditions hacendados in some areas could attract harvest labor by sponsoring a type of harvest fiesta called *mingaco*, thereby "paying" the workers only with food and drink.

With the sweat and blood of these workers and that of their families, a small wealthy elite initiated the physical modernization of Chile in the middle decades of the nineteenth century. Railroads built to carry minerals of the north to Caldera or the cereals of the central valley to Valparaíso permitted Chilean and foreign entrepreneurs to live an extravagant existence in the principal urban areas. Wealth accumulated in mining and commerce bought land and social status. To the list of traditional landed families like the Aguirre, Larraín, or Errázuriz, mining and commercial fortunes added British, French, and German surnames along with those of newly enriched Chileans. The economically integrated upper class that emerged treated the Chilean masses with contempt. Railroad and mining interests bewailed the drunken orgies of their workers, while landowners defended the practice of paying workers in company scrip on the grounds that it spared them the temptation of "foolish" consumption outside the haciendas.

Sumptuous houses and importation of luxurious European furnishings absorbed many of the windfall profits associated with wheat and flour exports, commerce, and mining. Santiago, Valparaíso, and even lesser central valley towns boasted new, lavishly decorated edifices. Upper-class gentlemen emulated the life styles of European capitalists and aristocrats. Prestigious social clubs and the National Agricultural Society (1869) brought together sociopolitical elites to decide matters of state and economy outside the public halls of the Congress. The best-endowed maintained haciendas near Santiago or Valparaíso as recreational retreats with ornamental gardens and well-furnished residences, or *casas de fundo.* With the extension of the railroad south to Talca, lesser properties, located farther from the capital, increased in value and, subsequently, in the ornamentation of the landowner's "big house."

No less impressive than the sumptuous buildings in the cities, the gracious country residences stood in stark contrast to the rude huts of the campesinos whose pitiful wages barely provided subsistence. Low labor costs inhibited the same landowners, so fond of modern urban convenience in their townhouses, from modernizing farm technology. Chilean landowners preferred labor-intensive, sickle-and-scythe harvesting of cereals long after most of North America and Australia had mechanized the wheat harvest. A minority of Chilean landowners adopted machinery, new crops, and new breeds of animals and pastures or began construction of irrigation canals; but the economics of Chilean agriculture—cheap labor and vast rural estates with uncultivated land—did not invite large-scale mechanization prior to the 1880s. The poverty of the Chilean masses limited internal demand for agricultural products; and by the early 1870s Chile's inability to compete with North American and Australian producers restricted expansion of its output despite the importance of the British market. Under these conditions, even without substantial mechanization, Chilean agriculture based upon the large haciendas could not provide year-round employment to the growing number of rootless rural laborers.

Industry offered no solution to the employment problem. Modernization and commercial expansion brought little industry to Chile. An American naval officer visiting the country at midcentury noted that Chile was "almost without factories of any description . . . dependent on foreign nations for every supply except food." This description ignored the numerous small-scale producers of household goods, cordage, rigging, tanneries, and the like, but it accurately portrayed the lack of any significant manufacturing establishment, apart from flour mills and breweries established by German immigrants in the south and the mining enterprises in the north. Major economic interest groups such as landowners, merchants, and mine owners generally opposed protective tariffs to encourage local industry. Dependent upon the export trade, albeit in different ways, landowners did not wish to pay taxes on imported European goods. Mine interests, closely linked to British firms, commercial houses, and shippers, supported "free trade"; merchants, like merchants everywhere, defended the right of the consumer to buy quality goods at low prices. Occasional editorials in Santiago or regional newspapers in the 1860s and 1870s supported, without notable success, some form of protective tariff to encourage domestic manufacturers. Debates in the legislature resulted in new tariff laws in 1872 and 1878, but conflict existed between the primary goal of increasing government revenues from custom duties and any effective tariff barrier to encourage Chilean industry. Protectionist sentiments existed but, with some notable exceptions such as special duties on imported sugar and beer, did not make significant gains until the tariff reforms in 1897. Even then, protectionism remained controversial. In response to economic crises, labor conflicts, and urban riots in the period 1903–07, President Pedro Montt led a movement to reduce tariffs on manufactured consumer goods and meat products. Not until the tariff reforms of 1928 would industrialization through protectionism become a dominant economic policy in Chile.

In the mid-1870s the overwhelming majority of Chilean manufacturing establishments were quite small, typically artisan producers of consumer goods or more durable items such as carriages and wagons. Rarely did firms employ large numbers of workers or operate anything like an industrial assembly process, although by 1874 some of the Talca flour mills were utilizing imported steam-powered machinery. Even shipbuilding, a likely enterprise given Chilean participation in the Pacific grain trade and the country's extensive mineral exports, experienced no significant growth. Of 259 Chilean-registered ships in 1865, only twenty-six were constructed in Chile, and all but six of these came from boatworks in the southern region. A brief war with Spain between 1864 and 1866 resulted in the loss of a number of these ships and a change in the registry of others. The Spanish blockaded Chile's main ports of entry, but lacked sufficient ships and troops to make the blockade effective along Chile's entire coast. Frustrated by the stalemate and Chile's refusal to provide the proper salute to the Spanish flag, the Spanish fleet bombarded Valparaíso, seriously damaging warehouses and port-works. Although the blockade caused temporary disruptions of commerce, it did nothing to stimulate Chilean shipbuilding even in the face of the obvious lesson of the nation's vulnerability to one of Europe's third-rate powers.

With no significant industry to occupy a growing population, the central valley sent its surplus labor into construction projects, the northern mines, or to foreign lands in search of employment. Mining depressions, reduction of public works, or decline in demand for the products of Chilean agriculture meant immediate crisis for the mass of the population, just as it meant bankruptcy for overextended entrepreneurs, landowners, or merchants. According to the census of 1875, more than 60 percent of the enumerated male labor force worked as unskilled laborers (*gañanes*) or "farmers" (*agricultores*). Of the more than 300,000 women reported in the census, approximately 85

Valparaíso, 1866: Evacuation before the Spanish Bombardment. (Courtesy Archivo Universidad de Chile.) Drawing by P. Blanchard.

percent worked as cooks, servants, washerwomen, seamstresses, or weavers. These figures obviously understate the contribution of women to the economy, especially in agriculture, but do provide a revealing glimpse into the economic opportunities open to most of Chile's female population during these years. Women achieved access to Chilean universities only after 1877, and as late as 1907, according to a group of Chilean historians reporting on the rise of the middle class in the country, there were only "3[women] lawyers, 7 doctors, 10 dentists, 10 pharmacists and 3980 school teachers." More generally, including the data for unskilled and semiskilled laborers in the countryside, construction crews, ports, and railroads, together with miners and various artisans (for example, 14,000 shoemakers, 250 candle and soap makers, etc.), the census suggests that 85 to 90 percent of all actively employed Chilean males corresponded to these working-class categories. Even with the most ample interpretation of *comerciantes,* or "merchants," of the professions, of industrialists of various sorts, of white-collar and public employees, and of miscellaneous non-"working-class" categories, substantially less than 10 percent of the enumerated actively employed corresponded to an emerging "middle" stratum or to the numerically tiny economic elite.

Thus the economic progress of the middle decades of the nineteenth century quite narrowly restricted wealth to an upper crust of society and allowed a thin veneer of ornamentation and physical modernization to cover the major urban centers. This veneer cracked with each economic recession or decline in prices for Chile's principal exports. Loss of the California and Australian markets after 1856, declines in copper prices, and the switch to a gold standard by European nations in 1873 shortly after the rich silver strike at Caracoles (1870), all drastically affected Chile's prosperity.

The economic recession of 1857–58 brought widespread unemployment and bankruptcies, followed by civil war in 1859. The worldwide economic depression of 1873 set in motion a train of events that looked even more disastrous for Chile. The shift to a gold standard by European powers was followed by a 50 percent drop in copper prices. Bad weather ruined the Chilean wheat crop of 1876–77. Famine followed. The economic depression seemed to climax forty years of economic "development." Government revenues, still dependent upon the devastated export sector, drastically declined. Budget reductions exacerbated employment problems with a cutback on public works and government personnel. Government borrowing to meet the crisis increased the fiscal deficit; in desperation President Pinto proposed direct taxation of income, real estate, and capital. Finally, as a last resort, the government shifted to paper currency— while the country now imported wheat to feed itself. Despite a favorable upturn in the balance of trade in 1878, the bubble seemed about to burst. The limits of the export-oriented economy had apparently been reached.

But then, much as the victory in the early nineteenth-century war against the Peru-Bolivia confederation had helped to consolidate the Chilean polity, another war against the same adversaries would now provide Chile with a new "golden goose"—the nitrate fields of the Atacama desert. As occurred with export booms throughout Latin America in the late nineteenth century—whether they were based upon coffee, sugar, wheat, minerals, or other primary commodities—exploitation of the nitrate fields would provide Chile with extensive export revenues which financed public works and modernization without coming to terms with the internal contradictions of the economy or the structural inequalities of Chilean society. At Santiago, Valparaíso, and other central valley cities and in the central valley countryside, landowners could patch the cracked veneer of prosperity and continue the beautification of their urban mansions and country estates while they postponed confrontation with the reality of the country's growing population of urban and rural poor.

With increased migration to the towns and cities came crude working-class neighborhoods, populated by "urban villagers," and mounting pressures on public health, education, police, and other urban facilities. Small shops, markets, service "industries," and bars, mostly without licenses, proliferated. Limited employment opportunities for migrant women increased the number of washerwomen, seamstresses, domestic servants, small illegal *cantina* operators, and also the visibility of prostitution in Santiago, Valparaíso, and provincial towns. Of 4158 female inmates in the Casa de Corrección from 1852 to 1860, 2972 (71%) had been sentenced for *"faltas al pudor"*: theft, drunkenness, vagrancy, prostitution, adultery, concubinage, and "public scandal." In a study of prostitution in Santiago, historian Alvaro Góngora Escobedo (*La prostitución en Santiago 1831–1931*) queried: "why did prostitutes (*rameras*) figure in the *Anuario Estadístico de la República Chile* until 1865, when there was no law against prostitution during these years? . . . Only after 1925, and then only briefly was prostitution criminalized." In fact, government authorities tolerated prostitution, then "regulated" the sex business (authorities in Santiago implemented a law, in the name of public health, to control the so-called "Casas de Tolerancia" in 1896). By 1879, when Chile went to war against Peru and Bolivia, the Intendente of Valparaíso, Eulogio Altamirano, claimed that venereal disease was a veritable "national calamity," affecting more than half the "volunteers" for military service. According to Altamirano, this incidence of venereal disease was typical of the poorer classes (*proles*). Most Chileans were poor in 1879; could half the young male adults be afflicted by venereal disease? No medical data are available to answer the question, but Altamirano's remarks reflected elite perceptions of the poor, *the other* 90 percent of Chileans who, if not literally "infected," constituted virtually a "race apart' from those who governed and those who controlled the country's wealth.

From its third number, the *Revista Médica de Chile,* which began publication in 1872, dealt with the scourge of venereal disease more than 250 times until 1930, emphasizing from the earliest articles its devastating effects on public health and its origins in the brothels, "coffee houses," bar-dance halls (*chinganas*), and hotels that rented rooms by the hour. Góngora's study of prostitution in Santiago, replete with maps on the growth and geographical dispersion of the sex business in the capital, makes clear that economic modernization and the evolution of a more complex occupational structure from the mid-nineteenth century incorporated thousands of young, illiterate, and barely educated female migrants into the world's "oldest profession." The 1896 law regulating the Casas de Tolerancia theoretically prohibited their operations within 150–200 meters of schools, convents, churches, and military bases. Political influence, bribes, and insufficient police personnel frequently made enforcement illusory. Not by chance, novelist Joaquin Edwards chose the brothel as a metaphor for much of "modern" Chilean society at the beginning of the twentieth century in his classic, *El Roto*. The architectural facades and technological glitz of modernization went hand-in-hand with the misery of the underclasses and the pervasive social malaise denounced by many Chilean intellectuals as the country approached the centennial of its independence in 1910.

The agro-commercial expansion of the mid-nineteenth century took on a special meaning for the population of the Concepción–southern region and the Araucanians to the south. In the southern area traders, farmers, and speculators maintained contact with local chieftains, but farms and settlements in the frontier territory remained subject to periodic raids or even relatively large-scale uprisings that wrought considerable destruction of property and loss of life. Araucania remained outside the Chilean nation. From the 1860s to the 1880s periodic military campaigns sought to "pacify" the territory of Araucanía, framed by debates that resonated of the colonial era over peaceful conversion and evangelization versus military conquest.

External demand for wheat, flour, and animal products made southern lands potentially more valuable. Expanded cereal cultivation accompanied by the growth of a prosperous flour-milling industry in the environs of Tomé put renewed pressure on the Indian lands. Partly in response to these pressures, an Indian insurrection from 1859 to 1860 coincided with the civil war that pitted Concepción forces against the central government, and caused much destruction in the areas of Negrete, Nacimiento, and Los Angeles. In April 1859 the periodical *El Correo del Sur* called in no uncertain terms for violent repression and blamed the Indians and "Indian territory" for numerous real and imagined evils:

> The necessity, not only to punish the Araucanian race, but also to make it impotent to harm us, is so well recognized that almost everyone desires that such measures be taken as the only way to rid the country of a million evils. It is well understood that they are odious and prejudicial guests in Chile. . . . The thousands of families that today find themselves in misery; the innumerable robberies committed by these savages . . . are clamoring for prompt and extreme measures, since conciliatory measures have accomplished nothing with this stupid race—the infamy and disgrace of the Chilean nation.

Once again the lure of quick profits and Indian land pitted the Araucanians in a struggle for survival against the superior firepower of "civilization." Now "odious guests" in their own land, the Indians desperately attempted to maintain their land and their autonomy against the encroaching outsiders.

The land rush occasioned by expansion of cereal cultivation—accompanied by government colonization schemes, legal chicanery, and corruption—necessitated troops to enforce the "property rights" of Chilean landowners. A new Indian uprising, led by a Frenchman who proclaimed himself King Aurélie Antoine I and swore to free the Indians from Chilean tyranny, spurred the government to renewed repression. Reminiscent of the military tactics of many colonial governors, the Chilean leaders established forts at Mulchén and Angol in 1863 and then "defense lines" near Malleco (1867–68) and Traiguén (1878–79), as troops drove the Indians further south and east. The official frontier shifted to the Malleco River in 1866, and in 1875 Biobío became a new Chilean province (see Map 11).

Chilean squatters, speculators, and would-be hacendados rushed to gain control of "empty" frontier lands. From 1852 to 1866 the national government attempted unsuccessfully to regulate land transactions in the southern territories. A ban on land deals with Indians in 1858 failed to stem the tide. Legislation defining as "public" all frontier lands that had not been "continually and effectively occupied for at least one year," set in motion thousands of legal conflicts between the government, Indians, squatters, and land speculators. Many of the conflicts were resolved outside the courts by force; others were decided by bribes or by influence exercised by powerful economic interests.

Finally in the mid-1870s Congress enacted a law that required public auctioning of all contested lands in a region bounded by the Renaico River to the north, the Malleco to the south, and the Vergara to the west (see Map 11). The down payments required were so high that they practically excluded peasants, workers, and artisans from acquiring these lands; incentives for private colonization companies to bring in "high quality"—that is, northern European—colonists discriminated against Chilean settlers. The government seldom sold properties of less than the legal maximum of 500 hectares. Instead of creating a frontier yeomanry, government policy allowed the frontier territory to become another domain of the large hacienda. In imitation of the central valley model, political and economic elites carved out new manorial possessions upon which ex-squatters, landless peasants, and Indians became *inquilinos* or peons.

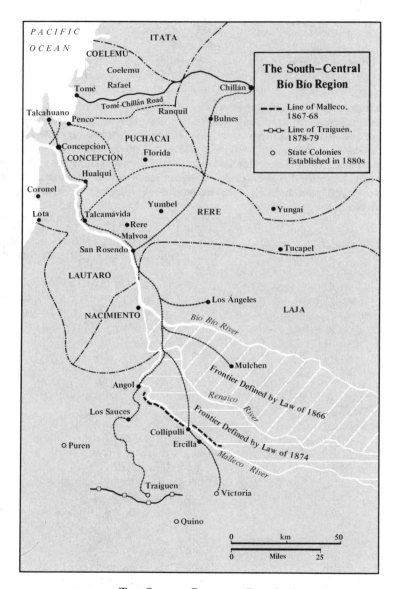

The South–Central
Bio Bío Region

- - - Line of Malleco, 1867-68
-□-□- Line of Traiguén, 1878-79
○ State Colonies Established in 1880s

MAP 11: THE SOUTH-CENTRAL BIOBÍO REGION

(*Source:* John Whaley, "Transportation in Chile's Biobío Region 1850–1915," Ph.D. dissertation, Indiana University, 1974.)

Between 1850 and 1875 ex-presidents and future presidents of Chile, along with such well-known entrepreneurs as Waddington, Bunster, Cousiño, and Smitmans, acquired large rural estates in the southern provinces.

Passage of the 1874 public lands legislation coincided with the maiden journey of the southern region's new railroad from Concepción to Chillán. Since the 1850s local elites in the frontier territory had struggled to obtain government support for a southern railway. At midcentury the region contained only two important urban centers: Concepción and Chillán. Agriculture and livestock entirely dominated the regional economy, though an incipient coal industry and a few fishing villages along the coast provided a hint of things to come. The gold strikes in California and Australia that stimulated demand for Chilean wheat and flour encouraged the export trade at Concepción-Talcahuano and brought notable growth to Tomé. Developing as the center of the milling industry and recipient of foreign investment and technology, Tomé accounted for more than 90 percent of the provinces' reported 842,000 quintals of flour by 1855. Expanded production and commerce also benefited Concepción and Talcahuano, which was the only legal port of entry for the entire southern region. But until railroads began to operate after 1874, high freight rates and the constraints of transport by oxcart seriously disadvantaged the southern region in relation to the central valley.

Loss of the California and Australia markets, economic depression in 1857, the havoc of civil war, and Indian uprisings (1859–63, 1868), all represented setbacks for the frontier provinces. With virtual completion of the Santiago-Valparaíso railroad in the early 1860s and its connection to San Fernando, southern agriculture faced the prospect of being unable to compete with the central valley. Until the early 1860s the southern mill industry supplied most of the flour exported by Chile; thereafter the southern share dropped off to somewhat less than 50 percent of the total, and what had been a modern industry in the 1850s failed to keep pace with rapid technological innovations in flour milling in the United States and Europe. By the late 1870s Chilean millers could not compete effectively in the international market, though trade with Peru, Ecuador, Argentina, and Brazil continued, along with less significant shipments to Europe or North America. Moreover, the share of the export market accounted for by shipments through Valparaíso rose from less than 25 percent between 1846 and 1850 to over 90 percent in 1880. Fortunately, after bumper crops in 1862–63 and a short-term decline in prices, increased Peruvian demand for Chilean wheat and the growing British market rescued the regional economy from disaster. Over the next ten years British purchases of Chilean wheat increased from approximately 340,000 pesos in 1863 to more than 2 million pesos in 1874—when the railroad connected Talcahuano to Chillán and the wheatlands of the interior.

Southern agriculture expanded by putting more and more land under cultivation by means of slash-and-burn technology. With large tracts of land available, high yields on virgin soil, and relatively cheap labor, southern agriculture could expand output with small amounts of capital investment. Agricultural workers received low wages along with food rations consisting of beans, potatoes, corn, and unleavened bread, or *galleta*. Peons rarely ate meat. Agricultural implements generally remained primitive: wooden plows, and weighted bramble-bush harrows. While labor supply remained plentiful and secure, no need to mechanize existed. Into the 1870s most hacendados of the south employed labor crews for the harvest, and paid temporary wages double or triple those paid to the resident labor force. Significant mechanization would come only later in the nineteenth century, when the supply of harvest laborers became less secure and workers less compliant due to the possibility of other employment in railroad and public construction projects or in the nitrate fields taken from Peru and Bolivia in the War of the Pacific.

Foreign markets for southern agriculture and the demand for coal by northern mines also stimulated the growth of some of the cities and towns of the region. Near Concepción the coal-mining enterprise of Matías Cousiño changed Lota from a rustic village into a mining town of some 5000 by the mid-1860s. Shortly thereafter the government extended telegraph service to Lota and from there to Nacimiento on the Araucanian frontier. Copper foundries, a brick factory, and other associated commercial establishments contributed to Lota's expansion. Coal mining also stimulated commercial development around Lebu and Coronel between 1862 and 1874. From 1865 to 1875 the population of Coronel increased from 2,132 to 5,568; by 1875 Lebu's population exceeded 5700.

The mining proletariat created in the 1860s and 1870s would eventually make the coal-mining region one of the most explosive areas of class conflict and union struggle in Chile. In the short run, development of the Chilean coal industry meant that despite the low quality of Chilean coal, the country could supply more than 50 percent of domestic consumption. Perhaps even more significant, the coal trade along with lumber and food exports expanded contacts between the two regions most hostile to policy emanating from Santiago and between workers in the most dynamic sectors of the Chilean economy.

By 1851 flour-milling and shipping activities at Tomé had transformed a tiny settlement of a dozen shacks into a mushrooming town with some 2000 residents. Favored by nearby sources of water power and an oxcart road connecting it to the wheat fields of the interior, the population of Tomé more than doubled in the next decade, reaching some 5300 in 1865. In contrast, Talcahuano's population declined from 2500 to 2000, and Concepción remained more or less stagnant, as Tomé took the fore in the cereal and flour-based commercial boom. After 1877 this situation would reverse itself as the favorable freight rates on the rail line between Talcahuano and Chillán killed off the oxcart traffic between Tomé and the interior.

Intraregional rivalries between Tomé interests and those at Concepción made even more discouraging the central government's neglect of the southern region. Limited economic progress, including the temporary booms of the early 1850s, did not fully incorporate the Concepción–southern region into the incipient process of modernization experienced by the central valley. The Indian frontier continued to limit southern expansion, while Santiago politicians and speculators treated the region as a vast opportunity for economic exploitation. Complicating this situation, some foreign interests even suggested that Chile had no effective control of or legal claim to Araucania. For example, a report by a British representative in Santiago to the Foreign Office in 1875 stated this position explicitly: "It seems to me that the Chilean government cannot claim any legal title to Araucania. It certainly has not had success in the conquest of this territory nor has it acquired rights to this territory through any treaty."

Only with the War of the Pacific and the nitrate boom of succeeding decades would the full importance of southern agriculture become apparent to the national government. Only then were the Araucanians finally subjugated—though not fully incorporated—into Chilean national life. For the Araucanians and for numerous Chilean landless peasants and squatters, the agro-commercial growth of the south in the mid-nineteenth century meant still another confrontation, and eventual defeat, by the economic and political forces associated with the expansion of Western European and North American capitalism. For the Araucanians it meant a final death struggle to maintain their land and autonomy. For most of the poor mestizo peasants and squatters it meant loss of the last opportunity to escape the poverty and lack of mobility inherent in the social structure of the central valley latifundia.

What most distinguished Chilean political development after 1830 from events in the other Spanish American republics was a remarkable constitutional continuity. Four elected presidents each served two consecutive five-year terms between 1831 and 1871. Congressional elections occurred on schedule with the repeated return of representatives of Chile's elite families to the Senate and Chamber of Deputies. Presidents and legislators of all political persuasions came overwhelmingly from a small number of intermarried, extended kinship groups with well-known surnames.

Oligarchy buttressed by endogamy and *compadrazgo** preserved the basic solidarity of a ruling elite whose economic interests extended from agriculture to mining, commerce, banking, and, later, industry. The geographical compactness of Chile's central valley—unlike the fragmentation or the greater size of Colombia, Mexico, Peru, or Brazil—facilitated national unity and elite consensus on fundamental social and economic institutions—even when philosophical disagreements or the clash of personalistic factions led to political conflict. To illustrate, a doctoral dissertation by Gabriel Marcella completed in 1973 found that one extended family—the Errázuriz—contributed four presidents and 59 parliamentarians from 1831 to 1927. On occasion as many as six served in the same legislature. Overall, Marcella reported that among 599 deputies and senators (out of 782 for whom some quantity of kinship data was available) there appeared 98 sets of brothers, 61 sets of father and son, 57 sets of uncle and nephew, 20 of cousins, 12 of father and son-in-law, and 32 of brothers-in-law. Moreover, the influence of kinship in the legislature *increased* rather than decreased between 1834 and 1888. Chilean political stability from 1831 to 1891 depended more than a little upon restricted suffrage, low levels of political participation, and maintenance of government positions in the hands of a small, intermarried, social, and economic oligarchy.

Notwithstanding these oligarchical features and the relative political stability of nineteenth-century Chile when compared with the rest of Latin America, there existed underlying tensions between economic interests in the outlying provinces and Santiago as well as between autocratic and oligarchic tendencies within the Chilean political system. These tensions, along with conflicts over the relationship between Church and State, fragmented the ruling elite. The Hispanic tradition of an authoritarian executive conflicted with the evolving desires of the leading families to rule Chile in their collective interest and to protect themselves from an overzealous president or an administration that took political debate outside the confines of salon, parliament, or the prestigious Club de la Unión.

Application of certain provisions of the 1833 constitution—in particular those requiring annual legislative action on the national budget, periodic approval of tax rates and tax collection, authorizations to maintain military personnel and to station troops within ten leagues of where Congress was in session—led gradually to an erosion of presidential dominance between 1841 and 1891—when a bloody civil war would confirm the victory of Congress over the executive.

The autocratic interpretation and implementation of the 1833 constitution by President Prieto (1831–41) could not eliminate entirely the influence of imported liberalism or the desire of certain Chilean elites to emulate British and Continental parliamentarism. Nevertheless, the presidential regime provided no formal mechanism for changing executive leadership through parliamentary elections or votes of no confidence. Instead, gradually but insistently—using the leverage of Congress' budgetary and tax

---

*Compadrazgo is a common form of fictive kinship prevalent throughout Spain and Latin America; literally "godmother" and "godfather" for baptism, marriage, etc.

authority—the foes of presidential dominance imposed constraints upon executive action and established the principle of ministerial responsibility to Congress. In the meantime, elections meant recurrent political violence and suppression of opposition newspapers. In two cases, in 1851 and 1859, conflict over government succession precipitated brief but bloody wars between the armies of rival factions, followed by elite political pacts to "reconcile" the contending parties. Both times Congress eventually legislated political amnesties (1857, 1861) in an effort to further "social peace."

As early as November 1841, Congress agreed to suspend consideration of legislation authorizing tax collection as well as the budget bill until the executive submitted an expanded legislative agenda—including legislation aimed at extending congressional oversight of public expenditures. Executive agreement to these demands meant de facto abrogation of an exclusive constitutional prerogative of the executive: designation of matters to be considered in the extraordinary sessions of the legislature. More important, President Bulnes' acceptance of the congressional demands was an implicit recognition of the legitimacy of legislative checks on government policy.

Influenced by Belgian procedures, legislators intent on asserting congressional authority also introduced the practice of "interpellation"—a questioning period to hold ministers accountable for their acts. Under this procedure individual deputies could request particular ministers to appear in the chamber to explain or justify government policy. Combined with delays on critical legislation, the practice of interpellation moved Chilean politics in the direction of quasiparliamentarism. Liberal intellectuals such as José Victorino Lastarria argued that interpellation and censure of ministers were rights inherent in the supervisory authority of Congress and served as guarantees against executive irregularities and abuses.

After bitterly contested congressional elections in 1849, during which the Bulnes government mounted a campaign of repression against the liberal forces, dissident conservatives, and the opposition political groups based on family ties or personal friendships, Lastarria submitted reform proposals to the new Congress. These proposals aimed to limit further presidential authority as well as to guarantee freedom of the press and the right of assembly. Though Congress did not approve these reforms, the attacks on executive dominance continued.

In 1850 a new political movement emerged called the Society of Equality. Headed by Francisco Bilbao and a number of personalities like Santiago Arcos and the Matta brothers who would play important roles as political reformers, the society held numerous public meetings and demonstrations against the government. Influenced by the revolutionary ideas and experience of France and Europe in 1848, as well as by British liberalism, the Society of Equality directly challenged the autocratic regime in the press and in the streets, copying to a certain extent the French Girondist tactics of 1848. It opposed the presidential candidacy of Manuel Montt, declaring that "proclaiming Montt as candidate for the presidency is authorization of revolution" and that "Montt signifies burial of the Republic." Attempting to forge an unlikely alliance between liberal patricians and the artisan community in Santiago, the Society of Equality's leaders mobilized some artisans and members of the National Guard against the government. These groups represented voters controlled by the government; they were a key prop of presidential control of Congress and presidential succession.

A virtual armed insurrection by the Society of Equality's "affiliate" in San Felipe in November 1850 brought a declaration of "state of siege" for Santiago and Aconcagua provinces, followed by full-on repression of the Society of Equality. The intendant of Santiago prohibited further meetings and declared the society "dissolved"; all similar organizations were outlawed. Government officials closed opposition newspapers, and many of the leaders of the reform movement fled into exile.

In April 1851 the government put down a military uprising in Santiago led by a liberal officer supported by the capital's *pipiolos.* The government election machine, based upon control of the votes of the militia, provided more than sufficient votes to make Bulnes' chosen successor, Manual Montt, the next president—despite support by liberals and regional interests in Concepción and La Serena for Bulnes' cousin and commander of the army stationed in the southern provinces, José María de la Cruz. Since the president appointed militia officers, and the officers handled distribution of the "certificates of qualification" that allowed the militiamen to vote, presidential intervention in elections generally spelled defeat for the opposition. Officers could also withhold certificates from unreliable militiamen and give them to more "trustworthy" citizens. Although this practice had become more or less expected, the increasing resistance to presidential dominance and the frustration of important economic interests in the provinces made it impossible for Bulnes' opponents to swallow the election results.

Opponents of the regime contested the legitimacy of the rigged elections and broke into armed revolt in Concepción and La Serena. Rebel forces in Coquimbo requisitioned the British ship *Firefly* and extorted contributions from wealthy government supporters. Before the intervention of the British squadron—encouraged by the Montt government—the northern rebel forces occupied the towns of Elqui, Huasco, Ovalle, Combarbalá, and Illapel. Miners from the important El Tamaya mine marched on Ovalle, and other groups occupied haciendas around Illapel. Miners, construction workers, and peasants mobilized to the rebel cause in other northern towns—an event in which some Marxist historians have discerned elements of an armed popular insurrection. Although this interpretation is not entirely inaccurate, the basic struggle in the 1851 revolt pitted the incumbent political machine against regional and liberal forces protesting the outcome of the elections and the more fundamental subordination of the southern and northern provinces to Santiago. Indicative of this underlying source of conflict was the leadership of the Concepción rebel forces in 1851 by would-be railroad entrepreneur, landowner, and liberal politico, Pedro Félix Vicuña. Vicuña's proposal for government subsidies of his project for a southern railroad had fallen upon deaf ears in Santiago shortly before he led the Concepción forces in support of the defeated liberal candidate. Vicuña also owned a major newspaper in the region and had himself named intendant of the province by the rebel forces. Thus the desire for political reform and frustrated economic interest, as well as personal ambition, motivated the rebel leadership in the civil conflict of 1851.

As in the north, the Montt government availed itself of British support to help quell the southern rebellion. In the words of the exiled Argentine Domingo Sarmiento, in a pamphlet he wrote supporting the Montt government, "British capital needs the guarantee of peace . . . to invest millions in the interior and to stimulate the export of cereals. . . . Montt is public tranquility, authority, good faith, and efficient administration." Within three months the Montt government reasserted control in both the northern and southern provinces.

Victory in the civil war in 1851, however, did not end the movement to put legislative checks on the presidency. President Montt's refusal to support a general amnesty for military and civilian adversaries in the recent war further embittered opponents. Debates over this issue again in 1857 failed to convince the government, which, faced with division among its supporters, ultimately accepted *conditional* amnesties. If the exiles requested forgiveness and promised good behavior, the government would permit their return to Chile on a case-by-case basis. Congress approved the amnesty law, but most of the Liberal leaders in exile rejected the Montt government's conditions. Congressional elections in 1858 rekindled the embers of hatred and resentment, moving the country toward another civil war in 1859.

By 1857 not only government policy but also the very composition of the president's cabinet became hostage to congressional approval. In August 1857 Congress approved an opposition senator's motion to postpone consideration of the budget until the president announced who would be appointed to the new cabinet. President Manuel Montt reluctantly acquiesced and, at congressional insistence, even named members of the liberal opposition to the cabinet. In effect this development put the Congress in control of the cabinet, making the Chilean political system a curious mixture of parliamentary and presidential government. The threat of congressional refusal to approve budget legislation or other critical government programs gradually transformed the autocratic presidential regime into a delicately balanced system of negotiation between government and opposition forces. On any particular issue, government supporters could defect and form an opposition majority to complicate further the life of the incumbent executive. Thus, by 1861 the institutional foundations of the multiparty "parliamentarism," for which Chile became well known after 1891, had substantially modified the autocratic regime installed by Portales and Prieto.

Erosion of presidentalism could not have occurred without a coincident ideological and political fragmentation of the Chilean elite. Introduction of liberalism as a political ideology in early nineteenth-century Chile threatened in two essential ways the hegemony of Iberian autocracy re-established by Portales: (1) rejection of Catholicism as the exclusive moral underpinning of the state and (2) acceptance of social pluralism, including freedom of association, freedom of the press, and the gamut of civil liberties associated with the British liberal tradition. As Chilean historian Cristián Gazmuri has demonstrated in El '48' chileno, the ideas and forms of collective action imported from revolutionary forces in Europe in 1848 combined with the liberalism of the "generation of 1842" to inspire the 1850–51 uprisings in Chile. The "spirit of 1848" also contributed new forms of social organization (sociabilidad), ranging from the spread of masonic lodges and volunteer fire departments (bomberos) to the establishment of the Radical party (1863–64) and Reform Clubs (Clubes de Reforma) in the late 1860s. These groups, often with overlapping memberships, typically included foreign merchants, bankers, and industrialists as well as up-and-coming Chilean mining magnates, professionals, and even military officers.

By the 1870s, what Gazmuri calls "the spirit of 1848" nourished a sort of political and mesocratic counterculture from which emerged the liberal forces that would reform the 1833 constitution. A generation of patrician and bourgeois rebels and political exiles forged in the conflicts bracketed by two civil wars, 1851 and 1859, would eventually transform the autocratic republic. Along the way, however, the gunpowder liberals of the 1850s would themselves be "renovated," coming to value "order and progress" much like Manuel Montt and Antonio Varas, their antagonists in the 1840s and 1850s. The liberal factions preferred a shift of political authority to congress from the president and diluting the influence of the Catholic Church in public affairs, but rarely went beyond vague populist rhetoric regarding changing the country's elitist political tradition and hierarchical social pyramid.

In the 1840s the "Generation of 1842" had arisen, as previously mentioned, from the new (1842) University of Chile. This liberal movement, headed by José Victorino Lastarria, brought an immediate response from the Church, which opposed any hint of religious toleration. Among the partisans of the national coalition surrounding President Bulnes (1841–51) as well as his successor, Manuel Montt (1851–61), were a number of personalities who favored a dilution of the Church's influence or at least a firmer exercise of the patronato by the State over the Church. Their efforts, together with liberal attacks on the Church and the intervention of foreign governments—especially the

British—on behalf of foreign nationals resident in Chile, resulted in a series of laws offensive to the Church and to devout Catholic politicians. Among other provisions, these laws expanded the power of civil authorities to supervise the activities of parish priests, and allowed non-Catholics to marry without conforming to Catholic ritual.

This politico-religious conflict divided the government coalition. Continued disputes between the Bulnes and Montt governments and the Church gave rise, in 1857, to the Conservative party, which gradually became the political voice of the Catholic Church. This meant that an integral part of future electoral battles and parliamentary debates would consist of issues related to the privileges and role of the Church in Chilean society. In addition, the Conservative party, finding itself in opposition to the incumbent executive, now supported the movement to shift the balance of power from the president to party coalitions in the Congress—albeit for different reasons than the liberals.

Approval of certain anticlerical measures by the Bulnes and Montt governments did not mean acceptance of the secular implications of liberalism. In the short run, the secular conservatives now known as the "Montt-Varistas," or the National party, continued to oppose social pluralism, unrestricted civil liberties, freedom of the press, and elections uncontrolled by the national executive machine. The Montt government, in particular, repressed opposition elements after facing civil war in 1851 and 1859.

Despite the outcome of the 1851 civil war, the formation of the Conservative party in 1857 seriously weakened the antiliberal government coalition. Now both Catholics and secular liberals favored further restriction upon presidential authority and institutionalization of "parliamentary" government. The Catholics desired a stronger Church role in government and society; the liberal program included expansion of the suffrage, prohibition of presidential re-election, and reform of the restrictive press laws. To complicate matters further, many liberals did not share the violently anticlerical positions of Bilbao or Lastarria. Indeed many Conservatives and Liberals came to take a common political stance against the incumbent regime.

Montt's apparent intention to impose the forceful minister of interior, Antonio Varas, as his successor, along with the government's hesitancy in granting a complete amnesty to those involved in the insurrection of 1851, pushed the Conservatives and the majority of Liberals into a "fusion" that sought to prevent Varas' election. A group of intransigent liberal anticlericals rejected this fusion, but nevertheless joined the opposition. Led by the future founders of the Radical party (1863), men like Guillermo Matta and Justo and Domingo Arteaga Alemparte, as well as other opposition forces, launched an antigovernment propaganda campaign across the nation.

The government response—declaration of a state of siege, arrests of prominent opposition leaders, closure of opposition periodicals—moved Pedro León Gallo, a rich miner and leader of the opposition in Copiapó, to send a private army against the government. As in 1851, the rebellion centered in the *norte chico* and spread to Concepción, but outbreaks also occurred in Valparaíso and the central valley. While the government eventually crushed the rebellion after both sides had sustained numerous casualties, Varas withdrew his candidacy, and Montt named José Joaquín Pérez as the government-supported candidate. Neither the moderate liberals nor the clericals in the Conservative party had any serious objections to Pérez as Montt's successor.

By 1861, therefore, the ruling elite had fragmented into at least four major groups: National party, Conservative party, Liberals, and militant liberals, who eventually formed the Radical party in 1863. The new President formed a cabinet composed of Nationals, Liberals, and Conservatives. Soon after taking office he promulgated an amnesty law for all political exiles. Despite Pérez' effort to conciliate long-standing animosities, personal and political differences made the coalition ineffective. Pérez then turned the cabinet over to the Liberal-Conservative "fusion" which gained a congressional majority through the expected executive intervention in the 1864 congressional elections. The National party (the party of Montt) and the Radicals now formed the opposition. Pérez declared his government to be "of all and for all" political factions. He governed for ten years without declaring a state of siege. At the end of his term in 1871 a constitutional amendment prohibited immediate presidential re-election.

During the next presidential term (1871–76) further legislative reforms consolidated the congressional-oligarchic system. Control of elections passed to juntas, or committees of wealthy taxpayers—a reform that assured significant minority representation in Congress, as well as the predominance of the landed elite in the central valley. It did not, however, settle the ongoing "religious question" including controversies over secularizing cemeteries, civil marriage, public education, and, more generally, separation of Church and State. This "religious question" remained the most prominent political schism in Chile until 1891, nearly a decade after the War of the Pacific (1879–83), when efforts by President Manuel Balmaceda (1886–91) to reverse the course of over half a century of political evolution by reasserting executive dominance, led to a bloody civil war. Indeed, the oligarchic "parliamentary" regime that had evolved between 1841 and 1876, and entrenched itself after 1891, would continue to wrangle over the "religious question" into the twentieth century, long after the social and economic issues of industrialization, class conflict, and democratization seemed to portend more profound and radical changes in Chilean politics and society.

In 1876 newly elected President Aníbal Pinto faced not only the "religious question" but also the economic depression that had begun in 1873. Policies suggested to combat the economic situation, such as working on Sundays and fiesta days, antagonized the Church. Government attempts to exert control over public education and proposals to secularize the cemeteries added fuel to the fire. The economic crisis heightened tempers. Clericals promised rebellion if the religious reforms passed; anticlericals accused priests of hoarding food while others starved. The death in 1878 of the conservative archbishop Ramón Valdivieso further divided opposition forces when the president refused to consult with the Church hierarchy before choosing Valdivieso's successor. When President Pinto selected a priest notorious for his illegitimate birth and liberal politics, clerical forces successfully petitioned the Pope to oppose his appointment. The issue remained unresolved for years.

Confronted by the mounting difficulties of the economic situation and the hostility of the ultramontane opposition, Pinto's situation seemed ever more impossible. While prosperity could provide the grease to make the delicately balanced political machine function, an end to the windfalls of the export economy and foreign investment typical since the 1840s spelled disaster. Fortunately for Chile's elites, Bolivia shortly provided the Pinto government with a pretext for declaring war and for the subsequent annexation of the nitrate fields of the Atacama desert. The nitrate fields would provide the means to nourish the Chilean economy and political apparatus for some years to come. They would also spawn a militant proletariat and new political parties that would force Chile to confront directly the "social question" and the politics of industrial class conflict.

6 Nitrate

Plagued by economic difficulties and internal political dissensions, Chile faced the possibility of war with Argentina, Bolivia, and Peru. Owing to poorly demarcated boundaries in Patagonia, a territorial dispute with Argentina had simmered since Chile's creation of the Punta Arenas colony in the early 1840s. A flare up of this dispute in the late 1870s menaced peaceful relations between the two nations. To the north, investments of Chilean capital and the migration of thousands of Chilean workers to extract guano, nitrates, copper, and silver from the Bolivian desert of Antofagasta created increasingly tense relations between Bolivia and Chile.

Skillful negotiations avoided war with Argentina, but the vast economic stakes in the north made a peaceful settlement with Bolivia impossible. A new Bolivian government contravened the provisions of the 1874 treaty prohibiting Bolivia from increasing export taxes on the Chilean nitrate operations for a period of twenty-five years, and imposed a surtax on nitrate shipments of ten centavos per metric quintal (100 kg). The Chilean government's support of the Anglo-Chilean owned Antofagasta Railroad and Nitrate Company (whose stockholders included Chilean congressmen and cabinet members) in its refusal to pay the tax led ultimately to war.

In the course of the Chile-Bolivia dispute in the 1870s, Peru entered into a secret alliance with Bolivia in February 1873. The alliance provided for mutual guarantees of independence and territory against aggression by a third party. According to the terms of the alliance, neither nation could conclude a peace, a truce, or an armistice without prior approval of the other; nor could either cede territory or privileges that would reduce or limit independence or sovereignty. Peru's interest in such a treaty stemmed from its almost total economic dependence upon the export of guano and nitrates to Europe. The expansion of European agriculture led to a spectacular increase in demand for fertilizer, which, in turn, stimulated intensive economic activity in Peru's southern provinces, particularly Tarapacá, and in Antofagasta in Bolivia. This activity, on top of the silver strike at Caracoles and the extensive copper mining in the 1870s, made the Peruvian and Bolivian deserts suddenly highly prized economic assets.

Depletion of the guano deposits that had provided Peruvian governments with most of their revenues between 1830 and 1870 led to increased emphasis on nitrates. In contrast to the Peruvian government's monopoly on guano, however, the nitrate industry developed under the control of private capital. Prior to the War of the Pacific (1879–83) foreign interests (Chilean, British, German, and French) acquired almost 50 percent of the productive capacity of the Tarapacá nitrate fields. Perhaps just as important, more than half the population of the province of Tarapacá consisted of foreigners (57%); further south in the district of Iquique this figure reached almost 70 percent. In the municipality of Antofagasta, Chileans constituted 85 percent of the population. Thus, in the nitrate fields, Peru's principal economic resource, both much of the ownership and the labor force owed their principal allegiance to other nations.

Responding to financial difficulties, the Peruvian government in 1875 decreed "nationalization" of many of the nitrate plants, or *oficinas,* issuing payment certificates redeemable in two years and bearing 8 percent interest. In reality this "nationalization" was a mixed venture associating the Peruvian government and international finance capital in an effort to create a nitrate monopoly. Unable to float bonds to finance payments, the Peruvian government failed to redeem the certificates. Eventually, many of the certificates changed hands as speculators in Lima paid from 10 to 60 percent of face value. Mismanagement by the Peruvian government, poor coordination between government and those operating the nitrate plants, coupled with a devastating earthquake in 1877 that destroyed numerous coastal loading platforms, brought a 25 to 30 percent decline in nitrate exports. Peruvian certificate holders and guano creditors put great pressure upon Chile to annex Tarapacá, but the Chilean government made no effort to contest Peru's sovereign right to nationalize property within its territory.

New Bolivian taxes on nitrate exported from the province of Antofagasta proved to be a different matter. Here a treaty protected Chilean economic interests, and most of the population was Chilean. In Antofagasta a Chilean company produced all of the nitrate, and of the port's 8000 inhabitants more than 75 percent were Chilean. When Bolivia ordered enforcement of the new nitrate tax in December 1878, and the Antofagasta Company refused to comply, Bolivian officials ordered the arrest of the company's manager and seizure of company property sufficient to cover the debt owed for the new tax. The manager took asylum with Chilean authorities. Relations between the two countries deteriorated rapidly. In February, Bolivian officials notified the company that its confiscated property would be auctioned to pay the nitrate tax; in the meantime the captain of the port prohibited further nitrate exports, causing suspension of operation and unemployment for more than 2000 workers. In response to Chilean protests, Bolivia revoked the company's nitrate concession—putting the company out of business—and then eliminated the nitrate tax.

After Bolivia rejected arbitration, a Chilean military expedition landed at Antofagasta and took control of the city. Chilean forces also occupied Caracoles and Salar del Carmen, while a warship went to Cobija to protect Chilean interests. Bolivia shortly declared war upon Chile, decreed confiscation of all Chilean property, and gave Chilean citizens ten days to leave the country. Peruvian diplomats hurried to Santiago in a final attempt to prevent full-scale war, but public revelation of Peru's secret alliance with Bolivia undermined the Peruvian role as mediator. In early April, Chile declared war upon Bolivia and Peru.

None of the belligerent nations were prepared to go to war. The Chilean army, quite small throughout the middle decades of the nineteenth century, numbered less than 2500 men, most of whom were stationed on the Indian frontier. Though somewhat better equipped and provisioned than Bolivia's or Peru's forces, the Chilean army lacked training in modern warfare, had no experience with large-unit maneuvers, and was practically without auxiliary services. The national guard, even more so than the army, had been seriously affected by the government's recent economy moves. Never a well-trained military organization, even the national guard's significant political role seemed threatened when the government in 1878 reduced it to approximately 7000 men—a 70 percent decline. Chilean naval forces, depleted by the sale of a transport and a corvette for economic reasons, consisted of six ships—only two of which the director of arsenals considered seaworthy. Although the addition of the merchant marine and vessels purchased during the war would allow Chile to move troops by sea to the war zone, at the outbreak of hostilities Chile's naval posture was dismaying. Having closed the Naval Academy and School for Mariners in 1876, the Chilean government had to hire foreigners to man its tiny armada.

Peruvian and Bolivian forces, though they outnumbered the Chileans, suffered from the effects of a half-century of political disorganization and internal strife. Neither Bolivia nor Peru were equipped to fight a modern war or to provision a large army over any considerable period of time. Peru's navy, relying upon two sound ironclads and a number of far less seaworthy wooden and iron vessels, appeared to be a match for Chile's anemic fleet. Foreigners also manned the Peruvian navy, though their quality as described by a contemporary—"the offscouring of the foreign merchant and naval services"—left something to be desired.

Notwithstanding their lack of preparedness, both the Chileans and their adversaries mobilized relatively large armies, reaching in Chile's case over 45,000 men by the end of the war. In the first months of the war Chilean forces successfully occupied most of the Bolivian desert. Rugged terrain made it extremely difficult for Bolivia to send troops across the Andes to Antofagasta. Following a series of Chilean-Peruvian naval encounters, Chile dominated the seas by the end of 1879. When its armies took Pisagua and Iquique, the resultant political disorders in Peru and Bolivia ousted the presidents of both these nations. In early 1880 Chilean forces moved into Arica and Tacna. A bloody battle, during which the opposing forces left 5000 casualties on the field, gave Chile control of Tacna in May 1880. Twelve days later the port of Arica also fell to the Chilean invaders.

After efforts by United States diplomats to mediate the conflict in late 1880 failed, Chile sent an army of 25,000 men to Lima. Chilean soldiers crushed the Peruvian defenders in mid-January 1881, and Lima became an occupied city. Though a guerrilla campaign continued until 1883, Chile controlled Lima and Callao, confiscated considerable Peruvian property, and levied taxes to support the army of occupation. The Chileans also imposed port duties and encouraged increased production by the nitrate industry.

The victorious Chileans dictated a harsh settlement to Peru and Bolivia. By virtue of the Treaty of Ancón (October 23, 1883), signed by a president imposed upon Peru by the Chileans, Peru ceded Tarapacá to Chile and agreed to a ten-year Chilean administration of the provinces of Tacna and Arica. A plebiscite, which was never held, was to decide which nation ultimately retained these territories. Of the fourteen articles in the peace treaty, nine referred in some way to guano or nitrates—a clear indication of the underlying issues of the "fertilizer war." Bolivia, though not a party to the treaty, eventually signed a truce with Chile in March 1884; it stipulated that confiscated property be returned to Chilean citizens. Antofagasta passed into Chilean hands, and Bolivia acquired access to the then Chilean-administered port of Arica. Chile conceded to Bolivia 35 percent of the import duties on goods passing through Arica destined for Bolivia. No peace treaty was signed between Bolivia and Chile for twenty years, when Bolivia recognized Chile's absolute and perpetual dominion of Antofagasta.

The victor in the war that was ostensibly fought over a ten-centavo surtax on nitrate exports, took as spoils the single most important source of Peruvian and Bolivian national wealth—the mineral-rich Atacama desert—along with Bolivia's access to the Pacific. For the next century this desert wealth would be the most important factor in Chilean socio-economic and political development. The manner of its acquisition remains a source of bitter resentment. Neither Peru nor Bolivia has forgotten their loss; they remain unresigned to Chile's "absolute and perpetual dominion" over the conquered territories. Numerous Peruvian generals still desire to recapture the battle monument at the Morro de Arica and redeem Peru's national honor. Similar sentiments in Bolivia have led the three nations to continue one of the most costly arms races in Latin America and have led Chile to put mine fields in strategic northern areas.

The War of the Pacific enlarged Chilean territory by more than one-third. It also had

Early nitrate works in Tarapacá, circa 1860. (Courtesy Archivo Universidad de Chile.)

Transport of coal to boilers at nitrate works, circa 1890.
(Courtesy Archivo Universidad de Chile.)

MAP 12: CHILEAN EXPANSION NORTHWARD

A. Original Chile-Bolivian boundary. B. Claimed by Chile in 1842. a. Established by treaty in 1866, but in A-B nitrate revenues were divided equally. C. Original Peru-Bolivian boundary. D. Boundary of Chile as a result of the War of the Pacific, 1883, with D-E to be occupied by Chile ten years. d. Chile-Peruvian boundary by settlement of 1929. (*Source:* W. J. Dennis, *Tacna and Arica*, New Haven: Yale University Press, 1931.)

immediate and profound effects on Chilean national life. The war itself significantly increased demand for foodstuffs and wine, thereby stimulating agriculture and livestock production in the south, the central valley, and the *norte chico*. Coastal shipping dramatically expanded as merchants contracted to supply the army in the north. Industry also responded positively to the war, particularly those firms producing foodstuffs, beverages, tobacco, footwear and leather goods, and other materiel for the military. According to a report of the National Manufacturer's Society (*Sociedad de Fomento Fabril*), founded in 1883, more factories were founded between 1880 and 1889 than had existed in Chile prior to the war. The enormous quantity of capital investment in the nitrate sector and the gush of tax revenues flowing to the national government from the nitrate companies helped to pull Chile out of the prewar economic stagnation. The merchant marine quintupled in size between 1880 and 1883, and coastal shipping, or *cabotaje*, expanded dramatically, since shipments to Antofagasta or Tarapacá had become domestic commerce.

The Chilean victory not only provided an economic bonanza but added to the pantheon of national heroes military leaders such as Manuel Baquedano and Arturo Prat. The war also reinforced the prevailing Chilean belief in the nation's racial and cultural superiority over its northern neighbors. Chile *was* special in Latin America, and after the War of the Pacific, Chileans of all classes believed more than ever in their national destiny.

With the end of the war a new spirit of nationalism contributed to renewed concern for Chile's lack of significant industry. In the first issue of its *Boletín*, the Sociedad de Fomento Fabril proclaimed that "Chile can and should be an Industrial Nation." The same proclamation went on to say that "only by dedicating its energies to industrialization will Chile achieve the stable base of political and economic equilibrium of the most advanced nations. . . . To contribute to this great objective, to make Chile an industrial nation, the Sociedad de Fomento Fabril has been founded under the protection of the government." Committed to encouragement of Chilean industry through moderate protective tariffs and government subsidies, the SFF represented a potential threat to the economic policies favored by the integrated elite triumvirate of landowners, merchants, and miners. In the short run, however, the fact that the act of foundation of the SFF occurred in the principal salon of the National Agricultural Society, at the behest of a minister of the national government, suggested that the new industrialists would not be far removed from the traditional holders of power. The list of the officers and members of the executive committee of the new industrial society revealed also the disproportionate influence of immigrants and their offspring in Chile's economic elite and its industrial life. Only three Spanish surnames accompanied those of the other members of the directorate: Edwards, Subercaseaux, Hillman, Tupper, Tiffou, Mitchell, Gabler, Lanz, Klein, Muzard, Lyon, Bernstein Crichton, Osthaus, Stuven.

In addition to stimulating industry, the War of the Pacific also affected labor supply throughout the republic. Military recruitment with appeals to patriotism, bounties, or through impressment depleted the work force in the nitrate fields, the northern mines, and the countryside. As the Chilean army moved north, desertions helped repopulate the nitrate fields, and demobilization after the war let loose thousands of potential laborers for employment in the desert, the *norte chico*, or public works. Mobilization of thousands of Chilean miners, campesinos, and laborers not only disrupted the labor supply but also changed the world view and long-term aspirations of the war veterans. Most had little inclination to return to the subordination of the central valley haciendas. Some acquired land in the southern frontier regions, but those who did not increase the ranks of vagabonds, beggars, and criminals sought their fortunes in the nitrate fields and the booming towns of the conquered territory, or went south to Coquimbo, Valparaíso, and Santiago. Wartime experiences and the opening of the northern desert as a *Chilean* mining region portended a radical transformation in the character of the Chilean work force and the beginnings of a truly industrial wage proletariat.

Rapid military victories against Bolivia and Peru also made available a large army capable of subjugating the people of Araucania. At the onset of the war some Indian groups took advantage of troop movements to the north and carried off a small-scale uprising in the region around Traiguén. In response President Pinto ordered the conquest of the Araucanians and the establishment of a new frontier line at the Cautín River. Closing off the Andean passes that linked the Araucanians to their brethren in Argentina, Chilean troops gained control of Indian territory in a concerted offensive. Simultaneous campaigns against the Indians by Argentine troops, modern weapons, and troop mobility resulting from the newly constructed southern railroad finally integrated the frontier territory into the Chilean nation. Roads, bridges, telegraph lines, and the army brought Carahue, Villarrica and Temuco—regions lost since the days of Pedro de Valdivia—into the national patrimony. Reduced to wards of the Chilean state on shrinking tribal lands, the Araucanians faced cultural and economic destruction at the hands of corrupt government officials, traders, speculators, and Chilean settlers seeking land to farm.

The national government tried to ensure orderly and rapid development of the frontier territory by claiming the right to dispose of all the *terrenos baldíos,* or "vacant lands." Influenced by theories of racial superiority, some Chilean authorities looked to northern Europe for colonists to populate the newly opened frontier territories. More than 10,000 colonists from Germany, France, and Switzerland settled at Victoria, Ercilla, Quillén, Temuco, Traiguén, Galvarino, Contulmo, and other frontier outposts in the 1880s. Instead of setting an example of European yeomanry, however, the colonists took quick advantage of Chilean and Indian sharecroppers and rural laborers, adapting thereby to the convenience of Chile's exploitive rural labor systems. The immigrant colonists who prospered in agriculture found *inquilinaje* a useful device to promote their interests, just as did the Chilean landowners in the central valley. Some colonists also contributed greatly by establishing artisan manufactures and even some industry, but most preferred towns or cities to the hardships of peasant pioneer farming in the Chilean south.

In any case, the government was unable to compete with Argentina, Brazil, or Uruguay in attracting the numbers of Europeans it desired to "upgrade" the Chilean race. Instead, it fell back on public auctions to deliver the frontier lands into private hands. Spontaneous colonization, squatting, and speculation continued as the major instruments of settlement in the southern region.

Conquest of the Araucanians ended the most important pre-1879 rationale for maintenance of a standing army in Chile. The frontier had provided a genuine military mission for Chilean armed forces since the time of independence, making them a necessary and valued element of national life. Acquisition through war of the northern territories and the persistent Argentine border dispute now gave a new mission to the Chilean military. The threat of conflict with Peru and Bolivia or with Argentina made military preparedness a national concern. In 1885 the Chilean government contracted the German lieutenant colonel Emil Körner to become subdirector of the Escuela Militar and to direct the modernization of Chilean military education. In the same year a military periodical first appeared, and shortly thereafter a military club, the Círculo Militar, was established in Santiago. Both periodical and club received government subsidies.

Under Körner's leadership Chile founded the Academia de Guerra, or War College, in 1886 with the stated purpose of improving the technical and scientific education of army officers. The Academia de Guerra nurtured a new Chilean junior officer military elite; critical of outdated methods, political patronage, and government inefficiency, it would eventually (in the 1920s) challenge the traditional political parties for control of the Chilean state. In the short run, only five years after establishment of the Academia de Guerra, Körner and his small core of followers would play a key role in the Chilean civil war of 1891. From the outset, therefore, the professionalization and modernization of the Chilean military on the Prussian model entailed serious consequences for Chilean politics—just as similar Prussian or French military missions soon affected civil-military relations in Argentina, Bolivia, Peru, and other Latin American nations. The War of the Pacific proved a turning point in Chile's civil-military relations as well as being the most important economic watershed in its history.

A mere seven years after termination of the War of the Pacific, Chile faced its most serious and bloody civil war of the nineteenth century. Chilean historians still debate the causes of this civil war, with explanations ranging from narrow political interpretations to those that attribute it to President Balmaceda's (1886–91) tragic confrontation with British imperialism and its Chilean lackeys. Events in Chile between 1970 and 1973 led many people to draw analogies between Balmaceda and President Salvador Allende as nationalists and reformers who met defeat at the hands of foreign interests and the Chilean oligarchy. As with most such historical controversies, there is evidence to support all versions of the conflict. No understanding of the civil war of 1891, however, can ignore the complex relationships between the changes in Chile's political economy wrought by the War of the Pacific and the persistence of long-standing political issues, such as the "religious question" and the constant tension between the Congress and the executive.

The nitrate fields of the Atacama desert added an entirely new factor to Chilean political economy. Basic questions had to be answered about how to integrate the wealth of the desert into the economy. Should the state operate the fields as a national industry, as the Peruvians had attempted? Should private capital be allowed to exploit the nitrate deposits and control the transportation networks, especially railroads, that shipped the nitrates to the ports? To what extent should foreign capital be permitted to invest in the nitrate industry?

Imbued with a fundamental commitment to liberal economic ideology, the government of President Pinto set the direction for the next four decades of nitrate policy by imposing an export tax of 40 centavos per metric quintal upon the nitrate company at Antofagasta. After Chilean troops seized Tarapacá, thereby bringing the richest deposits of nitrate also within Chilean control, the government increased the tax to $1.50 pesos. Considering that the original dispute between the Antofagasta Company and the Bolivian government—the dispute that precipitated war between Chile, Bolivia, and Peru—had arisen over an additional 10-centavo levy by Bolivia on nitrate exports, President Pinto's policy hardly made the nitrate producers happy.

Meanwhile President Pinto created a commission to consider long-range nitrate policy. This commission recommended return of the nitrate concessions to the holders of the Peruvian certificates, along with an export tax of $2.20 pesos per metric quintal. This recommendation established the basis for Chilean political economy for the next four decades. Private enterprise, foreign and national, would exploit the nitrate fields, and export taxes on nitrate would constitute more than 50 percent of all Chilean government revenue.

The Chilean government's decision to allow substantial foreign participation in the nitrate industry and the sale of certain Chilean-held certificates to foreigners soon placed thousands of Chilean workers in large nitrate complexes, or *oficinas,* controlled by foreign administrators. By 1883 the work force in Tarapacá alone had increased to 7000, with similar increments in the ranks of dock workers, construction and railroad crews, prostitutes, merchants, and industry related to nitrate production. Investments in public services in Iquique and Antofagasta provided jobs for still more, as demobilized troops returned from Peru. Nitrate mining depended upon pick and shovel; as the industry expanded in the last decades of the nineteenth century, it required more and more workers in the *oficinas.*

Caliche, the ore of the nitrate industry, consists of sodium nitrate and varying amounts of potassium nitrate, trace metals, iodine, and insolubles. Variation in nitrate content made some deposits more valuable, but the basic refining process was relatively uniform. Found in deposits up to two meters thick, the ore was blasted from the desert crust, crushed, and boiled in caldrons or dissolving tanks until it formed a solution and precipitated out impurities. When cooled, the evaporation formed *salitre,* or nitrate crystals. In the 1850s and 1860s coal-fueled furnaces that piped steam to dissolving tanks began to replace the fire-heated caldrons, thereby increasing the efficiency and scale of the *oficinas.* Mechanical ore crushers also made their appearance, but the industry remained highly labor-intensive. Laborers blasted the desert crust, crushed the *caliche,* loaded the ore for hauling, manned the catwalks over the open tanks, cleaned the pipes and machinery, and performed numerous specialized jobs in the production process. Women sewed the bags of fertilizer and served as cooks, laundresses, and seamstresses. Nitrate companies took few safety precautions; workers frequently suffered burns or mutilations by machinery. Amputees and otherwise disabled nitrate workers became a common sight in Iquique, Antofagasta, and other nitrate towns where displaced laborers drifted in search of subsistence.

Though the nitrate industry employed a large number of unskilled workers, the market for nitrates proved extremely volatile. Producers responded to short-term contractions in sales or declines in price by reducing output or laying off workers. Consequently the labor force of the nitrate fields periodically faced unemployment, and the Chilean government's revenues, increasingly dependent on nitrate export duties, could decline or increase precipitately over very short periods of time. In good times the nitrate companies could not always count upon sufficient workers to meet demands; in bad times thousands of displaced workers departed from the nitrate pampa to the northern cities and south to Coquimbo, Valparaíso, and Santiago. Fluctuations in international demand for nitrates, therefore, caused periodic political crises as Chile struggled to manage the consequences of large-scale movements of unemployed workers out of the nitrate fields into the ports, the *norte chico,* and the central valley.

The War of the Pacific also marked the onset of long-term price inflation. Paper money issued to finance the war, and the usual rise in prices associated with the artificial demand of a wartime economy, introduced serious inflation as a permanent facet of Chilean economic life. In the nitrate regions the companies controlled both the workers' income, usually paid in company scrip called *vales* or *fichas,* and the price of consumer goods at the company store, or *pulpería.* Thus, inflation pitted workers against the nitrate capitalists at the most basic level of subsistence. When labor was relatively scarce, the companies could use "low prices" at the *pulpería* to attract workers; when labor was more abundant or demand for nitrate slackened, the workers received less favorable treatment by the companies. Payment in company scrip limited the workers' ability to purchase consumption goods from independent merchants or peddlers. In order to maintain the workers as captive clients of the *pulpería,* the nitrate companies attempted to restrict independent traders from entering the nitrate *oficinas.* If a worker wished to use the company scrip in the "outside" world, storeowners typically discounted the scrip 10 to 30 percent. Under these conditions there emerged among the workers a sense of exploitation and a list of quite concrete demands for improvement of their situation. The militant expression of these demands in a strike in 1890 would play a key role in the civil war of 1891 when nitrate workers joined congressional forces to defeat President Balmaceda.

In the decade after the War of the Pacific these conditions in the nitrate industry and the industry's sensitivity to the international market made themselves felt quite strongly. By 1885 nitrate prices declined from their wartime high of 12 shillings to 5s. 4d. In an effort to control the decline in prices, the major nitrate companies formed a "combination," or cartel, assigning quotas according to installed capacity. This first of several "combinations" (1884–86) over the next thirty years had some success in reversing the price trend; but as conditions improved, the more efficient producers relied on their technological advantage or the richness of the deposits they exploited, and the "combination" disappeared. Rapid increases in output and in exports—1886, 451,000 metric tons; 1887, 713,000 metric tons; 1890, over 1,000,000 metric tons—unaccompanied by a corresponding increase in demand again placed pressure on the companies to control the level of supply. Given the bulky nature of the "ore," storage could quickly become a problem if exports slackened off, leaving production shutdowns as the most obvious instrument for dealing with the fickle market.

Limiting production or exports favored neither the Chilean government nor the labor force. Government revenues were tied to the total tonnage exported—not to price. Production cutbacks or shutdowns meant unemployment for the workers. Complicating this picture further, enterprising British capitalists who had made a financial killing by acquiring the Peruvian nitrate certificates, sought to consolidate control over the industry, including the railroad networks that linked the pampa with the coastal cities. The most ambitious, like John Thomas North, who became known as the "Nitrate King," also invested in related commercial ventures. In North's case investments included a company that controlled the water supply at Antofagasta and the region's principal bank. Competition among foreign capitalists for control of the nitrate railroads, for workers, for nitrate concessions, and for other favors from the Chilean government further enmeshed the evolution of the nitrate industry in Chilean politics. Meanwhile a growing nationalist sentiment in Chile publicly condemned the increasing foreign influence over the nation's new economic resources.

Revenues from the nitrate fields permitted the Chilean government to embark on a most ambitious program of public works, including impressive extension of the rail and telegraph network as well as significant expansion of the educational system. In 1888 a newly created Ministry of Industry and Public Works absorbed more than 20 percent of the national budget, and investments in education accounted for another 15 percent of government expenditures. Military spending also increased significantly. With increased expenditures came new public jobs, and new opportunities for the national government to distribute patronage positions to its supporters. Control over government contracts and over large deposits of government funds in private banks gave the president increased leverage in national politics. More generally, as public resources expanded, the role and perceived importance of the State grew immensely both in relationship to the economy and in regard to social and political opportunities within Chilean society. Personal and party feuds over the spoils of the new wealth, job opportunities, and government contracts made nitrate prosperity almost as much a political liability as an asset for the incumbent administration. At the same time, both the administration and the Chilean economy faced extraordinary vulnerability to international markets and prices for nitrates. Chilean politics and economy depended critically upon foreign demand for fertilizer, upon foreign bond-markets, and upon decisions made by foreign investors and commercial interests.

Nor did economic expansion eliminate fundamental conflicts within the Chilean polity. President Domingo Santa María's (1881–86) Liberal government steamrollered anticlerical legislation through a Liberal-dominated Congress. Engineered through the legislature by Minister of Interior José Manuel Balmaceda, laws establishing secular cemeteries, civil marriage, and civil registry of births profoundly offended Conservative interests, now in a decided though still influential minority. The latter, losers in the congressional debates, would not lose the opportunity to avenge themselves when Balmaceda took office as president and faced Chile's worst political crisis of the nineteenth century. Santa María's government also extended the suffrage to all literate, adult males—and then intervened in congressional elections in the most overt fashion to secure a compliant legislature. In power, liberals like Santa María proved just as enamoured of presidential discretion and just as likely to abuse presidential power as any of the Conservative or National party presidents of the mid-nineteenth century. Such inconsistency between action and previously proclaimed principles divided the Liberals into numerous factions and personalist cliques based upon animosity toward Santa María, Balmaceda, or other government ministers, the desire for a public post, or ideological commitment to particular reforms.

Santa María's choice of Balmaceda as his successor—and the knowledge that through presidential intervention in the elections Santa María could impose his choice—totally disrupted the Congress. An alliance of independent Liberals, or *sueltos*, Conservatives, and Radicals tried to obstruct passage of the tax bill that permitted the government to collect revenues to carry out its program. The opposition sought in this way to persuade Santa María to withdraw his support for Balmaceda. Though they failed to carry the day, this action set the tone for Balmaceda's difficulties in his next five years as Chile's president. If Santa María's own authoritarian bent as president seemed to conflict with his liberal record in Congress, Balmaceda's confrontation with Congress would be even more ironic inasmuch as throughout his long and distinguished public career he had been a champion of the parliamentary system and especially of congressional checks on the executive.

President Balmaceda took office at a time when public revenues were increasing dramatically as a result of the nitrate duties. Between 1886 and 1890 government revenues rose from 37 million pesos to over 58 million. Although Conservatives criticized the government for its failure to re-establish the convertibility of the Chilean currency, Balmaceda's policy of investing the windfall nitrate revenues in social and transport infrastructure, public works, and education produced quite positive results. Despite a general prosperity and visible evidences of the government's progress in realizing its program, personal rancor and political infighting over ministries and patronage weakened Balmaceda's coalition. Formation of a new political party, the Partido Demócrata (1887), to support artisan and working-class demands, and a wave of violent urban protests in 1888–89 hinted at the intensification of the "social question" in the 1890s. At the same time the President faced a number of issues concerning the financial manipulations of John T. North and other entrepreneurs in the northern provinces.

From 1888 on Balmaceda delivered a number of ominous speeches hinting at an increased state role in the nitrate industry or, at the least, at an effort to enlarge the role of national producers in the nitrate regions. In March 1889, Balmaceda traveled to the northern provinces. At Iquique the president publicly blamed foreign monopolists in control of the nitrate railroad and nitrate production for difficulties in the industry. He also stated that the state ought not to create an industrial monopoly but should prevent private monopolies from controlling production or restricting output. In short, Balmaceda sought to defend the government's stake in the revenues of the nitrate industry and to encourage further national investment without injuring the rights of foreign investors. In addition, he sought to balance the conflicting pressures from a variety of British firms and their Chilean supporters and retainers, including congressmen and cabinet members seeking new nitrate, railroad, and commercial concessions.

Other voices in Chile called for more radical measures, including complete nationalization of the nitrate industry. But Balmaceda himself never made this proposal or supported it. In his annual address to Congress in June 1889, Balmaceda proposed public auctions of certain state-owned nitrate fields limited to Chilean bidders. The president further recommended that foreign purchase of nitrate properties be limited to one-half of new concessions. Though certainly nationalistic in orientation, this policy proposal—never adopted by Congress—hardly constituted an attack on existing foreign investment in nitrates or exclusion of further foreign participation in the nitrate industry. And though certain historians see in Balmaceda a "decided antiimperialist," Balmaceda never took actions considered universally hostile to foreign investment in Chile. Indeed, in a manner of questionable propriety, he supported the associations of certain of his congressional adherents with foreign interests. On the other hand, Balmaceda's commitment to a program of internal modernization and national development depended upon a continuous flow of nitrate revenues, and he certainly opposed any private program that might artificially restrict nitrate production and hence decrease the government's ability to finance public programs. In this sense, the interests of the large British investors sometimes directly conflicted with those of the Chilean state and the policies of the incumbent government. Despite Balmaceda's careful *actions* in regard to foreign investment, his public *statements* made British interests wary, thereby creating powerful potential allies for the president's domestic adversaries.

Toward the end of 1889 the nitrate industry again faced a situation of surplus; stockpiling began, and prices declined. It looked as though another producers' "combination" would form to withhold production until the adverse market reversed itself. Balmaceda's government not only sought to avert this development and prevent layoffs, but also moved against John North's Nitrate Railway Company which monopolized nitrate hauling in Tarapacá. The government correctly recognized the burden on the industry of the monopoly prices charged by the Nitrate Railway, and therefore entered into negotiation with other entrepreneurs for the construction of other nitrate lines. Significantly, the greatest threat to North's railway came from the potential competition of other British investors, including the long-established commercial house of Gibbs and Sons.

When the government canceled the Nitrate Railway's monopoly concession, and entered into negotiations with Campbell, Outram and Company to construct a railroad from the *oficina* of Agua Santa to Caleta Buena, the Nitrate Railway interests appealed the decision in an effort to preserve their economic dominance in the region. President Balmaceda's Council of State ruled against the Nitrate Railway. North's company claimed that the executive had exceeded his constitutional authority, in that appeal of the monopoly concession was a matter for the courts. Influential domestic political opponents of Balmaceda supported North's constitutional arguments as further ammunition in the struggle against the president, though this did not necessarily mean support for the Nitrate Railway's monopoly. Nitrate Railway interests, playing on the executive-legislative tensions to press their claims, sent a memorandum to the Senate calling upon that body to hold Balmaceda accountable for violations of the constitution. Not only did this controversy intensify internal political dissension, but North's allies persuaded the British Foreign Office to raise the matter with the Chilean foreign minister despite objections by competing British companies within Chile. British diplomatic pressure added to Balmaceda's woes.

The complexity of the situation increased still further with the upcoming presidential elections of 1891, the spread of labor conflicts across the nitrate fields, and the deteriorating economic situation. Balmaceda, despite public disclaimers, seemed to favor as his successor a personal friend and wealthy landowner, Enrique Salvador Sanfuentes. Despite election reforms in the 1870s, the overriding influence of the president, in congressional elections as well as presidential elections, continued unabated. This meant that presidential blessing and mobilization of the presidential electoral apparatus generally guaranteed victories at the polls. Illustrative is a letter to Balmaceda in 1890 from a would-be congressional candidate, cited by Harold Blakemore in his brilliant study *British Nitrates and Chilean Politics 1886–1896*.

> I recollect that Your Excellency told me to write to you when I thought it was time for my re-election to the Deputies, and since I think that time has now come, I take the liberty of writing to Your Excellency to say that I wish to continue in my post as Deputy for the next period, with the sole aim of serving Your Excellency's policies at all times and with the same loyalty as always and with the unshakeable resolve of not missing a single day of the sessions.

Once elected, of course, the president could neither control the deputy's actions nor guarantee his loyalty—as Balmaceda discovered. Nevertheless, the president's control over elections through the cabinet, the intendants, and the governors, made selection of ministers and administrative officials prior to elections of primordial political significance. Since Sanfuentes counted numerous personal enemies among his Liberal colleagues, Balmaceda's ministerial appointments from 1889 on were subjected to ever more intense congressional scrutiny.

Partisan politics couched in the rhetoric of fundamental constitutional issues concerning presidential authority polarized the opposing forces. Policy regarding the volatile nitrate economy pushed the opposing factions toward violent confrontation. The president came to view interpellation or censure of his ministers—a practice well-established by this time and strongly supported by Balmaceda during his legislative career—as antipatriotic or "political" attacks on his program for national development. Gradually Balmaceda hardened his position against congressional manipulation, acting ever less diplomatically toward the growing number of congressional critics. In January 1890 the president closed the special session of Congress and appointed a new cabinet without reference to party alignments in the legislature. Contrary to custom, he refused to reconvene the Congress upon the appropriate request by the *Comisión Conservadora* of the legislature. When the next ordinary session of Congress convened in June 1890, Balmaceda's message to it focused mainly upon the need to reverse the trend toward weakening of the executive authority by a "bastard parliamentary system" that led to "the dictatorship of Congress." These remarks and the particulars of the president's reform proposals represented a direct attack upon the very principles liberal politicians, including Balmaceda, had fought for since the 1830s.

Three days later the Senate overwhelmingly censured Balmaceda's cabinet, headed by Enrique Sanfuentes; the Chamber of Deputies took similar action on June 7, 1890. In a move totally without precedent, Balmaceda refused to accept the resignation of his ministers, and Congress countered with the now traditional device of refusing to discuss the law authorizing tax collection until the president had appointed ministers acceptable to the legislature. Balmaceda persisted in his refusal, and tensions mounted.

Only mediation by the archbishop of Santiago brought a temporary compromise in August, with the appointment of a Supreme Court judge to head the cabinet.

Precisely as the political crisis heightened, a cyclical downturn in the nitrate industry fueled discontent among workers in the northern provinces. Continued monetary inflation reduced the workers' real income as prices rose, and unemployment even threatened subsistence. Isolated incidents of violence and work stoppages had reflected growing dissatisfaction among the workers between 1884 and 1889. In early July 1890 a strike by dockworkers in Iquique spread to rail and foundry workers, the mines at Huantajaya, throughout the nitrate pampa, north to Pisagua and south to Antofagasta. The workers' petitions varied from one work site to another, but typically they demanded an end to payment in company scrip, monthly cash settlements in silver or the equivalent in currency, freedom of commerce in the nitrate fields and mining camps (an end to monopolies by the company store), and elimination of the arbitrary fines or discounts from their wages which the companies imposed. For the first time in Chilean history workers carried off a "general strike" that threatened production from Tarapacá to the coal fields of Concepción.

Balmaceda received urgent appeals from employers in Tarapacá to use troops to restore order. Initially hesitant to intervene and seemingly supportive of the workers' demands in his public pronouncements, Balmaceda nevertheless dispatched warships with troops to the north. Violence, looting, and repression by company police or soldiers in some *oficinas* left dozens of casualties; at other locations the strike evolved more or less peacefully. Within ten days employers agreed to most of the workers' demands, thereby ending the strike—though in most of the *oficinas* and the cities employers failed to live up to their promises. Having temporarily squelched the strike by agreeing to meet the workers' terms, the employers gained time for the troops to arrive and deploy themselves. The presence of military units discouraged the workers' further efforts to revive the conflict, though it spread as far north as Arica and south to Valparaíso.

In the port of Valparaíso rioting and extensive looting brought harsh reprisals from police and military units sent from Santiago. Other military units arriving from Concepción stifled militancy in the coal mines, but lesser movements or isolated incidents of violence occurred at Quillota, Los Andes, Santiago, and Talca. With the restoration of order employers across the nation fired leaders of the strike movement and reinstituted the traditional practices on the work sites against which the workers had protested. A glut of nitrate stocks in relation to world demand allowed employers to rid themselves of "undesirable" laborers at the same time as negotiations continued to establish another "combination" to depress output until market conditions improved.

The timing of the labor crisis—Chile's first experience with a truly national, if spontaneous, labor movement—coincided exactly with the political crisis between Balmaceda and Congress. According to the 1833 constitution, Congress had to authorize tax collection every eighteen months. Refusal to authorize tax collections left the government, in theory, without revenues to carry on its daily operations. Instead, Balmaceda responded by notifying banks with government deposits held at thirty days' notice of intended withdrawal, to consider these accounts henceforth as "deposit accounts on call." This measure startled the financial community and escalated further the conflict with Congress. Feelings were so polarized that it became difficult to remember that the supposed issue at stake remained Balmaceda's refusal to accept congressional demands that he appoint a new cabinet.

By this time the opposition attacked Balmaceda's increasingly "dictatorial" and unconstitutional behavior, while Balmaceda reacted with insults in kind concerning the opposition's lack of patriotism and their political motivation. Seeking to create a personalist political machine apart from the old Liberal party upon which he could no longer rely, Balmaceda entangled himself in the jealousies and intrigues of local politics and patronage. Naturally the single most important issue continued to be designation of his successor, and this gave added importance to the distribution of patronage around the country and the appointment of "reliable" administrators in the provinces.

Balmaceda proved unable to negotiate an acceptable compromise with the opposition. Progressively bitter charges of antinationalist, unpatriotic activities punctuated the running battle with the growing legislative opposition. Throughout the entire year of 1890, Congress refused to pass the budget bill or to authorize force levels for the military. Undaunted, the president illegally decreed that the 1890 legislation would remain in effect. In quick response to this overtly unconstitutional act, Congress called upon *capitán de navío* Jorge Montt and the navy to support it against the president's usurpation of power. The fleet sailed north to occupy Iquique and gain control of the nitrate revenues for the congressional insurrectionists. Balmaceda, who had the loyalty of most of the regular army, imposed a state of siege, instituted highly repressive policies against the press, and suspended civil liberties in an effort to suffocate the rebellion.

Civil war continued for seven months with severe losses on both sides. Ultimately, control of the nitrate revenues, financial and material support by British and other foreign interests, and the military advice of Emil Körner left congressional forces victorious. Congressional agents successfully delayed arrival of two new ironclads the government had ordered from France, and obtained Mannlicher repeating rifles which helped carry the day for the congressional army. Ironically, the nitrate revenues Balmaceda had counted on to carry out his development program bought arms and equipment abroad for his enemies. The congressional army, recruited largely among the nitrate workers, received training under the direction of the Prussian officer contracted by presidents Santa María and Balmaceda to modernize Chile's army and defend the newly acquired nitrate regions. Since railroad construction in the north had been dominated by private interests, the civil war found Santiago unconnected to the north by a longitudinal rail line. Defection of most of the navy, which had received large amounts of money from the Balmaceda government for modernization, prevented Balmaceda from transporting sufficient forces north to overcome the insurgents. After his army was defeated at Concon and Placilla by an amphibious assault directed by Körner and a number of Chile's new professional, Prussian-trained officers, Balmaceda took refuge in the Argentine embassy. He left in charge in Santiago General Baquedano, the hero of the War of the Pacific, who had remained neutral in the civil war. The day after his presidential term ended—September 19, 1891—Balmaceda shot himself. In October, Jorge Montt was elected Balmaceda's successor, and Chilean politics entered a new era of congressional dominance.

The outcome of the civil war shifted the balance of Chilean politics from the executive to the Congress but did little to change the nation's dependence on nitrates. Population in the northern provinces more than doubled between 1885 and 1907; workers traveled from the *norte chico*, the central valley, and even further south to seek their fortune in the nitrate fields. Average levels of employment in the nitrate fields jumped impressively from nearly 6500 in the 1880s to almost 50,000 between 1910 and 1920. Cyclic downturns continued to inflict periodic depression, shutdowns, attempts to form production cartels, and massive unemployment. Economic depression between 1896 and 1897 saw nitrate production reduced to 40 percent of capacity. Large-scale unemployment followed. Financial panic associated with the government's unsuccessful experiment with a return to convertible currency (1895–98) and increased defense expenditures—25 percent of the budget—exacerbated the crisis, but still only provided a relatively mild hint of the more severe crises that would occur during the next three decades of nitrate dependence. As the labor force increased, the misery inflicted by the downturns of the economy became more severe. Instead of 5000 jobless workers, the nation now periodically faced the desperation of tens of thousands of laborers temporarily without work, means of subsistence, or domicile. The workers retained by the companies experienced wage cuts.

The linkage of the nitrate economy to the agriculture of the central valley and the Concepción–frontier region further integrated the regional economies into a national economy. Downturns in nitrate affected agriculture, coal mines, commerce, and a slowly growing industrial sector. Led by food and primary product-processing firms—canneries, flour mills, breweries, match factories, sugar refineries—along with foundries, cement, and even a nascent locomotive works, Chilean industry expanded during the last decade of the nineteenth century and into the first years of the twentieth. Forty percent of Chilean factories in 1895 dated from no earlier than 1890—almost 60 percent of these were located in Santiago or Valparaíso. Imported technologies made some of Chile's new industries—for example, cement, modernized flour mills, and wineries as efficient, by the first decades of the twentieth century, as any in the world. Increasingly integrated in their economic relationships, domestic firms produced input—alcohol, wood, paper, containers—for other national industries as well as consumer articles for the growing cities and nitrate districts. Moderate protective tariffs adopted in the 1890s reflected the effective lobbying by industrial interests like the SFF and the growing concern of certain Chileans to make Chile an industrial country. The Errázuriz Echaurren administration (1896–1901) also directed its ministries to give preference to Chilean manufactures in public projects, so long as domestic manufacturers charged no more than 10 to 15 percent more than foreign competitors.

Urbanization in the years after 1885 increased Valparaíso's population to over 120,000 and that of Santiago to more than 250,000 by the turn of the century. Iquique grew into a bustling nitrate port of 33,000 inhabitants, and Antofagasta's population rose to 14,000. Housing, sanitation, and public-health conditions in the growing urban concentrations remained sorely inadequate. Feeble government responses to smallpox epidemics in the early 1880s and to a catastrophic cholera epidemic in 1888, which according to official estimates took over 30,000 lives, reflected both the sorry state of public-health programs and the incapacity of the Chilean state to respond effectively to the problems of an urbanizing, modernizing society.

To the south, rural migrants continued their exodus out of the countryside to Concepción, Talcahuano, and Talca. By 1907 the Chilean census classified 43 percent of the population as urban. Though the crude definition of "urban"—as concentrations over 1000—gives a somewhat misleading impression, it cannot be denied that ever more Chileans were potential customers for Chilean agriculture and manufacturers as they left the rural estates and settled in towns, mining camps, or nitrate fields. And it was to this internal market that Chilean manufacturers largely dedicated their attentions. Of the total value of exports in 1900 (162 million pesos), only 3.3 million corresponded to manufactures—less than wealthy Chileans spent on imported perfume, jewelry, liquor, and fine textiles.

If nitrates brought uncertainty to the Chilean economy and much of the labor force, it also brought great wealth to a small number of capitalists and stock speculators. It allowed Chilean governments to avoid serious examination of the internal tax structure and to eliminate taxes on wealth or income. Balmaceda himself proposed abolition of the income and inheritance taxes introduced in the late 1870s. Nitrate financed public works, railroad construction, private mansions, and construction of irrigation canals for Chile's agricultural heartland. The nitrate industry's expansion generated secondary and support industries in the north and in the central valley and also provided a market for Chilean agriculture and coal mines while stimulating coastal shipping. More than anything else, however, the nitrate industry altered the character of the Chilean labor force. The conditions in the nitrate fields spawned an increasingly militant labor movement which carried its struggle against exploitation south to the countryside and the cities. The plight of the northern work force became a platform for political reformers and a school of leadership for a new generation of labor leaders.

A select group of Chilean intellectuals joined the battle with short stories, novels, and plays depicting the misery of Chile's masses in contrast to the decadence and pedantry of the nation's political elite and the splendor of the manor house on the hacienda or the urban mansion of the northern mining magnates. Publication of *Casa Grande* in 1908—by a member of Chile's oligarchy who scathingly attacked the character of his brethren—and of *Sinceridad: Chile íntimo en 1910*—by a schoolteacher writing under the pseudonym Dr. Julio Valdés Cange—focused attention in Chile upon the reality of what became known as the "social question."

The "social question" or "workers' question" by any other name still meant industrial class conflict combined with serious concern by some Chilean leaders with mass poverty, educational backwardness, and the whole range of issues associated with social and economic development. The War of the Pacific and the nitrate economy had ushered Chile into the industrial age. Unfortunately the civil war of 1891 reaffirmed the oligarchic tradition of Chilean politics, even reinvigorated the power of central valley landowners with legislation granting municipal autonomy and extending responsibility to local government for administration of congressional and presidential elections. The contradiction between the politics of parliamentary stalemate, and the evolution of an industrial labor movement influenced by imported socialist and Marxist ideology, would undermine the political system created by the 1833 constitution and radically alter class relations. Finally, in the 1920s this process would culminate in a military coup d'état when Chilean parliamentary government would prove unable to confront head on the reality of twentieth-century industrial society.

7 Politics, Labor, and the Social Question

In 1927, thirty-six years after congressional forces imposed parliamentary government upon Chile, José Manuel Balmaceda's son presented the presidential sash worn by his martyred father to an ambitious military officer named Carlos Ibáñez. Balmaceda's son delivered an emotional speech, claiming that Ibáñez represented the "perfect incarnation" of *Balmacedismo*—the principles for which his father had died.

Whether or not Ibáñez rightfully belonged to the tradition of Balmaceda or sympathized beyond convenient political rhetoric with Balmaceda's programs of the late 1880s, he explicitly rejected the interminable, parliamentary squabbles and the restrictions on executive authority that had frustrated his predecessors. More than had any Chilean president since the era of Portales, Ibáñez returned to Hispanic authoritarianism and condemned the imported liberalism that dominated Chilean political life in the late nineteenth and early twentieth century.

A prominent military officer trained in the Prussian tradition established in Chile by Emil Körner, Ibáñez led a new generation of Chilean military officers who despised parliamentary practices, politicians, and, above all else, politics. They blamed politics for Chile's economic problems, for the increasing class conflict, for the corruption and venality of public life, and for all else that ailed the nation. These views were epitomized in 1924 by a Chilean officer writing to a civilian government minister:

> Even though you, at this time and place, represent for us the most disgusting element in our country—politicians—that is, all that is corrupt, the dismal factional disputes, depravities and immoralities, in other words, the causes of our national degeneration, we recognize that you, despite the fact that you must defend sinecures, hand out public posts, and support avaricious ambitions, that you are one of the few honest politicians.

If the sentence was long, the sentiments it expressed reflected the frustration of the professional military with more than three decades of congressional neglect of Chile's most pressing problems. It also expressed the utter contempt for politics and politicians held by the military and by Chile's growing class of technicians and professional people. The professional military nurtured by Balmaceda's successors through the first decade of the twentieth century (and then neglected, to the Congress's ultimate regret) would no longer tolerate the sterile politics of salon, intrigue, and immobility that had both weakened the military institution and made the armed forces shock troops for oligarchical repression.

Whatever the objections to Ibáñez' dictatorial regime, it is easy to understand the disdain of a moralistic professional soldier for the type of political system that functioned in Chile after 1891. Even apart from the immediate issues of 1924 prior to the September 5 coup that brought the military into the government—Congress's decision to pay its representatives a salary contrary to constitutional prohibitions, while salaries due civil servants and military personnel were in arrears; its constant meddling in military personnel matters; its failure to pass social legislation in the midst of growing labor conflict—Ibáñez and his followers could no longer brook the political charade called parliamentary government in Chile.

Manuel Rivas Vicuña, one of the country's most respected politicians—and eventual political enemy of Ibáñez—captured the fundamental character of the Chilean political process during the post-1891 years. He described his "Election Memories of 1918":

> Would I again have a seat in Congress? We could hardly wait for the train to arrive in Curicó.
>
> What happened here?—I asked the first person I encountered in the station.
>
> The same as usual, *patrón*, the bosses [*futres*] got together and stole the money sent by the government for the elections.
>
> Afterward I found out from my friends that an agreement had been reached. My name and that of the Conservative candidate had triumphed without opposition; they had made no use of the blank check that I left in the event of an electoral struggle, and they had made only small payments to the voters.
>
> The bosses had stolen the money sent by the government for the elections.
>
> I've been lucky to avoid the necessity of buying votes for my campaigns. I've had no competition the four times I was elected deputy, and my friends generously took care of my electoral expenses.
>
> The general rule, I've been assured, is the opposite and reveals that from the worker to the great proprietors, all believe that elections are a business that provide those elected not just with honor but also with [material] benefit.
>
> Vote buying [*cohecho*] is a habit so deeply rooted it will be very difficult to eradicate.

The men who acquired offices in the Congress through vote buying debated interminably while Chilean society underwent profound socio-economic changes. In 1915 an ex-president of the Federation of Chilean University Students gave a funeral oration for the nation's political leaders—at the end of a presidential term in which President Ramón Barros Luco told his compatriots that "there are only two types of problem: those without solution and those that solve themselves." The military intervention of 1924 and Ibáñez' authoritarian regime (1927–31) were reactions to this type of political thinking and to the politics of parliamentary stalemate.

Ibáñez' usurpation of presidential authority and subordination of Congress also temporarily halted more positive trends during the parliamentary period—institutionalization of respect for civil liberties and political liberalization in the Chilean polity. Whatever the defects of the parliamentary period, it had allowed for the evolution of freedom of the press, for a growing, if not complete, recognition of the legitimacy of opposition movements and parties, and for a formal respect for the procedures of liberal democracy. Despite electoral corruption and empty political rhetoric, along with Congress's failure to deal with pressing social issues, the country's political institutions permitted expanded suffrage and a more open pattern of recruitment to public office. The military intervention of 1924 and the subsequent Ibáñez administration not only temporarily ended this trend toward political liberalization, but it represented a resurgence of the traditional Hispanic intolerance for liberalism, intensified by a military ideology of national regeneration.

In 1887 the recently organized Partido Demócrata brought a new political ideology and style into Chilean politics. Led by Malaquías Concha, the party proclaimed as its objectives "political, economic, and social liberation of the people [*pueblo*]" and proposed numerous reforms, including direct election of the president, municipal administration of the departments (eliminating the presidentially appointed governors), taxes on land and capital, compulsory public education, and support for industrialization through protective tariffs. Appealing especially to artisans and the lower middle class, the party also promoted policies designed to improve the lot of the urban poor.

The Partido Demócrata evolved as Chile's first populist political party, electing its first deputy to Congress in 1894. By 1903, it had obtained representation from Valparaíso, Santiago, and Concepción. The most progressive elements within the Partido Demócrata later emerged as leaders of the ever more militant labor organizations of the cities, the nitrate and mining camps, and the southern coal mines, as well as of the Socialist Workers Party (POS) formed in 1912. The party sponsored mass rallies, supported the workers' press and cultural centers, and generally provided a legitimate voice of political opposition on behalf of the working classes. Though it never became a truly proletarian-based organization and continued to recruit its leadership from artisans and the middle class, the Partido Demócrata nevertheless challenged the assumptions and policies of the landowning, commercial, and industrial interests that dominated Chilean politics.

The hypocrisy and the contradictions of the parliamentary era permitted greater latitude for political and social organization by workers and the urban poor than could have occurred under a more authoritarian civilian regime or a military government. Chilean elites believed themselves to be progressive. With the exception of the Conservatives who insisted still on the prerogatives of the Church or opposed universal education, they identified with the civil libertarian tradition of Britain. After all, Congress had only recently won a victory for liberty against the threat of executive tyranny! The constant changeovers of cabinets, punctuated by acrimonious debates in the legislature and the press, provided a milieu in which the political system could usually tolerate the worker press and even moderate representatives of the working class. This did not mean acceptance of all elected representatives of the working class. The Congress refused to seat Luis Emilio Recabarren, the most important labor leader in the country, after his electoral victory in 1906, on the pretext that he refused to swear the customary oath. One deputy commented that "even if it were not strictly in accord with justice to expel Mr. Recabarren from the Chamber, it would be necessary to do so for social morality . . . since it is not tolerable that the ideas of social dissolution sustained by Mr. Recabarren be represented in the Chamber." Nevertheless, the parliamentary system did allow increased political influence for middle-class and provincial interests. Before the parliamentary era ended (1924), Recabarren and other self-declared revolutionaries had also gained seats in the Congress.

Parliamentary politics tended to diffuse and weaken governmental authority. The multiplicity of political parties and factions and the electoral reforms that placed supervision of elections and registration in the hands of 267 "autonomous" municipal administrations, decentralized national politics. The Congress became a creature of local political machines which were frequently dominated by landowners, mining interests, or industrialists in accord with the economy of each congressional district. Executive intervention through use of the police or military could still influence electoral outcomes, but generally money to buy votes became much more important than naked force. In these respects the Chilean political system shared the corruption that accompanied expansion of the suffrage and democratization throughout most of the Western world, though expansion of the suffrage came much more slowly in Chile than in the United States or Argentina. As late as 1920, only 5 percent of the population cast ballots despite electoral reforms in 1874 and 1888 that removed property qualifications and extended the vote to adult, literate males. Still, dishonesty in public life and patronage as a principal instrument of assembling and maintaining local political machines reached no more distressing levels in Chile than it did in the United States or Argentina during the same period.

Unlike the United States, in Chile no wave of immigrants served the elite as urban "voting cattle"; government remained largely in the hands of a small clique of "political families" with aristocratic pretensions and a political base in the countryside—in an increasingly complex urbanizing society. Overt military intervention in Chilean politics in 1924 and the subsequent Ibáñez dictatorship (1927–31) meant, above all else, an end to an era in Chilean national life when socio-economic changes moved the country rapidly into the twentieth century, yet political leaders clung to a bastardized version of imported nineteenth-century liberalism.

No other problem so dominated Chilean development after 1891—and received so little meaningful attention by Chilean political leaders—than the continued growth of the urban and industrial proletariat and the intensified struggle between labor and capital called the "social question." Modest but persistent industrial growth in Chile from the 1890s until the world depression of the 1930s gradually increased the number of workers employed in factories, workshops, construction industries, and other urban manual jobs. This urban working class remained unprotected by social legislation or a strong labor movement.

Liberal philosophical and economic doctrine current in Europe and transplanted to Chile condemned associations of workingmen that attempted to negotiate collective agreements with employers as contrary to "liberty" and the "right to work." In England, where the Industrial Revolution first made itself felt and gave rise to the social question, laws against workers' "combinations" and repression of labor organizations were the common reaction by government and employers to labor activism. Only after years of organized struggle, protests, violence, and the resultant political reform did the English working classes obtain legislation that limited the duration of the work day, protected child labor, set minimum wages, or guaranteed the right of organization.

As the industrial age advanced, the same type of struggle eventually developed in the rest of Europe, the United States, and Latin America. Thus the social question in Chile, as in the rest of the Western world, consisted of political, social, and economic issues derived from the technological and demographic effects of industrialization during the nineteenth and early twentieth centuries.

Prior to 1924 Chilean laws provided no institutionalized procedure for dealing with conflicts between worker and employer. In theory a worker sought employment from an individual employer and came to an agreement concerning wages, conditions of work, and length of employment. Each worker had to reach his or her own agreement with the employer. No collective agreement or written contract existed, and prevailing custom defined as subversive strikes or work stoppages. According to this classic liberal interpretation of the worker-employer relation, the worker could freely come and go as he or she pleased, and could work or not work, depending upon the attractiveness of the employment offered. Likewise employers, competing for workers in the free labor market, would offer conditions of work and sufficient pay to attract and retain workers.

In reality, of course, this highly idealized conception of the labor market—imbued with the legitimacy of prevailing law and enforced as necessary by the police or the military from country to country—ignored the tendency for industrial ownership to become gradually more concentrated, for owners of factories to cooperate in holding down wages, and for the threat of unemployment in the cities to pose a life-and-death dilemma for the growing proletariat.

This liberal formulation also failed to recognize that the extensive political influence of the propertied classes had shaped the laws restricting labor organization but allowing employers' associations that effectively lobbied legislatures and administrators in their own behalf. For example, the Sociedad de Fomento Fabril (SFF) in Chile, which opposed labor organizations and collective labor agreements, attempted to protect its own interests with constant lobbying for protective tariffs. Its members also were sent to Congress, staffed government bureaucracies, or acted as ministers of state. Between 1883 and 1930, 36 percent of the association's executive council members served as congressmen, senators, or ministers of state. During the same period the monopolistic or oligopolistic structure characteristic of Chilean industry in the 1990s had begun to emerge. By 1918, 3.3 percent of all manufacturing firms employed 43.2 percent of manual workers in industry. A small number of firms dominated most of the important manufacturing sectors, including textiles, sugar, breweries, wineries, foundries, tobacco, cement, paper, glass and bottles, chemicals, vegetable oils, and coal. Collusive marketing and supply agreements reinforced the lack of competition as the larger firms attempted to freeze potential competitors out of the market. In a fashion compatible with both Hispanic and the liberal capitalism of the late nineteenth century, Chilean entrepreneurs sought to eliminate competition throughout the economy except in the labor market. Here they enthusiastically accepted the principles of British liberalism long after the advent of labor legislation and the recognition of the legitimacy of labor organizations in Britain. Although the industrialists strongly supported protective tariffs, government subsidies, monopoly profits, and influential industrial associations working closely with the government, they staunchly opposed organized collective action on the part of workers to improve their living conditions or to demand higher wages.

Likewise, Chile's wealthiest landowners, organized in the National Agricultural Society (SNA) since 1869, actively lobbied to restrict the negative effects of "free trade" on cattle interests. Highly influential in Chilean politics—from 1873 to 1901, 25 to 33 percent of the members of Congress belonged to the SNA—the landowners sponsored legislation in 1888 to establish a protective tariff on imported cattle. Landowners thus hoped to insulate Chilean cattle producers against the more modern cattle industry of Argentina. The proposed legislation indirectly provided incentives for landowners to revert land to pasture, even as the country proved unable to supply sufficient foodstuffs at reasonable prices to feed the growing cities and northern mining districts.

The cattle tax issue infuriated the leadership of the newly formed Partido Demócrata and became a symbolic rallying point for lower-class protests against the general inflation which was eroding an already precarious standard of living. Landowners responded that the lower classes ate little meat anyway and that in any case beans were healthier. A wave of protests and strikes in Santiago and the provinces, along with the other issues facing the Balmaceda government in 1888–89, led to withdrawal of the proposed cattle tax by its sponsors. A decade later, however, the landowners successfully put through legislation that imposed a duty on imported cattle in conjunction with the protective tariffs supported by the SFF for manufactured goods. Meat prices rose considerably from 1897 to 1902 amidst continual political conflict over a "tax on poor people's stomachs." Finally, in late October 1905, urban unrest related to the spiraling inflation culminated in two days of mob violence, looting, and destruction. This period, known since then as the "Red Week," found the army out of Santiago on maneuvers. To put down the violence the government and private groups distributed arms to members of Chile's most prestigious social club, the Club de la Unión, and to youths from elite families. These white guards massacred hundreds of people in the streets of Santiago. The SNA and other social leaders blamed the riots on agitators "stirring up class hatred." In reality, as the movement developed, usurious merchants, retail shops, and other symbols of the exploitation and deprivation of the poor, all felt the spontaneous wrath of the urban underclass.

Despite the events of October 1905, the cattle tax remained in effect until the economic crisis of 1907, when the government "suspended" its operation for two years. Congress reinstituted the cattle tax in December 1909, and it remained in effect until 1918—when almost 50 percent of all congressmen owned large haciendas. Whatever the real contribution of the cattle tax to increasing food prices and the widespread nutritional deficiencies among the urban poor, its survival until the end of World War I reflected the influence of the SNA and the ambiguity of the Chilean elite's commitment to the "free market" of liberal doctrine. Though seasonal competition between agriculture, public works, and the nitrate producers sometimes forced employers to sweeten the pot, only the labor force was truly expected to compete in the "free" market—for jobs!

By 1920 more Chileans worked in manufacturing than in the mining sector. Other urban employment, in construction, commerce, services, on the docks, and in transport, further enlarged the non-rural work force. It also added to the number of Chileans out of the immediate influence of the owners of large rural estates. Manufacturing itself had achieved moderate diversification, although it still lacked heavy industry and a significant capital goods sector. Diversification meant specialization of the work force and a growing pool of skilled laborers. Urban life for these workers pitted them against the continual inflation and periodic recessions generated in great part by the country's vulnerability to fluctuations in the nitrate market. These business cycles subjected much of the labor force to a grinding poverty that contrasted markedly with the prosperity and economic modernization that surrounded them.

Workers saw the palatial mansions of Santiago politicians and their extended families, along with the evident affluence of the new industrial elites. Technological innovations brought streetcars, automobiles, electric lights—even airplanes—to a nation where the best urban transport only a decade earlier consisted of elegant horse-drawn carriages. Workers could also not fail to notice the overwhelming influence of immigrants and their offspring in the nation's new factories, for by the outbreak of World War I foreign-born industrialists owned slightly more than half of all the country's manufacturing establishments, and foreigners filled more than half of the technical positions in industry.

Unlike the situation in neighboring Argentina, European immigrants did not swell the ranks of Chile's working classes. Whereas by 1914, some 40 percent of Argentina's agricultural labor force and 60 percent of the urban proletariat had been born abroad, in 1907 only 1 percent of Chile's rural labor force and fewer than 4 percent of industrial workers were foreigners. This meant that before World War I the labor movement in Chile was influenced far less by immigrant leadership and imported ideology than its counterpart across the Andes. Chilean authorities and political leaders did sometimes blame the labor agitation prior to the 1920s upon "waves of human scum thrown upon our beaches by other countries," but such hyperbole could not deceive government officials and employers who knew that the flow of immigrants to Chile hardly reached "wave" proportions. Only after the Russian Revolution of 1917 did Chile pass a Residence Law (1918) allowing the government to forbid entry into the country or to deport "foreigners who preached violent change in the social or political order." In contrast,

Argentina passed much harsher legislation in 1902 in response to a more serious participation by immigrants in a growing labor movement. Even in 1918, however,
Chilean leaders, who wanted to use the immigrants as scapegoats for mounting social
tensions, had to admit that the leadership and the rank and file of the Chilean labor
movement, as well as of the socialist-oriented political movements, consisted overwhelmingly of Chileans.

Historical treatments of the origins, character, and evolution of the Chilean labor movement in the early nineteenth century remain fragmentary. Historian Sergio Grez's
monumental study (*De la 'regeneración del pueblo' a la huelga general, Génesis y evolución
histórica del movimiento popular en Chile, 1810–1890*) of popular movements, social
protest, and labor conflicts lists numerous collective efforts by fisherman, artisans and
craftspeople, port workers, miners, peons, and other "workers" of many sorts to improve working and living conditions through protests, strikes, "uprisings," and even
minor rebellions from 1810 to 1890. Grez indicates that his list is "surely incomplete"
and suggests that until 1859 the most important movements involved miners, often in
"violent rebellions." Artisans and craftsmen engaged in urban protest movements, demanding tariff protection against imported manufactures. Although rare, urban strikes
also occurred and increased in number from the 1860s. Violent protests and strikes in
the ports, mines, and sometimes other sectors typically elicited energetic government
repression, including deployment of military units and police as strike breakers and to
"restore order."
    These patterns persisted until the 1890s. Railroad construction and nascent indus-
trialization added railway and factory workers to the list of strikers and organized
labor. Typographers, tailors, carters, workers in the urban tramways and slaughter-
houses, and many others organized in mutual aid and artisan associations (*organizaciones mutualistas, sociedades de artesanos*) and guilds (*gremios*) from the 1850s into the
1880s to defend their collective interests. These organizations became forerunners of a
modern labor union moment.
    Incipient industrialization also incorporated women into the labor force, particu-
larly but not exclusively in the textile sector. Women also organized separate mutual
aid societies (*sociedades obreras*) in the major cities from the 1880s that eventually gave
rise to organizations dedicated to defending women's rights and seeking to improve
their working conditions.
    Efforts to identify the first strike by Chilean workers face insurmountable obstacles.
Chilean historians often cite the rebellion of miners at Chañarcillo in 1834 as a starting
point in the story of the Chilean labor movement, but this rebellion certainly had an-
tecedents in the northern mining camps of colonial times and the early national period.
Whatever the specific chronology of significant events in labor history, the sporadic,
spontaneous protests, rebellions, and strikes prior to the 1880s clearly preceded the
more integrated, politically significant movements of the parliamentary era. A study
published in 1971 by Manuel Barrera documented 299 strikes in Chile's first century
(1810–1910) in addition to numerous other "movements, rebellions and incidents." Of
the 299 strikes, only 42 occurred before 1890, while the remainder took place between
1901 and 1910. Even if this study underestimates the number of strikes before 1890, the
Chilean labor movement as an organized, militant, *national* socio-political force dates
essentially from the last decade of the nineteenth century.
    Beginning with the general strike of 1890, described in Chapter 6, the Chilean labor
movement developed impressively, if unevenly, until World War I. A heterogeneous
collection of mutual aid societies, cooperatives, anarchist-oriented resistance societies,
and brotherhoods, or *mancomunales*, of the nitrate regions brought together thousands

of workers in a struggle to better living conditions, to provide minimal levels of security, or to petition Congress for legislation improving their lot. Tactics and objectives varied from one organization to another. Many of the mutual aid societies limited their attention to self-help efforts, such as burial expenses, and temporary relief in time of unemployment, sickness, or disability. Sometimes, however, an organization that began as a mutual aid society or a cultural group evolved into a more militant labor organization or engaged in explicitly political activities. In this sense, workers' organizations constituted an extremely diversified agglomeration conforming to no unified ideological, political, or social pattern. Paternalistic Conservative politicians, following in the steps of the earlier Catholic workers' circles of the 1870s, patronized the formation of Catholic workers' clubs while anarchists, socialists, and Democrats spread contradictory reformist and revolutionary propaganda among the workers.

The disunity of the workers' organizations and their geographical separation did not prevent the evolution of an increasingly hostile attitude among laborers toward capitalists and landowners. Shortly after the civil war of 1891, with the general strike of 1890 still fresh in mind, the leader of congressional forces and new Chilean president, Vice Admiral Jorge Montt proposed legislation outlawing strikes and other disruptions of economic activity. In justifying the legislation to Congress, its authors noted that "strikes promoted in the name of freedom to work are often the pretext adopted by demagogues to disturb order, cause injury or ruin to industry and misery to the workers." Significantly, the Congress did not pass this legislation, perhaps indicating an authentic commitment to freedom of association by certain parliamentary leaders, despite their abhorrence of movements menacing the flow of nitrate revenues or public order.

More important than legislative proposals, the Montt government moved to enlarge the army and intensify the German-oriented modernization begun before the civil war. In 1895 General Körner contracted thirty-six foreign officers (33 Germans, 2 Swedes, and 1 Dane) to serve as instructors in the Chilean army. Supported by calls from the most influential newspapers to expand the armed forces in the nitrate districts to convince the capitalists that the government would defend their property, as well as by the still more reactionary attacks on the very legitimacy of any political party representing lower-class interests, the Montt government acquired modern military hardware and made clear its commitment to law and order. If border disputes with Argentina or threats of renewed conflict with Peru and Bolivia were the main stimulus for modernizing the armed forces, in practice the Chilean labor movement became the principal target of military operations.

Successive governments through the first decade of the twentieth century maintained this commitment; by 1902 the permanent army had grown to 17,500, compared with its theoretical size of 2500 in 1879. The combination of a rapidly developing labor movement, the resistance by the government and ruling classes to acknowledge the legitimacy of such a movement, and a larger, modernizing military set the stage for a series of well-remembered tragedies that became symbols of struggle and forged a heritage of martyrdom for the modern Chilean labor movement. These include the maritime strike in Valparaíso in 1903, the dockworkers' strike in Antofagasta in 1906, and the massacre of workers at Santa María de Iquique in 1907. Both the army and the navy became instruments of repression of the labor movement.

Labor conflict and political crisis followed trends in the nitrate economy. Following the general strike of 1890 and the subsequent civil war, the cyclic depressions of the nitrate industry, upon which the Chilean state increasingly depended for revenues, led to the periodic unemployment of thousands of workers in the northern deserts. In turn, the nitrate recessions caused economic downturns throughout the Chilean economy.

TABLE 7–1. WORKERS IN THE NITRATE INDUSTRY

Year	Workers Employed	Year	Workers Employed
1895	22,485	1923	41,099
1896	19,345	1924	59,649
1897	16,727	1925	60,785
1898	15,955	1926	38,118
1907	39,653	1927	35,788
1908	40,825	1928	59,963
1909	37,792	1929	58,493
1912	47,800	1930	44,464
1913	53,161	1931*	
1914	43,979	1932	8535
1915	45,506	1933	8486
1916	53,470	1934	14,133
1917	56,378		
1918	56,981		
1919	44,498		
1920	23,542		
1921	33,876		
1922	25,462		

*No data for 1931.
Source: Laurence Stickell, "Migration and Mining: Labor in Northern Chile in the Nitrate Era, 1880–1930," unpublished Ph.D. dissertation, Indiana University, 1978.

As the size of the nitrate work force and the level of production increased from decade to decade, so did the human misery occasioned by recessions. Table 7–1 illustrates the cycles of boom and bust in the nitrate fields as reflected in the variations in the numbers of workers employed in the *oficinas*.

Until the disastrous depression of the 1930s, the nitrate industry expanded continually, with periodic depressions (1896–98, 1907, 1909, 1914–15, 1919–20, 1922, 1926–27) which inflicted unemployment upon the northern workers and forced them to migrate out of the nitrate camps to the ports and toward the central valley. Government commissions routinely documented the plight of the workers and urged reforms, but official action before 1924 consisted of minor social legislation—a workers' housing bill in 1906, a law establishing Sunday as a day of rest in 1907, and a law establishing a mandatory scheme for insuring against industrial accidents in 1917. Meanwhile, the level of conflict, the strength of organized labor, the spread of working-class militancy, the diffusion of anarchist and socialist ideology, and a mushrooming worker press turned the "social question" from the paternalistic concern of a select number of benevolent intellectuals into the most critical political issue confronting the country. Table 7–2 indicates the mounting participation of workers in strikes between 1911 and 1920, though official statistics clearly underestimate the size of the organized labor force and the number of strikes that occurred.

Not only the northern mining districts and urban centers experienced the effects of labor conflict. In 1911 the *Boletín de la Oficina del Trabajo*—the official organ of the Labor Office created in the first decade of the century to collect and publish labor statistics—recorded for the first time a strike in the countryside by forty rural workers. Earlier labor conflicts between landowners and rural workers had certainly occurred in the nineteenth century, but now an official government publication noted the emergence of

TABLE 7–2. STRIKES IN CHILE, 1911–20

Year	Strikes	Workers Involved
1911	10	4762
1912	18	11,154
1913	17	10,490
1914	5	829
1915*		
1916	16	18,523
1917	26	11,408
1918	30	24,392
1919	66	23,529
1920	105	50,439

*No data reported for 1915.
Source: Boletín de la Oficina del Trabajo, No. 18, 1922, p. 263.

class conflict in the rural sector. By 1921 the SNA was so concerned by the possibility of the organization of rural workers and *inquilinos* that it sent a letter to the Chilean president, Arturo Alessandri, urging him to take vigorous action to prevent further labor disturbances in the countryside and to protect private property.

In great part the extension of class conflict to the countryside responded to the efforts of the Chilean Workers' Federation, or Federación Obrera de Chile (FOCH). Indeed, the history of the Chilean labor movement to this day is heavily influenced by the origins, development, political alliances, and ideological orientation of FOCH prior to 1927. Founded in 1909 among the railway workers of Santiago under the aegis of a Conservative lawyer, FOCH gradually evolved into a radical, militantly anticapitalist, working-class organization. Under the influence of Luis Emilio Recabarren, who initially charged the organization with being an instrument of the bourgeoisie but helped to wrest it away from more moderate leadership, FOCH linked sympathizers of the Partido Demócrata and the Partido Obrero Socialista (POS), socialist, anarchists, and syndicalists.

Intra-organizational struggles for power eventually forced reformist elements to leave the movement; by 1921 FOCH had affiliated with the Red International of Labor Unions (RILU), and in 1922 the POS became the Chilean Communist Party. Overlapping membership and leadership between FOCH and the Communist party divided the labor movement as non-Communist Marxists, socialists, and reformers left both the POS and FOCH. Combined with the economic crisis of the early 1920s, these internal divisions reduced FOCH membership from 60,000 to perhaps 30,000 in 1922. Weaker in Santiago and Valparaíso than the anarchists, FOCH continued to be a major force among the nitrate, copper, and coal miners, as well as among the maritime workers, tram workers, and rural labor in certain regions.

In addition to FOCH, anarchists and anarcho-syndicalists played a highly significant role among the Chilean work force through the mid-1920s. Especially influential on the docks, among artisans, and in the construction trades, the anarchists also competed for workers' loyalty in the coal mines, the nitrate fields, and other industries. Rejecting compromise with the capitalist state, the anarchists identified government, church, and capital as the principal enemies. Anarchists played a key role in the formation of "resistance societies" and fomented strikes with varying degrees of success in the first decades of the twentieth century. In 1913 anarchist-inspired labor organization and job actions led to a general strike involving railway workers, port workers, construction and metal workers, tram workers, foundrymen, and workers in the Viña del Mar sugar refinery and the Chilean Tobacco Company. From 1913 to 1921, anarchist unions, mutualist societies, and resistance societies participated in the ebb and flow of labor's efforts to improve working conditions and to challenge antilabor legislation and policies. In addition, they encouraged tenant organizations in their struggle against the rising cost of housing. In the period 1917–20 they also joined in a wave of strikes and, allied with FOCH and other working-class organizations, in the Workers Assembly on National Nutrition (AOAN). AOAN demanded that President Sanfuentes introduce property and income taxes, free meals for schoolchildren, minimum wage legislation, and government regulation of food prices. When AOAN pressed its demands and strike activity continued, the Congress first passed a residence law aimed at the anarchists and then granted the president emergency powers. The president declared a state of siege in Santiago and Valparaíso, the first use of the state of siege authority since 1894.

In Magallanes, the rapid expansion of the meat-packing and sheep-ranching industry after 1910 had been accompanied by episodic violent protests and labor conflicts. Confrontations between workers and employers in Puerto Natales in 1919, characterized as an "occupation of the city" by government authorities, left numerous dead, wounded, and jailed among the workers. Business interests organized vigilantes (*guardias blancas*) to restore order. Coal miners in the region also declared strikes, exacerbating the tension between government authorities and the labor movement. Into 1920 the *Federación Obrera de Magallanes* continued the battle for higher wages and better working conditions on the Patagonian pampa and southern islands. The year began with a strike of port workers in Punta Arenas, followed by another strike at the Loreto coal mine, then by workers at the Calcutta and Fariña noodle factory. Conflicts persisted through May in various sectors; in July 1920, troops in Punta Arenas shot down striking workers after first setting fire to their union building, giving title to Carlos Vega Delgado's detailed account of this tragedy in *La massacre en la Federación Obrera de Magallanes*. Worsened by a lengthy strike in the coal fields near Concepción, the political and economic situation seemed on verge of breakdown.

Throughout the country, security forces attacked union headquarters, arrested labor leaders, and shut down worker newspapers such as *Verba Roja* and *Acción Directa*. Particular attention was focused on the IWW headquarters in Valparaíso, where police arrested some 200 people. Government-encouraged crowds also attacked the headquarters of the Chilean Federation of Students (FECH), known for its pro-labor stance. While other labor groups and working-class parties (FOCH, POS) also experienced the repression, the elite newspapers and the government highlighted the "antipatriotic" and "subversive" character of anarchism. Viewed as an even more serious threat to established order than FOCH, the anarchists suffered serious repression at the hands of government and were again a special target of the Ibáñez regime from 1927 to 1931.

The anarchists emphasized direct action and rejected alliances with politicians or political parties—in marked contrast to FOCH. They also violently opposed the alliance between FOCH and the Communist party, arguing that the labor movement should not be dependent on any political party or any government. The anarchists' militancy and competition with FOCH or workers' groups supporting the Partido Demócrata occasionally led to physical confrontations and even murder within the labor movement. The coal mines of Lota, in particular, were the scene of bitter conflicts among opposing labor factions.

Unrelated to any of the larger labor organizations, there also developed a "socialist" movement in the far southern province of Magallanes among the workers of the enormous cattle and sheep ranches and meat-processing plants dominated by British capital. Here migrants from Argentina played an important role in the battle against employers, making the Punta Arenas labor organizations in part an extension of the Argentine socialists. Nevertheless, both the Radical party and the Partido Demócrata exercised a certain influence in Magallanes, as did FOCH and to a lesser extent the anarchists. With time the unions in Magallanes ranked among the most aggressive in the Chilean labor movement and were brutally repressed by British firms and Chilean authorities on more than one occasion in the decade 1910–20.

The evolution of a militant labor movement in the context of a political system catering to the aristocratic tastes of Santiago high society had produced an intolerable situation by the early 1920s. Congress repeatedly refused to adopt labor legislation or even to enact piecemeal reforms to ameliorate the worst abuses of labor contractors and unscrupulous employers. Meanwhile, the Chilean economy continued to depend upon export and import duties, particularly revenues from nitrate. Inheritance taxes, as well as taxes on land and capital had practically ceased to exist. A study published in the *Revista Chilena* by Alberto Edwards in 1917 concluded that taxes on land, capital, and income had declined from 18 percent of government revenue in 1880 to almost nothing in 1913.

The economic crisis precipitated by the outbreak of World War I led to reintroduction of a small "temporary" income tax on public employees and to an inheritance tax. These measures raised the proportion of government revenue derived from internal taxes to almost 10 percent. As soon as new economic relations with the Allies, especially the United States, produced an economic upswing in 1916, property tax rates declined, and Congress deleted the income tax on public employees; only 4 percent of government revenues came from internal taxes, while 89 percent originated in export taxes (61.5%) and import duties (27.1%). Five years after publication of Edwards' study, Raul Simón, later an Ibáñez adviser, concluded in an article entitled "Our Financial Situation" that "the war of [1879] gave us a military victory that subsequent governments converted into a diplomatic and financial defeat." Noting the debilitating inflation that devalued Chilean currency by more than 70 percent between 1880 and 1922, Simón called for new taxes on imports and proportionate increases in other taxes to replace the disproportionate dependence on export duties. But the Congress had no more intention of taxing landowners, industrialists, and property owners to finance the nation's development than it did of dealing effectively with the social question. Yet unlike the political conflicts and civil wars of the nineteenth century, the political strife of the 1920s would not be limited to intra-elite factionalism, nor could temporary political pacts resolve the pressing socioeconomic and political exigencies. Still, the dominant political parties and most important social institutions, including the Catholic Church, avoided addressing directly the profound changes occurring in Chilean society.

With the exception of a small number of progressive churchmen, the leadership of the Catholic Church reinforced the prejudices of conservative interests. In the first decade of the century the Chilean archbishop even attacked popular education and universal suffrage, while senators blamed the tide of labor protests upon "the campaign for compulsory public education that represents the wave of socialism threatening to overwhelm us." These attitudes hardly portended great hope for the future in a country barely 38 percent literate and where, in the capital city, fewer than one-third of the population aged five to fifteen were enrolled in schools.

Despite the poverty and illiteracy of the masses, the physical modernization and beautification of Santiago, Valparaíso, and other leading cities allowed the well-to-do to immerse themselves in a charming, comfortable, even pretentious lifestyle. The modernity and elegance of certain parts of Santiago, Valparaíso, or Viña del Mar contrasted markedly with the continued backwardness of much of the country and the squalor of urban slums, or *conventillos*. Social life for the wealthy centered in the aristocratic social clubs, the racing season, the opera, weekly or biweekly strolls along the Alameda between Cochrane and Ejército streets, or outings in fancy carriages in the exclusive Parque Cousiño. In the words of one Chilean historian of the period, "These outings represented an imitation of the customs of the times of the Spanish nobility in El Retiro, the French in the Bois de Boulogne or the wealthy bourgeoisie in Buenos Aires in the wide Avenida Alvear." For a theatre-box (*palco*) at the *teatro municipal* the affluent paid 1000, 5000, even 20,000 pesos. These *palcos* served as meeting places of the political factions, for as much political activity went on at the theater, the opera, and the social clubs as in the Congress, which often simply formalized decisions made at social affairs.

The "good families" were few, and for them Santiago was a small world turning on the axis of the "high life." The society pages of the newspapers avidly reported the *vida social* of the elite and the goings and comings of the guests at the artistic or literary circles patronized by aristocratic women of the capital. Chile was governed by gentlemen who valued civility, tradition, and lineage—but who could also accept new blood and new money into their ranks when need be. Summer vacations at a country estate or near Valparaíso, trips to Europe where their sons and daughters were educated, and competition among the damsels to stay abreast of European fashions rounded out the good life for the masters of Chile.

For most Chileans another reality prevailed. More than half of all deaths recorded in 1913 were of infants and children under five years of age. The infant mortality rate more than tripled that of the United States, or the United Kingdom, and significantly exceeded the rates in Egypt, Mauritius, Japan, Argentina, and even Mexico. Children from eight to fifteen years old represented from 10–40 percent of the workers in many of the industries established since the 1880s. They labored under apalling health and safety conditions for meager pay. Historian Jorge Rojas Flores describes in *Los niños cristaleros*, for example, "the glass dust, the faulty ventilation, the humidity, the heat, the accidents (cuts, burns, mutilation by machines), and the dehydration . . . that put the children at risk" in Santiago's National Glass Factory and other glass manufacturers, where children made up 25–30 percent of the labor force from the early 1900s until 1930. Despite Chile's participation in the International Labor Organization and signing the conventions on child labor after World War I, in 1936 a worker delegate to the Pan American Labor Conference would still reveal that "to the venomous lead fumes are added the infernal heat in the factory, the fans don't function; they are for show when the labor inspectors appear. . . . [W]ater is not brought to the workers and the youngsters must put up with heat and thirst for eight hour shifts. If they can't resist and leave work, they are beaten by the foremen. . . . If they complain their wages are reduced or they are fired." Conditions in breweries, sugar and textile industries, mines, and the nitrate fields were no better. The "social question" was not abstract; mangled, broken, ill, and desperate discards of the incipient industrial age added pressures for government regulation of industrial relations, for social security and industrial safety legislation, for protection of child and female workers, and for industrial accident insurance.

The oligarchy that dominated Congress responded minimally to these demands before the 1920s. Revolutionary labor organizations and political parties would up the ante after World War I. Chile was not alone with its child labor force in the dawning of the industrial age; European and North American factories and mines had set the example. Even so, photos in the worker press of children and women strikers who had joined anarchist and communist-oriented labor organizations added a special dimension to the struggle for "social laws" that only bore fruit after the military coups of 1924–25 and implementation of the Labor Code imposed by decree in 1931.

The emergence of the social question as Chile's most pressing national problem coincided with truly dramatic demographic, technological, and economic changes in Chilean society. Population movements to the south and north and out of the rural areas into the cities intensified the trends initiated in the middle decades of the nineteenth century. From an essentially rural nation of 2 million people in 1880, Chile became an increasingly urban country of over 3.7 million in 1920 and of 4.2 million ten years later. Santiago's population mushroomed from 275,000 residents in 1900 to 700,000 by 1930, while Valparaíso reached a population of 200,000 in the same year. By 1930 almost one-fourth of Chile's population lived in Santiago or Valparaíso.

More important even than the advancing urbanization of the population, Chilean society and the economy became truly national with the extension of rail lines, telegraph networks, and steamship service and the evolution of a national labor market. Not only did the population of the provinces of Tarapacá and Antofagasta, which more than doubled between 1885 and 1920, became increasingly Chilean,—in 1885, 40 percent "foreign"; in 1920, 11 percent; in 1930, 8 percent—but the mobility of labor also created a nationally integrated labor market. The periodic ups and downs of the nitrate industry, with the associated ebbs and flows of workers between the northern deserts, coastal towns, and southern provinces, contributed to increasing articulation between the country's regional economies. In a sense, though the patterns of trade characteristic of the mid-nineteenth century still prevailed, regionalism itself declined as a meaningful political force. In search of relief or work, workers shifted from southern agriculture to the northern mines or nitrate districts, then with recessions in the north, migrated to the ports of the *norte chico*, Valparaíso, Santiago, or into the central valley and beyond.

The longitudinal railroad that by 1915 connected Puerto Montt to Coquimbo linked the urban markets and the northern mineral districts to the central valley and southern producers. Steamship lines and the transverse, privately owned railroads of the nitrate regions made Chile's most dynamic economic sectors, along with the urban centers, the most important markets for Chilean agriculture and industry. With the exception of the northern railroads and the trans-Andean line, the Chilean state controlled the railroad system and deliberately extended it north and south with strategic and developmental, rather than strictly commercial, objectives in mind. Cheap freight rates subsidized Chilean agriculture. In particular the railroad's penetration south allowed greatly expanded shipments of cattle, wheat, wine, lumber, and processed goods from the southern provinces to Santiago, Valparaíso, and north by ship to the nitrate and mining districts. This encouraged increased cultivation and modernization of southern agriculture, even as the seasonal competition for labor and hints of labor activism motivated southern landowners to mechanize the harvest.

The government also used the railroad, in times of recession, as a safety valve to funnel unemployed workers south or, in good times, to siphon labor north to nitrate and copper production centers. Fearing the concentration of unemployed workers in the northern ports, authorities issued free rail passes so that the unemployed could seek work or temporary quarters with relatives in other parts of the country. This policy somewhat ameliorated the immediate danger of a large-scale uprising, but it also spread throughout the entire country, in extremely visible human terms, the effects of each nitrate recession. Creation of the government employment service (*Servicio de Colocaciones*), in response to the recession at the outset of World War I, further nationalized the labor market. In its efforts to place unemployed nitrate workers in agriculture, public works, or industry, the Servicio de Colocaciones soon found that landowners often rejected nitrate hands who, in any case, resisted the low wages and poor working conditions on the haciendas. Labor Department officials became accustomed to seeing complaints by landowners that nitrate workers placed in agriculture "stirred up" the *inquilinos,* refused to eat the food provided by the farm's administrator, or simply ate a meal and left. Thus, integration of the labor market began to erode the extensive traditional authority of the hacendados.

Unlike a true economic enclave, the nitrate economy spurred national economic integration. Though foreign investors remitted many of the industry's profits abroad, operation of the industry created markets for Chilean agriculture and lumber, coal, and processing industries and induced development of service and support activities. In turn, Chilean industries developed product lines intended as inputs for other domestic manufacturers as well as supplying consumer demands. Coastal shipping greatly expanded to provision the northern districts, while tax revenues from exports and imports yielded resources for extensive public works, modernization of the military, public education, and other government expenses. In addition, after 1900 Chilean capital made steady gains in the nitrate industry, and by 1920 national capital controlled over 50 percent of the nitrate sector.

If an enclave could be said to exist in the Chilean economy in the mid-1920s—in a political and social sense, only agriculture would qualify. The extreme concentration of good agricultural land, especially in the central valley, kept 60 to 75 percent of the region's rural labor force culturally isolated on the vast haciendas that dominated the countryside. In 1924 only 2,650 rural estates (2.7% of all farms) contained almost 80 percent of the agricultural land in the central valley. On these large estates the resident labor force remained at the mercy of the landowners for access to land, housing, and daily sustenance. Their votes belonged to the landowners who used them to install themselves in the Congress and to maintain the prevailing system of rural land tenure as well as to exert their influence more generally on Chilean national life. Congressmen from the provinces depended for their election upon landowners who mobilized their peons to vote and controlled the counting of ballots in the municipality. Frequently the most important landowners of a district virtually "owned" its congressional seat. In the 1920s the initial penetration by FOCH or political agents into the rural areas challenged this arrangement, but not until the 1950s and 1960s would political reforms destroy the hacienda as a political enclave that separated tenant labor from the national community.

In economic terms, however, the Chilean haciendas did not constitute an enclave but had participated in international commerce ever since the colonial era. The economic evolution of Chile from the late nineteenth century through the depression of the 1930s more completely incorporated agriculture into the national economy. Domestic markets became the primary consumers of the countryside's wheat, livestock, dairy products, lumber, fruits, and processed foodstuffs. This meant that domestic economic conditions, rather than European, North American, or Australian markets, became the primary determinants of economic opportunities for Chile's agricultural interests. Rapid urbanization and the population growth in the northern provinces also pushed food prices upward. Higher food prices exacerbated the social question facing the country and created pressures for political regulation of the prices of food and basic necessities to mitigate the decline in real wages received by urban labor between 1890 and 1914. After 1932 efforts to retain the hacienda system and at the same time to pacify the urban labor force by regulating retail food prices would produce a curious political "arrangement" (see Chapter 8), which ensured the continued exploitation of the rural labor force. Such efforts did nothing, however, to increase production and productivity in Chilean agriculture.

National economic integration accompanied by political immobility and the intensifying social question concerned not only Chilean intellectuals but also leading Chilean military officers. The army's professionalization under Prussian leadership instilled in it a new sense of nationalism and a belief that its duty included regeneration of the country. Military writers like Carlos Soto Alvarez (1905) and Jorge Boonen Rivera (1917) emphasized the role of the armed forces in teaching patriotism and acting as agents of order and progress. Boonen Rivera went so far as to suggest that the army should be directly responsible for the revitalization of the nation. Two years later Captain Tobías Barros claimed that the army was the personification of the national ideal and that through active political intervention it must act to prevent further disintegration of the national situation. By 1921–22 some military leaders argued that the army should participate in all government policymaking. In 1922 an army captain published a speech delivered at the military club, in which he urged the army to exercise political influence to unify the diverse forces of the nation, to restore morality to public life, and to end the parliamentary chaos and immobility. According to this officer, the army alone of all Chilean institutions could rise above petty self-interest to save the nation.

The army had every reason to be concerned with Chile's social crisis. Political leaders had constantly called upon the armed forces to repress the mounting number of strikes and demonstrations during the first two decades of the twentieth century. A compulsory military service law (1900) brought large numbers of illiterate recruits to both army and navy, since the well-to-do generally managed to avoid the draft. Both services created primary schools to provide instruction to their personnel. Military service brought thousands of Chileans into a national institution, instructed them in the military's view of patriotism and national history, deployed them in regions far from their homes, and even provided training that could serve them when they left the service. Military schools for machinists, telegraphists, blacksmiths, construction workers, and miners as well as military participation in public works and disaster relief—for example, after the 1906 earthquake at Valparaíso—further engaged the army in "nonmilitary" projects.

Military dissatisfaction with the politics of the parliamentary period and with Chile's seeming economic decline manifested itself early in the twentieth century. In 1907 officers of the Santiago garrison established a "Liga Militar" as a lobby to secure better conditions and benefits for the army. Four years later leaders of the Liga Militar broached the subject of a military coup with Gonzalo Bulnes Pinto—son, grandson, and nephew of former presidents. Bulnes refused to go through with the plans for such a *golpe,* but not before the Liga Militar had expressed its opinions on matters ranging from government corruption, public education, crime, and economic policy to the need for increased benefits for the armed forces. Another abortive military movement in 1915, aimed at placing in power "a strong government able to end the political anarchy preventing the progress of the nation"; and in 1919 still another conspiracy among high-ranking officers to "avoid political chaos" and end the "dangers of communism" failed to end the parliamentary regime.

Especially disconcerting to the new generation of professional officers was the continual intervention by congressmen in the process of military promotions and assignments. Likewise, the apparent congressional favoritism of the more aristocratic,

British-influenced navy over the middle-class officer corps of the army created inter-service rivalries and frustrations. Gradually the military, and especially a group of pro-fessionally oriented army officers, resolved to end the regime of *politiquería* which they believed was debasing the army and weakening the fatherland.

World War I set in motion economic and political forces that doomed the parliamentary regime in Chile and ushered in the revival of copper as a principal source of foreign ex-change and government revenues. It also shifted Chile's international economic orien-tation toward the United States and away from Britain and Germany. Between 1900 and 1914, American investments in Chile increased from approximately $5 million to almost $200 million—almost two-thirds the value of British investments in Chile. In particular, American investors acquired nitrate and mining properties, especially cop-per and iron. By the end of World War I (1918) American investors controlled over 87 percent by value of Chilean copper production, which increased fourfold from 31.4 million pesos to 132.8 million pesos during the course of the war. Modern technology, which allowed economic mining of low-copper content ore at El Teniente in Rancagua and the giant open-pit mine at Chuquicamata in Antofagasta province, along with other deposits in the environs of Copiapó and near Santiago, resulted in good profits from the Chilean mines for the Chile Exploration Company, American Smelting, Ken-necott Copper, and Braden Copper Mining, among other companies. United States Steel and Bethlehem Steel also established themselves in Chile prior to World War I and expanded operations during the war. For the first time commerce with the United States exceeded 50 percent by value of Chilean foreign trade; by 1930 United States cap-ital would account for some 70 percent of all foreign investment in Chile.

   This fundamental reorientation of the Chilean economy toward the United States in-cluded large-scale introduction of American technicians, capital, machinery, and cul-tural influence into a country where North Americans had previously exerted little in-fluence. Indeed, support by American diplomats for President Balmaceda during the civil war of 1891 and, earlier, Secretary of State Blaine's inept efforts to mediate the War of the Pacific had made Chile's relations with the United States less than cordial. Now the rapid "Americanization" of critical sectors of the economy, the intensified economic relations with the United States, and the latter's role in the termination of World War I meant the gradual replacement of British dominance of Chile's economy by that of the United States. It also brought a pervasive influx of North American consumer goods, popular culture, and prejudices.

   The outbreak of the European war brought disaster to the Chilean economy, as it pit-ted Chile's two leading trading partners, England and Germany, against each other. Dis-ruption of shipping lanes and diversion of British and German shipping to wartime du-ties drastically reduced nitrate exports in 1914 and early 1915. Thousands of workers lost their jobs; subsequently nitrate companies and the railroads cut wages between 10 and 15 percent. Government subsidies to finance stockpiling allowed continued pro-duction at a reduced level, and thus avoided a complete collapse. Nevertheless, nitrate production declined by 60 percent, and in Tarapacá alone over half of the 23,500 nitrate workers lost their jobs. In the city of Antofagasta *ollas del pobre,* the equivalent of soup lines, fed more than 4,500 people a day. By late 1914 more than 48,000 people had left the nitrate region. Many Peruvians and Bolivians returned to Tacna or farther north to their native lands; Chileans dispersed southward. In the rest of Chile bankruptcies, runs on banks, and economic contraction resulted from the nitrate depression. In addition, the early war years led to shortages of consumer goods and raw materials for Chilean in-dustries resulting in a reduction in economic activity and generalized price increases.

Quickly, however, Allied control of the seas permitted Chilean minerals to reach European and United States markets. Demand in the United States for Chilean nitrate and copper contributed to an economic upswing. American bankers followed United States investors. With official American entry into the war in 1917, demand for Chilean raw materials, especially nitrate, more than doubled from the 1915–16 levels. Though German development of synthetic nitrates during the war presaged even worse problems for Chile at the war's termination, a temporary boom permitted a renewed splurge of public works, road construction, port modernization, and political patronage. Taking advantage of wartime demand, selected Chilean industries such as cement, textiles, and sugar refineries responded well to opportunities for import substitution. At the war's end, however, traditional industries still accounted for most of the value of industrial production, with food (44%), beverages (5.2%), textiles (4.7%), tobacco (4.7%), clothing and footwear (18.7%), and wood and wood products (6.5%) contributing over 80 percent by value of industrial output.

The temporary wartime boom ended almost as quickly as it began. German policymakers prohibited imports of Chilean nitrate to protect the manufacturers of synthetics. American and European markets found themselves with a temporary overstock— and a developing synthetic nitrate industry of their own. Though prices for copper remained high for another year, by 1919 the nitrate industry had entered another severe depression. For the second time in five years massive unemployment threatened the northern regions, and the economic side effects afflicted the rest of the country.

During the wartime prosperity Minister of Interior Eliodoro Yáñez decreed the creation of a *voluntary* conciliation and arbitration system to deal with labor conflict. With the authority of this decree the government intervened "informally" in several strikes to procure negotiated settlements between 1918 and 1920. The Yáñez decree represented an important recognition by the Chilean government of the necessity for establishing a system for managing industrial relations, but government authority remained quite limited due to the Congress' refusal to legislate in the field of industrial relations. As labor conflict intensified during 1919 and 1920, along with the postwar national depression, the social question became the major national issue before the presidential elections. With a paragon of the old elite opposing a self-declared reformer for the presidency, with strikes breaking out all over the country, and with electoral violence at a new peak, Chile appeared headed for another civil war—this time an explicit confrontation between the political and economic oligarchy and the supporters of reform. The events following the 1920 elections, however, made the frustrations and aspirations of the Chilean military, rather than the new President or the Congress, the real key to Chilean development in the next decade.

Amidst the post–World War I economic crisis, Chile faced a presidential election in which one of the candidates, Arturo Alessandri Palma, proclaimed "I want to be a threat to the reactionary spirits, a threat to those who resist all just and necessary reforms." His opponent, Luis Barros Borgoño, represented the tradition of Santiago's political families. Alessandri, an upper-middle-class lawyer who had considerable political experience in the Congress and the Senate, carried his campaign to "the people." His incendiary speeches attacked the oligarchy and promised to alleviate the misery of the working classes. Accompanied by a high level of violence and intimidation, the election results proved so close that Congress turned the matter over to a "tribunal of honor" to sort out the charges of fraud and to verify the credentials of electors as well as vote totals. As Alessandri's supporters feared that Barros Borgoño might "steal" the election in Congress, they carried out demonstrations in Iquique, Antofagasta, Santiago, Valparaíso, and Concepción, despite Alessandri's agreement to accept the decision of the tribunal of honor.

Three weeks after the election the war minister, Ladislao Errázuriz, mobilized the armed forces and sent army and navy units north to meet a supposed threat from Bolivia. The mobilization itself proved to be a greater threat to the soldiers than the illusory Bolivian invasion. Disease spread among ill-fed troops who lacked munitions and other supplies. Rumor suggested that the war minister and his associates were profiteering in provisioning the troops. Others believed that the mobilization was a political move to attempt to divert national attention from the recent presidential elections or even to remove military officers who supported Alessandri from Santiago. Although the electoral tribunal gave the election and the presidency to Alessandri, anger over their role as political pawns further heightened the professional officers' discontent with parliamentary politics.

President Alessandri governed Chile from 1920 to 1924 in the face of hostility and obstructionism from the Congress. Ministerial changes, threats to delay budget and tax bills, and failures to authorize the military garrison to remain in Santiago—in short, all the now traditional parliamentary practices for the frustration of presidential programs—continued despite the economic crisis and the spread of labor conflicts. Congress refused to pass the paternalistic social laws sponsored by the Conservative party or those introduced by the Alessandri administration. And only forty days after assuming office, the president, notwithstanding his proclaimed commitment to reform and social justice, used troops brutally to repress workers' movements. At the nitrate *oficina* San Gregorio a massacre of workers in early 1921 added still another group of martyrs to the northern proletariat's struggle for decent treatment by the nitrate industry and recognition of labor rights by the Chilean state.

Even when the president managed to obtain a Liberal majority in the congressional elections of 1924, he could not unite his supposed supporters or persuade them to act on the critical legislation delayed for over four years. Alessandri's use of police and military at the polls to "maintain order" marred the legitimacy of the electoral victory in any case. At the same time it further involved the armed forces in immediate political questions. By mid-1924, with government salaries in arrears, a mounting budget deficit, rampant inflation, and failure to deliver on even the most modest of his campaign promises, Alessandri supported legislation to provide a salary for congressmen.

In August 1924 Congress dropped its consideration of urgent legislation for creation of a national bank, for social welfare laws, for military appropriations, and for other pressing matters, in order to deal with what many judged to be an unconstitutional proposal for it to vote its members a salary, or *dieta*. On an afternoon in early September when Congress appeared ready to approve the particulars of the salary measures, a group of more than fifty junior officers filed ominously into the gallery of the Congress. Newspapers in the capital the next day reported that the government intended to discipline the officers, though no regulation prohibited military personnel from attending congressional sessions. In support of their colleagues a larger group of officers attended an evening session of the Senate, where they heard legislators criticize their behavior and then were asked to leave the building by the minister of war.

Agitation within the army led high-ranking generals to inform President Alessandri that any disciplinary action taken against the junior officers might lead to a collective reaction by the army. Alessandri downplayed the incidents, draping them in the letter of the law that allowed military personnel to attend congressional sessions except when military matters were being debated. The matter could not be disposed of so easily. On September 4, 1924, some 400 lieutenants and captains gathered at the Club Militar, to "strengthen the unity and comradeship among the elements of the army in these difficult times the armed forces are experiencing." The officers roundly attacked the minister of war, present at the meeting, and applauded General Luis Altamirano's words of support for the junior officers.

The next day high-ranking military officers presented a list of "petitions" to President Alessandri. These included action on the budget, social security laws, income tax legislation, social laws, payment of back salaries to public employees, and reformed pension, salary, and promotion schedules for the military. In addition the officers demanded the ouster of three ministers who had insulted them publicly in the Congress. According to one account, Alessandri had met the night before with certain officers and told them: "Request in writing the dispatch of specific projects [de tales y cuales proyectos]; I will sponsor them in Congress and close the Congress if they do not approve them." Alessandri's brother subsequently denied this account; but whatever the precise details, President Alessandri knew in advance about the military movement and had met with representatives of the protesting officers during the evening of September 4. On September 7, Alessandri vetoed the congressional salary bill and invited General Altamirano to head the cabinet; one day later Congress passed all the laws contained in the military petition. The military junta, though its petitions had been approved, refused to disband. A week later Alessandri resigned and left for Italy.

Prior to September 5, 1924, senior officers of the Chilean army and opposition politicians had seriously considered a coup against Alessandri who, according to the conspirators, had unconstitutionally intervened in the March 1924 elections, usurped power by dictatorial means, and dishonored the army. This conspiracy, organized by a secret society called TEA (tenacity, enthusiasm, abnegation), involved certain conservative elements of the armed forces in alliance with the opposition to Alessandri. When the movement of September 5, 1924, occurred, however, junior officers precipitated an essentially leaderless protest that evolved into a military coup. The more conservative, high-ranking officers—such as Luis Altamirano and Juan Pablo Bennett, who ultimately appeared as the leaders of the government junta—supported the junior officers in their professional demands such as for an improved salary schedule, for broadening of promotion opportunities, and for less political meddling in internal army affairs. They did not, however, support entirely the rest of the petitions on the list the younger officers presented to President Alessandri.

President Alessandri's resignation left the junta with no constitutional authority; the officers decided to request that Alessandri ask Congress for permission to absent himself from the country, and to accord him full presidential honors on his departure. When the President sought asylum in the American embassy, the junta faced the dilemma of devising an interim instrument for governing the country. Congress refused to accept Alessandri's resignation but voted him permission to leave the country for six months. The military junta then closed Congress and accepted Alessandri's resignation with the expectation of forming a provisional government. Behind the scenes, divisions within the armed forces made consolidation of the military government an impossibility. The junta announced a return to civilian politics and seemed to support the candidacy of Ladislao Errázuriz, the ultraconservative minister who had sent the armed forces on a wild goose chase to the northern deserts in 1920; but a group of officers headed by Ibáñez and Marmaduque Grove led a coup to "show . . . that the oligarchs are not masters of Chile." The golpistas called upon Alessandri to return and reassume the presidency. As a condition for his return, Alessandri demanded a return to civilian government, creation of a constituent assembly to consider constitutional reform, and return of the armed forces to their normal duties.

Alessandri returned to Santiago in March 1925 and resumed the duties of the presidency. Bowing to the influence of the armed forces and especially his war minister, Carlos Ibáñez, he failed to reconvene the Congress. In April, Alessandri named a commission to develop procedures for selecting members to a constitutional convention. When no satisfactory solution emerged, Alessandri commissioned a subcommittee to write a draft constitution for subsequent approval by plebiscite. From late May to July 22, the subcommittee worked on the constitutional proposal; in August a national plebiscite approved the new constitution under which Chile would be governed until 1973.

The new constitution shifted the balance of power from Congress to the executive. Included among its reforms were direct popular election of the president, an independent electoral tribunal to review election results, and prohibitions against congressmen serving as ministers or government employees. The presidential term was extended to six years with no immediate re-election permitted. Congress retained important budgetary authority and could override vetos, but it lost the traditional instruments used during the parliamentary era to immobilize executive policymaking—such as control over the cabinet, authority to prevent collection of taxes, and refusal to enact an annual budget.

Notwithstanding a shift of authority toward the executive, the new constitution officially recognized the role of political parties in national politics. By providing that the president and members of the House of Deputies and the Senate had overlapping and different terms of office, the constitution practically assured that no president could come into office in control of the legislative branch of government. Another provision in the constitution assigned the Congress the responsibility to choose the president "from among the citizens who have received the two highest relative numbers of votes"—if no candidate received a majority of the popular vote. In Chile's multiparty system, this provision gave Congress considerable leverage in "preconfirmation" bargaining with the two candidates who got the most votes in presidential elections. This leverage would prove significant time and time again in constraining or compromising the action of in-coming Chilean presidents. Thus while the 1925 constitution did decrease congressional authority and remove some of the traditional instruments whereby the Congress had controlled executive initiatives, it did not emasculate the Congress or eliminate its critical role and that of the political parties in Chilean politics.

Shortly after Alessandri returned to Santiago, he presided over still another massacre of northern workers. At La Coruña, in June 1925, soldiers machine-gunned hundreds of workers, destroyed their living quarters with field artillery, and brutally murdered a number of prisoners and wounded. A leading socialist, historian, and politician, Alejandro Chelén Rojas, coldly notes that "San Gregorio in 1921 and Coruña in 1925 stamped with workers' blood the administration of the caudillo who [instead of] a 'threat to reactionary spirits' was [a threat] for the dispossessed that had so many hopes for his government." Other historians have noted that Alessandri attempted to prevent Ibáñez from using force against the workers, but Ibáñez ignored Alessandri's orders, just as he had rejected the president's order to resign his ministerial post before the presidential elections. This interpretation ignores that Alessandri had close relations with British diplomats in Chile who heavily influenced the decision to send troops to confront the labor unrest and strikes in the nitrate region in 1925. It also ignores that Alessandri enthusiastically congratulated General Florentino de la Guarda immediately after repression of the workers and the "clean-up" operation that followed. In the words of Chilean historian Alejandro Soto Cardenas, in a study based on exhaustive research in British archives (*Influencia Británica en el salitre, Origen, naturaleza y decadencia*):

[T]he Chilean government, headed until October of 1925 by Arturo Alessandri, did everything possible to satisfy British demands tending to impose law and order in the nitrate camps in 1925. It closed the worker press, it detained labor leaders in the nitrate works and the ports, in Santiago and Valparaíso, it sent a regiment and various warships to the nitrate ports; it approved the military action taken at La Coruña, that ended in spilling blood and the embarkation of workers in Chilean warships who were thrown into the sea near the Juan Fernández Islands.

When Ibáñez published a public letter to Alessandri on October 1, 1925, explaining his refusal to resign, including his role as "chief of the revolution," Alessandri resigned the presidency for the second time. Before resigning, he appointed Luis Barros Borgoño—his opponent in the presidential elections of 1920—minister of the interior, and thus Barros Borgoño was the vice president after Alessandri's departure.

In the face of Alessandri's resignation, Ibáñez declared he would renounce his own candidacy if the major parties could agree upon a compromise candidate and avoid the spectacle of a complete return to politics as usual. The labor movement and leftist parties refused to comply, fomenting strikes and supporting their own candidate for the presidency, José Santos Salas. The traditional parties selected Emiliano Figueroa Larraín, a nondescript politician from a good family.

Figueroa Larraín easily won the election but failed to implement the spirit or the letter of the new constitution. Sensing his inability to deal with the realities facing the country or to control the minister of interior, Carlos Ibáñez, Figueroa Larraín requested permission to take a leave of absence from the country. This left affairs of state in the hands of Ibáñez. In May 1927, Figueroa Larraín officially resigned, whereupon Ibáñez had himself elected president in a carefully controlled election. Ibáñez obtained more than 222,000 of the slightly more than 230,000 votes cast.

Ibáñez's assumption of the presidency was blessed with far more auspicious economic developments than those confronting Alessandri in 1920. By 1924–25 international demand for nitrate had again strengthened. An all-time employment record, with more than 60,000 workers in the nitrate fields, brought renewed prosperity to the Chilean economy. Despite a recession in 1926–27 that briefly interrupted recovery, the final years of the decade saw a major boom in Chilean nitrate exports. Indeed, Ibáñez and his chief economic adviser, Pablo Ramírez, could take credit for the economic recovery that put most of the 70,000 unemployed in mid-1926 back to work by 1928. In the meantime, police monitored political and union activity and reported to Ibáñez and his ministers on the speeches or meetings of congressmen, politicians, and union leaders who seemed to oppose the regime. Reorganization of the national police (*carabineros*) under the minister of defense provided Ibáñez with a new, direct instrument for control of the opposition and a counterpoise to would-be challengers within the army.

Expanded production of copper added to the government's sources of revenue and to the economic recovery. So, too, did a large-scale influx of foreign capital in the form of private investment and loans. Total foreign investment in the country increased from $723 million in 1925 to more than $1 billion in 1930—exceeding domestic investment in both mining and industry. Taking advantage of increasing government revenues and the inflows of private foreign capital, the Ibáñez government embarked upon the largest public works program in Chilean history. Docks and port works, roads, sewage systems, water systems, and irrigation projects dotted the landscape from north to south. Construction of public buildings and paving of urban streets altered the faces of the nation's principal cities and employed thousands of workers. Impressive expansion and reform of the educational system meant that in a decade Chile's schools had doubled their capacity. In an effort to encourage industry, the government pushed protective tariffs through Congress and founded the Institute for Industrial Credit. Previously the emphasis upon real estate as collateral for loans had seriously restricted access by domestic industrialists to investment capital. Industry responded to the new incentives with increased output and even some diversification.

This flurry of economic activity distracted most Chileans from the political repression of the Ibáñez regime. Also obscured was the growing indebtedness as a result of the large loans the government had contracted to finance the expansion of public sector activity. After years of sterile parliamentary debate and indifference, Ibáñez even managed to squeeze legislation on agricultural colonization and "land reform" out of the Congress in 1928. Establishment of the Caja de Colonización Agrícola as an agency to administer land purchases and subdivision of large estates marked an important first step, at least symbolically, in dealing with the structural defects of the Chilean agrarian economy. Despite the Caja's limited activity, even this innovation was rabidly denounced by leading Chilean landowners.

In additional ways also the Ibáñez government represented a break with the parliamentary era. Explicit concern with a positive role of the state in encouraging industrialization, technological progress, and administrative reforms to consolidate and regularize procedures in the public administration evidenced the passage from a predominantly rural, oligarchical society to a modernizing urban polity. Educational reforms, including establishment of national standards for professional and technical degrees from the private and public universities, indicated the gradual emergence of nonaristocratic, universalistic norms in recruitment to an expanding civil service. Technicians and middle-class professionals staffed growing ministries and public agencies previously manned overwhelmingly through political patronage by the traditional parties. A growing middle class challenged the traditional "political class" for control of the state; the "social question" and a changing socio-economic structure made restoration of the parliamentary republic unlikely. In 1931 intellectuals and professional administrators in the Labor Department produced the Labor Code which incorporated the "social laws" of 1924 and created an elaborate framework for a modern industrial relations system. The Labor Code of 1931 served as the foundation for Chilean industrial relations for the next four decades.

Adoption of the "social laws" of 1924 regulating unionization, labor contracts, cooperatives, and social security had been followed by confusion. Following civil code tradition, all legislation required implementing provisions. These came slowly. Government officials and employers interpreted the laws pushed through Congress by the military coup quite differently from place to place. The Labor Code of 1931 consolidated existing legislation, including the "social laws" of 1924, and added regulations concerning agricultural workers and domestics, both of whom had been excluded from the earlier legislation. The code also established a national system of labor courts, as well as institutions to administer mandatory collective bargaining and arbitration (*juntas de conciliación*).

In general the Labor Code created a highly paternalistic and authoritarian system of government-worker relations. The code limited worker petitions and strikes to individual firms and restricted severely the activity of union federations. It gave authority to the government to order a "return to work" whenever a strike or lockout endangered public health or the economic or social life of the nation. Any labor conflict that failed to meet the rigorous requirements specified in the code could be declared illegal, and the unions were liable for any damages or losses under such circumstances. In practice these restrictive regulations meant that from 1932 on, illegal strikes outnumbered legal ones by a wide margin.

Notwithstanding the Labor Code's defects from the perspective of labor, it represented formal recognition by the Chilean state of the right of workers to organize, to petition employers for improved working conditions, to strike, and to have the work place regulated by an official agency—the Labor Department. Employers now had the obligation to enter into written contracts with workers, to bargain with unions, to obey labor legislation and social security laws and, more generally, to adopt a more limited view of the privileges of proprietorship. The Labor Code ended the classical liberal view of unrestricted property rights. The resistance of employer associations and landowners to the code's provisions testified to their awareness of its profound implications. Above all else, the Labor Code meant that the state recognized its role as an active agent in regulating class conflict and in institutionalizing procedures for managing the social question.

Ibáñez did not undertake these reforms out of benevolence or a desire to win the support of the labor movement. As with labor codes in Brazil under Vargas or later in Peronist Argentina, the Labor Code was seen as a means to control the labor movement, to subordinate it to the state, and to cleanse it of leftists and Marxists. Ibáñez used the police and army to persecute FOCH, the Communist party, and the anarchists. He also exiled leaders of the major political parties who objected to his restriction of civil liberties, to his intimidation of the press, his overt manipulation of Congress, and his disdain for the old politics. Many conservative Chileans, to whom the fascist-corporative governments of Primo de Rivera in Spain or Benito Mussolini in Italy seemed to offer a welcome relief from liberal democracy, fully supported Ibáñez's repression of popular movements and organizations. They applauded government officials who praised fascism in Italy and the ability of fascist regimes to direct economic growth and to curtail the corruption of liberal democracy. They also appreciated the regime's emphasis on work, order, and discipline. Ibáñez seemed to offer a version of the Portalian state adapted to the conditions of the twentieth century. Initially, many middle-class reformers also supported Ibáñez due to his emphasis on economic modernization, industrialization, agricultural colonization, and labor legislation.

An explicitly authoritarian, corporative orientation combined with a commitment to reform the apparatus of the Chilean state led both to significant policy innovations and lamentable abuses. Ibáñez transformed Congress into a captive, generally compliant assembly, thereby eliminating the central axis of traditional politics. He also created a government-controlled organization, the Republican Confederation for Civic Action, or CRAC, to replace existing labor organizations and the multiplicity of political parties of the pre-1927 period and thus sought to eliminate the influence of traditional and reformist political parties and to control the labor movement in an authoritarian style which later became common among the populist regimes in Latin America. In this effort Ibáñez ultimately failed, but there can be no question that his presidency represented a brief return to the ideals and methods of Portales—a swing of the pendulum away from liberalism and constitutional government. Eschewing "politics" and concentrating upon "cleansing" Chile by "cauterization," in both economic and political policies he established a precedent for another military dictatorship—much more brutal—in the mid-1970s. Like his successors in the 1970s, Ibáñez rejected liberal democracy, detested radicalism, and blamed politics for Chile's decadence.

If in many respects Ibáñez broke with the old order, the dependence of his government programs upon nitrate and copper revenues, along with increased levels of foreign investment and loans, made the regime as vulnerable to fluctuations in international markets as any Chilean administration since 1879. The stock market crash of 1929 soon paralyzed Chile's finances and wreaked havoc on the economy. Government efforts to form a new cartel called the Compañia de Salitre de Chile, or COSACH, in cooperation with the Guggenheim interests, brought criticism from economic nationalists and opponents of the government. It also failed to stem the effects of the depression. The value of copper and nitrate exports declined from over 200 million pesos in 1929 to 18.1 million in 1932; over 50,000 workers lost their jobs in the nitrate fields alone. Imports declined by over 75 percent in the same period, making Chile in this respect the country most seriously affected by the international depression. The government could not service outstanding loans or obtain new lines of credit. In February 1931, Congress extended Ibáñez's emergency powers to deal with the economic crisis; in May, Ibáñez declared he would maintain order by force of arms. Wage cuts for government personnel and the military followed, along with new income taxes, an increase in inheritance taxes, a moratorium on public works, and dismissals of public employees. These economy moves simply worsened the effects of the depression and added to unemployment. In July the government suspended service on the foreign debt in foreign currency—since the country's reserves were practically depleted. The Ibáñez government would fall a month later, but poor harvests in 1931–32 added to the misery.

By late 1931 government programs to disperse the northern unemployed in the agricultural regions or to shelter them in temporary barracks called *albergues* in the urban areas seemed a dreadful failure. The nation simply did not have the resources to provide relief for the thousands of unemployed and their families. Illustrative is the following excerpt from a report by the intendant of Talca to the minister of interior in January 1932:

> Apprised of government plans to begin shortly the distribution of 2000 families of unemployed workers throughout the central and southern provinces, I hasten, with all due respect, to make the following observations. . . .
>
> In Talca, without counting those unregistered by the Secretaría de Bienestar Social, there are more than 5000 unemployed, of which more than 700 along with their families are in the *albergues;* others are camped in emergency shelters along the roads and at the sites of public works, living off the small amount that good-hearted people can supply.
>
> In the countryside the poverty is much worse. The landowners have cut back their work to the minimum. . . . With the lack of capital, poor harvests, and drastic decline in prices, agriculture faces a total collapse. Many have no way to pay salaries, but they give their *inquilinos* milk in the morning and hot meals at noon, though they don't work.
>
> . . . I visited nearby zones some days ago and saw tragedies of hunger and misery that can't be described.
>
> . . . For this reason it seems unlikely to me that the efforts by the government to place the unemployed in agriculture will have any success.

By the end of 1931 the director of the Labor Department reported to the minister of social welfare that "The situation of the unemployed is simply terrible in Iquique, Coquimbo, Ovalle, Calera, Santiago, Talca, and Talcahuano. . . . The city of Santiago is so congested with unemployed—that, with all the efforts we have made, there are an enormous quantity of families that, as in the rest of the Republic, have been violently evicted from their dwellings and live in unhealthy makeshift shelters [*ranchos*]." In the same letter the director noted that the government's cutbacks in public works and rail-

Carlos Ibáñez del Campo, president 1927–1931, 1952–1958. (Courtesy of Chilean Army.)

road activity aggravated the crisis; the latter decision also negatively affected coal production in the Lota region.

The concentration of unemployed in urban areas not only stretched government relief efforts but also threatened public order. Intermittent attempts by the government to eradicate particular *albergues* and disperse more workers into the rural regions met stiff resistance. In turn, industrial and commercial interests in some cities petitioned the government for more protection against "ill-intentioned individuals [*maleantes*] who sought to subvert public order."

Civilian and military opposition to the Ibáñez regime became bolder with the government's apparent weakness. In late July 1931 a "general strike" by professional associations, white-collar workers, and students demanded a return to constitutional government. As the cabinet decided to close all banks to prevent conversion of money into foreign currency and to impose controls on foreign exchange, doctors in Santiago went out on strike and vowed not to resume practice until Ibáñez resigned. Violence in the streets, resurgence of political opposition in all sectors including the military, and the insoluble economic dilemma forced Ibáñez to resign from office on July 26, 1931.

The Congress "elected" under Ibáñez's tutelage next organized an *acusación constitucional*, a combination impeachment proceeding and public trial that denounced the abuses of the dictatorship. The *acusación constitucional* procedure dated from the period after independence and had roots in the colonial *residencias* that examined the performance of colonial officials after they left office. Over the years, this procedure came to be used to impeach incumbent ministers, to obstruct government policy initiatives, and as a way to exact political judgment against ex-presidents and government officials. In his defense Carlos Ibáñez sent Congress a letter from his Argentine exile. He told the legislators:

> When misgovernment, anarchy and corruption had led to national stagnation, when the people, defrauded and abandoned, was the constant victim of professional politicians and agitators, when those responsible for the destiny of la patria, . . . justified inaction with the appearance of respecting the Constitution, . . . the youth of the Armed Forces, supported by the good citizenry of this country, put an end to a period of national history that I need not further characterize. Whether I did well or badly, history will judge, and that judgment will not be twisted by the campaign of hate and falsehoods, that with obvious [political] motivation seeks to besmirch the regime I served.

Ibáñez told the Congress that he had saved the country from anarchy; he should be applauded, not maligned. Congress disagreed, approving the acusación constitucional with the ex-president in exile. Like others before him and after, Ibáñez soon benefited from political amnesty. He would play an important role in Chile politics into the 1950s when the voters returned him to the presidency (1952–58).

For the seventeen months following Ibáñez' resignation, the country suffered through several civilian and military governments of varying political tendencies, including the famous "100 days" of a Chilean "Socialist Republic," under the alternating leadership of Marmaduque Grove, Carlos Dávila, and an alliance with the newly formed socialist movement called Nueva Acción Pública, or "New Public Action." International economic conditions put unmanageable strains on any national government, while lack of political consensus denied all the military and civilian-military coalitions sufficient support to impose order or to direct economic recovery. In September 1931 conservative civilian politicians and the commander of the Chilean armed forces requested military assistance from the United States in order to put down a naval mutiny supposedly inspired by "communistic" elements. In conversations with the American ambassador, the Chilean commander emphasized the serious nature of the "imminent danger of social war" and referred to the continental, rather than local, character of the communistic activities that he believed threatened the nation. Handcuffed by a 1922 treaty limiting transfer of naval armaments, the United States nevertheless expressed a willingness to supply other materiel should the Chilean government make a formal request. United States representatives also expressed their "appreciation of the desires of the Chilean government to maintain order and stable institutions and to protect American interests in Chile. . . ."

Using airpower to defeat the naval mutiny, the Chilean government withdrew its request for American military assistance but, according to the American ambassador, subsequently asked for "a specialist in communistic propaganda and activities in order to assist in ferreting out the ramifications and origins of the movement in Chile." The State Department replied that "this Government regrets that there is not available in the Government service a specialist whose services it could offer."

The confusion following Ibáñez's ouster ultimately produced a significant realignment of political forces on an explicitly Left-Right ideological continuum. Small socialist movements merged to form the Socialist party (1933); a split between Trotzkyists and Stalinists divided the Communist party; splinter groups from existing parties created the Radical Socialist party (ex-Radicals), the Democrat party, or, Partido Democrático (ex-members of the Partido Demócrata), and the center-right Agrarian party (ex-Liber-

TABLE 7–3. POLITICS, AMNESTIES, AND PARDONS: 1925–42*

Political Chronology	Year	Amnesty Law or Other Policy	President
Break in constitutional stability	1924–32		
Military coup (September)	1924		
Labor laws	1924		
Military coup (January)	1925		
Alessandri returns from exile, resumes presidency (March)	1925		
New Constitution (September)	1925	Decree Law 535	Alessandri
Alessandri resigns (October)	1925		
Interim government	1925–27		Emiliano Figueroa
Ibáñez dictatorship	1927–31		
Ibáñez ousted (July)	1931		
Acusación Constitucional against Ibáñez approved in Senate			
Montero presidency (five months)	1932	Law 4977	Montero
Montero ousted by coup	1932	(4 June coup, "República Socialista" proclaimed)	
Various military and civil-military juntas		Decree Law 23	Military Junta
		Decree Law 75	Dávila
		Decree Law 180	Dávila
		Decree Law 437	Dávila
		Decree Law 504	(res) Dávila
Arturo Alessandri reelected	1932		
(governs with periodic use of facultades extraordinarias, state of siege)	1933–36		
Massacre at Ranquil	1934	Law 5483 (covers coup of 4 June 1932, Ranquil, etc.)	Alessandri
Railroad strikes	1935–36		
State of siege	1936	Law 5950	Alessandri
Popular Front created	1936		
Law of Internal Security of the State	1937	Law 6.026	
Massacre at Caja de Seguro Obrero	1938		
Pedro Aguirre Cerda elected president	1938		
Acusación Constitucional against Alessandri (fails in House of Deputies)	1939	Pres. Aguirre Cerda pardons persons involved in events at Caja de Seguro Obrero	
Failed coup by Gen. Ariosto Herrera (25 August)	1939		
	1941	Law 6885	Aguirre Cerda
	1942	Law 7159	Méndez (interim president)

*All laws and decrees listed in this table are amnesties for events related to political conflicts from 1925–42; amnesties cover a variety of "political crimes," including violation of the Law of Internal Security of the State. Amnesties for failing to vote or complying with obligatory military service are excluded.

TABLE 7–4. POLITICAL AMNESTIES IN CHILE, 1943–78*

Political Chronology	Year	Amnesty Laws
Death of President Ríos Interim presidency, A. Duhalde		
	1943	Law 7.425 (collective pardon)[†] (List of prisoners in Temuco jail)
"Massacre" at Plaza Bulnes	1946	
	1946	Law 8.526 Persons processed or sentenced for violations of Law 6.026, 1937 (Internal Security of the State) and Decree Law 425, 1925 ("abuses of media,—basic censorship law)
President González Videla	1946–52	
New law on peasant unions Wave of strikes in mines, farms Communist party outlawed Law for Permanent Defense of Democracy (Law 8.987)	1947	
	1948	
	1950	Law 9.611 Persons charged with crimes due to the strike of public health workers
	1950	Law 9.665 Persons charged with crimes due to the strike of postal and telegraph workers
Presidential elections	1952	Law 10.957 Persons processed or sentenced for crimes against the internal security of the state, under the law for the permanent defense of democracy, under the law against "abuses of the media" DL 425, election law; those sentenced or processed as a consequence of work stoppages or strikes, until 3 September 1952 (and various others, with exclusions stipulated)
Reconfiguration of party system End of Radical party presidencies (1938–52)		
Carlos Ibáñez	1952–58	
Molina peasant strike	1953	
Labor and peasant activism Coup plotting and scandals Debates on repeal of Law 8.987 Thousands of pardons granted Urban "insurrection"	1953–57	
	April 1–2, 1957	

(continued)

TABLE 7–4. POLITICAL AMNESTIES IN CHILE, 1943–78* (*continued*)

Political Chronology	Year	Amnesty Laws
	1955	Law 11.773 Persons responsible for any crimes or infractions sanctioned by Law 8.987 (Law for Permanent Defense of Democracy) [lists certain exclusions, e.g., homicide]; persons processed or sentenced for "desacato" by provoking a duel and those who served as seconds; also for various public sector workers (e.g., railroad workers, for missing work or strikes).
	1956	Law 12.004 Persons responsible for crimes or infractions under Law 8.987, committed prior to 18 October 1955 [excludes homicide, arson, and several crimes specified in article 480 of the Penal Code]; also covers government workers and workers in autonomous and semi-autonomous agencies; eliminates also administrative sanctions for the same violations (essentially illegal work stoppages or strikes, forbidden under Law 8.987).
	1958	Law 12.886 Persons responsible for crimes or infractions committed before December 1, 1957, under Law (8.987), and for all infractions or crimes committed "for political reasons;" prior to the same date; for those processed or sentenced, and those responsible for crimes under DL 425 (censorship law); specifies that coverage extends to members of the armed forces, police, and "investigations" (civilian political police) for crimes committed to repress acts against public order and social peace, committed prior to December 1, 1957; to persons who participated in the strike in December 1957, in the provinces of Tarapacá and Antofagasta and the Dept. of Chañaral; persons who engaged in illegal work stoppages from the Ministry of Agriculture and the Consejo de Fomento e Investigaciones Agrícolas, on February 7, 1958; government workers, and workers in semi-fiscal agencies, municipal, maritime, and railway workers, etc., who received administrative sanctions for the events of April 1–7, 1957.

(*continued*)

TABLE 7–4. POLITICAL AMNESTIES IN CHILE, 1943–78* *(continued)*

Political Chronology	Year	Amnesty Laws
Electoral reform (Australian ballot) Derogation Law 8.987 Allende and leftist coalition almost win presidency; Jorge Alessandri assumes presidency	1958	
Jorge Alessandri	*1958–64*	
Economic austerity, IMF model, return of inflation	1961	Law 14.629 Persons charged in process 2419 in the jurisdiction of the Naval courts-martial of Valparaíso, related to indiscipline, "sedition," and "insurrection" of personnel at the Escuela de Ingeniería Naval in May 1961.
Congressional elections; first time political right loses veto (1/3 + 1) over constitutional reform; realignment with Radical party, Liberals, and Conservatives Moderate agrarian reform law Pressures by Alliance for Progress Christian Democrats and left organize in countryside	1963	Law 15.576 Persons processed or sentenced for crimes committed within national territory covered by DL 425 and Title I of Law 12.927 (updated Internal Security of the State Law); Title II, Section III of the Military Code of Justice; and Title I of Section II of the Penal Code, committed prior to June 1, 1963; all those benefitting by this amnesty have their pension rights reinstated
"Ley Mordaza" (reformed censorship law: Law 15.576)	1964	Law 15.632 Persons charged or sentenced for crimes covered by Title III of Law 12.927, committed prior to 6 August, 1964 (*Delitos contra el orden público*)
Eduardo Frei M.	*1964–70*	
"Revolution in Liberty" Peasant unions organized Agrarian reform Political mobilization	1965	Law 16.239 Journalists processed or sentenced for violations of Law 15.576, 1964
	1965	Law 16.290 Persons processed or sentenced for violation of the Law of Internal Security of the State (excludes persons involved in an explosion at the Brazilian Embassy in Santiago)
	1966	Law 16.519 Persons responsible for violations of Law 15.576 committed prior to June 21, 1966. Includes also civil liability for these violations (excludes civil law suits by party parties)

(continued)

TABLE 7–4. POLITICAL AMNESTIES IN CHILE, 1943–78* (continued)

Political Chronology	Year	Amnesty Laws
		Law 16.604 Amnesty for mayors and municipal councilpersons for unauthorized use of funds (wrong budget categories) prior to July 1, 1966 (excludes personal enrichment and corruption)
Socialist party declares itself in favor of violent revolution; Splits in Christian Democratic Party; MIR and socialists carry out land occupations and first "armed expropriations" of banks Government called on to use police and armed forces to remove illegal occupants of land	1967–69	
	1968	Law 16.975 Amnesty for Intendentes and Gobernadores who refused to use force to execute court orders against illegal occupants of public and private property; journalists responsible for crimes covered by Law 12.927 (Internal Security of the State); restores worker benefits, denied due to the circumstances of the strike in 1966 at Potrerillos, El Salvador, Barquitos y Chuquicamata
"Massacre" of urban squatters in Puerto Montt; Acusación Constitucional against Interior Minister E. Pérez Zucovic	March 1969 June 1969	
	1969	Law 17.234 Amnesty for mayors and city council persons, ex-mayors, and ex-municipal employees who illegally transferred funds from one budget category to another prior to June 30, 1969. Eliminates civil liability in the same cases
Presidential elections: Salvador Allende wins plurality with Unidad Popular coalition	September 4, 1970	
Salvador Allende	1970–73	
Allende grants pardons to various Miristas	1970	
Ex-minister E. Perez Zucovic assassinated	1970	
Proposed political amnesty laws fail	1970–71	

(continued)

TABLE 7–4. POLITICAL AMNESTIES IN CHILE, 1943–78* (*continued*)

Political Chronology	Year	Amnesty Laws
	1971	Law 17.553 Mayors, city councilpersons and municipal employees, and ex-officials who have illegally transferred funds from one budget category to another prior to July 1, 1971; includes municipal and provincial treasurers (excludes cases of personal enrichment and corruption)
Political polarization/military coup	September 11, 1973	
Military government	1973–90	
		Decree Law 2.191 (April 1978)

*Excludes periodic amnesties for draft evaders and for violations of election laws (mandatory voting requirements) and individual amnesties (amnesties not involving at least two persons). Does not include thousands of individual pardons (*indultos*).

†Collective pardon (*indulto general*) requires legislation; individual pardon by presidential decree, Ministry of Justice.

als and Radicals). These divisions and realignments introduced new personalities and new energy into Chilean politics while setting the stage for political struggle during the next four decades.

In the short term, however, six different governments "controlled" the country within a 101-day period in 1932. Each government promulgated amnesty decrees and pardons in an effort to restore stability and to "reconcile" the antagonists of recent conflicts, just as had occurred from the late 1820s until 1925. Indeed, the nineteenth-century pattern of cyclic political violence and political ruptures followed by amnesties and other policies of "reconciliation" was converted into a common political tactic that would characterize Chilean politics from 1932 to 1973. The routinization of this pattern of political conflicts followed by pardons, amnesties, and other modes of "political reconciliation" is illustrated in Tables 7–3 and 7–4.

Seeking to end the chaotic situation—and with much of the officer corps disillusioned with the military role in politics—General Bartolomé Blanche assumed provisional executive authority and scheduled the presidential election for October, 1932. Contested among candidates representing the spectrum of political opinion, the presidential elections restored civilian government to Chile and returned Arturo Alessandri to the presidency. Alessandri obtained 184,754 of the 339,709 votes cast, while 20 percent of the electorate supported the socialist (Marmaduque Grove) or the Communist (Elías Lafertte) candidate. Subsequently the Left pressed Alessandri for social reforms, thereby restoring the social question to center stage in Chilean politics. In turn the Right sought restoration or reaffirmation of their status and privileges—which had been challenged by certain policies of the Ibáñez administration as well as by the "Socialist Republic."

At the depths of the depression and in the midst of political uncertainty, no one could have forecast that for the next forty years Chile would be the only Latin American nation without illegal changes of government. Neither could anyone have predicted, despite increasing American economic interest in Chile, the major role United States policy would play in Chile's internal political development over the next four decades.

8 Chilean Democracy

Chile's political instability between 1920 and 1932 gave way to four decades of legally elected civilian governments. From 1932 until September 1973 Chile was the only Latin American nation in which competitive party politics, uninterrupted by coups, assassinations or revolutions, determined the occupants of the presidency, Congress, and higher policymaking positions in the national bureaucracy. The same political parties competing at the national level also vied for control of local government institutions and for influence in national and regional student federations, labor unions, and other community or class organizations. Direct election of the president according to the provisions of the 1925 constitution made the selection of the chief executive a truly national event.

Incorporation of women (1949) and illiterates (1970) into the electoral registers increased by more than 30 percent the population eligible to vote. Improved literacy rates (50%, 1939; 75%, 1960), increased political awareness among working classes, and mandatory registration and voting did much to increase the number of voters in national elections. Important electoral reforms in 1958 and 1962 liberated the votes of rural workers from the control of landlords and reduced the possibility of vote buying and election fraud, thereby extending effective suffrage to practically the entire adult population.

The Chilean political system during these years combined multiparty politics with presidential government. Unlike a parliamentary system, governments did not "fall." Presidents served six-year terms, and during these six years cabinet shifts could reflect new party alliances or an executive decision to govern with a "nonpolitical" cabinet of technical experts or even a cabinet of personal loyalists. But the extreme fragmentation of the party system made it difficult for presidents to control legislative action or even to maintain the total support of their own party. Congressional and municipal elections which did not coincide in time with presidential elections added to legislative independence and to the unlikelihood that presidential electoral coalitions could be translated into majoritarian *governing* coalitions. Thus despite the increased authority of the president under the 1925 constitution, the old tensions between the legislature and the executive characteristic of the parliamentary period still played an important role in national politics.

Political tension between the president and the Congress did not mean total stalemate, but it did impose a certain constraint on the ability of presidents to implement the electoral platform upon which they campaigned. Since presidential electoral platforms generally contained more "Left" or populist planks than the Congress would accept, the growing frustration among leftist members of presidential coalitions meant their eventual collapse, and a gradual drift of policy toward the Right during each president's term of office. Thus Congress allowed Conservatives, Liberals, moderate and traditional Radicals, and certain middle-class business interests to limit the reformist projects of presidential coalitions.

Ceremony celebrating women's suffrage in national elections, 1949.
(Courtesy Archivo Universidad de Chile.)

Control over the votes of rural labor assured the Conservative and the Liberal parties, along with some Radicals, of enough congressional seats to retain important veto power over presidential programs. The "stability" of Chilean formal democracy, therefore, depended on considerable political bargaining, the use of political patronage, and shifting government coalitions undergirded by the continued dominance of the landowners over the votes and the political activity of their farm work force. This dominance, in turn, depended upon maintenance of the hacienda system through the prevention of rural unionization and the exclusion of outside political influences.

Recurrent challenges to the hacienda system after 1930 threatened to upset Chile's political stability. The urban labor movement and Marxist political parties made periodic efforts to encourage agricultural unionism and to wrest control of rural votes from the landowners. Every national administration, however, relied upon a complex system of economic and political subsidies to the landowners, including the repression of the rural labor movement, in order to install and preserve Chilean formal democracy. And, much to their later, self-confessed distress, Communists and Socialists colluded in elaborating an "arrangement" that made maintenance of the hacienda system and exploitation of rural labor the cornerstone in the edifice of Chilean formal democracy.

The world depression of the early 1930s marked the beginning of a period in Chilean history when even more than before internal developments responded to international economic and political movements. Disruption of foreign trade radically reduced the nation's import capabilities. According to League of Nations' estimates, no other nation in the world suffered a more severe impact from the international economic collapse than Chile. By 1932, imports, in real terms, stood at only one-sixth their 1929 levels. The Chilean government declared a moratorium on debt repayments and adopted a series

Vote-buying (cohecho), 1946. Buying votes influenced elections into the 1950s.
(Courtesy Archivo Universidad de Chile.)

of policies intended to alleviate the consequences of the abrupt decline in government revenues from taxes on exports, an extreme balance of trade deficit, lack of foreign credits, and a deterioration in the terms of trade (36% from 1929 to 1932). With imports down in real terms by over 80 percent (1929–32) and gross domestic product reduced in real terms by almost 40 percent during the same period, Chilean manufacturers rejected liberal economic principles in regard to international trade and urged upon the government policies to encourage local production. Import quotas, licenses, tariff barriers, currency devaluation, and a complicated system of multiple exchange controls discriminated against foreign commodities.

These conditions accelerated greatly the uneven process of industrial development that had been under way since before World War I. Led by the textile sector, Chilean manufacturers of chemicals, metal products, machinery, furniture, paper, non-metallic minerals, along with current consumer goods, achieved a significant increase in output and, by 1940, had altered the *structure* as well as overall contribution of industry in the national economy. Import-substitution industrialization reduced manufactured goods from 50 percent of the value of Chilean imports in 1925 to only 16 percent in 1969—with imports in the later year largely capital goods and high technology items.

In the years after 1930, utilizing imported foreign technology, capital goods, and primary or semiprocessed inputs for industry, Chile created a significant industrial sector, whose structure and composition altered as the predominance of agricultural-based firms (60 percent of total manufacturing income and 47 percent of employment in 1938) ended. Growth of the textile, chemical and petrochemicals, cement, and metal sectors—among other non-agricultural-based manufacturers—reduced the employment share

TABLE 8–1. GROWTH OF VOTER PARTICIPATION IN
PRESIDENTIAL ELECTIONS, 1925–70

Year	Total Votes Cast	Voters Registered	Percent of Population Registered to Vote	Population Total
1925	260,895	302,212	7.4	4,073,000
1927	233,103	302,142	7.2	4,188,000
1931	285,810	388,959	8.8	4,429,000
1932	343,892	429,772	9.0	4,495,000
1938	443,898	503,871	10.2	4,914,000
1942	466,507	581,486	11.1	5,244,000
1946	479,019	631,527	11.2	5,643,000
1952	955,102	1,105,029	17.6*	6,303,000
1958	1,250,437	1,521,272	20.8	7,316,000
1964	2,530,697	2,915,121	34.3	8,503,000
1970	2,954,799	3,539,747	37.0	9,566,000

*Including women for the first time in a presidential election.

Source: Instituto Nacional de Estadísticas, Demografía, Chile, 1969; and Fernando Silva Sánchez, Los Partidos Políticos Chilenos, Viña del Mar, Chile: Imprenta Lourdes, 1972. After Edward W. Glab, Jr., "Christian Democracy, Marxism and Revolution in Chile: The Election and Overthrow of Salvador Allende," unpublished doctoral dissertation, Northern Illinois University, 1975, p. 148.

of the agricultural-based firms to 35 percent in 1961. Overall, though the employment share of industry rose only from 17 percent in 1940 to approximately 20 percent in 1970, the absolute number of workers in industry almost doubled. By 1970 more than 560,000 Chileans earned their living in industrial employment, and this industrial labor force was becoming more significant in Chile's political life.

Government measures to stimulate industrialization led also to a significant increase in the size of the state bureaucracy. New credit institutions, exchange control commissions, and boards to regulate agricultural exports and establish retail price controls, added a network of governmental intervention in the national economy. Creation of a national development corporation (CORFO) in 1939 and the subsequent establishment of public and mixed-venture enterprises, as well as semi-autonomous "decentralized" public agencies in housing, school construction, agricultural extension, and social security entailed an even more significant amplification of the role of the state in defining the direction and character of national economic development.*

Not only did new state institutions indicate the changing role of national government in Chilean society, but they also created new employment opportunities for a growing group of salaried professionals and white-collar workers. The political implications of thousands of attractive government jobs were not lost on the political parties in their efforts to capture legislative majorities or to form government coalitions. By the early 1940s the public sector accounted for more than 50 percent of all internal investment capital, and in the years 1930–49 public employment more than doubled—a rate

*Between 1942 and 1952 these semi-autonomous, decentralized agencies gradually acquired their own legal identity and varying incomes derived from their own activities, apart from additional appropriations from the national budget.

of increase twice that in mining or agriculture and 32 percent above even industry and construction. These developments provided the basis for the consolidation of a bureaucratic "middle class" associated with an interventionist state. It would mean that a large proportion of the middle groups in Chilean society, both civilian and military, would support a further expansion of public activity in welfare, health care, education, and government-owned enterprises. If government activism meant marginal benefits for the working classes, it meant employment for the graduates of secondary schools, technical schools, and universities. Employment in the central administration more than tripled between 1925 and 1965, while national population barely doubled; this 300 percent increase in public employment did not include those holding positions in the semi-autonomous public enterprises such as the national airline (LAN) or national petroleum industry (ENAP).

In contrast to the aspirations and predictions of Chilean proponents of industrialization, however, significant industry did not mean increased economic independence. Wars in Europe, Korea, and Vietnam, international business cycles, and a complex, sophisticated network of multinational enterprises operating within a still more complicated international metals market limited Chilean economic performance. American, European, and multinational financial institutions determined the availability of credit and foreign investment for Chilean development.

Foreign corporations owned the principal enterprises that earned foreign exchange for the nation. Since intricate bargaining procedures among industrial consumers, the copper firms, and the United States government fixed the prices for these companies' copper output, production of increasing quantities of manufactured consumer goods did little to alter the historical reliance by Chile upon the export of one or several minerals. Indeed the combination of copper dependency and dependence upon foreign technology, capital goods, credit, investment funds, and technicians to carry out the process of industrialization made Chilean domestic development ever more vulnerable to external economic forces and to foreign manipulation.

Meanwhile, the policies that encouraged import-substitution industrialization through protective tariffs and nontariff barriers to imports both subsidized and encouraged the inefficiency of Chilean manufactures. These same policies created jobs for a labor force that was organized largely by leftist unions and political parties. Thus Chilean political economy gradually created a network of inefficient firms, to the detriment of consumers, and of domestic enterprises forced to suffer monopoly pricing for oftentimes lesser-quality inputs. It also nurtured a politically mobilized labor movement whose members owed their jobs to these government policies and to the expansion of the government bureaucracy. This volatile policy concoction generated cycles of inflation and political conflict, subject to the overall dependency of the economy on international prices and on the decisions made by foreign private investors and foreign governments. U.S. firms and government officials had largely replaced the British investors, merchants, bankers, and consuls of the nineteenth century. But Chile still gouged its lands; polluted its rivers, streams, and air; depleted its forests; and exploited its people to export minimally processed natural resources—even as its leaders sought to overcome this historical pattern with the schemes for industrialization.

Not only economic dependence increased in the period after 1930. International power struggles and ideological divisions conditioned Chilean politics. In the early 1930s a clear Left-Center-Right system of political cleavage replaced the old politics of factions, personalist cliques, and traditional party alignments. Marxism, liberalism, social Catholicism, and fascism all had supporters in Chile. The popular front, the Spanish Civil War, and nazism all influenced Chilean politics in the 1930s and 1940s. After

TABLE 8–2. EMPLOYMENT IN PUBLIC SECTOR,
CENTRAL ADMINISTRATION

Year	Number
1925	32,877
1935	41,266
1945	59,645
1955	75,542
1965	109,699

Source: Germán Urzúa Valenzuela and Ana María García
Barzelatto, Diagnóstico de la burocracia Chilena 1818–1969,
Editorial Jurídica, Santiago, 1971.

World War II the so-called Cold War drew United States agents and diplomats directly into Chilean politics in efforts to influence elections, manipulate labor organizations, disseminate American policy perspectives, and defend American investments. Likewise, the Soviet Union and Eastern European nations contributed funds and ideological orientation and direction for the country's Marxist parties and labor organizations. Although Soviet expenditures and influence in Chile never approximated that of the United States, the effects of Cold War rhetoric and the global confrontation between capitalist "free world" nations and the Soviet bloc gradually permeated Chilean society at all levels.

If the process of industrialization between 1932 and 1964 did not free Chile from dependence upon copper exports, foreign investment, or the fluctuations in the international economy, it did accelerate the trends toward urbanization and rural stagnation evident in the first decades of the twentieth century. Employment opportunities in industry attracted migrants from the countryside to major manufacturing centers in Santiago, Valparaíso, Concepción-Talcahuano, and other provincial centers such as Temuco and Talca. Even more than expanded economic opportunity in industry, however, the worsening conditions of labor in Chilean agriculture motivated rural workers and youths to flee the countryside. Real wages for rural workers declined by approximately 18 percent between 1940 and 1952 and by another 38 percent between 1953 and 1960. Tenant agricultural laborers (inquilinos) suffered a decrease in quantity and/or quality of land allotments and other non-cash perquisites such as rights to pasture animals, firewood, and food rations. Landlords supplied a lesser share of seed, fertilizer, or other inputs. In the period 1940/44–1950/54 the real earnings of sharecroppers and tenants declined by 27 percent, while landowners achieved a real gain in earnings of 33 percent. Indeed, the price of labor in agriculture declined relative to all other inputs between 1940 and 1960. Combined with the declining real income of agricultural labor, the rising real wages of blue-collar workers in manufacturing during the same period (1940/44–1950/54) accelerated the exodus from the countryside. Whereas total population approximately doubled from 1920 to 1960 (see Table 8–2), rural population increased by less than 18 percent. By 1960 more than half of all Chileans lived in cities of 20,000 or more, well above the comparable figures for all major world areas except North America and Oceania.

Underlying these demographic and economic trends could be found a complex, contradictory set of political arrangements that permitted the most traditional social and economic institutions in the nation, the large rural estates, to survive intact through

TABLE 8–3. DEMOGRAPHIC CHANGES IN CHILE, 1920–60

	1920	1930	1940	1950	1960
Total population	3,785,000	4,365,000	5,063,000	6,295,000	7,628,136
Rural population		2,185,800	2,421,300	2,530,400	2,650,500
Population in cities, 20,000 plus, as percent of total population in Chile	28	32	35	43	51
Population in cities, 20,000 plus, as percent of total population in Latin America	14	17	20	25	33

four decades of dramatic social change and economic modernization. To a great extent the survival of the hacienda system and its extensive subsidization by the state represented the trade-off between Marxists, reformers, and traditional political interests that permitted the establishment and maintenance of Chile's vaunted "stability" and "democracy." Whenever this trade-off was threatened, political toleration ended. When the large estates finally faced their demise in the period after 1964, so too did Chilean formal democracy. For Chile in the 1960s, agrarian reform would imply not only dramatic social and economic change, but also destruction of the long-enduring political arrangements that underpinned the country's record of institutional stability.

Arturo Alessandri returned to the presidency in 1932 determined to implement the 1925 constitution, to establish the legitimate prerogatives of the presidency detailed in that document, and to carry out the main provisions of the Labor Code. In contrast to his earlier administration, Alessandri now eschewed incendiary rhetoric in favor of appeals to national unity. He appointed ministers without the traditional overriding concern with party coalitions and managed to retain key ministers for four or five years of his six-year term—a feat almost unheard of in the days of parliamentary government. The emphasis on national unity, order, economic recovery, and constitutional rule gradually pushed the president into an ever more explicit alliance with the Right—the forces that had the most to gain from "law and order."

Faced with the depression-induced unemployment crisis, the continual threat of new military intervention, and the growing militance of socialist and communist movements, Alessandri allowed, even encouraged, the activity of white guards, called the "Republican Militia." According to the United States State Department files, in May 1933 President Alessandri personally reviewed a public parade of forty-two regiments of well-armed and equipped militiamen as it passed La Moneda, the presidential palace. As both a temporary counterbalance to the military and a threat to leftist movements, the militia played a significant role in polarizing Chilean politics until 1936 when the president ordered its dissolution. By then, the president's trusted military commander, General Oscar Novoa, had crushed an attempted coup in December 1933 and, through careful duty assignments and retirement of officers deemed too "political," had gradually brought the officer corps under presidential control.

Neutralizing the military threat eliminated one of the most difficult problems facing the administration. An upturn in the international economy and cautious domestic policy ameliorated the economic situation. Notwithstanding the government's extremely conservative fiscal policies, greater demand for copper and nitrates, the surge of industrial growth, and incentives to the private construction industry pulled the country out of the depths of the depression. Under the direction of arch-conservative Minister of Treasury Gustavo Ross, the administration reduced expenditures upon public works by almost 50 percent from 1932 to 1934; nevertheless official unemployment had practically disappeared by the end of 1935. In response to legislation passed at the end of 1933 allowing tax exemptions for a period of ten years on all buildings initiated before December 1935, construction increased by 40 percent in 1934 alone. This incentive not only balanced the deflationary effect of reduced public works but also renewed confidence in the private sector concerning the government's attitude toward private investment. Following on this legislation, a new public works program in 1936, focusing especially upon construction of roads, hospitals, and schools, accelerated economic recovery. Combined with construction in industry and the upturn in the export market, these projects alleviated most of the unemployment existing when Alessandri took office in 1932.

Inflation accompanied recovery. Price increases seemed to outpace salary gains, and a government freeze on salaries in the public sector alienated public employees. Failure of agriculture to provision adequately the urban centers and mining regions confronted the government with a dilemma that would underlie the contradictions in domestic political economy for the next forty years. With an ever more politicized and expanding urban labor movement, rising food prices spelled trouble for the incumbent government. Efforts to control food prices without a significant per capita increase in agricultural production required administrative controls on retail prices. Decree Law 520 of August 1932 created the General Commissariat of Subsistence and Prices, or Comisariato General de Subsistencia y Precios. Although this decree was promulgated during the brief reign of the "Socialist Republic," its major provisions remained in effect into the 1970s. It gave the General Commissariat authority to set prices for a wide range of goods considered of "basic necessity." It also extended authority to the General Commissariat to take charge of distribution of basic commodities, to expropriate or intervene in the administration of firms that refused to cooperate with government economic policies, to requisition production under specified conditions, and otherwise to regulate the operation of private firms. The more drastic provisions of this decree rarely were utilized from 1932 until the 1970s—when the Unidad Popular government, headed by President Salvador Allende, resorted to the terms of the 1932 decree to accelerate a program to transform Chile into a socialist society. From 1932 on, however, the government's authority to regulate the price of basic necessities created an expectation among the population that incumbent governments would control the rate of inflation.

Along with the General Commissariat, the Junta de Exportación Agrícola was created to promote agricultural exports and otherwise to benefit producers; it also soon came under pressure from urban political forces. In times of rising prices and "food shortages" the labor movement and leftist political parties demanded restrictions on exports of agricultural commodities, much as had occurred in colonial Chile when short-term grain shortages raised prices and royal officials sought to control prices in Santiago and other towns by prohibiting exports to Peru. In addition, the Junta de Exportación Agrícola, theoretically taking into account changing production costs, set floor prices for wheat. Inevitably, decisions on wheat prices were reflected in the price of bread—the basic food of the Chilean working classes. This made every price decision by the junta critical politically: it angered either producers or consumers.

Meanwhile, the increasing strength of the Socialist, Communist, and Radical parties and the growth of the labor movement during the second Alessandri administration made it politically impossible to ignore entirely pressures for price controls in urban areas. President Alessandri strongly favored the development of the *legal* union move-

TABLE 8–4. LEGAL AND ILLEGAL STRIKES IN CHILE,
1932–57

Year	Legal Strikes	Personnel/ Workers Involved	Illegal Strikes	Personnel/ Workers Involved
1932	3	500*	3	100*
1933	7	648	3	100
1934	2	100	11	3000
1935	10	1197	20	4236
1936	4	4781	16	2977
1937	4	460	17	2569
1938	6	7954	9	3419
1939	20	5674	6	5249
1940	20	8235	25	10,576
1941	15	2041	16	890
1942	7	671	12	2062
1943	26	1897	101	46,832
1944	38	14,039	53	17,249
1945	36	32,334	112	66,612
1946	27	18,262	169	76,475
1947	37	17,887	127	51,652
1948	20	7172	6	1203
1949[†]	23	6533	24	8711
1950	28	12,058	164	41,833
1951	30	12,718	150	47,443
1952	45	28,073	156	89,566
1953	60	54,628	148	68,480
1954	61	25,009	247	49,687
1955	62	23,062	212	104,370
1956	25	5138	122	95,300
1957	12	8722	68	17,616

*Approximate figure.
[†]Year after implementation of Law for Permanent Defense of Democracy.
Source: Chilean Labor Department, Annual Report 1948, and yearly, 1949–1958.

ment under the terms of the Labor Code, since he saw the code as a major result of his own zeal in the 1920s. Accordingly the administration supported efforts by the Labor Department to encourage the organization of legal unions. The unions in turn pressed for lower food prices. This meant a clash with agricultural interests.

Successful implementation of price controls and a restrictive agricultural export policy depended upon artificial depression of producer prices for agricultural commodities. Only gradually did succeeding administrations elaborate a complex array of direct and indirect subsidies to the landowners—including negative interest rates on credit, low freight rates on state railroads, exemption from import duties on farm machinery, export bounties, and exceedingly low tax rates on land and income. However, the most important trade-off in the arrangement that came to reconcile the conflicting interests of industrialists, urban workers, salaried middle-class groups, and landowners emerged quite soon after Alessandri assumed office. Discrimination against the rural

labor movement and repression of agricultural unionism would allow a superficial reconciliation of the contradictory interests of urban labor, reformist political movements,
and the traditional landed elite.

From the end of 1932 until December 1938 the number of legal unions in Chile more
than doubled, and membership rose from 54,000 to more than 125,000. At the same
time, industrial relations gradually conformed to the provisions of the Labor Code as
the technocrats of the Labor Department successfully channeled class conflict within
the institutions established by the code. An exception to this trend, the predominance
of illegal strikes over legal strikes, reflected the overly restrictive nature of the legislation regulating work stoppages; this exception did not prevent effective institutionalization of the procedures for labor disputes. Whereas prior to 1924 labor disputes
represented a revolutionary challenge to the parliamentary system, the Alessandri administration (1932–38) most effectively established administrative capabilities for *routine* handling of worker-employer collective bargaining. The underlying revolutionary
issues of the social question seemed to evaporate as unions and their political allies accepted the legitimacy of the *juntas de conciliación* and the labor courts.

Only in agriculture did employers *en masse* refuse to recognize the legitimacy of
unionization and the very applicability of the Labor Code. In sharp contrast to his generalized commitment to implement the Labor Code, President Alessandri also discouraged agricultural unionization. Unfortunately for Alessandri, leading officials
within the Labor Department, among them some who had helped to write the Labor
Code, attempted to fulfill their duty by applying the terms of the code in the countryside. This included efforts to force landowners to introduce written contracts with all
their workers, to pay social security taxes as the law required, and, most significant, to
unionize agricultural labor.

The implications of a unionized agricultural labor force associated with reformist
and Marxist political parties threatened not only the economic basis of Chilean agriculture but also the control of landowners over the votes of their agricultural tenants,
sharecroppers, and resident laborers—votes that guaranteed the presence of rightist
forces in the Congress.

The response to this threat by the Alessandri administration and the National Agricultural Society (SNA) provided the foundation for the political "solution" to the problems posed by rapid urbanization, industrialization, growth of the urban labor movement, and inflation. If rural labor could be forced to bear most of the costs of price
controls discriminating against agriculture, and if landowners could be spared the inconvenience and cost of compliance with labor laws—while maintaining political control over the rural work force—then political "stability" could be maintained and the
threat of discontent or violence in the cities could be reduced.

In response to initial unionization efforts in vineyards in Talca province and a small
number of farms near Santiago in 1932 and 1933, the SNA protested to the Labor Department and to President Alessandri that the unionization provisions of the Labor
Code did not apply to agriculture. Significantly, both the Labor Department and the
Consejo de Defensa Fiscal, a kind of administrative supreme court, ruled against the
landowners. The Labor Department concluded that "there is no doubt that the agricultural worker has the complete right to unionize." Taking its case directly to President
Alessandri, however, the SNA secured a reversal of the Labor Department's decision in
the form of an ambiguously worded telegram sent to all the department's offices:

> This Department, in conjunction with the government, is studying activities related to
> the unionization of workers in rural properties. Since there exist complex difficulties

in carrying out these legal provisions, this Department orders you to refrain from assisting in the constitution of organizations of this type until you receive definite and precise instructions.

Since formation of a legal union required the presence of a labor inspector, this telegram effectively prevented organization of legal agricultural unions. No "definitive and precise" (or any other) instructions were forthcoming. True to the declarations made in his first presidential term (1920–24, 1925) when he noted the disadvantages of agricultural unionization, Alessandri's decision launched four decades of administrative, legislative, and physical repression of rural labor by successive national administrations. This repression served as the foundation of the political economy of Chilean formal democracy.

In June 1934—as if an omen of the future—*carabineros* massacred more than one hundred peasants protesting their eviction from their land in the frontier region of the upper Biobío. Rising in armed rebellion, the peasants of Ranquil looted stores and threatened landowners before the national police murdered the movement's leaders and restored order. Shortly thereafter the Alessandri administration urgently requested Congress to approve new legislation on agricultural colonization, but the events at Ranquil and the earlier action on rural unionization made clear the government's commitment to maintenance of the existing order in the countryside.

With the shift of the Alessandri government toward the Right, the most important reformist, middle-class party in Chile, the Radicals sought alliances with the Socialists and the Communists. At the urging of an agent of the Comintern, sent to Chile by the Soviets to influence the ideological orientation of the Chilean Communist party, the Chilean Communists adopted a popular front strategy. Comintern's new policy, enunciated in August 1935, told communist movements around the world that "the formation of a joint People's Front, providing for joint action with Social Democratic parties is a necessity. . . . Comrades, you will remember the ancient tale of the capture of Troy. The attacking army was unable to achieve victory until, with the aid of the Trojan Horse, it penetrated to the very heart of the enemy camp. We, revolutionary workers, should not be shy of using the same tactics."

In line with this new tactic Chilean Communists sought contacts with the ideologically divided Radical party, made efforts to reduce tension between themselves and the Socialists, and worked to form a united front against the Alessandri government. In December 1936, the Communists supported the formation of a unified national labor organization, the Confederación de Trabajadores de Chile (CTCH), headed by a Socialist secretary general, with a Communist serving as assistant secretary general. According to the agent sent by Moscow to Chile to direct the formation of the popular front movement, small favors and promises of support to selected leaders of the Radical party gradually created a nucleus of Radicals willing to include the Communists in a coalition aimed at capturing the presidency in 1938.

President Alessandri, governing with emergency powers (*facultades extraordinarias*), hardened his line toward the Left, declared a state of siege, and harshly repressed railroad strikes in 1935 and 1936. A growing willingness among leftist elements in the splintered Partido Demócrata, among Trotskyists, and other leftist fragments to oppose the government, produced a skeletal popular front executive committee in March 1936. Ideological diversity and the underlying distrust by Socialists and Radicals of the Communists dictated a mild declaration of objectives: restoration of democratic liberties, economic nationalism, socio-economic justice for the middle and working classes. Nevertheless, the alliance of organized labor with the popular front parties seriously

TABLE 8–5. ELECTIONS, CHAMBER OF DEPUTIES, 1937

Party	Deputies Elected	Votes	Percent of Total Vote
Conservador	35	87,845	21.3
Liberal	35	85,515	20.8
Demócrata	7	20,026	4.9
Agrario	3	9721	2.3
Socialista	19	46,050	11.2
Radical	29	76,941	18.7
Nacista	3	14,564	3.5
Democrático	5	18,676	4.5
Independientes	3	17,040	4.0
Acción Rep.	2	9802	2.3
Comunista	6	17,162	4.2
Sin representación	—	9217	2.3
Totals	147	412,812	100.0

Source: Germán Urzúa Valenzuela, Los Partidos Políticos Chilenos, Editorial Jurídica, Santiago, 1968, p. 81.

threatened the political position of the Alessandri administration. One month later, by-elections for a vacant Senate seat from the provinces of Biobío, Malleco, and Cautín gave a surprising victory to the candidate of the Radical party.

Although the new senator was one of the wealthiest landowners in the region, national political analysts interpreted his victory as an initial indication of the viability of the popular front strategy. Despite continued reservations by more traditional leaders of the Radical party, including the party's eventual presidential candidate of 1938, Pedro Aguirre Cerda, most of the party's regional leaders sought to strengthen the popular front coalition. With upcoming congressional elections in March 1937, majority elements in the Radical party hoped through the popular front tactic to increase Radical influence. However, an intervening by-election in the northern provinces of Atacama and Coquimbo gave an unexpected victory to the Alessandrista candidate after a campaign that depicted the popular front as "a consortium organized by Moscow-bought Communists." Shortly thereafter, Radicals opposed to the popular front accepted ministerial posts in the Alessandri government.

The congressional elections of 1937 maintained rightist control in the legislature, though certain electoral trends encouraged supporters of the popular front. Both the Conservatives and the Liberals obtained higher vote totals than the Radicals, who again obtained approximately 19 percent of the ballots cast. The Communists polled only slightly more votes than the Chilean Nazi party. However, while the hold of the rightist parties over the rural districts combined with vote buying and coercion guaranteed their continued dominance in Congress, significant gains by the Socialist party helped persuade many Radicals to maintain the popular front for the up-coming presidential elections of 1938.

At Alessandri's request, Congress enacted a law to protect the internal security of the state (Ley de Seguridad Interior del Estado, Law 6.026). Modified on various occasions from 1937 into the 1970s, this law, modeled on decrees enacted in the 1931–32 period, would be the permanent basis for repression of leftists, journalists, and other dissidents declared "enemies" of la patria. The law's provisions were so ample, and so ambiguous, that anyone "who propagates by word of mouth, in writing, or any other medium, whether in the country, or outside the country, tendentious or false information tending to destroy the republican democratic regime, or to perturb the constitutional order, the security of the country, the economic or monetary regime, price stability [etc.] or spreads such information outside the country" would be guilty of a crime against the "internal security of the state." Henceforth, illegal strikes, subversive propaganda, revolutionary rhetoric, leftist political movements, indeed, criticizing the government while visiting a foreign nation, might be crimes against internal security punishable by imprisonment or exile. The new law contained a list of many more such crimes (among them, insulting the flag; slandering, defaming, or libeling the president, ministers, judges, senators, or deputies in Congress; and vandalism or damage of public property). In some cases, those charged with violating this law were subjected to military tribunals rather than civilian courts.

As the presidential election of 1938 approached, the Right chose as its standard bearer Alessandri's ex-treasury minister, Gustavo Ross Santa María. No doubts existed concerning Ross's ideological or political orientation; he represented the interests of the propertied classes. He was reputed to have answered an appeal for legislation to benefit the middle class with "for me there are but two classes, upper and lower. To the first belong those who have gotten ahead in life; to the latter, those who, for whatever reason, have been failures." Ross's candidacy made clear the issues at stake in the 1938 election. An editorial in a leftist paper, *Claridad*, declared: "No one hates the people as he [Ross] does; no one is more likely to implement a 'strong' government, a government of hunger and the lash. . . . In choosing Ross, the Right has declared war on the Chilean masses." Not unexpectedly Ross's supporters compared him to Portales; the candidate's campaign slogan "Order and work" supported the historical parallel.

Divisions within the popular-front parties appeared to preclude their choosing a single candidate to contest the election against Ross. The Radical party claimed the "best right" to select a popular-front candidate; Socialists asked the front to support Marmaduque Grove, one of the leaders of the short-lived "Socialist Republic" of 1932. In a convention arranged through tough bargaining, each party nominated its candidate: Radicals, Pedro Aguirre Cerda; Socialists, Marmaduque Grove; Communists, Elías Lafferte; Demócratas, Juan Pradenas Muñoz. Six ballots later the convention appeared deadlocked. The next day, April 16, 1938, the Demócratas shifted their support to the Radical candidate; and early on April 17 the Socialists withdrew Grove, and the convention unanimously nominated Pedro Aguirre Cerda. A leader of the Radical party's anti-popular-front faction, ex-minister of interior under Alessandri in the 1920s, wealthy landowner, experienced politician—Aguirre Cerda now found himself the presidential candidate of the antifascist, popular-front movement he had originally opposed. His reluctance to accept Communist support consoled the moderate elements of the Radical party who hoped that his victory would allow them to increase their share of congressional representation and would give them access to public employment.

A bitter, violent, shrill electoral contest gave the popular-front candidate a narrow victory. Only when key military leaders and the commander of the national police (*Carabineros*) informed Ross that he could not count on their support in preventing Aguirre Cerda's inauguration did the rightist candidate concede victory. The distribution of votes in the election revealed the basic sources of rightist political and economic power, as well as the critical role that continuation by the supposedly leftist government of the repression of rural labor would play in maintaining "social peace" during the next ten years. The rightist candidate defeated Aguirre Cerda overwhelmingly throughout the agricultural heartland of the central valley. Importantly, however, Communist and Socialist agents in the countryside broke enough votes away from the landlords to reduce the Right's expected margin of victory in Talca from 10,000 votes to less

TABLE 8–6. PRESIDENTIAL ELECTION, 1938

Province	Aguirre Cerda	Ross Santa María
Tarapacá	6164	4162
Antofagasta	11,339	4984
Atacama	4834	2580
Coquimbo	10748	7874
Aconcagua	4001	7474
Valparaíso	22667	19,105
Santiago	64297	50,998
O'Higgins	7091	11,095
Colchagua	2542	9789
Curicó	1950	4805
Talca	5717	8485
Maule	1934	4817
Linares	3592	8764
Nuble	7813	13,853
Concepción	17,417	9734
Arauco	2481	2318
Bío Bío	6054	6797
Malleco	5978	7929
Cautín	13,125	12,228
Valdivia	12,982	10,811
Llanquihue	2854	5784
Aisén	412	440
Chiloé	2513	3257
Magallanes	4215	526
Total	222,720	218,609

Source: Germán Urzúa Valenzuela, Los partidos políticos Chilenos, Editorial Jurídica, Santiago, 1968, p. 83.

than 3000 and to achieve victory in Cautín. In the major cities and mining districts the popular-front candidate emerged victorious with the support of middle- and working-class voters. Radical party and Demócrata votes in parts of the frontier provinces and the lake district provided a slim margin of victory for Aguirre Cerda or prevented a landslide for Ross. Significantly, the base of Radical power in the south consisted of landowners, industrialists, bureaucrats, and their clientele. Loss of these essentially conservative voters by the popular front, and others like them throughout the country, would have spelled defeat. To maintain their support the government would be forced to make important concessions in contradiction to its own populist rhetoric during the next three years.

Even more important, in the short run, the victory of Aguirre Cerda owed much to the unlikely last-minute support of Chilean Nazis and ex-dictator Carlos Ibáñez. In the 1938 presidential election Ibáñez again attempted to regain the presidency, railing against politicians and disorder. Supported by the Chilean Nazi party (Movimiento Nacional Socialista de Chile), Ibáñez never adopted Nazi rhetoric or uniform but could easily accept the Nazi vision of a strong state that ruled a disciplined people for the "common good." Among the Radicals and the Socialists, minority factions still remembered the Ibáñez presidency fondly. This meant that the popular-front candidate could lose enough votes to Ibáñez to permit the election of Ross.

Salvador Allende in uniform of Socialist Militia. (Photo courtesy of Baltazar Robles, gift to author, 1971.)

Events leading up to the election produced an unlikely, indeed unique, alliance between the Nazis and the popular front. Disorders at the Congress when Alessandri read his last state of the union message were punctuated by shots fired toward the president by Nazi leader and deputy González von Marées. When the government applied an internal security law against the Nazis and other demonstrators, the Ibáñez forces and the leftists united in attacking Alessandri and the Ross candidacy. Meanwhile, Ibáñez attempted to secure popular-front support for his candidacy and the withdrawal of Aguirre Cerda.

Unable to undermine Aguirre Cerda's candidacy and equally unable to muster widespread popular support for the Ibáñez candidacy, the Nazis decided to overthrow the Alessandri government with a coup. Nazi plans called for occupation of key buildings in Santiago, support from sympathetic army units, and the assassination of both rightist politicians, including Alessandri and Ross, and leaders of the popular front. Facing imprisonment by September 8, 1938, on conviction for his role in the shooting incident in Congress, the Nazi leader set September 5 as the day for the coup. Nazi youths occupied the university and seized the Social Security building.

Now after six years of constitutional government, Alessandri faced still another threat to his overriding objective: institutionalizing the 1925 constitution and maintaining political order. He responded harshly, authorizing the use of artillery against the occupants of the university. Soon after, the Nazi youths in the Social Security building surrendered to *carabineros*—who killed them with submachine guns and small arms. More than sixty bodies were later removed from the building. A week later Alessandri requested authority from Congress to impose a state of siege for the remainder of his term. Ibáñez, who apparently had not actively participated in the coup attempt, surrendered almost immediately to army units and was jailed.

A week later Congress authorized President Alessandri to impose a state of siege and newspaper censorship and to employ other "extraordinary powers" to maintain public order. Prevented from carrying on his campaign, and promised influence in a popular-front government by Aguirre Cerda, Ibáñez withdrew his candidacy two weeks before the election. From his jail cell González von Marées endorsed the candidate of the popular front. Thus a popular front proclaiming its antifascist inspiration received part of its margin of victory from supporters of ex-dictator Carlos Ibáñez and from Chile's Nazi party.

The heterogeneous electoral support that gave Aguirre Cerda the presidency, involved political contradictions incapable of resolution within the framework of formal democracy. Ibáñistas, Nazis, Communists, Socialists, and Radicals could not ultimately agree upon general policy or political methods.

President Aguirre Cerda faced several immediate crises shortly after assuming office. In January 1939 a disastrous earthquake in south-central Chile devastated Chillán, Concepción, and the neighboring provinces. Official reports counted over 50,000 deaths and many times that number of casualties. Aguirre Cerda reacted quickly, declaring martial law in the affected provinces and organizing relief efforts. International assistance from Europe, the United States, and neighboring countries permitted quick restoration of basic services and transport. A week later, taking advantage of the urgent need to provide for reconstruction, the president presented Congress with a six-year plan for national development and reconstruction.

The enormous amount of money Aguirre Cerda indicated would be necessary to carry out the popular-front program along with the costs of reconstruction after the earthquake frightened the rightist majority in Congress. Conservatives and Liberals recognized the need to provide for reconstruction, but the remainder of Aguirre Cerda's ambitious program for national development, including large sums for low-cost housing and stimulation of industrial development, portended accelerated inflation, higher taxes, and expansion of the state bureaucracy. Congressional rejection of the development program, despite support for a massive reconstruction appropriation, sent Aguirre Cerda on a speaking tour to the devastated provinces to rally popular support.

In an effort to achieve a compromise, the president's minister of finance, Roberto Wachholtz, devised a new package for Congress, which proposed two separate agencies—the Relief and Reconstruction Corporation to deal with the immediate problems occasioned by the earthquake, and the National Development Corporation (CORFO) to carry out the longer-term economic objectives. In addition, the new proposal called for heavy reliance upon foreign loans instead of internal financing of the development projects. To prevent the popular-front parties from using CORFO for political advantage, its board of directors would represent producer groups as well as government officials; a single representative of the Chilean Workers Confederation (CTCH) would be included to make known labor's views.

This new plan angered many of the government's leftist supporters, particularly Socialists, whom the President mollified with promises of more patronage. In March 1939, after overcoming the rightist opposition through pressure on selected congressmen from the devastated provinces, Aguirre Cerda won a narrow victory for his development and reconstruction legislation. After further jockeying between the president and Congress, Law 6334 went into effect in late April 1939. This victory for Aguirre Cerda and the popular front would provide the basis for greatly expanded state intervention in national development. It also subordinated Chilean economic policy to the main source of capital for CORFO—the United States Export-Import Bank (Exim Bank).

While Aguirre Cerda was fighting for approval of the reconstruction and development program, his popular-front allies, especially the Socialists and Communists, carried out a national campaign among urban and rural workers to mobilize support for the government. Labor conflicts, strikes, unionization efforts, and industrial violence created an atmosphere bordering on insurrection. For members of the President's own party, as well as for the Conservative-Liberal opposition, the most serious threat to maintenance of the fragile social order came from the massive wave of labor conflict and unionization in the countryside. An extension of the electoral campaign in the countryside directed by Communist functionaries, rural conflict and unionization in the first months of the popular front administration reached alarming levels. In 1939 the Labor Department officially registered 170 labor petitions from groups of rural laborers and *inquilinos*—compared to six the previous year. During the same period campesinos organized more than 200 agricultural unions.

The National Agricultural Society and local groups of landowners appealed directly to President Aguirre Cerda to halt rural unionization and labor conflict in agriculture. In the middle of March 1939 some of the country's most influential landowners informed the president that they confronted "the initial elements of a state of revolution . . . produced under the pretext of the right of rural workers to organize." In agreement with all the parties of the popular front and the CTCH, President Aguirre Cerda illegally ordered suspension of rural unionization, using the same administrative device employed by President Alessandri in 1933. Despite the supposedly "temporary" nature of this suspension, it remained in effect until 1946.

Taking advantage of the vulnerability of agricultural workers, and of the willingness of popular-front parties to trade the welfare of the campesinos for "social peace" and support of the government's reconstruction and development legislation, landowners carried out a purge of union leaders and evicted large numbers of "troublemakers" from their tenancies. By the time the CTCH and the Communist party had repudiated this sacrifice of the rural work force to political expediency, Aguirre Cerda's new minister of interior, Arturo Olavarría Bravo, had already devised his system of "judgment day," or *juicio final*, to deal with rural militancy. As described by Olavarría himself,

> A group of carabineros [police] would arrive at a farm accompanied by a convoy of trucks. When the inquilinos were assembled in the area, the carabinero officer would order those who wished to continue the strike to stand on his left. The officer would then order that the strikers gather their families, cats, dogs, chickens, and belongings and get in the trucks to be evicted. . . . This tactic I converted into a system. General Oscar Reeves Leiva, Director General of Carabineros, called it *el juicio final*, as the good ones went to the right and the bad ones to the left, as it is hoped will occur one day in the valley of Jehosaphat. Of course, I did not have to use the *juicio final* many times.

Only the Trotskyists rejected Aguirre Cerda's sacrifice of the rural work force. In particular, Emilio Zapata, the leader and organizer of Chile's first national peasant league, *Liga Nacional de Defensa de Campesinos Pobres* ("National Poor Peasants League"), protested the government's acquiescence to landowner demands. Zapata delivered an angry critique of the government in the Congress and gradually broke with the popular-front coalition. Recalling the situation of 1939, Zapata remarked in 1971:

> What Aguirre Cerda had to do was tell the *patrones* that they couldn't use lockouts or sabotage production, and that they couldn't throw people off the land in political reprisal. . . . Neither Aguirre Cerda nor his ministers were responsive. They were

walls without ears. . . . Although they possessed the legal means to prevent it, they did nothing while the landowners threw the campesinos "into the streets" for the crime of voting for Aguirre Cerda or for joining *ligas* or unions.

Rural workers had no means to resist landowner reprisals. The popular-front government provided police to enforce court orders for evictions, to break the newly formed unions, and to allow the landowners to retain control of the countryside. This was one of the costs Aguirre Cerda was willing to pay to gain support for the rest of his program in Congress and to maintain "social peace." Socialists, Communists, and the CTCH likewise agreed to the terms of the bargain. In exchange, the industrialization program emerged from Congress, and the Socialists occupied high-level administrative posts.

Aguirre Cerda's concession to the landowners did not end the Right's campaign against the government. Neither did it prevent Emilio Zapata's National Peasant League from carrying out its "First National Congress of Chilean Peasants" in Santiago in April 1939. Rejecting the popular front's policies, leaders of the Trotskyist-oriented organization called for intensification of class struggle and the end of the latifundia. Two months later the Communists sponsored a highly visible "First National Congress of Rural Unions," preceding the National Congress of the CTCH. In the meantime (late April) Socialist leaders called for a purge of the bureaucracy of all "traitors," so that the public administration could be put completely at the service of the masses.

Tensions increased as rumors circulated that Socialist leader Marmaduque Grove had prepared a May Day speech calling for dissolution of Congress, recognition of the Socialist militia as an official arm of the government, and other revolutionary measures. The rightist press, in a fashion remarkably similar to the campaign that would later precede the military coup of September 1973, emphasized the precarious nature of Chilean democracy, the growing Communist threat, and alluded to the military role

Emilio Zapata (center) leading procession of peasants and farm workers, Santiago, 1939. (Photo courtesy of Baltazar Robles, gift to author, 1971.)

in preventing leftist extremists from destroying constitutional government. Aguirre Cerda responded by applying the internal security law against a leading rightist paper, *El Diario Ilustrado,* thereby preventing the paper's circulation outside of Santiago. Congress, in turn, censured the minister of the interior for violating freedom of the press in the *El Diario Ilustrado* case.

In the annual military parade honoring Arturo Prat, Chile's naval hero of the War of the Pacific, the Right found its military sympathizer when, according to the rightist press, General Ariosto Herrera Ramírez jumped from his horse to order removal of a Communist banner from a balcony of the presidential palace. In early July *El Diario Ilustrado* published a supposedly confidential circular detailing plans by the Socialists for an internal coup, or *autogolpe,* including provisions for formation of a red army, elimination of opposition politicians, and infiltration of the armed forces. (Again, we have a striking parallel with the "white paper" and the so-called plan zeta denounced by the Chilean Right and the military in 1973.)

In turn, the government announced discovery of a plot to oust the President. The rightist press made light of the government's claims, but investigations led Aguirre Cerda to request General Ariosto Herrera to resign. Herrera refused, and his military colleagues elected him president of the Club Militar in August 1939. Emerging as a hero of the Right, Herrera also supported the officers punished by the government for their supposed participation in the plot of early July. Ignoring orders from the minister of defense, he overtly insulted Aguirre Cerda with a decision to reinstate the officers in question. Thereupon the government relieved him of his command and asked him to resign his commission. On August 25, 1939, instigated by comrades of the second division he commanded and by the rightist press, General Herrera led an abortive coup attempt, in which the ever present hand of Carlos Ibáñez again was apparent. With the movement's quick collapse, Ibáñez sought asylum in the Paraguayan embassy.

The abortive coup passed the initiative back to the popular-front government. Congress allotted the president state-of-siege authority for a period of twenty days, during which time Aguirre Cerda purged the military of conspiratorial officers. Now, however, the latent divisions within the popular front itself surfaced with vengeance. Competition between Socialists and Communists to gain control of student movements and the CTCH exacerbated the traditional hostility between the country's two major Marxist parties. Internal divisions within the Socialist party, between those favoring the moderate policies of Aguirre Cerda and the more militant *inconformistas* and ex-Trotskyists, led to a party split and formation of the Socialist Workers party (PST) in 1941. Aguirre Cerda's own party remained divided between the would-be populists and the more conservative advocates of middle-class-oriented reform.

By the end of 1939 Congress passed only two major pieces of legislation, including the reconstruction-CORFO package; by early 1940 Aguirre Cerda reorganized the cabinet, relying upon wealthy, respected, personally loyal appointees rather than designees of the popular-front parties. In July 1940 the president publicly announced that labor conflicts in the countryside could not be tolerated, because they diminished agricultural production. A month later the minister of the interior instructed the *carabineros* to repress the activity of "professional agitators who provoke problems in the countryside and industrial centers." The president's effort to conciliate the rightist parties coincided with mounting conflict between Socialists and Communists, as well as with the internal split in the Socialist party. Communist attacks upon the Socialist minister of development, who negotiated for loans in the United States, increased the level of conflict and precipitated a rupture in the coalition.

In January 1941, Socialists demanded the ouster of the Communists from the popular front; refusal by the popular-front executive committee to expel the Communists led to Socialist withdrawal. The CTCH, divided between Communists and Socialists, also voted by a narrow margin to leave the popular-front government. Finally, after an impressive victory of popular-front parties and Socialists in the congressional elections of 1941, the president's own Radical party withdrew its support from him when he refused to accept party dictates in regard to ministerial appointments and patronage. To embarrass the president, his party colleagues now opposed legislation that he sent to the Congress. This opposition destroyed Aguirre Cerda's power, and he died, a broken man, in late 1941. In his own words, "the Chilean working classes were just as poor . . . and just as miserable as when I became President." True to his own democratic principles, however, Aguirre Cerda vetoed legislation passed by Congress that outlawed the Communist party.

Two Radical presidents and one interim president followed Aguirre Cerda. Juan Antonio Ríos, who had been a critic of Aguirre Cerda's cooperation with the Communists, served from 1942 to 1946, when he, too, died in office. Ríos renewed Radical contacts with Conservatives and some Liberals as the Right recognized the benefits of state support for *private* industrial enterprise. They also appreciated Ríos' anticommunist position and his decision to sustain the administrative order against rural unionization. Rapprochement between moderate Radical party factions and the Right coincided with a growing middle-class conservatism; at the same time the Radicals were trying to reconcile their own internal cleavages with the shifting trends in national politics. Positioned in the center of the political spectrum, the Radicals opportunistically entered in alliances with the Left or the Right, as expediency required, in order to retain their hold on the presidency and the patronage of a growing bureaucracy.

A new, most unlikely, coalition of Radicals, Communists, and Liberals brought Radical leader Gabriel González Videla to office in 1946. The policies of industrialization through CORFO loans to private investors and heavy borrowing from the Exim Bank continued. Shortly after González Videla assumed office, the Communist party unleashed a campaign of labor conflict and strikes even more extensive than the movement of the first years of Aguirre Cerda's presidency. During the 1946–47 harvest, rural workers engaged in more than 650 labor conflicts and formed more than 300 agricultural unions. Again, organization of rural labor threatened to destroy the underlying trade-off reconciling the socio-economic consequences of urbanization and industrialization and the political power of the landowners.

Fulfilling a campaign promise, González Videla rescinded the order issued by Aguirre Cerda in 1939 to restrict rural unionization. Quickly, however, the new president also fulfilled a bargain made with his rightist supporters in the Liberal party, and supported new legislation (Law 8811) that made agricultural unionization practically impossible. In contrast to the Labor Code regulating the majority of Chilean workers, the new law outlawed agricultural strikes and severely limited the rights of rural workers to present labor petitions and to engage in collective bargaining. Now, instead of an illegal administrative order, congressional legislation sanctified the arrangement whereby rural labor bore a disproportionate share of the costs of Chilean industrialization and continued to serve as "voting cattle" for the owners of the large rural estates. This legislation remained in effect until 1967.

In contrast to their performance in 1939, Communist leaders in 1946 and 1947 persisted in their unionization efforts and in their leadership of industrial conflicts despite the opposition of the president. From their ministerial positions in González Videla's government, the Communists refused to acquiesce in the renewed repression of rural labor. They carried the struggle to the mines and the cities, and thus incited fierce rightist opposition while also alienating themselves from the president. As landowners and industrialists called for cooperation with the president, to "extirpate the Communist

President Juan Antonio Ríos and vice president Alfredo Duhalde, 1945.
(Courtesy Archivo Universidad de Chile.)

President Arturo Alessandri and President-elect Pedro Aguirre Cerda, 1938.
(Courtesy Archivo Universidad de Chile.)

Arturo Alessandri and President Gabriel González Videla, 1946. (Courtesy Archivo Universidad de Chile.)

menace," Congress first extended González Videla's extraordinary powers to deal with subversion (Law 8837) and followed, in 1948, with the so-called Law for the Permanent Defense of Democracy (Law 8987). This legislation outlawed the Communist party, excluded its members from participation in the labor movement, and set up zones of banishment or "relegation" for subversives. This temporary elimination of the Communists from overt political activity and a "cleansing" of the labor movement restored political stability. It also reflected the integral relationship between the Cold War, American foreign policy, and Chilean domestic development.

American investment in Chile during the 1930s increased, as did Chilean awareness of the significant impact of foreign control over the copper and nitrates that provided most of the country's foreign exchange. Leftist political movements sought continually to undermine the position of United States firms, attacking the exploitation of Chilean resources by international monopolies and imperialism—already, by then, a synonym for the United States. The advent of a popular-front government with Marxist participation presented American interests with a delicate situation. To finance development projects the Chilean government needed resources; higher taxes on the copper industry appeared the most likely source of such capital. Further, the initial outline of the CORFO project, whether under Marxist or nationalist direction, threatened to expand significantly the state sector of the economy, to the detriment or even the elimination of American investments in oil, public utilities, mining, and basic industry.

The political compromise that had allowed the popular-front government to create CORFO shifted emphasis from internal to external financing for economic modernization and industrialization. Rather than greatly increased taxes on wealth and income in Chile, or taxes on the copper firms which would discourage further investment, moderate Radicals and industrial leaders opted for loans, credits, and foreign private investment as the source of risk capital. United States diplomats in Santiago and Washington, D.C., saw that it was possible to protect American interests through a careful lending policy and, at the same time, to support the anti-Marxist elements of the popular-front coalition; they developed a highly successful cooperative strategy for dealing with Aguirre Cerda's government. Despite Chile's hesitance to declare war against the Axis powers, the initial success of the policy American interests had elaborated gradually subordinated both Chilean economic policy and domestic political events to American needs during the Second World War and, in the aftermath, the Cold War.

Recognizing American credit policy's potential for influencing the popular front government, an embassy official made the following assessment of the alternatives open to United States policymakers:

> If we negotiate with Wachholtz [the moderate, Radical minister of finance in the first Aguirre Cerda cabinet] . . . we will strengthen the moderate elements in the popular front here; whereas if we deferred the negotiations in the expectation that the dissensions in the popular front here would come to a head we would be taking a long chance.

By the end of 1940 the United States Export-Import Bank had arranged credits totaling $17 million for CORFO—to be used exclusively to pay for materials, machinery, technical assistance, or consultants from the United States. During the next eight years Exim Bank and other American-dominated financial institutions continued to bankroll CORFO's large-scale investment program in housing, industry, agriculture, and commerce. Whereas CORFO's policies directly threatened the position of selected American firms, its overall effect was to greatly expand the market for imports of United States capital goods, in addition to placing Chilean policymakers in a vulnerable position vis-à-vis decisions made in Washington, D.C.

World War II raised international prices for copper. Practically all of Chile's copper, however, was marketed through subsidiaries of United States copper firms established in Chile—for whom the Allied governments fixed a ceiling price upon copper products during the course of the war. Different Chilean sources estimate that the loss Chile sustained by its "contribution" to the Allied war effort was between $100 million and $500 million. Further, Chilean dollar reserves accumulated from exports to the United States during the war were unfrozen at a time when postwar inflation substantially reduced their purchasing power. Moreover, in the United States recession of 1949–50 production by American copper firms in Chile was reduced after four years of deterioration in the terms of trade. When the outbreak of the Korean War quickly snapped the United States out of the recession, the American government and the copper companies reimposed price controls on copper.

American control of Chile's principal economic resources accompanied intensified involvement in Chilean politics. Cold War intrigue made post-World War II Chilean politics a confrontation zone for "Communism" and the "Free World." American policy-makers considered the presence of Communist ministers in the González Videla government to be dangerous, and so allied with the Chilean Right in an active campaign to weaken, then destroy, Marxist political parties and the labor movement. Simultaneously the United States provided financial support for Socialist factions of the CTCH which opposed the rapidly increasing Communist influence. The United States gave badly needed financial assistance to the Chilean government on the condition that the Communist menace be eliminated. A split in the labor movement and the breakup of the CTCH were preliminary successes; a mounting anticommunist campaign by the rightist press and eventually by the González Videla government further heartened American diplomats and business interests.

Doubt still remained that González Videla would totally break his alliance with the Communists. Communist control of the labor movement, especially in copper and the coal mines, made any frontal offensive quite risky. Communist-inspired mobilization of rural labor and hundreds of agricultural labor conflicts in the 1946–47 harvest threatened the very foundation of the political arrangement elaborated by Aguirre Cerda and his Radical successors. Labor conflict in the northern provinces and a crippling coal strike panicked the Radical administration. In the meantime a representative of the Chilean government sought further economic assistance from the Exim Bank and the International Bank to bolster the Chilean economy. For, despite increased copper production, the declining terms of trade between Chile and the industrial nations significantly reduced the nation's import capabilities, even as the industrialization process necessitated greater quantities of capital goods, high technology, and raw materials.

Chile's suspension of foreign debt payments after the earthquake of 1939, complaints by American businessmen that Chile's request for loans to finance hydroelectric development threatened American private interests, and rumors of nationalization of American oil and power companies, all delayed approval of the requests for new assistance. Despite the secret assurances by González Videla's special emissary to the State Department that the Chilean president did not favor communism and would oppose Argentine President Juan Perón's efforts to undermine American influence in the southern cone, no quick commitment on financial assistance was forthcoming. To the

TABLE 8–7. NET TERMS-OF-TRADE RELATIONS:
PRICE INDEX FOR CHILE (1938 = 100)

	Exports	Imports	Terms of Trade
1936	100.5	88.5	113.6
1937	129.7	96.9	133.8
1938	100.0	100.0	100.0
1939	107.5	94.7	113.5
1940	105.4	104.2	101.2
1941	109.2	113.1	96.6
1942	118.4	150.1	78.9
1943	120.9	168.7	71.7
1944	125.6	179.6	69.9
1945	129.7	183.2	70.8
1946	151.1	200.6	75.3
1947	201.1	245.4	81.9
1948	221.1	250.8	88.2
1949	220.3	246.1	89.5
1950	222.1	237.0	93.7
1951	279.4	276.9	100.9

Source: Theodore H. Moran, Multinational Corporations and the Politics of Dependence, Copper in Chile, Princeton University Press, 1974, p. 71.

contrary, the State Department officials involved in the negotiations made clear the department's concern that Chile "adjust its debt situation" and improve the tax situation of the American copper companies.

Disappointed by the results of the economic mission to the United States, González Videla reportedly threatened the American ambassador with a deterioration in Chilean-American relations. In response, Ambassador Claude Bowers cabled a confidential message to the secretary of state, noting that "Chile is [a] key country in the struggle against Communism, and I feel that we should make every effort to overcome present impasse." As the Communist campaign of labor agitation mounted, so also did American concern with Chile as a Cold War battleground. Accounts of the rising Communist menace dominated correspondence from the American embassy in Santiago to Washington, D.C., from May 1947 on.

Anticipating a showdown with his ex-political allies, President González Videla requested an emergency shipment of coal from the United States in case of Communist shutdowns of the coal mines. Ambassador Bowers recommended to the secretary of state, "I suggest situation set forth above [reference to a general strike scheduled for late June 1947] be taken into consideration in connection with Chile's request for coal stockpile in its struggle to combat Communism." In September 1947, Bowers reported to Washington that González Videla was gradually eliminating Communists from the administration, and on October 6, 1947, the ambassador cabled that "González Videla declared war on Communism as a result of what he claims is a Communist plot to overthrow the Government and obtain control of the production (in order to deprive the United States of the use in an emergency) of strategic raw materials, namely copper and nitrates." Despite heavy commitments to Europe and other Latin American nations, the United States assured the Chilean president that emergency coal shipments would be available. Three days later Ambassador Bowers cabled: "Our war with Communists is on two fronts, Europe and South America." After another four days had passed, the ambassador added: "The issue is clear as crystal—Communism or democracy."

With American assurances of coal shipments to break the coal miners' strike, the government moved in police and military units to restore order and terminate the labor conflict. Subsequently Chile broke off diplomatic relations with the Soviet Union, Yugoslavia, and Czechoslovakia, nations that the Chilean president accused of engineering political chaos through their domestic agents, the Chilean Communist party. The Law for the Permanent Defense of Democracy, passed in 1948, outlawed the Communist party, eliminated almost 30,000 voters from the electoral registers, provided authority to purge the labor movement, and allowed the president to restore "democracy" to Chile. Implementation of Law 8811 on agricultural unionization, along with the Law for the Permanent Defense of Democracy, destroyed the impressive network of rural labor unions created from 1946 to 1947 and ended the threat to the hegemony of the political Right in the countryside. Thus the "arrangement" initiated by Alessandri and elaborated by the popular-front government could remain intact.

Appropriately, González Videla called upon Jorge Alessandri, the ex-president's son, to act as his finance minister. Anaconda announced plans for an additional $130 million investment in their copper properties at Chuquicamata. And despite the effects of the United States recession on a worsening Chilean economy, Exim Bank and the international lending agencies agreed to provide substantial economic assistance to the Chilean government. In the next four years Exim Bank not only financed the creation or expansion of a large number of Chilean industries, it also ensured, through its lending policies, that American machinery, technology, and patent holders participated in the process of industrialization. Exim Bank loans required the exclusive use of United States purchased capital goods for the Chilean industries receiving Bank credits and even that American carriers ship the goods to Chile. Further, whereas the Chilean government guaranteed the loans and even provided much of the capital, Exim Bank demanded that only private investors hold a majority of the industries' voting stock.

American influence in the development policies of the Chilean government benefited Chilean private investors as well as United States interests. Credit to agricultural and industrial interests from CORFO often entailed negative real interest rates; that is, inflation more than counterbalanced the interest rates, making credit a subsidy to debtors. Externally financed economic modernization was oriented toward importing capital goods for industry and labor-saving farm machinery and thereby strengthened the position of employers, especially in agriculture, vis-à-vis the labor force. Moreover, private investors achieved a dominant voice in the three major industrial complexes originating from CORFO initiative—the Pacific Steel Corporation (CAP), the National Petroleum Corporation (ENAP), and the National Electric Corporation (ENDESA). Key stockholders included Kennecott Copper Corporation and influential members of the National Society of Manufacturers. Even enterprises in which CORFO had a majority interest acted more like private firms than public enterprises, since entrepreneurs and bankers on the various government policymaking agencies assured a favorable attitude toward private business.

The growing economic, political, and cultural influence of the United States in Chile in the early post-World War II years did not eliminate certain basic contradictions between Chilean national interest and the interests of American companies or foreign policies dictated by the Cold War. Among some Chilean leaders and businessmen there developed a conscious awareness of the disadvantages of subordinating Chilean copper policy, industrialization, and domestic politics to changes in United States policy. Efforts to establish particular industries through CORFO brought Chilean officials and industrialists into direct conflict with U.S. corporations. Economic assistance conditioned with requirements to buy higher-priced American products or to ship in costlier United States carriers provided obvious examples of differences in American and Chilean national interests. Most of all, the disparity between what copper exports might bring the nation and what they actually provided in foreign exchange led groups on both the Right and the Left to resent, if not attack openly, the American copper firms.

Notwithstanding increased taxation of the copper industry in the early 1950s, pressures to exact greater benefits for Chile from the country's most valuable natural resource increased gradually in that decade and resulted, in the 1960s, in policies to nationalize the major United States copper companies. The Chilean Right gratefully accepted American support for an anticommunist campaign, credits for industrialization, cooperation in infiltrating the Chilean labor movement with "responsible" unionists, and educational exchanges, but they remained in their own way Chilean nationalists. This nationalism and their anger with American support for *agrarian reform* would ally them in the 1960s and early 1970s with middle-class and leftist political parties in efforts to eliminate American control over Chilean copper.

During three Radical administrations (1938–52), the combination of deficit-financing of industrialization, real salary gains for middle-class groups without proportional increases in internal taxation or government revenues, and the stagnation of agriculture heightened inflationary pressures. Despite government promises of progressive income redistribution and better educational opportunities, most urban workers along with the rural labor force actually lost ground in real income from 1938 to 1952, and more than one-third of the school-age children did not attend school. Worse, rather than gaining the "economic independence" promised by González Videla, the country had become increasingly dependent upon private foreign capital, loans, and marketing decisions made by the United States copper firms. Most strikingly, it had become more dependent upon imports of *food*. Domestic agricultural production did not keep pace with population growth and fell even further behind a rate of urbanization more than double that of population increase. Poor performance by agriculture necessitated a growing quantity of foreign exchange to feed Chile's people. It also meant further inflationary pressure added to currency emissions, deficit financing, and growth of the government bureaucracy.

Inflation meant frustration for the salaried middle classes and government employees even when periodic upward wage adjustments somewhat ameliorated the full impact of the price increases that caused suffering for most blue-collar workers and the rural labor force. By the 1952 presidential elections, with renewed labor agitation and González Videla's vacillating application of anticommunist and internal security legislation, Chile had a highly fragmented, weary, and frustrated electorate. Carlos Ibáñez took advantage of the population's exasperation with party politics and again emerged as an authoritarian, "above politics," antiparty candidate for president. Supported by a heterogeneous coalition of Socialists, middle-class groups, dissident Radicals and Conservatives, and the ascendant Agrarian Labor party (*Partido Agrario Laborista*), and also by a newly organized "Feminist Party," in the first presidential election after extension of suffrage to women in national elections in Chile, Ibàñez swept into office with a broom as a symbol of his intensions to "clean house." Promising electoral reforms, an end to corruption, and eventual elimination of the anticommunist legislation, the ex-dictator overwhelmingly defeated the divided opposition.

As in the 1927–31 period, Carlos Ibáñez' lack of commitment to formal democracy or to the Chilean party system made his second administration highly personalistic, authoritarian, repressive—and in some ways quite innovative. As in his earlier administration (1927–31), Ibáñez sought to utilize the state apparatus to encourage industrialization and to stimulate national development. Creation of the Banco Central, through consolidation of existing credit institutions, and support for public enterprise and semi-autonomous entities in various sectors of the economy, such as IANSA (sugar), CAP (steel), ENDESA (energy), and ENAP (petroleum), reaffirmed Ibáñez' activist, technocratic vision of the state. Loyal to neither party nor ideology, Ibáñez filled government posts with upwardly mobile politicians from splinter parties or ethnic minorities, such as Arab-Chileans. Indifferent to the long-term strength of the traditional parties, the president cooperated with the Falange (later Christian Democrat) deputy, Jorge Rogers Sotomayor, in adopting a far-reaching electoral reform (1958) that would drastically curtail the power of the landlords in Chilean politics. Further, after using Law 8811 and the anti-communist legislation to repress agricultural unionism and the urban labor movement throughout his term of office, Ibáñez fulfilled his campaign promise to eliminate the Law for the Permanent Defense of Democracy prior to leaving office. This paved the way for consolidation of a new electoral coalition between Socialists and Communists, the Popular Action Front (FRAP), which almost captured the presidency in the 1958 elections.

The electoral reform of 1958 introduced an Australian ballot (a single official ballot) and increased penalties for electoral fraud and bribery. A public ballot meant that landowners could no longer effectively control the votes of rural workers through distribution of party ballots and monitoring of the polls to assure that workers voted "correctly." In addition, the new election law made voting compulsory and provided for jail terms or fines for nonvoters. This inducement to electoral participation combined with the official secret ballot ended the hegemony of the landowners in the rural districts. It also meant that the cornerstone of Chilean political stability, the hacienda system, would come under mounting pressure from 1958 on as the availability of rural votes

TABLE 8–8. PRESIDENTIAL ELECTION, 1952

Candidate	Vote Totals
Carlos Ibáñez	446,439
Arturo Matte (Liberals & Conservatives)	297,357
Pedro E. Alfonso (Radicals & Falange)	190,360
Salvador Allende (Socialists & Communists)	51,975
Total	954,131

sent Marxists, Christian Democrats, Radicals, and other smaller political parties into the countryside in search of rural votes.

If the eventual political consequences of the Ibáñez administration proved beneficial to rural workers and eroded the power of the Right, the immediate results of the administration's political and economic policies gravely affected the urban and rural poor throughout the nation. The end of the Korean War, and with it the plunging demand for Chilean copper, reduced Chile's import capabilities by almost 30 percent in 1953. At the same time, the country approached the limits of easy import-substitution industrialization. Investment as well as growth in economic output declined. In turn, government revenues decreased, but a system of automatic readjustment of salaries in response to inflation inhibited cutbacks in government expenditures. Stagflation that brought the annual inflation rate (86% in 1956) to the highest levels in Chilean history (before 1970–73) and international pressure on the government concerning debt payments moved the government to call in an American economic mission to design a program of stabilization. Hoping that the good relations between the Klein-Saks Mission and the International Monetary Fund would reopen international lines of support for the Chilean economy, the Ibáñez government attempted to implement the mission's recommendations.

The Klein-Saks recommendations conformed closely to what now is considered conventional, hard-line, antiflationary policies favored by the International Monetary Fund: elimination of "excess demand" through wage controls, restrictions on credit, cutbacks on government expenditures, elimination of subsidies by public services such as water and transport, reduced currency emissions, replacement of multiple exchange rates for a single "floating" rate, and removal of price controls except for "essential commodities." This program entailed suspension of automatic wage readjustments and efforts to ensure that wage increases did not exceed the rate of inflation. In addition, the administration adopted a generally favorable attitude toward development through incentives to private domestic investors and the American copper companies. So-called New Deal, or *nuevo trato*, legislation (1955), intended to attract further investment through "profit stimulus," reduced effective tax rates on Anaconda and Kennecott, as well as providing the companies with a number of commercial, accounting, and exchange control benefits.

The Copper Department created as part of this legislation eventually gave the Chilean government much-needed technical capabilities to monitor the copper industry; but the immediate effect of the *nuevo trato* was higher profits for Anaconda and Kennecott without the desired further investments by the companies in Chile. Worse still, from the Chilean perspective, Chile's share of the world market barely remained stable and the percentage of copper refined in Chile by the companies actually declined from a high of 89 percent in 1951 to merely 45 percent in 1958. In practice, the copper companies profited and private businesses adjusted to the inflationary situation, while salaried and wage-earning Chileans bore the brunt of the government's program. The administration imposed readjustments in remuneration substantially below the rate of inflation to "depress demand." Workers and salaried employees consequently found themselves with less money to spend on food, clothing, and shelter. To carry through on the program, the Ibáñez government was forced to deal harshly with the resultant labor agitation (1955–57) and rioting in Santiago (1957); among other measures labor leaders and "communists" were confined in detention camps under the terms of the Law for the Permanent Defense of Democracy.

Inflation rates declined; so did the standard of living of the majority of Chileans. When restrictions on credit and subsidies to industrialists and landowners also angered the groups who, with the middle classes, had helped bring Ibáñez to power, the government lost the base of support it had briefly captured in the years from 1952 to 1955. As the 1958 presidential elections approached, unification of the leftist parties and total rejection of Ibáñez policies by the mass of the Chilean electorate set the stage for another close contest in which the Socialist-Communist candidate, Salvador Allende, fell just short of victory.

TABLE 8–9. PRESIDENTIAL ELECTION, 1958

Province	J. Alessandri (supported by Liberals and Conservatives)	Bossay (Radical)	Zamorano ("leftist" priest)	Allende (FRAP)	Frei (Christian Democrat)
Tarapacá	3558	3859	529	8299	4922
Antofagasta	5670	5866	1083	14954	6567
Atacama	2533	5423	247	6167	3621
Coquimbo	10,460	8886	1280	14,283	7952
Aconcagua	10,018	4233	1530	7290	5953
Valparaíso	35,680	17,192	5727	26,611	29,913
Santiago	151,797	51,984	11,194	121,452	91,305
O'Higgins	16,753	4517	2175	14,537	8426
Colchagua	13,556	3435	477	6190	4379
Curicó	6509	2458	704	6067	3107
Talca	9763	4163	7206	8584	6377
Maule	5823	4551	830	2749	3375
Linares	10,674	4044	4156	7927	5912
Ñuble	11,988	11,164	811	10,947	11,290
Concepción	17,418	13,091	624	34,594	18,154
Arauco	1932	3125	61	6258	1616
Biobío	7660	4670	200	7360	3611
Malleco	10,133	5592	187	7485	4951
Cautín	21,228	8979	920	11,921	12,587
Valdivia	12,387	6791	637	11,559	7545
Osorno	8318	5524	156	5542	2770
Lianquihue	7430	4304	219	4056	6075
Chiloé	6146	4621	157	3689	1559
Aisén	1229	1027	44	1261	953
Magallanes	1285	2791	151	6708	2857
Total	389,948	192,110	41,305	356,499	255,777

The presidential elections of 1958 brought to office Jorge Alessandri, son of ex-President Arturo Alessandri and an experienced conservative economic minister. Having won the presidency with a scant plurality over Salvador Allende, Alessandri could not count upon a docile Congress or even the temporary popular base achieved by Ibáñez in 1952. A year after he took office, the Cuban Revolution injected a whole new concern into Chilean politics and American foreign policy. In an effort to counteract the appeal of the Cuban Revolution throughout the rest of Latin America, the United States proposed the Alliance for Progress, which included commitment to agrarian reform—the single policy most bitterly resisted by the Chilean Right during the previous thirty years. Although Alessandri attempted to maintain the essential administrative and legislative impediments to agricultural unionism and rural labor conflict, he found himself under rapidly mounting pressure from Marxist and Christian Democratic political organization among the rural labor force.

The electoral successes of the FRAP coalition in the countryside in the 1958 presidential election and the disappearance of the Law for the Permanent Defense for Democracy renewed interest among Socialists and Communists in political mobilization of rural workers. In addition, the growing strength of the Christian Democratic party in the early 1960s sent groups of Catholic organizers to rural areas to compete with the Marxists. Penetration of Marxist parties and Christian Democrats into the countryside, combined with the electoral reform of 1958, produced a fundamental alteration in Chilean politics in the 1961 congressional elections. For the first time in the twentieth century the Conservatives and the Liberals failed to gain one-third of the seats in Congress. FRAP obtained more votes than any other single party list and controlled 27.5 percent (40) of the seats in the Chamber of Deputies and elected thirteen senators (of a total of 45). The Christian Democrats, originally a small group that had broken away from the Conservative party in the late 1930s, for the first time polled more votes than the Conservatives.

The outcome of the 1961 congressional elections left the incumbent Alessandri administration dependent upon the Radical party. The Radicals, hoping to win back the presidency in 1964, demanded ministerial participation in exchange for support of the government in the legislature. In addition, the Radicals now became advocates of "land reform." United States diplomats also put pressure on the Alessandri government to adopt a land reform program as part of the Alliance for Progress.

Alessandri, a firm believer in the benefits of private enterprise and diminishing government "interference" in the economy, opposed the reformist elements that demanded sweeping social and economic changes in Chilean life. However, loss of congressional influence by Conservatives and Liberals, along with pressures from the Alliance for Progress and mounting Marxist/Christian Democratic political activity, forced certain changes upon the administration. In defense of their political base in the countryside, Conservatives and Liberals attacked the Alliance for Progress and argued that increased Chilean participation in the profits of the copper industry would do far more for the country than land reforms, tax reforms, or other redistributionist measures sponsored by the Alliance. In language that would become more familiar after the military coup of 1973, one Conservative senator cautioned that the potential for demagoguery in the Alliance for Progress threatened the basic values of the "Western and Christian world."

Attacked by both the Left and the Right, the American copper companies felt the impact of the first tentative measures that ultimately resulted in nationalization. Taxes on the industry increased by 10 to 15 percent, and a Conservative minister proposed a plan whereby the companies would be forced to raise production considerably as well as to increase drastically (to 90 percent) the amount of copper refined in Chile. Although this plan was blocked through cabinet reshuffles and negotiations between the

TABLE 8–10. SUMMARY OVERVIEW OF LANDOWNER-GOVERNMENT
RESPONSE TO RURAL LABOR ACTIVISM IN CHILE, 1932–57

Presidential Election	Landowner Reaction
1932–33	
Presidential election (1932). First legally organized rural unions formed in Chile; several rural labor conflicts.	Pressure from SNA and other landowner associations on President Alessandri, claiming unionization in countryside not legal.
1938–39	
Popular-front candidate Pedro Aguirre Cerda elected.	Landowner associations publish numerous editorials railing against communist agitation send letters to Pedro Aguirre Cerda. (Example: Landowners of Pirque claim: "Professional agitators have created discontent among workers and are forming unions, inciting social indiscipline. We have initial stages of a State of Revolution. Request that the government suspend for now all procedures leading to rural unionization.")
First large wave of rural unionization, labor conflicts.	
1946–47	
Gabriel González Videla elected President with Communist support.	Numerous editorials in SNA journal, *El Campesino,* denouncing agitations in the country. (Examples: November, December, 1946; March, 1947).
Communists occupy ministries; massive wave of rural (and urban-mining) labor conflicts, strikes, unionization.	Move in Congress to pass "special law" to regulate rural labor—with support of Gabriél González Videla.
1952–53	
Carlos Ibáñez elected President with support of Socialists; campesino strike at Molina; march on Santiago; isolated conflicts elsewhere.	Calls for government intervention; application of Law 8987.

Government Responses	*Landowner Follow-up*
Circular 4060-4061 "temporarily" suspends rural unionization; remains in effect until 1937–38.	Workers involved in first legal unions around Molina (Talca Province) dismissed and evicted; workers presenting labor petitions (1934–35) arrested, dismissed, evicted.
Ministerial Order 34* "temporarily suspends" rural unionization; remains in effect until 1946. * Clearly illegal, unconstitutional.	*Intendente of Curicó:* "Due to labor petitions presented by agricultural workers, the majority of affected land-owners in this province are dismissing workers who participated. Workers whose families have lived on these farms for generations being forced to leave." *Intendente of Linares:* "Landowners have organized movement to evict on a massive scale rural workers from farms in this region."
Law 8811 (1947) restricts rural labor conflicts; outlaws strikes in agriculture; makes rural unionization almost impossible Law 8987 (Law for the Permanent Defense of Democracy) outlaws Communists; "cleanses" labor movement—destroying most rural labor organizations.	Labor Department receives communications from all over the country reporting massive dismissals and evictions of rural workers—especially those active in labor conflicts or labor leaders.
Application of Law 8987 against leaders of Molina strike; eventual negotiated settlement.	Dismissal of labor leaders in Molina farms—but during 1953–57 conflicts continue, in gradually reduced number.

companies and Alessandri, the political position of both the American copper companies and the Chilean landowners seemed ever less tenable.

The growing need to import food, inflation, and a mounting press campaign by leftist and reformist newspapers and intellectuals isolated the landowners politically and identified them in the public mind as the group largely responsible for Chile's social and economic backwardness. Intensified organizational activity by Marxists and Christian Democrats in the countryside reminded landowners of the labor crises and union struggles of 1939–41 and 1946–47. Once again editorials appeared in the major SNA publication warning of the threat of communism and anarchy if rural workers were allowed to unionize. Now, however, landowners lacked the political strength in Congress and the urban alliances necessary to prevent the first step toward transformation of the Chilean countryside.

In 1962, the year after the Right lost its veto power in Congress, and under pressure from Alliance for Progress officials who controlled the American "foreign aid" program, Chile adopted an agrarian reform law that began a decade-long assault upon the hacienda system. Law 15020 created three government agencies to administer programs of land reform, agricultural extension, and agricultural planning. Though under the Alessandri administration the government failed to carry out extensive agrarian reform, the legislation did provide a legal basis for more extensive transfers of land from large estates to small holders. In addition, two of the new government agencies—the Agrarian Reform Corporation (CORA) and the Institute for Agrarian and Livestock Development (INDAP)—would later play a revolutionary role in transforming Chilean agriculture and Chilean politics. In the short run (1962–64), the Alessandri government carried out what many Chileans called a "flower pot reform" (*reforma de macetero*), converting 60,000 hectares of public lands and well-recompensed private estates into small and medium-size farms.

By the end of the Alessandri administration a three-way battle was shaping up for the 1964 presidential election. FRAP again supported the candidacy of Salvador Allende. The Christian Democrats, who obtained extensive financing from covert American sources, offered Eduardo Frei. The Right (*Frente Democrático*) presented Julio Durán, a member of the conservative wing of the Radical party. In March 1964 a congressional by-election to replace a popular Socialist congressman in Curicó was interpreted by the three contending forces as a barometer of electoral strength for the upcoming presidential elections. However accurately the Curicó by-election reflected national political sentiment, FRAP's decisive victory disheartened the Right which finished third behind the Christian Democrats. The Frente Democrático dissolved and, in an effort to prevent a "communist" victory, threw its support to Eduardo Frei.

In the presidential campaign that followed both the Christian Democrats and FRAP promised agrarian reform, rural unionization, and enforcement of labor law in the countryside. Both Marxists and Christian Democrats courted rural votes, supported rural strike committees, helped organize rural unions, and promised an end to the hacienda system. To the landowners the Christian Democrats were the lesser of two evils.

When the Christian Democrats won the presidential election, and found themselves in competition with the Marxists for rural votes in the upcoming congressional elections of 1965, the viability of the new government came to depend upon greatly increasing party representation in Congress. To achieve this, some Christian Democratic candidates adopted the most drastic tactics previously used by Marxists in the rural sector, including sponsorship of illegal agricultural strikes and land occupations. The rural votes that had guaranteed the political power of the hacendados in national politics now provided the impetus for a frontal attack on the hacienda system by the Christian Democratic administration, as well as by the Marxist opposition.

This attack on the hacienda system would first erode the political and economic arrangement that had held the Chilean party system together between 1932 and 1964, and would then intensify polarization of political conflict and so bring to an end Chile's vaunted political stability and to its special version of democracy.

9 Christians and Marxists

Competition for the presidency in 1964 pitted against each other the Christian Democrats and the Marxist Frente de Acción Popular, both of which rejected the basic assumptions of capitalist liberal democracy. The Marxist-dominated FRAP coalition offered the ultimate prospect of creation of a socialist society in Chile. The Christian Democrats proclaimed that Chilean society required fundamental, even revolutionary, changes, but that these changes could be carried out through legal, peaceful means. To emphasize the difference between themselves and the Marxists, they adopted as the slogan of their program, "Revolution in Liberty."

The Christian Democrats criticized the evils of capitalism and materialistic socialism, offering in their stead a vaguely defined "communitarian" society or Christian socialism. Based upon writings of the French philosopher Jacques Maritain and upon Catholic social doctrine, a communitarian society would supposedly end class conflict through new types of "worker enterprises" that harmonize labor and capital. It would combine social pluralism and civil liberties with a just redistribution of wealth and income. But just as Marxist-Leninists lack any detailed description of the works of a truly communist society, Christian Democrats had various visions of a communitarian society.

Marxist parties had played an active role in Chilean politics since the second decade of the twentieth century. Communists, Socialists, and Trotskyists could trace their ancestry to the labor movement of the late nineteenth century, the Partido Demócrata (1887), and the Partido Obrero Socialista (POS) led by Recabarren and his comrades after 1912. Although the Communist party dated only from 1922 and the Socialist party from the early 1930s, an indigenous Marxist movement linked to international Marxism had struggled for at least half a century to reform or destroy Chilean formal democracy.

In the labor movement the Marxists had created a firm base of popular support. Just as some families passed Catholicism from generation to generation, so other families transmitted loyalty to the Communist or the Socialist party. Party-oriented youth movements, retail shops, sports clubs, doctors, and even barber shops allowed most of such people's daily lives to go on within a network of party loyalists. Of course, not all party members or sympathizers so restricted their lives or committed themselves to party work, but both Communists and Socialists had established strong roots in Chilean soil.

The FRAP coalition's presidential candidate in 1964, Salvador Allende, was a savvy, well-known politician. During the popular-front years Dr. Allende served as minister of health and subsequently gained valuable political experience in the Congress. In 1952 and 1958, respectively, Allende lost presidential elections to Carlos Ibáñez and Jorge Alessandri. The slim margin of his loss to Alessandri in 1958 badly scared the traditional political parties, the Catholic Church, and policymakers in the United States.

In contrast to the Marxist parties, the Christian Democrats could trace their official existence back only to 1957. Prior to that time, however, the ideological and organizational evolution of Christian Democracy stemmed from Catholic social doctrine and from dissident and more progressive elements within the Chilean Conservative party. In particular, the papal encyclicals *Rerum Novarum* (1891) and *Quadragesimo Anno* (1931) established the foundations of official Catholic response to the dilemmas of industrial society and the international challenge of Marxism. Pope Leo XIII noted in *Rerum Novarum* that the process of industrialization and capitalist development concentrated production and wealth into the hands of "a small number of opulent and wealthy men and put upon the innumerable multitude of proletarians a yoke that differed little from slavery." Without organizations to defend them the workers found themselves "alone and defenseless . . . against the inhumanity of their masters." This critique of capitalist development did little immediately to influence the Latin American or Chilean Catholic hierarchy, but nonetheless provided doctrinal justification for initial efforts by progressive Catholic laypersons and clerics to improve the lot of the working classes.

Forty years later, at the depths of the world depression, Pope Pius XI reconfirmed the Church's concern for the plight of the working classes in a harsh attack on capitalism and international imperialism. Pius XI's *Quadragesimo Anno* went further than Leo XIII and specifically referred to the misery of the landless laborers of the countryside, indirectly placing the Church on the side of those advocating agrarian reform to bring about social justice.

These encyclicals and other doctrinal statements placed the Church in opposition to the economic and political liberalism upon which the institutions of Western capitalist democracy rested. Progressive Catholic social theorists rejected the legitimacy of labor market determination of wages, insisting upon a just wage sufficient to guarantee a decent standard of living for the worker and the worker's family. The Church also officially recognized the importance of workers' organizations—not as vehicles of class struggle, but as "instruments of concord and peace," guided by Christian principles in the solution of the social question. Despite this pacific orientation, *Rerum Novarum* recognized that harsh working conditions, long hours, and low pay sometimes justified workers in resorting to strikes or other forceful means to better their conditions.

In the first two decades of the twentieth century a small number of Catholic politicians and churchmen in Chile responded to the social question with proposals for reform inspired by the social doctrines elaborated in *Rerum Novarum*. Based in the Jesuit college of San Ignacio, Father Fernando Vives Solar and Father Jorge Fernández Pradel influenced a group of future political leaders, priests, and bishops who later played a leading role in the development of Chilean Christian Democracy. By 1917 Father Vives and his colleagues had established a "Social Secretariat" and were engaged in unionization efforts among small numbers of workers in industry, transport, and commerce in Santiago. Objections by leading Conservative politicians undermined these first efforts and periodically forced the temporary European exile of controversial clerics.

Against the background of the post-World War I economic crisis in Chile, and the growing sentiment favoring separation of Church and State, the Chilean archbishop and prominent historian Crescente Errázuriz delivered a pastoral message entitled "On Social Action." Archbishop Errázuriz took note of the misery of many Chilean workers and, in particular, of the lamentable condition of the campesinos. Speaking several years before the military coup of 1924 forced the "social laws" upon a recalcitrant Chilean Congress, the archbishop accepted the necessity of workers' organizations in order "to obtain for the workers the benefits to which they have a right."

Coincident with the Church's increased concern with the plight of Chilean workers and campesinos after World War I, it also faced pressures for separation of Church and

State. In June 1923 President Alessandri proposed legislation to Congress intended to protect religious freedom for all Chileans and to insulate the Catholic Church from its traditional role in partisan politics. Quoting Bishop Valdivieso (1859), the president pointed to the dangers associated with linking the "future of the Church, the most precious interests of religion, . . . to the fortunes of a [political] party." Negotiations between Church officials and the Alessandri administration assured the former title to its extensive property holdings, financial assistance, and the right to maintain or expand its role in education, public health, and charitable activities. Thus, when the Constitution of 1925 officially separated Church and State, the archbishop of Santiago could comment in his pastoral that "It is just to note that the authorities in Chile, in establishing this separation, have not been motivated by the spirit of persecution which characterizes other countries where Catholicism has been attacked. . . . The State is separated from the Church; but the Church is not separated from the State, and will always be ready to serve it."

Archbishop Errázuriz' effective leadership in the Church-State separation matter left the Church in a relatively unblemished political position. He averted direct confrontation between Liberals, Radicals, and Conservatives, thereby allowing these groups, along with the Church, to focus upon the threatening implications of the social question.

Pastoral messages and other doctrinal statements on the social question by leading intellectuals of the Chilean Church derived both from a real concern for the condition of the Chilean poor and also from the growing Marxist influence among the country's working classes. Catholic leaders, grounded in the Church's philosophical and theological rejection of "individualistic liberalism," attempted to forge a response to the social question that would be an alternative to the millenarian Marxist vision of a classless society. Indicative of this anti-Marxist motivation for part of the Church's concern with the social question, the bishop of Temuco in 1933 presented a paper at the Third Congress of Catholic Men entitled "A Study of the Practical Manner of Combatting Communisn in Chile."

Anticommunism and sincere commitment to Catholic social doctrine provided the foundation of the education received at San Ignacio and Santiago's Catholic University by the generation of students in the late 1920s and early 1930s who would become the principal leaders of Chilean Christian Democracy. These young progressive Catholics— Bernardo Leighton, Manuel Garretón, Ignacio Palma, Radomiro Tomic, Eduardo Frei— served their political apprenticeship in the youth movement of the Conservative party. They became so active in carrying out the social doctrine of the Church that finally the Conservative party could not tolerate them, and in 1938 they broke away to form a new party, the Falange Nacional.

In the year that the Falange emerged as an independent political party, the Catholic Church created the Secretariado Nacional Económico Social (National Economic and Social Secretariat) in response to the social agitation associated with the growing strength of the Chilean popular front. Under the direction of Oscar Larson, who had previously worked with the Catholic Students Federation (ANEC), the Secretariat moved into direct social action, including organization of rural workers. Emilio Tagle, later the archibishop of Valparaíso, and Oscar Larson supported the formation of the Unión de Campesinos among rural workers in the region around Buin (Santiago province). By 1941 this Catholic rural labor union was reported to have 300 members in twelve rural estates. It was hardly a massive organizational drive, especially when compared with the national effort to unionize rural workers by Communists and Socialists from 1939 to 1941. Nevertheless this first Catholic support of rural workers' organizations infuriated the Conservative party, traditionally the Church's closest political ally.

In Fundo Huelquén, owned by a deputy of the Conservative party, a Falange lawyer and clerics assisted the workers in presentation of a labor petition to the landowner. The landowner attacked the clerics who participated in the workers' movement, suggesting that they leave determination of the workers' salaries to God and the conscience of the *patrón*. Subsequently the Conservative party demanded that the efforts of Larson, Tagle, and their colleagues be stopped and that the Unión de Campesinos be disbanded. The Church hierarchy acquiesced; Larson left for missions outside of Chile. Despite their immediate victory, the landowners recognized the threat of social movements inspired by Catholic social doctrine. They complained that "the *falangistas* are worse than the Communists, since we know how to defend ourselves against the Communists, but not so against the *falangistas*. . . ."

During the next decade the Falange remained a small, elitist social Christian party with a populist orientation. Occasionally Falange deputies made the critical difference in forging electoral or legislative coalitions or gave dramatic speeches in the Congress. For example, in 1947 Falange deputy Jorge Rogers Sotomayor bitterly denounced the rural unionization law (Law 8811) that reaffirmed the repression of rural workers. From time to time also, Falange leaders served in cabinet posts, beginning with Bernardo Leighton's brief stint as minister of labor (1938) in the second Alessandri administration. Progressive elements within the Church also continued with small-scale leadership-formation programs among workers and youth organizations. Neither in the political nor labor arena, however, did these progressive Catholics gain a mass following or exercise great national influence.

Complicating further the evolution of social Catholicism as a political force, new divisions within the Conservative party led to the foundation in the 1940s of the Partido Conservador Social Cristiano (Conservative Social Christian party). Somewhat more conservative than the Falange, and led by more established ex-Conservative politicians, the Conservative Social Christian party outpolled the Falange in national and local elections into the 1950s. The eventual dissolution in 1957 of the Partido Conservador Social Cristiano, however, united most progressive Catholics, along with ex-members of the Agrarian Labor party, into the Christian Democratic party (PDC) in anticipation of the 1958 presidential election.

After World War II a concern on the part of the Holy See and the United States about the advance of Marxism in Chile gave new impetus and financial support to Catholic organizations among workers, students, women, and peasants. Middle-class reformers, professionals, and technicians found in the Falange an alternative to the unmoving conservatism of the traditional parties and to the opportunism of the Radicals. With a heterogeneous base, the Falange developed as a multiclass movement under the continued direction of the generation of leaders who had founded it in the late 1930s. Slowly the Falange gained in national prestige and visibility, as it advocated extensive reforms consistent with the social doctrine of the Church.

Before 1953 the Falange was more active in urban areas and universities than in the countryside, but it would be the rural organizing activity of the Falange and Catholic labor leaders that did the most to boost the political credibility of the Catholic reformers. In 1952 Falange politician Emilio Lorenzini began to organize rural labor around the town of Molina in Talca province with the Federación Sindical Cristiana de la Tierra. The vineyards of the Molina region had seen a number of rural labor conflicts between 1919 and 1952. As late as 1946–47 headline-making legal strikes occurred in the region's farms—before Law 8811 and the Law for the Permanent Defense of

TABLE 9–1. ELECTORAL EVOLUTION OF FALANGE NACIONAL,
PARTIDO DEMÓCRATA CRISTIANA, CHAMBER OF DEPUTIES

Year	Total Votes	Percent of Electorate	Number of Deputies Elected
1941	15,553	3.5	3
1945	10,527	2.2	3
1949*	18,221	3.9	3
1953	22,353	2.8	3
1957	82,710	9.2	17
1961†	213,559	16.	23
1965	989,626	41.6	82

*In 1949 the Social Christian Party polled 2,018 votes without electing a deputy.
†Christian Democrats.
Source: Adapted from Germán Urzúa Valenzuela, Los Partidos Políticos Chilenos, Santiago, Editorial Jurídica, 1968, pp. 124–25.

Democracy suppressed the rural labor movement. It was ironical that in applying the latter law the government had banished Communist leaders, such as José Campusano, to the Molina district. Tense cooperation in the fields between Falange and Communist cadres set the stage for fierce competition in later years.

Emilio Lorenzini affiliated the Federación Sindical Cristiana de la Tierra with the major Catholic labor organization, Acción Sindical Chilena (ASICH). Formed in 1947 under the leadership of Jesuit Alberto Hurtado—after special authorization by the Jesuit general and Pope Pius XII—ASICH was a thorn in the side of both the Marxists and the traditional political parties in Chile. In the rural district around Molina, supported by Bishop Manuel Larraín (an early colleague of Father Hurtado in the awakening of the Catholic labor movement in the 1920s), ASICH and the Federación Sindical Cristiana de la Tierra provided campesinos with legal services, literacy and leadership training, and assistance in labor conflicts.

In October 1953, Lorenzini organized the Primer Congreso Sindical de los Obreros Campesinos de Molina, where rural workers and union leaders drew up labor petitions to present in the vineyards of Molina in November (prior to the harvest). When the landowners refused to negotiate in good faith with the workers, the campesinos declared a strike. Illegal under the terms of Law 8811, the strike brought government repression. Lorenzini and other union leaders went to jail for offenses specified in the Law for the Permanent Defense of Democracy; the government dealt with progressive Catholics by applying legislation intended to control "communist" activities.

Unwilling to accept defeat, ASICH organized a march to Santiago by the Molina campesinos. The political effect of this march in the early days of the new Ibáñez administration forced the government to release Lorenzini and other union leaders as well as to pressure the landowners to negotiate with the farm workers—despite the fact that the strike was clearly illegal. For both the numbers of workers involved and its psychological impact on national politics, the Molina strike is generally cited as the most important rural labor conflict in Chile prior to 1964. More important in the long run, however, were the campesino leaders who emerged in the Molina region, and the spread of the Catholic rural labor movement throughout the central valley, which provided Falange and Catholic reformers with a growing base in the Chilean countryside. In addition, after years of sporadic Marxist political and labor activity in the rural districts, the Church, Falange politicians, and Catholic-oriented rural labor unions had carried out the most important agricultural strike in Chilean history. The Molina strike and the subsequent activism of Catholic rural organizations gave credibility to Falange claims that they favored land reform, social justice, rural unionization, and sweeping social change.

Only four years after the Federación Sindical de la Tierra emerged in Molina, the Jesuit general in Rome, at the request of the Chilean Church, sent to Chile the Belgian Jesuit and social scientist, Roger Vekemans. The Chilean Church wanted help in the battle against communism; Vekemans would spearhead the anticommunist offensive for the next decade. Vekemans recruited Belgian businessman J. N. A. Sierens to begin social research in Chile. Sierens put together a systematic survey of Chilean institutions, with special attention given to "communist penetration." Noting the slim defeat of Allende in the 1958 presidential elections, Sierens recommended coordinated action by the Church to prevent a potential Marxist victory in 1964.

Vekemans, at the head of the Centro Bellarmino, directed an intellectual, organizational, and political campaign under the aegis of a "research and development foundation," called by its acronym DESAL. Large grants from Western European governments, private foundations, and Christian Democratic parties, as well as funds from the United States Central Intelligence Agency, via the conduit of the International Development Foundation, funded DESAL and other Catholic intellectual and organizing efforts. Vekemans, along with Father Mario Zañartu (affiliated with the University of Notre Dame in the United States) and other Jesuits, gave doctrinal direction to the campaign against Marxism in Chile. A thorough study of this international politico-religious penetration of Chilean politics by David E. Mutchler* documented an intricate web of financial arrangements and organizational ties emanating from Vekemans and his colleagues. In this web were entangled the mass media, labor, business, the American AID mission, CIA, Western European governments, political parties, and private foundations.

Complementing its research activities and elaboration of a new "development ideology," the Catholic Church's anti-Marxist offensive resulted in the creation of numerous neighborhood organizations, unions, farm committees, discussion groups, women's organizations, and quasi-political groups that could be mobilized for the 1964 election campaign. In the meantime, ASICH formed the Unión de Campesinos Cristianos in 1960 to unite isolated farm unions and worker's committees and to expand the rural labor movement. Moreover, parallel operations by Acción Católica Rural (Rural Catholic Action) and the Institute for Rural Education (IER)—also partially financed with American funds and partially staffed with Peace Corps volunteers—gave rise to the Asociación Nacional de Organizaciones Campesinas (ANOC), or the National Association of Campesino Organizations. After completing their training at the IER, ANOC leaders received salaries from the institute while they led rural labor conflicts, created Christian-inspired rural organizations, and opposed communism in the countryside.

These Catholic-oriented rural labor leaders mobilized thousands of Chilean campesinos into new organizations and inspired a growing rural activism. Though some leaders of the movement may have understood the international and the national political implications of their ties with IER, ACR, and the Christian Democrats, later events would demonstrate that many participants were more independent and more

---

The Church as a Political Factor in Latin America (New York: Praeger, 1971).

militant than their unknown patrons desired. Internal debates and conflicts over strategy and direction of the movement in the mid-1960s and after made clear that these
campesino organizations were far more complex and less manipulable than their early
directors had imagined. In the short term, however, these organizations proved an important resource in the campaign against Marxism in Chile.

As the political situation of the Alessandri government deteriorated after 1961, the
rising Catholic rural labor movement, in alliance with the newly founded Christian
Democratic party, represented a major alternative to the Marxist-dominated FRAP
coalition of Communists, Socialists, and smaller reformist parties. The most prominent
Christian Democratic leaders, including Eduardo Frei, had been schoolmates of important officials of Vekemans' Centro Bellarmino. Personal ties reinforced doctrinal and
ideological connections between the Christian Democrats and the Jesuit intellectuals.

In 1962 the Chilean bishops entrusted Vekemans and Renato Poblete, an old school-
mate of Eduardo Frei, with preparation of a "pastoral plan" that would help Frei
against Allende in the 1964 election. Also in 1962 the Chilean bishops initiated their
own land reform experiments, anticipating the legislation passed by the Alessandri
government later that year. Almost simultaneously the Church distributed a pastoral
letter entitled "The Social and Political Duty." This pastoral made clear that "communism deprives man of his liberty, suppresses all dignity and morality of the human person; it denies to the individual all natural rights. . . . Communism destroys any bond
between mother and child." During the 1964 election campaign Christian Democrats
distributed thousands of copies of this pastoral letter and papered the walls of Chile
with posters depicting the foreheads of Chilean children being branded with the ham-

Political rally for Eduardo Frei Montalva, Curicó, 1964.
(Courtesy Archivo Universidad de Chile.)

mer and sickle. The international Catholic offensive (1957–64) thus contributed to the domestic political campaign against the Marxists.

Meanwhile, Fidel Castro's sister, Juana Castro, came to Chile to tell the Chilean people, especially Chilean women, of the horrors of communism in Cuba. These developments combined with the psychological effect of the by-elections of Curicó—that prompted support by the Right for Frei's candidacy—and with millions of dollars in covert campaign contributions from American agents and European Christian Democrats, to give the Christian Democrats the presidency in 1964.

If anticommunism was the rationale for massive U.S., West German, and Church support for Chile's Christian Democrats, there existed within the Christian Democratic party many sincere reformers and even a small number of committed revolutionaries. President Frei's call for "Revolution in Liberty" was not empty rhetoric. The Christian Democrats intended to alter dramatically the very foundations of Chilean society, to redistribute income and wealth, to improve the living standards of, and to broaden opportunities for, the nation's workers and peasants, and to democratize the country's political and social life.

Faced with the many social and economic problems inherited from the process of economic development after 1930 and the historical legacy of a highly stratified class society, the Christian Democratic administration attempted to carry out a sweeping reform program encompassing every area of Chilean life. All the persistent problems of the Chilean economy received government attention—including efforts to control inflation, to improve the nation's balance of payments through stimulation of exports, to carry out large-scale agrarian reform, to enact meaningful tax reforms, and to make significant investments in public health, education and vocational training, and to expand the services of the Labor Department.

Almost every aspect of the government's program threatened either the political and economic privileges of the traditional elite or menaced leftist influence over organized labor and the urban and rural poor. No way existed for the Christian Democrats to implement their program without alienating the support of the rightist parties whose votes had elected President Frei. Similarly, no matter how successful the government was in implementing social and economic reforms, the FRAP parties could urge more rapid or more extensive changes, pointing to areas of policy failure and push working-class and peasant organizations into direct action that impelled the administration to move either faster than it desired or to use police to halt illegal land occupations or strikes.

Unfortunately for the Christian Democratic government, official policymakers clearly and precisely outlined the administration's short- and long-term goals in overly optimistic terms. Even with the Christian Democrats' stunning victory in the 1965 congressional elections, which gave them majority control of the House of Deputies, FRAP and rightist representatives in the Senate still managed to delay passage of key legislation. Every major component of the government's program—"Chileanization" of the copper industry, agrarian reform/agricultural unionization, tax reform, wage-price stabilization, and proposals to stimulate industrial growth—faced the scrutiny and obstructionism of the opposition. This was, of course, merely a new version of the historical struggle between executive coalitions and Congress that had characterized Chilean politics in the parliamentary period and also after 1932—complicated now by the facts that a single party rather than a coalition controlled the executive and that traditional political forces considered some Christian Democrats *prepotentes*, or uncompromising.

Only in 1966–67, after considerable negotiation and compromise, did the copper legislation, agrarian reform, and agricultural unionization legislation clear the Congress. Predictably, the Marxists opposed any effort by the government to restrain inflation through limitations on wage readjustments. The Right, enraged at the government-sponsored mobilization of rural workers into unions and cooperatives as well as at the prospect of a real agrarian reform, held hostage the copper legislation in an effort to weaken the administration's agrarian program. The Right also exacerbated relations with the United States by joining the Marxists in a call for outright nationalization of the copper industry instead of the acquisition by the Chilean government of majority interest in the companies that the government called "Chileanization." Only half face-tiously, leading Conservative and Liberal politicians suggested compensating the companies just as the United States-approved agrarian reform would compensate Chilean landowners for their expropriated holdings—with government bonds payable in thirty years.

The ambitious scope and the specificity with which the Christian Democrats set out their program made its effective implementation through legal means in a six-year period a practical impossibility. Notwithstanding greatly increased copper prices, due in part to the war in Vietnam, and substantial assistance from the Alliance for Progress, internal political opposition and the structural constraints of the Chilean socio-economic situation prevented total success. Thus, even the sometimes impressive accomplishments of the regime fell far short of its publicly announced objectives. Moreover, the severe drought of 1967–68 disrupted agricultural production, thereby adding to the nation's economic difficulties. The discrepancy between stated objectives and actual attainment allowed both the rightist and the FRAP opposition to point to the failure of the Christian Democratic administration.

In one area, especially, Christian Democratic policies led to dismal failure. Rather than decreasing Chile's economic dependence and reducing the influence of foreign capital on its economy, the Frei government created numerous incentives to attract for-

TABLE 9–2. COMPARISON OF POLICY OBJECTIVES AND PERFORMANCE OF "REVOLUTION IN LIBERTY"

Policy Objectives	Time Frame	Targeted Increase	Actual Increase
Retail prices	1965	25%	29%
Retail prices	1966	15%	23%
Retail prices	1967	10%	18%
Nonagricultural prices	1965	Less than 20%	28%
Money supply	1965	25%	65%
Real GNP	1964–70	23%	30%
Exports	1964–70	94%	94%
New farm ownerships	1964–70	100,000	28,000
New housing units	1964–70	360,000	260,000
Copper output	1964–70	90%	10%
Real GDP	1965–70	31%	18%
Per capita real GDP	1965–70	20%	5%
Gross investment	1965–70	70%	22% (through 1969)
Domestic saving	1965–70	100%	52% (through 1969)
Exports	1965–70	55%	68%
Copper exports	1965–70	70%	107%
Imports	1965–70	31%	63%

Source: After Thomas L. Edwards, Economic Development and Reform in Chile: Progress Under Frei, 1964–1970, Latin American Studies Center, Michigan State University, 1972, p. 50.

eign investors and subordinated public policy to conditions imposed by United States and international lending agencies. The incentives to foreign capital included generous profit-remittance arrangements and liberalized import regulations for firms establishing themselves in Chile. Promise of tax stability and exchange-control advantages also served to encourage foreign investment. In response to these incentives multinational enterprises substantially increased their investments in Chile, especially in the industrial sector. By 1970 over one hundred United States corporations had investments in Chile, among them twenty-four of the top United States-based multinationals.

Foreign investment brought with it high technology, capital-intensive production units that made little contribution to the government's efforts to reduce unemployment. Indeed, for the decade 1960–70, industry provided an average of only 15,000 new job opportunities per year—nowhere near enough to absorb the continuing tide of migrants from the countryside to the urban areas. This migration enlarged the rings of misery surrounding Santiago and other major cities, as the shantytowns and squatter settlements (*callampas,* or "mushroom towns") grew at alarming rates. In Santiago alone the *callampas* and squatter settlements sheltered nearly one-half million people, or 20 to 25 percent of the city's population.

Living conditions in these urban settlements varied from poor to deplorable. Most lacked basic urban services and amenities, including sewers and potable water. Unemployment levels ranged well above the official national figure of 8 percent, and underemployment disguised the desperate situation of families without any steady, dependable source of income. As in the rest of Latin America, these urban poor lacked meaningful unemployment insurance or welfare services that might guarantee even a "floor to misery." They endured a daily struggle for survival. Lacking also the protection of unions or private charitable relief, thousands of slum dwellers and residents of the shantytowns of Santiago received the political messages of the "Revolution in Liberty" without obtaining the material benefits it promised.

When the government did respond to the physical needs of the urban poor with self-help housing projects (*operación sitio*), encouragement of *centros de madres* ("mothers' centers") or *juntas de vecinos* ("neighborhood councils"), construction of waterworks or installation of electric lines, there always remained those who felt left out. The admittedly partisan process that determined which groups of urban poor would benefit from government programs, whether because of party affiliation or the high visibility of political mobilization in particular settlements, further undermined the government's efforts. For every successful program there were more people left out than included. The backlog of need and poverty made even significant improvements in the living conditions of some groups of the urban poor a political defeat for the incumbent administration, just as distribution of land to some 30,000 campesinos alienated many times that number who did not receive land from the government program.

In part, the extremely favorable treatment afforded the multinationals by the Frei administration, and the constraints on the government's program of reform, stemmed from the negotiated "solution" to Chile's immediate balance of payments crisis facing the Christian Democrats when they came to office. Chile's accumulated international obligations in 1964, over $1 billion, required almost 40 percent of copper export earnings for debt service alone. To support the Frei government's "Revolution in Liberty," the United States and ten other creditor nations agreed to a "rollover" or credit relief plan of approximately $100 million for a two-year period and a grace period that allowed for a five-year repayment schedule beginning in 1968. Chile pledged in exchange to facilitate transfer of payments on the renegotiated debt and also to relax controls on foreign exchange for purchase of certain types of imports. In turn, USAID provided large loans and other assistance to the Chilean administration; in 1964–65 USAID accounted for almost 15 percent of Chile's national budget. Thus the financial feasibility of the Christian Democratic reforms depended not only upon the hope for better copper prices, but also upon the good will of U.S. policymakers and the cooperation of the multinational enterprises. Touting the "Revolution in Liberty" as a positive alternative to the Cuban revolutionary model, United States policymakers sought to buttress the Christian Democrats as well as to support American business interests in Chile. This strategy, reminiscent of the American decision to underwrite the initial CORFO projects in 1939 and 1940—only now on a much grander scale—entangled the Christian Democratic administration in the web of American foreign policy, including the war in Vietnam. It also exacerbated the internal divisions within the government party as the Christian Democratic youth movement and the more populist elements of the party rejected any identification with foreign capital, imperialism, the American embassy, or the Vietnam War.

Apart from its uneven record with respect to its announced social and economic objectives, the Christian Democratic government mobilized hundreds of thousands of women, students, workers, and campesinos into new unions, cooperatives, and community organizations. These organizations depended upon government encouragement or subsidies and came to expect continual economic benefits or expanded government services. Distribution of consumer goods, credit, agricultural inputs, and jobs through political agencies like Promoción Popular (Popular Promotion) and INDAP created a vast network of patronage and spoils tying bureaucrats, party hacks, slum dwellers, and campesinos to government pursestrings. Immediate benefits such as new sewing machines for a *centro de madres* or seed and fertilizer for a campesino cooperative helped convince the underclasses of the government's concern for their plight. Accompanied by promises of increasing material benefits by government enthusiasts who staffed the mushrooming public sector, these initial spoils of reform also created high expectations of rapid, often unobtainable, changes in lifestyle and of economic opportunities.

To a great extent the Christian Democratic program of political mobilization and deliberate "consciousness raising" (*concientización*) made impossible the attainment of its other major economic objectives such as control of inflation, increases in productivity, and higher levels of domestic savings and investment. With their hopes aroused by both the government's propaganda and the even more alluring Marxist vision in which redistribution of wealth and land would greatly improve the lot of the masses, Chilean workers and peasants could hardly be expected to accept government proposals for wage restraints, forced-savings plans, and moderation in labor disputes.

Moreover, as the government generally refused to use police or the military against slum dwellers, organized labor, or campesinos, illegal land occupations and even worker-declared "expropriation" of farms and factories occurred more frequently. Whereas the leftist press indignantly publicized the small number of cases in which the government did use force to halt labor conflicts or to remove trespassers—especially when workers died or were injured as in Puerto Montt in early March 1969—the political Right noted the government's reluctance to guarantee private property rights and organized white guards to defend its interests. No administrative decree or government policy could effectively limit popular mobilization once set in motion; only police or the military sufficed. With its unwillingness to adopt clearly repressive tactics, especially given the numerous divisions within the Christian Democratic party itself, the government found a lawful "Revolution in Liberty" to be illusory. If the government chose to uphold the law, it necessarily employed force against workers, peasants, and students acting illegally to accelerate the program of reform.

TABLE 9–3. DISTRIBUTION OF LABOR FORCE BY ECONOMIC SECTOR, 1960–70 (1000s)

	1960	1961	1962	1963	1964	1965	1966	1967	1968	1969	1970	Percent
Agriculture	711.1	668.6	687.7	704.0	680.8	709.8	717.7	750.0	736.4	731.7	738.0	24.2
Mining	92.5	94.9	91.7	88.7	91.7	93.4	93.6	94.0	94.5	97.7	99.2	3.3
Industry	412.6	1439.7	450.4	464.5	477.9	506.7	527.7	534.4	544.6	550.7	562.9	18.8
Construction	130.5	135.6	158.6	158.5	188.8	183.1	186.3	169.0	168.5	172.0	177.5	6.0
Electricity, gas, and water	10.8	11.0	11.1	11.8	12.3	12.5	11.9	11.9	11.8	11.8	11.8	0.3
Commerce	260.3	265.5	279.0	294.1	311.1	330.0	351.0	375.0	1404.2	428.5	451.5	15.1
Transport	121.2	126.0	135.0	139.0	143.8	148.0	149.5	156.2	161.8	167.4	175.6	5.9
Services	578.0	587.6	592.5	613.6	630.9	640.0	665.0	721.4	757.5	761.3	777.7	26.0
Total	2317.0	2348.9	2406.0	2474.2	12546.3	2623.5	2702.7	2811.9	2879.3	2921.1	2994.2	100.0

Source: Odeplan, Chilean Planning Agency.

TABLE 9–4. ILLEGAL STRIKES, URBAN LAND INVASIONS,
FACTORY SEIZURES, AND FARM SEIZURES, 1966–1970

	1966	1967	1968	1969	1970
Urban land invasions		13	8	73	220
Factory *tomas*	n.d.	n.d.	5	24	133
Illegal strikes	936	878	901	771*	1085
Farm *tomas*	36†	9	27	148	271

*First nine months only.
†1960–66.
Source: Chilean Labor Department Annual Report for each year; Solon Barraclough and J. A. Fernández, *Diagnóstico de la reforma agraria Chilena*, Mexico, Siglo Veintiuno, 1974; Walden F. Bello, "The Roots and Dynamics of Revolution and Counterrevolution in Chile," unpublished doctoral dissertation, Princeton University, 1975.

The Marxist parties, recognizing this dilemma, lost no opportunity to exacerbate it by proclaiming their support for land occupations, farm seizures (*tomas*), and widespread illegal strikes. If in order to demonstrate its commitment to reform, the government invariably refused to halt these activities, then legal reform would have given way to an uncontrolled and uncontrollable revolutionary situation. Just as the leftists deliberately confronted the government with this choice between suppression of popular movements and chaos, so the rightists challenged the legality of the agrarian reform process and organized sometimes violent resistance to the government's legal reforms.

Complicating this situation, a minority element within the Christian Democratic party encouraged mass mobilization and political activism beyond the limits officially set by the Frei administration. In particular, Jacques Chonchol, director of INDAP, believed it necessary to go beyond the bounds of existing law in the unionization of rural labor and in support for agrarian reform. While the government sought to squeeze new legislation out of Congress (1964–67), Chonchol, via INDAP, promoted large numbers of agricultural labor conflicts and organized multifarm unions in direct violation of existing legislation. Not to be outdone, Communist and Socialist organizers competed with INDAP in the effort to mobilize the rural labor force against the landowners and to accelerate agrarian reform.

These efforts overwhelmed the Labor Department, which lacked sufficient personnel and resources to administer properly the mounting number of requests to form agricultural unions or to process efficiently the hundreds of agricultural labor disputes. After frequent appearances in its offices of INDAP organizers (*promotores*) representing campesino groups, the Labor Department ruled that INDAP officials "do not have the legal right to intervene in the presentation of labor petitions and in the process of negotiation of labor conflicts in the agricultural sector." In response, INDAP personnel received instructions to limit their intervention in rural labor conflicts to "informal" support or assistance. In addition, the new peasant organizations and even the Catholic rural labor movement, generated by ASICH and the Institute for Rural Education, pressured CORA, the agency responsible for implementing land reform, to speed up the expropriation and redistribution of agricultural land. Administrative inability to keep pace with the tide of popular mobilization and rising expectations made the government appear unwilling to fulfill its promises to the urban and the rural poor. It also made credible Marxist attacks on the government for failing to carry out completely its promised program. Added to criticism from the Right, united in the Partido Nacional after merger of Conservatives and Liberals in 1965, the dissident Christian Democrats and Marxist swamped the government reform program in sectarian politics and obstructionism.

The debate within the Christian Democratic party over the pace, character, and objectives of agrarian reform typified the basic contradictions that eventually proved fatal to the "Revolution in Liberty." The essential constraints on Chilean development could not be overcome without both improved distribution of wealth and income *and* increased production of goods and services. If redistribution occurred at the cost of current investment and reduced productivity, then any gains to the workers and peasants could only be temporary. Rising demands for goods and services without concomitant expansion of domestic production and export earnings could only lead to a renewal of the inflationary spiral. Under these conditions an ever more militant, politicized rural labor force became a serious obstacle to the government's overall economic program at the same time as it was a major social and political accomplishment of governmental policy.

More than any other aspect of the government program, official encouragement and often subsidization of the formation of thousands of organizations among Chile's urban and rural poor upset the equilibrium of Chilean society. It also created political forces that the government could not or would not control. Consistent with the ambiguity that characterized its reform program, the government sometimes did and sometimes did not call in police to squelch illegal rural labor conflicts, strikes in the cities or mines, or land occupations; sometimes it used a labor conflict as a pretext to place one of its representatives (*intervenor*) in the farm where the conflict was taking place and to organize the campesinos for eventual expropriation of the property.

Thus the "Revolution in Liberty" proved to be neither a revolution nor entirely lawful. It also failed to solve the fundamental economic problems the Christian Democrats themselves had identified in 1964: slow economic growth, instability of prices (inflation), dependence upon foreign markets and capital, and unequal distribution of wealth and income. Nevertheless, it did improve the living conditions of thousands of rural workers, tenants, and other beneficiaries of land reform; it did enact critical po-

TABLE 9–5. CHRISTIAN DEMOCRATIC AGRARIAN REFORM:
EXPROPRIATIONS, 1965–JULY 14, 1970

| Year | Number of properties* | Area in Hectares | | Total Area |
		Irrigated	Unirrigated	
1965	99	41,260.1	499,923.0	541,183.1
1966	265	57,877.4	468,326.0	526,203.4
1967 (Law 15.020)	131	20,141.8	115,155.4	136,297.2
1967 (Law 16.640)	86	30,443.1	119,285.4	149,728.5
1968	223	44,681.1	612,566.3	657,247.4
1969	314	54,478.8	807,361.8	861,840.6
1970 (to July 14)	201	30,986.6	604,181.5	635,168.1[†]
Total	1319	279,868.9	3,128,919.4	3,408,788.3

*Some *asentamientos* (land reform settlements) were formed by combining two or more properties.
[†]Error in original reads 535,163.1.

Source: CORA, *Reforma agraria chilena, 1965–1970*, Santiago, CORA, 1970, p. 36.

litical and administrative reforms; it instituted a tax system that generated substantial internal revenues; and it spread the belief that the Chilean state could offer real hope for improvement of the lot of the poor. In the areas of education and public health the Frei government also made impressive gains. Primary school enrollment increased by 46 percent, university enrollments doubled, and matriculation in technical schools quadrupled. Public health programs that established numerous rural clinics and trained community health leaders cut Chile's atrocious infant mortality rate and also bettered other general health conditions.

The reformist legislation of the Frei years and the massive organizational drive encouraged by the Christian Democratic administration provided substantial leverage for further fundamental reforms in Chilean society. In this sense the Christian Democrats definitively destroyed the cornerstone of Chilean formal democracy as it had functioned since 1932, without providing anything but the vaguely conceived notion of a "communitarian" society to replace it.

As the 1970 presidential elections approached, the Unidad Popular coalition, with Salvador Allende as its presidential candidate, offered a "transition to socialism" as their answer to this dilemma. The Christian Democratic candidate, Radomiro Tomic, urged an intensification of the "Revolution in Liberty." Jorge Alessandri, now an old man running as an "independent," appealed to the old elites and alienated middle-class sectors with the prospect of restoration of law and order.

From the perspective of the political Right the drastic nature of the Christian Democratic reforms between 1964 and 1970 prevented them from again supporting the Christian Democratic candidate as the lesser of two evils. In any case, most political analysts, including those in the American embassy in Santiago, predicted a victory for Alessandri. When Salvador Allende emerged with a slim plurality, Chile plunged into three years of dramatic change, punctuated by increasing polarization, political violence, and American intervention in Chilean politics. Christian Democracy's broad-front reformist projects proved to be both too much and too little of what Chile required to become a more Christian and more democratic society.

In the last year of the Christian Democratic administration political tension mounted. A "strike" (the so-called *tacnazo*, because it involved the Tacna regiment) among the officers and men of the Tacna and Yungay regiments of the army resulted in demands for the ouster of the minister of defense and for better pay and materiel for the armed ser-

TABLE 9–6. GROWTH OF CAMPESINO COOPERATIVE MOVEMENT, 1965–70

Year	Number	Members	Federations	Cooperatives Affiliated	Confederations	Federations Affiliated
1964	24	1718				
1965	43	3204				
1966	84	7802				
1967	123	11,452				
1968	171	18,456				
1969	222	30,034	7	51		
1970*	250	37,675	9[†]	81	1	9

*To October 22.
[†]Does not include five federations in formation which would include 45 affiliated cooperatives.
Source: INDAP, 1964/1970, n.p.

TABLE 9–7. UNION MEMBERSHIP IN CHILE — 1964 AND 1970

	1964		1970	
	Number	Members	Number	Members
Industrial or plant unions	632	142,958	1437	197,651
Professional or craft unions	1207	125,926	2569	239,323
Agricultural unions	24	1863	510	114,112
Totals	1863	270,542	4006	551,086

Source: Chilean Labor Department Annual Report for each year.

vices. Led by retired general Roberto Viaux, this military movement temporarily controlled the main arsenal, the non-commissioned officers' school, and the principal recruiting station; it reminded many Chileans of the events of 1924. Though the movement sputtered and dissolved after the resignation of the defense minister and government promises to attend to the military's economic demands, there was talk of a possible Viaux presidential candidacy after his incarceration—in striking parallel to the 1934 Senate campaign of Marmaduque Grove when the campaign slogan "From jail to the senate" inspired the Chilean Left. Members of the Socialist party took the opportunity to support military aspirations for improved pay and materiel despite their distrust of the reactionary tendencies of Viaux and his comrades.

Shortly thereafter the government pushed legislation through Congress to pacify the military. Even so, on November 19, 1969, the government felt compelled to issue an official declaration threatening severe sanctions against anyone seeking to subvert the discipline of the armed forces. The declaration also emphasized that the commanders of the armed forces and carabineros had reaffirmed their loyalty, discipline, and respect for democratic institutions. To confirm this, President Frei declared a "state of emergency" under the questionable authority granted to the executive in cases of "public calamity." This decree allowed the commander of the armed forces to take action to "prevent the commission of crimes or the occurrence of events affecting the security of the state."

At the same time that the Frei government was facing Chile's first major breach of military discipline since the popular-front period, revolutionaries and pseudorevolutionaries incited an already highly politicized population to take matters of economic

TABLE 9–8. IMPROVEMENTS IN PUBLIC HEALTH DURING THE FREI ADMINISTRATION

	1964	1969
General mortality (per 1000)	11.1	8.9
Infant mortality (per 1000 births)	102.9	79.0
Measles (per 100,000)	38.6	3.5
Typhoid fever (per 100,000)	2.1	0.9
Tuberculosis (per 100,000)	48.8	29.6

Source: Presidential message to the National Congress, Santiago, May 21, 1970; Sergio Molina, El Proceso de Cambio en Chile, Santiago, Editorial Universitaria, 1972, p. 89.

and social change into their own hands. The Movimiento de Izquierda Revolucionaria (MIR), or Left Revolutionary Movement, a relatively new revolutionary organization which rejected electoral politics, spread its inflammatory ideology among the Mapuche and the campesinos of southern Chile and into the *callampas* and *campamentos* of the urban centers. Favoring direct action, MIR cadres, often university students from the University of Concepción, joined with the Mapuche in land "recuperation" movements that were met, not unexpectedly, by landowner resistance. Elements of the Socialist party and MAPU (a radical splinter group from the Christian Democratic party) and even certain Communists also turned to overt attacks on the rights of landed proprietors, industrial enterprises, and owners of urban land and housing projects.

Part of this mass mobilization owed its inspiration to the usual prepresidential election rhetoric and vote seeking of the Marxist parties and the Christian Democrats. The Marxists, now in alliance with most of the Radical party and with a number of smaller parties, had again chosen Salvador Allende as their presidential candidate and formed a new version of the popular front called *unidad popular* (UP), or "popular unity." The popular unity electoral program called for revolutionary change. In the introduction to the UP electoral program, the parties of the coalition told the Chilean people that:

> Chile is a capitalist country, dependent on the imperialist nations and dominated by bourgeois groups who are structurally related to foreign capital and cannot resolve the country's fundamental problems—problems which are clearly the result of class privilege which will never be given up voluntarily.

The program criticized the Christian Democratic government as "nothing but a new government of the bourgeoisie, in the service of national and foreign capitalism, whose weak efforts to promote social change came to a sad end in economic stagnation, a rising cost of living, and violent repression of the people." According to the UP parties, the results of the Frei government demonstrated that reformism could not solve the problems of Chile's people.

To solve Chile's problems, the UP coalition proposed a peaceful transition to socialism. This required replacement of Chile's existing political institutions with a unicameral legislature, or people's assembly, to root out the evils of presidentialism and parliamentarism; reorganization of the judiciary and educational system; and greatly increased participation of workers and peasants through union and community organizations in national and local policymaking. Further, the program called for restructuring the economy by greatly increasing the scope of the "social" or public sector, by expropriating all agricultural estates of more than the equivalent of eighty hectares of irrigated land, and by nationalizing the financial system (banks and insurance companies) as well as "all those activities which have a strong influence on the nation's social and economic development." This last category seemed to open the door to a broad program of socialization of the means of production and of distribution channels. The UP indicated that with the dominant "social" sector of the economy there would coexist a "mixed" sector in which enterprises would combine public and private capital; and that, at least in the short run, small private firms could continue to operate. However, uncertainty among the country's small businesses concerning the eventual limits of the UP program, and the coalition's inability to reach internal agreement upon such limits, would produce serious political problems for the UP government (1970–73).

Opposing the UP coalition in the 1970 presidential election, the Christian Democrats chose as their candidate Radomiro Tomic. Tomic, ex-Chilean ambassador to the United States and one of the founders of the Falange, was considered an uncompromising leftist by the Chilean Right. Whereas other potential Christian Democratic candidates might have been able to reconstruct the alliance between the Partido Nacional, other conservative forces, and the Christian Democrats who elected Eduardo Frei in 1964, Tomic declared his unwillingness to cooperate with either the Right or the Radicals who refused to participate in the UP coalition. In a seeming attempt to appear even more revolutionary than Allende, Tomic highlighted his campaign with promises to complete agrarian reform by expropriating all the large rural estates "from the Andes to the sea" (*desde la cordillera hasta el mar*). Repeatedly Tomic emphasized that a victory in coalition with the Right was a victory *for* the Right. In contrast to his harsh attacks on the Partido Nacional and its candidate, Tomic's campaign speeches treated the possibility of an Allende victory as an alternative opportunity for progressive forces in Chile to unite and carry out fundamental social change.

If the Tomic candidacy, rather than that of a more moderate Christian Democrat, made rightist support for the Christian Democrats impossible, political polls showing ex-President Jorge Alessandri the likely victor in a three-way race for the presidency in 1970 whetted the appetite of the Chilean law-and-order forces for a return to "the stick" that Portales had once recommended to cure a nation's "bad habits." The combined support of the Partido Nacional, alienated middle-class groups, and a large number of urban and rural workers still attracted by the appeal of Alessandri's name, made his candidacy appear destined for success. Unfortunately for Alessandri and his supporters, his age and lack of vitality became embarrassingly evident in Chile's introduction to television politics. The image of a tired, inarticulate politician broadcast via television to many of the nation's voters reinforced the outhouse humor of UP election posters that caricatured Alessandri on a toilet with the caption "NICA" or *Ni cagando*, politely translated as "No way!"

Alessandri's weakness as a campaigner and the Christian Democratic decision to go it alone split the vote three ways. Salvador Allende received a slim plurality. Notwithstanding the addition of Radicals and other small parties to the old FRAP coalition, the UP's share of the vote actually decreased slightly from that achieved by FRAP in the 1964 election. More than a mandate for Allende or for revolutionary change, the election clearly demonstrated the extreme political divisions within Chilean society in 1970, with the "centrist" candidate finishing last.

According to the Chilean constitution, when no presidential candidate received a majority of the votes, Congress could choose as president one of the two candidates with the highest vote total. Since the Christian Democrats controlled the deciding votes in Congress, Alessandri proposed to exchange an immediate resignation for congressional designation of him as president. This would have allowed Eduardo Frei, ineligible to succeed himself immediately, to enter new elections and refashion a Rightist-

TABLE 9–9. PRESIDENTIAL ELECTIONS, 1964 AND 1970

Political Parties and Candidates	1964		1970	
	Total	Percentage	Total	Percentage
FRAP/UP (Salvador Allende)	977,902	39.5	1,070,344	36.3
Christian Democrats (Eduardo Frei, 1964 Radomiro Tomic, 1970)	1,409,102	55.5	821,801	27.8
Julio Durán*	125,233	5.0		
Jorge Alessandri			1,031,159	34.9

*Durán withdrew his candidacy before the election but still received 5 percent of the vote.

Christian Democratic alliance to prevent Allende from becoming president. While this plan attracted some Christian Democrats, most of the party's congressional representatives and Radomiro Tomic opposed it firmly. Instead, they demanded passage of a package of constitutional guarantees with UP support prior to the congressional vote on Chile's next president: among these, guarantees of the multiparty system, maintenance of civil liberties and freedom of the press, access by all parties to government-controlled TV stations, protection for the armed forces against political purges or the creation of militia, continued existence of, and public subsidies for, the private educational system, autonomy of the university system, protection for government employees—many added during the Frei administration—against dismissals or political persecution. In short, the Christian Democrats sought to buttress with constitutional amendments Chile's existing *political system* against the in-coming Allende administration's plans for a new institutional order. The Christian Democrats insisted that only approval of these amendments with the votes of UP deputies and senators would allow them to vote for Allende as president.

As the Christian Democrats bargained with the UP parties for constitutional amendments to limit the future course of an Allende government, Right-wing extremist groups, such as Patria y Libertad ("Fatherland and Freedom"), and United States business and diplomatic groups plotted to prevent Allende's inauguration. International Telephone and Telegraph, one of the largest American-based multinationals with interests in Chile, took the initiative in approaching the CIA with a plan to destabilize the Chilean economy through international economic pressure, delays, or cancellation of loans and credits, and by fomenting panic among Chile's private businesses. Covert efforts to bankrupt savings banks and to induce unemployment also figured in the American scheme to prevent Allende's confirmation by the Chilean Congress. Later, congressional hearings in the United States made clear that President Nixon and his closest foreign policy advisers, including Henry Kissinger, played an active role in this effort to subvert the work of Chile's Congress.

Despite the behind-the-scenes machinations of ITT and American policymakers, the UP bargain with the Christian Democrats on the package of constitutional amendments seemed to assure an Allende victory in the congressional voting. Two days before the Congress was to decide on Chile's next president, extreme right-wing groups, allegedly with CIA backing, made a desperate effort to kidnap the commander-in-chief of the Chilean army. Apparently they hoped to cast the blame for the abduction on MIR or on the UP—and thereby change the Christian Democratic votes in the Congress or provoke military intervention. This ploy backfired. General Schneider resisted his assailants, and they mortally wounded him in an exchange of gunfire. Schneider died on October 25, 1970, the day after the Chilean Congress confirmed Salvador Allende as Chile's next president.

Proclaiming that with him the people (*el pueblo*) of Chile entered into the presidential palace, Salvador Allende received the presidential sash on November 3, 1970. Less than three years later Allende's body would be carried from La Moneda, testimony to his unsuccessful struggle to take Chile down the peaceful road to socialism.

Salvador Allende inherited the political mythology and constitutional legitimacy of a system no longer viable without substantial modifications. The increasing violence, including political terrorism and "expropriation" of money from banks by *Miristas*, as well as the challenge to civilian authority represented by the *tacnazo* in the last year of the Frei administration, reflected the decomposition of the political arrangements that had held together the old order. President Allende lacked a revolutionary army to carry out his will; he headed a precarious multiparty coalition lacking both internal cohesiveness and underlying agreement on the pace and character of change to be implemented by the *unidad popular* government. Like all reformist Chilean presidents in the twentieth century, President Allende faced a hostile Congress and entrenched bureaucracy. And, with less than 37 percent of the vote, he lacked even the popular mandate President Aguirre Cerda had achieved after the election won by the popular front in 1938.

Worse still, Allende was a Marxist whose program evoked the intense hostility of the majority of the Chilean electorate as well as the uncompromising and active opposition of the United States. From the outset, American foreign policy, both covert and diplomatic, sought to disrupt the Chilean economy, to cut off or stifle credit from international lending agencies, to provide financial and moral support for the regime's opponents—and to maintain friendly relations with the Chilean military. Viewed as a "test case" of the viability of elected Marxist governments not only in Latin America but also in Western Europe (especially France and Italy), the Allende government potentially threatened the integrity of the NATO alliance as well as the southern cone of South America. Friendly and expanding relations with Cuba and Eastern Europe, when added to the government's eventual expropriation of American copper companies and other foreign investments, persuaded hard-line American officials that every effort be made to "destabilize" the Chilean economy and oust the UP government. The concentration in Santiago of numerous leftist intellectuals and political exiles from other Latin American countries made the Chilean capital a center of revolutionary activity, closely scrutinized by secret police and military intelligence agents from Brazil, Bolivia, Uruguay, and Argentina.

Ironically, the very successes of certain of the UP government's programs, and the economic consequences of these successes, so polarized Chilean society that less than three years after Allende's inauguration (August, 1973) the congressional opposition called upon the military to re-establish the "rule of the constitution and the law." In a setting quite different from the confrontation between President Balmaceda and Congress before the civil war of 1891, the confrontation between the UP coalition and the old order nevertheless adopted the familiar rhetoric and charges of Chilean politics: the president had violated his constitutional authority, and Congress sought to uphold its constitutional mandate, to assure respect for the constitution, and to prevent executive tyranny. Censure of government ministers and impeachment proceedings (*acusaciones constitucionales*) in Congress, so reminiscent of the structure of political conflict since the parliamentary period, now served as a reminder that the effort to implement socialism through legal means faced the challenge of the numerous checks and balances inherent in the Chilean political system. Less than three weeks after Congress appealed to the armed forces to preserve Chilean democracy from presidential excess, a military coup on September 11, 1973, splattered the peaceful road to socialism with blood.

The Popular Unity government's short-term economic policies attempted to effect a massive income redistribution program through differential wage and salary readjustments to benefit the poorest sectors of Chilean society. In marked contrast to the stabilization schemes of the Ibáñez or Alessandri periods, the UP policymakers hoped to stimulate demand by providing significantly higher-than-inflation salary increments to the urban and rural poor. Added to increases in real income for the mass of Chilean workers, impressive increases in government expenditures and monetary expansion stimulated the stagnant economy. The administration's policymakers expected these meaures to increase effective demand and, thereby, to convince Chilean entrepreneurs to utilize the excess capacity that idled numerous workers. Thus, through a combination of income redistribution, increase in effective demand, and reduction of unemployment, the UP government hoped to bring the country out of the economic recession inherited from the Frei government and to increase popular support for the Allende coalition.

Unfortunately for the government, the monopolistic structure of Chilean industry, rapidly expanding demands by workers for expropriation of farms and factories, and the corresponding distrust by private investors of the government's ultimate intentions toward private firms, all militated against substantial new private investment. This meant that despite short-term improvements in industrial production and in worker consumption, the UP's programs of income redistribution in the context of a "transition to socialism"—with capitalist owners still making investment decisions—led to shortages, rising prices, and black markets. Instead of investing for the future, private entrepreneurs sold off their inventory at speculative prices or, in agriculture, disposed of farm machinery and cattle herds. They invested in dollars, German marks, or other hard currencies. Under these conditions rising demand, escalating emissions of currency, and deficit spending fueled inflation. By mid-1973 the annual rate of inflation exceeded 300 percent and reduced the real income of workers and salaried employees to levels below those of late 1970 when the UP had taken office.

Every short-term success of government policy involved contradictions that led ever more rapidly to political and economic disaster. In part, this resulted from the disunity of the UP coalition. Acting as if the coalition were simply another executive-electoral alliance, each party demanded its share of the spoils. The government filled important administrative posts through an elaborate quota system which assigned personnel designated by the political parties to positions throughout the administration. Employment opportunities in the firms nationalized, "intervened," or requisitioned by the government became plums with which to reward party stalwarts or to combat unemployment. These difficulties led to precipitate declines in productivity throughout the economy.

In the rural sector, debate over the types of agricultural production units to establish on the expropriated farms created uncertainty among the campesinos and smallholders. Attacks on the *asentamiento* system introduced by the Christian Democrat administration alienated the beneficiaries of the Frei agrarian reform, while experiments with variations on collective farms, state farms, and regional production units resulted in virtual disorganization of the agricultural economy. After a good harvest in 1970–71, agricultural production declined seriously. As a result the government was forced to use scarce foreign exchange to import foodstuffs needed to meet the increased demand occasioned by higher worker incomes and to make up for the reduction in domestic production.

The government's methods for dealing with shortages, carrying out agrarian reform, and constructing the "social" or public sector of the economy exacerbated political tensions and intensified the economic crisis. In an attempt to minimize the problems of urban supply, the government organized public entities to compete with the private sector in wholesale and retail distribution. DINAC, a public enterprise constituted by the amalgamation of several large distribution agencies acquired by CORFO, made efforts to gain control of wholesale distribution, while thousands of private supply and price committees *juntas de abastecimiento y precios* (JAP) were organized to cooperate in local distribution of articles of consumption to urban neighbor-hoods. These JAP committees assisted inspectors from DIRINCO, the agency charged with enforcing price controls, in their efforts to prevent private retail merchants from evading such controls. Subsequently, the supply of "people's marketbaskets," or *canastas populares*, to

TABLE 9–10. THE AGRARIAN SECTOR: EXPORT OF GOODS AND AGRICULTURAL IMPORTS 1965–70 (YEARLY AVERAGE), 1971, AND 1972 (MILLIONS OF DOLLARS)

	1965–70	1971	1972
Total exports	$939	$964	$836
Agricultural exports	$ 24	$ 29	$ 19
Agricultural imports	$184	$311	$468
Agricultural imports as percentage of total export earnings	19.6%	32.2%	56.0%

Source: Stefan de Vylder, *Allende's Chile*, Cambridge University Press, 1974, p. 202.

the JAP for distribution to the people of the shantytowns and worker neighborhoods directly threatened the viability of Chile's more than 125,000 retail merchants and un-counted ambulatory vendors. The JAPs also served as a potential organizational mechanism for administering a direct, mandatory system of rationing as well as for monitoring the activities of opposition elements at the local level. None of these implications were lost upon the opposition which attacked the inefficiency, corruption, and "political criteria" with which the JAPs distributed the *canastas populares*.

Ideological and political fragmentation within the UP government heightened the economic uncertainty. Unable to control the activities of MIR, certain members of his own Socialist party, and the militant Mapucistas, President Allende failed to halt the acceleration of farm and factory seizures and illegal strikes in which workers demanded nationalization or expropriation of the enterprises where they were employed.

In the first eighteen months of the UP government, campesinos temporarily or permanently occupied some 1700 rural properties. In Article 171 of the agrarian reform law enacted by the Christian Democratic government, the Allende government found a legal mechanism to convert farm seizures or illegal strikes into de facto transfers of managerial responsibility for rural estates. Article 171 provided that "in case of lockout or illegal work stoppage that, for any reason, suspends exploitation of a rural enterprise, the President of the Republic can order resumption of labors [*reanudación de faenas*] with the intervention of the civil authority . . . and the support of police if necessary." The law gave the government official [*interventor*] assigned to "intervene" the farm "all the prerogatives necessary to continue operation of the enterprise." With this authority government *interventores* could hire new personnel, incur new liabilities or pay old debts, and decide what crops to plant or animals to sell. A short period of intervention could easily bankrupt any farm or at least make most owners quite willing to sell their farms to CORA on favorable terms. Thus, Article 171 of the agrarian reform law could be used by the Popular Unity government as a flexible legal tool to speed up the agrarian reform process—if only campesinos intensified the process of illegal farm occupations or strikes. In practice this tactic was used on so many farms that the administration soon ran out of party loyalists in the agrarian bureaucracies to assign as *interventores*.

In the urban sector the government resorted to application of the all-but-forgotten Decree Law 520, a vestige of the "Socialist Republic" of 1932. As indicated in Chapter 8, this decree law allowed the government to requisition, intervene, or expropriate any private enterprise that failed to comply with laws regulating price controls, speculation, stockpiling in anticipation of increases in official prices for particular commodities, interruption of production, or refusal to utilize efficiently installed capacity when the government decided there existed a "shortage" of a particular commodity. Legislation against lockouts also gave the government leverage in labor conflicts. As in the

TABLE 9–11. REQUISITIONS AND INTERVENTIONS,
NOVEMBER 1970–NOVEMBER 1972

Period	Interventions	Requisitions	Total
November–December 1970	37	1	38
January–February 1971	23	–	23
March–April 1971	1	5	6
May–June 1971	12	12	24
July–August 1971	9	6	15
September–October 1971	24	7	31
November–December 1971	21	9	30
January–February 1972	13	6	19
March–April 1972	14	7	21
May–June 1972	16	3	19
July–August 1972	7	18	25
September–October 1972*	23	48	71
November 1972	2	4	6
Total	202	126	328

*During the October strike a large number of enterprises were subjected to intervention or requisition for participation in the general lockout. Most of these companies were later returned to their owners.

Source: Based on Instituto de Economía, La Economía Chilena en 1972, pp. 116ff. After Stefan de Vylder, Allende's Chile, Cambridge University Press, 1974, p. 146.

agricultural sector, requisitions or interventions in industry could quickly bankrupt the legal owners and facilitate transfer of the affected industry to the public sector.

Under these conditions the predictions made in 1938 by Polish economist Oscar Lange proved entirely accurate. Indeed Lange's analysis is perhaps the most appropriate epitaph, as well as explanation, for the domestic economic failures of the UP government.

An economic system based on private enterprise and private property of the means of production can work only as long as the security of private property and of income derived from enterprise is maintained. The very existence of a government bent on introducing socialism is a constant threat to this security. Therefore, the capitalistic economy cannot function under a socialist government unless the government is socialist in name only.
. . . Owners threatened with expropriation have no inducement to make the necessary investments and to manage them efficiently. And no government supervision or administrative measures can cope effectively with the passive resistance and sabotage of the owners and managers.

No administrative device adopted by the government could cope with the resistance of the opposition. Black markets, shortages, and rampant inflation undermined confidence in the government and hardened the opposition forces against the de facto socialization of the economy. At the same time that the activities of MIR and the most radical members of the government coalition convinced the government's enemies that

TABLE 9-12. INDUSTRIAL ESTABLISHMENTS CONTROLLED BY THE CHILEAN STATE

Form of Control	November 1970	December 1971	December 1972	May 1973
State ownership*	31	62	103	165
Under intervention or requisition	–	39	99	120
Total	31	101	202	285

*Both social and mixed areas and including six new industries that were created by the Chilean state after November 1970.

Source: Stefan de Vylder, *Allende's Chile*, Cambridge University Press, 1974, p. 145.

only violent resistance could halt consolidation of a new political reality, the Communists and Allende sought to negotiate a de-escalation of conflict with the Christian Democrats in exchange for clearly defined limits on the extent of socialization in industry and agriculture. Neither those who believed that socialism could be established only through force and popular mobilization, nor the Partido Nacional and the growing movement of economic and professional associations (*gremios*) committed to violent counterrevolution, gave any breathing room to the government's efforts to arrive at a pacific resolution of the crisis.

As the political and economic situation deteriorated, supply and distribution problems in the urban areas sent into the streets thousands of women from upper-, middle-, and even working-class homes, banging on pots and pans to symbolize the government's inability to resolve the economic crisis. In response, organized workers and their families facetiously offered to share their food with the *momios* (literally, "mummy," a term UP sympathizers applied to the supporters of the old order) if they were really unable to feed themselves. Moving their struggle against the government to the streets, leaders of the major trade associations and economic interest groups such as the SNA and the SFF allied themselves with extreme right-wing political organizations such as Patria y Libertad, PROTECO, and Soberanía, Orden y Libertad (SOL). These recently organized movements established white guard vigilantes to resist farm and factory seizures and to recover occupied private property in *retomas*. By mid-1972 the opposition had united in a so-called *gremialista* movement. A massive strike in October of 1972 mobilized shopkeepers, professional and economic associations, bank clerks, students, and even certain working-class and campesino groups in an effort to shut down the Chilean economy. The strike was precipitated by the demand of the 40,000 members of the independent truckers' association that the government suspend its plans to create a state-owned trucking enterprise, but it quickly became openly political and directly challenged the UP government and its program.

Recognizing the critical political moment, ex-President Eduardo Frei personally influenced the Christian Democratic party to support the strike and mobilize its followers in opposition to the government. On October 15, 1972, the party's secretary general, Renán Fuentealba declared that the government was "acting openly in defiance of the constitution and the laws, as well as of fundamental human rights," and that this circumstance was "dangerous for all our citizens." In light of this danger, Fuentealba affirmed the Christian Democrats' adherence to the truckers' movement. Predictably, the

Partido Nacional aggressively supported the strike, maintaining that only organized civil disobedience could overcome the government's effort to impose communism on Chile.

Faced with a situation bordering on insurrection, the UP government declared a partial state of emergency. In resorting to this traditional use of regimes of exception to counter the opposition and appealing to the armed forces and police to uphold the constitution, the Popular Unity government followed the examples of Portales, Montt, Balmaceda, Ibáñez, Alessandri, Aguirre Cerda, and Frei. Chile had been governed under regimes of exception for much of its early history, and frequently from 1932 to 1970. The Popular Unity government was also typically Chilean in stretching the law to its limits and beyond for its own ends (what Chileans call *resquicios legales* and Americans call taking advantage of legal "loopholes"). This meant that military officers took over the responsibility for maintaining order, for enforcing temporary censorship on the opposition media, and, in effect, for shoring up the UP coalition's fragile position. By October 21, the newly created *comando gremial* confronted the government with a sweeping set of demands that, if accepted, would have amounted to abrogation of the UP program. Despite the serious economic effects of the strike (the government later estimated the loss to the country at almost $300 million), continued production in the factories and support by UP loyalists prevented a complete economic shutdown. The *gremialista* movement failed to win a definitive victory. In addition, the emergence of new working-class organizations, or *cordones industriales,* among the factory workers in Santiago's "industrial belts"—such as Los Cerrillos, Puente Alto, and Vicuña MacKenna—threatened the development of real popular militias and institutions of "parallel power." Pursuing a more revolutionary course than the leadership of the CUT, the Communist party, or President Allende, a nucleus of revolutionary workers in the *cordones industriales* began preparing for armed confrontation.

All the major parties of the Popular Unity coalition made some, generally haphazard, efforts to train armed cadres for the eventual confrontation. Cuban military advisers and other foreign sympathizers provided arms and training to some of these groups. Army, Navy, and Air Force intelligence services, aware of these initiatives, and perhaps overestimating the leftist cadres' military capabilities in 1972–73, took countermeasures, including purges within the armed forces themselves to eliminate leftist sympathizers. Formation of armed groups, stockpiling weapons, and training at isolated sites in the countryside and mountains seemed to validate beliefs by the opposition parties that the Popular Unity eventually intended to resort to force to impose its program. For the Christian Democrats, the National party, and the military institutions this belief would, by itself, justify the ouster of President Allende less than one year later, although this outcome was arguably still avoidable in late 1972. At the least, President Allende acted as if he believed a military coup could be prevented and took measures intended to prevent that outcome. These included renewed efforts to negotiate an overall compromise with the Christian Democrats on constitutional and economic issues and inviting military participation in the Cabinet.

Coincident with the October strike, the opposition moved on the legislative front to impeach four of Allende's ministers. Faced with a loss of key advisers and the resurrection of the political tactic of censure and impeachment of ministers, President Allende made a critical political decision. He invited the army commander-in-chief, Carlos Prats, to serve as minister of interior while at the same time continuing in his army post. The president also included an air force general and an admiral in his new cabinet. Jacques Chonchol, the ex-Christian Democrat who served as Allende's minister of agriculture and was probably the member of the Allende ministerial team most hated by the opposition (because of his leadership in the agrarian reform process), left the cabinet.

Inviting the military officers to participate as ministers in the cabinet, and particularly the appointment of Army Commander, Carlos Prats, as Minister of Interior, emulated the repeated use of military officers as government ministers in times of crisis since the early twentieth century. Despite the Popular Unity government's revolutionary program, most of its leaders shared the perception, cultivated since the 1940s, that when civilian political parties and movements reached an impasse that threatened institutional breakdown, the armed forces were an acceptable temporary arbiter. By "depoliticizing" the government with military ministers, Allende signaled his desire to achieve a political truce, with all sides theoretically confiding in the integrity and patriotism of the armed forces as guarantors of any agreements negotiated between the government and opposition parties. Implicitly, Allende and the opposition recognized the historical importance of the armed forces as occasional political arbiters—and of course this role had been formalized in the 1941 legislation assigning to the armed forces control and supervision of national elections.

Declaring their full confidence in General Prats, the leaders of the truckers' strike negotiated a settlement in early November that included promises by the government to return enterprises occupied by workers during the strike and also not to nationalize the transport and wholesale trade sectors of the economy. Although the government did not entirely fulfill these promises, the October strike had made the military the arbiter of the nation's political conflicts.

General Prats emphasized that the two most important tasks facing the new cabinet consisted of restoration of order and administration of peaceful, honest congressional elections in March 1973. In the aftermath of the truckers' strike, however, speculation abounded about the extent of American financial support and CIA involvement in the events of October. Meanwhile the opposition looked to the March 1973 elections as an opportunity to win the two-thirds majority in the Congress that would permit Allende's impeachment. The presence of General Prats in the interior ministry seemed to guarantee the integrity of the March elections, but it also inspired harsh condemnation from those on the left who proposed "getting on with the Revolution."

Concentrating their efforts on the upcoming elections, the Christian Democrats, the Partido Nacional, and other opposition forces forged an electoral alliance called the Democratic Confederation, or CODE. The results of the March elections, however, proved a victory for no one. CODE obtained 55 percent of the votes but actually lost seats in the Congress to the UP coalition. The opposition *was* a majority, but it now faced three years of the Allende administration before the presidential elections scheduled for 1976. Notwithstanding the veracity of CODE's claims of electoral fraud and the abnormal delay in reporting the election returns, there could be no doubt that the UP coalition retained significant popular support. Despite the economic crisis, shortages of consumer goods, and the opposition's media offensive against the government, the UP coalition still could count on more than 40 percent of Chile's voters—an increase over its electoral support in the 1970 presidential elections.

Between March 1973 and September 1973, intensified militancy by MIR and certain elements within the UP coalition, as well as public threats by Socialist leader Carlos Altamirano to infiltrate and subvert the armed forces, were juxtaposed to counterrevolutionary economic sabotage and terrorism. The galloping inflation rate increased the number of strikes, including an extremely costly work stoppage by the miners at the El Teniente copper mine in Rancagua. Workers who in the past had looked to Marxist union leaders now followed a Christian Democrat in a strike condemned by the UP government. Lasting more than two months, the strike drew support from thousands of university students and members of the Federation of Secondary Students in Santiago. It also directly pitted the UP government against an important group of organized workers—not against *momios.*

Amidst rampant inflation, political and economic crises, and the rising pitch of government and opposition rhetoric, unsuccessful negotiations between the government and the Christian Democrats continued—even after an abortive coup d'état by the second tank regiment in Santiago in June 1973. The quick defeat of this *tancazo* seemed to reaffirm General Prats' commitment to defense of the constitutional government. Gradually, however, Prats' apparent political ambitions, rumors that he would emerge as the UP presidential candidate in 1976, and an incident in which he reportedly threatened a woman driver with death for sticking out her tongue at him as he motored through Santiago, all combined to erode his support among fellow officers.

The political situation grew even worse in late July with new strikes by the truckers and the *gremialista* movement. After a temporary absence, representatives of the armed forces again returned to the cabinet to restore order (August 9, 1973). Now all three service commanders, as well as the commander of the national police force (*carabineros*), occupied ministries. Intensified implementation of the provisions of the gun control law, passed in 1972, sent military units to factories and shanty towns to disarm workers and forestall a popular insurrection. These searches for arms, or *allanamientos,* also served to collect intelligence on the quantity of arms available in the *cordones industriales,* and to train army units in tactics for confrontation with the civilian population at factory work sites, union halls, party offices, and in the *poblaciones.* The number of *alla-*

Demonstrations in favor of President Allende after failed coup of June 29, 1973.
(Courtesy of LOM Publishers.)

namientos increased gradually after early 1973. Less attention was given to the armed vigilantes organized by the *gremialista* and right-wing political movements. In July 1973, according to pro-*unidad popular* sources, only two of twenty-four *allanamientos* involved "groups of armed fascists"; all the rest were directed against factories, offices of *unidad popular* parties, government offices, or other supporters of the Allende government. By the first part of August, when the new military-based cabinet was organized, the *allanamientos* were coordinated operations of army, air force, and naval units moving against leftists throughout the nation.

In the meantime the *gremialista* strike movement continued, supported by the entire political opposition and students at the Catholic University. Unable to negotiate an end to the trucking strike and annoyed by obstacles put in his way by Allende's civilian supporters, air force General César Ruiz Danyau abruptly resigned from the cabinet only days after accepting the portfolio of transport and public works. President Allende's quick acceptance of Ruiz's resignation as minister *and as air force commander-in-chief* provoked a new political crisis, involving agitation among the general's air force colleagues.

Violence in the streets of Santiago, political terrorism by leftists and rightists, and an imminent state of political chaos elicited a call by the majority opposition in the Chilean Congress for the military to intervene to guarantee institutional stability, civil peace, security, and development. The same day, hundreds of wives of military officers gathered outside of General Prats' residence to demand his resignation. Prats resigned the next day and was followed by his military colleagues General Guillermo Pickering and Mario Sepúlveda (commander of the Santiago garrison). Now President Allende was at the mercy of General Augusto Pinochet Ugarte.

On September 11, 1973, General Pinochet and his fellow service commanders led a well-coordinated, brutal, and highly successful military movement that ended the UP government and resulted in the death of President Salvador Allende. According to the military, Salvador Allende committed suicide after surviving aerial bombardment of the presidential palace.

More has been written about Chile between 1970 and 1973 than about all the rest of Chilean history. The *unidad popular* experience raised important theoretical questions for socialist intellectuals and politicians concerning the viability and correct tactics of the "peaceful road to socialism." These leftists who believe(d) in the possibility of such a process have sought to determine where the Allende government went wrong, how the process could have been salvaged, how European Communists and Socialists can prevent the "fascization" of the middle class which was the social base of the counter-revolution in Chile.

Congressional investigations in the United States have made available incontrovertible evidence of extensive U.S. efforts to undermine the Allende government. Declassified government documents made public in 1999, although still heavily censored, revealed more fully the depth and range of covert operations by U.S. intelligence and military personnel in a plot to "neutralize" Army Commander General René Schneider in order to prevent Allende's inauguration as president. Handwritten notes, taken by CIA Director Richard Helms, recorded the orders of President Richard Nixon to foster a coup in Chile (September 15, 1970). The declassified documents confirm the Nixon administration and Secretary of State Henry Kissinger's instructions to CIA personnel to promote a coup in Chile: "It is firm and continuing policy that Allende be overthrown by a coup" (October 16, 1970). After Allende took office, U.S. policies, both covert and overt, contributed significantly to the government's economic woes and to the political polarization that eventually culminated with the military coup on Sep-

La Moneda palace, rocketed by Air Force planes, September 11, 1973.
(Courtesy of LOM Publishers.)

tember 11, 1973. U.S. military and intelligence personnel maintained contacts in the
Chilean armed forces and with their intelligence "assets" and employees in Chile.
Speculation that U.S. military and civilian personnel assisted in planning, coordinating, and even effecting the 1973 coup never entirely ended. Whether or not further declassification of U.S. government documents or personal testimonies will eventually
clarify the full extent of U.S. involvement in the overthrow of the Unidad Popular government, U.S. operations were one key factor of many in the tragic outcome of Chilean
politics from 1970 to 1973.

Nevertheless, from the first moments after the coup, many Marxists insisted that the
"real" key to the failure of the UP administration was the activities of the ultra-leftists."
Typical in this respect, an article in *World Marxist Review* (July 1974) noted that "the
working class was gradually forced into isolation and the intermediate strata became,
objectively, allies of the country's enemies. . . . The Chilean experience has reaffirmed anew that ultra-leftism is a boon for imperialism and reaction." In the year after
the military coup, leaders of the Chilean Communist party who escaped the military
intelligence's dragnet, still claimed that "at times of crisis we worked in alliance with
the patriotic part of the Army faithful to the constitution and this played a decisive role
in suppressing the October 1972 conspiracy [the truckers' strike]. This alliance could
have developed were it not for the spread of ultraleftism."

In contrast, Trotskyists and other militant revolutionaries have seen in the Chilean experience new evidence that there can be no peaceful road to socialism. They argue that Allende should have armed and unleashed the workers and peasants in a violent revolutionary movement to destroy Chile's liberal democracy and the capitalist state. How the military would have reacted to such a move by President Allende in 1970 or 1971—and the inevitable massacre that would have occurred—is usually omitted from these "revolutionary" postmortems.

For the Right and the Christian Democrats, of course, there was little interest in explaining why Allende failed to take Chile down the peaceful road to socialism. Like the Marxists and other UP supporters, however, they found soon enough that the military coup that ousted President Allende brought neither relief from economic crisis nor restoration of constitutional order. Instead, the Chilean military imposed a highly authoritarian, repressive political regime that effectively eliminated every basis of civil liberty and political freedom stipulated in the Chilean constitution of 1925.

The ultimate tragedy of *unidad popular*, then, was that President Allende lost the opportunity to carry out important social reforms while maintaining the political liberty that had evolved in Chile after 1932. United States diplomacy, economic pressure, and covert subversion of Chile's domestic politics played an important role in the failure of the UP coalition. However, American or other outside pressures could not by themselves have ensured this failure. Short of military intervention, the United States did not have enough leverage, even with the variety of economic and political screws it tightened, to guarantee Allende's failure. Whereas the Agency for International Development (AID), the Export-Import Bank, the Inter-American Development Bank, and the World Bank rejected Chile's requests for credit during 1971 and 1972, short-term credits from Western Europe, the Soviet Union, and the Socialist bloc more than made up for the withdrawal of financial support by the United States. A large foreign exchange surplus inherited from the Frei government even allowed temporary increases in imports to buttress the government's short-term emphasis on improved consumption for the working classes. This was so despite declines in copper prices that portended extreme balance-of-payment problems in 1971. By the end of 1971 the government's principal economic strategist, Pedro Vuskovic, alleged that lack of foreign exchange constituted the main constraint on further realization of the UP program. This constraint originated not in a net decrease in available foreign credits, but rather in circumstances occasioned largely by the government's own economic policies.

Whatever the full extent of United States complicity in the tragedy of September 1973, and whatever the impact of international economics, the most critical factor of all in the failure of the Allende administration was bad politics and unrealistic economic policies. Lacking internal cohesion, the support of the majority of the electorate, control of Congress, and the sympathy of most bureaucrats, judges, police, and military officers and confronted by a hostile administration in the United States, the Popular Unity government embarked on revolutionary socioeconomic and political initiatives. Bad politics—the spouting of revolutionary rhetoric without the force to impose a revolutionary program—produced a politico-economic crisis. Bad politics prevented conciliation and compromise with the Christian Democrats, the small shopkeepers, the truckers, the beneficiaries of the Frei agrarian reform—in short, with all the elements of the middle strata, working class, and peasantry who had nothing to lose and much to gain by an attack on economic monopolies and foreign corporations. President Allende failed because he lacked the power to impose a revolutionary socialist regime yet insisted on employing the rhetoric of revolution. He also failed because, unlike a transition to social democracy, there is no peaceful road to the socialism envisaged by

Burning "subversive" books, Santiago, September 1973. (Courtesy of LOM Publishers.)

Marxist-Leninists; Lenin's political vision, as he proclaimed, was always antagonistic to constitutional democracy. By aggressively pursuing an illusion dreaded and resisted since the 1930s by Chilean anti-Marxists and by threatening the basic values, beliefs, and interests of broad sectors of the population, President Allende's Unidad Popular coalition set the stage for a military government and counterrevolution.

For the opponents of the Popular Unity government, September 11, 1973, was a day of liberation; for most its supporters it was a day of grief and fear. For others it was a day that began an era of persecution, martyrdom, then disillusionment.

10 Dictatorship

Not even the shrillest political rhetoric of leftists and rightists between 1970 and 1973 prepared Chileans for the ferocity of the military coup of September 11, 1973. Accustomed as they were to the gross hyperbole of propaganda from all political parties and movements since the early 1930s, most Chileans did not really believe that a military *Putsch* would occur; fewer still anticipated installation of a military-dominated government that would become the longest-lived administration in Chilean history.

Called upon by opposition groups in the Congress to restore the constitutional order purportedly violated by the Popular Unity government, the military leadership instead closed the legislature, curtailed activities by political parties, and outlawed the political organizations that had supported the government of President Allende. Press censorship, suspension of civil liberties, and fierce repression of leading politicians, labor leaders, academics, and other supposed Marxist sympathizers merged into a "holy war" against what the military called the "Marxist cancer."

Initial resistance to the coup in factories, workplaces, homes, and in the streets proved hopeless against the overwhelming power and brutality of the military forces which hunted down and attacked Allende supporters and other "subversives." Accounts of torture in the improvised detention centers that held thousands of Chileans and hundreds of foreign "subversives" throughout the nation became so widespread as to be routine.

The military junta directed its avenging wrath not only at political leaders but also at symbols of the cultural and institutional foundations of Chilean democracy. When Chilean Nobel prize-winning poet and Communist party activist Pablo Neruda died of cancer—and grief—twelve days after the coup, his house was ransacked and the library vandalized. Though his funeral procession became a spontaneous protest against the junta, the circumstances of his death also symbolized the junta's determination to eradicate all vestiges of the political left. Literature, sculpture, painting, and even popular songs now became targets of the junta's violence. The murder of intellectual and folksinger Victor Jara after detention and torture at the Estadio Chile—which, like the Estadio Nacional and soccer stadiums in the provinces, was turned into a makeshift prison, torture, and murder center—initiated an era in which listening to records or tapes by "subversive" artists would be quiet acts of resistance.

General Augusto Pinochet justified the coup and the new government's repressive measures in part by alleging that the Allende coalition had a plot (*plan zeta*) to murder military and civilian opposition leaders in order to impose communism definitively upon Chile. Moreover, the general maintained:

> The greatest possible enforcement and highest respect for Human Rights implies that these must not be exercised by those individuals who spread doctrines or commit acts which in fact seek to abolish them. This makes it necessary to apply restrictions as rigorous as the circumstances may require to those who defy the juridical norms in

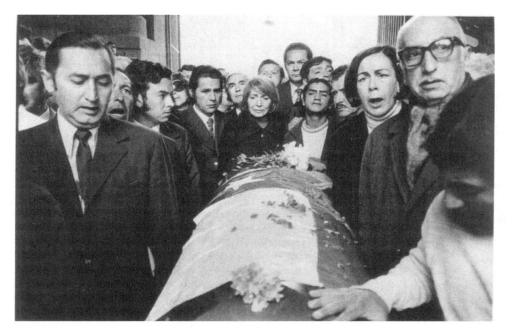

Funeral for Pablo Neruda, September 25, 1973. (Courtesy of LOM Publishers.)

force. . . . Our attitude must necessarily remain inflexible for the good of Chile and its people.

In addition to justifying its violent extirpation of subversives, the Chilean junta pointed to the international significance of its victory over communism. Reminding Chileans of the glories of independence, General Pinochet declared that "Chile was one of the first countries in the world to abolish slavery. Now our country has broken the chains of totalitarian Marxism, the great Twentieth-Century Slavery, before which so many bow their heads without the courage to defeat it. We are thus once again pioneers in Humanity's fight for liberation."

The military pioneers in "Humanity's fight for liberation" did not limit their attacks to supporters of the Allende government. Once the initial campaign of terror and assassination gave way to gradual institutionalization of a military-police state, the regime's leaders made clear that they intended to write the final epitaph for Chilean democracy and to transform the moral and intellectual foundations of Chilean life. Military rectors replaced academic administrators in the universities; Chilean higher education faced a thorough pogrom which practically wiped out departments and schools in the social sciences, philosophy, education, and other disciplines touched by Marxist or liberal influences. Social and ideological pluralism disappeared.

In a fashion reminiscent of the military's heroes—Portales and Ibáñez—the junta declared its contempt for "old style" democracy, for politics, and for politicians. Rekindling the embers of the military movement of 1924 and Ibáñez' theme of anti-politics in the 1952 election, the junta replaced Ibáñez' symbolic broom with torture and death—and promised to end forever the immorality, corruption, and ineptitude of civilian democratic politics which had allowed the assumption of the Popular Unity government.

As the initial fury of September 11, 1973 subsided, the military junta turned to the task of imposing a new social and political order upon Chile. In retrospect, it is possible to identify several overlapping stages in the evolution of the policies of the military junta and its civilian supporters in their efforts to carry out a thorough "modernization" and "cleansing" (*depuración*) of the Chilean polity. In the first stage, the government implemented essentially *ad hoc* measures of political repression and economic retrenchment to establish political control and achieve economic stabilization.

The military junta based its legitimacy in the "natural right of rebellion against tyrannical government," that is, the alleged tyranny of Allende's Popular Unity government. On this foundation, the junta initially ruled the country with military edicts (*bandos militares*) for the "duration of the emergency." On September 18, 1973, the junta decreed a state of siege throughout the country; Decree Law No. 5 (September 22, 1973) stipulated that the state of siege should be understood as if the country were "in a state or time of war." The prior publication of Decree Law 4 (September 18, 1973) had proclaimed a "state of emergency," thereby conferring authority on Military Zone Commanders to issues *bandos militares*, essentially the equivalent of government under martial law. This decision subjected civilians to courts-martial, rather than ordinary courts, and eliminated due process and the possibility that higher tribunals review the decisions of the rapid military "trials." For disobeying military orders, the penalty could be summary execution. Military and police personnel killed many prisoners "attempting to escape." Some were buried in mass graves, unidentified and unseen by next of kin.

Previous governments, including those of Eduardo Frei and Salvador Allende, had declared "states of emergency" and used constitutional regimes of exception to confront strikes, disorders, and other "emergencies." These political customs in Chile made the military junta's resort to emergency powers seem "natural"—even legally plausible. Nonetheless, the 1925 constitution did not authorize the junta to close Congress. Moreover, Decree 521 (1974), which officially created the new secret police agency (DINA), had secret articles conveying draconian authority for clandestine operations. In practice, the DINA had operated extra-officially from late 1973, directly responsible to the Junta de Gobierno as its instrument for "eradication" of leftist political parties and movements. There followed widespread detentions, arrests without warrants, torture, and murders. Prisoners "disappeared"; government officials denied knowledge of their whereabouts. In addition, the secret police and clandestine operations by other repressive agents of the government, such as the "Joint Command" (*Comando Conjunto*), confiscated money, jewelry, automobiles, real estate, and other property of their targets—an ironic feature of a government that proclaimed its commitment to "saving the country from communism" and protecting private property rights.

To the surprise of many Chileans, the Supreme Court and other tribunals denied requests for writs of habeas corpus (*recursos de amparo*) from the small number of lawyers willing to defend these persons' rights. According to a report in the last issue of *Solidarity* (N. 300, May 1990), the magazine published by the Vicaría de Solidaridad, the first *recurso de amparo* was presented on September 14, 1973, by telephone. Christian Democrat Bernardo Leighton sought to protect three cabinet ministers and other officials of the Allende government arrested by military authorities. (Two years later a failed assassination attempt in Rome, Italy, against Leighton and his wife left both political exiles seriously injured). Three Supreme Court judges denied the request the same day. In the years after the military coup, judges typically accepted at face value the word of government officials that the "disappeared" were not in custody. Of some

2500 *recursos de amparo* presented by the human rights organization Comité para la Paz, from September 11, 1973, until October 1975, the courts approved one. The government responded to the court by issuing a detention order against the person that the court intended to rescue.

Opposing the military regime in Chile or in exile could have high costs. Lawyers, employees, and collaborators of the Vicaría de Solidaridad, created on January 1, 1976, by Cardenal Raúl Silva Henríquez as an institutional effort by the Catholic Church to defend human rights in the country, risked imprisonment and exile: José Zalaquett was exiled in April 1976; Hernán Montealegre was detained seventeen days at the Cuatro Alamos interrogation center, then sent to Tres Alamos prison camp until the end of the year; medical doctors Manuel Almeyda, Patricio Arroyo, and Pedro Castillo were arrested in May 1981; and José Manuel Parada was assassinated in 1985 after receiving information from an ex–Air Force soldier who detailed for the Vicaría the clandestine criminal operations of the Comando Conjunto.

Fear, concerns for career and advancement in the court system, an initial disposition to believe the denials of government ministers and military officials, and, in some cases, an enthusiastic willingness to collaborate in the task of "extirpating the marxist cancer" all contributed to the inefficacy of the judicial branch in protecting civil liberties and rights. In retrospect, some critics compared the Chilean judiciary after 1973 to the German judges who applied, with professional literalism and diligence, the Nuremberg Laws and other juridical atrocities under Nazism. Others, more generous in their evaluation, pointed to a tradition of lethargy, conservatism, and hierarchy amongst Chilean judges that made them, and the judicial system itself, ill-suited to resist the dictatorship. In the several well-publicized instances when judges finally (in the 1980s) challenged the military regime, demanding to know the whereabouts of the "disappeared" or seeking to indict military and police personnel for crimes against citizens, the Supreme Court disciplined the dissenting magistrates and cases were switched from civil to military jurisdiction, thus assuring their dismissal by military judges (*fiscales militares*).

To "disappear" became an active verb with a direct pronoun object: "They disappeared him (her); "*lo desaparecieron.*" Most of the "disappeared" never reappeared; their murders by death squads and agents of the military junta, if not the whereabouts of their remains, would be confirmed by a "Truth Commission" organized after termination of the military regime in 1990.

By 1975, a second stage began as the regime institutionalized the new security apparatus and intensified repression against the leadership of the targeted leftist parties and movements. When the limited success of the economic measures became evident, the junta adopted a more drastic economic "shock treatment." This second stage—consolidation of General Pinochet's control through the secret police and security apparatus and adoption of the shock treatment—brought a radical application of orthodox monetary and fiscal policy combined with a number of politically motivated cuts in particular government agencies and public enterprises.

During these first two stages in the evolution of military policy, key leaders began to enunciate a longer term program for political and economic transformation of Chile. First, in a "Declaration of Principles of the Government of Chile" (1974), the junta proclaimed its intention to "take upon itself the historic mission of giving Chile new governmental institutions that [would] embody the profound changes occurring in modern times." In order to do this the government "guided by the inspiration of Portales, . . . [would] energetically apply the principle of authority and drastically punish any outburst of disorder or anarchy." Anticipating later policies, the "Declaration of Principles" also emphasized the task of "reorganizing the economy, destroyed to its very roots by Marxism," and "imposing authority and discipline in production and labor relations."

Further elaborating on these themes in 1975, the government published *National Objectives of the Chilean Government*. Once again emphasizing the linkage of its political vision with Chile's Portalian legacy and the country's national heritage, the junta declared that a new political system would require "formation of new generations steeped in the concepts of love of God, the Fatherland and the family." This declaration hinted at the strong push for a new curriculum that the junta would later introduce into the nation's primary schools, emphasizing patriotism, morality, and anti-communism. The new political system would also involve a strengthening of presidential authority and a "rationalized, modern and functional public administration purified of all political and party influence." Without specifying further the precise character of this new political system, the government made clear that it would be *depoliticized*, technocratic, efficient, and free from Marxist influence.

A third phase in the development of the military junta's political objectives began almost simultaneously with implementation of the "shock treatment." No longer satisfied with emergency decrees, and seeking to create an apparent juridical legitimacy, the junta introduced a series of "constitutional acts," which amended or eliminated certain parts of the Constitution of 1925—without fully replacing it. Lacking any legal basis, these "constitutional acts" proved of little use in legitimizing the military dictatorship. In a 1977 speech, General Pinochet announced the so-called "Chacarillas Plan": his intentions and a general itinerary for institutionalizing "authoritarian democracy" with a new constitution and complementary legislation to transform permanently Chilean government and society. Appointment of Sergio Fernández as the military government's first civilian Minister of Interior (1978), rescinding the state of siege (although a state of emergency remained in effect), and announcement of the "seven modernizations" (1979) set the stage for a plebiscite on the new constitution in 1980.

Changing economic and political conditions within Chile from 1976 to 1980 led, in 1980, to a fourth stage of post-1973 institutional development: a national plebiscite on a new constitution and its implementation in 1981. In the period after 1981, the government sought to institutionalize the program of socio-economic and political transformation initiated with the coup in 1973. This included the so-called seven modernizations announced in 1979 (see below) and implementation of the new constitution. In this stage General Pinochet sought to manage a resurgence of political opposition amidst an economic recession (1981–84) and then to complete the presidential term which ended in 1989 according to the 1980 constitution.

Though recognizable in retrospect as overlapping stages in the development of post-1973 Chile, the contradictory tendencies within the military government, among both military and civilian elites, as well as the concerted struggle of opponents against the dictatorship, made the everyday history of this evolution far from inevitable. Following that process in some detail provides a framework for understanding the conflictive, polarized society that emerged in Chile in the late 1980s.

In 1973 no fundamental consensus existed within the military regarding the appropriate duration of military rule or upon a comprehensive alternative political regime. Civilian supporters of the military government also disagreed as to the type of political system that ought to follow military rule. Some preferred a relatively quick restoration of civilian government under a more restrictive liberal democracy which excluded Marxist and leftist participation. Others favored replacing liberal democratic institutions with a more corporatist system based on functional representation through occupational associations or *gremios*. (The term *gremio* in Chile was used broadly to refer to professional and occupational associations as diverse as truckers, white-collar employees, and retail merchants. *Gremios* had constituted the main social base of opposition to the Popular Unity government.)

Despite lack of agreement on the type of political system with which to replace that established under the Chilean constitution of 1925, a general consensus within the military blamed "politics" and the "political class" for the crisis of 1970–73 and for the economic disaster the country had experienced. According to this view, the defects of Chilean democracy and the unpatriotic, self-interested maneuverings of politicians had permitted the penetration of Marxism into Chilean national life. This threatened the nation's historical traditions as well as its national security and sovereignty. The junta leadership and its supporters viewed the military coup as the beginning of a salvational crusade to wrest *la patria* from the abyss.

A narrower, technocratic critique of Chilean development from the 1930s until 1973 emanated especially from a group of economists influenced by conservative academics in the United States. Many of these Chileans had received advanced professional education at the University of Chicago or studied in Chile under Chicago-influenced professors as part of an exchange program with the Catholic University established in the 1950s. In Chile they were soon nicknamed "the Chicago Boys" or, more generically, the neo-liberal economists. These economists focused upon the inefficient allocation of resources that resulted from politicization of the economy, overregulation, excessive protectionism, and the burden of unprofitable public enterprises. Underlying these defects was a *political system* that spawned irresponsible demands and demagogic promises.

In the short run, a melding of anti-political sentiment, anti-Marxism, and the technocratic orientations of the junta's policy advisers led to a combination of ferocious repression of the opposition and, by 1975, to economic shock treatment.

In the period 1973 to 1975, the junta seemed to have the support of a majority of Chileans in the effort to restore political order and reconstruct the economy. Professional organizations, the *gremios*, a number of women's organizations sharing the banner of *poder femenino*, and the major non-Marxist political parties—in short, the social base of the opposition to the Popular Unity government—viewed the military junta as the only short-term solution to the political and economic crisis facing the nation. Even most religious leaders initially supported the military intervention. The hierarchy of the Catholic Church, at odds with the Popular Unity government over proposed educational reforms, called upon the Chilean population to cooperate with the new regime in restoring order, even though the Permanent Committee of the Episcopal Conference lamented the violence and bloodshed of the coup. In a 1975 study done by researcher Brian Smith, almost all of the bishops of the Chilean Catholic Church indicated that they believed the coup had been necessary.

Only slowly and with painful moderation did the majority of Chilean social and political groups begin to challenge even the most extreme measures of the military government. MIR, which had predicted a coup all along and criticized the naiveté of a "peaceful road to socialism," declared that socialism had not been defeated, but rather that a "reformist illusion" had come to an end. The military security apparatus made MIR activists a special target; penetration of the organization by military security, torture of captured *Miristas,* and murder of many militants significantly weakened the MIR organization by 1976. Likewise, the government targeted the Communist party leadership as well as party-affiliated labor union, student, and community organizations. Systematic persecution resulted in the deaths of many Communist party members and the capture of almost the entire internal leadership in 1976. By then, however, the party had created a clandestine apparatus within Chile. It had also created a parallel party organization in Europe, with the Central Committee leadership operating in the Soviet Union. Thus, the Communists, albeit with difficulty, maintained contacts with worker, peasant, student, and community organizations.

Divided even before the military coup, the Chilean Socialist party fragmented further after 1973. Debates over the cause of the coup and proper goals for the party under the dictatorship left two major factions—one supporting an alliance with the Communists and another favoring a more moderate role in alliance with non-Marxist Leninist democratic parties. In many ways, in the initial periods after the coup, the Socialist party suffered the most serious disintegration and divisions of all Chilean political movements.

In contrast to the leftist parties and movements, a majority of Christian Democrats initially approved of the military ouster of President Allende. While expressing their regret for the departure from Chile's constitutional traditions, party leaders nevertheless laid blame for the coup on "the economic disaster, institutional chaos, armed violence and the profound moral crisis to which the deposed government led the nation." Christian Democratic leaders called upon their supporters to "contribute to the new government their technical, professional, or functional cooperation." The Christian Democrats expected a brief military interlude and then elections which would allow ex-President Frei to assume again the executive office.

In its 1974 "Declaration of Principles," however, the military leaders affirmed that "it is imperative to change the mentality of Chileans. . . . The Government does not intend to be a mere caretaker. . . . The Government of the Armed Forces aspires to initiate a new era in the national destiny." This declaration and subsequent actions taken against Christian Democratic leaders and party members destroyed the illusions of Christian Democrats who had supported the coup. It also vindicated the judgment of a minority of Christian Democrats who denounced the coup from the first instance. Christian Democratic leaders finally understood that it would be impossible to implement their own programs through the junta, or to convince the military leaders to step aside. Gradually, the full scope of the military repression and the realization that democracy would not be restored pushed most of the Christian Democrats into active opposition to the military government. In turn, General Pinochet felt entrenched enough to dispense with the façade of a legal political party opposition. By 1977 the military would no longer tolerate Christian Democratic or other organized opposition and decreed the "dissolution" of *all* political parties.

Meanwhile, some groups and individuals within the Catholic Church also opposed and confronted military repression. In October 1973 the Committee of Cooperation for Peace (COPACHI) began to provide legal services, food, medical assistance, and sanctuary to victims of the persecution unleashed by the military and the new security apparatus, *Dirección Nacional de Inteligencia* (DINA). Gradually a national network of safehouses and underground resistance emerged, oftentimes using Church buildings or the homes of courageous Chileans willing to risk their lives to save others from death or torture. With the Church and Chilean Catholics sorely divided, however, some religious leaders withdrew from COPACHI after evidence surfaced of its linkages to clandestine activities. Under pressure from conservative Catholics and from General Pinochet, Cardinal Silva agreed to the dissolution of COPACHI in 1975.

Almost immediately Cardinal Silva Henríquez established the Vicariate of Solidarity, which from 1976 onwards became the single most important source of moral opposition to the dictatorship. At the same time, it provided a partial umbrella of protection for numerous community organizations, research institutes, and human-rights defense groups. In particular, small groups of women, partially sheltered against the regime's wrath by the moral umbrella of the Church and partially protected by their status as "women, mothers, and wives," became visible leaders in the struggle against human rights abuses. In practice, neither the moral umbrella of the Church nor the supposedly elevated role of mothers and wives in a society which the military and their civilian allies claimed was based on the privileged place of the family, entirely protected human rights activists and other women viewed as subversives from hideous psychological torture, rape, and worse in the regime's detention centers. Nevertheless, the permeable umbrella of the Church permitted *some* protection against the systematic campaign of political repression. The Vicariate also extended material support to the urban and rural poor, provided technical assistance to small farmers, published magazines for popular education, maintained records on political detainees and "disappeared" persons (people killed or detained and unaccounted for by the government), and offered legal services to families of the detained and disappeared.

Consolidation of the military junta's political power occurred simultaneously with the gradual evolution of a program of economic stabilization and deregulation. In the first eighteen months, economic policy, like the government's political initiatives, had an "emergency" character. Bringing a halt to hyperinflation along with deregulating the economy and reducing the entrepreneurial role of the state (thereby reducing the large losses in public enterprises) received primary attention. To achieve these objectives the government devalued the Chilean currency, removed price controls from almost all commodities (October 1973), postponed scheduled wage increases (and then adjusted wages in relation to a doctored consumer price index), freed interest rates for capital market transactions, and modified taxes. To encourage investment the government eliminated capital gains taxes and reduced taxes on corporate profits. A new value-added tax of 20 percent was introduced to raise revenue. In addition, the government returned to private ownership more than two hundred firms incorporated into the public sector under the Popular Unity government. The junta also took initial steps to liberalize trade and capital flows by reducing tariff barriers and passing a new foreign investment law (Decree Law 600, 1974) that gave foreign investors equal treatment with domestic investors. Reduced tariff barriers were supposed to make imported goods less expensive for the Chilean consumer and also to encourage efficiency and modernization of Chilean industry. Perhaps most importantly, the junta drastically reduced government expenditures and employment in the public sector.

Unfavorable international economic trends, including increasing prices for imported oil, sharply falling prices for Chilean exports, especially copper, and rising interest rates limited the success of the *junta's* economic policies. The unfavorable international trends, combined with the government's focus on reducing public sector expenditures, led to dramatic increases in unemployment, which exceeded 14 percent of the labor force by official estimates in 1975. Real wages declined sharply as did labor's share of gross domestic income. Inflation, though reduced, continued at levels over 300 percent per year in 1975. While still blaming the difficult economic situation on the legacy of the Popular Unity government, the military leadership and a group of civilian advisers decided to shift from its "gradualist" approach to the earlier mentioned economic "shock treatment."

In previewing the shock program, Minister of Economy Sergio de Castro declared that the misery and suffering experienced by Chileans in the period 1974–75 "[was] the result of the years of demagogy and erroneous economic policies, the consequence of an exaggerated statism, the result of exaggerated protectionism that guaranteed monopoly profits . . . the result of policies made to benefit special interest groups to the detriment of the majority of the population." The shock treatment was intended to eliminate inflation and institutional barriers to economic growth quickly and dramatically through intensification of the stabilization program already in place and the addition of new more radical policies. Minister of Finance Jorge Cauas, in announcing the shock program in April 1975, told the nation:

> The President of the Republic and the Honorable Government Junta have asked me to design and carry out an economic program with the fundamental purpose of eradicating the inflation that has affected our country for more than seventy years and which recently has become extreme as a result of the demagogical economic policy carried out by the former government.
>
> . . . The main objective of this program is, as we have already stated, to put a brake on inflation by the end of this year. For this reason, certain basic measures have been approved. Although these measures imply continued sacrifice on the part of the community in the coming months, the compensations will be economic stability which will permit adequate economic development. This will mean that in the not too distant future poverty will be stamped out and all Chileans will be able to benefit from the advantages of the modern world.
>
> . . . The way to recovery, although it is short and well known, is fraught with sacrifices and denials.

What followed included reductions of between 15 to 25 percent in government expenditures and large decreases in the size and role of the public sector; a temporary 10 percent increase in income taxes; a series of tax revisions to increase government income; and tightened monetary policy. Approximately 80,000 government employees lost their jobs and unemployment grew throughout the economy, while industrial output dropped 25 percent in 1975. However, inflation declined precipitously (from over 300 percent per year in 1974 to 84 percent in 1977) and the government deficit practically disappeared by the end of 1975.

In many respects these government policies achieved their short-term objectives. Declines in the rate of inflation, improvement in government revenue collection, and elimination of large government deficits all encouraged government policymakers. Hyperinflation disappeared, but inflationary expectations lingered. In 1976 the government resorted to revaluation of the Chilean peso by 10 percent, with subsequent pre-announced exchange-rate adjustments to convince the Chilean people that inflation was truly under control. Though very impressive improvement did occur, inflation remained above 30 percent per year.

Numerous technical critiques of the shock treatment emerged among opponents of the military government as well as among some supporters who disagreed both with the severity of the economic measures and with the impact these policies had on key sectors of the economy. The most evident and widespread impacts involved massive unemployment, reaching approximately 20 percent of the labor force, and a steep decline in gross domestic product—down officially by 13 percent in a single year. Grim, desperate impoverishment afflicted millions of Chileans.

The recession and unemployment also began to induce a restructuring of the labor force. More and more poor Chileans performed occasional services ("guarding" cars, wiping windshields, shining shoes, working as domestic servants) and/or became itinerant vendors (*ambulantes*) of combs, gum, candy, pens, foodstuffs, or other low value commodities. Increasing participation in small-scale commerce and services created a more isolated, disorganized labor force, while contributing to feelings of social dislocation and to a preoccupation with survival on a daily basis. Reinforced by the political repression, secret police raids on homes and *poblaciones*, and the intensity of government efforts to eradicate community, student, and labor organizations, these conditions cast a pall of despair over the urban shantytowns and small provincial towns. Restitution of farmland to former owners and dismantling of the agrarian reform cooperatives (see Chapter 1) pleased many recipients of the new farm properties, but also left 35,000 to 40,000 landless workers who failed to qualify for the military program of land parcelization. Scattered makeshift settlements or *villorrios* in the rural areas cropped up around the country, and rural-urban migration accelerated without providing either jobs or solace to the migrants.

As a result of the desperate economic situation, the growth of the informal and service sectors, and the loss of jobs in certain parts of the industrial sector of the economy, labor force participation by women—and particularly poor women—greatly increased. The recession made working outside the home a necessity for survival. This trend, which would continue after economic recovery later in the decade, contributed to a further breakdown in traditional family patterns, both by inducing an increased "independence" of many women and by eroding the self-esteem of men unable to perform their expected role of "protectors and providers" in the nuclear family. Thus, while the military government proclaimed its intentions to reaffirm and support the traditional patriarchal family as the basic unit of Chilean society, government policies and the economic crisis confronted many Chilean women and the families they sustained with quite another reality.

In efforts to palliate the urgent situation of hundreds of thousands of Chilean families, the military government introduced a program of make-work public works projects and miscellaneous jobs called the *Programa de Empleo Mínimo* (PEM). Initiated in March 1975 with some 19,000 participants, it had grown to over 150,000 by late 1976 (over 5 percent of the economically active labor force). These workers received small "salaries" and, in about 30 percent of the cases, food rations (funded by the U.S. AID program and Catholic Relief—*Caritas*) for janitorial, service, maintenance, reforestation, and construction jobs. They were not counted among the *officially* unemployed. For hundreds of thousands more Chileans the recession induced by the shock treatment allowed not even the meager buffer of PEM.

Economic stabilization, reducing the role of the public sector, deregulation, and "opening" of the economy merged gradually into a coherent neo-liberal program for restructuring the Chilean economy. Policies utilized to achieve these ends included monetary restraints, budget reductions, and privatizing public assets (selling most of the 492 firms owned by CORFO and almost all the previously nationalized banks as well as much publicly held agricultural land). Inasmuch as the divestiture program occurred in a depressed economic environment, a select group of national and foreign firms acquired these enterprises at very favorable prices. The process also led to concentration of financial and productive assets in the hands of a small number of new diversified financial groups such as Grupo Vial, Grupo Cruzat-Larraín, Grupo Yarur, Grupo Matte, Grupo Puig, and Grupo Edwards.

Implementation of the economic program and consolidation of the regime's political control brought efforts to legitimize the *junta's* authority with something beyond the original emergency decrees. By 1975 the junta and its civilian collaborators were actively planning a "new institutional order" to replace the outmoded institutions of Chilean democracy. Four "constitutional acts" adopted between December 1975 and September 11, 1976, moved Chile in the direction of a constitutional military dictatorship.

The apparent contradiction of this three-word characterization will not surprise readers familiar with *Alice in Wonderland* or George Orwell's *1984*. Only by reading these constitutional acts can one appreciate fully the unintentional irony promulgated into law by Chile's military dictators. To illustrate, Constitutional Act Number 3 (September 4, 1976) stipulated, among other intriguing provisions:

Article 1. Men are born free and equal in dignity. This constitutional act guarantees all individuals:

11. Liberty of conscience, and expression of all creeds and free exercise of all religions, as do not violate moral principles, good behavior or public order . . .

12. Freedom of opinion and information, in all ways and by all means, without prior censorship, notwithstanding responsibility under the law for offense or abuse as may be committed in use of these freedoms. However, the courts may prohibit publication or circulation of opinions or information affecting moral principles, public order, national security or the private life of individuals.

. . . Individuals who may have been at any time convicted or found guilty of threatening the institutional order of the Republic may not own, direct, or manage mass communications media, nor may they in any way participate in functions connected with the publication or broadcast of opinions or information.

Article 2. No individual may invoke any constitutional or legal precept whatsoever to violate the rights or freedoms established hereunder, or to threaten the integrity or operation of the state of law or the established regime.

Any act of individuals or groups directed to disseminate doctrines which threaten the family, or which promote violence or the concept of a society based on class struggle, or as may be otherwise contrary to the established regime or the integrity or operation of the state of law, is illicit and in violation of the institutional organization of the Republic.

If these sections read like a tongue-in-cheek Orwellian invention, Constitutional Act Number 4 (promulgated at the same time as the act above) seems to go further than even Orwell. To combat "latent subversion," this act authorized the president of the republic to declare "a state of defense against subversion." Under such conditions, the president "may only restrict personal freedom, freedom of information, and the right of assembly." If the president declared a state of "internal or external war" or a "state of internal commotion," his authority was still greater, including the power to deprive Chileans of their citizenship and "to suspend or restrict all of the rights or guarantees set forth in Constitutional Act Number 3. . . ."

By the end of 1976 the Chileans were living in a juridical Wonderland; but the enforcement mechanisms of the military junta could hardly be characterized as a house of cards. And no Chilean could merely wake up to escape the nightmare. Moreover, the reach of state terrorism extended to Europe and the United States as the Chilean government joined other military regimes in Argentina, Uruguay, and Paraguay in "Operation Condor." As revealed in declassified U.S. government documents, this "South American joint intelligence operation" was designed "to eliminate Marxist terrorist activities" with 'special teams which travel anywhere in the world' . . . to carry out sanctions up to assassination against terrorists or supporters of terrorist organizations." The Chilean military junta defined "terrorists or supporters of terrorist organizations" rather broadly; assassins killed ex–Army Commander General Carlos Prats and his wife in Buenos Aires (1974), attacked Christian Democratic leader Bernardo Leighton and his wife in Rome (1975), and murdered ex–Unidad Popular cabinet minister Orlando Letelier in Washington, D.C. (1976). Agents of Operation Condor hunted down, interrogated, tortured, and murdered leftists and other regime opponents throughout Latin America and elsewhere—sometimes with specialized collaboration from U.S. police and intelligence agencies, including surveillance and interrogation of subjects within the United States.

The "constitutional acts" remained emergency measures rather than a legitimate foundation of a new political order. With growing Church denunciations of the activities of DINA and the new focus of U.S. foreign policy under President Carter on human rights, supporters of the military government engaged in internal discussions concerning the desirability and need to establish a more permanent alternative political system. Within the military government, and among its civilian supporters, disagreement existed over the precise features of a new institutional order. Nevertheless, consolidation of the regime, weakness of the opposition (including abolition of all political parties in March 1977), and pressure for moderation of the repressive policies from the United States as well as some European nations, made expedient a vague commitment to a transition to a new constitutional order. Meanwhile the political architecture of the authoritarian regime left a complex structure of military edicts (*bandos*), decree laws, decrees, and "secret laws" that constituted an impressive, if surrealistic, juridical tyranny from 1973 to 1981. After implementing a new constitution in 1981, the military government defined its legislation as laws, rather than as decree laws, and began numbering the laws from the numeration existant in 1973. Table 10–1 summarizes the major "legal" foundations of the military regime from 1973 until 1985.

From 1973 onward, government-sponsored constitutional study groups and official agencies had debated a new institutional order, but General Pinochet had made no specific commitment to adopt a new constitution nor to a timetable for military withdrawal from a tutelary role in national politics. In July 1977, General Pinochet announced the "Chacarillas Plan," promising movement toward a new system of "protected democracy." Apparently acting without full consultation with other junta members, General Pinochet provided in the Chacarilla Plan a framework for gradual transition from military rule to a new political system. During a lengthy transition period basic legislative reforms in the areas of labor, social welfare, education, and public administration would provide the foundations for the new political order, while the military and selected civilian leaders would share responsibility for policymaking. Ultimately, the new system would use a restrictive and indirect system of electing a new president, and reserve to the armed forces the mission of protecting, guaranteeing, and supervising national security and modernization.

Shortly after announcing the Chacarillas Plan, General Pinochet abolished the DINA. This action served as a symbolic indication that the "emergency" situation of 1973–76 had ended and that the regime was moving toward institutionalization of a new political system. In addition, abolition of the DINA served to mollify critics in the United States and Europe, where this agency had carried out assassinations and attacks on prominent Chileans. In its place, however, Pinochet created the National Information Center (CNI), an agency with the same general purpose and practices—but now with formal, rather than secret, authority and jurisdiction.

The outlawing of the political parties, unilateral announcement of the Chacarilla Plan, and reorganization and institutionalization of the secret police all evidenced General Pinochet's emerging predominance within the junta. By combining political adeptness and skillful manipulation of internal incentives within the armed forces, he gradually achieved control over the junta, the security apparatus, and the main administrative centers of power. With the national budget as an instrument for policy initiatives, and for rewarding supporters, especially the armed forces which had long felt neglected and unappreciated by civilian politicians, General Pinochet astutely modified spending priorities and the perquisites of armed service personnel.

TABLE 10–1. "LEGAL" FOUNDATIONS OF MILITARY RULE, 1973–87

DL 3	September 11, 1973	State of siege, defined initially as "state of internal war"
DL 4		State of emergency in provinces and regions
DL 5		Interpretative decree regarding Code of Military Justice, affirming the existence of a "state of war"
DL 8		Delegation to military authorities of power to rule through military edicts (*bandos militares*) and to exercise judicial authority over civilians (*jurisdicción militar*)*
DL 81		Authority to expel (banish) persons from country during the state of siege (which lasted until 1978 and was reimposed several times thereafter)
DL 521	June 14, 1974	Official creation of the DINA (secret police, accountable to General Pinochet, which already functioned extraofficially in late 1973). This decree has "secret" provisions detailing the secret police's "authority"
DL 527	June 17, 1974	Charter of the military junta (*Estatuto de la Junta de Gobierno*)
DL 604	August 10, 1974	Prohibits entry into country of persons who spread or support doctrines that threaten national security or who are known to be "agitators of activists"
DL 640	September 2, 1974	Regulations defining the various "regimes of exception"
DL 788	December 4, 1974	Provides that the "decree laws" of the military junta have the effect of amending the 1925 constitution
DL 922	March 11, 1975	State of Siege Decree
DL 1.008 and 1.009	May 8, 1975	Increases period during which detainees may be held "incomunicado" in cases involving crimes against the security of the state (arrestees cannot see lawyers or obtain habeas corpus writs)
DS 890 (M. Interior)	August 26, 1975	Modifies the Law of State Security; greatly restricts civil rights and liberties (*garantías constitucionales*) and due process.
DL 1.281	December 11, 1975	Authorizes Military Zone Commanders to censure or suspend publication of up to six editions of magazines, newspapers, and other media
Constitutional Acts		
DL 1.319	January 9, 1976	
DL 1.551	September 11, 1976	"Essential Foundations of Chileanism"
DL 1.552	September 11, 1976	"Constitutional Rights and Duties"
DL 1.553	September 11, 1976	"On Regimes of Exception"
DL 1.877	1977	Modifies Law 12.927 (Internal Security Law), increased authority of the president during states of emergency
DL 1.878	August 13, 1977	Creates CNI (new secret police to replace DINA) and details its authority
	April 19, 1978	State of siege ends; country remains in "state of emergency"
DL 3.168	February 6, 1980	Authorizes internal exile (*relegación*) for persons who alter or seek to alter public order, for up to three months (Modification of DL 81 and DL 1.877, Internal Security of the State)
Plebiscite for new Constitución	September 11, 1980	Occurs under "state of emergency" Constitution adds a new regime of exception, "state of perturbation of internal peace," with special powers for president when such a circumstance occurs

(continued)

TABLE 10–1. "LEGAL" FOUNDATIONS OF MILITARY RULE, 1973–87 *(continued)*

		Article 24 ("transitory article") provides that until full implementation of constitution (in practice, this would be after 1989), president has virtually unlimited authority to assure internal security by suspending civil liberties and rights; declaring appropriate regime of exception, etc.
DL 3.451	1980	Extends to 25 days the period during which detainees may be held in centers "other than jails" when certain crimes against internal security are being investigated
DL 3.645	1981	Clarifies the application of transitory Article 24, regarding expulsion of citizens and foreigners; also regulates labor unions
	1981–84	Country under state of emergency (Transitory Article 24)
Ley 18.015	July 27, 1981	Details infractions covered by Transitory Article 24; modified by Law 18.150, July 30, 1982
	1984 (November)	Country declared under state of siege (7 months) and also state of emergency
Ley 18.313	1984	Law on "Abuses of the Media" (*Sobre abusos de la Publicidad*) amended; further restrictions on media
Ley 18.314	May 14, 1984	New "Antiterrorism Law" greatly broadens the definition of "terrorism" and increases penalties
Ley 18.415	June 15, 1985	New Law on "States of Exception"
DS 324	June 15, 1985	New Law on press censorship and rules governing the mass media
	June 1985	Country declared in state of siege
Ley 18.667	November 27, 1987	Modifications to the Military Code allow maintaing secret documents that might affect the security of the state

*The junta ruled initially with an uncoordinated raft of military edicts (*bandos*) whose legal status was, at the least, questionable. See Manuel Antonio Garretón, Roberto Garretón, and Carmen Garretón, *Por la fuerza sin la razón, Análisis y textos de los bandos de la dictadura militar,* Santiago: LOM Publisher, 1999.

In the first two years of the military *junta*, with public expenditures declining by some 40 percent, military expenditures *increased* by over 30 percent. Officers achieved great economic gains and privileges, while the national police (*carabineros*) gained in status and benefits with their transfer from the ministry of interior and "elevation" to co-equal participants in the junta with the other armed forces. International disputes and the potential for armed conflict with Bolivia and Peru in the mid-1970s and, later, with Argentina, focused national concern on re-equipping and modernizing the armed forces while providing narrow professional national defense missions for the military commanders. The government also encouraged development of a more diversified Chilean arms industry to protect the country against the vagaries of international supplies. In this context, the intelligence branches and *Investigaciones* assumed a more important role in domestic politics and came to serve as a key source of power and control for General Pinochet. The dictatorship became less a government *of* the armed forces and more a regime of military leaders and civilian technocrats, led by General Pinochet, supported *by* the armed forces. In this arrangement the security apparatus gained autonomy and became a key element in assuring political control.

Over time, however, disagreements within the military institutions over government policy and professional issues came to the surface. In 1973 the coup leaders had purged high ranking officers who appeared most likely to resist the coup and a number of others were killed, imprisoned, tortured, and retired. Enlisted personnel who refused to participate in the coup also suffered execution, incarceration, or other punishment. Later, General Prats, ex-commander-in-chief and a potential challenger to Pinochet's control, was assassinated in Buenos Aires.

Consolidation of General Pinochet's hegemony through the operations of DINA and, later, the CNI alienated certain sectors within the armed forces, but modifications of the career and promotion system in the army made officers increasingly reliant upon the patronage and good graces of Pinochet himself. Nevertheless, some officers resisted the neo-liberal economic program, favoring a more nationalist and populist alternative to resolve the country's crisis. Disproportionately large increases in expenditures for internal security and the army distressed some navy and air force officers. Before 1976–77, however, this distress did not translate into open challenges to General Pinochet or the military junta.

Announcement of the Chacarillas Plan opened the door to debate concerning the character of the regime, timing of movement to an alternative political model, and the role of political parties, labor, and other organizations in the new political system. This debate eventually involved high ranking military officers and even members of the junta. Conflicts with Air Force General Gustavo Leigh over the pace of political "normalization" and the process of junta decision-making resulted in the latter's removal from the junta and, in 1978, a number of forced retirements within the air force.

Meanwhile Chilean exiles around the world continued to wonder if they could ever return to their homeland, or if Chile would ever again be free of military rectors in the universities, military censors over the media, military masters over a civilian population. In the face of a United Nations charge of human rights violations in Chile, General Pinochet called a national referendum in the first week of 1978, in which Chilean citizens were asked to vote "no" or "yes" on the following resolution:

> In the face of the international aggression unleashed against the government of the fatherland, I support [General] Pinochet in his defense of the dignity of Chile, and I reaffirm the legitimate right of the republic to conduct the process of institutionalization in a manner befitting its sovereignty.

With the opposition repressed and the mass media muffled, the government claimed that more than 75 percent of the electorate had expressed support for Pinochet. Based on this overwhelming "mandate," General Pinochet announced that there would be no further elections for a decade, and he told Chile's politicians, "It's finished for you."

In response to the consolidation of the regime's position as well as to apparent support reflected in the January 1978 plebiscite, General Pinochet lifted the "state of siege" in March and replaced it with the somewhat less restrictive "state of emergency." Under the "state of emergency," the military tribunals were theoretically subject to review by the Supreme Court, and civil liberties were partially restored. The following month Pinochet announced a general amnesty in the name of political reconciliation. The April 19, 1978, amnesty decree (Decree Law 2.191) responded to international and bilateral pressures: investigations in the United States regarding the assassination by DINA agents of Orlando Letelier, ex–cabinet minister in the Allende government and leader-in-exile of the opposition to the military dictatorship; threats of a boycott of Chilean products by port workers and organized labor in the United States and Europe; the announced on-site visit of a United Nations commission investigating human rights violations in Chile; and growing concern about the possibility of war with Argentina over unresolved border disputes. The amnesty decree also emerged from the immediate political conjuncture in Chile: the recent referendum (*consulta nacional*) that overwhelmingly supported Pinochet's rule; the incessant denunciations of human rights violations by spokespersons of the Catholic Church; inquietude in the armed forces regarding the possible loss of impunity for the repressive measures taken after September 11, 1973, if political conditions changed; and the appointment of the first civilian Minister of Interior since 1973, with the self-proclaimed mission of consolidating a new institutional order.

The new Minister of Interior, Sergio Fernández, declared that the amnesty should be understood as a measure to promote "social peace" and "reconciliation." It covered "political crimes" (and others as well, due to careless drafting) between September 11, 1973 and March 10, 1978, but specifically excluded persons involved in the Letelier case. Article 1 of the decree extended amnesty to all persons (authors, accomplices, or those who concealed crimes [*encubridores*] who had engaged in criminal activity during the state of siege in effect from September 11, 1973, to March 10, 1978, unless currently charged or sentenced. Article 2 amnestied those persons who at the time the decree law took effect had been sentenced by military tribunals since September 11, 1973 (thus those charged but not "sentenced" were excluded; likewise those in prison or clandestine detention centers without charges against them). Article 3 excluded from the amnesty many "common crimes," such as parracide, infanticide, armed robbery, drug trafficking, corruption of minors, rape, and others. Imperfections in composing the list of exclusions produced some amusing categories of amnestied felons, whose amnesty the government left intact rather than "undo" it once conceded. As a result of promulgating the amnesty, according to the semi-official historian of the military government Gonzalo Rojas Sánchez (*Chile escoge la libertad, La presidencia de Augusto Pinochet Ugarte 11.IX.73-11.III. 1990*): "after completing five years in power, Pinochet could assure that his measures had continued a consistent and permanent line in the gradual reestablishment of the exercise of the rights of persons, . . . which revealed the success achieved by the authorities and the citizenry in their common efforts to secure social peace against those who sought to menace it."

In practice, Decree Law 2.191 was also a "self-amnesty" for crimes committed by agents of the government, both civilian and military, including the illegal detentions, torture, murder, and "disappearances" since the 1973 coup. From the time of its promulgation the amnesty would be controversial. Although initially hailed by Church leaders as an olive branch extended by the junta, human rights activists quickly rejected any possibility of amnesty for "crimes against humanity," for torture covered by international treaties, and for state terrorism. Within the armed forces and hardline political right, the amnesty also provoked dissent. How could Marxist "terrorists" be amnestied after driving the country to ruin, attacking, kidnapping, and killing police and military personnel? Why had the government seemingly eroded the country's sovereignty by bowing to foreign pressures? The junta and its ministers denied that foreign pressures had influenced the decision to decree an amnesty. Such denials convinced few Chileans, who expressed their opinion with traditional clichés: "If the river resounds, it's because there are rocks in it"; "where there's smoke, there's fire."

On March 21, 1978, General Pinochet had accepted ex-DINA Commander General Manuel Contreras' resignation from the Army. In early April the Chilean government expelled Michael Townley, a U.S. citizen working for the DINA and involved in the Letelier assassination. He left the country in FBI custody. Shortly thereafter the United States formally requested the extradition of Contreras; Colonel Pedro Espinoza, the second ranking officer in the DINA; and lieutenant Armando Fernández Larios. The president of the Chilean Supreme Court later rejected the extradition request, but in April 1978 the military government sought to soften its international image and promote internal "reconciliation."

To provide a political opening for the new cabinet, the government had declared an end to the "state of siege" (but not to the "state of emergency") and authorized return of high-profile Christian Democratic exiles Jaime Castillo and Bernardo Leighton. In addition, various persons processed by military tribunals received pardons in early April. Sergio Fernández believed that such measures might pave the way for approval and implementation of a new constitution to give more permanence and legitimacy to "authoritarian democracy." According to the Minister Secretary General of the Government, General René Vidal, the government hoped that "along with the general sense of pacification given by the amnesty, pardon and 'forgetting' (el olvido) would definitively calm the spirits, extinguishing hatreds and resentments." In addition, the growing threat of armed conflict with Argentina made urgent the quest for "national unity."

Que Pasa, a generally pro-government magazine, editorialized: "Hopefully, the recent amnesty decreed by the Military Junta will be the road to normalization." However, the editorial warned that the amnesty did not signify "a diminultion in vigilance of public order" and warned that the amnesty "should not allow resurgence of terrorism and violence." In any case, the government quickly clarified that the amnesty did not permit the return of exiles without specific authorization by the proper authorities. Such permission could only be obtained on a case-by-case basis.

On April 23, 1978, *El Mercurio's* editorial, titled "In the National Tradition," listed various previous amnesty laws from 1857 until the 1950s, connecting the military junta's 1978 amnesty with Chile's patriotic tradition of seeking national unity after internal conflict. The declared spirit of reconciliation, nevertheless, had its limits. The "political recess" remained in effect; party activity was still banned, and press censorship and intimidation continued. Moreover, the official translation of Pinochet's announcement distributed by the Chilean embassy in Washington, D.C., made clear the general's firm intentions to prevent renewed political opposition:

> I wish to announce tonight that I have decided to pardon prison sentences or commute them to exile—that is, abandonment of the country—for all persons sentenced by military courts for crimes against the national security committed before or after September 11, 1973.
>
> Although it is entirely improper to refer to persons found guilty of a crime as political prisoners, now, as a result of the amnesty decree which is inspired by humanitarian motives, no one will be able to say that there are persons deprived of their freedom in Chile because of political happenings.
>
> I hope that this decision by my Government will be understood as a sign of pacification and not one of weakness, for anyone who falls into error in that respect runs the risk from now on of suffering full application of the law.

As General Pinochet secured his control over the country, the economic shock treatment gave way to impressive economic growth based upon improved international prices for Chilean products, increases in agricultural, industrial, and mining exports, and large inflows of foreign investment and loans. A rush of financial and real estate speculation generated enthusiasm in elite circles in Santiago, Valparaíso, and other urban centers. New office buildings and shopping centers dotted both downtown Santiago and the fashionable neighborhoods of the capital. Luxury condominiums decorated the coastline at Valparaíso and Viña del Mar. Road and highway construction,

TABLE 10–2. AVAILABILITY OF GOODS AND SERVICES PER 10,000 POPULATION, 1970–81

	1970	1971	1972	1973	1974	1975	1976	1977	1978	1979	1980	1981
Automobiles	189	203	223	228	216	251	253	279	313	354	413	494
Television sets	138	186	197	129	242	167	139	418	435	459	477	454
Refrigerators	72	68	64	52	39	27	31	49	72	132	156	171
Washing machines	52	61	58	53	64	46	43	48	69	100	127	150
Telephones	415	438	455	461	466	466	475	483	523	536	541	555
Residential electricity consumption (thousand kilowatts)	988	1077	1269	1376	1397	1366	1344	1380	1476	1546	1625	1709
Liquefied gas	302	345	370	387	395	379	393	415	413	411	412	413

Source: Bela Balassa, "Policy Experiments in Chile 1973–1983" in Gary M. Walton, ed., The National Economic Policies of Chile, Greenwich, Conn., 1985, pp. 222–23.

port modernization, improvements in bus and rail transport, all seemed to justify the confidence of the junta and the neo-liberal economic team in the correctness of their program and in Chile's future. Import duties, initially reduced to an average of 15 percent, and then to 10 percent in 1979, spurred a consumption frenzy among Chileans able to purchase imported goods previously exorbitantly expensive due to tariff protection. Improving economic conditions reaffirmed support for the military government despite stories of torture and international criticism. Television sets, calculators, stereos, computers, and more esoteric imports were justification enough for many Chileans of the overthrow of the Popular Unity government.

Selected macroeconomic indicators also affirmed the government's success: inflation reduced from over 600 percent per year to 30 percent in 1979; solid growth of domestic production after 1977; dramatic decreases in budget deficits; impressive expansion of non-traditional exports to a diversified list of European, Asian, and Western Hemisphere markets; positive balance of payments after 1978; and increasing levels of foreign investment and international confidence in the Chilean economy.

With the economic recovery Chile's affluent and middle-class sectors enjoyed what came to be called "the Chilean Miracle." Boasting of its success in *Chile, 1980 Economic Profile*, the government declared: "Five years ago Chile boldly embarked on a course to revitalize its weakened economy, replacing protectionism with free-market policies . . . the average GDP growth rate over the last five years has been 7.3%. . . . A diversified economy capable of functioning at an internationally competitive level has now been established, thereby assuring economic stability and offering excellent opportunities for domestic and foreign investors."

In contrast to the government's pride in "the miracle," a number of dissident intellectuals, artists, and writers such as Fernando Alegría, Poli Délano, Ariel Dorfman, Antonio Skármeta, and Hernán Valdés produced work with subtle ironies and/or horrific detail which focused on the human cost of the supposed economic miracle. In the press, magazines, and dramatic presentations seemingly innocuous messages encoded scathing critiques of the military dictatorship, as regime opponents attempted to walk the precipice between the wrath of censors and secret police and the temptations of self-censorship. In some cases folk art in the *poblaciones* or provincial towns served both to earn a survival wage for artisans who created decorative appliqué and embroidered pieces (*arpilleras*) while expressing resistance to the government's programs. In a less subtle effort, Chilean writer Pablo Huneeus published "The New Economist's Creed." This satirical spoof offended some readers with its seeming parody of religious beliefs, but it also reflected the cynical claims by the Pinochet government of defending the "Western-Christian Tradition." The "New Economist's Creed" read, in part:

I believe in the all powerful dollar, creator of heaven and earth;

I believe in Milton Friedman, His only son, our God, conceived by the grace of the University of Chicago;

Born of the Stock Market . . . expropriated, died and buried;

Descended into the hell of Socialism;

In the Third Year, returned to life, ascending the 11th [day of the military coup in September 1973]

I believe in the Holy Spirit, sacred private enterprise and Japanese cars;

I believe in the capital markets, the *financieras* and Pierre Cardin shirts;

I believe that Adam Smith lives, Keynes is dead, and Marx was a nightmare

Viviana Díaz, daughter of a "disappeared" person, chains herself to the Tribunals of Justice, 1979. Díaz became president of the Agrupación de Familiares de Detenidos Desaparecidos in 1999 with the death of longtime leader Sola Sierra. (Photo courtesy of Archivo Vicaría de la Solidaridad.)

I believe in selling the factories, mines and forests of the country

I believe there are too many journalists and public opinion counts for nothing

I believe that sociologists are a plague and the poor a necessary evil

I believe in tennis, long lunches and comparative advantage;

I believe in international prices, domestic salaries and Argentine shoes;

I believe Carter is a communist, the Cardinal is a communist and the communists are communists;

I believe in the communion of the market, forgiveness for our sins, the appearance of the "disappeared" [unaccounted for political prisoners] and in the eternal Junta.

     Amen.

Opponents and critics of the military government pointed out that while the so-called miracle amounted to economic recovery, it was a recovery in which unemployment remained over 15 percent, the gains in consumption were concentrated among the top 20 percent of income earners in the country (though real wages were improving), and the foreign debt was burgeoning. Wild financial and real estate speculation

TABLE 10–3. SELECTED ECONOMIC INDICATORS, 1973–82

Year	1973	1974	1975	1976	1977	1978	1979	1980	1981	x73–81	1982
Growth rate real GDP (%)	-5.6	1.0	-12.9	3.5	9.9	8.2	8.3	7.8	5.7	2.6	-14.3
Inflation (%)*	508.1	375.9	340.7	174.3	63.5	30.3	38.9	31.2	9.5	156.5	20.7
Government deficit as % of GDP	24.7	10.5	2.6	2.3	1.8	0.8	-1.7	-3.1	-1.7	4.0	2.3
Exports FOB (millions of dollars)	1309	2151	1590	2116	2185	2460	2835	4705	3836	2687	3706
Imports FOB (millions of dollars)	1288	1794	1520	1473	2151	2886	4190	5469	6513	3032	3643
Commercial balance (millions of dollars)	21	357	70	643	34	-426	-355	-764	-2677	-344	63
Balance of payments (millions of dollars)	-21	-55	-344	414	113	712	1047	1244	67	353	-1165
Long- and medium-term foreign debt (millions of dollars)	3261	4026	4267	4274	4510	5923	7507	9413	12,553	6193	13,815

*Change in Consumer Price Index (INE), December–December each year.

x = average, 1973–81.

Source: Banco Central de Chile, Informe Económico de Chile, 1983, p. 46.

provided a façade of "boom" while portending disaster. The traditional industrial sector, battered by competition from imports, failed to recover its vigor despite stimulation of export-oriented industries such as wood and paper products, fishmeal, minerals, and processed fruit. With financial intermediation between the domestic economy and foreign commercial banks among the most profitable of enterprises, *real* interest rates remained very high while domestic investment stayed very low. Indeed, the most profitable sector of the economy seemed to be in the ever more complex pyramid of financial speculation which utilized paper assets as security for secondary and tertiary credit lines. The same financial groups at the center of the speculative boom also controlled over 60 percent of total private exports by 1980. Critics also pointed to the growing foreign indebtedness—particularly short-term loans attracted by the high *real* domestic interest rates—and the increased vulnerability of the economy to fluctuations in the international marketplace. And although the military regime emphasized private enterprise, it benefitted considerably from the previous nationalization of the major copper enterprises (the *gran minería del cobre*). In 1976 the junta decreed the Ley Reservada del Cobre, allocating 10 percent of the value of copper exports (in dollars) directly to the armed forces for arms purchases and other items. A minimum level for these funds was established; if copper prices declined the national treasury would cover the difference. In 1987 the floor level for these funds was linked to the consumer price index in the United States. In practice, approximately 42 percent of the increase in value in the Chilean economy from 1970 to 1990 originated in copper exports (and 75% of that amount from the *gran minería del cobre*). Obviously the military regime and its civilian allies and advisors did not entirely trust "the market" to protect their own vital interests. As economist Patricio Meller facetiously commented in *Un siglo de economía política chilena (1890–1990):*

> From the standpoint of microenomic or macroeconomic rationality, it is not obvious that Chile should spend more on armaments whenever the price of copper goes up. Or, will our "enemies" have a greater incentive to attack us when this occurs? What would a private entrepreneur opine if taxes on his business were linked to sales, independent of profit or loss? Why did none of the pro-government economists question the rationality of the Ley Reservada del Cobre? In synthesis, the benefits resulting from the nationalization of the GMC [*gran minería del cobre*] by the Popular Unity government were perceived during the military government.

In 1980, however, this list of defects in the economic model paled in comparison with the highly visible "miracle." As economic growth and the glitter of new construction and public works bolstered the government's confidence and base of support, General Pinochet announced further institutional initiatives. In September 1979 he declared that the government would adopt a program of national modernization, involving radical changes in the areas of labor policy, education, social security, health, regional decentralization, justice, and agriculture. What came to be called "the seven modernizations" paved the way for the eventual institutionalization of the authoritarian system in a constitutional plebiscite in 1980.

Most important of the seven modernizations was the 1979 "Labor Plan." The culmination of a six-year attack on organized labor, the new labor plan focused on permanent depoliticization and demobilization of labor in Chilean society. From an economic standpoint, the neoliberal model prescribed "labor flexibility," that is, an end to job security and to government "overregulation" of working conditions. In the first months after the coup, the military government had banned strikes, prohibited collective bargaining, and suspended the processing of all labor petitions. It outlawed the CUT, prohibited union elections, and assigned military officers to mediate labor disputes between workers and employers. Other measures barred union meetings held without prior approval by the police.

From the outset, the military junta defined these innovations as "emergency measures" that would be revised as the regime developed a program to modify the old Labor Code. The Minister of Labor declared in 1976 that "it is not possible to introduce a new industrial relations system until the evils that brought us to this social crisis are extirpated. For this reason collective bargaining and union elections have been suspended." The emergency measures remained in place until the Labor Plan of 1979.

Organized labor's initial responses to the military government involved primarily non-Marxist groups which the junta allowed to function as evidence that government policy was not antilabor, but rather anticommunist and antipolitical. In 1974, public employees, maritime workers, bank employees, health workers, and even some members of the metallurgical federation, who were affiliated with the National Workers' Central (CNT), attempted to obtain government recognition as the official voice of labor. The CNT, which included Christian Democrats and *gremialistas*, failed to achieve any immediate mass support. It also failed to reconcile the conflicts between those who wholeheartedly supported the junta and those who preferred the role of "responsible" (versus Marxist) opposition. The existence of the CNT initially served the government's need to establish alternative procedures for industrial relations and to demonstrate to the International Labor Office that labor rights and interests in Chile were being respected. In addition, the junta's second labor minister, Air Force General Nicanor Díaz, and some of his colleagues sought to put into place a corporatist and populist model of industrial relations rather than merely repress labor for the benefit of employers.

Meanwhile, the CUT constituted an external directorate in Paris and made efforts to maintain clandestine contacts with the outlawed political parties and their supporters in the workplace. Illegal strikes in 1974, by both ex-Popular Unity supporters and more conservative workers, challenged the military's policies but they also provoked harsh reactions against union leaders and rank and file. Speaking at the May 1, Labor Day celebration in 1975, the minister of labor proclaimed that "September 11 detained Marxism, it did not destroy it; we must now destroy Marxism."

In June 1975 a group of labor federations previously affiliated with the CUT, including Christian Democrats who rejected collaboration with the military regime, created a loosely organized alternative to the CNT which they called the National Union Coordinating Committee (CNS). The government, however, viewed the CNS as an effort to resurrect the politicized, leftist labor movement of the past; its leaders suffered periodic arrests, harassment, and sometimes death or "disappearance."

Toward the end of 1975, a so-called Group of Ten, predominantly Christian Democratic labor leaders, also became active. This group included relatively moderate labor opponents to the military regime, and even some personalities whom the dictatorship had designated to represent Chile at International Labor Organization (ILO) meetings outside the country. In May 1976 the Group of Ten published an open letter criticizing the government's labor policies, and in 1977 took the lead in rejecting General Pinochet's proposals for a "protected democracy" in the Chacarillas Plan.

In response to the renewed activism of labor, and emulating in some ways the labor policies of General Ibáñez's first administration (1927–31), the junta attempted to establish a heterogeneous base of *gremios* in a new National Gremialist Secretariat (1976) and a National Unity Labor Front. It also sponsored parallel unions within firms or economic sectors where labor opposition existed, for example, among copper and port workers and within the National Electricity Industry (ENDESA). Most of these efforts fell short of government aspirations, although certain labor leaders and workers repeatedly manifested support for the junta. Finally, in 1978, the military government attempted to create a new officialist labor organization called the National Union of Chilean Workers (UNTRACH), but this organization could not garner any mass support despite its moderate criticisms of government policy.

Renewed strike activity from 1977 to 1978, including job actions, absenteeism, and hunger strikes in the copper mines, ports, and among textile, chemical, metallurgical, and transportation workers, was met with a variety of repressive measures. Authorities arrested numerous labor leaders, fired participants in the job actions, sentenced some activists to internal exile (relegación), and dissolved seven union federations affiliated with the CNS. Not only did these measures fail to end the strikes before the workers attained some of their goals, but, more importantly, the high visibility of the strikers and of the government response focused international attention anew on Chilean politics and provoked both official and grass roots support for the opposition in Europe and the United States. President Carter's emphasis on human rights in U.S. foreign policy collided directly with the Chilean government's practices, and the possibility of a boycott by the AFL-CIO in the United States threatened the very basis of the export-led economic recovery promoted by the government.

Inability to control workers in government-owned copper mines, together with the threat of isolation from U.S. markets by refusal of American workers to offload Chilean cargoes, pushed the Pinochet government toward new labor policies. Beginning with an abrupt call for union elections in 1978 and Decree Law 2200, the Chilean military regime redesigned the Chilean industrial relations system. Thus, the Labor Plan, heralded as one of the seven modernizations initiated in 1979, represented the Pinochet government's efforts to clarify and codify the role and limits of labor in the evolving system of "protected democracy."

The new labor regimen legalized a system of collective bargaining and guaranteed yearly wage readjustments tied to the official rate of inflation. Union organization and bargaining between employers and workers were recognized as basic to modern industrial relations. However, the new regulations limited collective bargaining and strike action to individual plant unions or, in agriculture, to unions in individual farms. Strikes were limited to sixty days, after which time employees who refused to return to work "are considered to have resigned . . . but will be eligible for unemployement subsidies." (This provision led eventually to a number of 59-day strikes, followed by brief interludes and then subsequent return to strike action.) In contrast to previous legislation which allowed for federations and confederations to act at regional or national levels, the new labor laws forbade these types of organizations from participating in collective bargaining and a number of other "political" activities. To avoid the possibility of simultaneous labor disputes or strikes, the new regulations specified a timetable for labor negotiations in particular firms or sectors of the economy, and published a long list of firms and sectors where strikes were prohibited. The laws authorized the government to dissolve labor organizations for participating in "monopolistic practices" (presenting similar labor petitions in several firms at the same time), engaging in "political" activities, or carrying out activities beyond the scope of "union functions."

In the case of agricultural unions this meant the loss of all the gains achieved during the Christian Democratic and Popular Unity administrations. Permitted to organize unions only in farms with fifteen permanent workers (or nine in some special cases), farmworkers faced restrictions on organization more severe than those enacted in 1947 and were subject to layoff at the whim of the employer. Simply by refusing to hire more than fourteen *full-time* workers, agricultural employers could avoid unionization. As a result, in 1981, agricultural workers unions claimed fewer than 30,000 members nationwide—approximately 15 percent of the membership they had at the end of 1973. In addition, agricultural policies which both reversed the agrarian reform and added to rural unemployment made the plight of rural labor and the problems of the rural labor movement even more difficult. Indeed, no group of workers suffered more, or lost more, under the military regime than the Chilean campesinos.

Supplementary labor decrees allowed work days of up to twelve hours, without overtime scales, so long as total hours worked per week did not exceed forty-eight. The government also eliminated the traditional system of labor courts and even abolished the old *colegios profesionales,* essentially professional associations of doctors, lawyers, pharmacists, or journalists, and replaced them with *gremialista* associations. Officially, these policies were adopted to eliminate restraints on the market and inefficiencies in the economy; in practice they coincided with the government's ongoing efforts to depoliticize Chilean society by fragmenting organized labor and professional associations and limiting their activities to narrow, geographically specific actions.

In addition to the "Labor Plan," the other "modernizations" also had both economic and political objectives. Modernization of the educational system involved decentralization of educational administration by placing the primary schools under the direction of municipal authorities. The national government retained supervisory control over the content of education—emphasizing basic skills, Chilean history and geography, and civic duties and responsibilities. This emphasis had emerged early in the military administration with declarations in the *Objetivo Nacional del Gobierno de Chile* (1975) that "education should strengthen and transmit love for *la patria* and national values, . . . appreciation of the family as the basic cell of society, acceptance of the idea of national unity." Constitutional Act No. 3 (1976) had also emphasized "promoting among students a sense of moral, civic, and social responsibility, love of *la patria* and its fundamental values . . . and the spirit of brotherhood among people and among nations." This emphasis on morality and national values carried forward to the announced plan for educational modernization, set forth in the "Presidential Directive for Education" (March 5, 1979).

Beginning in 1980–81, municipal governments took over responsibility for administering the public primary schools, with curriculum and budgets supervised by the Ministry of Education. The government emphasized the need to strengthen primary education where, in 1973, fewer than 60 percent of the students enrolled in grade one completed grade eight (the last year of public, obligatory education). In addition, expanded preschool and day-care programs, coordinated with nutrition programs, greatly improved the situation of young children and some working mothers. The government also emphasized the need to expand technical and vocational education.

Transfer of responsibility for school administration to the municipalities practically destroyed the enormous political and social influence of the 90,000-member National Teachers Union (SUTE). Bargaining over salary and working conditions became essentially "local" matters, with teachers subjected to personnel policies at the municipal rather than the national level, as well as regulated by national labor law prohibiting strikes in the public sector.

Established in 1970 after many years of organizational development in the educational sector, SUTE affiliated teachers and administrators employed by the Ministry of Education. It had obtained legal recognition from the Popular Unity government and had participated actively in formulating educational policy. After the coup of 1973,

General Pinochet declared that it was necessary to purge public education of subversive elements. To achieve this objective new policies eliminated most of the employment security won for teachers over the last fifty years. In December 1973 the government ended payroll check-offs for SUTE and froze the union's funds. A year later, both SUTE and smaller teacher organizations lost their legal status (Decree Law 1284) and recognition.

To replace SUTE and other teacher organizations the government created a new association called the *Colegio de Profesores* (Decree Law 678, 1974). This organization would supposedly register all teachers in the public and private sector, regulate professional and ethical conduct of teachers, and set standards for teacher preparation and licensing. It would also assist in the government program to depoliticize the teaching profession in Chile. Many of the old headquarters and social centers of SUTE were transferred to the new Colegio. The Colegio de Profesores was itself subsequently dissolved when the government decreed abolition of all the professional *colegios* in 1981. Though the Colegio was replaced in late 1981 by a new Chilean Educators Gremialist Association (AGECH), teachers lost control over professional standards and national educational policy, while at the same time they faced a fragmented, localized labor market that fit the model of the economy favored by neo-liberal policymakers.

In the areas of secondary and university education, reforms introduced by the military government emphasized rationalization of the national system to eliminate competing and overlapping programs, more specialization, and reduction of subsidies for higher education. A decree law in December 1980 redefined the functions of Chilean universities, including the types of degrees they could award, while allowing other educational institutions, such as *centros de educación superior,* to offer programs previously reserved to the universities. Subsequent decrees refined and elaborated the new educational policies, with the general thrust toward *self-financing* and a relative shift of resources from higher education to primary and technical education prevailing. In 1974 higher education absorbed 47 percent of the national education budget. This share fell to 33 percent in 1978, 27 percent in 1980, and 20 percent in 1982. Thus, the corollary of the government's commitment to allocate increasing resources to preschool and primary education was the relative decline in support of higher education. In many ways this policy represented a highly positive redistribution of opportunities in favor of poorer sectors of the population; yet the increased fees at the level of secondary (and university) education frustrated the ambitions of those with lesser means as they graduated from the eighth year of free public education. Encouraging the proliferation of private educational institutions, institutes, and technical training, the government reduced expenditures on the university system, made fewer openings available to entry-level students, and gradually increased the extent to which student fees accounted for university income. By 1982, some 18 percent of university income came from student fees, which averaged over $1300 per year. Moreover, the technical universities, primarily catering to lower income students in the past, also raised fees to levels ranging from $600 to $1200 per year. These fees made higher education inaccessible to many thousands of students. The previous commitment to free or low-cost higher education had disappeared.

The military program for modernization of education entailed a fundamental contradiction between a long overdue focus on more resources for primary and technical education and a contraction of opportunities in the system of higher education. Educational "modernization" represented not merely a technical, rationalizing effort but also an integral part of the military government's move toward a new political order. An expanding system of preschools allowed the government to establish a presence in numerous neighborhoods and communities, as well as to deliver nutrition and health services, along with its political message, to thousands of poor families. In the primary schools, an emphasis on "basics," and also on morality and patriotism, clearly coincided with the regime's self-defined mission of preparing new generations of Chileans "steeped in a love of the fatherland." Military administrators in the universities, purges of the faculties and student bodies, more competitive admission policies, and increases in student fees all evidenced the concern with depoliticizing university life and refocusing student efforts on narrow professional and vocational goals. The "modernization" of the educational system, along with the political purges, also significantly reduced the traditional participation by students in national and university politics. Only after 1984, with the brief political opening or *apertura* tolerated by the government, did students re-emerge, along with labor and party activists, as a vocal force in opposition to the government.

Educational reform measures coincided with other policy initiatives in health and social security in shaping the social framework for "protected democracy." Modernization of the health care and social security systems also emphasized privatization and rationalization. Worker pension payments were shifted from a large number of specialized public funds to a relatively smaller number of private companies called pension administration funds (Administradoras de Fondos de Pensiones or AFP). The law required worker contributions, but allowed freedom of choice regarding where they deposited their money. Lacking good information about the new system and the companies involved, most participants chose the new large financial conglomerates which also managed pension funds. Older workers and the infirm remained under public plans, thus taking paying members of the system to the private sector and leaving the public sector saddled with already incurred obligations. Several public agencies retained responsibility for licensing and regulating the AFP; limited public liability existed in case of bankruptcy of the insurance companies or in cases when pensions did not amount to a legislated minimum. The pension system reform added greatly to concentration of financial assets within the economy. After two months of operation of the system the two largest financial conglomerates controlled 75 percent of the pension assets.

In the area of health policy, the military government inherited a relatively sophisticated National Health Service which paralleled a good quality system of private health care. To make the National Health Service (SNS) more efficient, the government adopted Decree Law 2763, "Restructuring of the Health Sector." This administrative reform created twenty-seven regional agencies, with directors appointed by the president, and with a mandate to reduce costs and to improve service. Priority was given to programs of maternal and infant care, along with nutrition education and feeding programs. Inasmuch as the new social security and pension system allowed workers to choose private health care providers under private insurance schemes, the SNS would become a provider of services to those least able to provide for their own health services—a provider of last resort.

Although the majority of doctors in Chile initially seemed to favor drastic reform of the National Health Service and the move toward privatization, some doctors and medical students protested the new system. These protests, along with the technical and administrative barriers to complete evisceration of the SNS, spared the health system total dismantlement. Public investment in new health facilities dropped as did refurbishment of old installations. Nevertheless, the SNS and other government agencies carried out effective programs of prenatal and postnatal care, as well as nutritional supplement programs, which allowed the country to reduce infant mortality and malnutrition-related disease. Redirection of health priorities toward these objectives by the military government, and the generally high quality training and performance of Chilean health professionals, overcame many of the constraints imposed by budget reductions. This was achieved despite economic conditions that might have led to increased malnutrition and nutrition-related disease among infants and young children.

In the area of judicial and criminal justice administration, the government also moved forward with "modernization." This program included building a number of new combination court-penal facilities, appointing large numbers of new judges, improving judicial compensation, and liberalizing rules of evidence to "allow all sorts of evidence useful in establishing the truth . . . photos, tapes, films, cassettes, videos, etc." New provisions regarding civil procedures, juvenile justice, and legal assistance also were implemented from 1981 to 1983. In 1983 the government claimed that 30 percent of all courts ever created in Chile had been established since 1973. The government also proudly displayed similarly impressive statistics for new offices of Civil Registry and Notaries which it claimed made civil and criminal justice administration more efficient and more accessible to the Chilean population.

With the "seven modernizations" under way and the economic recovery in full swing, General Pinochet moved toward the fourth stage of post-1973 development: efforts to legitimize both the political and economic initiatives of the regime through the adoption of a new constitution. Heralded as the "Constitution of Liberty," after the book written by the neo-liberals' intellectual hero, conservative economist Friedrich Hayek, the constitutional project enshrined the notion of "protected democracy" and gave constitutional protection to the basic features of the "seven modernizations." The government submitted the constitution to plebiscite on September 11, 1980 (the seventh anniversary of the coup of 1973) amidst forceful publicity campaigns and severe restrictions on opposition organization and access to the media. Claims of vote fraud and intimidation by opponents did little to mitigate the impact of the apparently overwhelming acceptance of the new constitution. The government reported that with 93 percent of Chile's eligible voters participating in the plebiscite, more than two-thirds of the voters had given their approval. The government also noted that some 30 percent of the voters rejected the new constitution, an indication that opposition claims of intimidation and fraud had not prevented large numbers of Chileans from voting against the government's proposal.

While it was impossible to know with certainty the extent of fraud or intimidation involved in the plebiscite, the size of the *negative* vote gave seeming credibility to the government's victory. General Pinochet and his advisers had either achieved an impressive electoral affirmation of their policies or they had proven themselves extraordinarily astute politicians in their reporting and manipulation of the plebiscite outcome. It was even possible that the government had both won the plebiscite *and* skillfully fabricated the reported results to enhance the credibility of the plebiscite process.

Most importantly, the new constitution marked the end of the *ad hoc* emergency decrees, defined the institutional character of "protected democracy," and established a new juridical framework for national life. Government policy now derived from a constitutional process apparently sanctioned by a majority of the Chilean electorate. Future changes in process or policy depended upon modification or elimination of this new legal system. The constitution also legitimized the continuation of General Pinochet's personalist administration until 1989, with the possibility of his re-election to a new term of office lasting until 1997.

Decree Law 1150 (October 21, 1980) promulgated the new Political Constitution of

TABLE 10–4. NUTRITION, HEALTH, AND EDUCATION INDICATORS, 1970–82

	1970	1971	1972	1973	1974	1975	1976	1977	1978	1979	1980	1981	1982
Nutrition													
Calorie consumption per capita	2282	2645	2819	2642	2243	2290	2565	2511	2603	2634	2655	2675	2627
Protein per capita (grams)	67.1	73.8	78.8	70.7	64.3	62.7	66.3	65.8	67.8	68.6	65.5	68.5	70.2
Health													
Physicians per 1000 population	75	76	77	78	80	83	85	90	92	94	95	97	n.a.
Hospital beds per 1000 population	3.8	3.8	3.9	3.8	3.8	3.8	3.6	3.6	3.5	3.6	3.4	3.3	3.3
Medical visits per capita	1.08	1.22	1.14	1.03	0.92	0.88	1.05	1.07	1.09	1.13	1.13	1.14	1.19
Adult visits per capita	0.99	1.12	1.00	0.87	0.73	0.70	0.86	0.87	0.89	0.93	0.93	0.93	n.a.
Pediatric visits per child	1.04	1.22	1.16	1.09	1.08	1.01	1.15	1.18	1.22	1.26	1.26	1.30	n.a.
Obstetrical visits per woman of child bearing age	0.26	0.26	0.33	0.31	0.27	0.27	0.27	0.33	0.35	0.35	0.35	0.36	n.a.
Crude death rate per 1000	8.9	8.8	9.0	8.2	7.8	7.3	7.8	7.0	6.7	6.8	6.7	6.2	6.1
Infant mortality rate per 1000	82.2	73.9	72.7	65.8	65.2	57.6	56.6	50.1	40.1	37.9	33.0	27.0	23.6
Life expectancy (years)	64.2	64.5	64.8	65.1	65.4	65.7	65.9	66.2	66.5	66.7	67.0	67.3	67.5
Education (per age group)													
Preschool (%)	11.8	13.9	16.0	16.6	19.9	20.0	21.7	23.8	25.3	25.2	26.8	26.5	26.7
Primary school (%)	107	114	117	120	121	119	117	118	119	120	118	115	111
Secondary school (%)	39.6	46.3	49.4	50.9	50.1	48.0	48.9	50.5	52.5	54.9	55.3	56.9	54.8

Source: Bela Balassa, "Policy Experiments in Chile, 1973–1983," Gary Walton, ed., The National Economic Policies of Chile Greenwich, Conn., 1985, pp. 222–23; INE, Compendio Estadístico, 1984, 1985.

the Republic of Chile. Implementation began in 1981. Much of the language of the constitution, as well as the basic concepts, had been drawn from the "Declaration of Principles" (1974), the National Objectives of Government (1975), the "Constitutional Acts" (1976), the decrees concerning regional administration, the Labor Plan, and the other "modernizations" undertaken in the late 1970s. Matters of continuing controversy within the government, or areas of implementation which required additional legislation or regulations, were treated in "interim provisions." For example, *all political party activity remained outlawed* until an "organic constitutional law" regulating party activity could be adopted. (No law appeared until 1987.)

The 1980 constitution institutionalized "protected democracy" and the new socioeconomic order. Chile was officially "modern," but even to 2000 it remained the only country in the Western Hemisphere without a divorce law. The patrimonial, even medieval, foundations of some aspects of family and property law continued in some respects to make women second-class citizens. The new constitution reaffirmed traditional Hispanic values and practices and explicitly emphasized the role of the patriarchal family as the basic unit of a hierarchically organized society. It did this in the name of Western-Christian values, patriotism, and national security, echoes of the Spanish conquest and the nineteenth-century wars to conquer and "civilize" the country's indigenous population. Every citizen was obligated to "honor the fatherland, defend its sovereignty, and contribute to the preservation of national security and the essential values of Chilean tradition (Art. 22). The same section of the constitution made military service obligatory and provided for mandatory firearms registration with the military authorities. While the constitution also provided a long list of civil rights and liberties of all Chileans (Art. 19), these were limited by the requirements of national security. For example, the right of free association was subject to the provision that "all groups contrary to morality, public order or security of the State are prohibited."

The Constitution nowhere specifically defined "national security," but the text assigned the armed forces the mission to "guarantee the institutional order of the republic" (Art. 90). Indeed, the new constitution officially made the armed services a dominant political force in Chile. This constitutional development paralleled the growth in personnel of the armed forces (especially the army) and their growing share of government expenditures. In addition, a National Security Council, responsible for a number of advisory and policymaking tasks (Arts. 95–96), inserted military officers into legislative and administrative functions. Each of the armed services received direct representation on the regional development councils which appointed mayors, thereby controlling or monitoring both municipal administration and the reformed educational system. Provision for eventual election of a new Congress, after adoption of a law regulating political parties, also included *designees* of the National Security Council as senators (ex-commanders of each of the three military branches and the *carabineros*). In short, the new constitution provided for permanent militarization of Chilean politics.

The constitution also ratified the social and economic initiatives of the period 1973–81. Article 19 required special legislative approval for the state to engage in entrepreneurial activities. Article 62 reserved to presidential initiative any law to impose, eliminate, or reduce taxes, or to create new public services or new positions in the public administration. This provision was intended to limit severely the role of a "political" legislature and also to focus attention on any efforts to increase the size or expand the functions of the government. The president also had such authority with respect to determination of remuneration in the public sector and in the contracting of foreign loans by any public entity. These provisions, along with a number of others, greatly enhanced the authority of the president and emasculated the legislative branch—a further irony of the military government since the overthrow of President Allende, like that of President Balmaceda in 1891, had been carried out partly in the name of limiting executive abuse of authority and re-establishing the balance between Congress and the president.

The constitution also reaffirmed and institutionalized the labor and social security "modernizations." Articles 8, 15, 16, and 19 prohibited "propagation of any doctrines that . . . advocate violence, or a conception of society or of the state, or of the juridical order of a totalitarian character, or founded on the idea of class conflict"; made unconstitutional all movements, organizations, or political parties that advocated such ideas; outlawed all political party participation in union affairs; and outlawed participation in political parties by labor leaders. In addition, any future congressman or senator who attempted to influence labor negotiations, administrative proceedings, or labor court cases could be removed from office.

The period between approval of the new constitution and March 1981 marked a high point in General Pinochet's administration. Economic expansion, political institutionalization, and the advent of the more supportive administration of President Ronald Reagan in the United States, all seemed to favor the continuity and the strengthening of the Chilean regime. Instead, between March 1981 and the end of the year a combination of international and domestic developments brought economic collapse and financial panic, erosion of political support both among the government's staunch supporters and the social base of the regime, and renewed pressures for rapid transition to a less authoritarian political system.

A complex interaction of international economic trends and internal economic developments provoked the worst economic depression in Chile since the early 1930s. Recession in the United States and Europe, along with tightened monetary and credit policies and sky-rocketing interest rates all affected Chile drastically. Chilean firms and private parties had contracted large amounts of dollar-denominated loans at a fixed exchange rate. Short-term foreign indebtedness more than tripled from 1979 to 1982; medium- and long-term debt doubled in the same period. Even more importantly, while public foreign indebtedness had represented more than 50 percent of such obligations in 1979, the private sector indebtedness reached more than 66 percent of the more than 17 billion-dollar total foreign debt by 1982. Since consumption, speculation in real estate, financial pyramids, and flight capital accounted for considerable portions of this private debt, investment and increased productive capabilities grew much too slowly to finance the growing interest payment burden. Shifting government policies on exchange rates (devaluation of 18 percent in June 1982, subsequent pre-announced mini-devaluations, until September 1982, with a floating exchange rate thereafter) exacerbated the crisis, with the result that the Chilean private sector all but collapsed.

According to the government's orthodox policymakers this collapse should have been allowed to "correct itself." Indeed, many of the doctrinaire "Chicago Boys" blamed the financial collapse to a great extent on the government's failure to implement more fully the neoliberal reforms. These critics pointed out that as early as 1976 the government had rescued the Bank of Osorno, rather than allowing bankruptcy, thereby undermining the discipline of the market in rationalizing the economy. Moreover, according to this viewpoint, fixing the exchange rate in 1979 discriminated against Chilean exporters (since internal inflation exceeded international inflation) and overvalued the Chilean peso. This made Chilean agricultural and industrial products uncompetitive. Further, indexing wages to the consumer price index in the new labor legislation had prevented Chilean employers from "bargaining freely" concerning the cost of labor. Thus, according to the neo-liberals, the reforms had neither been carried far enough nor implemented thoroughly enough.

Others pointed out that lack of careful regulation of the financial activities of the major conglomerates had allowed accumulation of an immense private foreign debt, secured only with fragile, sometimes clearly fraudulent, paper assets. Rising interest rates and drastic reductions in the inflow of foreign loans and investments that had fueled the financial "boom" made it impossible to continue the debt service. Declining prices for Chilean exports as a consequence of the international recession (including a decline in copper prices of over 40 percent from its peak in early 1980 to mid-1982) and a growing balance of payments deficit (15 percent of gross domestic product in 1981) contributed to the debacle. Tariff reductions that had practically eliminated protection for Chilean industries and agriculture allowed consumer goods to flood the country from nations whose industries received a variety of tariff and non-tariff protection from their own governments.

The highly visible sugar firm, Compañía Refinería de Azúcar de Viña del Mar (CRAV), part of the financial empire of a prominent businessman, collapsed in May 1981. A seemingly isolated event, this business failure was a warning of things to come. In mid-1981 the Pinochet government began responding to certain portents of the coming crisis. In part these responses stemmed from concern for illegal, corrupt financial practices and in part from the resurgence of a type of "interest group" politics in which sectors of industrialists, agricultural interests, and others lobbied for more favorable, special treatment. First, a new banking law prohibited loans by banks to their owners and affiliate firms; eliminated common stock as an acceptable part of bank capital, and otherwise sought to regulate the rash of financial pyramiding and Ponzi schemes. Too late to prevent the coming collapse, these new laws at least pointed at one source of the impending disaster. Meanwhile, four banks and finance companies went bankrupt in November 1981. The government responded by arresting the principals for financial irregularities and assumed control of the banks.

A largely symbolic change in finance minister, followed by further devaluation of the peso, did nothing to arrest the downward economic spiral. Significantly, the government directed the national sugar enterprise, IANSA, to adopt new price and subsidy policies for sugar-beet growers and imposed tariffs on specific goods to protect Chilean firms from "dumping" by foreign competitors. Agriculture and mining, in selected regions, also received energy subsidies.

In January 1983 the crisis forced the government to "intervene" (take over management and operations of) the largest private banks in the country, assume responsibility for privately contracted debt, and begin a public rescue of the mangled private sector. General Pinochet lamented his failure to deport the speculators and corrupt bankers whom he called "paper emperors," but it would be the hundreds of thousands of unemployed and homeless Chileans who would pay the highest price for the gigantic swindles.

The Chilean economy declined in gross domestic product by over 14 percent in 1982; unemployment rose to over 20 percent with an additional 450,000 Chileans participating in two government make-work programs—PEM, and the newly created Job Program for Heads of Household, or POJH. By the end of 1983 over 500,000 Chileans depended upon PEM or POJH for subsistence. With the interest burden of the debt almost 50 percent that of the value of annual exports, and rising, General Pinochet and his advisers called upon the people of Chile to tighten their belts and to make even more sacrifices for the future of their children and their nation. The private debts which had served to enrich small numbers of Chileans would now be collectivized. The nation would renegotiate the debt with international bankers and international financial organizations. Government control over the country's credit system, the "intervened"

TABLE 10–5. FOREIGN DEBT, DEBT AS PERCENT OF EXPORTS OF GOODS AND SERVICES, AND RATIO OF INTEREST PAYMENTS TO EXPORTS OF GOODS AND SERVICES

	1981	1982	1983	1984	1985	1986*
Debt (millions of dollars)	15,591	17,159	18,037	19,669	20,413	20,690
Interest payments/exports of goods and services (%)	38.8	49.5	38.9	48.0	43.5	39.2
Debt as percent of exports of goods and services	311	370	390	438	454	426

*Preliminary estimate.
Source: CEPAL, "Preliminary Review of the Latin American Economy," 1986.

TABLE 10–6. WORKERS INSCRIBED IN PEM, POJH

	PEM	POJH (begins Oct. 1982)	Percent of Labor Force
1975	72,695		2.3
1976	157,836		5.0
1977	187,647		5.9
1978	145,792		4.2
1979	133,933		3.9
1980	190,673		5.2
1981	175,607		4.9
1982	225,290	102,772 (Dec.)	9.0
1983 (Oct.)	286,751	225,264	14.0

Source: Jaime Ruiz-Tagle and Roberto Urmeneta, Los trabajadores del programa del empleo mínimo, 1984, pp. 24, 168; Instituto Nacional de Estadísticas, Compendio Estadístico, 1984.

(bailed out) banks, and major firms associated with financial conglomerates, along with continued government operation of public enterprises in the copper, petroleum, coal, and other sectors, the ports, telecommunication, transportation, and international trade, was a further irony of a program dedicated since 1973 to emphasis on market decision-making and privatization.

Mockingly, opponents of the Pinochet government, and even ex-supporters, termed this process the "Chicago road to Socialism." Government policymakers, in contrast, claimed that the interventions would be temporary and looked forward to "reprivatization." In reality, the extent to which government policymakers had determined the character of economic opportunities in the private sector, together with the official and unofficial participation of representatives of the major economic groups in making public policy, resembled much more closely the customary patterns of Hispanic capitalism in Chile than any brand of socialism. As in the past, private enterprise and profit depended upon government policies which allowed coercion of labor, concentration of wealth in a limited number of firms and families, and collusion between government authorities and a small number of private actors in managing the economy. Admittedly, the government had declared its intent to liberalize the economy, just as Chilean Conservatives and Liberals had done during the nineteenth century. In both cases, however, economic liberalism coincided with political authoritarianism and elitist processes of policymaking. General Pinochet, pragmatically repressing or sometimes co-opting opposition, imposed his policy initiatives in collaboration with civilian advisers and technocrats, while denying the value and denigrating the legitimacy of democratic institutions. As particular policies failed or proved defective, whether neo-liberal or otherwise, these could be dropped or modified. But as in colonial Chile, access to government officials determined economic opportunities. The military regime's not-so-invisible hand favored its supporters and also some officers and their family members in more than questionable economic ventures. Even the privatization of government enterprises, a key feature of the neoliberal economic plan, offered private benefits to "lucky" investors and bidders for public assets transferred to the private sector. As in the past, government authority remained the single most important *commodity* in Chile.

Beginning in late 1981, the collapse of the economic "miracle" precipitated widespread political realignment. *Gremialistas*—old-time members of the National party, middle-class professionals, and an array of small businessmen—suffered the consequences of the depression and expressed open, if cautious, opposition to government policies. Groups which had railed vociferously against President Allende, and which had been closely associated with the *junta* in its early years, now called the Pinochet regime "the worst government in the country's history." Prominent leaders of the truckers, Chamber of Commerce, retail merchants, and professional organizations verbally attacked General Pinochet in harsh, even insulting language. Some went to jail and others suffered harassment and beatings by unidentified "civilians." Still violently anti-Marxist and unwilling to form a coalition with Communists and Socialists, even for the limited and temporary purpose of ousting Pinochet, these groups now called for a change in government policies—and sometimes for a more rapid transition to democracy. However, many of these groups still preferred authoritarian government to the threatened "return to chaos" which the government-controlled media and propaganda constantly assured Chileans would follow if the military government passed from the scene. Although the occasion of ex-President Eduardo Frei's death in 1982 sparked a massive demonstration against General Pinochet's regime, it also underlined the lack of viable civilian opposition leadership with which to replace him.

With the political parties still outlawed and traditional political leaders unable to assemble an effective opposition movement to confront the dictatorship, organized labor took a new and central role in seeking to reactivate and mobilize opposition forces. The most important group of organized workers in Chile, the Copper Workers Confederation (CTC), notwithstanding internal divisions and parallel government unions within its membership, confronted the Pinochet regime head on in 1981. A lengthy strike at the El Teniente mine in Rancagua created extremely tense relations with the government. In 1982, copper workers joined with the Coordinadora Nacional Sindical (CNS), the Confederation of Private Sector Employees (CEPCH), and the independent Catholic-inspired Unitary Workers Front (FUT) in sending a letter to General Pinochet requesting modification of the Labor Plan and many of the government's economic policies. The Copper Workers Confederation threatened the government with another strike and even discussed the possibility of a call for a general strike in May 1983. After reconsideration, the CTC instead joined forces with other labor organizations, community organizations, and professional groups in sponsoring a national day of protest (May 11, 1983). All over Chile, and especially in Santiago, Chileans kept their children home from school, absented themselves from work, and—as the opposition had done in the time of protests against the Popular Unity government—banged on pots and pans, while screaming insults at Pinochet and calling for his ouster.

Following the success of this day of protest, labor made another effort at achieving a loose unity in the creation of a National Workers' Command (CNT). Though unable to overcome long-standing ideological and organizational conflicts, a broad spectrum of workers' organizations, ranging from the National Association of Public Employees (ANEF) to the Maritime Confederation and the Confederation of Private Sector Employees united in public opposition to the Pinochet government. In the process, some labor leaders suffered incarceration or even assassination, for example, Tucapel Jiménez, a leader of ANEF.

A second national day of protest on June 14, 1983, proved even more successful, but a national strike called for later in the month failed to achieve the desired impact. Repeated "days of protest" followed these initial acts of mass public opposition. Each protest left a small toll of dead and many injured in confrontations between civilians and the security forces. In August 1983, General Pinochet deployed thousands of troops in Santiago to control a mass demonstration called by a coalition of labor organizations and the outlawed political parties. *Pobladores* lit fires and built barricades in the shantytowns; the armed forces invaded neighborhoods of the poor, made mass arrests, and attacked protesters, while demonstrators in middle-class neighborhoods experienced the indiscriminate use of tear gas and random shooting. In addition to the mass demonstrations, small groups of Chileans organized numerous quick, mobile protests at designated times and places, with participants arriving on pre-arranged schedule and rapidly dispersing to avoid detention by *carabineros*.

Protesta Nacional, Plaza de Armas, 1983. (Courtesy of Archivo Vicaría de la Solidaridad.)

Having taken the initiative in 1983, labor organizations continued to resist government policy. In 1984 ten leaders of the CNT signed an open letter to Pinochet calling for a return to the constitution of 1925, repeal of the Labor Plan, and reversal of the government's economic policies—in short, a comprehensive change of regime and policy. Thus, the government's effort to depoliticize labor had actually resulted in an admittedly divided labor movement assuming a central role in national politics previously performed by the now outlawed political parties. As in the case of economic policy, the results of government labor policy proved in many ways contrary to government objectives.

As mounting public protests against the government occurred in 1984–85, labor groups played a key coordinating role. At the plant level, individual unions refocused their energies on demands for improved wages and working conditions. Outside the organized labor movement, which had lost many members to unemployment and repression, a variety of women's groups, local committees, agricultural cooperatives, and *ad hoc* shantytown associations carried on self-help and anti-regime activities all over Chile. Many of these groups maintained some connections with clandestine party networks, Church-related organizations, and labor unions. In other cases they operated in relative isolation, attempting to feed the hungry, hide the persecuted, improve local distribution of consumer goods, and maintain community or local solidarity.

Aware of the mounting frustration and, in some cases, political organization of hundreds of thousands of shantytown dwellers, the government carried out recurrent night-time raids to demobilize anti-government groups active in the *poblaciones*. The urban poor had long constituted a dilemma for Chilean political leaders, but now the cumulative effects of the military government's economic and internal security policies had the effect of radicalizing many shantytown dwellers, particularly the young and unemployed. The extreme social segregation between the urban poor and the residents of middle- and upper-class neighborhoods of Santiago made the apparent radicalization of these groups of great concern to many elements in the capital. Lack of knowledge and contact among rich and poor reached levels never before experienced in Chile, producing an eerie if imperfect analogue to racial ghettos in the United States. The fear of unleashing the stored-up hatred of the *pobladores* limited the willingness of many opposition groups with middle-class constituencies to adopt an insurrectionary style in efforts to replace General Pinochet with a more moderate administration.

At the same time, contradictory as it might seem, a significant minority of *pobladores* continued to support General Pinochet, whether because they had benefited directly from the government's public works and housing programs, or their children had received nutritional and day care services, or because they remembered negatively the intense politicization of daily life from 1970 to 1973. Support for the government within the *poblaciones* and elsewhere also resulted, in part, from General Pinochet's successful efforts to transform the pre-existing network of mothers' clubs (*centros de madres*) into a clientelistic base of support. Affiliated nationally in an organization called CEMA, headed officially by General Pinochet's wife (CEMA had customarily been headed by the wives of Chile's civilian presidents), CEMA provided an instrument for mobilizing a feminine social base for the regime. Wives of military officers were assigned to coordinate local groups, distribute patronage, carry out educational programs, and enlist women in the crusade to purify the nation and to restore the order and harmony so necessary for family life. These appeals to morality, patriotism, and feminine virtue, along with material benefits customarily distributed through the CEMA network since the 1960s, garnered significant, if minority, support for the regime from women of all social classes.

Differences of opinion within the *poblaciones*, as well as among women's organizations and community groups, were symptomatic of persistent political and ideological cleavages within Chilean society. The wave of protests initiated in 1983 eventually gave rise to the resurgence of the three major political blocks characteristic of Chile since the 1930s. On the political right, a so-called Group of 8 allied a range of *gremialista*, "nationalist," and more traditional conservative politicians who provided a civilian face for the social base of the Pinochet government. Eventually some of these groups would seek to distance themselves from the government and form a new united rightist political party (in 1987) so as to appear as likely participants in a transitional coalition when Pinochet passed from the scene. In the short term, however, the political right supplied ministers and advisers to the junta.

In 1983, in an effort to contain the wave of mass protests and demonstrations, General Pinochet appointed the ex-leader of the National party, Sergio Onofre Jarpa, as minister of interior. Feigning a willingness to negotiate with the "responsible" (non-Marxist) opposition, General Pinochet deftly utilized the rightist politicos as shills in a so-called political opening, or *apertura*. In reality, Jarpa had no power and certainly no ability to meet the most important demands of the opposition: General Pinochet's resignation and the immediate return to democracy. Nevertheless, the participation of civilian politicians from the rightist parties and movements as figureheads of the administration gave a veneer of legitimacy and a hint of flexibility to the Pinochet government. It also served to reinforce divisions between centrist and leftist opponents of the regime inasmuch as the government seemed to accept the existence of the Christian Democrats and their allies *de facto*, if not *de jure*, so long as the left remained excluded from dialogue or participation in the political process.

The political center, including the Christian Democrats, Social Democrats, Radicals, part of the Socialist party, and other smaller groups united in the Alianza Democrática (AD). The Alianza repeatedly called for Pinochet's resignation and favored rapid transition to a more democratic system. However, it rejected the use of violence to oust Pinochet and opposed a coalition with Marxist parties and movements in any transitional government alternative to the junta. With a diverse and multi-class social base, the parties and movements of the Alianza occupied a tenuous, shifting middle ground between the junta's program of anti-politics and their own desire to limit leftist influence in Chile while, at the same time, restoring most civil liberties, electoral politics, and a set of government initiatives closer to the developmentalist and redistributionist policies of the 1960s. Frustrated in its negotiations with Minister Jarpa, the parties and movements which had made up the Alianza Democrática, and particularly Christian Democrats, continued to view themselves as the obvious successors to Pinochet in any transition from authoritarian rule—either within the bounds of the 1980 constitution or through a return to the constitution of 1925.

On the left, the Communist party, MIR, and a part of the Socialist party identified with ex-Popular Unity Minister, Clodomiro Almeyda, formed the Movimiento Democrático Popular (MDP). The MDP called for all forms of resistance against the dictatorship and still insisted upon the ultimate goal of a socialist society in Chile. Operating both clandestinely and also "above ground," when conditions permitted, the MDP's revolutionary objectives and declarations gave credibility to General Pinochet's repeated warnings to Chileans of a "return to chaos" should his administration succumb to the demands of the politicians for a return to the past. Likewise, the MDP's tactics and strategic objectives separated the left from the political center just as had been the case since the 1930s. Between the MDP and the AD, a "Socialist bloc" (some socialists, left Catholics, and other smaller groups) represented an ideological transition between the revolutionary Marxist left and the political center.

After more than a decade of a dictatorship dedicated to depoliticizing Chilean society, the major ideological and organizational tendencies—which had emerged in the 1930s, dominated national life from 1930 to 1973, been blamed by the military and its supporters for the crisis of 1970–73, and suffered concerted attacks since 1973—survived, reasserted themselves, challenged the regime, and continued unable to draw forth a consensual basis for Chilean politics and society. Even among the groups firmly opposed to the new Constitution and to the thrust of government policies, historical animosities and basic disagreements over an alternative to the Pinochet government prevented formation of a unified opposition movement. General Pinochet well understood and skillfully utilized these divisions amongst the opposition to maintain himself in power.

To some extent, the new constitution assisted Pinochet in this effort, as did changes in internal politics and the foreign policies of the United States. United States policy toward Chile had shifted considerably from President Nixon's support and assistance in the early years of the military government—juxtaposed to congressional legislation restricting military and other aid—to President Carter's public condemnation of human rights abuses, to President Reagan's reemphasis on anti-communism. Never, however, had U.S. foreign policy prevented General Pinochet from obtaining private foreign loans or investments. This had proved especially important during the height of the economic "miracle," and it proved critical once again in the mid-1980s.

In particular, United States support for millions of dollars' worth of credits, loans, and loan guarantees by the World Bank, Inter-American Development Bank, and large syndicates of private commercial banks helped to buffer Chile's debt burden and financed public works, new investments, and palliative make-work programs. The earthquake of 1985 (see Chapter 1) complicated the country's economic recovery, but also justified major new loan programs from international agencies for reconstruction of ports, highways, bridges, housing, and other physical infrastructure. All these projects helped to alleviate social and economic pressures. They also allowed General Pinochet to claim the confidence of the international banking community in his efforts to maintain himself in power and to institutionalize the new political order.

Dramatic declines in oil prices, plunging international interest rates, and economic recovery in the United States and Europe in the mid-1980s also provided breathing space for Pinochet by bolstering the Chilean economy. Economic recovery, again based on export expansion and imported capital, allowed unemployment to drop to "only" 10 percent in 1987. As the value of exports climbed to over $4 billion and the country achieved a trade balance of approximately $1 billion, enthusiastic government policymakers reaffirmed the validity of the export-driven model of economic growth. Stimulation of nontraditional exports reached new "highs" in late 1986 when the government announced that "a company that markets bathroom fixtures under the Fanaloza trade mark, has just shipped a trial order of 2,175 toilet-and-tank units to the United States. . . . The company's general manager said that this is one of Fanaloza's most exciting export operations since it started shipping yacht bathroom fixtures in 1984." Exports of toilet tank units aside, the gradual diversification and expansion of manufactured exports and services would be a hallmark of the military government's economic policies that drove economic growth into the 1990s.

Along with renewed export growth, an innovative debt-equity conversion scheme enhanced the regime's international credibility. This scheme permitted investors to purchase government "foreign debt notes" at a discount, outside of Chile, and to exchange them at full face value in pesos to pay debts, acquire stock or fixed assets, or assets received in payment of foreclosure, or to finance new investments in Chile. The debt-equity conversion process which, according to official estimates, involved $1.96 billion from mid-1985 to June 1987, both helped to retire some of the 20 billion-dollar foreign debt and to *reprivatize* assets obtained by the government as a result of the collapse in the early 1980s. Hailed by officials of the United States Treasury and by international lenders as a model of innovation for other Latin American debtors, the Chilean government also persisted in its efforts to attract new foreign investment and to revitalize the private sector of the economy. Indeed, CORFO sold stock in government-owned companies to foreign investors and to the major private pension funds in order to raise money and to renew the divestiture program. Significant new investments from private companies and banks from Canada, New Zealand, Australia, West Germany, France, Spain, the United Kingdom, and the United States, together with new credit lines from the World Bank, InterAmerican Development Bank, and private foreign financial institutions, added to the Pinochet administration's optimism about the economy. Though a new United States ambassador to Chile openly discussed with members of the opposition the possibility of General Pinochet's departure from government, public and private economic policymakers in the United States provided encouragement and substantial leverage for General Pinochet in his efforts to survive the challenges to his administration.

By the time General Pinochet had successfully orchestrated the constitutional plebiscite of 1980, frustration and desperation had already led to escalation in the tactics used by some elements of the opposition in efforts to rid the country of an ever more personalist dictatorship. The evident ineffectiveness of the centrist and rightist opposition, along with the need to re-establish its own credibility, led the Communist party of Chile to call publicly for the use of *all* types of struggle against the dictatorship. A commitment to armed struggle, as a part of an overall resistance to the Pinochet government, allied the Communists with MIR and certain sectors of the Socialist party. The 1979 victory of the Sandinistas in Nicaragua against the Somoza dictatorship gave this tactic some credibility, despite the obvious differences between Nicaragua and Chile. In addition, the new Reagan administration in the United States shifted emphasis in U.S. policy away from a focus on human rights issues and clearly supported the Pinochet government in international forums. Lack of viable internal alternatives to Pinochet, and the loss of hope for U.S. pressures on the regime for changes in policies, made the new Communist tactic understandable, if very unlikely to achieve success. However, it also made it practically impossible for Christian Democratic leadership or other democratic movements to join in a unified opposition coalition even for the limited purpose of ousting General Pinochet.

Lack of unity did not prevent growing levels of opposition among all strata of the Chilean population after the collapse of the "miracle" in 1981. Reversals of economic policy and disputes among diverse entrepreneurial groups over corrective measures fragmented the "nonpolitical" social base of the government. The resurgence of labor protests and strikes, calls both for Pinochet's resignation and for restoration of democracy from all the old political parties (theoretically nonexistent under the new constitution), and increasing numbers of "days of protest" all raised the hopes of opposition forces that General Pinochet's regime had run its course. By mid-1984, expectations were high for a quick end to the dictatorship. Daring headlines in opposition newspapers even declared in bold print: "He doesn't want to leave"—and in smaller print— "We'll have to throw him out." A year later, in August 1985, a temporary opposition coalition hammered out a "National Accord for Transition to Full Democracy." This *Acuerdo* called for immediate termination to the states of "constitutional exception" (state of siege, state of emergency, state of internal commotion, etc.), restoration of university autonomy, an end to political banishment and exile, and constitutional reforms that eliminated the main elements of the "Constitution of Liberty." The *Acuerdo* also called for programs of economic reactivation, abandonment of the neo-liberal policies, creation of jobs, and *an active role for the state in reshaping the Chilean economy.* In short, the opposition asked General Pinochet to surrender both his office and the major changes he had introduced since 1973.

Surrender was not acceptable. Instead, Pinochet announced that the 1980 constitution would remain in effect, that he would complete his term of office scheduled to end in 1989, and that he had not yet decided whether he would be a candidate, as the constitution allowed, for the term which would end in 1997. Opposition newspapers, magazines, and other publications, which had appeared in the "political opening" allowed by Pinochet from 1983 to 1984, again were censored or closed down. Selective detentions and harassment reminded the opposition of the limits to the general's tolerance. On the political left, declarations that the *Acuerdo* was no substitute for armed struggle reinforced General Pinochet's determination and frightened many middle- and upper-class Chileans who were bombarded with the threat of "Cubanization" and "Nicaraguanization" of Chile. In fact, small groups of military cadres were being trained in Cuba, Nicaragua, and elsewhere for eventual return to Chile to fight against the dictatorship. Although never a military threat to the junta, the existence of these cadres and the publicized operations they carried out unintentionally served the military regime's purposes by demonstrating that "terrorists" and "guerrillas" were not merely an invention of government propagandists. Groups which preferred some measure of liberalization, *without Marxist participation* in Chilean politics, saw no obvious alternative to Pinochet's continuation in office. Christian Democratic, social democratic, and more conservative political groups found themselves without a concrete program for temporary or long-term replacement of Pinochet and the new system of "protected democracy." Nor could they patch together a workable formula for accommodating the reality of the persistence of the left in Chilean society and politics. General Pinochet had not succeeded in depoliticizing Chile, but the perpetuation and intensification of political polarization served his interests in the mid-1980s, if only by preventing the opposition from uniting effectively against him.

A key to General Pinochet's political survival remained his control over the military, and especially over the army and the internal security forces. Through manipulations of command assignments, modification of the career and retirement system, and personalist patronage, General Pinochet had established a base of support in the army. As commander-in-chief of the armed forces, he relied upon respect for hierarchy and military discipline to maintain formal control over the other services. Certain elements within the military had adopted a radical anti-Marxism as a collective political commitment, and this base of ideologically oriented officers provided further support for General Pinochet's stance against a return to the past. Further, Chilean sociologists Arturo Chacón and Humberto Lagos reported, in a study called *La Religión en las Fuerzas Armadas y de Orden,* that by 1986 some 15,000 members of the Chilean armed forces had joined evangelical churches, and become "zealous proselytizers, anti-Catholic, anti-communist and anti-Marxist."

These new trends within the military institutions after 1973 also introduced contradictions which led to difficulties for the Pinochet government. Disagreements over economic policy and over the permanent political role of key officers, if not the entire armed forces, under the new constitution, bothered some Chilean military professionals who still preferred a narrower focus on external defense, force modernization, and professional careers *apart from* responsibility for policymaking. Other officers resented the personalization of the government, the relative dominance of the army and security forces, and the civilian population's understandable antagonism for what ex-*gremialista* leader, Orlando Sáenz, now called Chile's military institutions: "an occupying force." A number of officers even held a real preference for civilian, democratic institutions, though most shared concern about the participation of the left in a democratic system.

By the early 1980s some officers were well aware of the advantages to the armed forces of negotiating some sort of extrication from the military's political role *at minimal damage to the military institutions.* But with whom could military officers negotiate such an extrication? And who could guarantee their lives and careers against revenge for the years of repression if the government changed? (These fears would be dramatically reactivated in 1999, when a renovated Supreme Court somewhat "reinterpreted" the 1978 Amnesty Decree and charged high-ranking officers for crimes against human rights.) No civilian coalition or political force had emerged that could effectively challenge General Pinochet, present an alternative program widely enough shared to offer some chance of success, or, most importantly, comply with any agreement negotiated with the military as a way to initiate a transition to a more democratic, civilian government. The profound ideological and organizational divisions of the Chilean polity, the lack of any obvious personage (after the death of Eduardo Frei in 1982) with whom to replace General Pinochet, and the lack of effective guarantees against persecution, trials, and loss of career (as occurred in some cases in Argentina after restoration of civilian government in 1983), all restrained the efforts of military officers who might otherwise have sought a gradual process of accommodation with certain civilian parties and movements. Nevertheless, dissent within the air force and navy took the form of public criticisms, leading to forced retirements and changes in command assignments. This public criticism continued even after an assassination attempt against General Pinochet in early September 1986 in which a number of his military escort were wounded or killed.

Responding to the assassination attempt, to dissent within the military institutions, to the discovery of a large Cuban-supplied arms cache in northern Chile, and to civilian calls for his ouster, General Pinochet unleashed a new campaign of repression, murder, and detentions against targeted civilians. He replaced the army member of the *junta* with the director of the secret police and forced a number of generals into retirement. General Pinochet reiterated his intention to remain in office until 1989 and to institutionalize the new political order. Providing a symbolic gesture to domestic and external critics, he ended the "state of siege" (reduced to a "state of emergency") and promulgated a new law on political parties in early 1987—with the expected limitations on party functions and the exclusion of Marxist and other "subversive" organizations.

Ultimately, only military acquiescence in the removal of General Pinochet, or an unexpected problem with his health, appeared to offer any chance of cutting short the constitutionally prescribed term ending in 1989. In a further irony of the military regime, civilian politicians once again looked to the military to remove a president by other than constitutional means, in order to achieve the objective they believed would be attained in 1973: restoration of democratic government with exclusions on participation by Marxists and the left. However, democracy without the participation of more than 30 percent of the Chilean population remained as much a contradiction in 1987 as it had forty years earlier with adoption of the "Law for the Permanent Defense of Democracy" in the administration of President González Videla.

Unable to unite, unable to provide the military with assurances of institutional integrity and immunity from prosecution for abuses of human rights, and unable to agree upon a formula for short-term transition or for a new political system, the opposition to General Pinochet was openly discouraged at the beginning of 1987. Groups on the political right sought to find some new common ground in anticipation of the politics of succession in 1989; the center continued criticizing government policies and seeking new temporary coalitions and agreements as a basis for restoring democracy, though the Socialist party withdrew from the Alianza Democrática at the end of 1986. The left, divided as always, gave some support to the centrist projects while the more revolutionary groups advocated political mobilization and, where possible, armed resistance against the regime.

An historic papal visit to Chile in early April, 1987, preceded by unprecedented levels of political posturing and maneuvering by government and opposition forces, focused the world's attention once again both on the abuses of the Pinochet government and the divisions among the opposition to the regime. At the behest of John Paul II, opposition forces from left to right, including the Communist party, signed a vague pledge to work for a peaceful transition to democracy and met together to consider the possibilities of the political moment. However, this unusual meeting of leaders from Chile's fragmented opposition had much less impact than the fierce military and police repression against regime opponents who defiantly protested government policies during a papal mass attended by hundreds of thousands of Chileans in Santiago. Televised around the world, the violent disruption of the papal ceremony symbolized the stalemate of Chilean politics in 1987. General Pinochet blamed the violence on Communist agitators; the opposition took heart from the Pope's message of peace and solidarity with those who suffered from injustice, unemployment, and misery, but were unable to agree on the "true" message of the Pope or to translate the Pope's spiritual solidarity into political power. Thus, in the short term, the Pope's visit to Chile did little to change the reality of the dictatorship's hold on the country.

By mid-1987, government and opposition preparations for the plebiscite to select a president for the term 1989–97, as required by the 1980 constitution, took center stage

Agrupación de Familiares de Detenidos Desaparecidos, Patio of the Vicaría de la Solidaridad, 1987. (Courtesy of Archivo Vicaría de la Solidaridad.)

in Chile's political drama. Even as destructive storms ravaged central Chile in July 1987, leaving a toll of human death and injury as well as extensive damage to roads, bridges, farms and housing, opposition groups debated the most effective tactics for confronting the dictatorship in the upcoming plebiscite. Some favored refusal to register, abstentionism, selection of an alternate candidate to oppose whomever the government selected (despite constitutional provisions for a single candidate in the 1988 plebiscite), or pressuring the government to allow "free and competitive elections." Others dismissed the feasibility of electoral opposition and urged continued armed resistance.

While the moderate opposition discussed electoral tactics, and the Manuel Rodríguez Patriotic Front carried out a variety of armed actions against the government, General Pinochet insisted upon compliance with the transitory provisions of the 1980 constitution. This meant exclusion of Marxists and other "subversives" from the political process and institutionalization of the authoritarian political order. In October 1987 the dictatorship again made clear its commitment to these objectives in new repressive legislation. In an obvious effort to limit political debate and bulwark the regime against a new wave of protests and labor activism, the military *junta* sought to bar employment of "Marxists" in education and journalism, provided for fines against news media which propagated "Marxist" ideas, and even threatened penalties against groups and individuals who cooperated politically or proposed coalitions with Marxist movements or parties.

In these circumstances, the insights reportedly offered by President Salvador Allende to opposition leader Orlando Sáenz, about a month before Allende's death, seemed ever more prophetic:

> Let me tell you something. . . . You are looking for a military dictatorship. And from somewhere, not that I believe there's anything after death, but still, if there is, I shall look down on you all and find you all together, casting about for ways to get out of power the military man you replace me with. I shall see you all there, plotting and planning it, but with a great deal more difficulty than you are having now, how to get rid of the soldier you put in my place. Because it won't cost you much to get him in. But by heaven, it will cost you something to get him out.

If these words were Allende's prophecy, he proved clairvoyant. Fifteen years had passed since September 11, 1973; the military junta still controlled the country.

The plebiscite provided for in the 1980 constitution to allow popular approval or rejection of the military junta's candidate for president from 1989 to 1997 created an opportunity for voter rejection of Pinochet. In February 1988, most of the opposition groups agreed to work together in the plebiscite in the form of a Concertación de Partidos por la Democracia; several months later the Communist party and some other leftist factions joined the anti-Pinochet *electoral* strategy to oust the dictator. Pinochet's advisers had convinced him in 1980 to accept the constitution to legitimate the new political order. Now the charter for Chile's *Alice in Wonderland* potentially threatened the reign of the Queen of Hearts. It also offered the possibility of changing the new political system *within* the law. Thus the opposition turned the plebiscite, intended as an instrument to perpetuate the military regime, into a device to defeat the dictator in an internationally observed electoral event and to initiate a year-long interim period before holding competitive presidential and congressional elections.

On August 30, 1988, the military junta named Pinochet the candidate for president, subject to voter approval in the plebiscite scheduled for October 5. The government ended the state of exception and allowed most exiles to return to the country. Under international scrutiny, the pre-plebiscite campaign enrolled 92 percent of eligible voters. More spectacularly, the government provided fifteen minutes per day for Pinochet and anti-Pinochet political spots on national television. The television campaign became an artistic, musical, testimonial, and commercial contest awaited every evening by millions of Chileans. The Concertación attempted to persuade voters that they had nothing to fear, that change was possible, that finally they could restore democracy to Chile. Television spots for the "No" campaign became so popular that a videocassette of the best segments was distributed and marketed throughout the country. The political jingle, "La alegría ya viene" ("Happy times are coming") was so contagious that Minister of Interior Sergio Fernández complained that even government supporters were "humming it despite themselves."

Pinochet's "Yes" campaign (yes to Pinochet for eight more years) emphasized the achievements of the military regime, that Chile was a successful nation (un país ganador), and that the supporters of the "No" campaign, if victorious, would take the country back to the horrors of political polarization of 1970–73. Televised images of strikes, riots, police with clubs and tear gas, and food lines told voters to vote Yes, to reaffirm Pinochet's and the military's salvation of the country from chaos and international Marxism. The Yes campaign's initial television spots lacked polish; responding to the No campaign's sophisticated political advertising, the Yes spin-masters belatedly delivered more effective Madison Avenue–style political spots.

The No campaign succeeded. Fifty-five percent of voters rejected another eight years of Pinochet, but even after seventeen years of dictatorship some 43 percent of the electorate favored continued authoritarian rule. Chileans held their breath to see if Pinochet would accept the voters' decision. After the three other junta members refused his late-night request for them to sign a decree granting him "extraordinary powers" and deploying the army in Santiago's streets, Pinochet reluctantly acknowledged the opposition's victory. It remained to be seen if the general would respect the 1980 constitution, govern for an interim year as the law specified, then call elections and hand over the presidential sash to his successor in March 1990.

After defeat in the plebiscite the military government turned its attention to redesigning the election system and gerrymandering electoral districts to suit their purposes before the 1989 elections. The new election law reduced the number of deputies in the Chamber of Deputies from the 150 in Congress prior to 1973 to 120 and created 60 electoral districts, each sending two deputies to Congress. This binomial (two seats per district) system would use a special version of proportional representation that allotted one seat in Congress to parties or coalitions that obtained the highest number of votes in the district, and the other seat to the second finisher, unless the winning party or coalition doubled the second finishers vote total. In practice, this meant that the rightist parties could elect a congressmen in each district where they obtained 33.4 percent of the vote. Indeed, the binomial system was designed to provide the rightist minority a long-term guarantee of overrepresentation in Congress. It also put internal stress on the Concertación because only two candidates could be presented in each district from the variety of parties that made up the coalition. Pre-election bargaining and horse-trading for future candidacies and government patronage were necessary to hold the coalition together. In contrast, the political right consisted essentially of two major parties, Renovación Nacional (RN) and Unión Demócrata Independiente (UDI), both of which could present one candidate in each electoral district and allow the voters to decide directly which party would send their candidate to Congress.

The 1989 elections gave the Concertación coalition 72 seats versus 48 for the pro-Pinochet parties. With their nine designated senators and sixteen elected senators, however, the rightists had a majority in the Senate (25–22), providing an insurmountable obstacle to constitutional reform and an effective brake on numerous policy initiatives contained in the Concertación program.

Before Aylwin was inaugurated and the new Congress began to function, the military government and the Concertación negotiated constitutional reforms, approved by plebiscite (July 1989). Among the some fifty reforms, approval of the 1989 constitutional plebiscite reduced the term of office to four years for the president who would take office in 1990, made subsequent constitutional reforms slightly easier (two-thirds in both legislative bodies instead of three-fifths in two consecutive congresses), and increased the number of elected senators (but retained nine senators designated by the president and representatives of the armed forces). In a free and fair election on December 14, 1989, the Concertación candidate, Christian Democrat Patricio Aylwin (who had bitterly opposed the Unidad Popular program in 1970 and had initially supported the military coup in 1973), garnered 55 percent of the vote against Pinochet's ex–Minister of Economy Hernán Büchi and the independent rightist candidacy of Franciso Javier Errázuriz.

The Concertación's slogan in the 1988 plebiscite, "happy times are coming," echoed

TABLE 10–7. CONGRESSIONAL ELECTIONS
(CÁMARA DE DIPUTADOS), 1989

	Votes	Percent*
Christian Democrats	1,766,347	26.74
Party for Democracy (PPD)	890,947	13.48
Socialist Party	210,918	3.19
Radical Party and PRSD	369,703	5.59
Other Concertación†	273,580	4.1
Total Concertación	3,511,495	53.1
Renovación Nacional	1,274,298	19.29
UDI	685,911	10.38
IND	194,911	2.95
INDPS	171,229	2.59
Total "Democracy and Progress" coalition	2,326,349	35.21
Other Parties (Non-Coalition)		
LIBSOC	206,138	3.12
U. Dem.	360,597	5.45
AL Centro	177,942	2.69
INDEP	127,941	1.93
NAC	53,819	0.81
Del Sur	47,387	0.71
Total valid votes	6,605,530	

Source: Germán Urzúa Valenzuela, *Historia política de Chile y su evolución electoral (desde 1810 a 1992)*, Santiago: Editorial Jurídica, 1992, p. 76.

*Percentages do not add to 100 because of rounding.

†The Concertación included seventeen parties, movements, and political groups. Small parties and movements included, among others, Humanists, Social Democrats, PADENA, USOPO.

TABLE 10–8. PRESIDENTIAL ELECTIONS, DECEMBER 14, 1989

	Valid Votes	Percent
Patricio Aylwin	3,850.023	55.2
Hernán Büchi	2,051,975	29.4
Francisco Errázuriz	1,076,894	15.4
Total	6,978,892	100.0

Source: Germán Urzúa Valenzuela, *Historia política de Chile y su evolución electoral (desde* 1810 a 1992), Santiago: Editorial Jurídica, 1992, p. 763; *Que Pasa*, December 16, 1999; p. 11.

the slogan of President Pérez in 1861 (see Chapter 6) as he inaugurated his "government of all, for all" in the transition from the Montt-Varas authoritarian regime to a more liberal polity (1861–71). The Socialist party's motto, "a Chile for all [Chileans]" (*"un Chile para todos"*) came even closer to Pérez's *"un Chile de todos, para todos."* But just as Pérez was constrained by the 1833 constitution and the political coalitions that controlled the Congress from 1861 to 1871, the Aylwin coalition government came to office by accepting the legitimacy of the 1980 constitution—which many of the parties and spokespersons for the Concertación had previously rejected. Rumors had it that many "informal" guarantees had also been afforded to General Pinochet and the armed forces regarding the 1978 amnesty decree, respect for the relative autonomy of military institutions, and promises not to pursue the human rights issue too vigorously—despite the official Concertación program's call for "truth and justice." Accepting the 1980 constitution meant, at least for the interim, accepting "protected democracy." This political reality provided the political right, the armed forces, business groups, and foreign investors with normative force to accompany their political and economic power. The constitutional and legal constraints on the incoming government reinforced the effects of the economic reforms that had divested the national government of most public enterprises through accelerated privatization from 1986 to 1988.

Major economic producer associations (fruit, mining, forestry, and fisheries, along with the traditional associations such as the SNA and SOFOFA) had become ever more important participants in policymaking and in determining the course of the economy. Creation of an independent Central Bank, on the model of the U.S. Federal Reserve, took monetary policy away from presidential control. And although the Concertación had gained a majority in the Chamber of Deputies, the nine designated senators gave veto power in the Senate to the major rightist parties, Renovación Nacional, and UDI (the party of Jaime Guzman, principal architect of the 1980 constitution).

In some ways General Pinochet (and, indirectly, foreign investors and domestic entrepreneurs) snatched victory from defeat. Pinochet would become the father of Chile's new "democracy," the army commander in the new civilian administration, the guarantor that the Concertación government would abide by the political formula that the junta and its supporters had imposed. He had the electoral system redesigned and assured himself and his allies veto power in the Congress and the continued tenure in office for the judges, bureaucrats, and military officers he had appointed. He had accepted the results of the 1988 plebiscite in an emotional televised address to the nation. He likewise accepted the 1989 constitutional reforms and the voters' verdict in the 1989 elections. He scoffed at those who called him "dictator," asking rhetorically, "What sort of dictator allows himself to be voted out of office, accepts constitutional reforms through plebiscite, and respects the outcome of presidential and congressional elections?"

Like Ibáñez from 1927 to 1931, Pinochet claimed that he had heard his nation's call, responded as a patriot, and rescued *la patria* from irresponsible and corrupt politicians, subversives, and international communism. He had saved the country from the Marxists; now he was orchestrating the return to democracy. As he put it, more than once, "Mission Accomplished" (*misión cumplida*).

On the anniversary of the 1973 coup, September 11, 1989, General Pinochet told Chileans: "The armed forces have reconstructed authentic democracy. They have definitively carried out their mission. . . . I love this country more than life itself." In the days before General Pinochet left office the military junta issued a spate of new decrees and "organic laws" (*leyes orgánicas*) further constraining the policy initiatives of the incoming government and protecting the armed forces, police, judiciary, and bureaucrats appointed by the military from dismissal by the new president. General Pinochet would bequeath not only his political system but also his political appointees throughout the government to the next administration.

The Concertación labeled these last-minute decrees *leyes de amarre* ("laws that bind"). General Pinochet proclaimed that he would leave the Concertación government *"todo atado y bien atado"* ("tied up, and well tied up"). The dictatorship was ending, but the "authentic democracy" bequeathed by the military junta and its civilian allies was on a very short tether. President Aylwin would take power with less constitutional authority to control the armed forces than any president in Chile's history. And the government coalition would be tightly bound by the new institutional order, by the *leyes de amarre,* and by the fear of an authoritarian resurgence during the next four years.

11 Concertación

THE PAST IN THE PRESENT

On March 11, 1990, Patricio Aylwin took office as Chile's first elected president since 1970. His Minister of Justice, Francisco Cumplido, had written in 1983: "The Constitution of 1980 does not meet, in its elaboration or the manner in which it was ratified, the essential conditions required by constitutional doctrine for the existence of a legitimate political order based on the rule of law." Aylwin, in a speech closing the meeting of the Grupo de Estudios Constitucionales in 1984, had insisted that "[following] the procedures for transition in the 1980 Constitution will only serve to consolidate a regime of permanent dictatorship. . . . On this road democracy is not reached. Accepting it is accepting the actual dictatorship and the authoritarian regime to which it leads. Doing this means renouncing the reestablishment of democracy." Aylwin continued: "We comply with this Constitution as part of the current reality. . . . We comply with it despite the fact that it is repugnant to us."

In 1990, Aylwin, Cumplido, and the rest of the cabinet, the newly elected legislators of the Concertación coalition, swore an oath to uphold the 1980 constitution and the political order that they had rejected as repugnant and illegitimate. They paid this tactical price for peaceful transition from military regime to elected civilian government.

Viewed retrospectively, the decision to pay such a price was consistent with Chilean political history. The victors at the Battle of Lircay (1830) overturned the 1828 constitution to impose, in 1833, an autocratic republic. From 1833 presidents routinely repressed political opposition, imposing regimes of exception and using "extraordinary authority" (*facultades extraordinarias*). Press censorship emulated the practices of the colonial Inquisition; censors burned banned books in public to mid-century.

Until the 1870s, when they finally managed to implement constitutional reforms, the factions defeated in internecine strife alternately struggled against and swore allegiance to the 1833 constitution. Writing in 1860, liberal politician and revolutionary Federico Errázuriz denounced the 1833 constitution as the foundation of tyranny. In 1871, as the newly elected president Errázuriz swore to uphold it until reforms were possible. In 1874, forty-four years and two civil wars after the battle at Lircay, constitutional reforms somewhat liberalized the 1833 charter. Even so, many of the authoritarian legacies dating from colonial times and the autocratic republic, both institutional and cultural, persisted into the 1890s.

In 1891 blood spilt in another civil war reaffirmed the liberal victory but also the authoritarian past. After a series of political amnesties from 1891 to 1894, the defeated advocates of presidentialism (the Balmacedistas) swore their loyalty to a system that they had spent the lives of thousands to overturn. The Balmacedista political party (Liberal Democrats) took center stage in political bargaining, coalition management, and the distribution of political patronage. Balmacedistas served in Congress, in presidential cabinets, in the judiciary, and in the armed forces. In 1915 a Balmacedista president took office without a hint of constitutional crisis.

By the 1920s different social forces, including a modernized and more professional army officer corps and a rising labor movement, challenged the reformed 1833 regime. Bayonets once again imposed a new constitution. A military coup in September 1924 (and a second coup in January 1925) precipitated an end to the "parliamentary republic." Some months later, after first orchestrating a plebiscite to legitimate the work of an ad hoc constitutional commission, the government promulgated the constitution of 1925, a constitution no more legitimate in its manner of elaboration or its manner of approval than its predecessors of 1828 and 1833. After the brief presidency of ex-Balmacedista Emilio Figueroa Larraín (December 1925–April 1927), Carlos Ibáñez del Campo, the most prominent military officer in the 1924–25 military movements, arranged his own "election" to the presidency, receiving approximately 98 percent of the votes cast.

Ibáñez governed as virtual dictator until 1931, when the world economic crisis provoked economic collapse in Chile and he was forced from office by student demonstrations and strikes by white-collar professionals, including doctors and bureaucrats. During his presidency Ibáñez enjoyed the support of key civilian technocrats and of many politicians from the centrist and rightist political parties. Congress continued to function after legally avoiding elections by handpicking a "consensus slate" of legislators at the Termas de Chillán. In the tradition of Bernardo O'Higgins' abdication in 1823, Ibáñez chose resignation and exile in 1931 rather than unleashing the army against the civilian population in Santiago.

After an interval of political chaos and military unrest (1931–32), the 1925 constitution became effectively the law of the land. The country experienced almost four decades of institutional stability. From 1932 to 1970 Chile was the only Latin American country without a single irregular presidential succession. Elections occurred as scheduled, supervised after 1941 by the armed forces as stipulated in the election law approved by the congress. But always there were significant minorities who rejected the legitimacy of the 1925 constitution and the existing political order, who called for an end to capitalism, "formal democracy," and social injustice. As in the past, those who called for an end to the existing regime served in Congress, the bureaucracy, the judiciary, the armed forces, and government agencies. They swore loyalty to the constitution and promised to uphold the laws, even as they sought to overturn them: a Socialist colonel, Marmaduque Grove, led the battle in 1932 to establish a *"república socialista"*; in the late 1930s a Nazi congressmen called for an end to the corrupt liberal regime from his seat in the legislature, then headed a coup attempt in 1938; in the 1940s and 1950s, Falangist and Christian Democratic deputies and senators denounced the injustices of capitalism and promoted creation of a "communitarian society." Communists, Socialists, Trotskyists, and others elected to Congress, appointed as cabinet ministers and judges, and teaching in the country's schools proclaimed the need for revolution, while they worked within the system to destroy it.

By the 1960s the leading political figures in Chile openly called for an end to the existing socioeconomic regime and for political revolution, whether accomplished peacefully or with violence. Forty years after the 1924 military coup, recently inaugurated President Eduardo Frei Montalva (1964–70) proclaimed a "Revolution in Liberty" that he hoped would create, through peaceful reforms, a more just social order. This effort, and the ensuing Popular Unity government (1970–73) with its "Chilean way to socialism" provoked another violent rupture in the body politic.

On September 11, 1973, bayonets prevailed. The victors imposed another constitution (1980); the vanquished, even another decade later (1990), could only return to the political arena by promising to respect the constitutional order imposed by the military junta at the same time that they proclaimed its illegitimacy and their intentions to "reform" it. So began the transition from military to civilian government in 1990, much as had the battle to liberalize the autocratic regime from the mid-1830s until 1874.

The Concertación's electoral slogan in the 1988 plebiscite campaign that defeated General Pinochet was *"la alegría ya viene"* ("happy times are coming"). An end to routine repression, to pervasive fear, to the arbitrary brutality of the military government understandably inspired joy in the majority of Chileans. So too did the return to electoral politics, congressional debate, and legislation instead of decrees by a military junta, a chance for a freer press and to exercise the rights of freedom of association, movement, and speech. Chileans could celebrate a government that would rule according to law and without regimes of exception—even if "the law" still meant the 1980 constitution. Aylwin's inauguration in 1990 was a time of hope, of great expectations—perhaps of too much hope and too many expectations. The pent-up frustrations and demands of almost seventeen years of dictatorship could hardly be satisfied in a four-year presidency, particularly since the military government and its civilian supporters had installed a political system intended to impede "a return to the past" and to provide them with a range of vetoes over institutional reform and policy initiatives for the future.

Beyond the constitutional and institutional constraints on the Aylwin government, the explicit threat of "another September 11" framed the newly elected government's policymaking. The armed forces' commanders, the armed services' representatives in the senate, and the right-wing political parties took seriously the military's role as "guarantors of the institutional order"; General Pinochet declared at the end of 1990 that if the circumstances demanded it, he would lead another "September 11." Aylwin sincerely desired to restore civilian rule and to redress the "social debt" left by the dictatorship, but his number one priority was to prevent such an authoritarian reversion and to assure that after four years Chileans would *elect* his successor.

The Concertación's official program was an eclectic wish list written by committees of intellectuals, politicians, and activists from political parties and the multifarious nongovernmental organizations (NGOs) (known by the acronym "ONGs" in Chile) that had served as a surrogate political opposition and acted clandestinely in the 1970s and 1980s when the military government outlawed even non-Marxist political parties (1977). The program served various purposes: creating a viable electoral coalition in 1989 by establishing a minimal list of shared objectives for parties and movements that had, both from 1970 to 1973 and during the dictatorship, often been at odds; persuading independent voters and the undecided that a Concertación government would not be too great a risk that socialists, Christian Democrats, Radicals, and assorted Catholic reformers would not provoke a "return to chaos"; and providing a minimal consensus for policy initiatives during Aylwin's four-year presidency.

Among many other initiatives, the Concertación program proposed constitutional and legal reforms to democratize the 1980 constitution; human rights policies that included overturning the military's 1978 self-amnesty and initiatives to assist victims of state terrorism from 1973 to 1990 and their families; and extensive reforms of the judicial system, penal code, military code of justice, election law, national security and arms control laws, and the quasi-constitutional provisions (organic laws) regulating the armed forces and police. Rewriting the military regime's health, social security, pension, forestry, and foreign investment laws was also on the agenda. In addition, the Concertación promised to enact legislation to assure the "full incorporation of women" into society; protect families and guarantee equal opportunity for females in the work force; protect the environment; enhance educational opportunities, reduce "extreme poverty," and overcome the "social debt" of the dictatorship; redemocratize municipal government; reform the dictatorship's labor code; and create an ombudsman (*defensor del pueblo*) to represent persons claiming abuse by government authorities.

As with most electoral platforms worldwide, the Concertación made many more promises to voters than would likely be achieved, especially given the special circumstances of Chile in 1990 and the last-minute shortening of Aylwin's term from eight to four years. By publicly accepting the 1980 constitution as the legal foundation of the transition, the Concertación also acknowledged the political reality that further democratization depended on negotiating piecemeal agreements with the pro-Pinochet opposition. One of President Aylwin's key advisers, Eduardo Boeninger, repeatedly warned of the dangers of moving too fast, offering too much, and mobilizing social movements to push forward the program: "The main threat is populism, by which I mean the danger of responding to widespread social demands by making promises that outstrip the resources available to fulfill them." Indeed, Boeninger and other key policymakers in the presidential inner circle decided, *sub rosa*, to suppress or postpone many of the most sensitive policy initiatives in the Concertación program, especially in the area of human rights, constitutional reform, and changes in legislation affecting the armed forces.

Others in the coalition, including some congressmen, objected that this approach conceded too much to the political right, the military, and private business interests; underestimated the government's ability to mobilize support for its program; and allowed the legacy of fear to limit unnecessarily the Concertación's policies. This objection certainly applied to civil-military relations and human rights concerns but overlooked one of the most important changes in Chile since 1973: many activists and members of the Socialist party, the Party for Democracy (PPD), and the Christian Democratic party had been transformed ideologically and now accepted much of the neoliberal economic program. Indeed, hardly anyone in Chile offered an alternative to continuing the overall economic policies of the military government. Moreover, they valued decision-making by consensus to avoid the polarization of the past. Political learning by party and union leaders (others called it recantation of their values and submission to military threats) had largely removed revolutionary rhetoric and objectives from public discourse.

Aylwin's cabinet included ex-revolutionaries who now expressed more concern about maintaining macroeconomic equilibria and promoting foreign investment and export earnings than about promoting any sort of social utopia. The military regime had not only imposed its version of "protected democracy," but had also largely won the battle of ideas, especially in the economic realm, epitomized by what was referred to in Chile as the "renovation" of socialists (*renovación socialista*). Thus the *leyes de amarre* and the 1980 constitution that impeded implementation of the Concertación program were reinforced by the changes wrought by the dictatorship in everyday political discourse and public opinion regarding possibilities for the future. Other laws adopted by the military government in 1989 assured tenure for bureaucrats appointed before March 1990. Pinochet bequeathed not only the system of "protected democracy" to the Aylwin government but also most of its administrative and judicial personnel. In many government offices after 1990, policymakers viewed their secretaries, office workers, and even custodians with suspicion. More than 40 percent of the electorate had favored Pinochet in the 1988 plebiscite and over 40 percent had voted against the Concertación in 1989. Significant social support remained for the authoritarian neoliberal regime, impressive evidence that the military government from 1973 to 1990 neither existed in a vacuum nor imposed itself without deep roots in civil society. Pinochet and the military junta had not invented authoritarian institutions and political practices in Chile.

In an imaginary letter from Pinochet to a Chilean psychiatrist, written by Sergio Marras (*Carta apócrifa de Pinochet a un siquiatra chileno*)—really a response to an open letter written previously by a Chilean psychiatrist, Marco Antonio De la Parra, to Pinochet (*Carta abierta a Pinochet: monólogo de la clase media chilena con su padre*)—the "fictional" Pinochet tells "the doctor":

> I am the continuation of the authoritarian vein bequeathed to us by Mapuches and Spaniards, of this inevitable insanity of being democrats on the surface (*de la boca para afuera*). Where do you think I found my authoritarian vein if not from the atavistic lessons of this country? . . . I have not been the Teacher, as you suggest. I am simply the Good Student. . . . Mine was not the first dictatorship in this country, nor will it be the last in which bodies are hidden. . . . Neither me, nor my work, has been extinguished. And they shall not be extinguished. You all carry me [and my work] inside yourselves like Captain Riley and the Alien embryo. . . . You [all] have been defeated and you remain defeated. You live with my legacy [*bajo mi herencia*]. But when I die things won't change much.

Sergio Marras' apocryphal letter angered many Chileans and saddened others. Pinochet did not respond, not even a lawsuit against the author for defamation of character. When Marras published the book in June 1998, four years after Aylwin left office, he could not know that only months later Pinochet would be arrested in London, at the request of a Spanish judge, on charges of violation of human rights. Still less could the policymakers in the Aylwin government have imagined such a scenario. Pinochet's presence as army commander and defender of his legacy dominated Chilean politics and newspaper headlines from 1990 to 1994.

Perhaps nothing more clearly illustrated the constraints facing the Aylwin government than General Pinochet's continued command of the army. Some commentators compared this circumstance to an imaginary, if imaginable, political transition in Spain without General Francisco Franco's death in 1975. What would a "transition to democracy" have been like if Franco had stepped down as head of state but continued to command the Spanish army for the following decade? Pinochet not only continued as commander of the army; he and the other armed services' commanders could not be removed by the elected president as a result of the Organic Laws of the Armed Forces decreed by the outgoing military junta in 1989. And the Concertación lacked sufficient votes in the senate to reform these laws owing to the designated senators and the binomial district electoral system that overrepresented the political right in Congress.

In August 1990, celebrating Bernardo O'Higgins' birthday, president Aylwin extolled the example of the independence hero's patriotic abdication of the "Supreme Directorship of the Nation" in 1823, rather than provoking civil war and rejecting the will of the people (*voluntad de su pueblo*). Aylwin reminded Chileans that Captain General Bernardo O'Higgins had gone into voluntary exile to spare his country further grief. This less than subtle appeal to Pinochet went unanswered. Other informal spokespersons reminded the country that ex-general Carlos Ibáñez, serving as "elected" president in 1931, had done the same, taking flight to Buenos Aires rather than turning the army on demonstrators in the streets of Santiago who demanded his resignation from the presidency. In case Pinochet did not understand the hints: the father of the nation, O'Higgins, and the country's greatest military "antipolitician" before 1973, Ibáñez, had both sacrificed their personal position for the good of the nation.

And what about Captain General Augusto Pinochet in 1990? Pinochet left the presidency as stipulated in the 1980 constitution, proclaiming that he had saved the nation from communism: "mission accomplished." Still, he insisted that there was danger of a leftist resurgence, of vengeance against the armed forces, of backsliding toward socialism, of efforts to dismantle the new institutions. Pinochet could leave the presidency, but regarding the command of the army he was unmoved and unmovable. In any case, Pinochet told Chileans on the anniversary of his appointment by president Salvador Allende as army commander-in-chief that he had been called to that position "by divine providence." In 1990, on the anniversary of the September 11, 1973, coup, Pinochet proclaimed, "If the conditions of 1973 were to occur again, I would act in the same fashion." The message to the Concertación government and to the nation was clear: Chile still needed his guiding presence, just in case.

In practice, by 1994, the Aylwin government had accomplished almost none of the promised constitutional and institutional reforms. It proved impossible to change the constitutional provisions affecting the armed forces, the designated senators, or the electoral system. The 1978 amnesty (Decree Law 2.191), which the Concertación program promised to derogate, remained in place. Indeed, the Concertación leadership decided not to ask Congress to derogate the amnesty for fear of provoking a violent response by the armed forces. For the moment, the armed forces' de facto veto held the government hostage.

Between 1990 and 1994, the army's "Advisory Committee to the Commander in Chief" (CAS), created several years before by Pinochet, became a virtual shadow government. Headed by General Jorge Ballerino, the CAS carried out political intelligence, coordinated communications campaigns (anti-government media programs) to counter government initiatives, and negotiated in private with designated government officials when displeased with the formal decisions of the Minister of Defense. Military spokesmen made known their views both behind the scenes and in several overt challenges to government authority, most notably in the so-called "security, readiness and coordination exercise" (*operación de enlistamiento y enlace*) in December 1990 and the *boinazo* of 1993, when combat-ready troops wearing black berets (*boinas*, thus the name given the operation) backed by armored vehicles deployed in downtown Santiago while President Aylwin traveled in Europe. This operation coincided with a "routine" meeting of army generals with Pinochet, emphasizing the armed forces' displeasure with various government policies and with the "inefficiency" of the Defense Ministry in processing promotions, duty assignments and other matters of professional concern. Congressional debates and press coverage regarding human rights policies, investigations into corruption in the armed forces, conflicts over budgets, scandals regarding arms sales to Croatia, military intelligence's tapping of phone lines and surveillance of prominent politicians, and congressional investigations affecting members of General Pinochet's family all contributed to the periodic flare-ups in civil-military relations.

According to presidential adviser Edgardo Boeninger, who had direct contacts with General Ballerino during the *ejercicio de enlace* episode, "the [December 19, 1990] *ejercicio de enlace* was a threat. And while there was a general discontent that framed it, the principal detonator was the case of the checks [involving Pinochet's son]." When General Ballerino made this known, the Concertación government and the investigating committee in Congress "deactivated the '*pinocheques*' scandal." Put another way, the government decided to suppress investigation and prosecution of General Pinochet's son in the name of social peace.

The *boinazo* of 1993 took place after the semi-official newspaper *La Nación* headlined "Check case against Pinochet's son reopened," with another headline reading "Eight

generals subpoenaed to testify before Court [regarding violations of human rights]."
With Aylwin out of the country, and Pinochet refusing to negotiate with the Defense
Minister, an "informal" meeting with the Minister of Interior at General Ballerino's private residence (May 30, 1993) began to defuse this new threat to political "normality."
Pinochet wanted a *"ley de punto final"* (an end to the human rights issue and to judicial
investigation of the cases involving "the disappeared"), better treatment for himself and
the army, and definitive suppression of the financial scandal (the *pinocheques* case) involving his son, among other concessions. Presidential advisers sought also to influence
the content of the headlines in *La Nación* the next day to lower the political temperature.

To quell the virtual military sedition, the government again promised to drop the
check case and to attempt a more global "solution" to the human rights issue. It also
agreed to personnel changes in the Defense Ministry and to work toward more "efficiency" in processing army requisitions, promotions, and duty assignments, as well as
to arranging less onerous (less public) circumstances for military personnel testifying
in ongoing court investigations. The government also gave up on its behind-the-scenes
efforts to encourage Pinochet's early resignation as army commander. Aylwin proposed a modified *ley de punto final,* a law intended to end judicial processes and investigations of the military government's abuses. The government partially disguised the
proposed *punto final* law as judicial and penal code forms.

Opposition to the proposed law from within the Concertación coalition and from
human rights organizations eventually forced its withdrawal from congressional consideration. Opponents asked how the government could support still another amnesty
law when it had promised to derogate the 1978 amnesty decree. Unable to provide a
punto final to the human rights issue, the government nevertheless made repeated efforts to appease the armed forces until 1994. Meanwhile, nonstop headlines regarding
civil-military relations in the press and attention to pronouncements of active-duty and
retired officers on radio and television highlighted the ongoing battle over the control
by civilian authorities of the armed forces. Retired military officers, obvious surrogates
for their active-duty brethren, repeatedly complained that the press was subjecting
them to a "campaign intended to erode their prestige." They also objected to the "constant parade" of officers called to testify in the courts.

Tensions in civil-military relations remained a permanent topic in the press and television news throughout the Aylwin presidency. No amount of pressure, however,
forced General Pinochet or the other armed services commanders to resign before they
were ready to do so; no threats of impeachment (*acusación constitucional*), investigations
into corruption, or even the graphic revelations of massive human rights violations removed the tether placed on the government by the legacy of the military regime. General Pinochet and the armed forces made clear for all Chileans from 1990 to 1994 that
they had not accepted subordination to the Minister of Defense nor did they intend to
resume the military's pre-1973 lower profile role in Chilean politics. When Aylwin left
the presidency in 1994, Pinochet remained as the Commander of the Army—a poignant
symbol of the limits of a transition constrained by the 1980 constitution and the armed
forces' more prominent role in national politics.

General Ballerino would pay a price for his role as the army's most visible political
operative, failing to succeed Pinochet as army commander and retiring to a private
conservative think tank. But despite the personal price by Ballerino, from 1990 to 1994
his work in the CAS effectively limited the Concertación government's policy initiatives, especially in the area of human rights, military budgets, and other policies perceived as affecting the armed forces' institutional interests, including defense of General Pinochet's image and that of his family. (After General Pinochet retired as army

commander in 1998 the new commander quietly folded the CAS into another intelligence and research agency; it lost its high political profile and virtually disappeared from the mass media).

President Aylwin failed to achieve the constitutional reforms promised by the Concertación program, just as president Pérez's "government of transition" had failed to extrude constitutional reform from the congress in the decade of 1861–71. With the exception of the Organic Law of Municipalities (Law 18.695), which replaced appointed mayors with elected councillors (concejales) and mayors, no significant constitutional reform passed during Aylwin's presidency. Like Pérez in the 1860s, however, Aylwin attempted to promote a politics of consensus that gradually made other political initiatives feasible, from tax reform and social programs focused on reducing poverty to creation of new government agencies to promote policies ostensibly favoring environmental protection, improvement in the conditions of indigenous peoples, and an end to gender discrimination.

Despite the veto power of the political opposition, Aylwin duly sent proposed legislation to Congress to implement much of the Concertación program, including proposed constitutional reforms, modification in the laws regulating the armed forces and national police (leyes orgánicas de las Fuerzas Armadas y de Orden), changes in the Military Code of Justice, and proposals to restrict the jurisdiction of military tribunals over civilians. He created a National Commission on Truth and Reconciliation in 1990 (nicknamed the Rettig Commission, for its director, longtime Radical party politician Raúl Rettig) to investigate human rights abuses during the dictatorship and to achieve "justice, within the possible."

President Patricio Aylwin (far right), with members of the Agrupación de Familiares de Detenidos Desaparecidos, announces creation of Rettig Commission, January 1990. (Courtesy of Archivo Universidad de Chile.)

The Rettig Commission delivered its report to Aylwin in February 1991. It validated the victims' claims of abuse and state terrorism in agonizing detail and provided the rationale for reparations. During the commission's investigations, newspapers reported on discovery of mass graves of victims of the military regime; gruesome photos of the mummified bodies shocked even supporters of the military government.

After reviewing the report for almost a month, Aylwin addressed the nation on March 4, 1991. He apologized to victims on behalf of all Chileans, offered moral and economic reparation, and "solemnly appealed to the armed forces and police, and all those who participated in excesses committed to acknowledge the pain they caused and make efforts to lessen it." In Rancagua assassins killed an army doctor and his wife; he had been accused by the FPMR (Manuel Rodríguez Patriotic Front) of collaborating with the secret police and monitoring victims during torture sessions. El Mercurio featured a picture of General Pinochet at the funeral for the army martyr juxtaposed to a story on Aylwin's message to country regarding the Rettig Report.

General Pinochet, who had referred to the Rettig Commission as a "sewer," declared that there was nothing to ask pardon for, that the armed forces had saved the country from terrorism and international communism, and that the Army rejected the fundamental findings of the commission and its premises. The Navy took a similar, if less offensive tack; the National Police and Air Force Commanders expressed somewhat more conciliatory responses. Some leaders on the political right sarcastically referred to the "Commission on Resentment and Revenge" (a play on the "Truth and Reconciliation" in its official name). On the other side of the political spectrum, the Communist party newspaper, El Siglo, headlined: "Rettig Report: Crimes without Punishment?", and the Agrupación de Familiares de Detenidos-Desaparecidos (family members of the victims) objected to the "one-sided" (sesgado) report that ignored the thousands of torture victims, political prisoners, and exiles and underestimated the number of human rights violations that resulted in death: 2279, including 132 members of the armed forces and security services.

Shortly after public release of the Rettig Commission report (an instant best-seller), assassins killed Senator Jaime Guzmán, a principal author of the 1980 constitution and Pinochet confidant, near the Oriente campus of the Catholic University in Santiago. The Rettig Commission report passed from front-page news; the war against terrorism and violent crime replaced the military regime's human rights violations in public discussion. Periodically the human rights issue resurfaced, when authorities announced the discovery of newly found human remains in mass graves, when victims and family members protested government policies, when congressmen made speeches denouncing the military regime's crimes in the legislature, when the government could not avoid an issue that it wished to bury permanently with a law specifying a statute of limitations for prosecutions for crimes committed after 1970 (a so-called ley de punto final). Divisions within the Concertación prevented passage of such a law during Aylwin's presidency; a minority of Christian Democrats and many Socialists and PPD leaders made clear that approval of such a law, as had occurred in Argentina, would risk dissolution of the coalition and affect chances for a single Concertación candidate in the 1993 presidential elections. Nevertheless, with some important exceptions, such as the ex-commander and second-in-command of the DINA, the military successfully resisted trials during Aylwin's presidency. Congress killed the government's proposals for constitutional reforms and amended other legislative proposals beyond recognition.

In contrast to the failures of the Aylwin government in the area of constitutional reform, the politics of consensus permitted numerous policy initiatives whose long-term impacts would go far beyond Aylwin's four-year term, among them:

- An increase in the value-added tax (IVA) that accounted for approximately 40 percent of government revenue, from 16 to 18 percent, with additional revenue to be used for social programs

- Creation of a national environmental commission, the Comisión Nacional de Medio Ambiente, CONAMA (1990), and promulgation of a comprehensive law on the protection of the environment (Law 19.300, 1994)

- Establishment of the Fondo de Solidaridad e Inversión Social, FOSIS, a Fund for Solidarity and Social Investment to fight poverty through grassroots development projects, often by subcontracting with municipal governments and hundreds of the NGOs that had been key elements in the campaign against the dictatorship); FOSIS operated within the newly created Ministry of Planning and International Cooperation, MIDEPLAN (Law 18.989, 1990)

- Creation of the Agency for International Cooperation, AGCI, to coordinate international and private development assistance with the hundreds of NGOs operating in the country (1990)

- Creation of a ministerial level agency dedicated to "women's issues" and legal reforms to promote more gender equality and erase gender discrimination, the National Women's Service, SERNAM (Law 19.023, 1991)

- Reform of labor laws to provide slightly better job security and severance pay (Law 19.010, 1990) and liberalized requirements for unionization and collective bargaining (Law 19.049, 1991; Law 19.069, 1991)

- Creation of the Corporación Nacional de Reparación y Reconciliación to carry out the recommendations of the Rettig Commission regarding human rights and victims of the dictatorship (Law 19.123, 1991)

- Creation of the National Indigenous Development Commission, CONADI, to promote integration and development of Indian peoples under the new Indigenous Peoples Law (Law 19.253, 1993)

In addition, the Aylwin government committed new resources to health services, housing subsidies, and income supplements for low-income households, created Servicio País (a sort of Chilean domestic peace corps employing recently graduated professionals in development projects), and established the Integral Health Provision Program, PRAIS, to provide health services to victims of human rights abuses.

The verdict remained uncertain on the long-term impact of these and numerous other policy initiatives. Initial assessments ranged from complaints about favoritism, corruption, inefficiencies, and "political manipulation" in FOSIS, CONADI, and CONAMA operations to highly favorable evaluations of the extent to which careful program targeting reduced poverty and indigence. In most areas the record was mixed; costly environmental investments in ENAMI's Ventanas facilities made after 1992, for example, significantly reduced air and water pollution in the Punchuncaví region that had been afflicted by toxic clouds and soil and water pollution for many years. Emissions of sulphur had been reduced by 1998 to "only" 28,000 tons. In other northern mining regions, however, levels of contamination increased and accidental chemical spills dumped toxins into rivers that flowed to the sea. Similar stories could be told for the Santiago metropolitan area, the major ports, the internal waterways, and lakes. Gradual implementation of an environmental review system and the action of courts in the environmental sphere significantly delayed major public works and industrial projects and made environmental concerns a more routine aspect of policymaking. On balance, however, the bulldozer of "progress" still carried more weight than arguments about mitigating environmental externalities. Poorer urban neighborhoods were particularly affected by air pollution and environmental contamination, as evidenced by casual reading of any of Santiago's newspapers. Wealth and income "trickled down" to the underclasses much more slowly than did the environmental hazards and filth of the "economic miracle."

In retrospect, the quantity and diversity of the Aylwin government's social and environmental policy initiatives were impressive, creating enough new government agencies and the corresponding alphabet soup of acronyms to remind observers in the United States of Franklin Roosevelt's "New Deal" in the 1930s. Denied the possibility of enacting constitutional reforms, the Aylwin government nevertheless took many initiatives to overcome what was called the "social debt" of the military regime and worked to liberalize the political ambience. Perhaps most importantly, Aylwin sought to restore decency, civility, and morality to public life; his supporters and leftist critics hoped that the institutional reforms they sought would not require the forty years that liberals had fought to modify the 1833 constitution or even the fourteen that passed from initiation of the Pérez transition government to the constitutional reforms of 1874.

In other areas the Aylwin government also made strides: gradually pardoning, on a case by case basis, the some 400 political prisoners left by the dictatorship; providing health care, pensions, and scholarships for families of torture victims and political exiles; enacting labor reforms that somewhat loosened restrictions imposed by the military government on union organization, collective bargaining, and strikes; and, perhaps most important in terms of negotiations with the political right and sustaining the elected government, establishing competent management of the economy by the administration's economic team. Indeed, spokespersons for the political opposition and ex–cabinet members in the military regime repeatedly applauded the technical capacity and performance of the Aylwin economic team headed by Finance Minister Alejandro Foxley. Foxley proved an able administrator of the neoliberal model; he insisted on the need to avoid a return to "populism" and the importance of macroeconomic stability.

Like president Pérez (with the legacy of the 1859 civil war discussed in Chapter 5), Aylwin faced the legacy of the 1973 military coup and the repression that followed, dividing the country into bands of "enemies." In 1861 Pérez confronted the legacy of the traumatic civil war of 1859, government repression of the liberal opposition, the memory and living reminders of dead and wounded of the opposing armed forces, and the flight of numerous political exiles. Pérez began his presidency with a general amnesty approved unanimously in Congress. Aylwin's task in 1990 was much more arduous than had been Pérez's in 1861. Agreements among elites reached in semi-private negotiations (what Chileans call the *política de cúpulas*) no longer could ensure social peace and political reconciliation. There would be no "ample amnesty" in 1990; it would not be possible to "erase the memory" of past convulsions. At the end of the twentieth century Chile was a much more complex, heterogeneous, and internationalized society than it had been in 1861; the Internet, international law, human rights organizations, and CNN beamed through the "weight of the night" that Portales and the Conservatives had relied on to maintain their hegemony until the 1870s. Moreover, the number and variety of political actors made it impossible to arrange a quick deal in Congress among the "political class," as had occurred in 1861 and again from 1891 to 1894.

New economic realities also influenced politics and policymaking, most especially the enormously increased de facto power of foreign investors, international consortia, and the influence of the major economic groups that controlled the key sectors of the Chilean economy. Opening Chile's economy as a primary strategy to promote economic growth had been enormously successful. It also made the economy extremely sensitive to decisions by actors from Asia to northern Europe, from Africa to Oceania. Once "open to the world," lack of control over the influences that entered made the country and its government ever more vulnerable to the vicissitudes of the international political and economic systems.

Added to the power of foreign investors, the dictates of the international economy, the scrutiny of international communications networks, and the demands of international human rights organizations, Aylwin encountered the challenge of coalition management. The various political parties that constituted the Concertación disagreed on many policy issues. Internal divisions and personalist factions within the parties further complicated the president's task, as did the almost constant jockeying for position by party leaders for the upcoming 1993 legislative and presidential elections.

The first strictly political test of the Aylwin government's performance came in the 1992 municipal elections which gave the Concertación 53 percent of the vote, the political right (UDI, RN, UCC) 37 percent, and the newly relegalized Communist party 6.6 percent of the vote, a surprise to many in the Concertación and a mild concern to the political right. Abstention combined with null and blank ballots cast reached almost 20 percent of the 7.8 million registered voters. The Communists and others who rejected the government's hesitant human rights policies, its failure to achieve significant labor reforms, and its perpetuation of the military regime's economic policies called for more rapid and comprehensive implementation of the Concertación electoral program.

Congressional elections in 1993 slightly reduced the Concertación's delegation in the Chamber of Deputies (from 72 to 70) and in the Senate (from 22 to 21). Thus from 1989 to 1993 the historical "three-thirds" pattern of Chilean elections (right, center, left) reemerged, albeit with a much more moderate left (at least within the Socialist party and the PPD), a much less influential Radical party, and a weaker "revolutionary" left, *unrepresented in Congress* (Communists, MIR), complemented by a smattering of environmentalists, "humanists," and independent leftists. Unlike the highly politicized and partisan past of Chilean politics, however, more Chileans declared themselves "independents" or refused to register. Under the new election laws, voters who refused to register were not required to vote; those who registered and did not vote potentially faced fines. Disaffection with "politics" and the political parties more generally, manifested by low voter turnouts and deliberately spoiled ballots, distinguished the post-1990 system from pre-1973 patterns despite the apparent similarities in vote distribution.

Before the 1993 elections the political right agreed to a reduction in the term of the next president from eight to six years (thus returning to the presidential term fixed in the 1925 constitution). Everyone recognized that the Concertación candidate, Eduardo Frei Ruiz-Tagle, son of ex-President Eduardo Frei Montalva (1964–70), would be the victor. On December 11, 1993, Frei and the Concertación obtained 58 percent of the vote; the leading rightist opposition candidate was Arturo Alessandri Besa, the nephew of ex-president Jorge Alessandri (1958–64) and the grandson of two-time president Arturo Alessandri (1920–24, 1924–25; 1932–38). Frei took office in March 1994. Not only was the political rights' historical one-third of the electorate approximately replicated, but so too was Chile's tradition of political families, of sons and grandsons following their parents and extended family members into the presidency, the Chamber of Deputies, the Senate, the judiciary, and the government bureaucracy. Nepotism rivaled clientelism and political patronage as a dominant factor in the 1990s. A "political class" still ruled Chile, although its aristocratic origins and patrician habits had somewhat altered.

Congressional elections in 1997 again reaffirmed the same pattern: Concertación over half of the votes; rightist parties and independent rightist candidates from 36 to 40

TABLE 11–1. PRESIDENTIAL ELECTION, DECEMBER 11, 1993

Candidate	Party/Coalition	Votes	Percent
Eduardo Frei Ruiz Tagle	Christian Democrat, Concertación	4,008,654	58.0
Arturo Alessandri Besa	RN/UDI/UCC (led by Errázuriz)	1,685,584	24.4
José Pinera Echenique	Non partisan	427,286	6.2
Mafredo Max-Neef	Independent/environmentalist	383,847	5.6
Eugenio Pizarro Poblete	Communist party, but not party member	324,121	4.7
Cristián Reitze	Green party	81,905	1.2
Total		7,314,890	

Source: APSI December 13–26, 1993. Percentages rounded; total does not equal 100%.

percent, depending on how individual independents were characterized on a left-right spectrum, with a slight gain for the Communist party and other ideological leftists, at close to 10 percent. The binomial system again slightly overrepresented the right and discriminated against the left parties and movements not included in the Concertación coalition. The Communists and other non-Concertación leftists, despite obtaining 7 percent of the vote, elected not a single deputy because of their exclusion from either major coalition. In contrast, the Concertación allocated four seats to the PRSD (which obtained fewer votes than the Communists), and the Unión por Chile allocated seven seats to independents and a regional rightist party, the Partido del Sur, which, together, obtained 5 percent of the votes.

Overall, electoral trends since the 1988 plebiscite lost by General Pinochet confirmed that more than half of the electorate favored the Concertación parties and that 35–40 percent supported the political right. The Communist party, despite garnering 5–8 percent of the vote, by its exclusion from either coalition lacked any representation in the congress from 1989 to 2000. Neither the Socialists (PS) nor the Party for Democracy (PPD) represented, by themselves, 15 percent of the electorate (although together they closely approximated the historical voting strength of "socialists"), and support for the Christian Democrats (DC) had slightly eroded by 1997. Moreover, shifts within the Concertación and the opposition parties, especially the loss of support by Christian Democrats by 1997 and the candidacy of Ricardo Lagos against the UDI's populist Joaquín Lavín made the outcomes of the 1999 presidential and legislative elections less certain. Nevertheless, in certain respects the historical "three-thirds" distribution of the electorate had survived. The vote of the rightist parties (UCC, RN, UDI) and "independent" rightists in municipal, legislative, and presidential elections from 1989 until 1997 varied from 35 to 42 percent of the electorate; the rightist presidential candidate in 1970, Jorge Alessandri, had obtained 34.9 percent. Likewise, the Christian Democratic party presidential candidate, Radomiro Tomic, had received 27.8 percent of the vote in 1970; Christian Democrats within the Concertación coalition received 23–29 percent of the votes in the period 1989–97. Although more difficult to "track" because of the creation of new small parties and fragmentation of the "old left," a rough tally of the votes of the groups that more or less corresponded to the parties of the Popular Unity coalition, including the Communist party and the PRSD, yields 30–38 percent of the electorate from 1989 to 1997, compared with the Popular Unity vote of 36.3 percent in 1970. These calculations are inherently imperfect. The "same" groups espoused different ideologies and occupied different places in the political coalitions of 1997 than in 1970. Comparing political party percentage of votes in presidential, congressional, and mu-

TABLE 11–2. ELECTIONS: CHAMBER OF DEPUTIES, DECEMBER 11, 1997;
SENATE, DECEMBER 11, 1997*

Coalition	Party	Deputies (120)			
		% Votes	Deputies, 1997	Senate, % Votes	20/38[†], 1997/Total
Concertación	Christian Democrats	23.0	39	29.2	10/14
	Party for Democracy (PPD)	12.6	16	4.3	0/2
	Socialist Party	11.1	11	14.6	1/4
	Radical Social Democrats (PRSD)	3.1	4	1.8	0
	Nonpartisan	0.8	70	–	0
	Total (Concertación)	50.6			
Unión por Chile (political right)	Renovación Nacional	16.8	23	14.8	2/7
	Unión Demócrata Independiente	14.4	17	17.2	7/9
	Partido del Sur	0.4	1	–	–
	Nonpartisan	4.7	6	4.6	0/1
	Total (UPC)	36.3	47		
Left	Communist Party	6.9	0	8.4	0
	Nueva Alianza Popular	0.2	0	–	0
	Nonpartisan	0.5	0	0.2	0
	Total (Communist/left)	7.6	0		
Chile 2000	Humanist Party	2.9	0	2.0	0
	Unión de Centro Centro Progresista	1.2	1	0.4	0/1
	Nonpartisan	0.9	0	2.2	0
	Total	4.3			
Nonpartisan candidates, no coalition		0.7	2	–	0

*In 1997 the Senate consisted of 48 members, 38 elected and 9 "designated" as stipulated in the 1980 constitution. Senators were elected for eight-year terms from two-seat (binomial) constituencies, half the seats renewed every four years. The designated senators included 4 ex–commanders in chief of the armed forces and police (one each branch); 1 ex–comptroller general, 2 ex–Supreme Court Justices, 2 ex–university presidents. Former presidents who filled that position for six uninterrupted years were ex–oficio senators for life (*vitalicios*). General Augusto Pinochet became a *senador vitalicio* en 1998.

[†]The numbers in the last column of the table refer to senators elected in 1997/total number of elected senators, by party. The Chamber of Deputies consisted of 120 members, elected in two-seat constituencies for a four-year term. The Chamber of Deputies was renewed in entirety every four years. Due to the allocation of seats *within coalitions* and the mechanics of the Chilean D'Hondt electoral system in binomial districts, parties that obtain lesser vote percentages may obtain seats in the legislature, while other parties unaffiliated with coalitions receive none. This occurred with the Communist party in 1993 and 1997.

nicipal elections is in some ways misleading. Nonetheless, despite different voting laws, changes in party ideology and coalitions, and different political circumstances, certain underlying patterns in distribution of voter preferences are striking.

The Left Revolutionary Movement (MIR) had called on its supporters and on the "real left" to cast spoiled ballots (*votos nulos*) in the 1997 elections as "the only useful and dignified vote for workers and popular sectors," proclaiming further that "only political and social organization and spoiled ballots are an alternative to the political

TABLE 11–3. ELECTORAL TRENDS, BY PARTY AND BY COALITION,
1988–97, PERCENT OF VOTE*

Party	1988 Plebiscite	1989 (leg)	1992 (mun)	1993 (leg)	1996 (mun)	1997 (leg)
DC		26.19	29.03	27.20	26.66	22.98
PRSD		4.35	5.34	3.77	6.58	3.12
Ind (PDC-PR)		2.59	0.00	0.00	0.00	0.79
PPD		16.94	9.48	12.01	12.28	12.55
PS		0.09	8.80	12.44	11.13	11.10
PC		5.35	6.56	6.36	5.97	7.48
PHV		0.94	0.82	1.41	1.60	2.91
RN		19.24	17.60	17.64	18.74	18.82
UDI		15.22	11.23	15.07	13.08	17.06
UCC		2.64	8.26	3.78	2.80	2.14
Indend.		1.90	2.62	0.10	0.84	0.70
Others		4.56	0.24	0.20	0.32	0.36
Total		100.0	100.0	100.0	100.0	100.0
Coalition						
Concertación	55.98	51.10	53.49	55.42	56.65	50.55
RN-UDI/Opp.	44.02	39.02	29.06	36.70	32.14	36.24
PC	5.35	6.56	6.36	5.97	7.48	
PH	–	–	1.41	1.60	2.91	
UCC	2.64	8.26	–	2.80	2.14	

*mun, municipal elections; leg, congressional elections.
Source: The Electoral Websites (Elections in Chile):
www.agora.stm.it/elections/chile.htm; www.elecciones. gov.cl (Ministerio del Interior).

right and the Concertación!" MIR declared that "the votes of thousands of citizens are worth less than a group of military officers who impose designated senators. . . . The principal human rights victimizer [General Pinochet] is being imposed as a senator for life." On its Internet Web site and in its publications MIR urged "the return [from the hands of foreign investors and the Chilean economic groups, obtained via privatization] of our mineral, maritime, forestry and agricultural wealth, that cost so many generations to accumulate. . . . We have joined together to initiate an alternative political road, truly democratic, constructing the ideas and the force for a more just society."

In addition to MIR, this manifesto was also sponsored by a collection of tiny leftist groups and dissidents, dissatisfied with the human rights, economic, and social policies of the Frei government. In October 1997 MIR denounced the "Concertación's policies of collaboration with the political right, the armed forces, and the ruling classes." In large block letters it urged: VOTO DIGNO = VOTO NULO. POR UNA VIDA DIGNA PARA TODOS LA LUCHA CONTINUA (A dignified vote is a spoiled ballot; The struggle continues for a dignified life for all [Chileans]). The Humanist party also called for "a social revolution that drastically changes the lives of the people, a political revolution that changes the structure of power, and a human revolution that creates new paradigms to replace the reigning decadent values."

The Socialist Party Web site, in contrast, proclaimed its program of *"Chile para todos"* ("A Chile for all [Chileans]") and told voters that the Socialists promised "to continue working alongside President Frei and the future government [referring to the year 2000] that we hope will be presided over by Ricardo Lagos [Socialist party leader, minister in the Aylwin and Frei cabinets]." The Socialists offered twelve proposals as their agenda; most were recycled from the moribund Concertación platform of 1989, beginning with an end to the designated senators and other reforms of the 1980 constitution. Other proposals included reforming the labor code; educational and university reforms; better health care; improved social programs; more attention to youth and infants; support for policy initiatives to stimulate music, film, and audiovisual projects; eliminating the sales taxes on books; improving opportunities for women; protecting citizens against abuses by public officials; upgrading the National Environmental Commission (CONAMA); and developing a fairer and more efficient tax system. No part of the program proposed establishing socialism in Chile; to the contrary, the Socialists seemed to support the neoliberal economic model, with some adjustments to achieve a more "just and equitable" society. Within the Socialist party, some activists retained their commitment to prosecuting military personnel guilty of human rights violations or, at the least, "discovering the truth" before applying the 1978 amnesty in accord with the Supreme Court's repeated rulings that upheld the validity of Amnesty Decree Law 2.191 for most of the crimes committed between 1973 and 1978.

For MIR, the Communist party, and other small leftist groups the Socialist, Christian Democratic, and PPD programs amounted to "selling out" (*entreguismo*) to the armed forces, the political right and the weight of the authoritarian past. It also meant that the Concertación offered no real alternative to the neoliberal model, no end to the exploitation of natural resources and the labor force. They asked, rhetorically, why they had all struggled against the dictatorship only to accept its constitution, its laws, its economic model, its "protected democracy." After all the spilt blood, the torture, the years of exile, the humiliation and sacrifice, how could this facade democracy be the fruit of "victory" in 1988 and 1990?

With the votes counted in the 1997 elections, the Humanist party declared: "In 1993 the Concertación obtained the vote of 3,733,276 Chileans and the Right the vote of 2,255,150. On December 11, 1997, the Concertación obtained 2,898,362 votes and the Right 2,077,442. Thus 900,000 Chileans less supported the Concertación and nearly 200,000 less supported the Right." According to the Humanists' calculations, more than 50 percent of the potential electorate "voted" against the Concertación and against the Right, that is, against the existing political order: 1,600,000 potential voters who did not register, 1,000,000 who abstained, 300,000 who voted blank ballots, and 950,000 who spoiled their ballots, combined with the votes obtained by the Humanists (2.91%) and the Communists (7.48%). The Humanist manifesto claimed that only by eliminating the "institutional straitjacket" imposed by the Right and the Military junta and managed by the Concertación could the discontent be overcome.

The Humanists proclaimed that

> a constitutional convention and a new constitution are the only option. . . . [continued application of] the neoliberal model will only deepen the problems in health care, education, housing, work, and nutrition of the majority of Chileans. We will also see the further deterioration of our environment and our personal liberties. . . . This system is not fixable (*perfectible*), only its replacement with one that makes human beings and not money the central value . . . will permit overcoming this situation. . . . There is nothing worse than a people with no future.

The Humanist party criticisms were also reminiscent of the literature of national decline so evident in Chile in the early 1900s: the Humanists seemed to echo Enrique Mac-

Iver's memorable "Speech regarding the moral decline of the Republic" delivered at the Club Ateneo in August 1900. Mac-Iver began: "It seems to me that we are not happy; one notes a malaise not limited to a particular class nor to particular regions of the country, but which extends to the entire country and to all who inhabit it." After consideration of the reasons for the widespread discontent, Mac-Iver asked in 1900, "What are we today?" The answer: "I think the best answer is silence," for what most contributed to this dismal situation is "lack of public morality, what others might call public immorality."

The Humanist party in 1997 represented the electoral choice of a tiny minority of Chileans; it nevertheless expressed the social discontent, the frustration, the disappointment, and the impatience of many Chileans with the course of the political transition after 1990. The evident cynicism of some Concertación leaders, the permanent internal wrangling of both major coalitions, the public insults traded by politicians and military officers, the barely disguised jockeying for position in the next congressional and presidential elections—all these features of daily life had corroded the spirit of sacrifice and enthusiasm of the 1988–90 campaigns to oust General Pinochet.

In 1990 there had been a change of government but not of the political regime. The 1980 constitution, the electoral system, and the other *leyes de amarre* ("laws that bind") decreed by the military government remained in place. The Concertación leadership administered the economic system and political order inherited from the military government, the very economic and political order that it had resisted since 1981. But it did not do so entirely by choice; nor did many of its supporters give up on the possibility, in the longer term, of creating a more democratic and justice society. State terrorism had ended; the numbing chill of fear that cut to the quick for so many years was wearing off, although it was still not entirely overcome by 1994 or even 1999. It was too much to expect that the new programs initiated by the Aylwin government would eliminate the legacy of centuries of impunity for the powerful, social inequalities, and environmental degradation, but they definitely set a new tone, whether to be followed, altered, or scrapped by those who followed. Chileans chose their national legislators and municipal councilors in free and fair elections (even if the operation of the electoral law slightly distorted representation). Human rights violations dramatically declined; press censorship was less heavy-handed. For all its limitations, the Aylwin government made important changes for the better in the lives of millions of Chileans.

As expected, the Concertación candidate had easily won the presidential elections in December 1993. Inaugurated in 1994, president Eduardo Frei Ruiz-Tagle called for further modernization of the state; consolidation of the economic model, labor, health care, and educational reforms; and increased "insertion" into the world economy. Frei and his advisers lowered the profile on demands for constitutional reform and democratization; human rights virtually disappeared from the official public agenda. Frei sought unsuccessfully in 1995 to negotiate among the political elite a *ley de punto final*, disguised as an omnibus reform package, to "finish" with the human rights issue. In this effort the Frei government, like its predecessor, failed. The victims' families, human rights organizations both in Chile and internationally, cadres of lawyers, journalists, medical professionals, religious leaders, journalists, student leaders, the Communist party, and a minority of dedicated politicians in the Socialist and Christian Democratic parties resisted the government's efforts to negotiate a legislated amnesia and impunity.

Like the Aylwin government, Frei could not put an end to the human rights issue. Memories of the victims' anguish and current evidence of the victimizers' lack of contrition, even their publicly expressed pride in the inquisitorial salvation of the *patria* after 1973, impeded "turning the page" before the full story had been told. Beginning with the initial civil-military tensions in 1990 and the initial efforts by Aylwin to promote national reconciliation through "truth and justice"—to the extent possible—the Concertación governments failed in this endeavor. For four years (1994–98) Frei used private and public channels, dinner parties, meetings with Church officials, quiet negotiations with the opposition parties, and conversations between the defense minister and armed forces' political liaisons—all to no avail. The military and its civilian allies could not make the demands for "truth and justice" disappear as they had the bodies of the victims.

In March 1998 General Pinochet stepped down as army commander and took his seat in congress as "Senator for Life" (*vitalicio*). For some Chileans, Pinochet's investiture in the senate was an important reaffirmation of the institutional framework imposed in 1980. For others, Pinochet's entry into the senate was an intolerable reminder of his (and the military regime's) impunity for crimes against humanity. Shortly thereafter a group of Concertación legislators presented an *acusación constitucional* against Pinochet for "gravely compromising the honor and security of the nation" during his tenure as army commander. In accord with the 1980 constitution, if the Chamber of Deputies approved the *acusación* and the Senate upheld it, Pinochet would lose his congressional privilege (*fuero*), exposing him to criminal and civil prosecutions in a variety of cases. Fearful that such an outcome would destabilize the political system and discredit the previous administration, the Frei government opposed approval of the *acusación*.

General Augusto Pinochet in his last year as commander of the army.
(Courtesy of Archivo Vicaría de la Solidaridad.)

The Chamber of Deputies acrimoniously debated the *acusación* for almost a month. Congressmen supporting the accusation against Pinochet presented numerous "proofs" of the charges, ranging from the numerous skirmishes between the armed forces and government during the Aylwin government to Pinochet's use of the "illegal" CAS to engage in political operations regarding the economy, diplomacy, and social policy. They also recalled his speech to the Rotary Club in 1990, in which he said that the German Federal Republic's army was full of "long-haired, marijuana-smoking homosexuals" (*"un ejército de marihuaneros, o sea, drogadictos, melenudos, homosexuales"*). That Congress could openly debate a constitutional accusation against general Pinochet indirectly confirmed the gradual resurgence of civilian political institutions even without modification of the 1980 constitution. Such a debate would have been risky in 1990. Nevertheless, in a highly divided and divisive vote (62–55), the Chamber of Deputies rejected the *acusación.* Many Concertación congressmen defected; had the government not controlled key Christian Democratic legislators the Chamber of Deputies might have approved the accusation against the ex–army commander, although its defeat in the Senate was assured. Ex-president Aylwin, in words that may have influenced some of the key votes (and which he later claimed to regret), declared that Pinochet had never *really* constituted a threat to the institutional order from 1990 to 1994. To the contrary, Aylwin suggested that Pinochet had helped to smooth over some situations in which the true military hardliners might have upset the consolidation of democratic government. Some Aylwin supporters believed that approval of the *acusación* would be viewed as a backhanded acknowledgment of the chilling effects on policymaking of Pinochet's threats and pressures from 1990 to 1994, thus criticism of Aylwin's emphasis on "prudence" and "moderation."

Pinochet retained his seat in the Senate. He could not ensure that September 11, the day of the military coup in 1973, remain a national holiday. Shortly after the debates on the *acusación constitucional,* Senator Pinochet agreed to replace the annual celebration of the 1973 coup with a face-saving "day of national unity" to be celebrated the first week of September each year. Pinochet and the Frei government acclaimed the agreement as an "historic accord"; some groups on the political left characterized it as a "day of national shame rather than national unity." Cartoonists drew caricatures of a calendar with September 11 missing, and the Communist newspaper, *El Siglo,* featured pictures of Pinochet and Andrés Zaldívar, Christian Democratic president of the Senate and potential presidential candidate, with the headline: "The coupmakers [of 1973] reunited" (*"Se vuelven a juntar los golpistas"*). Whatever the subplots and notwithstanding the criticism from the political left, the main storyline was that the country would no longer officially celebrate the day that Air Force planes rocketed the La Moneda palace. No one could predict whether the "day of national unity" would catch on as an annual event, or even be celebrated.

Andrés Zaldívar, like Patricio Aylwin, had initially supported the military coup in 1973. Many of their now-coalition partners from the Socialist party and Party for Democracy (PPD) had been arrested, brutalized, and exiled. (Zaldívar had also been temporarily forbidden reentry into the country). The Communists' criticisms struck a nerve in the coalition. Pinochet, the Christian Democrats, and the "renovated" Socialists seemingly had agreed to bury memories of the 1973 coup and the crimes of the dictatorship under a tombstone reading: *Day of National Unity.* A Communist party spokesperson put it simply: "The marriage of Zaldívar and Pinochet confirms that the model of the Concertación differs hardly at all from that imposed by the dictatorship. . . . It demonstrates that they share the political project that subjects the country and its people to instability and misery."

No such "marriage" or shared project existed in practice. The Communists and the radical political left exaggerated the Concertación's affinity with supporters of the military regime. But the Concertación government *had* postponed, if not largely abandoned, its own programs of 1988 and 1989. And the Frei government was looking for almost *any* way to resolve politically, rather than through the court system, the legacy of human rights violations. Government leaders remained unsure if the political system would resist the hundreds of trials of retired and active duty officers implied by the demands of the human rights organizations and the *agrupaciones* of the victims' family members.

On September 11, 1998, the country commemorated the twenty-fifth anniversary of the 1973 military coup and the death of Salvador Allende. Diverse public ceremonies and private social gatherings reflected the persisting antagonisms amongst those who had supported the coup and the military government and those who came to oppose it. The country witnessed processions to the nation's cemeteries, masses in the churches, protest marches, vandalism, violence, sabotage against public utilities, power outages, bonfires, and barricades in the streets, leaving a toll of dead, wounded, and incarcerated. Most of those participating in the violence were less than twenty years old; they had not been born on September 11, 1973. A small group of Miristas (Movimiento de Izquierda Revolucionaria) enacted a midday ceremony at the Monument to the Detained, Disappeared, and the "Executed for Political Reasons" (*Ejecutados Políticos*). A speaker at the ceremony asked for a moment of silence for the "dead, disappeared, and absent." After an extended silence he added: "None of them or us was innocent. We all knew the risks and we decided to fight against repression and death, not only for an ideal, but 'for *la patria*.' Across town, at small gatherings and dinner tables, similar discourse among military comrades and civilian supporters of the military government justified the repression against the "subversives" that had "saved *la patria*" from international communism.

A bit more than a month later the country was shocked by Senator Pinochet's arrest in London (October 17, 1998) and the request by a Spanish judge, Baltasar Garzón, for his extradition to Spain. Pinochet's arrest and the subsequent international press coverage rekindled the embers of moral outrage against the military regime for events after 1973. The international media and the proceedings in the British House of Lords upset the Concertación's continued efforts to gradually negotiate pacts with center and right-wing parties to consolidate the transition to civilian rule. Santiago's political climate altered dramatically; pro- and anti-Pinochet rallies resurrected the battle lines and rhetoric of the late 1980s. Debates over how to return Pinochet to Chile, how much effort to make on his behalf, to what extent Chilean sovereignty was at stake—and the obvious glee of human rights groups and some members of the Concertación coalition that justice might finally be done, even if by foreign courts—reinforced the fundamental distrust across the country's main political divide.

Pinochet's fate, and the exposure of the armed forces to future censure, or even trials for hundreds of retired and active-duty officers, again became a critical concern for the armed forces and, potentially, an important issue in the presidential elections scheduled for December 1999. Which other Latin American officer corps, besides Argentina and Guatemala, had high-ranking officers who could not travel to Europe or the United States for fear of arrest on charges of human rights violations? For how long would officers be called before Chilean courts to testify about "the past?" When would the "vanquished" finally accept the permanence of the 1980 constitution, the armed forces' "guardianship" over Chile's "protected democracy?" When would the Concertación party leaders finally express gratitude to the armed forces for having saved the country from the clutches of international communism in 1973? Helpless against the British Law Lords, a Spanish judge, the denunciations of international human rights organizations, and now, it seemed, the independence of several Chilean judges, the armed forces and the political right threatened, cajoled, bargained in private, and appealed to Chilean sovereignty and to nationalism. Joaquín Lavín, the presidential candidate of the political right, counted a distant cousin among the "disappeared" killed in 1973. He preferred to distance himself from the unsavory emotional and moral legacy of the military junta, but would not, and could not, abandon his party's identification with the 1980 constitution and the construction of "protected democracy."

The Chilean military and the rightist parties persuaded the Frei government to object to Pinochet's arrest on grounds that it violated Chilean sovereignty and Pinochet's supposed diplomatic immunity. Chile's foreign minister, a political exile during the Pinochet government, argued this case in England, Spain, and elsewhere. For many Chileans the world seemed topsy-turvy; in the words of Colombian novelist Gabriel García Márquez in *One Hundred Years of Solitude*, it seemed that "the liberals and masons were defending the Church, the Catholics burning it down." By August 1999, as a visibly aged and infirm Pinochet languished in England, almost thirty criminal and civil lawsuits had been filed against him in Chile (This number would increase to over 140 by mid-2000.) Prospects increased for reopening "closed" cases and investigating the murders and widespread torture after 1973. Newspaper headlines, magazine articles, and television talk shows returned to the crisis of 1973—and before. Why was there a coup in 1973? What was the role of the United States? (Declassification of thousands of documents by the Clinton administration on the 1970–78 period during the U.S. summer of 1999 added fuel to the fire.) Was there a "war" or "civil war" in 1973 and after? Or did the military regime target opponents in extermination operations, like "hunting rats"?

In late July 1999, the Chilean Supreme Court, with a newfound independence, ruled that retired and active duty officers could be tried in cases involving "kidnaping" (*secuestro calificado*) from the pre-1978 period, where the kidnaping had not resulted in death or where there existed no definitive evidence that the victim was deceased. According to the court, since the crimes were "ongoing," no amnesty could be applied. This legal theory had been advanced in the early 1990s but had usually been rejected by military courts, appeals courts, and by the Supreme Court, which applied the amnesty decree to "close" the cases that came before it (*sobreseimiento*) or rejected the human rights organizations' legal pleas (*recurso de casación, recurso de queja, recurso de inaplicabilidad*) to reopen cases on procedural grounds. Almost all Chileans believed that the "disappeared" were dead; the legal theory resurrected by the Supreme Court in 1999 invited the armed forces to acknowledge the crimes and, most importantly, indicate what had happened to the victims' bodies.

Five high-ranking officers who had been direct subordinates of General Pinochet in 1973 were charged in the so-called "caravan of death" case. Hundreds of other military personnel potentially faced testifying or being charged with human rights violations in other cases. On the other hand, the court had upheld the validity of the amnesty decree in cases of "extrajudicial execution," murder, torture resulting in death, and so on. The ruling reaffirmed the legitimacy of the 1978 amnesty and that only the "ongoing crime" of *secuestro calificado* was not covered by the amnesty. Human rights organizations still objected to this interpretation. It meant that crimes that had been the result of state terrorism, defined as crimes against humanity by international law, would be permanently amnestied.

Military commanders organized "private retreats" to consider the consequences of the Supreme Court's decision. After a three-day meeting with thirty-seven of the forty-one active-duty army generals at a resort hotel in Pichidangui, Commander Ricardo

Izurieta made public the army's concerns regarding the "new interpretation" of the amnesty law and the reopening of the human rights violations cases. He again expressed indignation over the ongoing "kidnapping" of Pinochet in England and reasserted the need for increased salaries and resources for the armed forces. *El Mercurio* reported, menacingly, that during this three-day retreat, "extra-official sources suggested that the army generals reflected on their role as the guarantors of constitutional order, and whether these legal actions [by the Supreme Court] against military personnel to some degree affected this constitutional role."

Glaring headlines on the same day in the afternoon tabloid, *La Hora*, proclaimed: "ONE THOUSAND BODIES THROWN INTO THE SEA"—reporting an interview with the son of ex DINA commander General Manuel Contreras. The milder version in *La Tercera* headlined: "Contreras' son reveals abuse of the 'disappeared'" (*detenidos-desaparecidos*), but also reported that Contreras had revealed that after Aylwin took office in 1990 "some bodies in mass graves were dug up, so that they could be made to disappear into the sea." The next day *La Tercera's* Internet edition headlined: "Connection between DINA and Pinochet Demonstrated." Lawyer Carmen Hertz, representing victims in the "caravan of death" case, made public a document signed by Pinochet as president of the government junta, dated January 5, 1974, months before DINA's official creation. The document informed government agency heads, "the DINA has been created with personnel of the armed forces and police. . . . [I]t will advise the junta on all matters regarding internal and external security, and will depend exclusively on

La Hora, July 23, 1999. [Ex-commander of DINA's son claims,] "One thousand bodies thrown into the sea."

the junta, over which I preside." Pinochet had ordered as early as January 1974 that government agencies provide full cooperation with the DINA and that they "maintain the maximum secret (*sigilo*) regarding DINA activities." Hertz claimed that this document demonstrated that DINA had operated prior to its official creation, that it was clearly an instrument of the government, that Pinochet had instructed other agencies of government to cover up the DINA's operations. Further, that since DINA's crimes had been "organized and perpetrated by agents of the State," international law regarding crimes against humanity "prohibited application in such cases of amnesty laws." Finally, it seemed, a smoking gun had been put in Pinochet's hand, and all this with the *Senador Vitalicio* still in England, awaiting a decision regarding his extradition to Spain for trial on charges of crimes against humanity.

Chilean politics was trapped in the recent, and not-so-recent, past, even as actors from left to right of the political system sought some way to "finish" the current story. In retrospect, conflictive civil-military relations and the living phantoms of the tortured, murdered, and disappeared, interspersed with efforts to "close the book" on a past that operated in the present, were the most indelible features of the 1990–2000 decade. (Table 11–4 lists the most important "moments of conflict" in civil-military relations from 1990 to 1999. Most of them focused at least partially on the legacy of human rights violations after 1973).

In late July the government and the political opposition continued maneuvering in hopes of negotiating some sort of *punto final*. But as political cartoonist Guillo so devastatingly depicted, neither the armed forces, the rightist parties, nor the government could find the right people with whom to negotiate such a "finish" to the human rights questions. Meanwhile Pinochet's health declined and he hinted that he would accept release from Britain on "humanitarian grounds." He now claimed that while he could accept "political responsibility" for any "excesses" that had occurred during the military government, he had no criminal responsibility because such things "happened behind my back." Once again Guillo's political cartoons satirized Pinochet's claims of "ignorance" regarding human rights violations. This was the same Pinochet who had boasted as the country's ruler that "not a leaf moved in the country without his knowledge" (or in some versions, his *permission*). (Cartoons available at www.guillo.cl; scroll to N.62 and 63.)

CODEPU (Corporación de Promoción y Defensa de los Derechos del Pueblo), an NGO dedicated to defending human rights cases throughout the dictatorship, declared publicly in mid-August 1999 that the human rights violations in Chile had not been limited to the "disappeared" and that resolution of the human rights question could not be limited to the "archaeological quest" for human remains. According to CODEPU, justice must be sought for the thousands of political executions, for the hundreds of thousands of tortured, for almost a million political exiles, for the crimes against humanity committed by the military regime, "which have no statute of limitations nor are they subject to amnesty" according to international law. The CODEPU proclamation continued: "We reject any effort [by the government, the political right, and the armed forces] to mount a political operation to impose a 'punto final.' In Chile, resolving the pending human rights issues requires justice. . . . Independent and autonomous courts must investigate, process, and judge, in accord with the law, and in these cases, specifically, justice requires application of the principles of international human rights law." After almost ten years of "political transition," hundreds of military personnel still faced the threat of prosecution for crimes against humanity–among them Senator-for-Life Augusto Pinochet, still under house arrest outside London. Pinochet's arrest in London had inalterably changed the short-term course of Chilean politics and, perhaps, even the long-term course of efforts to promote respect for human rights in the international com-

TABLE 11–4. MAJOR EPISODES AND TENSION POINTS IN CIVIL-MILITARY RELATIONS, 1990–2000

Attack on ex–junta member General Leigh	March 21, 1990
Human remains discovered in Colina, fundo Las Tórtolas, until 1980 an army firing range; remains identified as those of three "disappeared" Communist party members	March 21, 1990
Aylwin publicly names members of "Truth and Reconciliation Commission, created by Supreme Decree 355	April 24, 1990 April 29, 1990
Pinochet meets with Aylwin at La Moneda; protestors shout insults as he arrives; Pinochet complains about treatment by Minister of Defense and concerns about Rettig Commission	May 3, 1990
Retigg Commission begins to function	May 9, 1990
Colonel(r) Luis Fontaine, ex–director of Dicomar, assassinated (accused of responsibility for 1986 "degollados" case); understood as vigilante justice by FPMR	May 10, 1990
More human remains located: Pisagua, Chihuío, Tocopilla	June and ongoing in the months while Rettig Commission was functioning
"Secret" meeting of Pinochet's Political Advisory Committee (CAS) and several Deputies from *Concertación* at a dinner at the home of President of House of Deputies	August 6, 1990
Pinochet gives interview critical of the Rettig Commission created by government to investigate human rights violations	August 19, 1990
Aylwin speech on O'Higgins birthday; reminds country of Captain General O'Higgins patriotic sacrifice in abdicating power (insinuating Pinochet should follow the example)	August 20, 1990
Funeral of ex-president Allende	September 4, 1990
Pinochet insults the German army with comments about "long-haired, marijuana-smoking homosexuals" in speech at the Club de la Unión; story breaks on *pinocheques* case involving General Pinochet's son	September 5, 1990
Pinochet publishes his "autobiography," *Camino recorrido, memorias de un soldado;* calls Allende an incarnation of the devil	September 6, 1990
Pinochet affirms that if the occasion arose, he would do the same as he had on September 11, 1973	September 11, 1990
Retired General Alejandro Medina Lois detained and charged with "defamation" (*injuria*) against Pres. Aylwin	September 14, 1990
Minister of Defense notifies Pinochet that Army must return the "Pharaonic House" at Lo Curro to the Presidency	September 14, 1990
Aylwin orders Pinochet to meet with him the following week at the Palacio Moneda	September 14, 1990
Publicity on *pinocheques* case involving multimillion-dollar transaction between Army and General Pinochet's son, Augusto Pinochet H.; 51 deputies ask information from Defense Minister on case.	September 16, 1990–
Aylwin insulted at annual Military Parade; Aylwin later (November) rejects promotion of General Carlos Parera, who had not asked permission to begin the parade, as required by protocol	September 19, 1990
Pinocheques case involving one of Pinochet's sons; financial scandal involving Pinochet's daughter, Lucia; "Cutufa" case (Ponzi scheme in army); Minister of Defense Rojas tries to negotiate with General Ballerino, Pinochet's representative, his early retirement as army commander (suggests 4 months). Results in *"Operación de enlistamiento y enlace"* ("coordination exercise," no communication to Defense Ministry, Army in barracks; Santiago fearing a coup	December 19, 1990

(*continued*)

Leyes Cumplido (3 laws that reform Penal Code, Law of Internal Security of the State, Military Code of Justice, Arms Control law)	January 1991
Aylwin presents Rettig Commission Report publicly; next several weeks armed forces respond formally, rejecting findings and reaffirming their salvation of *la patria* in 1973 and after	March 4, 1991
Jaime Guzman assassinated	April 1, 1991
Cristián Edwards, son of owner of *El Mercurio*, kidnapped (returned after ransom payment, February 1992)	September 7, 1991
Aylwin proposes reforms in civil-military relations allowing president to force retirement of officers; Congress considers army intelligence (DINE) budget (reform proposal rejected)	November 1991
Law 19.123 creates Corporación Nacional de Reparación y Reconciliación	January 3, 1992
Aylwin proposes "double dependency" for Carabineros (Min. Defense and Interior); reform proposal rejected	January 1992
Retired army general in charge of *Investigaciones* (civilian secret police) fired; Army complains that he was "spying" on military personnel	March 1992
Government proposes reform of Organic Law of the Armed Forces and Carabineros, including modification in regulations regarding promotions, appointments, and retirements	March 1992
Army infiltration of *Investigaciones* denounced; calls for ouster of Army intelligence chief General Eugenio Covarrubias	
Aylwin proposes constitutional reforms, including modification in National Security Council and authority to fire armed services chiefs (rejected)	June 1992
Public revelation of Army telecommunication office surveillance of civilian politicians and phone taps; includes potential RN presidential candidate, Sebastián Piñera; tapes leaked to national television and played on the air; case goes to Supreme Court but transferred to military justice system and later quashed	August, 1992
Aylwin proposes reforms in military justice system; (proposal never moves out of congressional committee)	November 1992
Security Council meets at request of Pinochet, Navy commander, and Supreme Court justice; topic: *acusacion constitucional* against three members of Supreme Court and the Army General Counsel; *acusación constitucional* against one supreme court justice approved with support of 3 senators from Renovación Nacional— provokes concern among military institutions because neither the Supreme Court nor the National Security Council remain secure bastions	November–December 1992
Supreme Court, for first time, accepts the theory that the 1978 amnesty does not apply to the "disappeared" because the crime is "ongoing" (*secuestro—kindnapping*); also accepts the doctrine that the amnesty does not impede investigation into human rights cases—though the amnesty would ultimately apply to perpetrators.	December 30, 1992
Rockslide kills over 100 persons in Santiago; Aylwin refuses to declare "state of catastrophe" to avoid military control over affected part of city as as stipulated in 1980 constitution	May 1993
Genaro Arriagada denounces "lack of control over intelligence services," reveals hidden microphones discovered in government offices; Army charges Arriagada under Article 276 of Military Code of Justice for "revealing information that affects troops attitudes toward service"; charges later dropped	May 1993

(*continued*)

TABLE 11–4. MAJOR EPISODES AND TENSION POINTS IN CIVIL-MILITARY RELATIONS,
1990–2000 (*continued*)

Army criticizes delays in processing promotions, duty assignments, salary increases, foreign travel requests, etc.; accuses Defense Ministry of deliberate bureaucratic harassment	May 1993
Council of Generals meeting in Santiago; *La Nación* headlines reopening of *pinocheques* case; pressure for Pinochet to resign; Aylwin traveling overseas; *boinazo* occurs in downtown Santiago; Krauss seeks to manage crisis; fear of military coup; Army presents lists of concerns, ranging from the *pinocheques* case to a *punto final* on the human rights issues to informal government committee	May 28, 1993
Aylwin develops plan for law of *punto final;* requests press to exercise restraint in covering civil military relations and human rights issues; seeks to prevent airing on television of interview with Michael Townley regarding Letelier case	May 28, 1993–mid-June
Aylwin withdraws *ley Aylwin* from congressional consideration	June–August 1993
	September 1993
Supreme Court opens case against General Manuel Contreras, ex-chief of DINA for Letelier case	November 1993
Frei assumes presidency	March 11, 1994
Judge Milton Juica convicts 17 carabineros in *degollados* case; implicates General Stange as derelict in case; government requests Stange's resignation as Carabinero commander; Stange refuses; given administrative leave two weeks later	April 1994
Frei refuses to process Carabinero promotion list	1994–1995
Supreme Court upholds convictions of Manuel Contreras and Pedro Espinoza; Contreras resists incarceration, goes to naval hospital in Talcahuano; Espinoza goes to the Army's telecommunication headquarters in Santiago, Army negotiates with Defense Minister; Espinoza goes to Punta Peuco prison;	May 30, 1995
Contreras appeals to court in Concepción to be allowed to remain "imprisoned" in Naval hospital; Military "protests" regarding Contreras case	June 1995
Frei orders the Consejo de Defensa Fiscal to cease further investigation into *pinocheques*	July
Courts apply 1978 amnesty to cases involving 22 officers	July 1995–January 1996
Concepción Court rules against Contreras; Army insists his condition fragile, appeals to Supreme Court; meanwhile Pinochet suggests transferring the Punta Peuco prison to Army control and raising army salaries 14 percent	August 1995
Frei proposes change in National Security Council and designated senators, to increase civilian role; modified in October (proposal rejected April 1996)	August 1995
Frei proposes ample accord in name of "national reconciliation": changes in organic laws, increased presidential authority to fire armed services commanders, and a *punto* final to human rights issues; armed forces oppose change in organic laws	September 1995
Minister of Defense Pérez Yoma announces his resignation for failure to end stalemate; Army accepts "mixed custody" and given an 8 percent raise	September 1995
General Stange agrees to retire	October 1995

(*continued*)

TABLE 11–4. MAJOR EPISODES AND TENSION POINTS IN CIVIL-MILITARY RELATIONS, 1990–2000 (*continued*)

Eight carabineros convicted in *degollados* case; army major and sub-oficial convicted in murder of bus driver	November 1995
Army captain sentenced to 600 days jail for the *caso de los quemados,* burning to death one person and maiming another	January 1996
Argentine police announce arrest for murder of General Carlos Prats (Buenos Aires, 1974)	January 1996
Contreras interred in Punta Peuco; 23 army officers assigned to special duty as prison guards; no civilians in ostensibly civilian prison; Senate rejects Frei's reform proposals regarding National Security Council and elimination of designated senators	April 1996
Army captain sentenced to 6 years for homicide	June 1996
Army launches Internet Web site; first Latin American army to appear in cyberspace	September 1996
Frente Patriótico Manuel Rodríguez assaults high security prison; liberates "political prisoners" with helicopters, including assassin of Jaime Guzmán	December 1996
Air Force launches Internet Web site	December 1996
Frei forced to call meeting of National Security Council to discuss terrorism	January 1997
Christian Democratic deputies propose reforms of military justice system, limits on jurisdiction of military tribunals; military resists and reforms "postponed"	July 1997
Frei rejects promotion to Brig. Gen of Jaime Lepe, ex-functionary of DINA, linked to murder of Spanish diplomat Carmen Soria; army officially objects	November 1997
Deputies announce constitutional accusation against Pinochet; he postpones retirement until March 10, last possible day as stipulated in constitution	January 1998
Army names Pinochet "Commander-in-Chief Benemérito"; does not inform Ministry of Defense	
Constitutional accusation presented; Frei government argues against it, but some Christian Democrats and most Socialists favor approving the accusation; Minister of Defense Edmundo Pérez Yoma resigns; divisions in Concertación threaten coalition	March 11, 1998
Acusación constitucional fails in secret vote, 62–55, 1 abstention	April 9, 1998
Pinochet arrested in England	October 1998
Army Commander makes various speeches complaining about government's lack of energy in defending Pinochet; pushes for higher salaries and more resources and organizes seminars in the *Escuela Militar* and bases throughout the country on the "real history" of 1973–90; sparks "conversations" with Minister of Defense	April–May 1999
Supreme Court rules that officers involved in "Caravan of Death" in 1973 can be prosecuted for "kidnapping" (*secuestro calificado*) as an ongoing crime, not for murder and illegal execution, crimes covered by 1978 amnesty; Army holds special "retreat" with 37 of 41 generals, expresses concerns to Minister of Defense; Navy, Air Force, Police, and Army commanders meet with Minister of Defense to seek *punto final*, request higher salaries, and demand more effort to obtain Pinochet's release from England and return to Chile	July 1999

(*continued*)

TABLE 11–4. MAJOR EPISODES AND TENSION POINTS IN CIVIL-MILITARY RELATIONS,
1990–2000 (*continued*)

Defense Minister Pérez Yoma organizes a national roundtable (*mesa de diálogo*) in effort to find a way to achieve "national reconcilia-tion"	August 1999
Mesa de diálogo meets with individual presentations	September 1999
First "Day of National Unity" Holiday, marred by protests, vio-lence, "acts of repudiation"	September 6, 1999
After 25 years, Sept. 11 no longer a national holiday	September 11, 1999
British judge rules Pinochet should be extradited to Spain	October 8, 1999
Pinochet returned to Chile for "humanitarian reasons", too ill to stand trial	March 4, 2000
Richard Lages inaugurated as president	March 11, 2000
Santiago Appeals Court removes Pinochet's congressional immu-nity (Lawyers appeal)	June 5, 2000
Monument to Salvador Allende inaugurated in Plaza de la Consti-tución	June 23, 2000
Ex-dictator potentially faces 140 criminal proceedings	July 2000
Pinochet supporters attempt to place black wreath on monument	July 16, 2000
Supreme Court strips Pinochet of Congressional immunity in "caravan of death" case	August 8, 2000

munity. At the least, few Chilean officers who served in the military government in the 1970s and early 1980s were planning international travel.

During the course of his presidency Eduardo Frei Ruiz-Tagle came more and more to be viewed as a technocratic administrator of the legacy bequeathed by the dictatorship, albeit with some commitment to reducing poverty and providing enhanced opportunities for working people and the middle class. From 1996 leaders of the Socialist party and the Party for Democracy, publicly and in private, asked themselves whether their continued participation in the Concertación was justified—and what alternatives might exist. The Christian Democrats, apparently decided on another of their own in the 1999 presidential race, flirted with the idea of a center-right coalition, with Reno-vación Nacional, and resisted the efforts by Ricardo Lagos, the most prominent Social-ist presidential contender (and Minister of Public Works) to get agreement on his can-didacy for the next go-around. Party politics and personal ambition took precedence; the crusading spirit of 1988–89 had given way to political horse-trading, patronage, and everyday politics. Sociologist Tomás Moulian's best-selling *Chile Now: Anatomy of a Myth* (*Chile Actual: Anatomía de un Mito*) captured the generalized disappointment with the moral and cultural defects of the "new Chile." Asked about his book, Moulián commented, "It's a book that tries to understand how we came to this mockery, this sham democracy (*simulacro de democracia*), this ever more depoliticized society, this ever more individualist society. . . . This is a society with more comfort than before, but with much less felicity and happiness than before."

Even some businessmen read Moulián's book, but consistently good economic growth (until the 1998–99 recession), low inflation and unemployment rates, and an orgy of public and private construction projects seemed to make the low level of polit-ical debate and the social malaise less important. Like the weather, everyone com-plained about the politicians, about the superficiality of modernization, and about the "culture of silence" and rampant individualism, but few Chileans did anything about these complaints. Notable exceptions existed, of course: students protesting and striking against government policies; health workers and government employees opposing privatization (ENAMI, CODELCO, ENAP, EMPORCHI); and environmentalists and Indian peoples resisting the forestry and energy megaprojects in the northern deserts, the southern coastal mountain regions, and the Andes cordillera.

At the beginning of 1997 Minister of Finance Eduardo Aninat boasted of sustained positive growth for the last ten years, the lowest inflation rates in the twentieth century (1994–96, single-digit inflation), historic levels of domestic savings (25%), thousands of new jobs created, decline in the percentage of the population in poverty (down to 27%), exports at over 16 billion dollars—in short, perpetuation of the "miracle." By 1998 the government pushed forward with privatization of services in the major ports, seeking bids by concessionaires who would modernize these doors to the international market, increasing the efficiency of container unloading to match that in neighboring Argentina, the United States, and Europe. Bids from private investors in 1999 for the port concessions exceeded greatly the government's projections, and despite major strikes by port workers in July and August 1999, the privatization schemes moved forward.

Flies in the ointment annoyed the government: auxiliary health care workers virtually shut down the public hospitals at the end of 1996 (they were earning less than $175/month). During 1997 the Copper Workers' Federation threatened nationwide protest movements if the government decided to privatize the publicly owned mining and energy sectors; in the major universities the Communists made gains in student elections. A year later Mapuche representatives at the United Nations denounced the Frei government's violation of indigenous rights and violation of its own environmental and Indian people's legislation. In July 1998 Pehuenche Indians, environmentalists, students, and sympathizers blocked roads in the Alto Biobío region to stop work by ENDESA subcontractor Besalco on initial stages of the controversial Ralco Hydroelectric project. Violent confrontations between Mapuche protesters, private security guards, and police multiplied from the end of 1998 to mid-1999. The most militant Indian groups demanded restoration of ancestral lands lost after the military campaigns of the 1880s and some form of political autonomy. Police arrested and jailed activists who damaged the property of forestry and energy firms.

These signs of social movement resurgence were dramatic but limited. The government closed the coal mines at Lota in 1997 despite violent protests in Santiago and the Concepción-Talcahuano region. It proceeded with port privatization despite resistance that required police intervention in Valparaíso, San Antonio, and elsewhere. Triumphalism remained the dominant sentiment of the governing parties until 1998, despite internal frictions within the coalition. The political right, ever wary of any backsliding toward "socialism" or "statism," urged "finishing" the privatization process, less bureaucracy, less regulation, and more market-oriented policies, except where particular economic groups had created their own special subsidies: forestry, fisheries, mining, and traditional agricultural producer groups. And, despite the low incidence of taxes on profits, they demanded further reduction of the tax burden.

The Asian economic crisis hit Chile in 1997, put a crimp in economic expansion, and forced the government to announce some belt-tightening. The crisis also made clear, again, the vulnerability of "the miracle" to international market conditions and decisions of foreign investors. Few Chileans wished to resurrect the critique of capitalism made by "dependency" theorists, a discarded concept associated with the "old left" and the nationalist policies that rejected an open economy with massive foreign investment. But Chile was still a highly dependent economy: dependent on fluctuations in prices for its exports, especially copper; dependent on foreign sources for oil, coal, and natural gas to fuel the economy; dependent for its competitiveness, in part, on nonenforcement of environmental regulations, insecure working conditions, and low wages for its labor force; dependent on decisions made by international consortia and transnational financial conglomerates; and dependent on actions by policymakers in Asia, Europe, and the United States.

There were, of course, some important differences in the "new Chile": Technological innovation; entrepreneurial initiative; a more highly qualified and internationalized professional, business, and academic community; and an active government role in promoting Chilean exports distinguished the Chilean economy in 2000 from the Chile of thirty years earlier. Shifts in employment patterns also reflected the economic transformations of the last three decades. Agriculture now employed approximately 15 percent of the labor force versus almost 25 percent in 1970; the service sector, including financial services, had expanded from 25 percent to almost 35 percent. Female labor force participation rates had increased significantly, jumping from perhaps 25 percent in 1970 to almost 40 percent by 1999.

Government statistics in the late 1990s demonstrated that poverty and indigence was on the decline, that living conditions and opportunities were improving, and that the country continued on the path of modernization and development. The United Nations Development Programme's *Report on Human Development,* published annually since 1990 to measure comparative socioeconomic opportunities around the globe, seemed to confirm Chile's progress, ranking it higher on its summary measure of "human development" than all other Latin American countries (31 of more than 170 countries included in the study). Due to "technical adjustments" in calculation Chile fell to number 34 in 1999, but it still remained highest on this indicator of all Latin American countries. On some other measures Chile still lagged behind other Latin American countries, especially in reducing social and economic equalities. In particular, Chilean women saw less improvement in their economic opportunities and political participation than their counterparts in many countries of Latin America. According to the United Nations Development Programme, several Latin American countries scored better both on the "gender-related development index" and the "gender-empowerment index," imperfect but suggestive measures of improvement in "human development" for females around the globe. In short, Chile ranked higher on the overall "human development index" than for both of these summary measures of gender-related development and opportunities.

Major marketing firms offered a slightly different perspective on Chile in 1999. A special report by Sandra Novoa in the June 27, 1999, Sunday edition of *El Mercurio* detailed the discussions at a marketing conference in Santiago two weeks earlier. Advertisers, market research firms, and academics specializing in business administration agreed that the old indicators used to target consumers—having a phone, television, automobile, and even a small house, were no longer useful in characterizing Chile's socioeconomic map. The advertisers required a different "socioeconomic alphabet" (*abecedario socioeconómico*) for better identifying target markets in the new consumer society. Based on survey research, the marketing firm ICARE argued that "due to the economic and political changes in Chile during the last twenty years that have modified life style and values, the old tools for segmenting markets are obsolete." The doubling of incomes and the higher educational levels in the 1990s had changed consumer tastes and opportunities. Cable and color television, household telephones, automobiles, and other items previously limited to high income groups were now common "even in lower strata household." While the marketing firms disagreed about which of the more discriminating variables were most useful in "modern" Chile, the schematic "socioeconomic alphabet" presented by the Adimark-J. Walker Thompson study was a revealing snapshot of Chile, 1999.

According to this marketing snapshot, after more than a decade of sustained eco-

TABLE 11–5. HUMAN DEVELOPMENT INDEX (HDI), 1998,
UNITED NATIONS DEVELOPMENT PROGRAMME

	Life expectancy at birth (years) 1995	Adult literacy rate (%) 1995	Combined first-, second-, and third-level gross enrollment ratio (%) 1995	Real GDP per capita (PPP$) 1995
High human development	73.52	95.69	78.68	16,241
1 Canada	79.1	99	100	21,916
2 France	78.7	99	89	21,176
3 Norway	77.6	99	92	22,427
4 USA	76.4	99	96	26,977
8 Japan	79.9	99	78	21,930
11 Spain	77.7	97.1	90	14,789
30 Korea, Rep. of	71.7	98	83	11,594
31 Chile	**75.1**	**95.2**	**73**	**9930**
34 Costa Rica	**76.6**	**94.8**	**69**	**5969**
36 Argentina	**72.6**	**96.2**	**79**	**8498**
38 Uruguay	**72.7**	**97.3**	**76**	**6854**
45 Panama	**73.4**	**90.8**	**72**	**6258**
46 Venezuela	**72.3**	**91.1**	**67**	**8090**
49 Mexico	**72.1**	**89.6**	**67**	**6769**
53 Colombia	**70.3**	**91.3**	**69**	**6347**
62 Brazil	**66.6**	**83.3**	**72**	**5928**
63 Belize	**74.2**	**70**	**74**	**5623**
Medium human development	67.47	83.25	65.61	3390
65 Suriname	70.9	93	71	4862
66 Lebanon	69.3	92.4	75	4977
72 Russian Federation	65.5	99	78	4531
73 Ecuador	**69.5**	**90.1**	**71**	**4602**
84 Jamaica	74.1	85	67	3801
85 Cuba	75.7	95.7	66	3100
86 Peru	67.7	88.7	79	3940
88 Dominican Republic	70.3	82.1	73	3923
91 Paraguay	**69.1**	**92.1**	**63**	**3583**
100 Guyana	63.5	98.1	64	3205
111 Guatemala	**66.1**	**65**	**46**	**3682**
114 El Salvador	**69.4**	**71.5**	**58**	**2610**
115 Swaziland	58.8	76.7	77	2954
116 Bolivia	**60.5**	**83.1**	**69**	**2617**
119 Honduras	**68.8**	**72.7**	**60**	**1977**
Low human development	56.67	60.85	47.09	1352
131 Myanmar	58.9	83.1	48	1130
138 Pakistan	62.8	37.8	41	2209
139 India	61.6	52	55	1422
159 Haiti	54.6	45	29	917
174 Sierra Leone	34.7	31.4	30	625
All developing countries	62.2	70.44	57.49	3068
Least developed countries	51.16	49.2	36.42	1008
Industrial countries	74.17	98.63	82.81	16,337
World	63.62	77.58	61.59	5990

Adjusted real GDP per capita (PPP$) 1995	Life expectancy index	Education index	GDP index	Human development index (HDI) value 1995	Real GDP per capita (PPP$) rank minus HDI rank
6193	0.8087	0.9002	0.9809	0.8966	–
6230.98	0.9008	0.9933	0.987	0.96	10
6229.37	0.8948	0.9567	0.987	0.946	12
6231.96	0.8758	0.9667	0.987	0.943	5
6259.29	0.8562	0.98	0.992	0.943	–1
6231	0.9142	0.92	0.987	0.94	2
6187.12	0.8783	0.9473	0.98	0.935	19
6139.72	0.779	0.9298	0.972	0.894	6
6115.55	0.8355	0.8765	0.968	0.893	9
5968.72	0.8603	0.8613	0.945	0.889	28
6090.16	0.7938	0.9045	0.964	0.888	11
6048.8	0.7943	0.9016	0.958	0.885	14
6022.74	0.8065	0.8439	0.954	0.868	14
6081.66	0.7885	0.829	0.963	0.86	2
6045.81	0.7853	0.8213	0.957	0.855	5
6027.8	0.7557	0.8389	0.954	0.85	4
5928.15	0.693	0.795	0.938	0.809	1
5622.82	0.8198	0.7119	0.889	0.807	1
3390	0.7078	0.7737	0.5297	0.6704	–
4862	0.7657	0.8566	0.767	0.796	9
4977.44	0.7377	0.8644	0.785	0.796	7
4530.9	0.6745	0.92	0.713	0.769	5
4602.45	0.7415	0.8359	0.725	0.767	3
3800.69	0.8183	0.7909	0.596	0.735	9
3100	0.8448	0.8592	0.483	0.729	18
3939.71	0.7117	0.8567	0.618	0.729	2
3922.62	0.7542	0.7906	0.615	0.72	1
3582.6	0.735	0.8248	0.561	0.707	5
3204.74	0.6423	0.8665	0.5	0.67	1
3682.08	0.6842	0.5854	0.577	0.615	–16
2610.09	0.7397	0.6686	0.404	0.604	–2
2954.33	0.5628	0.7697	0.46	0.597	–10
2616.72	0.5918	0.7834	0.405	0.593	–6
1976.99	0.7298	0.6855	0.302	0.573	7
1362	0.5278	0.496	0.2032	0.409	–
1130.24	0.5645	0.7129	0.166	0.481	22
2209.13	0.6295	0.3887	0.34	0.453	–16
1421.99	0.6098	0.529	0.213	0.451	1
917.38	0.4932	0.3967	0.132	0.34	3
624.85	0.1622	0.3089	0.084	0.185	–3
3068	0.62	0.6612	0.4778	0.5864	–
1008	0.436	0.4494	0.1462	0.3439	–
6194	0.8195	0.9336	0.9811	0.9114	–
5990	0.6437	0.7225	0.9482	0.7715	–

TABLE 11–6. TRENDS IN HUMAN DEVELOPMENT,
1998 UNITED NATIONS DEVELOPMENT PROGRAMME

HDI rank	Life expectancy at birth (years) 1960	Life expectancy at birth (years) 1995	Infant mortality rate (per 1000 live births) 1960	Infant mortality rate (per 1000 live births) 1996	Population with access to safe water (%) 1975–80
High human development	55.91	70.15	97.87	29.28	58.71
23 Cyprus	68.64	77.22	29.8	9	–
24 Barbados	64.22	76.01	74	11	–
25 Hong Kong, China	66.2	79.04	43.4	–	–
28 Singapore	64.49	77.12	35.65	4	–
30 Korea, Rep. of	53.89	71.74	85	6	66
31 Chile	57.13	75.13	113.65	11	–
32 Bahamas	63.22	73.17	49.65	19	–
34 Costa Rica	61.6	76.62	84.5	13	72
36 Argentina	64.9	72.63	60.05	22	–
38 Uruguay	67.71	72.66	50.45	20	–
45 Panama	60.65	73.39	68.8	18	77
46 Venezuela	59.5	72.31	80.9	24	79
49 Mexico	56.86	72.12	94.75	27	62
53 Colombia	56.54	70.34	98.7	26	64
62 Brazil	54.67	66.58	115.65	44	62
63 Belize	61.42	74.19	73.5	36	–
Medium human development	47.09	67.47	145.24	40.42	–
Excluding China	47.11	65.95	138.66	42.53	–
65 Suriname	60.13	70.94	69.85	25	–
73 Ecuador	53.07	69.49	124.3	31	36
84 Jamaica	62.73	74.1	62.85	10	86
85 Cuba	63.82	75.69	64.65	10	–
86 Peru	47.71	67.7	142.15	45	–
88 Dominican Republic	51.76	70.25	124.85	45	55
91 Paraguay	63.86	69.1	66	28	13
111 Guatemala	45.61	66.05	125.05	43	39
114 El Salvador	50.47	69.38	129.85	34	53
116 Bolivia	42.67	60.51	166.65	71	34
119 Honduras	46.28	68.79	144.7	29	41
126 Nicaragua	47.04	67.53	141	44	46
Low human development	42.15	56.67	167.13	90.02	–
Excluding India	40.01	53.18	169.55	102.11	22.38
131 Myanmar	43.74	58.87	158	105	17
159 Haiti	42.14	54.59	182	94	12
174 Sierra Leone	31.5	34.73	218.8	164	14
All developing countries	46.04	62.2	148.92	64.76	–
Least developed countries	39.06	51.16	170.21	109	–
Industrial countries	68.57	74.17	39.16	13.03	–
World	50.22	63.62	128.6	60	–

Population with access to safe water (%) 1990–96	Under-weight children under age five (%) 1975	Under-weight children under age five (%) 1990–97	Adult literacy rate (%) 1970	Adult literacy rate (%) 1995	Gross enrolment ratio for all levels (% age 6–23) 1980	Gross enrolment ratio for all levels (% age 6–23) 1996	Real GDP per capita (PPP$) 1960	Real GDP per capita (PPP$) 1995
82.66	20.96	11.5	76.42	89.51	58.3	69.59	1944	7835
–	–	–	–	–	–	–	2039	13,379
–	–	–	92.1	97.4	67	76	–	–
–	–	–	78.7	92.2	59	72	2323	22,950
–	–	–	74	91.1	53	72	2409	22,604
93	–	–	86.7	98	66	82	690	11,594
–	2	1	87.7	95.2	65	72	3130	9930
–	–	–	94.8	98.2	70	75	–	–
96	10	2	87.7	94.8	55	68	2160	5969
–	–	–	92.6	96.2	65	77	3381	8498
–	6	7	92.5	97.3	63	75	4401	6854
93	14	7	79.1	90.8	66	70	1533	6258
79	14	6	76.4	91.1	58	68	3899	8090
83	19	14	74.7	89.6	68	66	2870	6769
85	19	8	80.8	91.3	53	70	1874	6347
76	18	6	68.4	83.3	54	72	1404	5928
–	–	–	–	–	–	–	–	–
–	29.54	19.4	53.35	80.57	50.7	64.44	864	3355
–	36.18	23.2	56.51	79.04	51.9	64.96	1172	3945
–	–	–	81.8	93	–	–	2234	4862
68	20	17	74.7	90.1	69	72	1461	4602
86	14	10	69.6	85	67	65	1829	3801
–	–	–	81.7	95.7	72	63	–	–
–	17	8	71.3	88.7	65	81	2130	3940
65	17	6	67.9	82.1	60	68	1227	3923
60	9	4	81	92.1	49	62	1220	3583
77	30	27	43.8	65	35	46	1667	3682
69	22	11	56.3	71.5	47	55	1305	2610
63	17	8	58.2	83.1	54	66	1142	2617
87	23	18	54	72.7	47	60	901	1977
61	20	12	57.3	65.7	53	62	1756	1837
–	59.67	45	30.99	50.85	37.1	47.09	657	1362
54.76	44.49	37.3	27.21	49.41	33.5	39.47	717	1296
60	41	43	71.6	83.1	39	48	341	1130
37	26	28	23.8	45	–	–	921	917
34	22	29	12.9	31.4	30	28	871	625
71	40.21	30.3	47.73	70.44	46.5	57.49	915	3068
57	–	39	29.68	49.2	31.6	36.42	562	1008
–	–	–	–	98.63	–	83	–	16337
–	–	30	–	77.58	–	62	–	5990

TABLE 11–7. CHILE 1998 AND THE UNITED NATIONS DEVELOPMENT PROGRAMME: GENDER EMPOWERMENT MEASURE

	Gender empowerment measure (GEM) rank	Seats in parliament held by women (%)	Female administrators and managers (%)	Female professional and technical workers (%)	Women's share of earned income (%)	GEM value
High human development	–	14.1	–	–	35	–
1 Canada	7	21.2	42.2	56.1	38	0.72
2 France	31	9	9.4	41.4	39	0.489
3 Norway	2	36.4	31.5	61.9	42	0.79
4 USA	11	11.2	42.7	52.6	40	0.675
8 Japan	38	7.7	8.9	43.3	34	0.472
11 Spain	16	19.9	31.9	43	30	0.617
18 Denmark	3	33	19.2	46.8	42	0.739
19 Germany	8	25.5	25.8	49	35	0.694
31 Chile	61	7.2	20.1	53.9	22	0.416
34 Costa Rica	28	15.8	23.4	45.4	27	0.503
36 Argentina	–	–	–	–	–	–
38 Uruguay	59	6.9	28.2	63.7	34	0.422
45 Panama	44	9.7	27.6	49.2	28	0.46
46 Venezuela	62	6.3	22.9	57.1	27	0.414
49 Mexico	37	14.2	19.8	45.2	26	0.474
53 Colombia	41	9.8	31	44	33	0.47
62 Brazil	68	6.7	17.3	62.6	29	0.374
63 Belize	40	10.8	36.6	38.8	18	0.471
Medium human development	–	–	–	–	36	–
65 Suriname	53	15.7	12.1	61.8	26	0.434
73 Ecuador	69	3.7	27.5	46.6	19	0.369
84 Jamaica	–	–	–	–	–	–
85 Cuba	25	22.8	18.5	47.8	31	0.523
86 Peru	54	10.8	23.8	41.3	24	0.433
88 Dominican Republic	58	10	21.2	49.5	24	0.424
91 Paraguay	67	5.6	22.6	54.1	23	0.374
100 Guyana	39	20	12.8	47.5	27	0.472
111 Guatemala	35	12.5	32.4	45.2	21	0.479
114 El Salvador	34	15.5	25.7	44.1	34	0.48
116 Bolivia	65	3.7	28.3	42.2	27	0.393
159 Haiti	71	3.6	32.6	39.3	36	0.356
All developing countries	–	8.6	–	–	32	–
Least developed countries	–	–	–	–	–	–
Industrial countries	–	15.3	–	–	37	–
World	–	11.8	–	–	33	–

nomic growth, almost half of Chilean households had average monthly incomes of U.S.$ 600/month or less in 1999, although the government, using official definitions of poverty and indigence, classified only 27 percent of households as "poor" or "indigent." Automobiles, most household appliances, and consumer durables cost more in Chile than in Europe or the United States. Credit was much more costly, if gradually more available to middle- and lower-income groups. Many government subsidies for health, education, and transportation had been eliminated after the military government's "modernizations" and privatization of most of the social security and public health systems.

A growing number of households had two wage earners, and Chileans now work much longer hours than they did in the 1960s. In 1997–99, the Asian crisis and rising unemployment levels threatened to erode "the miracle." Chileans of all socioeconomic strata were experiencing the stress of modernization. Rising use of drugs, higher levels of street crime, and a feeling of hopelessness and alienation among low-income youth marred "the miracle," emulating a pattern familiar in more developed capitalist societies, including Great Britain and the United States, as well as in much of Latin America in the 1990s.

Electrical power rationing imposed in 1999 by the multinational firms that now controlled the energy sector, when drought reduced the availability of hydroelectric power, added to the economic woes, angered all political sectors, and worried the government as the country approached the primary elections organized by the Concertación to select a candidate for the presidential elections of December 1999. For the first time since 1990, public opinion polls showed less than 50 percent support for the incumbent president. The Ministry of Planning (MIDEPLAN) periodic survey on social and economic conditions (*Encuesta Casen*) in 1998 highlighted one overriding trend: despite declines in the incidence of indigence and poverty since 1990, the degree of income inequality had slightly *increased*.

According to MIDEPLAN, results of the *Encuesta Casen* demonstrated a significant decline in the levels of indigence and poverty from 1990 to 1998. This positive trend–at the beginning of the decade the Casen survey classified almost half the population as poor or indigent–stalled after 1996. The incidence of poor and indigent households remained higher in rural areas (23% of all poor and indigent households), but since approximately 85 percent of the population resided in urban places, most poor and indigent households were urban.

With careful macroeconomic management, the neoliberal "trickle down" model had generated increased employment and real income as long as there existed favorable external conditions. Even under these circumstances, however, no improvement occurred regarding income distribution. The ratio between the top 20 percent of income earners and the bottom 20 percent remained at about 14:1 (see Table 11–11). If not for government income transfers and subsidies to low-income families, income concentration would have been slightly worse. Thus despite robust economic performance and well-intentioned social policies, the *Concertación* governments from 1990–2000 failed to improve the patterns of social and economic inequality inherited from the military regime. Some observers argued that, indeed, intensification of the neoliberal policies, especially privatization; deemphasis of public health and education; and weak regulatory policies worsened the tendencies engendered by the dictatorship.

The chasm separating upperclass Chileans from those at the bottom of the social hierarchy remained the principal feature of the social topography. The top 10 percent of households accounted for a bit more than 41 percent of income; the bottom 30 percent

TABLE 11-8. CHILE 1998 AND THE UNITED NATIONS DEVELOPMENT
PROGRAMME GENDER-RELATED DEVELOPMENT INDEX

	Gender-related development index (GDI) rank	Life expectancy at birth (years) 1995, Female	Life expectancy at birth (years) 1995, Male	Adult literacy rate (%) 1995, Female	Adult literacy rate (%) 1995, Male
High human development	–	76.79	70.27	95.23	96.16
1 Canada	1	81.78	76.28	99	99
2 France	7	82.64	74.37	99	99
3 Norway	2	80.48	74.65	99	99
4 USA	6	79.69	72.99	99	99
8 Japan	13	82.83	76.71	99	99
11 Spain	19	81.34	74.08	96.1	98.2
30 Korea, Rep. of	37	75.43	68.05	96.69	99.28
31 Chile	**46**	**78.01**	**72.16**	**94.96**	**95.4**
34 Costa Rica	39	79.01	74.34	94.95	94.72
36 Argentina	48	76.23	69.12	96.19	96.23
38 Uruguay	31	75.94	69.45	97.67	96.89
45 Panama	42	75.56	71.42	90.22	91.37
46 Venezuela	43	75.28	69.51	90.34	91.79
49 Mexico	49	75.12	69.19	87.41	91.84
53 Colombia	41	73.07	67.67	91.38	91.23
62 Brazil	56	70.72	62.76	83.21	83.32
63 Belize	72	75.57	72.86	70	70
64 Libyan Arab Jamahiriya	79	66.26	62.78	63.01	87.93
Medium human development	–	69.68	65.35	76.93	89.53
65 Suriname	63	73.44	68.45	90.96	95.1
72 Russian Federation	53	72.08	59.18	99	99
73 Ecuador	78	72.16	66.99	88.22	92.04
84 Jamaica	65	76.34	71.91	89.11	80.81
85 Cuba	69	77.64	73.86	95.29	96.17
86 Peru	80	70.19	65.33	82.96	94.54
87 Jordan	90	70.84	67.02	79.36	93.39
88 Dominican Republic	81	72.39	68.3	82.24	82.01
91 Paraguay	89	71.36	66.83	90.61	93.5
100 Guyana	95	67.05	60.26	97.49	98.65
111 Guatemala	113	68.67	63.65	57.2	72.8
116 Bolivia	110	62.13	58.89	76	90.51
119 Honduras	114	71.2	66.49	72.7	72.63
126 Nicaragua	115	69.93	65.16	66.62	64.65
Low human development	–	57.46	55.9	38.34	62.96
131 Myanmar	120	60.55	57.25	77.69	88.73
158 Senegal	149	51.3	49.3	23.2	43.05
159 Haiti	144	56.28	52.9	42.2	48.05
174 Sierra Leone	163	36.27	33.25	18.19	45.39
All developing countries	–	63.67	60.78	61.82	78.86
Least developed countries	–	52.3	50.03	39.3	59.19
Industrial countries	–	77.9	70.36	98.5	98.76
World	–	65.37	61.92	71.48	83.71

Combined first-, secondary-, and third-level gross enrollment ratio (%) 1995, Female	Combined first-, secondary-, and third-level gross enrollment ratio (%) 1995, Male	Share of earned income (%) 1995, Female	Share of earned income (%) 1995, Male	GDI value (1995)	HDI rank minus GDI rank
79.03	75.51	34.41	65.59	0.8604	–
100	100	37.958	62.042	0.94	0
91	87	39.115	60.885	0.925	–5
93	92	42.356	57.644	0.935	1
98	93	40.301	59.699	0.927	–2
77	79	34.053	65.947	0.902	–5
94	87	29.7	70.3	0.877	–8
78.43	65.92	29.192	70.808	0.826	–8
72.06	64.71	22.02	77.98	0.783	–16
68.3	59.49	26.873	73.127	0.818	–6
80.62	68.69	22.097	77.903	0.777	–13
79.57	65.1	33.731	66.269	0.841	6
73.06	63.35	27.837	72.163	0.804	1
68.43	57.95	27.143	72.857	0.79	1
66.14	63.97	25.734	74.266	0.774	–2
70.66	62.74	33.489	66.511	0.81	8
71.8	69.1	29.267	70.733	0.751	–1
74.11	72.87	18.462	81.538	0.689	–16
89	85.48	16.297	83.703	0.664	–22
63.67	64.93	36.38	63.62	0.6559	–
71	71	26.11	73.89	0.735	–5
82	75	41.309	58.691	0.757	12
68.86	64.27	18.618	81.382	0.667	–12
68.85	63.43	39.171	60.829	0.724	12
67.26	62.12	31.456	68.544	0.705	9
76.13	72.03	23.801	76.199	0.664	–1
66	66	19.093	80.907	0.647	–10
73.95	63.61	24.022	75.978	0.662	0
63.02	61.07	23.243	76.757	0.651	–5
65.76	58.79	26.929	73.071	0.63	–3
41.71	46.54	21.325	78.675	0.549	–10
63.47	65.83	26.806	73.194	0.557	–2
61.32	56.23	24.383	75.617	0.544	–3
65.69	59.74	28.329	71.671	0.526	1
39.51	52.22	28.64	71.36	0.388	–
47.53	46.42	42.328	57.672	0.478	1
27.89	36.51	35.096	64.904	0.326	–1
27.99	29.55	35.982	64.018	0.335	5
23.68	35.66	29.211	70.789	0.165	0
53.06	58.9	32.42	67.58	0.564	–
30.85	40.32	34.29	65.71	0.3324	–
83.98	81.57	38.02	61.98	0.8879	–
58.07	62.51	33.71	66.29	0.7365	–

TABLE 11–9. CHILE 1999: A MARKETING PERSPECTIVE OF THE SOCIAL PYRAMID*

A: High, 4% B. Upper middle, 10%	Average family monthly income: U.S.$8000	Professionals, business executives, entrepreneurs, businessmen, diplomats, officials of international organizations; average educational levels, 17–20 years; 100% have modern automobiles, especially Mercedes Benz, BMW, Volvo, etc; 100% have private phones, often with unlisted numbers; usually at least 2 domestic household workers, often servants and a chauffeur, who dress well and are educated
C1: Middle, 6%	Average monthly income: U.S.$4700	Professionals, doctors, lawyers, engineers, middle-level business executives, small business proprietors, small commercial farm operators; 14–17 years of education; 95% have an auto no more than 4 years old; most have two cars; 100% with private phones; 80% have domestic household workers, generally "live-in," sometimes more than one
C2: Middle, 20%	Average monthly income: U.S.$1,700	Young professionals and business executives, technicians, proprietors of small businesses, salesmen, merchants, salaried employees; 10–12 years of education; 80% have relatively modern cars, worth up to U.S.$12,500; 85% have private phones; if they have domestic household workers, usually not "live-in" and often "by-the-day"
C3: Middle, 4%	Average monthly family income: U.S.$1,000	Salaried employees in public or private sector, specialized workers, teachers, taxi owners; 10–14 years of education; 55% have an automobile, usually worth no more than U.S.$8000; 75% have a private phone, usually no domestic household workers, unless both spouses employed
D: Lower, 35%	Average monthly family income: U.S.$600	Workers, low-level white collar; janitors, messengers, domestic workers, seamstress; 6–10 years education; 15% have cars 10 year old or less, usually valued at less than U.S.$5000; 45% have private phones; almost never have domestic workers
E. Poverty level, 10%	Average monthly family U.S. income: U.S.$250	Day workers; earn less than minimum wage; education 2–4 years; no car; no private phone; no domestic workers

*Percentages in table do not add to 100% (rounded to 99%).

for less than 10 percent. (Of course, Chile shared this general pattern of increasing income inequalities in the 1990s with the United States, most of Latin America, and parts of Europe). Added to the failures of constitutional and political reform and the inability to resolve the human rights legacy of the dictatorship, the persistent social and economic inequalities made ever more poignant the often-asked question, "*What sort of democracy is this?*" It also made more understandable the unwillingness of youthful vot-

TABLE 11–10. CHILE: INCIDENCE OF POVERTY AND INDIGENCE, 1990–98,
BY PERCENTAGE OF POPULATION AND HOUSEHOLDS

Year	Indigents (1000)	Percent	Poor (1000)	Percent	Indigent households	Percent	Poor households	Percent
1990	1,659,300	12.9	4,965,600	38.6	336,300	10.6	1,056,500	33.3
1992	1,169,300	8.8	4,331,700	32.6	242,400	7.2	932,500	27.7
1994	1,036,200	7.6	3,780,000	27.5	219,300	6.2	820,500	23.2
1996	813,800	5.8	3,288,300	23.2	178,800	4.9	706,800	19.7
1998	820,000	5.6	3.160,100	21.7	173,900	4.7	666,000	17.8

Source: MIDEPLAN, División Social, Resultados de la Encuesta CASEN, 1998.

TABLE 11–11. CHILE: PERCENT DISTRIBUTION OF HOUSEHOLD
MONEY INCOME, BY DECILES, 1990–98

Deciles	Distribution of Money Income (%)				
	1990	1992	1994	1996	1998
1	1.6	1.7	1.5	1.4	1.4
2	2.8.	2.9	2.8	2.7	2.7
3	3.7	3.8	3.6	3.6	3.6
4	4.5	4.7	4.6	4.6	4.6
5	5.4	5.6	5.6	5.5	5.4
6	6.9	6.6	6.4	6.4	6.4
7	7.8	8.0	8.0	8.1	8.3
8	10.3	10.4	10.5	11.0	10.9
9	15.1	14.7	15.3	15.4	15.9
10	41.8	41.6	41.6	41.3	41.0
Total	100.0	100.0	100.0	100.0	100.0
20/20	12.9	12.2	13.2	13.8	13.9

Source: MIDEPLAN, Encuesta CASEN, 1998.

ers to register, the rising abstention rates and spoiled ballots in the 1997 elections, and the increased number of protest movements among university students and environmental activists (1997–99).

Further concentration of ownership of the mass media also accompanied increased concentration of income and economic power in the 1990s. The magazines that had resisted the military dictatorship gradually disappeared: *Cauce, Análisis, Apsi.* Market forces also eliminated *La Época* and *Fortín Mapocho,* the newspapers that had challenged the ideological dominance of *El Mercurio,* and its late afternoon sister, *La Segunda. Que Pasa,* which had become the most important political and economic weekly, passed into the hands of the newer media conglomerate, Copesa, which controlled *La Tercera* (the most widely read newspaper) and *La Cuarta* (a popular tabloid). Although Copesa competed with the El Mercurio group, still controlled by the Edwards family, between the two they controlled almost 90 percent of newspaper advertising. Television news likewise was homogenized and broadcasters routinely exercised self-censorship.

In contrast, while the transition to civilian government seemed to reduce journalistic pluralism, it also brought a spate of new book publishers and a vigorous output of history, social science, and social commentary by younger scholars and others denied the possibility of making their views known in the 1980s. Research centers and academic departments expanded work on nineteenth-century and modern Chile, a development unforeseeable in the mid-1980s. For their controversial and critical views, none of these authors suffered imprisonment, torture, or exile, though Alejandra Matus, a journalist who wrote a critical book on the court system (*The Black Book of Chilean Justice*) found the study censored and herself subject to arrest for defamation of a Supreme Court Justice. She fled the country. In accord with the times, the book circulated widely on the Internet. Matus requested, and received, political asylum in the United States—a bitter pill for a Chilean government that had proclaimed its commitment to democratization.

Dissatisfaction with the pace, style, and achievements of the political transition could not be equated with "no change at all." The pervasive fear that the dictatorship had spread through the country dissipated, despite the ongoing battles over impunity for human rights violations and tensions in civil-military relations. Economic recession encouraged renewed criticism of the neoliberal model, especially its impact on the most vulnerable groups in society. Few Chileans longed for the return of military rule. As the country approached its third presidential election since 1989, general Pinochet's fate in England, or Spain, remained uncertain, as did the long-term survival of the particular version of "protected democracy" that he had imposed. But even as Chileans looked toward the future, they daily confronted unfinished business with the past.

Epilogue

Living *with the legacies* of the military regime was not the same as living *under* the military regime. The country approached September 11, 1998, with a new army commander and General Pinochet ensconced in the Senate—a "senator for life" (*senador vitalicio*) as provided for in the 1980 constitution. Congress had eliminated September 11 as a national holiday, although it had been replaced with the "day of national unity" scheduled for the first week of September each year. Chileans hardly lived in the best of all possible worlds, but they seemed to be doing better than most other Latin Americans.

On the occasion of president Eduardo Frei Ruiz-Tagle's last state of the nation message to Congress on May 21, 1999, legislators of the right-wing UDI party delivered a note to the British ambassador protesting her presence in the Congress, unfolded a banner protesting Pinochet's detention in England, and unceremoniously abandoned the building, amidst fisticuffs between themselves and pro-government legislators. International television broadcast these embarrassing images of the Chilean legislature as protesters insulted each other and stoned police outside Congress in downtown Valparaíso. Nine days remained before the primary elections. For the first time since 1990 fractures in the Concertación coalition threatened the political framework that had evolved since 1988. Political propaganda distributed in upperclass neighborhoods ominously reminded voters of the "mistake" the country had made in 1970 and of the terrible consequences that followed: Allende, Popular Unity, shortages, violence, a military coup. A new campaign of fear and terror seemed in the making in anticipation of the presidential elections of 1999. Rumblings in the barracks and the military academies regarding the detention of Pinochet and economic issues affecting the armed forces elicited memories of the 1969 coup attempt against Frei Ruiz-Tagle's father, then-president Eduardo Frei Montalva.

In May 1999, the political ambience was almost as dense as Santiago's polluted air, which once again had forced the government to declare an "environmental alert" the week before the state of the nation message. If many Chileans wanted to take a deep breath and restore the calm, they literally choked as increasing levels of particulates and ozone exacerbated the effects of the first flu epidemic of the approaching winter. Television news broadcasters interviewed women waiting in long lines at the overloaded public health clinics and hospitals for health professionals to attend their children. The "Chilean miracle" seemed flawed. Chileans asked themselves why public services and utilities betrayed their trust, why environmental conditions continued to deteriorate, when the economy would recover, and whether the government coalition could survive the results of the primary election. They also wondered out loud if the armed forces would "tolerate" a victory in December 1999 by Socialist party candidate Ricardo Lagos, the same Lagos who had pointed his finger at Pinochet and denounced him on television during the media campaign accompanying the 1988 plebiscite.

No one in Chile doubted the military's continued influence in politics, although disagreement existed over its reach and prospects for the future. Army commander General Ricardo Izurieta scheduled meetings with the high command and "private" encounters with retired officers of the Círculo de Oficiales en Retiro de las Fuerzas Armadas in which he lambasted government policies toward the armed forces, complained of erosion of salaries and resources, and denounced the government's lack of energetic efforts to rescue Pinochet and uphold Chilean sovereignty. Shortly after the president's May 21 state of the nation address to congress, Izurieta scheduled a seminar for 1200 young officers at the Escuela Militar to remind them of the "real history" of the military regime, a history that military sources claimed was being denigrated by the very groups who had caused the tragedy of 1973. The army scheduled similar seminars in bases across the country as the armed forces explicitly and directly re-engaged in the important battle for the definition of the country's official history. Army officers publicly declared that controlling the interpretation of the country's recent past was a critical task in defining its present and its future.

On the left, adding to the rising tensions, demonstrators in anti-Pinochet rallies and political campaigns chanted pro-Allende slogans and resuscitated the menacing rhetoric of the recent past: *avanzar sin transar* (advance without compromise). Labor conflict increased; protesting students occupied universities for days or weeks at a time, suspending classes and demanding more government support for education, scholarships, and student loans. Indian activists and their supporters damaged property and vehicles of lumber companies in the south, renewing historical claims on thousands of acres of land lost to the onslaught of the Chilean army and settlers from the late nineteenth century until the present. Human rights organizations demanded information on the fate of the "disappeared," for "the truth" on the crimes of the dictatorship, for "justice" and repentance. Plaintiffs brought new criminal and civil charges against military officers for human rights violation, and a renovated Supreme Court modified its interpretation of the 1978 amnesty to allow the reopening of investigations into certain cases—a signal to the armed forces that could not be ignored.

President Frei did nothing to challenge the general's "seminars" for the officer corps nor to discipline him for outspoken remarks on the status of Pinochet, the role of the army in politics, and the barely veiled threats to civilian politicians. Of course, the Armed Forces Organic Laws, a last-minute legacy of the military regime (March 1989), prevented Frei, even had he wished to, from firing General Izurieta or commanders of the other armed forces. As Pinochet had intended, the civilian government was constrained (*"atado y bien atado"*). But rumblings in the ranks concerned the high command. New and reactivated judicial inquiries into high profile cases of human rights abuses and the expanding investigation against Pinochet himself by Spanish Judge Baltasar Garzón and by Chilean judge Juan Guzmán, who was assigned the numerous cases brought against the ex-dictator by human rights organizations and victims' families, augured poorly for continued military solidarity.

Amongst the older generation, some retired officers sought peace with themselves, and perhaps with God and society, by breaking the vows of silence, acknowledging their crimes, and providing information regarding the fate of the "disappeared." Among younger officers, especially in the Air Force and Navy, there existed a desire to be done with "the past." Even in the army the shadow of Pinochet and his hard-core loyalists generated some resentment. In June 1999 the Spanish newspaper *El País* reported that a retired Chilean colonel had revealed that Pinochet's personal helicopter pilot had told him that many of the "disappeared" had been thrown into the sea; others, still alive, were dropped from helicopters into the Andes. The colonel also claimed that bodies of some of the "disappeared" were buried on military bases (*terrenos militares*).

In response, rightist politicians and military officers of all branches attempted again to negotiate a "final settlement" of the human rights issue. Could they trade information and the "truth" for a *ley de punto final?* Would the victims' families, the human rights organizations, the political left, and the Concertación government accept a South African solution: truth for impunity? Could the 1978 amnesty law be expanded to include crimes committed until March 1990 or even until the assassination of Jaime Guzmán in 1991? If so, at what price? If not, were there groups in the armed forces that would put a stop to the resurgent demands for truth and justice by force?

Both the Aylwin and Frei governments had sought unsuccessfully to "close the book" on the crimes of state terrorism. Nevertheless, the smoldering embers that Pinochet declared should be "doused with a bucket of water" in an 1989 interview threatened to burst anew into flames in mid-1999. Pinochet granted an interview in England to journalist Dominic Lawson, which was published in the *Guardian* and translated in *El Mercurio de Valparaíso* and *La Tercera.* He denied that he had authorized torture during his government, accepting "political responsibility" for any excesses but not "criminal responsibility." He claimed that he hadn't had time to supervise the methods used to save the country from the scourge of international communism. When Lawson commented that Pinochet had been a general all his life, but had answered the interview questions like a politician, Pinochet responded: "I am a General of the Republic of Chile. I never liked politicians." And with that,

> Pinochet moved slowly and stiffly, his back absolutely rigid and upright, into the garden to join his grandchildren. Captain Torres [his aide] dutifully began blowing up an inflatable paddling pool. As I watched the general sitting playing with his grandchildren, the thought kept coming into my mind that he reminded me very much of someone else, someone I had seen, but never met. The strangely hoarse, muffled voice; the great stress, at all times, on "respect"; the somewhat courtly manner of expression; the Catholicism; the ruthless paternalist in great old age, much loved by his grandchildren. And then I realised who it was that Pinochet reminded me of: the aged Don Corleone, in *The Godfather,* as acted by Marlon Brando. Augusto Pinochet Ugarte, however, is the genuine article.

On May 30, 1999, the Concertación coalition sponsored the first-ever national primary election to select the coalition's presidential candidate for the December elections. Voters overwhelmingly supported Ricardo Lagos (71%) over the Christian Democratic candidate, Andrés Zaldívar (29%). As election day got under way, a massive power black-out affected Santiago and the central valley for three hours; government spokespersons and politicians speculated that the outage was not accidental but rather a less than subtle reminder that the real centers of "power" in the country had serious concerns about Lagos' possible election as president. Two days later, Pinochet's most important adviser from 1990 to 1994, retired General Jorge Ballerino, appeared in a television interview to express his displeasure with the possibility of a "Marxist" president; another retired general asserted that Lagos' candidacy threatened the "return of Allendismo and the Unidad Popular."

Lagos attempted to convince the Armed Forces, private investors, and public opinion that times had changed, that his previous support of Salvador Allende and participation in the Popular Unity Government (1970–73) posed no threat to them in the year 2000. As expected, the political right initiated a propaganda campaign associating Lagos with "the past"—seeking to use the lingering fear in Chilean society of renewed polarization as a barrier to his election. But Chilean voters were more concerned with the present: the recession, rising unemployment rates (over 600,000 officially unemployed in July 1999, exceeding 10% of the work force for the first time in over a decade), lack of affordable health insurance and medical services, and fear of street crime. From the left, the Communist party candidate, Gladys Marín, accused Lagos of being merely a continuation of the last ten years, a "renovated" socialist who would do nothing to overcome the misery generated by the neoliberal model imposed by the dictatorship and managed for the last ten years by the Concertación.

Ten years of truce, of conflict management via "prudence and moderation," had mitigated some of the ills afflicting the body politic, but the recent past still haunted the present. On September 6, 1999, the country "celebrated" the new "Day of National Unity" with small protest demonstrations, "acts of repudiation," scattered barricades, and bonfires in poor neighborhoods in Santiago. Government spokespersons barely mentioned the holiday. Not even presidential candidates showed their faces, choosing private meetings or "prayers for unity" rather than public ceremonies. Ugly incidents occurred between members of the Agrupación de Familiares de Detenidos-Desaparecidos and two senators—one an ex-commander of the Carabineros—who went to place a floral wreath on the monument dedicated to the *detenidos-desaparecidos*. The senators were insulted and chased out of the cemetery, accused of defiling the memories of the "victims of fascism." Army commander General Ricardo Izurieta managed to be in the far south with the Minister of Public Works inaugurating the last section of the Carretera Austral ("the southern highway") that "unified" the Aisén region to the north after eight years of work by the army's engineer corps (Cuerpo de Trabajo Militar). Izurieta artlessly compared the symbol of unity of the highway with the "army's ongoing commitment to national unity."

In Santiago, one of the two main "inventors" of the new holiday, Andrés Zaldívar, lamented the incidents in the cemetery and concluded: "the conditions and spirit necessary for reconciliation still don't exist in Chile; there is too much pending business regarding truth and justice." The other "inventor" of the holiday, General Pinochet, remained detained in England. Confirming Zaldívar's affirmation, the Communist party presidential candidate, Gladys Marín, declared that "the 'Day of National Unity' doesn't exist and it is a step backward that they have decreed it when the country has yet to resolve such fundamental issues as those regarding human rights." Outside Santiago, *El Mercurio* reported that "in the Valparaíso Region there were no public celebrations of the Day of National Unity and in Temuco human rights organizations scheduled a nighttime vigil outside the Tucapel army regiment's headquarters, opposite the Plaza Recabarren." Further south, the Bishop of Osorno, Alejandro Goic, called on Chileans and all believers to make every effort so that the new holiday would really be an "occasion for promoting unity" (*jornada de unión*). Four days later came September 11, then the annual "independence day" celebration on September 18. The country waited for the always eventful month of September to unfold and looked toward the December presidential elections.

On September 11 the country saw the usual processions to the cemetery, the wreaths placed at Morandé 80 (the former location of the door to La Moneda palace used by Allende), and also the reaffirmations of the military coup by the Augusto Pinochet Ugarte Foundation and other loyal partisans of Pinochet and the military government. Fewer deaths and injuries resulted on September 11, 1999, than in years past, but the bitterness remained.

Antagonistic memories of the recent past still divided the country in the present. Yet the Navy Commander had finally acknowledged in public statements that human rights abuses had occurred during the military government—although he insisted that they were not government policy but simply "individual excesses." The Army still resisted the gesture made by the Navy, but in an interview published in the Concepción newspaper *El Sur* on September 12, 1999, Senator José Viera-Gallo claimed that in private conversations some generals had referred to those involved in the "caravan of death" case in 1973 as "murderers and psychopaths." In contrast, ex–Minister of Justice during the military government and author of the 1978 amnesty, Monica Madariaga, called on the government to cancel the annual military parade (September 19) because of Pinochet's detention in England and the "state of grief" within the armed forces. Two days later the president of the Senate read a letter sent from Pinochet to Chileans, calling for "reconciliation and national unity"; the same day newspapers headlined the arrest of the ex-director of the CNI and ex-member of the military junta, General Humberto Gordon. Gordon, who retired as a four-star general, the same rank held by army commander General Ricardo Izurieta in September 1999, was charged in the murder of labor leader Tucapel Jiménez in 1982—a crime not covered by the 1978 amnesty decree. (Gordon died in June, 2000 with the case still unresolved.) On September 18, 1999, Archbishop Francisco Javier Errázuriz's homily told attendees at the Te Deum mass in Santiago's Cathedral: "We shall soon celebrate the 2000th anniversary of the arrival to this world of Jesus Christ, Word of the Father to Humanity. We pray that he inspire our gratitude and our communication with God, . . . and that with Him and Our Lady of Reconciliation, we construct a Nation of brothers."

In less spectacular, but perhaps equally important news reports, Chileans learned that a court, for the first time, had temporarily stopped worked on a major hydroelectric project (the Ralco dam) because conditions of the environmental impact report had not been met. The stoppage was successfully appealed by the contractor and by CONAMA, but it represented an important milestone in environmental and ethnic politics. Those protesting the project in this case were a small group of Mapuche Indians. A week later the Temuco Appeals Court sanctioned a municipal government official for "racial discrimination" against a Mapuche social worker, Bernardita Calfuqueo. The growing autonomy of the judicial system was beginning to make a difference, however small, not only in civil-military relations, but also in the application of environmental, anti-discrimination, and indigenous legislation. As the 1990s ended, the historical impunity of the powerful and wealthy no longer seemed absolutely secure in Chile.

On October 8, 1999, a British judge ruled that General Pinochet should be extradited to Spain for trial on charges related to torture, murder, and the cases of the *detenidos-desaparecidos*, defined by the judge as ongoing torture of the victims' families.

I find that the information before me relating to allegations after 8th December 1988 constitutes a course of conduct amounting to torture and conspiracy to torture for which Senator Pinochet enjoys no immunity. . . . I take the view that information relating to the allegation of conspiracy prior to 8th December 1988 can be considered by the court, since conspiracy is a continuing offence. However, this would not be my ruling relating to the substantive offences.

Whether the disappearances amount to torture; the effect on the families of those who disappeared can amount to mental torture. Whether or not this was intended by the regime of Senator Pinochet is in my view a matter of fact for the trial court.

On the basis of my findings I am therefore satisfied that all the conditions are in place which oblige me under the terms of Section 9(8) of the Extradition Act 1989 to commit Senator Pinochet to await the decision of the Secretary of State.

By November, General Izurieta and the army high command grew more than impatient with the spectacle of officers testifying in criminal proceedings. Izurieta objected publicly to the reinterpretation of the amnesty decree that permitted investigation into the "ongoing cases" (cases where no bodies had been found). At mid-month the Conference of Catholic Bishops called on the British government to return Pinochet to Chile for "humanitarian reasons"—he was old and infirm.

Meanwhile the social and economic legacy of the military government also exerted its continued influence. On November 14, 1999, *El Mercurio de Valparaíso* reported that the Port of Valparaíso had passed into private hands. With no government officials in attendance and punctuated by violent protests by approximately fifty port workers who burned tires on Avenida Errázuriz, Terminal 1 began a new era controlled by the German-Chilean consortium: Terminal Pacífico Sur, S.A., a partnership of the Ultramar Group and Hamburger Hafen und Lagerhaus Aktiengesellshaft (HHLA). Police broke up the protests. A spokesman for the new port enterprise claimed that within eighteen months efficiency of container debarkation would greatly increase, creating benefits for all Chileans by modernizing the port operations. He acknowledged that some workers would have to look for jobs elsewhere.

A month later Chileans went to the polls to select a new president. On December 12, 1999, no candidate received the necessary majority to be elected. The rightist candidate, Joaquín Lavín, ran a surprisingly strong campaign, appealing to what he called the voters' "real needs" in a highly populistic and costly media blitz that featured the slogan *"viva el cambio"*—"Long live change!" Ricardo Lagos, candidate of the Concertación coalition, was saddled with the recent legacy of the recession and the frustration of some voters with the two post-1990 governments' inability to reform the 1980 constitution and their unwillingness to modify the economic system introduced by the military regime. Lavín, author of a book praising the "silent revolution" achieved after 1973, promised to replace traditional politics with a government that worked for "all Chileans." His energy, youthfulness (age 46), and promises appealed especially to the feminine vote, as evidenced by his margin of approximately 5 percent over Lagos among women voters. Overall, Lavín obtained some 47.5 percent and Lagos 48 percent. The relatively small percentage of votes for minor party, environmental, and personalist candidates was enough to force a run-off election, scheduled for January 16, 2000.

The Concertación coalition and its supporters faced the prospect of a return to government of officials and consultants of the Pinochet government. Many of Lavín's advisers and supporters had worked in the military government, as had Lavín himself. Associating himself with the "economic miracle" and seeking to dissociate himself from the human rights abuses of the military regime, Lavín successfully appealed to voters tired of the "politics of the past" and focused on concrete issues such as jobs, health care, crime, and housing. In contrast, Lagos' slogan "growth with equity" did not catch on; many voters wondered why the Concertación had not done a better job for the last ten years. Lagos also bore the burden of the "natural" attrition of a governing coalition after a decade in power. For some sectors, including some Christian Democrats, he also still symbolized the conflicts of the Allende years—something not to be repeated.

Shortly before the January run-off, the British government announced that a team of doctors had found General Pinochet medically unfit to stand trial, that he would likely be returned to Chile rather than extradited to Spain. Both Lavín and Lagos attempted to skirt the "Pinochet issue," taking the tack that it was an issue for courts to resolve, not the presidential candidates—although both affirmed that it was a matter for Chile and Chileans to settle rather than for British, Spanish, or other foreign authorities.

Faced with a virtual tie between Lavín and Lagos in the opinion polls, the Concertación electoral organization appointed a prominent Christian Democratic woman, Soledad Alvear, to direct the run-off campaign. Lagos promised voters jobs, housing, better health care, more police protection for their neighborhoods, improved educational opportunities from pre-school through the university, and a sports field and cultural center in every neighborhood. On his Internet Web site, below these electoral promises, Lagos signed his name and wrote "I give my word" (*"Te doy mi palabra"*). Critics said that Lagos had "Lavínized" his campaign, succumbing to populist promise-making.

If so, it worked. Ricardo Lagos obtained 51.3 percent of the votes on January 16, 2000. He declared that he would be "the president of all Chileans" and the third president of the Concertación coalition (rather than the second socialist president of Chile). Lagos still lost among women voters, although the margin was reduced to only 3 percent: Ricardo Lagos E. (48.65%), Joaquín Lavín I. (51.35%). Among male voters, the Concertación outdistanced Lavín's Alianza por Chile coalition by almost 10 percent: Ricardo Lagos E. (54.27%), Joaquín Lavín I. (45.73%). Political pundits speculated that fear of a "return to the chaos of the past"—a political code for the shortages, rationing, food lines, and political violence of 1970–73—had most influenced female voters because the burden of dealing with "the past" had fallen disproportionately on women, especially in the poorest neighborhoods, where the Lavín campaign had been surprisingly successful. But Lavín also won an important victory in the Valparaíso region—and in that district the female vote for Lavín was almost 10 percent greater than for Lagos (54.95% versus 45.05%).

Clearly, the immediate concerns of the Chilean electorate had changed since 1989, although the "Pinochet issue," the "human rights issue," and the underlying lack of consensus regarding the political system imposed in 1980 persisted. All these concerns now reflected the blurring of international and national politics and political economy. The Chile of 2000, more than ever before, faced the opportunities and challenges resulting from the erosion of its geographical isolation and its intensified incorporation into diverse global networks.

Chileans experienced a moment of hope as Joaquín Lavín immediately congratulated Lagos on his victory and offered to cooperate with the newly elected president in the task of national reconciliation. Lavín also reaffirmed his campaign messages: "I am at Ricardo Lagos' disposition to help overcome the real problems of our people, to defeat crime, to end unemployment, to improve the living conditions of the poorest Chileans, in concrete ways, without the meanness of petty politics, and without questioning the consensus on the nature of our economic system. I am also at his disposition to work for the unity of Chileans." Lagos responded with a call for Chileans to "leave behind the hatreds and rancor of the past," urging them to put the interests of the *Patria* above "politics" and private interests. Both the victor and the defeated candidate seemed to share the dream of national unity and political reconciliation.

Ricardo Lagos had written in 1993 (*Después de la Transición*) that "the triumph in the plebiscite [the defeat of Pinochet in 1988] was the most important historical event in Chile in the second half of the twentieth century. . . . We won the right to dream again and to construct the future." In early 2000, Chileans awaited Lagos' inauguration and

TABLE E–1. PRESIDENTIAL ELECTIONS, 1999/2000

	December 12, 1999	January 16, 2000 (Run-off)
Ricardo Lagos Escobar (Concertación)	48.0%	51.3%
Joaquín Lavín Infante (Alianza por Chile)	47.5%	48.7%
Gladys Marín Millie (Communist party)	3.2%	
Tomás Hirsch Goldschmidt (Humanist party)	0.5%	
Sara Larraín Ruiz-Tagle (Environmentalist)	0.4%	
Arturo Frei Bolívar (UCC, ex–Christian Democrat)	0.4%	

Source: Ministry of Interior.

speculated on the possible implications of Pinochet's return to the country. The last day of January an Associated Press report, like many that flashed across the Internet, informed readers that "Pinochet, who has diabetes and suffered two small strokes last fall, remains under police guard at a rented mansion west of London. A Chilean air force Boeing 707 sent to fetch him is parked at a military base northwest of London." Two months later, a week before Lagos' inauguration on March 11, the British government decided, for "humanitarian reasons," to return Pinochet to Chile. Received triumphantly by the armed forces, Pinochet almost immediately faced a legal challenge (*proceso de desafuero*) to his congressional immunity from prosecution (*fuero parlamentario*) extended to him as a result of his position as "senator for life." The *desafuero* process rekindled the embers of discord, dividing Chileans once again over the proper historical interpretation of the recent past and the course for the future.

As Lagos approached his first address to congress (May 21, 2000), the legacy of the military regime's human rights abuses and the determined opposition of victims, family members, and anti-Pinochet political groups to forgetting the past in the name of the future held hostage the government's program of constitutional and political reform. The *desafuero* process and the criminal prosecutions threatened to open a veritable Pandora's box. Tensions intensified when the Santiago Appeals Court ruled against Pinochet, removing his immunity from prosecution; his lawyers immediately appealed to the Supreme Court. By mid-July Pinochet faced over 140 separate criminal actions. The hardcore human rights movements and their lawyers were prepared to fight Pinochet's impunity until his death, determined to make sure that history remembered him as a tyrant and a criminal.

In June 2000 the "Mesa de Diálogo" reached an agreement regarding a new process for searching for the remains of the disappeared. Congress rapidly passed legislation protecting potential informants, and the armed forces' commanders agreed to cooperate in the investigation. As part of the agreement, for the first time, the armed forces officially recognized that "agents of the state" had engaged in human rights violations during the military government and that measures should be taken to guarantee that this never occur again. Some of the *agrupaciones* and human rights lawyers denounced the agreement negotiated in the Mesa de Diálogo as a prelude to confirming impunity, especially if the 1978 amnesty decree were eventually applied to cases in which human remains were found—ending the legal fiction of "ongoing kidnappings" (*secuestros calificados*). But most Chileans had finally accepted the impossibility of repealing or annulling the 1978 amnesty; they hoped that the victims' families could somehow learn the "truth" regarding their loved ones' deaths, and that the past could be put behind, if not forgotten.

The mounting number of criminal cases against retired officers and Pinochet himself held hostage any meaningful political reconciliation. Although Church officials and some politicians still used the term "reconciliation," the public statement issued by the Mesa de Diálogo appealed instead to *convivencia*, a mixture of political civility and tolerance, rather than the more utopian goal of reconciliation.

The Lagos government preferred to allow the courts to handle the Pinochet matter and other criminal cases, to separate the issues of constitutional and institutional reform from Pinochet's personal fate, and to move forward with social and economic policies designed to improve income distribution and the living conditions of the majority of the population. The political right and the leaders of the armed forces hesitated to entirely unlink support for constitutional reform, however limited (for example, eliminating the designated senators and the *senadores vitalicios*), from the government's possible influence over the Supreme Court in the Pinochet case. Some UDI and RN politicos called for a *political* solution—perhaps another all-inclusive amnesty or general pardon, perhaps rejection of the legal fiction of the ongoing kidnappings, acknowledging the murders from 1973 to 1978, and thereby applying the 1978 amnesty.

By admitting the murders and other crimes committed before April 1978, Pinochet and the others would be beneficiaries of the amnesty provisions. Pinochet supporters and the armed forces found this "solution" distasteful if not abominable. In their view, almost three decades after saving the country from Marxism, Pinochet (and other military personnel) were being asked to confess to torture, murder, mass executions, and disappearing the victims in order to be beneficiaries of the amnesty decreed by the military regime in 1978. This was hardly the historical legacy they wished to bequeath their beloved Chilean *patria*. The inauguration in June 2000 of a monument to Salvador Allende in the Plaza de la Constitución, on a corner between La Moneda Palace and the Ministry of Justice, further embittered Pinochet's supporters and those who blamed Allende for seeking to impose Marxism on the country in the early 1970s. One particularly irate columnist, Fernando Moreno Valencia, wrote in *El Metropolitano* (June 30, 2000): "We now have [a monument to] the person responsible for the 1000-day effort to install totalitarian Marxism [in Chile] in the Plaza of the Constitution. . . . The effort to bury Pinochet implies resuscitating Allende."

Worse still, on the legal front, even if the legal fiction of kidnapping were replaced with acknowledgment of the murders and the 1978 amnesty applied to pre-1978 cases, all criminal cases after 1978, including many operations of the CNI and the UAT (*unidad anti-terrorista*), directly responsible to Pinochet, would still fall outside the coverage of the 1978 amnesty decree. Continued investigations, prosecutions, newspaper, magazine, and television coverage were besmirching the honor of the armed forces and the historical image of their salvational mission. Retired officers and civilian supporters of the military regime battled to protect and diffuse their version of Chile's recent past, what they regarded as the "true history" of the country's escape from the clutches of international communism.

As the Supreme Court began hearing the appeal by Pinochet's lawyers of the decision by the Santiago Appeals court to strip him of his congressional immunity, the seventh chamber of the same Santiago appeals court sentenced the ex-operations chief of the secret police (CNI), retired army major Alvaro Corbalán, to life-imprisonment for the murder in 1983 of Juan Alegría Mondaca, a carpenter. Other ex-CNI agents were also sentenced for their role in the crime, including Dr. Osvaldo Pincetti Gac, known by prisoners as "doctor torment," who was convicted as an accomplice. Alegría had been killed in 1983, as part of the CNI's effort to cover up its role in the assassination of labor leader Tucapel Jiménez. The Jiménez case was still open, with the responsibility of various officers and agents of the CNI under continuing investigation. Whatever the outcome of the Pinochet *desafuero* appeal, the courts and criminal justice system seemed intent on penetrating the veil of impunity that had protected those guilty of human rights violations during the military government, at least for crimes committed after the amnesty decree of 1978. Conviction for murder and long prison terms for Corbalán and other CNI agents would have been virtually impossible in 1990. The struggle for justice was not without setbacks, but by mid-2000 there existed a growing momentum against impunity and for making *Nunca Más* ("never again") a shared goal of the vast majority of Chileans.

On July 25, 2000 the Supreme Court voted 11 to 9 to deny consideration of Pinochet's health status until after making the decision on the substance of the *desafuero* appeal. The president of the Supreme Court announced that the court would reconvene on Tuesday, August 1, to discuss Pinochet's appeal on the *desafuero* case. Chileans faced another week of judicial limbo on "the Pinochet case"; they also faced another week of "bad to critical" air quality in the capital. SESMA (the Metropolitan Environmental Service) declared an "environmental preemergency," ordering certain private vehicles off the streets and dedicating several main traffic arteries exclusively to public transportation. This measure, called the Red Vial de Emergencia (RVE), was becoming a familiar routine in Santiago in the winter of 2000. Far to the north in Arica, the Ministry of Health announced that dangerous levels of lead were found in blood samples from ninety children, among the first to be tested in a region where over twenty-one tons of industrial wastes, including lead, mercury, arsenic, and cadmium, had been dumped during the last fourteen years. Clearly, the capital's and the country's environmental challenges would endure long after Pinochet's fate was sealed.

The same week that the Supreme Court met to consider Pinochet's appeal, René Ríos Boettiger died. Ríos, who signed his cartoons "Pepo," created Chile's most famous cartoon character, *Condorito*, a half century earlier in 1949. "Pepo" claimed that Condorito was a response to the Walt Disney movie "Saludos Amigos," in which Chile was depicted as a small airplane unable to cross the Andes. Condorito would be a personality that represented Chile's "idiosyncracy," its national spirit and popular culture. The little condor represented "every man" and the common man—sports referee, policeman, astronaut, millionaire, fireman, farmer, lion tamer, waiter, bus driver, bureaucrat, volunteer in the foreign legion. He was too clever by half, lazy, broke, picaresque, versatile, and inept, a country bumpkin and an urban schemer. Condorito's adventures, his family and in-laws, his buddies and his working life transversed frontiers, making the little condor as beloved in Bolivia, Peru, and Argentina as in Chile. Condorito's half-century paralleled Chile's dramatic transformation from a country dominated by the hacienda and rural traditions to a highly urbanized, modernizing society. The little airplane that couldn't cross the Andes now jetted its products all over the world. The death of "Pepo," the end of an era, paralleled the end of the long career of the rustic, clever, scheming, *"huaso"* general Pinochet, whose immediate future was in the hands of the Supreme Court. Long term, however, Pinochet's place in Chilean history could not hope to compete with that of Condorito, a figure beloved by generations of Chileans across ethnic, class, regional, and political lines. Typical of the "new" Chile, in 1999 Condorito had his own website on the Internet, and Microsoft had selected the little condor as an image for its Windows 98 in Ibero-America.

On August 8, 2000, the Supreme Court upheld the ruling of the Santiago Appeals Court, removing Pinochet's congressional immunity by a vote of 14-6. This decision cleared the way for possible prosecution in the "caravan of death" case, and maybe others, depending on Pinochet's medical condition. As expected, the decision reopened debates about the past as well as the future amongst Pinochet's supporters and detractors.

Military officers and leaders of the political right insisted on the need to interpret the past, especially the military coup of 1973 and the repression of opponents by the military government, in light of the grave threat faced by the country in 1973: international communism and its domestic allies. Senator Sergio Diez, the military regime's ex-ambassador to the United Nations who had publicly denied that there existed *detenidos-desaparecidos*, declared that "there is a moral obligation to present the complete truth . . . it wasn't just a case of military officers that set out to destroy democratic governments. . . ."

President Ricardo Lagos insisted again, "I have an agenda and I am going to pursue it. I was elected to govern for the future, not to reconsider what happened in the past. All Chile knows what I think about what happened in the past, but my obligation as president is the future, and that's what I am about." Rhetoric aside, the effort by supporters of the military regime and their adversaries to "interpret" the past was a central part of the present debate—and a key to the country's political future.

Lagos's commitment to administer the future also faced some difficult short-term obstacles, despite his resolute support for the independence of the judiciary and his commitment to tip the balance toward the civilian government in civil-military relations. September, the traditional "month of the Army," unfolded with soap opera-like drama: protests on the "day of national unity" (this year, September 4); the usual demonstrations on September 11, the day of the military coup in 1973; periodic contradictory announcements regarding the human rights cases against various military officers; and warnings by military spokespersons that the decision against Pinochet would derail the agreement reached by the Mesa de Diálogo. New revelations of CIA involvement in Chile in the 1960s and 1970s, along with charges that the ex-commander of the DINA, Manuel Contreras, had been on the CIA payroll added to the drama. Slow economic recovery, rising unemployment (over 10% again in early October), discord within the Concertación coalition, and scandals involving more than generous pensions and severance pay given to political appointees in government and semi-public enterprises between 1990 and 2000 provided grist for the opposition press mill. As the October municipal elections drew near, the Lagos government found itself in apparent disarray. It had temporarily lost much of the moral high ground and floundered in efforts to turn the economy around.

The opposition now agreed to eventual constitutional reforms, in particular to eliminate the designated and lifetime senators—but continued to insist on the need to "close the book on the past." No legislation or political agreement, however, not even a new amnesty law could keep the book on the past firmly shut. Even Pinochet's eventual passing would require reopening the book and making new entries as his contemporaries sought to rewrite and reinterpret "what happened" in Chile in the last three decades of the twentieth century. A poignant sign of what might come was the public statement in early October by ex-junta member and air force general Fernando Matthei, revealing that Pinochet had requested emergency powers from the Junta on the night of the October 5, 1988 plebiscite. According to Matthei, Pinochet intended to send the army into the streets and overturn the victory of the "NO" coalition. Ex-commander of the Carabineros, retired general Rodolfo Stange, remembered the events slightly differently; he *had* also refused to sign the document that Pinochet had prepared on October 5, 1988, but only because the police had the situation under control and the army's help was not needed to maintain order.

More of the "real story" of October 5, 1988 and the events during the year that preceded President Aylwins' inauguration would gradually be made public. Likewise, journalists, historians, and others would continue to research, revise, and rewrite the country's recent political history. Public speculation by members of the Frei family that the DINA had murdered former president Eduardo Frei Montalva in the hospital in 1982 reopened still another unhealed wound. Thousands of documents taken by police from the notorious *Colonia Dignidad,* a redoubt of neo-Nazis whose leaders collaborated with the military regime's secret police and that served as a torture center, would also contribute to a rewriting of Chilean history.

Meanwhile, the past lived in the present, influencing government and opposition decisions on constitutional reform, the economy, social justice, and civil-military relations. Beyond the Pinochet case, the course of civil-military relations, and president Lagos's reform agenda, Father Alberto Hurtado's calls in the 1940s and 1950s for social justice retained their currency as the country entered 2001. Likewise Cardinal Jules Gerard Saliege's words of 1942 that had inspired Father Hurtado remained an inspiration and challenge for Chileans in the twenty-first century: "The future will be whatever our faith, our hope, and our efforts to overcome human misery make it."

Political Chronology

1534	King of Spain names Diego de Almagro governor of Nueva Toledo, extending approximately from Ica to just north of TalTal.
1535–36	Almagro expedition enters Chile and reconnoiters into the central valley. Finding no great source of wealth as in Peru, Almagro returns to Cuzco to contest the spoils of conquest with the Pizaros.
1539	Pizaro authorizes Pedro de Valdivia to lead expedition of conquest to Chile, which he baptizes Nuevo Extremo or Nueva Extremadura.
1540–41	Pedro de Valdivia's expedition arrives at the Mapocho river in December; Santiago founded February 12, 1541, and within the month Valdivia creates the first cabildo. September 11, 1541, local Indians attack the new town, practically destroying it and most of the settlers' provisions.
1540–53	Initial settlement and warfare with indigenous population under leadership of Valdivia. First towns founded: La Serena (1544); Concepción (1550); La Imperial, Valdivia, Villarrica (1552); Los Confines (1553).
1553	Battle of Tucapel, Valdivia killed by Indians led by cacique Lautaro—his ex-groom.
1553–57	Disputes among Valdivia's lieutenants over control of the colony. Continued warfare with Indians. Spanish defeated at Marigueñu (1554), settlements abandoned. Three years later Spanish destroy Lautaro's forces at Peteroa (1557).
1557–61	Viceroy at Lima names his son, García Hurtado de Mendoza, governor of Chile and sends an army financed out of the royal treasury to secure Chile. Alonso de Ercilla y Zúñiga, author of the epic poem, *La Araucana,* arrives with this expedition to Chile.
1557–59	Exploration of territory from Concepción to the south. Osorno founded (1558), and expedition under command of Juan Ladrillero penetrates to the Strait of Magellan. Fort at Tucapel reconstructed and Concepción resettled.
1559	Tasa de Santillán—ordinances seeking to regulate Indian labor and personal service to the Spanish—prohibits use of Indians as beasts of burden and require sufficient daily food for Indian workers. Ordinances largely ignored, despite application in mines at Quilacoya near Concepción.
1561–63	Administration of Governor Francisco de Villagra. Creation of Diocese of Santiago (1561). Bartolomé Rodrigo González Marmolejo appointed first Bishop. Fray Gil de González preaches "defensive war," unsuccessfully seeking to defend Indians.

1563–65   Interim administration of Pedro de Villagra. Pope Paul IV creates Diocese of La Imperial (1563). Philip II decrees establishment of Chile's first *audiencia* at Concepción (1565).

1565–67   Interim administration of Rodrigo de Quiroga. Audiencia installed at Concepción and town of Castro founded (1567) after expedition of exploration and conquest to island of Chiloé.

1567–75   Chile governed by Bravo de Saravia. Bishop of La Imperial advises king to suppress the audiencia (1570) because of its failure to help pacify the territory and deal firmly with abuses against the Indians. Despite continued efforts by the Bishop and royal decrees, *encomenderos* continue to evade regulations. Audiencia at Concepción abolished (1573).

1575–80   Rodrigo de Quiroga, one of the area's first conquistadors and lieutenant of Valdivia, assumes political leadership, supports encomenderos, and urges king to approve "personal service" of Indians to Spaniards. Carries out large expeditions of war against Indians in southern region. Prisoners are maimed to prevent their escape.

1580   Chillán founded.

1580–83   Interim administration of Ruiz de Gamboa, Quiroga's son-in-law. In effort to secure permanent appointment, Ruiz de Gamboa cooperates with Bishop Medillín in promulgation of Tasa de Gamboa (1580) which sought to abolish "personal service." Gamboa fails to win decisive victory over Araucanians, and the Spanish king sends Alonso de Sotomayor, a veteran soldier, as governor of Chile.

1583–92   Administration of Alonso de Sotomayor. Gradual revocation of Gamboa's reforms; forced labor—personal service reinstated. Stimulation to mining economy in Quillota and Choapa valleys. Despite harsh campaigns against Araucanians, Indians remain unsubdued. Sotomayor's secret marriage to a Creole woman leads to his downfall.

1592–99   Administration of Martín García Oñez de Loyola, nephew of the viceroy of Peru and relative of Ignatius de Loyola, founder of the Society of Jesus (Jesuit order). Renewal of official concern with conditions of Indians. Outlaws sale of Indian captives or their transport from the south to northern mines or to Peru.

1598   Indian uprising under cacique Pelantaru. Oñez de Loyola is killed and decapitated in valley of Curalaba. Nine years later his head is returned by Indians to Governor Alonso García Ramón. Philip II dies.

1599–1601   Several interim administrations. Abandonment of Spanish settlements in the south. Beginning of permanent royal subsidy (*situado real*) to finance war against Araucanians (1600).

1601–05   Administration of Alonso de Ribera. Permanent army is established in Chile (1603). Diocese of La Imperial moves to Concepción (1603). Indian offensive continues with Spanish defeats at Santa Cruz, Valdivia (1599), La Imperial and Angol (1600), Villarrica (1602), Osorno and Arauco (1604). Spanish respond with renewed sorties south. Southern economy totally disrupted.

1605–10   Administration of García Ramón. Accompanied to Chile by the Jesuit, Luis de Valdivia. Luis de Valdivia preaches "defensive warfare." García Ramón continues offensive against Indians, suffering humiliating defeat in 1606. King authorizes perpetual slavery for captured Indian rebels (1608). Pope Paul V authorizes war against the Araucanians. Jesuit Luis de Valdivia arrives in Spain to seek official acceptance of "defensive warfare" (1609). In the same year a new audiencia established in Santiago.

1610–11   Interim administrations of Merlo de la Fuente and Jaraquemada. Luis de Valdivia's influence results in reappointment of Alonso de Ribera as governor of Chile. Valdivia named as *visitador general*.

1612–17   Administration of Alonso de Ribera. Political intrigue between governor and Luis de Valdivia. Murder of Jesuit missionaries at Elicura provides pretext for renewed warfare (1614) despite official policy to the contrary.

1617–24   Interim administration of five different governors. Luis de Valdivia leaves Chile in 1619. "Defensive warfare" largely discredited. Tasa de Esquilache (1620) again seeks to regulate Indian labor—generally unsuccessful.

1625–29   Administration of Fernández de Córdoba. King of Spain authorizes renewed warfare against Araucanians and slavery for captives. Governor allows branding of Indian captives. Spaniards suffer new military defeats, notably at Las Cangrejeras near Yumbel.

1629–39   Administration of Lazo de la Vega. Spanish defeat Araucanians at La Albarrada (1631) and Philip IV officially abolishes "personal service" (1633). New regulations—Tasa de Lazo de la Vega (1635)—issued concerning Indian labor. Abolishes personal service but "allows" Indians to pay tribute in labor and "rent" their services. Widespread abuses.

1639–46   Administration of the Marquis de Baides. Governor attempts to negotiate with Araucanians. Pact of Quillín recognizes sovereignty of Araucanians. In exchange Indians agree to receive missionaries. Peace treaty terms violated. Warfare resumes, though Indians help Spaniards repel invasion of southern Chile by Brouwer expedition (1643).

1646–49   Administration of Martín de Mujica. Earthquake destroys Santiago (1647). Followed by typhoid epidemic. Viceroy at Peru temporarily suspends certain taxes in Chile. Pact of Quillín renewed.

1650–56   Administration of Acuña y Cabrera. Cunco Indians kill crew of ship carrying situado to Valdivia (1651). Punitive expedition destroyed by Indians (1653). Nepotism and corruption weaken Spanish military. Indian uprising in 1655; vecinos of Concepción "depose" Acuña y Cabrera. Indians again push Spaniards out of southern settlements. Southern economy in shambles.

1656–63   Three interim administrations. King Philip IV prohibits future slave raids and military expeditions into hostile territory without prior approval. Viceroy at Lima appeals decisions to protect Peruvian labor supply.

1664–68   Administration of Francisco de Meneses. Governor in disputes with Church and audiencia. Corruption prevails as governor and supporters loot public administration, sell favors, and engage in slave raids (*malocas*) and trade. Peruvian viceroy, Count of Santistéban, supports continued enslavement of Araucanians.

1668–70   Two interim administrations succeed Meneses after he leaves Chile in disgrace.

1670–81   Administration of Juan Henríquez. Debate over treatment of Indians continues. Writings of Diego de Rosales gain influence. Queen Regent Mariana of Austria officially abolishes slavery in 1674. Henríquez and audiencia develop *depósito* system to circumvent abolition (1676). King Charles II reaffirms abolition decree of 1674 and orders freed Indians transported for their "care" to Peru (1679). King reverses his decree in response to Governor Henríquez's letters defending Chilean interests (1683). Pirates under Bartholomew Sharp sack La Serena (1680).

1682–92   Administration of José de Garro. Governor proposes massacre of Araucanian leaders. Viceroy and King reject Garro's proposal (1686). New pirate attacks at Coquimbo and La Serena (1686). Earthquake at Lima (1687) stimulates Chilean wheat production, increase in prices and temporary economic expansion.

1692–1700   Administration of Tomás Marín de Poveda. Royal decree of 1693 authorizes Indians to pay tribute in money or kind instead of personal service. Decree evaded as others in the past. Renewed efforts to pacify Araucanians through negotiations and missions—unsuccessful as in the past.

1700   Death of Charles II. Beginning of Bourbon era for Spanish America. Charles II leaves no successor. Throne is willed to Philip of Anjou (Philip V of Spain), grandson of Louis XIV of France.

1701–14   War of the Spanish Succession ended by the treaties of Utrecht and Rastadt. Philip V, King of Spain, renounces claim to French throne.

1713   England granted the *asiento* or monopoly on slave trade with Spain's colonies.

1701–08   Administration of Governor Francisco Ibáñez de Peralta. Corruption involving the situado. Civil war with rebels calling for ouster of governor. Rebellion suppressed. Increasing levels of contraband trade. Numerous complaints against governor lead to his removal by Philip V.

1709–16   Administration of Governor Juan Andrés de Ustáriz. Large scale commercial corruption involving French merchants after Ustáriz buys post of Chilean governorship for 24,000 pesos. Pirates under Captain Rogers find Alexander Selkirk ("Robinson Crusoe") on the island Más a Tierra in the Juan Fernández Archipelago.

1717–33   Administration of Governor Gabriel Cano y Aponte. Moderate policies pursued toward Mapuches. Period of relative peace with exception of rebellion in 1723. Earthquake provokes great damage to Santiago (1730) and affects seriously most of central Chile. Earthquake is followed by tidal wave at Valparaíso causing serious losses. Smallpox epidemic (1731).

1734–37   Interim administration of Manuel de Salamanca.

1737–45   Administration of Governor José Antonio Manso de Velasco. Founding of new towns in mining and agricultural districts, including San Felipe (1740), Los Angeles, Canquenes, San Fernando (1742), Melipilla, Rancagua, Curicó (1743). In recognition of his service, Manso de Velasco is made viceroy at Lima.

1745–55   Administration of Governor Domingo Ortiz de Rozas. Real Universidad de San Felipe inaugurated (1747) and La Moneda begins to function (1749). For his service in founding new settlements—Quirihue and Coelemu (1749), La Florida (1751), Casablanca and Petorca (1753), and Ligua (1754)—the king confers title upon Ortiz de Rozas. Ortiz de Rozas dies (1756) on return to Spain.

1751   Earthquake and tidal wave destroy Concepción.

1755–61   Administration of Governor Manuel de Amat y Junient. University of San Felipe begins operation (1757). Violent repression of prison rebellion in Santiago (1758). Amat y Junient becomes viceroy at Lima upon leaving Chilean post.

1761–68   Administration of Governor Antonio de Guill y Gonzaga. Foundation of Rere (1765). Yumbel (1766), and Tucapel el Nuevo (1765). Jesuits expelled from Chile (1767). Governor delegates much authority to *corregidor* Zañartu who imposes a reign of repression against criminals and indigents in Santiago. According to Francisco Encina, the slogan for Zañartu's program "By Reason or by Force" anticipated the slogan on the Chilean national escutcheon.

1768–73   After the death of Guill y Gonzaga, several interim administrations follow. New Indian uprisings and Spanish losses force negotiation of still another treaty (Paz de Negrete, 1770) in which Spanish give Indians compensation in money and cattle.

1773–80   Administration of Agustín de Jáuregui. Establishment of viceroyalty of Buenos Aires (1776), opening of direct commerce to Chile (1778), separation of Cuyo from Chile (1779). Governor introduces Draconian criminal legislation in efforts to curb violence, robberies, cattle rustling, and drunkeness. First significant census taken in Chile (1778). Like several of his predecessors, Jáuregui leaves Chile to become viceroy at Lima.

1780–87   Administration of Governor Ambrosio de Benavides. Administrative reorganization—introduction of intendant system (1782) with Chile divided into two intendencies: Santiago and Concepción. Upon the death of Benavides, the Intendant of Concepción, Ambrosio de O'Higgins, becomes governor of Chile.

1783   Earth tremor and flooding in Santiago as Mapocho River rages through the city. Entire neighborhoods disappear.

1787–96   Administration of Governor Ambrosio O'Higgins. Foundation of numerous new towns and mining centers. Public works, road construction, and beautification of Santiago. Encomiendas abolished (1791). New treaty with Indians in south (Parlamento of Negrete, 1793). Foundation of the *Consulado* (1795). O'Higgins becomes viceroy at Lima in 1796.

1796–1802 Administration of Governor Gabriel de Avilés y del Fierro and several interim administrations. Threat of war against England preoccupies the colony with preparations for defense against invasion. After brief tenure in Chile, Avilés becomes viceroy at Buenos Aires and then at Lima. Interim governors follow until 1802.

1802–08   Administration of Governor Luis Muñoz de Guzmán. Continuation of public works programs in Santiago. Buenos Aires occupied by English (1806). Beginnings of political unrest in Chile. Vaccinations introduced in Chile (1805). Muñoz de Guzmán dies in 1808.

1808–10   Interim administration of Francisco Antonio García Carrasco. Unrest intensifies and governor is replaced by Mateo de Toro y Zambrano.

Sept. 18, 1810   Cabildo Abierto creates first junta, beginnings of Chilean independence movement.

1811–13   "Dictatorship" of José Miguel Carrera. Offspring of slaves born in Chile declared free (1811). Appearance of Chile's first newspaper, La Aurora de Chile (1812). Civil war in Chile.

1814   Treaty of Lircay. Patria Vieja ends after defeat of insurrectionists at Rancagua. Chilean forces retreat to Mendoza.

1814–17   La Reconquista—temporary restoration of Spanish authority as military expeditions from Peru defeat rebel forces.

1817   General San Martín and Bernardo O'Higgins lead army from Argentina into Chile and defeat Spanish forces at Chacabuco (February 12, 1817).

1817–23   Dictatorship of Bernardo O'Higgins. Continued war against Spanish forces south of Santiago. Expeditionary force leaves Chile to liberate Peru (1820). Peruvian independence declared (1821) as San Martín occupies Lima. Titles of nobility abolished (1817).

1823–30   Period of chaos and political uncertainty dominated by liberal, federalist experiments and personality of Ramón Freire. Slavery abolished (1823). Federalist experiment (1826–28).

1828–30   Renewed civil war.

1830   Battle of Lircay (April 17, 1830). Conservative forces emerge victorious.

1831–41   Two five-year terms of President Joaquín Prieto. Constitution of 1833 adopted. Chile defeats Peru-Bolivia Confederation (1836–1839). Initiation of "Portalian State."

1842   University of Chile founded.

1849   Emergence of Liberal party.

1850   Sociedad de Igualdad established under leadership of Francisco Bilbao to contest election of Manuel Montt.

1841–51   Two five-year terms of President Manuel Bulnes, hero of the war against Bolivia and Peru. Civil War of 1851 mars succession, but Bulnes successfully defends his chosen successor, Manuel Montt.

1851–61   Two five-year terms of President Manuel Montt. Civil wars in 1851 and 1859 fragment ruling elite. Formation of Conservative party (1857). Economic boom as a consequence of gold strike in California. Expansion of Chilean commerce, mining and agriculture. Political challenge to clerical forces and old Conservative elite.

1861–71   Two five-year terms of President José Joaquín Pérez. Coalition governments incorporate Liberals and Conservatives into government as President breaks with party that elected him. Radical party formed in 1861 by Pedro León Gallo and the Matta brothers. Radical party becomes proponent of political reforms. "Theological Question" becomes a key issue in Chilean politics.

1871–75   Administration of President Federico Errázuriz Zañartu. Errázuriz dismisses Conservative members of coalition (1873) and forms cabinet entirely of Liberals, Radicals, and Nationals—the so-called Liberal Alliance. Religious question dominates domestic politics.

1876–81   Administration of President Aníbal Pinto. Severe economic crisis facing country "alleviated" by victory in the War of the Pacific (1879–1883). Chile acquires nitrate fields from Peru and Bolivia, increasing territory by more than one-third.

1883   Creation of the Sociedad de Fomento Fabril.

1881–86   Administration of President Domingo Santa María. Attempted renewal of political authoritarianism and anticlericalism. Suffrage extended to all males over 25 years of age.

1886–91   Administration of José Manuel Balmaceda. Growth of nitrate and export trade accompanied by expansion of public works programs, government bureaucracy, educational opportunities. Conflict between President Balmaceda and Congress over government policies and constitutional issues leads to civil war. Balmaceda commits suicide as term ends. Congressional victory inaugurates period of "parliamentary republic" (1891–1924).

1887   Formation of Partido Demócrata.

1888   Establishment of the Catholic University.

1889   Creation of Pedagogical Institute.

1890–91   Civil war.

1891–96   Administration of Jorge Montt. Leader of the opposition against Balmaceda, Montt attempts to restore peace in Chile. Incipient industrialization brings pressures for protectionist legislation. Partido Demócrata, elects first deputy to Congress (1894).

1896–1901   Administration of Federico Errázuriz Echaurren. Diplomacy avoids conflict with Argentina. Tariff legislation and cattle tax (1897) provoke intense opposition. "Social question" emerging in Chilean politics with growth of workers' press and labor organizations. First electric trolley in Santiago (1900). President dies in office (1901).

1901–06   Administration of Germán Riesco Errázuriz. Campaigns with slogan "I am not a threat to anyone." Promulgation of Code of Civil Procedure (1902) and Criminal Procedure (1906). Peace treaty signed with Bolivia (1904). Strikes in Valparaíso (1903) and "meat strike" protesting cattle tax erupt into violence in Santiago—"Red Week" 1905. Earthquake devastates Valparaíso (1906).

1906–10	Administration of Pedro Montt. Worker protest, wave of strikes in 1907–09. Stockmarket crash (1907). Massacre of workers at Santa María de Iquique (1907). TransAndean railroad completed (1910).
1907	Massacre of workers at Santa María de Iquique.
1909	Organization of Gran Federación de Obreros de Chile. By 1917 becomes a militant labor organization (FOCH) and eventually affiliates with RILU.
1910–15	Administration of Ramón Barros Luco. Famous for his remark "There are only two kinds of political problems, those that solve themselves and those without solution." Barros Luco faces military conspiracy (1912). Initial impact of World War I on economy brings recession and worker activism.
1912	Creation of Socialist Workers Party (POS) founded by Luis Emilio Recabarren and supporters.
1913	General strike in Valparaíso, led by anarchists.
1915–20	Administration of Juan Luis Sanfuentes. World War I impacts Chilean society and economy, increasing industrialization and labor organization. Economic crisis after war brings urban protests in Santiago and labor activism.
1917	Port strike in Valparaíso. Government declares martial law; Yáñez decree seeks to regulate industrial relations.
1918	AOAN rally in Santiago.
1919–20	Wave of labor activism, AOAN rally in Valparaíso (January); Congress gives President Sanfuentes emergency powers; tram strike in Santiago; ADAN rally in Santiago (August); Police raid IWW headquarters in Valparaíso and attack Student Federation (FECH) headquarters in Santiago. Arrests and detention of labor and POS leaders. Workers and police die in labor conflict in Puerto Natales (1919) and Magallanes (1920).
1920	Arturo Alessandri assumes Presidency (December).
1920–24	First administration of President Arturo Alessandri. Alessandri, after populist campaign, is unable to move reforms through Congress. Military "coup" pushes social and labor legislation through Congress with a "rattling of sabers." Alessandri leaves the country.
1922	Establishment of Chilean Communist party.
1925	New Constitution approved. President Alessandri returns to Chile only to leave again after conflict with Defense Minister, Carlos Ibáñez.
1925	Massacre of striking nitrate workers at Oficina La Coruña in Antofagasta.
1927–31	Ibáñez takes control of government after a period of "tutelage." Controlled elections provide a compliant congress. Massive public works program induces temporary prosperity as Ibáñez represses opposition. Stock market crash and depression bring Ibáñez's downfall.
1932–38	Arturo Alessandri returns to presidency after more than a year of juntas, insurrections, and uncertainty which includes the 100 days of a Chilean "Socialist Republic." Alessandri restores order, imposes the 1925 constitution, and utilizes fiscal conservatism to improve public finances. In departure

from earlier (1920s) rhetoric, Alessandri presides over a Conservative regime.

1933	Creation of Socialist Party of Chile.
1934	Massacre of peasants at Ranquil.
1935–38	Formation of the Falange Nacional with splinter of Conservative youth group from Conservative party. Falange eventually (1957) becomes the Chilean Christian Democratic Party.
1936	Formation of Popular Front as prelude to 1938 presidential elections.
1938	Massacre of Nazis involved in protest movement (September 5) and incarceration of their leader, González Von Marées.
1938–41	Administration of Pedro Aguirre Cerda with support of Popular Front coalition. Reformist programs follow, including creation of Chilean Development Corporation (CORFO). Rural activism frightens political right; Popular Front parties agree to "suspend" rural unionization. Aguirre Cerda dies in 1941.
1942–46	Administration of President Juan Antonio Ríos. Popular Front dissolved but variety of coalitions follow. Communists and Socialists dominate labor movement but competition for control eventually divides leftist parties. President Ríos dies in 1946; new elections bring fellow Radical, González Videla, to the presidency.
1946–52	Administration of President Gabriel González Videla. Initial coalition of Radicals, Liberals, and Communists breaks up. González Videla, with support by the United States, moves against Communists. Communist party outlawed in 1948 and labor organizations purged. Chile becomes Cold War battleground.
1947	New legislation restricts rights of rural labor. Conflicts in labor movement lead to divisions between Communist- and Socialist-led unions.
1948	Coal strikes and labor agitation. Law for the Permanent Defense of Democracy outlaws Communist party.
1952–58	Administration of President Carlos Ibáñez. Ibáñez elected on "anti-political" platform. Economic difficulties after the Korean War plague Ibáñez. High inflation rates and foreign advisers' stabilization programs undercut Ibáñez's popularity. Ibáñez approves electoral reform and relegalization of Communist party before leaving office.
1958–64	Administration of President Jorge Alessandri. After barely winning election over Salvador Allende, the candidate of the Leftist Coalition (FRAP), Alessandri presides over a conservative administration that introduced a number of minor reforms. Anti-inflation programs are relatively successful, but alienate workers, peasants, and part of the middle class. Under pressure from Alliance for Progress, a land reform law passes in 1962.
1964–70	Administration of President Eduardo Frei Montalva. Frei presides over the Christian Democratic "Revolution in Liberty" that dramatically alters Chilean politics and society. Mobilization of workers, peasants, slum-dwellers,

and women destabilizes Chilean politics—and the government is unable to deliver on all its promises. Renewed inflation, economic stagnation, and seizures of farms, urban lots, and housing projects punctuate the last years of Christian Democratic government.

1970–73   Unidad Popular administration of President Salvador Allende. A program to put Chile on the peaceful road to socialism is met with bitter resistance by domestic and international opponents. Political polarization finally results in a bloody military coup, September 11, 1973.

1973–90   Military dictatorship directed by General Augusto Pinochet. Political parties outlawed and civil liberties restricted. Severe repression of opposition. Military regime seeks to create new political system; 1980 constitution "institutionalizes" new regime of "protected democracy." Drastic economic and social policy changes emphasize privatization and foreign investment. Economic boomlet (1977–81) followed by intense recession (1982–85). Support for military government erodes but opposition unable to forge unified coalition. Assassination attempt on Pinochet in late 1986. Country remains under "state of emergency" into 1987.

1988   General Pinochet defeated in plebiscite in bid for eight more years as president.

1989   Constitutional reforms, *leyes de amarre*, congressional and presidential elections.

1990–94   Administration of Patricio Aylwin and the Concertación coalition. Sustained economic growth; tense civil-military relations. Rettig Commission (1990–91) investigates human rights violations, but 1978 amnesty remains in place. Government unable to enact constitutional reforms; major social and economic policy initiatives. Presidential and congressional elections in 1993 reaffirm support for the Concertación.

1994–2000   Administration of Eduardo Frei-Ruiz Tagle. Second government of the Concertación coalition. Economic growth continues until recession in 1998–99; civil-military relations less conflictive but still no resolution of human rights issue. Pinochet arrested in England, 1998; Supreme Court "reinterprets" 1978 amnesty decree in 1999. Primary elections won by ex-supporter of Salvador Allende, Ricardo Lagos. Presidential elections, December 1999. Runoff January 2000.

2000   Administration of President Ricardo Lagos Escobar. Pinochet returns to Chile (March). Has congressional immunity removed by Supreme Court, August 8, 2000; Lagos tells country, "I was elected to govern for the future, not to consider what happened in the past." Tensions continue in civil-military relations; economic recovery slower than expected during 2000.

Selective Guide to the Literature on Chile

History-writing in Chile begins virtually with colonization in the sixteenth century. Sergio Martínez Baeza, *El libro en Chile,* 1982, goes back further, relating the history of printing, its introduction to Spain and the Spanish colonies, the development of private and public libraries, laws regulating the press and book censorship, and the book trade. Martínez identifies three major publications on Chile covering the colonial period and nineteenth century; they remain benchmarks for historiography on the country: Claudio Gay, *Historia física y política de Chile,* 30 vols., 1844–65, covering "history," zoology, botany, agriculture, and two volumes of documents; Diego Barros Arana, *Historia general de Chile,* 16 vols., 1884–1902, more than 9000 pages; Francisco Antonio Encina, *Historia de Chile desde la prehistoria hasta la revolución de 1891,* 20 vols., 1940–52, almost 12,000 pages. In some ways, the differences in interpretation and methods of the liberal nineteenth-century historian Barros Arana and the conservative, twentieth-century historian Encina set the polemical and politicized tone for much of the history-writing in Chile to the present. Martínez Baeza's history of "the book in Chile" also offers a useful synopsis of the publishing industry and the development of the National Library, "born with *la patria.*"

The bibliography that follows emphasizes published books, especially those with helpful bibliographies. Manuscript sources, archival and government documents, professional articles, and theses are listed where I have relied on particular works in this volume or where they are essential sources on special topics. For this edition, I have added reference to a number of Internet Web sites where information may be easily obtained (1999–2000) on Chilean history, government, politics, socioeconomic conditions, and other more specialized topics. No doubt some of the website "addresses" will change after publication of this volume; at the time of publication these sites were active.

BASIC GEOGRAPHIC, DEMOGRAPHIC, AND SOCIOECONOMIC INFORMATION

The communication revolution of the last two decades makes statistical and descriptive material of all sorts regarding Chile more accessible than ever before. Chilean government agencies, private businesses, producer associations, and interest groups have rushed to the Internet. The Internet's dynamic character and rapid change of Web site addresses and content are challenges to scholars preparing bibliographies and citing "sources" that literally disappear in cyberspace. For that reason I have noted the date and Web address for material directly cited in the text. Three exceptionally valuable websites for accessing government, media, university, and private sector information in Chile are www.lanic.utexas.edu/la/chile; www.brujula.cl/, and www.estado.cl. The Instituto Nacional de Estadísticas (INE, the National Statistical Institute) manages an extensive data collection and publication program that includes a lengthy list of basic data sources and more specialized information. The annual *Compendio Estadístico,* published since 1971, provides demographic, social, and economic data, but the INE's publication program ranges from specialized volumes (e.g., *Women and Men in Chile, Figures and Reality,* 1995) published in English and Spanish to compilations of statistical series (e.g., *Chile: Series Estadísticas,* beginning in 1981) on environment, demography, housing, labor, education, culture, communications media, public health, police services, and all sectors of the economy. A list of the INE publications can be found in the *Catálogo de Publicaciones.* At the time this book was published, the most recent publications regarding the census were. *Resultados oficiales, Censo de población 1992: Población total del país, regiones,* 1993, and *Censo de Población y vivienda: Chile 1992 Resultados generales,* 1992.

Most Chilean government ministries provide relatively up-to-date information, as do both branches of Congress, the armed forces, and the specialized agencies, for example, the National Environmental Commission (Comisión Nacional de Medio Ambiente), the National Development Corporation (CORFO, *Chile Economic Report*), ProChile (which maintains English and Spanish Web sites with information on business in Chile, international trade, and trade agreements), the ministry-level agency responsible for policy and research on issues related to women (SERNAM), and even Chilean embassies in Europe, Asia, and Australia. Public health data, social services information, and electoral information are also easily accessed. The Ministry of Interior has maintained up-to-date information on electoral law and recent electoral results (by party and candidates, disaggregated by region and municipality). In some cases government officials go beyond providing published data; in preparing this book I inquired via email whether the Ministry of Mining had more recent data than was displayed on the Web site and I received an update within two days, truly an indication of the professional and collaborative spirit of an individual government official (whom I had never met), Eduardo Quiñones M., but also of the futility of including a longer list of rapidly dated sources of official statistical material on Chile in this bibliography.

The most important business associations, lobbies, and interest groups, ranging from environmental organizations and think tanks (CODEF, TERRAM, RENACE) and human rights groups to the Furious Bicyclist Movement (Movimiento Furioso de Ciclistas, promoting the use of bicycles in urban zones) also maintain Web sites and publish periodicals and newsletters. The Sociedad de Fomento Fabril (SFF, National Manufacturers Association) maintains a Web site displaying "The Chilean Economy in Figures," with an array of charts, tables and graphs ranging from population growth to destination of Chilean exports. The Sociedad Nacional de Minería (SONAMI) does the same for the mining sector and also maintains a documentation center and library with an archive of media coverage of the mining economy. Many Chilean newspapers and magazines also maintain Web sites. It is possible to read daily news and even see Chilean television on the Internet. In addition to Chilean sources, the United Nations (FAO, ECLAC, UNESCO, UNPOP), the InterAmerican Development Bank (Chile, Basic Socio-Economic Data—http://database.iadb.org/), the World Bank (*Social Indicators of Development*), International Monetary Fund, Organization of American States (OAS), and the U.S. Embassy in Santiago (e.g., *Country Commercial Guide, Fiscal Year* 1998, Chile) periodically publish useful macroeconomic and sectoral reports on Chile, much of which is also partially accessible via the Internet. For a sense of Chile in global comparative perspective the United Nations Development Programme, *Human Development Report* (published since 1990) is excellent. The most recent reports available online in 1999 could be found at the UNDP home page: http://www.undp.org/. For a helpful annual overview of the Chilean economy see the U.S. State Department, "Country Report on Economic Policy and Trade Practices," accessible in 1999 both through the State Department Web site, www.state.gov/www/issues/, and the Web site maintained by the U.S. embassy in Chile (www.usembassy.cl/epol.htm).

The most important sources for geological, geographic, and meteorological information are also government agencies, with the collaboration of Chilean academics in various universities and private research organizations. The Servicio Nacional de Geología y Minería de

Chile (SERNAGEOMIN), created in 1980, oversees mining concessions, mine safety and security, environmental regulation,and research regarding the mining industry. It also compiles information on mining production based on data from producers and exporters; these data are published in *Anuario de la Minería de Chile*. SERNAGEOMIN publishes a variety of geologic maps of Chile and sustains a regular publication program on geological research. Other departments of the Ministry of Mining, the Comisión Chilena de Cobre (COCHILCO), the Corporación Nacional del Cobre de Chile (CODELCO), the Empresa Nacional de Minería (ENAMI), the Empresa Nacional del Petróleo (ENAP), the Comisión Chilena de Energia Nuclear (CCHEN), and the Centro de Investigación Minera y Metalúrgica (CIMM) also publish useful information, not only on mining, but also on the labor force, economic conditions, foreign investment, and trade. The publication lists for SERNAGEOMIN, and for most other entities within the Ministry of Mines, are available on-line. Also on-line is the magazine *Minería Chilena*, a montly update and wealth of news on investment, production, and other aspects of the international mining industry in Chile. A statistical series for fisheries, *Anuario estadístico de pesca*, is published by the Servicio Nacional de Pesca; in agriculture and forestry the Oficina de Estudios y Políticas Agrarias (ODEPA) publishes numerous periodical data sources on land use, crop patterns, prices, markets, and technical topics, including *Mercados Agropecuarios, El Pulso de la Agricultura, Boletín de Comercio Exterior Silvoagropecuario,* and *Revista de Comercio Exterior Silvoagropecuario;* for forestry data within the Ministry of Agriculture, the Corporación Nacional Forestal (CONAF) is the indicated source. The Planning Ministry (MIDEPLAN) also provides extensive macroeconomic and regional data on development projects. MIDEPLAN's *Prospectiva y Población, 1998,* offers social statistics for the 1990s.

For geographical information, maps, and economic geography the Instituto Geográfico Militar, successor of the Servicio Geográfico del Ejército de Chile (1891), is indispensable. The IGM's *Atlas geográfico de Chile para la educación* 4th ed., 1994, contains excellent maps, by region, with extensive data on flora, fauna, communications, transportation, production, climate, and census data from the 1992 census, along with a very useful bibliography on related government and private sources, including the Central Bank's *Indicadores económicos y sociales,* 1960–. Rafael Sagredo B., Fernando Gutiérrez A., and Pilar Aylwin J., *Geografia de Chile ilustrada,* 1997, includes excellent maps and discussions of resources, demographic change, economic geography, and environmental issues in development. The Central Bank's *Chile, crecimiento con estabilidad, 1997,* summarizes recent economic policy and results. In English, *Chile, A Country Study, Area Handbook for Chile,* 3rd ed., 1994, has basic information on land, society, politics, and economy. A most useful source for social science research (especially economics, politics, and public opinion) is the Centro de Estudios Públicos, which in 1999 maintained a Web site at www.cepchile.cl/. Many articles from the CEP quarterly journal, findings and tables from opinion polls, and list of publications are also available on-line. Other basic sources are: Instituto Geográfico Militar, *Atlas de la República de Chile,* 2nd ed., 1983; *Geografía de Chile,* 8 vols., 1983–84: I. *Fundamentos geográficos del territorio nacional;* II. *Geomorfología;* III. *Biogeografía;* IV. *Población y sistema nacional de asentamientos urbanos;* V. *Geografía de los suelos;* VI. *Geografía de los fondos marinos;* VII. *Geografía industrial;* VIII. *Hidrografía;* Instituto Nacional de Estadísticas (INE), *Anuario de Demografía* (demographic yearbook); *Compendio Estadístico* (annual statistical compendium with demographic, economic, and social data).

For biographical and biohistorical information, see Salvatore Bizzarro, *Historical Dictionary of Chile,* 2nd ed., 1987; Mario Céspedes, *Gran diccionario de Chile: biográfico-cultural,* 1988; Lía Cortés and Jordi Fuentes, *Diccionario político de Chile: 1810–1966,* 1967; *Diccionario biográfico de Chile,* 5th ed., 1944; Pedro Pablo Figueroa, *Diccionario biográfico de Chile: 1550–1887,* 3 vols., 1897–1902; *Diccionario biográfico de extranjeros en Chile,* 1900; Virgilio Figueroa, *Diccionario histórico, biográfico y bibliográfico de Chile: 1800–1931,* 5 vols., 1925–31; Jordi Fuentes,

Lía Cortés, Fernando Castillo I., and Arturo Valdés P., *Diccionario Histórico de Chile*, 7th ed., 1982; Armando de Ramón, *Biografía de Chilenos, Miembros de los poderes Ejectivo, Legislativo y Judicial, 1876–1973* (letras A–K), 1999.

Historical statistics, census data, and presidential messages are provided in Markos Mamalakis, "Historical Statistics of Chile: An Introduction" *Latin American Research Review* 13:2 (1978), 127–37, which provides a brief summary of source material on historical statistics, including national accounts, demography, agriculture, industry, mining, the public sector, money and banking, trade and balance of payments, accompanied by a useful list of specific references. Mamalakis has contributed greatly to historical research in Chile with *Historical Statistics of Chile: National Accounts*, 1978; *Demography and Labor Force*, 1980; *Forestry and Related Activities*, 1982; *Money, Prices and Credit Services*, 1984; *Money, Banking and Financial Services*, 1985.

For official census data before the 1970s, see República de Chile: *Dirección de estadística y censos* (census for 1940, 1952, 1960, 1970); *Dirección de estadística y censos: síntesis estadística*, 1968; *Dirección de estadística y censos: población total por provincias, Chile: 1885–1960*, 1964; and *Dirección general de estadística: estadística chilena* (monthly 1960–70); República de Chile, Oficina Central de Estadística, *Censo de 1854, 1865, 1875, 1895, 1907* (19th- and early 20th-century census reports). *El pasado republicano de Chile: o sea Colección de discursos pronunciados por los presidentes de la República ante el Congreso nacional al inaugurar cada año el período legislativo*, Concepción, 1899 (collection of state of the nation addresses by presidents 1832–99);

BASIC GENERAL HISTORIOGRAPHICAL AND BIBLIOGRAPHICAL SOURCES

Fidel Araneda Bravo, "Los estudios históricos en Chile," *Atenea 113*, Nov.–Dec. 1953; Horacio Aránguiz Donoso, *Bibliografía histórica: 1959–1967*, 1970 (surveys of literature in 50 journals and books published between 1959 and 1967); Ramón Briseño, *Estadística bibliográfica de la literatura chilena*, 2 vols., 1862–79 (includes a listing of newspapers by city and public documents arranged by presidential administration); the Bibilioteca Nacional published a fascimile version of the original, 1965–66, 3 vols., with a very useful introduction: "Estudio preliminar de Guillermo Feliú Cruz. Edición facsimilar de la principe de 1862, realizada por la Biblioteca Nacional bajo los auspicios de la Comisión Nacional de Conmemoración del Centenario de la muerte de Andrés Bello"; Harold Blakemore, comp. *Chile*, 1988; *Historiografía colonial de Chile*, I, 1796–1886, 1958; Paul Drake, "El impacto académico de los terremotos políticos: investigaciones de la historia chilena en inglés, 1977–1983," *Alternativas*, Jan.–April 1984, 56–78; Herminia Elgueta de Ocsenius, *Suplemento y adiciones a la bibliografía de bibliografías chilenas*, 1930 (updates Laval's work (see below) to 1930, bringing total of titles reviewed to almost 600); Guillermo Feliú Cruz, *Historia de las fuentes de la bibliografía chilena*, 3 vols., 1956–58 (evaluates contributions of all major bibliographers to 1958); Hernán Godoy Urzúa "El ensayo social: notas sobre la literatura sociológica en Chile," *Anales de la Universidad de Chile*, No. 120, Oct.–Dec. 1960; *Historia de las fuentes de la bibliografía chilena, ensayo crítico*, 3 vols., 1966–68; *Historia, fichero bibliográfico* (decades of citations from a leading history journal); Julio César Jobet, "Notas sobre la historiografía chilena," *Atenea 291–292*, Sept.–Oct. 1949; *Temas históricos chilenos*, 1973 (historiographical interpretation of selected themes in Chilean historical literature); Ramón Laval, *Bibliografía de blibliografías chilenas*, 1915; Luis Montt, *Bibliografía chilena*, 3 vols., 1904–21; Robert Oppenheimer, *Chile: A Bibliography*, 1977; Julio Retamal and Sergio Villalobos R., *Bibliografía histórica chilena, Revistas chilenas 1843–1878*, 1993; Nicolás Enrique Reyes and L. J. Silva Arriagada, *Ensayo de una bibliografía histórica y geográfica de Chile*, 1902 (lists works published to 1900; good source for locating local or regional studies); William Sater, "A Survey of Recent Chilean Historiography 1965–1976," *Latin American Research Review* 1979 (an extensive overview and synthesis of recent scholarship on Chile); Peter J. Sehlinger, *A Select Guide to Chilean Libraries and Archives*, 1979; John Tepaske, ed., *Research Guide to Andean History*, 1981; Jack Ray Thomas, "The Impact of the Generation of 1842 on Chilean Historiography, *The Historian* 41:4 (Aug. 1979); Emilio Vaisse, *Bibliografía general de Chile*.

A number of anthologies and critical surveys offer introductions to Chilean art, literature, journalism, and music as well as biographical material on Chilean intellectuals and artists. Since 1945 the *Revista Musical Chilena* (Universidad de Chile) has published scholarly articles on Chilean music in international perspective, ranging from classical music to folkmusic and the "Nueva Canción" of the 1970s and 1980s. A particularly interesting article on the national musical festivals since 1947 and the prize winners is Luis Merino, "Los festivales de música en Chile, propósitos y transcendencia," in the *Revista Musical Chilena*, 149–150 (1980): 80–105. Fernando Alegría, *Literatura chilena del siglo XX*, 2nd ed., 1962; and *La poesía chilena; orígenes y desarrollo del siglo XVI al XIX*, 1954; Homero Castillo and Raúl Silva Castro, *Historia bibliográfica de la novela chilena*, 1961; Samuel Claro and I. Urrutia, *Historia de la música en Chile*, 1973; Luis E. Délano and Edmundo Palacios, *Antología de la poesía social de Chile*, 1962; Julio Durán Cerda, *Panorama del teatro chileno: 1842–1959*, 1959; David William Foster, *Chilean Literature: A Working Bibliography of Secondary Sources*, 1978; Gaspar Galaz and Milan Ivelić, *La pintura en Chile desde la colonia hasta nuestros días*, 1981; Mario Godoy Quezada, *Historia del cine chileno*, 1966; Cedomil Goic, *La novela chilena*, 1968; Mariano Latorre, *La literatura en Chile*, 1941; Samuel A. Lillo, *Literatura chilena*, 7th ed., 1952 (official text on Chilean literature for secondary schools); Hugo Montes and Julio Orlandi, *Historia de la literatura chilena*, 10th ed., 1982; Eugenio Pereira Salas, *Historia de la música en Chile: 1850–1900*, 1957; Arturo Torres Rioseco, *Breve historia de la literatura chilena*, 1956; Manuel Rojas, *Historia breve de la literatura chilena*, 1964; Antonio Romera, *Historia de la pintura chilena*, 1960; Vicente Salas Viu, *La creación musical en Chile: 1900–1951*, 1951; Raúl Silva Castro, *Panorama literario de Chile*, 1961; and *Prensa y periodismo en Chile: 1812–1956*, 1961; *Evolución de las letras chilenas, 1810–1960*, 1960; *Antología general de la poesía chilena*, 1959; *Antología de cuentistas chilenos*, 1957; Gastón Somoshegyi-Szokol, *Contemporary Chilean Literature in the University Library at Berkeley*, Berkeley, 1975 (partially annotated bibliography, and bibliographical guide to general anthologies and literary studies); Arturo Torres Rioseco and Raúl Silva Castro, *Ensayo de bibliografía de la literatura chilena*, 1935; Fernando Uriarte, "La novela proletaria en Chile," *Mapocho* 4, 1965; José Zamudio, *La novela histórica en Chile*, 1949; Hernán Godoy (ed.), *El carácter chileno*, 1981, and *La cultura chilena*, 1982, provide a number of views of popular culture and intellectual development in Chile from colonial times to the 1980s.

GEOGRAPHY, POPULATION, AND NATURAL RESOURCES

From the time Pedro de Valdivia wrote to the Emperor Charles V in 1545 that, "this land is such that there is none better in the world for living in and settling," the role played by Chilean geography in shaping the territory's socio-economic and political development has been apparent to many writers on Chile. Early, now classic, accounts are Abbé Don J. Ignatious Molina, *The Geographical, Natural, and Civil History of Chile*, 2 vols., trans. from the Italian with notes from the Spanish and French versions by the English editor, 1809; and Claudio Gay, *Historia física y política de Chile: documentos sobre la historia, estadística y la geografía*, 26 vols., 1844–55. The best short summary of the relation between Chilean geography and historical development is Harold Blakemore, "Chile," in Harold Blakemore and Clifford T. Smith (eds.), *Latin America: Geographical Perspectives* 1971. Other useful geographic and demographic summaries include George Pendle, *The Land and the People of Chile*, 1964; Preston

James, *Latin America*, 4th ed., 1964; Gilbert J. Butland, *Chile: An Outline of Its Geography, Economics and Politics*, 1956; Francis Maitland, *Chile: Its Land and People*, 1941; Benjamín Subercaseaux, *Chile: A Geographic Extravaganza* (trans. *of Chile: o una loca geografía*), 1943. Robert McCaa has added concern for methods and sources for social and demographic history in "Chilean Social and Demographic History: Sources, Issues and Methods," *LARR* 13:2, 1978, 104–26. Dated, but historically essential, is the classic by Enrique Espinosa, *Geografía descriptiva de la república de Chile*, 5th ed., 1903. Standard geographical treatments are provided in Elías Almeyda Arroyo, *Geografía de Chile*, 1955; Sociedad Chilena de Historia, *Geografía de Chile: física, humana y económica*, 1968; Pedro Cunill, *Geografía de Chile*, 7th ed., 1978. Many descriptions of selected Chilean regions are also available. The most well known deal with the desert north, the central valley, and Antarctica: Isaiah Bowman, *Desert Trails of Atacama*, 1924; W. J. Dennis, *Tacna and Arica*, 1931; George McBride, *Chile: Land and Society*—the classic description of Chile's central valley agriculture and hacienda system 1936; O. Pinochet de la Barra, *La antártica chilena*, 1948. None of these last works is strictly speaking a geography, but all contain geographical information in addition to considerable historical, social, and economic material. Two useful works that treat Chilean boundaries are: Jaime Eyzaguirre, *Breve historia de las fronteras de Chile*, 4th ed., 1973, and Robert D. Talbott, *A History of the Chilean Boundaries*, 1974.

INDIGENOUS PEOPLES

Although pre-Hispanic Chilean history is not thoroughly researched, a number of basic contributions in the field provide detailed and often conflicting information. Julio M. Montané's *Bibliografía selectiva de antropología chilena: Primera parte—Araucanos, Pehuenches, Chiloé y territorios adyacentes; Segunda parte—generalidades: Zona norte y central*, 2 vols., 1963–64, contains approximately 400 references on Chilean Indians. Julian H. Steward (ed.), *Handbook on South American Indians*, Vol. II, 1957, offers the best summary in English of Chilean indigenous civilization. Other well-known studies are Agustín Edwards, *People of Old*, 1929; F. L. Cornely, *Cultura diaguita chilena y cultura de El Molle*, 1956; René León Echaíz, *Prehistoria de Chile Central*, 1957; Tomás Guevara, *Historia de Chile prehispánico*, 2 vols., 1925–27; *Historia de la civilización de Araucanía*, 7 vols., 1898–1913; Ricardo Latcham, *La prehistoria chilena*, 1936, and *Organización social y creencias religiosas de los antiguos araucanos*, 1924; Alejandro Lipschutz, *La comunidad indígena en América y en Chile*, 1956; José T. Medina, *Los aborígenes de Chile*, 1952; Greta Mostny, *Culturas pre-colombinas en Chile*, 1960. Another very useful and readable overview of pre-Hispanic Chilean peoples appears in Francisco Esteve Barba, *Descubrimiento y conquista de Chile*, 1946, along with a somewhat more extensive bibliography. As is the case with the study of pre-Columbian peoples in general, Julian Steward and Louis Faron, *Native Peoples of South America*, 1959, offers a brief but helpful summary of knowledge on the natives of Chile, as does Wendell C. Bennett and Junius B. Bird, *Andean Culture History*, 1965. A more recent overview of pre-Columbian Chile by Osvaldo Silva appears in the first volume of a 4-volume work edited by Sergio Villalobos, *Historia de Chile* (a 1983 edition makes all four volumes available in a single book).

The Araucanian Indians' heroic resistance to the Spanish conquest inspired the first epic poem of Latin America, Alonso de Ercilla's *La Araucana*. Much of the historical work, chronicles, and other literature of the colonial period (see below) reflects this interest in the Araucanian people and their war against the Spanish. Several 19th-century descriptions of the Araucanians provide insight into the social and economic conditions prevalent after centuries of warfare: Ignacio Domeyko, *Araucanía y sus habitantes*, 1st ed., 1845, 2nd ed., 1971; Pedro Ruís Aldea, *Los araucanos i sus costumbres*, 1st ed., 1856, Vol. 5, 1902; Edmund Reuel Smith, *The Araucanians, or Notes of a Tour among the Indian Tribes of Southern Chile*, 1855.

Scholarship in English on the Araucanians and Mapuche has been dominated by the work of Louis Faron: *Mapuche Social Structure*, 1961; *Hawks of the Sun*, 1964; *The Mapuche Indians of Chile*, 1968. All provide additional references. A mid-20th-century study by Mischa Titien, *Araucanian Culture in Transition*, 1951, provides insight into the dilemma of Chile's Indians in the 20th century; Alejandro Saavedra's *La cuestión mapuche*, 1971, presents a much more dismal picture twenty years later—with significant political implications. José Bengoa and E. Valenzuela's *Economía Mapuche. Pobreza y subsistencia en la sociedad Mapuche contemporánea*, 1983, is even more depressing.

TRAVEL ACCOUNTS

Observations of travelers provide information and insight often lacking in other sources. For an overview of travel accounts see Guillermo Feliú Cruz, *Notas para una bibliografía sobre viajeros relativos a Chile*, 1965. Accounts by Chileans, North Americans, Latin Americans, and Europeans from the 17th century onward are both interesting reading and valuable resources for the historical study of Chile. Among the most useful are:
  Henry Willis Baxley, *What I Saw on the West Coast of South and North America*, 1865; R. Nelson Boyd, *Chile: Sketches of Chile and the Chilians 1879–1880*, 1881; Henry M. Brackenridge, *A Voyage to South America, performed by order of the American Government in the years 1817, and 1818, in the Frigate Congress*, 2 vols., 1819; Alexander Caldcleugh, *Travels in South America during the Years 1819, 1820, 1821, 1825*; Vicente Carvallo y Goyeneche, "Descripción histórico-geográfica del reino de Chile," *Colección de Historiadores 10*, 1879; Richard J. Cleveland, *A Narrative of Voyages and Commercial Enterprises*, 2 vols., 1842; Charles Darwin, *The Voyage of the Beagle*, 1962; Thomas Cochrane Dundonald, *Narrative of Services in the Liberation of Chile, Peru and Brazil from Spanish and Portuguese Domination*, 2 vols., 1859; George Alexander Findlay, *A Directory for the Navigation of the South Pacific Ocean*, 1863; M. Frezier, *Relation du voyage de la mer du sud aux côtes du Chili et du Pérou*, 1716; Lt. J. Gilliss, *The U.S. Naval Astronomical Expedition to the Southern Hemisphere during the Years 1849–1852*, 1855; María Graham, *Journal of a Residence in Chile during the Year of 1822*, 1824; Thaddaeus Peregrinus Haenke, *Descripción del reyno de Chile*, 1942; Samuel Haigh, *Sketches of Buenos Ayres and Chile*, 1829; Basil Hall, *Extracts of a Journal Written on the Coasts of Chile, Peru, and Mexico in the Years 1820, 1821, 1822*, 2 vols., 1826; Adolph E. Howard, *A Handbook or Guide to British Shipmasters and Others Trading to the Coast of Chile*, 1882; Daniel J. Hunter, *A Sketch of Chile, expressly prepared for the use of emigrants from the United States and Europe to that country*, 1866; Samuel Burr Johnston, *Cartas escritas durante una residencia de tres años en Chile*, trans. José Toribio Medina, 1917; and *Diario de un tipógrafo Yanqui en Chile y Perú durante la guerra de la independencia*, 1919; Gabriel Lafond de Lurcy, *Viaje a Chile*, 1970; Mrs. C. B. Merwin, *Three Years in Chile*, 1863; John Miers, *Travels in Chile and La Plata*, 2 vols., 1826; Fray Diego de Ocaña, "Relación del viaje a Chile: año de 1600," *Anales de la Universidad de Chile*, No. 120 (1960); Vicente Pérez Rosales, *Recuerdos del pasado*, trans.; John Polt as, *Times Gone By* with an Introduction by Brian Loveman (forthcoming, 2001); Eduardo Poeppig, *Un testigo en la alborada de Chile: 1826–1829*, 1960; Ignacio Richard, *A Mining Journey Across the Great Andes*, 1863; William S. W. Ruschenberger, *Three Years in the Pacific: 1831–1834*, 1834; W. H. Russell, *A Visit to Chile and the Nitrate Fields of Tarapacá*, 1890; Domingo F. Sarmiento, *Chile: descripciones-viajes-episodios-costumbres*, 1961; Peter Schmidtmeyer, *Travels into Chile over the Andes in the Years 1820–1821*, 1824; Juan G. Serrato, *A través de Chile*, 1898; William Bennet Stevenson, *A Historical and Descriptive Narrative of Twenty Years' Residence in South America*, 3 vols., 1825; Thomas Sutcliffe, *Sixteen Years in Chile and Peru by the Retired Governor of Juan Fernández*, 1841; Paul Turetler, *Andanzas de un alemán en Chile 1851–1863*, trans. by Carlos Keller, 1958; *Useful Information for Captains of Merchant Vessels and Others Trading to the Port of Valparaíso*, 1872; George Vancouver, *A Voyage of Discovery to the North Pacific Ocean*

and Round the World, 3 vols., 1789; *Viajeros en Chile: 1817–1847*, 1955 (Samuel Haigh, Alexander Caldcleugh, Max Radiguet).

CHILEAN HISTORY

Two historians, Diego Barros Arana and Francisco Encina, establish the framework for Chilean historical studies. The foremost Liberal historian of the 19th century, Diego Barros Arana produced the *Historia general de Chile*, 16 vols., 1884–1902, the starting point for almost all Chilean historiography through 1833, including the conservative, revisionist *Historia de Chile desde la prehistoria hasta 1891* by Francisco Encina, 20 vols., 1940–52. A 3-volume summary of the Encina history by Leopoldo Castedo—*Resumen de la historia de Chile*—has gone through several editions and makes the Encina history somewhat more acessible to readers unwilling to read or to acquire the 20-volume edition (1st ed., 1954). Charles C. Griffin, "Francisco Encina and Revisionism in Chilean History," *HAHR* 36, Feb. 1957, is an important critical review of the Encina history. Ricardo Donoso's *Barros Arana: educador, historiador y hombre público*, 1931 provides a bibliography of Barros Arana's historical scholarship, including works on the independence movements and the Portalian period. Also useful are Domingo Amunátegui Solar's 2-volume *Historia de Chile*, 1933—intended as a secondary school textbook—and Jaime Eyzaguirre's *Historia de Chile*, 2 vols., 2nd ed., 1973, covering the period from pre-Columbian times until 1861. Also of importance are Eyzaguirre's earlier works, *Fisonomía histórica de Chile*, 1948 and *Historia de Chile: génesis de la nacionalidad*, 1965. More recent general histories are Sergio Villalobos R., Osvaldo Silva G., Fernando Silva V., and Patricio Estellé M., *Historia de Chile*, 4 vols. 1983; and Gonzalo Vial Correa, *Historia de Chile (1891–1973)*, 4 vols., 1981–97 (volumes cover to 1931; Vial was working on the post–1931 period in 1999). Luis Galdames, *Estudio de la historia de Chile*, 8th ed., 1938, translated into English as *A History of Chile*, 1941, is a one-volume survey ending shortly after the Great Depression. An earlier narrative in English, A. U. Hancock, *History of Chile*, 1893, is largely a political history, ending with the civil war of 1891. Ricardo Donoso's *Breve historia de Chile*, 1963, is the briefest general history in Spanish. A secondary school text by Francisco Frías Valenzuela, based on the author's longer multivolume work, provides an important indication of what Chilean students learn of Chilean history, *Manual de historia de Chile*, 5th ed. 1960. Jay Kinsburner's *Chile: A Historical Interpretation*, 1973, is an interpretation of key developments in Chilean history. In English, Simon Collier and William F. Sater, *A History of Chile, 1808–1994*, 1996, and Leslie Bethell, ed., *Chile Since Independence*, 1993, offer alternative narratives and analyses of Chilean development since 1808. A group of conservative historians published a new interpretative history in 2000: Álvaro Góngora, Patricia Arrancibia, Gonzalo Vial and Aldo Yávar, Chile (1541–2000). Una interpretación de su historia polític.

In general, 20th-century history is not well developed in the available Chilean histories. However, one collection of articles edited by Hernán Godoy, *Estructura social de Chile*, 1971, offers an excellent selection of materials on Chilean society, economy, and politics from the time of the conquest to the 1970s. In addition, this anthology contains a good topical bibliography organized by historical period. A collaborative effort by Mariana Aylwin, Carlos Bascuñán, Sofía Correa, Cristián Gazmuri, Sol Serrano, and Matías Tagle, *Chile en el siglo XX*, 3rd ed., 1990, offers a fresh interpretation of Chilean history from 1900. In 1999 the first two volumes of a 4-volume interpretative social history appeared: Gabriel Salazar and Julio Pinto, *Historia contemporánea de Chile, I, Estado, legitimidad, ciudadanía; II, Actores, identidad y movimiento*. Ideologically framed histories and historiographies with extensive bibliographies for the period 1958–1999 are (from the left) Luis Vitale, Luis Moulian, et al., *Para recuperar la memoria histórica, Frei, Allende y Pinochet*, 1999; Luis Vitale, *Interpretación marxista de la historia de Chile, De Alessandri P. a Frei M. (1932–1964) Industrialización y modernidad* 1998; and (from the right) Alberto Cardemil, *El camino de la utopía, Alessandri, Frei, Allende. Pensamiento y obra,* 1997.

CONQUEST AND THE FORMATION OF CHILEAN SOCIETY

The single most important source of primary materials on the conquest of Chile is the series "Colección de historiadores de Chile y documentos relativos a la historia nacional (CH)," 51 vols., 1861–1953. This collection of chronicles, documents, and histories of the conquest has received priority from a number of Chile's most prominent historians and includes most of the key contributions to Chilean history in the early colonial period. Newer editions of some of the more salient works have been reissued in paperback in abbreviated form in a series called "Escritores coloniales de Chile," including Alonso de Góngora Marmolejo, *Historia de Chile desde su descubrimiento hasta el año 1575;* Alonso de Ovalle, *Histórica relación del reyno de Chile;* Alonso González de Nájera, *Desengaño y reparo de la guerra de Chile;* Francisco Núñez Pineda y Bascuñán, *Cautiverio Feliz* (an account of life among the Araucanians by a captured Spaniard); and Diego de Rosales, *Historia general del reino de Chile.* Other key works in the "Colección de historiadores" are Vicente Carvallo Goyeneche, *Descripción histórico-geográfica del reino de Chile;* and Miguel de Olivares, *Historia militar, civil, y sagrada de Chile.* As in the rest of Spanish America, many of these early writers on Chile were members of religious orders, especially the Society of Jesus (Jesuits).

A major figure in the creation of the "Colección de historiadores," José Toribio Medina, also made available large quantities of primary materials to scholars through his energetic archival research. Major published contributions include: *Cartas de Pedro de Valdivia que tratan del descubrimiento y conquista de Chile,* 1953—letters from Valdivia to Charles V; *Colección de documentos inéditos para la historia de Chile desde el viaje de Magallanes hasta la batalla de Maipo, 1518–1818,* 30 vols., 1888–1902; and *Cosas de la Colonia,* 1952. Other sources of primary materials include the *Archivo de la Capitanía Jeneral; Archivo de la Real Audiencia; Archivo del Arzobispado de Santiago;* and the *Archivo Nacional de Chile.* In addition, the "Actas del cabildo de Santiago de 1541 a 1557 y de 1558 a 1577" can be found in the "Colección de historiadores," vols. 1 and 17.

Historical treatments of the period of conquest are numerous, ranging from biographies of Pedro de Valdivia and other conquistadores to comprehensive and detailed monographic studies. Among the most useful of the latter, Francisco Esteve Barba's *Descubrimiento y conquista de Chile,* 1946 stands out as a reliable summary with helpful bibliography following each chapter. The set of histories from the Catholic point of view, by Catholic historian Crescente Errázuriz offers a comprehensive treatment of the period from the conquest to the late 16th century and an interpretation somewhat different from the Liberal orientation of Barros Arana, whose volumes—*Historia de Chile, Pedro de Valdivia,* 2 vols., 1911–21; *Historia de Chile sin gobernador 1554–1557,* 1912; *Historia de Chile, Don García de Mendoza: 1557–1561,* 1914; *Historia de Chile, Francisco de Villagra 1561–1563,* 1915; *Historia de Chile, Pedro de Villagra 1563–1565,* 1916; and *Seis años en la historia de Chile, 1598–1605,* 1908—contain a wealth of detailed information. A doctoral dissertation at the University of Florida, Thomas Braman, *Land and Society in Early Colonial Santiago,* 1977, synthesizes much of the older materials on the early years of conquest and includes a good working bibliography for this period.

On Pedro de Valdivia, his companions, and the conquest of Chile, a handful of well-known studies summarizes existing knowledge: Rosa Arciniega, *Don Pedro de Valdivia: Conquistador de Chile,* 1943; Jaime Eyzaguirre, *Ventura de Pedro de Valdivia,* 1963; Hugh R. S. Pocock, *The Conquest of Chile,* 1967; Joaquín Santa Cruz, *Problemas históricos de la conquista de*

Chile, 1902; Luis Silva Lezaeta, *El conquistador Francisco de Aguirre*, 1953; Ida W. Vernon, *Pedro de Valdivia: Conquistador of Chile*, 1960. A sympathetic treatment of Valdivia's mistress, later wife of another Chilean governor, is Stella B. May, *The Conqueror's Lady: Inéz de Suarez*, 1930. Other historians have taken the biographies of major Indian chiefs as a point of departure, for example, René León Echaíz, *El toqui Lautaro*, 1971.

The ongoing warfare between Spaniards and the Araucanians of Chile gave to Chilean colonial society a unique character. The best single volume interpreting the relationship between the frontier status of Chile and the evolution of Chilean society is Alvaro Jara's *Guerra y sociedad en Chile*, 1971, translated from a French edition published ten years earlier. Jara's other work on colonial labor systems and Spanish-Indian relations complements the monograph and serves as a basis for colonial labor history: "Fuentes para la historia del trabajo en Chile," *BACH 54, 55, 58, 51,* 1956–57, 1959; *El salario de los indios y los sesmos del oro en la Tasa de Santillán*, 1961; *Los asientos del trabajo y la provisión de mano de obra para los no-encomenderos en la ciudad de Santiago: 1586–1600*, Estudios de historia económica americana, trabajo y salario en el período colonial, No. 1, 1959; "Salario en una economía caracterizada por las relaciones de dependencia personal," *RCHG 133,* 1965. The only available interpretation of Spanish-Indian confrontation in English is Eugene H. Korth's, *Spanish Policy in Colonial Chile*, 1968. An earlier article by Louis de Armond, "Frontier Warfare in Colonial Chile," *Pacific Historical Review*, May 1954, is still an interesting introductory reading on the Chilean frontier. An important contribution to the literature on Spanish-Mapuche conflicts and evangelization, with an extensive bibliography on colonial issues that includes theses done in Chile on these topics, is Rolf Foerster G., *Jesuitas y Mapuches, 1593–1767,* 1996. Leonardo León Solís, *Maloqueros y conchavadores en Araucanía y las Pampas, 1700–1800,* 1991, and Sergio Villalobos, *Vida fronteriza en la Araucanía. El mito de la guerra de Arauco*, 1995, challenge conventional interpretations of the Chilean Indian frontier. Andrea Ruiz-Esquide Figueroa, *Los indios amigos en la frontera araucana*, 1993, provides a more specialized look at the "pacified" Indian peoples. An important article by Guillaume Boccara in 1999 reviews the genesis and evolution of the "Mapuche" (a term not used widely, according to Boccara, before the mid-eighteenth century) and includes a valuable collection of source citations: "Etnogénesis mapuche: resistencia y restructuración entre los indígenas del centro-sur de Chile (siglos XVI–XVIII)," *Hispanic American Historical Review*, August 1999, 425–61.

Among the most valuable secondary sources on the Indian question and early colonial society are Domingo Amunátegui Solar, *Las encomiendas de indíjenas en Chile*, 2 vols., 1909; Miguel Luis Amunátegui, *Descubrimiento y conquista de Chile*, 1862; Guillermo Feliú Cruz and Carlos Monje Alfaro, *Las encomiendas según tasas y ordenanzas*, 1941; Kalky Glauser R., "Orígenes del régimen de producción vigente en Chile," *Cuadernos de la Realidad Nacional*, No. 8, 1971; Mario Góngora, *El estado en el derecho indiano, época de fundación: 1492–1570,* 1951; "Vagabundaje y sociedad fronteriza en Chile: Siglo XVIII a XIX," *Cuadernos del Centro de Estudios Socioeconómicos*, No. 2, 1966; *Encomenderos y estancieros, estudios acerca de la constitución social aristocrática de Chile después de la conquista: 1580–1660,* 1970; Néstor Meza Villalobos, *Políticas indígenas en los orígenes de la sociedad chilena*, 1951; *La formación de la fortuna mobiliaria y el ritmo de la conquista*, 1941; María Isabel Gonzáles Pomes, "La encomienda indígena en Chile durante el siglo XVIII," *Historia 5*, 1966; Jorge Randolph, *Las guerras de Arauco y la esclavitud*, 1966; Manuel Salvat Monguillot, "El régimen de encomiendas en los primeros tiempos de la conquista," *RCHG*, No. 132, 1964; Fernando Silva Vargas, *Tierras y pueblo de indios en el reino de Chile*, 1962.

The most important Marxist contribution to conquest historiography is Luis Vitale, *Interpretación marxista de la historia de Chile: Tomo 1: Las culturas primitivas, la conquista española,* 1957. One Chilean historian, Tomás Thayer Ojeda, has given special attention to the origins of the so-called "raza chilena" more generally. Major works include: *Elementos étnicos que han intervenido en la población de Chile,* 1919; *Formación de la sociedad chilena y censos de la población de Chile entre los años 1540 a 1565, con datos estadísticos, biográficos, étnicos, y demográficos,* 3 vols., 1939–41; *Los conquistadores de Chile,* 2 vols., 1908; with Carlos J. Larraín, *Valdivia y sus compañeros,* 1950.

COLONIAL SOCIETY AND CULTURE

Central to the development of Chilean society, as in the rest of Spanish America, the Catholic Church and its representatives played a critical role in conquest, social organization, education, and public policy. Eugene Korth's already mentioned study is a basic source in English for an overview of the role of the Church in shaping Spanish colonial policy in Chile. Among the numerous Spanish-language sources are: Diego Barros Arana, *Riquezas de los antiguos jesuitas de Chile,* 1872; Francisco Enrich, *Historia de la compañía de Jesús en Chile,* 2 vols., 1891; Crescente Errázuriz, *Los orígenes de la iglesia chilena: 1540–1603,* 1873; José Ignacio Víctor Eyzaguirre, *Historia eclesiástica, política y literaria de Chile,* 3 vols., 1959; Elías Lizana and Pablo Maulen (eds.), *Colección de documentos históricos recopilados del archivo del arzobispado de Santiago,* 4 vols. 1919–21; José Toribio Medina, *La inquisición en Chile,* 2 vols., 1890; Policarpo Gazulla, *Los primeros mercedarios en Chile; 1535–1600,* 1918; Carlos Silva Cotapos, *Historia eclesiástica de Chile,* 1925.

Insight into colonial art, literature, and music in Chile can be found in Fernando Alegría, *La poesía chilena; orígenes y desarrollo del siglo XVI al XIX,* 1954; Luis Alvarez Urquieta, *La pintura en Chile durante el período colonial,* 1933; Alfredo Benavides Rodríguez, *La arquitectura en el virreinato del Perú y en la capitanía general de Chile,* 2nd ed., 1961; Alejandro Fuenzalida Grandón, *Historia del desarrollo intelectual de Chile: 1541–1810,* 1903; *Historia de la literatura colonial,* 3 vols., 1878; Eugenio Pereira Salas, *Los orígenes del arte musical en Chile,* 1941; *Historia del arte en el reino de Chile: 1541–1776,* 1965; Luis Roa Urzúa, *El arte en la época colonial de Chile,* 1929; Tomás Thayer Ojeda, "Las bibliotecas coloniales en Chile," *Revista de bibliografía chilena y extranjera 1,* No. 11, 1943.

Colonial education and pastimes are treated in Miguel Luis and Gregorio Amunátegui, *De la instrucción pública en Chile,* 1856; José Toribio Medina, *La instrucción pública en Chile desde sus orígenes hasta la fundación de la universidad de San Felipe de Santiago de Chile,* 2 vols., 1928; Eugenio Pereira Salas, *Juego y alegrías coloniales en Chile,* 1947.

Nineteenth-century treatments of the colonial economy reflect the struggle between liberalism and the Hispanic-Catholic tradition. More recent interpretations reflect the global confrontation between supporters of capitalism and Marxism. Articles on specialized themes on colonial society and economy as well as documents with commentary appear periodically in *RCHG, BACH,* and *Historia.*

Marxist interpretations of colonial society include José Cademártori, *La economía chilena,* 1968, esp. chaps. 2 and 3; André Gunder Frank, *Capitalism and Underdevelopment in Latin America,* 1969; Julio César Jobet, *Ensayo crítico del desarrollo económico-social de Chile,* 1955; Hernán Ramírez Necochea, *Antecedentes económicos de la independencia de Chile,* 1959; Marcelo Segall, *Desarrollo del capitalismo en Chile,* 1953; "Las luchas de clases en las primeras décadas de la República de Chile," *Anales de la Universidad de Chile,* No. 125, 1962; Luis Vitale, *Interpretación marxista de la historia de Chile: La colonia y la revolución de 1810,* 1969.

A survey of historiographical literature on colonial Chile in the 19th century, with portraits of the most well-known Chilean historians and facsimiles of the title pages of important works, is Guillermo Feliú Cruz, *Historiografía colonial de Chile,* Tomo I, *1796–1886,* 1958; Armando de Ramón and José Manuel Larraín's *Orígenes de la vida económica chilena, 1659–1808,* 1982, adds a wealth of empirical data on prices, production, commerce, and patterns of economic change in the 17th and 18th centuries. To this must be added the studies of Rolando Mellafe, *Las primeras crisis coloniales, formas de asiento y origen de la sociedad chilena, siglos XVI y XVII* in *Siete Estudios,* Homenaje de la Facultad de Ciencias Humanas a Eugenio Pereira Salas, 1975, and *Latifundio y poder rural en Chile en los siglos XVII y XVIII,* 1980.

The insertion of the Chilean colonial economy in international commerce is well treated in Eduardo Cavieres F., *El comercio chileno en la economía mundo colonial,* 1996. Among the great number of works on colonial society and economy, including social and economic institutions and patterns of commerce, are the following basic studies: Sergio Bagú, *Economía de la sociedad colonial,* 1949; and *Estructura social de la colonia,* 1952; Marcello Carmagnani, *Les Mécanismes de la vie économique dans une société coloniale: le Chili (1680–1830),* 1973; Miguel Cruchaga, *Estudio sobre la organización económica y la hacienda pública de Chile;* Mario Góngora, "Los 'hombres ricos' de Santiago y La Serena a través de las cuentas del quinto real," *RCHG,* No. 131, 1963; Eugenio Pereira Salas, *Buques norteamericanos a fines de la era colonial: 1778–1810,* 1936; Demetrio Ramos, *Trigo chileno, navieros del Callao y hacendados limeños,* 1967; Ruggiero Romano, *Una economía colonial: Chile en el siglo XVIII,* 1965; Agustín Ross, *Reseña histórica sobre el comercio de Chile en la era colonial,* 1894; René Salinas, "Raciones alimenticias en Chile colonial" *Historia* 12 (1974–75); Sergio Sepúlveda, *El trigo chileno en el mercado mundial,* 1959; John Tepaske and Herbert Klein, *The Royal Treasuries of the Spanish Empire in America: Chile and the Río de la Plata,* 1982; Sergio Villalobos, *El comercio y la crisis colonial: un mito de la independencia,* 1968, and *Comercio y contrabando en el Río de la Plata y Chile: 1700–1811,* 1965.

On mining in particular, the reader may consult: J. Bruggen, *Bibliografía minera y jeológica de Chile,* 8 vols., 1919–27; Alberto Herrmann, *La producción en Chile de los metales y minerales más importantes de las sales naturales, del azufre y del guano desde la conquista hasta fines del año 1902,* 1903; Augusto Orrego Cortés, *La industria del oro en Chile,* 1890; Francisco San Ramón, *Reseña industrial e histórica de la minería y metalurgia de Chile,* 1899; José Joaquín (Jotabeche) Vallejo, *Costumbres mineras,* 1943; Benjamín Vicuña Mackenna, *El libro de la plata,* 1882; *El libro del cobre y del carbón de piedra,* 1883; and *La edad del oro en Chile,* 2 vols., 1932.

Studies on social themes in the colonial period, including the role of ethnic and cultural minorities in colonial Chile, are: Domingo Amunátegui Solar, *Historia social de Chile,* 1936; and *La sociedad chilena del siglo XVIII: mayorazgos y títulos de castilla,* 3 vols., 1903–04; Gunter Bohm, *Nuevos antecedentes para una historia de los judíos en Chile colonial,* 1963; Marcello Carmagnani, "Colonial Latin American Demography: Growth of Chilean Population, 1700–1830," *Journal of Social History,* No. 2, 1963; and *El salariado minero en Chile colonial, su desarrollo en una sociedad provincial: el norte Chico; 1690–1800,* 1963; Guillermo de la Cuadra Gormaz, *Origen de doscientas familias coloniales de Santiago,* 3 vols., 1941–47; *Origen y desarrollo de las familias chilenas,* 1948–49; and "Censo de la capitanía general de Chile en 1777," *BACH,* No. 12, 1940; Enrique Eberhardt, *Historia de Santiago de Chile,* 1916; Guillermo Feliú Cruz, *La abolición de la esclavitud en Chile,* 1942; Della M. Flusche, *Two Families in Colonial Chile,* 1989; Alejandro Fuenzalida Grandón, *La evolución social de Chile: 1514–1810,* 1906; Mario Góngora, *Origen de los inquilinos de Chile central,* 1960; and "Urban Social Stratification in Colonial Chile," *HAHR* 55, 1975; with Jean Borde, *Evolución de la propiedad rural en el valle del Puange,* 2 vols., 1956; Eugene Korth and Della M. Flusche, *Forgotten Females: Women of African and Indian Descent in Colonial Chile, 1553–1800,* 1983; Elías Lizana, *Colección de documentos históricos de archivo del arzobispado de Santiago,* 4 vols., 1919–21; Rolando Mellafe, *La introducción de la esclavitud negra en Chile,* 1959; Humberto Muñoz, *Los movimientos sociales en el Chile colonial,* 1945; William F. Sater, "The Black Experience in Chile," *Slavery and Race Relations in Latin America,* R. Toplin (ed.), 1974; Gonzalo Vial Correa, *El africano en el reino de Chile,* 1957.

On the cabildo and the effects of administrative reforms in the colonial period, see: Julio Alemparte, *El cabildo en Chile colonial,* 1940; Miguel Luis Amunátegui, *El cabildo de Santiago desde 1573 hasta 1581,* 3 vols., 1890–91; Jacques Barbier, "Elite and Cadres in Bourbon Chile," *HAHR,* Aug. 1972 (clearly the most important recent revisionist work on the effects of the

Bourbon reforms on colonial administration and society); *Reform and Politics in Bourbon Chile, 1755–1796,* 1980; Della M. Flusche, "The Cabildo and Public Health in Seventeenth Century Chile," *TA* 29, 1972; and "City Councilmen and the Church in Seventeenth Century Chile," *Records of American Catholic Historical Society of Philadelphia* 81, No. 3, 1970; Carlos Ugarte, "El cabildo de Santiago y el comercio exterior del reino de Chile en el siglo XVIII," *Estudios de las Instituciones Políticas y Sociales,* Vol. I, 1967.

INDEPENDENCE AND THE AUTOCRATIC REPUBLIC

Simon Collier, *Ideas and Politics of Chilean Independence: 1808–1833,* 1967, is the most important source in English on late 18th-century Chile, the independence movement, and the formation of the Portalian state. Collier's bibliography lists manuscript sources, contemporary newspapers and journals, as well as contemporary and modern scholarship on the period. I have relied heavily on Collier's work in my own discussion of this period in Chapter 4 and will not attempt here to replicate his bibliography. In addition, Collier's article "The Historiography of the Portalian Period 1830–1891 in Chile," *HAHR,* Nov. 1977, adds an important and systematic treatment of traditional and revisionist history on the independence period, formation of the Portalian state, and 19th-century Chilean historiography more generally.

Review of the historiography of the independence period is found in Gonzalo Vial, "Historiografía de la independencia de Chile," *Historia,* No. 4, 1965. Recent studies by American scholars have considerably expanded our knowledge of post-independence commercial affairs and the social composition of the Chilean oligarchy; Stanley Frederick Edwards, *Chilean Economic Policy Goals 1811–1829: A Study of Late Eighteenth Century Social Mercantilism and Early Nineteenth Century Economic Reality,* Ph.D. diss., Tulane Univ., 1971; and John Rector, *Merchants, Trade and Commercial. Policy in Chile: 1810–1840,* Ph.D. diss., Indiana Univ., 1976; and "Transformaciones comerciales producidas por la independencia de Chile," *RCHG,* No. 143, 1975. The work of Roger Haigh, *The Formation of the Chilean Oligarchy: 1810–1821,* 1972, and of Mary Felstiner, *The Larraín Family in the Independence of Chile: 1789–1830,* Ph.D. diss., Stanford, 1970; "Kinship Politics in the Chilean Independence Movement," *HAHR* 56, Feb. 1976, offers insight into the nature and behavior of the Chilean oligarchy in the early 19th century. For accounts of the evolution of Chile's political elite in the 19th century see the classic work by Alberto Edwards Vives, *La fronda aristocrática,* 1936 and Gabriel Marcella, *The Structure of Politics in Nineteenth Century Spanish America: The Chilean Oligarchy 1833–1891,* Ph.D. diss., Univ. of Notre Dame, 1973.

The independence period and formation of the "Portalian" state have produced a voluminous literature. On the independence movement and its leaders see: Julio Alemparte, *Carrera y Freire,* 1903; Miguel Luis Amunátegui, *La crónica de 1810,* 3 vols., 1876; *Don Manuel de Salas,* 3 vols., 1895; *Los precursores de la independencia de Chile,* 3 vols., 1919; with Benjamín Vicuña Mackenna, *La dictadura de O'Higgins,* 1920; *La revolución de la independencia,* 1945; and *Nacimiento de la república de Chile: 1808–1833,* 1930; Stephen Clissold *Bernardo O'Higgins and the Independence of Chile, 1960;* 1960; Agustín Edwards, *The Dawn,* 1931; Francisco Antonio Encina, *Portales: Introducción a la historia de la época de Diego Portales: 1830–1891,* 2 vols., 1934; Federico Errázuriz, *Chile bajo el imperio de la constitución de 1828,* 1861; Jaime Eyzaguirre, *Ideario y ruta de la emancipación chilena,* 1957; and *O'Higgins,* 3rd ed., 1950; Guillermo Feliú Cruz, *El pensamiento de O'Higgins,* 1954; Antonio Huneeus Gana, *La Constitución de 1833,* 1933; Jay Kinsbruner, *Bernardo O'Higgins,* 1968; William R. Manning (ed.), *Diplomatic Correspondence of the United States Concerning the Independence of Latin American Nations.* 3 vols., 1925; José Toribio Medina, *Actas del cabildo de Santiago de Chile durante el período llamado de la patria vieja: 1810–1814,* 1910; Néstor Meza Villalobos, *La actividad política del reino de Chile entre 1806 a 1810,* 1968; Bartolomé Mitre, *Historia de San Martín y de la emancipación sudamericana,* 3 vols., 1887–88; Ricardo Montaner Bello, *Historia diplomática de la historia de Chile,*

1961; Francisco José Moreno, *Legitimacy and Stability in Latin America: A Study of Chilean Political Culture*, 1969 (the study by Moreno emphasizes the conflict between the "authoristic" tradition and the liberal principles espoused in the independence period and the 19th century); A. Orrego Luco, *La patria vieja*, 2 vols., 1935–57; Eugenio Orrego Vicuña, *O'Higgins: vida y tiempo*, 1946; Hernán Ramírez Necochea, *Antecedentes económicos de la independencia de Chile*, 1959 (a Marxist interpretation of the independence movement); Raúl Silva Castro, *Egaña en la patria vieja*, 1959; *Ideas y confesiones de Portales*, 1954; and (ed.), *Escritos políticos de Camilo Henríquez*, 1960; Benjamín Vicuña Mackenna, *El ostracismo de los Carrera*, 1938; and *Tradición y reforma en 1810*, 1961; Donald E. Worcester, *Sea Power and Chilean Independence*, 1962.

For post-1810 political development until the Constitution of 1833, the following sources are a good foundation: Diego Barros Arana, Benjamín Vicuña Mackenna, et al., *Historia de la república de Chile: 1810–1830*, 5 vols., 1866–82; Ricardo Donoso, *Desarrollo político y social de Chile, desde la constitución de 1833*, 2nd ed., 1942; *Las ideas políticas en Chile*, 2nd ed., 1967 (this last work is perhaps the most important statement by a Chilean author of the struggle between liberalism and Hispanic values as a constant issue in Chilean history); Alberto Edwards, *La organización política de Chile: 1810–1833*, 2nd ed., 1955; Jaime Eyzaguirre, "Las ideas políticas en Chile hasta 1833," *BACH* 1, 1933; Jay Kinsbruner, *Diego Portales: Interpretive Essays on the Man and Times*, 1967; Daniel Martner, *Estudio de política comercial chilena e historia económica nacional*, 2 vols., 1923; Paul V. Shaw, *The Early Constitutions of Chile*, 1930; Ramón Sotomayor Valdéz, *Historia de Chile bajo el gobierno del general don Joaquín Prieto*, 4 vols., 1900–03; Benjamín Vicuña Mackenna, *Don Diego Portales*, 2 vols., 1863; Sergio Villalobos, *Portales, Una falsificación histórica*, 1989; Carlos Walker Martínez, *Portales*, 1879; José Zapiola, *Recuerdos de treinta años: 1810–1840*, 5th ed., 1902.

NINETEENTH-CENTURY CHILE

Simon Collier's "The Historiography of the 'Portalian' Period: 1830–1891 in Chile," *HAHR*, Nov. 1977, must be consulted when treating this period of Chilean history. Allen Woll's *A Functional Past: The Uses of History in Nineteenth Century Chile*, 1982; summarizes the ideological currents influencing 19th-century Chilean historiography and offers important insights into 19th-century Chilean society. Iván Jaksić's *Andrés Bello: Scholarship and Nation Building in Nineteenth Century Latin America* (forthcoming, 2001), will be a basic source for Chilean intellectual history in the first half-century of independence. This biography is much more ambitious than Miguel Luis Amunátegui, *Vida de don Andrés Bello*, 1882; Raúl Silva Castro, *Don Andrés Bello, 1781–1865*, 1965; and Rafael Caldera, *Andrés Bello*, 7th ed., 1981. Jaksić's *Selected Writings of Andrés Bello*, 1997, makes many of Bello's most important contributions accessible to readers in English. For those not satisfied with selections, see Andrés Bello, *Obras completas de Andrés Bello*, 26 vols., 1981–84. On Bello's liberal intellectual adversary, José Victorino Lastarria, see Bernardo Subercaseaux, *Cultura y sociedad liberal en el siglo XIX (Lastarria, ideologia y literatura)*, 1981, and José Victorino Lastarria, *Recuerdos literarios: Datos para la historia literaria de la América española i del progreso intelectual en Chile*, 2nd ed., 1885; *Diario político, 1849–1852* (with an introduction by Raúl Silva Castro), 1968. Finally translated into English is Lastarria's *Literary Memoirs*, R. Kelly Washbourne, trans., with an introduction by Frederick Nunn, 2000.

In general, historical studies on nineteenth century Chile, prior to the 1980s, came less to rely on the classical Chilean sources and turned to work by European and North American researchers. A resurgence and modernization of Chilean historical studies in the 1980s somewhat changed this trend. Scholars such as Cristián Gazmuri, *El "48" Chileno: Igualitarios, reformistas, radicales, masones y bomberos*, 1992; Alfredo Jocelyn-Holt Letelier, *El peso de la noche, Nuestra frágil fortaleza histórica*, 1997; and Bernardino Bravo Lira, *Portales, El hombre y su obra*, 1989; *El absolutismo ilustrado en Hispanomerica, Chile (1760–1860) De Carlos III a Portales y Montt*, 1992; *El estado de derecho en la historia de Chile*, 1996; and Gonzalo Vial Correa, *Historia de Chile, 1891–1973*, multiple volumes, 1981–97, offered differing and controversial interpretations of Chile's nineteenth century history. New encyclopedic history manuals also reflected an updating and variously framed revisionist versions of Chilean history. Two competing alternatives are *Nueva historia de Chile, Desde los orígenes hasta nuestros días*, 3rd ed., 1997; Alejandro Concha Cruz and Julio Maltés Cortez, *Historia de Chile*, 12th ed., 1998. In 1997 Zig Zag also published the 59th edition of Walter Millar's school text, *Historia de Chile*, a highly stylized, illustrated primer that has sold over a million copies. Millar's history ends in 1974; telling the reader that "it is especially moving how women all over Chile donate their jewelry and other objects of value to the Fund for National Reconstruction [established by the military junta after 1973]." The Department of History at the University of Santiago (USACH) contributed greatly to the resurgence in Chilean historical studies with their journal *Contribuciones Científicas y Tecnológicas*, a gold mine of new approaches, new sources, and new thinking on Chilean social and economic history. Juan Guillermo Muñoz, Luis Ortega, Julio Pinto, Alfredo Joceyln-Holt, Gabriel Salazar, Leonardo León, Jorge Pinto, Sergio Grez, and their colleagues at USACH have been important catalysts in this movement that has focused on issues ranging from gender relations, migration, and labor history to new looks at colonial social and economic history. A parallel renaissance took place at the Instituto de Historia, Pontificia Universidad Católica de Chile, where historians such as Nicolás Cruz, Cristián Gazmuri, Ricardo Krebs, and Sol Serrano contributed to innovative studies of socioeconomic and political history. *Historia*, founded by Jaime Eyzaguirre, continues as the leading professional history journal. *Mapocho*, a review of the humanities and social sciences founded in 1963 by Guillermo Feliú Cruz as the cultural extension medium of the Dirección de Bibliotecas, Archivos y Museos, is a treasure chest for historians as well as students of literature, arts, and the social sciences. As the Director of the Centro de Investigaciones Diego Barros Arana in the late 1990s, historian Rafael Sagredo encouraged creative and specialized historical studies in several new series published by DIBAM, ranging from documentary collections to social and labor history. Other especially important history and social science journals include: *Cuadernos de Historia, Estudios Públicos, Estudios Sociales, Revista de Ciencia Política*, and the *Anales de la Universidad de Chile*.

On Chilean social and economic development in the 19th century, Arnold J. Bauer, *Chilean Rural Society from the Spanish Conquest to 1930*, 1975, provides a useful overview along with a valuable bibliography. Eduardo Cavieres, *Comercio chileno y comerciantes ingleses 1820–1880: un ciclo de historia económica*, 1988, is an insightful look at Chile's incorporation into the international economy and the influence of British merchants and foreign policy. On trade policy, see Sergio Villalobos R. and Rafael Sagredo B., *El proteccionismo económico en Chile siglo XIX*, 1987. Harold Blakemore's *British Nitrates and Chilean Politics: 1886–1896*, 1974, a much broader work than its title suggests, offers a crucial interpretation of socio-economic development and Chilean politics, including a controversial treatment of the martyred president Balmaceda. For a radically different view, readers should consult Hernán Ramírez Necochea, *Historia del imperialismo en Chile*, 1960; *La guerra civil de 1891: antecedentes económicos*, 1953; and *Balmaceda y la contrarrevolución de 1891*, 2nd ed., 1969. Frederick Pike's *Chile and the United States: 1880–1962*, 1962, interprets much of 19th- and early 20th-century Chilean history. A controversial revisionist interpretation of political and economic development in the 19th century is Maurice Zeitlin, *The Civil Wars in Chile*, 1984. On the role of women viewed through the educational system, see Gertrude M. Yeager, "Women's Roles in Nineteenth-Century Chile: Public Education Records, 1843–1883," *Latin American Research Review 18*, No. 3, 1983.

It is difficult to overestimate the role of the Catholic Church in nineteenth-century Chile (or to the present, for that matter). Basic sources are Fidel Araneda Bravo, *Breve historia de la*

Iglesia en Chile, 1968; *Historia de la Iglesia en Chile,* 1986; Marciano Barrios Valdés, *La Iglesia en Chile, sinopsis histórico,* 1987; *Chile y su iglesia: una sola historia,* 1992; Academia Filosófica de Santo Tomás de Aquino, *Estudio sobre la Iglesia en Chile desde la independencia,* 1878; José Ignacio Víctor Eyzaguirre, *Historia eclesiástica, politica y literaria de Chile,* 3 vols., 1850; Carlos Silva Cotapos, *Historia eclesiástica de Chile,* 1925. Marciano Barrios Valdés, "Historiografía eclesiástica, 1848–1988. La Iglesia: Una visión de los laicos," *Historia 28,* 1994: 5–35 assesses the view of secular historians on Church historians and the role of the Church in Chilean history, a topic that has been central since Miguel Luis Amunátegui published the *Compendio de la historia política y eclesiástica de Chile* in 1881. For a survey of work on the "social question," see Patricio Valdivieso Fernández, "'Cuestión Social' y doctrina social de la Iglesia en Chile (1880–1920): Ensyo histórico sobre el estado de la investigación," *Historia 32,* 1999: 553–73.

On 19th- and early 20th-century Chilean politics, Pike's work cited above is a useful summary. A more recent, revisionist view of post-1861 political developments is Julio Heise González, *Historia de Chile: el período parlamentario 1861–1925,* vol. I, 1974, vol. 2, 1982. This study is essential for understanding institutional evolution, the issues and myths surrounding the civil war of 1891, and early 20th-century political history. Heise's bibliography lists most of the important primary and secondary works on Chilean political and constitutional development from the early 19th century to the 1930s. Fernando Campos Harriet, *Historia constitucional de Chile,* 6th ed., 1983, covers the institutional development of the country from precolonial times until 1970, with detailed accounts of the 19th-century administrations, legislation, public policy, and extensive bibliographical references in the notes. A basic source on Congress, political parties, and government cabinets that also reprints Chile's constitutions since 1810 is Luis Valencia Avaria, comp., *Anales de la República, Tomos I y II Actualizados,* 1986. Ricardo Anguita, *Leyes promulgadas en Chile desde 1810 hasta el 1 de junio de 1912,* 5 vols., 1912–13 reprints and systematically indexes legislation by topic from independence until almost the outbreak of World War I. A revisionist look at Chilean political history in the nineteenth century, focusing on civil wars, political crises, and amnesties, is Brian Loveman and Elizabeth Lira, *Las suaves cenizas del olvido, Via chilena de reconciliación política, 1814–1932,* 1999.

In *Diagnóstico de la burocracia chilena: 1818–1969,* Germán Urzúa Valenzuela and Ana María García Barzellatto provide a synthesis of the growth of the Chilean state apparatus since independence and the political implications of bureaucratic expansion, including developments in the 19th century. Also of value is Germán Urzúa Valenzuela, *Evolución de la administración pública chilena (1818–1968),* 1970. Ricardo Donoso's polemical *Desarrollo político y social de Chile desde la constitución de 1833* and *Las ideas políticas en Chile,* 2nd ed., 1967 are both among the key secondary works on the 19th century. For a Marxian interpretation, also the source of much revisionist history on the 19th century, see Julio César Jobet, *Ensayo Crítico del desarrollo económico-social de Chile,* 1955. Another important contribution to social history is Guillermo Feliú Cruz, "Un esquema de la evolución social de Chile en el siglo hasta 1891," in *Chile: visto a través de Agustín Ross,* 1950.

In general, studies on the 19th century are much more specialized. In the broad area of socio-economic evolution, including works on particular areas of the Chilean economy, social stratification and class conflict, the social question, technological change and international economic relations, one school of historical scholarship has emphasized the "dependency" of Chilean development upon events in Europe and North America. Complementing more traditional Marxist treatments of Chilean socio-economic trends in the 19th century and Francisco Encina's earlier laments concerning the direction and character of Chilean development in *Nuestra inferioridad económica,* 1955, the dependency theorists trace most problems facing Chile to this pattern of international exploitation in the past centuries. Key works in this tradition include Ramírez Necochea's already mentioned study, *Historia del imperialismo* en Chile, 1960; Marta Harnecker and Gabriela Uribe, *Imperialismo y dependencia*, 1972; and three doctoral dissertations: Roger Burbach. *The Chilean Industrial Bourgeoisie and Foreign Capital 1920–1970*, Indiana Univ., 1975; Charles G. Pregger Román, *Dependent Development in Nineteenth Century Chile*, Rutgers Univ., 1975; and Jacqueline Spencer Garreaud, *A Dependent Country: Chile 1817–1861*, Univ. of California, San Diego, 1981. A related but more balanced approach is Aníbal Pinto Santa Cruz, *Chile: un caso de desarrollo frustrado*, 1959.

Markos J. Mamalakis's *The Growth and Structure of the Chilean Economy: From Independence to Allende*, 1976, offers a significant counter to the dependency theorists. Carmen Cariola Sutter and Osvaldo Sunkel, *Un siglo de historia económica de Chile, 1830–1930*, 1982, offers interpretive essays on a century of Chilean economic evolution, useful statistical appendices, and an important annotated thematic bibliography. Patricio Meller's *Un siglo de economía política chilena (1890–1990)*, 1996, brings this topic to the transition from the military regime to an elected government in 1990.

Henry W. Kirsch, *Industrial Development in a Traditional Society, The Conflict of Entrepreneurship and Modernization in Chile*, 1977, reassesses Chilean industrial development and includes a wealth of descriptive material and bibliographical references. Other key sources on industrialization include Oscar Alvarez A., *Historia del desarrollo industrial de Chile*, 1936; special issue of *Colección Estudios CIEPLAN*, No. 12, March 1984, "Perspectivas históricas de la economía chilena: del siglo XIX a la crisis del 30" (includes a suggestive article by Carlos Hurtado R. T., "La economía chilena entre 1830–1930: sus limitaciones y sus herencias," which re-evaluates Chilean economic policy and the role of the state in the 19th century). Another important contribution to the reassessment of Chilean industrial and economic development is J. Gabriel Palma, *Growth and Structure of Chilean Manufacturing Industry from 1830 to 1935: Origins and Development of a Process of Industrialization in an Export Economy*, Ph.D. diss., Univ. of Oxford, 1979. Also of use on the 19th-century development of the Chilean economy are Harold Blakemore, *Dos estudios sobre salitre y política en Chile (1870–1895)*, 1991; Luis Ortega and Julio Pinto, *Expansión minera y desarrollo industrial: un caso de crecimiento asociado (Chile 1850–1914)*, 1990; Luis Ortega, *Change and Crisis in Chile's Economy and Society, 1865–1879*, Ph.D. diss., Univ. of London, 1979; "Acerca de los orígenes de la industrialización chilena, 1860–1879," *Revista Nueva Historia*, No. 2, 1981; and P. S. Conoboy, *Money and Politics in Chile, 1878–1925*, Ph.D. diss., Univ. of Southhampton, 1977.

For particular sectors or regions of the Chilean economy, development of transport, and communication networks in the 19th century the following sources are of considerable value: Marcello Carmagnani, *Sviluppo Industriale e Sotto-Sviluppo Económico: il caso cileno 1860–1920* (Turin, 1971); C. W. Centner, "Great Britain and Chilean Mining: 1830–1914," *Economic History Review*, No. 12 (1942); Santiago Machiavello Varas, *El problema de la industria del cobre y sus proyecciones económicas y sociales*, 1923; Markos Mamalakis and Clark Reynolds, *Essays on the Chilean Economy*, 1965; Santiago Marín Vicuña, *Los ferrocarriles en Chile*, 1912; Max Nolff, "Industria manufacturera," CORFO, *Geografía económica de Chile*, 1967; Robert B. Oppenheimer, *Chilean Transportation Development: The Railroads and Socio-economic Change in the Central Valley*, Ph.D. diss, Univ. of California, Los Angeles, 1976; "National Capital and National Development: Financing Chile's Railroads in the 19th Century," *Business History Review*, 54, Spring 1982; Luis Ortega, "The First Four Decades of the Chilean Coal Mining Industry," *Journal of Latin American Studies 14*, May 1982; L. R. Pederson. *The Mining History of the Norte Chico: Chile*, 1966; Ian Thomson and Dietrich Angerstein, *Historia del ferrocarril en Chile*, 1997; John Whaley, *Transportation in Chile's Bío Bío Region: 1850–1915*, Ph.D. diss., (Indiana Univ., 1974. Whaley's work, an excellent economic history of the Biobío region, also discusses primary sources and railroad statistics.

On nitrates, the most important sector of the economy in the late 19th century, see in addition to the Blakemore work already mentioned, Oscar Bermúdez, *Historia del salitre desde* sus orígenes hasta la guerra del Pacífico, 1963; G. Billinghurst, Los capitales salitreros de Tarapacá, 1889; Manuel Cruchaga, Guano y salitre, 1929; J. R. Brown, "Nitrate Crisis: Combinations and the Chilean Government in the Nitrate Age," HAHR, No. 63, 1963; "The Chilean Nitrate Railways Controversy," HAHR, No. 38, 1958; Ronald Crozier, "El salitre hasta la Guerra del Pacífico. Una revisión," Historia (Santiago) 30, 1997: 53–126; M. B. Donald, "History of the Chile Nitrate Industry," Annals of Science 1, Jan. 1936; and 2, April 1936; Manuel A. Fernández, Technology and British Nitrate Enterprises in Chile 1810–1945, 1981; Roberto Hernández C., El salitre: Resumen histórico desde su descubrimiento y explotación, 1930; Historia del salitre, desde la guerra del Pacífico hasta la Revolución de 1891, 1981; Thomas F. O'Brien, The Nitrate Industry and Chile's Crucial Transition: 1870–1891, 1982; Michael Monteón, Chile in the Nitrate Era, The Evolution of Economic Dependence, 1880–1930, 1982; Charles Bergquist, Labor in Latin America, Comparative Essays on Chile, Argentina, Venezuela and Colombia, 1986; Enrique Reyes Navarro, Salitre de Chile: Apertura, inversión y mercado mundial, 1880–1925, 1994; Alejandro Soto Cardenas, Influencia británica en el salitre, Origen, naturaleza y decadencia, 1998 (an impressive study of the nitrate industry from the mid-nineteenth century until 1930, based on extensive review of British public and private archives); J. F. Rippy, British Investments in Latin America: 1822–1949, 1966. A doctoral dissertation at Indiana University (1978) by Laurence Stickell, Migration and Mining: Labor in Northern Chile in the Nitrate Era, 1880–1930, is a most important social and labor history of the nitrate industry.

Each of the "major" events and international conflicts of Chile's 19th-century history has occasioned its own historical literature. This includes, of course, the war against the Peru-Bolivia confederation early in the century, participation in the gold rushes of California and Australia, the civil wars of 1851 and 1859, the War of the Pacific, the civil war of 1891, and the effects of each economic boom or depression.

On the California gold rush's impact on Chile see Jay Monaghan, Chile, Peru and the California Gold Rush of 1849, 1973. A Marxist treatment of the civil wars of 1851 and 1859 is Luis Vitale's, Las guerras civiles de 1851 y 1859 en Chile, 1971. Useful specialized studies on fiscal, financial, and public-sector performance include: Roberto Espinoza, Cuestiones financieras de Chile, 1909; La reforma bancaria y monetaria, 1913; Carlos T. Hamud, El sector público chileno entre 1830–1930, 1969; and Agustín Ross, Chile: 1851–1910: sesenta años de cuestiones monetarias y financieras y de problemas bancarios, 1911. Another ostensibly specialized study in Claudio Véliz, Historia de la marina mercante de Chile, 1961, a work which goes well beyond history of the merchant marine, representing a basic source for Chilean economic history in the 19th century.

Immigration to Chile in the 19th century has also received limited, but careful attention in Carl Solberg, Immigration and Nationalism: Argentina and Chile 1890–1914, 1970; Jean Pierre Blancpain, Les Allemands au Chili: 1816–1945, 1974—a massive study of the German experience in Chile and the German contribution to Chilean society; Francia y los franceses en Chile, 1987; Carlos Díaz and Fredy Cancino, Italianos en Chile, 1988; Mark Jefferson, Recent Colonization in Chile, 1921; N. Vega, Album de la Colonie Français au Chili, 1903; La inmigración europea en Chile, 1882–1895, 1896; George Young, The Germans in Chile: Immigration and Colonization 1849–1914, 1974. A more comprehensive look at immigration, with brief summaries of the immigration to Chile of most ethnic groups (Germans, British, French, Italians, Swiss, Jews, Yugoslavs, Scandanavians, etc.) and relevant bibliography, is René A. Feri Fagerstrom, Reseña de la colonización en Chile, 1989. On internal and cross-border migration, see Carmen Norambuena Carrasco, ed., Faltan o sobran brazos? Migraciones internas y fronterizas (1850–1930), 1997.

For the most systematic and detailed discussion of Chile in world affairs in the 19th century, and the domestic impact of these events, see the award-winning volume by Robert N. Burr, By Reason or Force: Chile and the Balancing Power in South America 1830–1905, 1965.

Burr's bibliography lists a wide range of official publications and other primary sources for Chilean international relations in the 19th century as well as materials on domestic development. An earlier but still useful look at Chilean diplomacy in the 19th century is Henry Clay Evans, *Chile and Its Relations with the United States*, 1927. Evan's book also surveys domestic socio-economic development in the 19th century. Other diplomatic studies include the classic by Mario Barros, *Historia diplomática de Chile 1541–1938*, 1970, which provides an overview from the colonial period to the Popular Front; William R. Sherman, *The Diplomatic and Commercial Relations of the United States and Chile: 1820–1914*, 1926. The war with Spain in the 1860s is treated in William Columbus Davis, *The Last Conquistadores*, 1959. Of great value for the War of the Pacific and late 19th-century Chile is William Sater's careful study, *The Heroic Image in Chile: Arturo Prat,Secular Saint*, 1973. Sater's bibliography and notes contain numerous references to primary sources and government documents related to the War of the Pacific and Chilean economic and political development in the 19th century as well as newspaper and journal sources. Sater's article, "Chile during the First Months of the War of the Pacific," *Journal of Latin American Studies* 5, 1973, is helpful for background on the Chilean situation as the country entered the War of the Pacific. Sater has also contributed *Chile and the War of the Pacific*, 1986, which details conditions in Chile during the war and its effect on domestic politics and economy and a lively, controversial new look at U.S.-Chilean in *Chile and the United States, Empires in Conflict*, 1990. Joaquín Fermandois offers a particular Chilean view of domestic politics and U.S.-Chilean relations in the 1930s and the 1970s in *Abismo y cimiento: Gustavo Ross y las relaciones entre Chile y Estados Unidos, 1932–1938*, 1997, and *Chile y el mundo, 1970–1973: la política exterior del gobierno de la Unidad Popular y el sistema internacional*, 1985. On the period since 1960 see Paul Sigmund, *The United States and Democracy in Chile*, 1994.

The War of the Pacific and the subsequent diplomatic conflicts involving Chile, Peru, and Bolivia are the subjects of a large number of patriotic diatribes and some scholarly study. For varying interpretations of the war and polemical discussion of culpability the following list of sources may be consulted: Pascual Ahumada Moreno, *Guerra del Pacífico*, 8 vols., 1884–1891; Jorge Basadre, *Historia de la República del Perú*, 6th ed., 1968 (Basadre is Peru's most eminent historian); Gonzalo Bulnes, *Guerra del Pacífico*, 3 vols., 1911; Andrés A. Cáceres, *La Guerra del 79: sus compañas. Redacción y notas por Julio C. Guerrero*, 1973 (the memoirs of Peru's leading general and hero of the War of the Pacific); and *La guerra entre el Perú y Chile: 1879–1883*, 1924; Edmundo H. Civati Bernasconi, *Guerra del Pacífico: 1879–1883*, 2 vols., 1946; W. J. Dennis,*Tacna and Arica: An Account of the Chile-Peru Boundary Dispute and the Arbitration of the United States*, 1931; Francisco García Calderón, *Memorias del cautiverio: prólogo y notas de Ventura García Calderón*, 1949 (account of this Peruvian expresident's capture and imprisonment by the Chileans after the occupation of Lima); V. G. Kiernan, "Foreign Interest in the War of the Pacific," *HAHR* 35, 1955; Sir Clements R. Markham, *The War between Peru and Chile: 1879–1882*, 1882; Herbert Millington, *American Diplomacy and the War of the Pacific*, 1948; Mariano Felipe Paz-Soldán, *Narración histórica de la guerra de Chile contra el Perú y Bolivia*, 1884.

LABOR AND THE SOCIAL QUESTION

The last decades of the 19th century brought the social question to Chile. In addition to the numerous contemporary accounts, political proclamations, and other writing, the following works are useful to the understanding of the social question and the labor movement in Chile. Robert Alexander, *Communism in Latin America*, 1957; and *Labor Relations in Argentina, Brazil and Chile*, 1962; Alan Angell, *Politics and the Labour Movement in Chile*, 1972; Jorge Barría Serín, *Breve historia del sindicalismo chileno*, 1967; *Trayectoria y estructura del movimiento sindical chileno*, 1963; and *El movimiento obrero en Chile*, 1972; Peter DeShazo, *Urban Workers and Labor Unions in Chile, 1902–1927*, 1983; Julio César Jobet *Recabarren, los orígenes del movimiento obrero y del socialismo chileno*, 1956; Eduardo Devés, *Los que van a morir te saludan: Historia de una masacre. Escuela Santa María de Iquique, 1907*, 1998; Mario Garcés, *Crisis social y motines populares en el 1900*, 1991; Sergio González Miranda, *Hombres y mujeres de la pampa*, 1991; Sergio Grez Toso, *De la 'Regeneración del Pueblo' a la huelga general. Génesis y evolución histórica del movimiento popular en Chile (1810–1890)*, 1997 (an 800-page tome on popular organizations such as mutual aid societies, artisan groups, and proto-labor unions since independence); Guillermo Kaempffer Villagrán, *Así sucedió, Sangrientos episodios de la lucha obrera en Chile*, 1962; Patricio Manns, *Breve síntesis del movimiento obrero*, 1972; James Oliver Morris, *Elites, Intellectuals, and Consensus: A Study of the Social Question and the Industrial Relations System in Chile*, 1966—this book provides the most complete list of references to newspaper, periodical and contemporary literature on the social question as well as secondary sources—; Fernando Ortiz Letelier, *El movimiento obrero en Chile 1891–1919*, 1985; Crisóstomo Pizarro, *La huelga obrera en Chile*, 1986; Julio Pinto Vallejos, *Trabajos y rebeldías en la pampa salitrera*, 1998 (perhaps the most carefully researched history of the nitrate labor force, the emergence of the labor movement, and social change in northern Chile); Hernán Ramírez Necochea, *Historia del movimiento obrero en Chile: siglo XIX*, 1956; Luis Emilio Recabarren, *Los albores de la revolución social en Chile*, 1921—the author is the most well-known early leader of the Chilean labor movement—; and *Ricos y pobres a través de un siglo de vida republicana*, 1910; Jorge Rojas Flores, *Los niños cristaleros: Trabajo infantil de la industria. Chile, 1880–1950*, 1996 (an important study of child labor in Chilean industry); Gabriel Salazar, *Labradores, peones y proletarios*, 1985; Carlos Vega Delgado, *La masacre en la Federación Obrera de Magallanes, El movimiento obrero patagónico-fueguino hasta 1920*, 1996. Alberto Varona, *Francisco Bilbao: revolucionario de América*, 1973. For debates and other materials on the social question, see Sergio Grez Toso, *La 'cuestión social' en Chile, Ideas y debates precursores*, 1995.

A useful sample of contemporary sources on the social question and early labor histories includes: Juan Enrique Concha, *Cuestiones obreras*, 1899; Luis Malaquías Concha S., *Sobre la dictación de un código del trabajo y de la previsión social*, 1907; Javier Díaz Lira, *Observaciones sobre la cuestión social en Chile*, 1904; Marcos Gutiérrez Martínez, *La cuestión obrera i el derecho de propiedad*, 1904; "Informes de los Señores Concha y Quezada," *Boletín de la sociedad de fomento fabril 20*, 1903; Tulio Lagos V., *Bosquejo histórico del movimiento obrero en Chile*, 1947; J. Lawrence Laughlin, "The Strike at Iquique," *The Journal of Political Economy 17*, 1909; Augusto Orrego Luco, "La cuestión social en Chile," *Anales de la Universidad de Chile 119. Primero y segundo trimestre*, 1961, No. 121 y 122; Moisés Poblete Troncoso, *El derecho del trabajo y la seguridad social en Chile*, 1949; J. Valdés Cange (pseudonym used by Alejandro Venegas), *Cartas al Excelentísimo Señor Don Pedro Montt*, 1909; Benjamín Vicuña Subercaseaux, *Socialismo revolucionario y la cuestión social en Europa y Chile*, 1908.

Political histories of Chile of the 19th century are numerous. Available to a lesser extent are summaries of the terms of individual presidents. Simon Collier's earlier cited article on the historiography of the Portalian period, *HAHR*, Nov. 1977, reviews the major work on this period while Harold Blakemore's "The Chilean Revolution of 1891 and Its Historiography," *HAHR 45*, Aug. 1965, is the single most important review of sources on the civil war of 1891, Balmaceda, and Chilean society at the turn of the century. Among the most important Chilean treatments of the period 1831–71, along with specialized work on reform movements and organizations are: Diego Barros Arana, *Un decenio de la historia de Chile 1841–1851*, 2 vols., 1905–06 (perhaps the best historical treatment of any period in Chilean history); Agustín Edwards, *Cuatro presidentes de Chile, 1841–1876*, 2 vols., 1932; José Victorino Lastarria, *Diario Político 1849–1852*, 1968; Benjamín Oviedo, *La masonería en Chile, bosquejo histórico*, 1929; Fernando Pinto, *La masonería y su influencia en Chile*, 1966; Daniel Riquelme, *La revolución del 20 de abril de 1851,* 1966; Luis A. Romero, *La Sociedad de Igualdad, Los artesanos de Santiago de Chile y sus primeras experiencias políticas, 1820–1851,* 1978; Gabriel Sanhueza, *Santiago Arcos,* 1956; Ismael Valdés, *El Cuerpo de Bomberos, 1863–1900,* 1980; Benjamín Vicuña Mackenna, *Los Girondinos chilenos,* 1902; *Historia de los 10 años de la administración de don Manuel Montt,* 5 vols., 1862–63; *Historia de la jornada del 20 de abril de 1851,* 1878; *Historia jeneral de la República de Chile desde su independencia hasta nuestros,* 5 vols., 1866–82; Luis Vitale, *Las guerras civiles de 1851 y 1859,* 1971. Carlos Foresti, Eva Löfquist, and Alvar Foresti, *La narrativa chilena, Desde la Independencia hasta la Guerra del Pacífico, I 1810–1859,* 1999, offer analysis of the political press and literature in the pre-1879 period with extensive bibliography.

Many of the Chilean histories of the 19th century represent Liberal attacks on Conservative or Portalian administrations or vice versa.

On individual presidential administrations see: Juan Bautista Alberdi, *Biografía del general Don Manuel Bulnes: presidente de la República de Chile,* 1846; José A. Alfonso, *Los partidos políticos en Chile,* 1902; Agustín Edwards, *Cuatro presedentes de Chile, 1841–1876,* 2 vols., 1933; Alberto Edwards Vives, *El gobierno de don Manuel Montt: 1851–1861,* 1932; Isidoro Errázuriz, *Historia de la administración Errázuriz,* 1935; Jaime Eyzaguirre, *Chile durante el gobierno de Errázuriz Echaurren: 1896–1901,* 1957; Germán Riesco, *Presidencia de Riesco,* 1950; Ricardo Salas Edwards, *Balmaceda y el parlamentarismo en Chile,* 1914; Ramón Sotomayor Valdés, *Historia de Chile durante los cuarenta años transcurridos desde 1831 hasta 1871,* 2 vols., 1875–76; Benjamín Vicuña Mackenna, *Introducción a los diez años de la administración Montt, Don Diego Portales.* 2 vols., Valparaíso, 1863; Cristián A. Zegers, *Aníbal Pinto: Historia política de su gobierno,* 1969.

The evolution of 19th-century political thought, parliamentary institutions, electoral reform, the crisis of the Balmaceda presidency, and the character of the Chilean oligarchy are treated in: José A. Alfonso, *El parlamentarismo i la reforma política en Chile,* 1909; Justo and Domingo Arteaga, *Los constituyentes de 1870,* 1910; Abdón Cifuentes, *Memorias,* 2 vols., 1936; Malaquías Concha, *El programa de la democracia,* 1908; Ricardo Donoso, *Alessandri, agitador y demoledor: cincuenta años de historia política de Chile,* 2 vols., 1952, 1954; and *Historia de las ideas políticas en Chile,* 1946; Alberto Edwards Vives, *La fronda aristocrática,* 1936; Rafael Egaña, *Historia de la dictadura y la revolución de 1891,* 1891; Pedro Pablo Figueroa, *Historia de la revolución constituyente: 1858–1859,* 1889; Maximiliano Ibáñez, *El régimen parlamentario en Chile,* 1908; Abraham König, *La constitución de 1833 en 1913,* 1913; José J. Larraín, *El derecho parlamentario chileno,* 2 vols., 1896–97; José Victorino Lastarria, *La constitución política de la República de Chile comentada,* 1856; José Maza, *Sistemas de sufragio i cuestión electoral,* 1913; Hermógenes Pérez de Arce, *El parlamentarismo,* 1901; Paul Reinsch, "Parliamentary Government in Chile," *APSR,* June 1909; Manuel Rivas Vicuña, *Historia política y parlamentaria de Chile,* 3 vols., 1964—a key figure in Chilean parliamentary politics provides valuable insight into the parliamentary era—; Ramón V. Subercaseaux, *Memorias de ochenta años,* 1936.

THE CIVIL WAR OF 1891

The civil war of 1891, with its relationship to the nitrate economy, and also the symbol of President Balmaceda, has generated considerable historical literature. Harold Blakemore's "The Chilean Revolution of 1891 and Its Historiography," *HAHR 14,* 1965, reviews this literature and offers the reader the benefit of Professor Blakemore's astute interpretation of the Balmaceda years. Blakemore's book *British Nitrates and Chilean Politics: 1886–1896,* 1974, is by far the most important work on the Balmaceda period. Among the most important treatments of the Balmaceda period and the civil war of 1891 are: J. Bañados Espinosa, *Balmaceda: su gobierno y la revolución de 1891,* 2 vols., Paris, 1894; Aníbal Bravo Kendrick, *La revolución de 1891,* 1946; J. Díaz Valderrama, *La guerra civil de 1891,* 2 vols., 1942; Maurice Kervey, *Dark Days in Chile,* London, 1891–92; Luis Ortega, ed., *La guerra civil de 1891, 100 años hoy,* 1993;

Fernando Pinto Lagarrigue, *Balmaceda y los gobiernos seudo-parlamentarios*, 1991; Crisóstomo Pizarro, *La revolución de 1891*, 1971; Hernán Ramírez Necochea, *Balmaceda y la contrarrevolución de 1891*, 2nd ed., 1969 (a Marxist interpretation of the Civil War of 1891); J. Rodríguez Bravo, *Balmaceda y el conflicto entre el congreso y el ejecutivo*, 2 vols., 1921, 1926; Edwards R. Salas, *Balmaceda y el parlamentarismo en Chile*, 2 vols., 1914, 1925; J. Sears and B. W. Wells, *The Chilean Revolution of 1891*, 1893; Bernardo Subercaseaux S., *Fin de siglo, La época de Balmaceda*, 1988; Ximena Vergara and Luis L. Barros, "La guerra civil del 91 y la instauración del parlamentarismo" *Revista Latinoamericana de Ciencias Sociales* 3, June 1972; J. M. Yrarrázaval, *El presidente Balmaceda*, 2 vols., 1940.

ECONOMY AND SOCIETY IN THE TWENTIETH CENTURY

It is very difficult to find a discussion of the Chilean economy that fails to include discussion of Chilean politics. In an effort to provide a bibliographical overview of Chilean political economy in the 20th century, I have compiled a list of works covering the economy to approximately 1970. The works on this list include both general treatments and studies with a more specialized focus. In addition, separate lists of references follow for the agricultural sector, copper, and mining, due to the special importance of these sectors of the Chilean economy both in strictly economic terms and in regard to Chilean politics.

In addition to the recent work of Mamalakis (*The Growth and Structure of the Chilean Economy: From Independence to Allende,* 1976) mentioned earlier, the best synthesis of Chilean political economy and economic issues for the period 1952 to 1970 is Ricardo Ffrench Davis, *Políticas económicas en Chile: 1952–1970*, 1973, which examines stabilization programs and economic policy from the time of the Klein-Saks missions to 1970. It also includes extremely useful data series and an excellent bibliography of technical literature on the Chilean economy. For general treatments of Chilean economic development and economic issues see: Jere R. Behrman, *Macroeconomic Policy in a Developing Country: The Chilean Experience,* 1977; José Cademártori, *La economía chilena: un enfoque marxista,* 1968; Alvin Cohen, *Economic Change in Chile: 1929–1959,* 1960; ECLA (CEPAL), *Antecedentes sobre el desarrollo de la economía chilena: 1925–1952,* 1954; Enrique Figueroa Ortiz, *Carbón: cien años de historia (1848–1960),* 1987; Instituto de Economía de la Universidad de Chile, *Desarrollo económico de Chile: 1940–1956,* 1956; and *La economía de Chile: 1950–1963,* 2 vols., 1963; Julio César Jobet, *Ensayo crítico del desarrollo económico social de Chile,* 1955; Santiago Machiavello Varas, *Política económica nacional: antecedentes y directiva,* 2 vols., 1931; Markos Mamalakis and Clark Reynolds, *Essays on the Chilean Economy,* 1965; Daniel Martner, *Estudio de política comercial chilena e historia económica nacional,* 2 vols., 1923; Aníbal Pinto et al., *Chile hoy,* 1970; *Chile: una economía difícil,* 1964; *Tres ensayos sobre Chile y América Latina,* Buenos Aires, 1971; and *Hacia nuestra independencia económica,* 1963; Universidad de Chile, *Desarrollo de Chile en la primera mitad del siglo XX,* I. 1953; Stefan de Vylder, *From Colonialism to Dependence: An Introduction to Chile's Economic History,* Stockholm, 1977; Roberto Zahler et al., *Chile 1940/1975 Treinta y cinco años de discontinuidad económica,* 2nd ed., 1978; Mario Zañartu and John Kennedy (eds.), *The Overall Development of Chile,* Notre Dame, 1969. A fascinating study of the image of Balmaceda as portrayed in popular poetry is Micaela Navarrete Araya, *Balmaceda en la poesia popular 1886–1896,* 1993.

Public finance, monetary issues, and the continuing debate over inflation and stabilization policy are discussed in: César Araneda Encina, *Veinte años de la historia monetaria de Chile: 1925–1945,* 1945; Banco Central de Chile, *Evolución de las finanzas públicas de Chile: 1950–1960,* 1963; Jorge Cauas, "Políticas de estabilización: el caso chileno," *Estudios monetarios* 2, 1970; Tom E. Davis, "Eight Decades of Inflation in Chile: 1879–1959: A Political Interpretation," *Journal of Political Economy 81,* No. 4, 1963; David Felix, "An Alternative View of the 'Monetarist-Structuralist' Controversy," *Latin American Issues: Essays and Comments.* A. Hirschman (ed.), 1961; Frank Fetter, *Monetary Inflation in Chile*, 1931; Herman Finer, *The Chilean Development Corporation*, 1947; Joseph Grunwald, "The 'Structuralist' School in Price Stabilization and Economic Development: The Chilean Case," *Latin American Issues: Essays and Comments*, A. Hirschman (ed.), 1961; Albert O. Hirschman, "Inflation in Chile," *Journeys Toward Progress*, 1963; Rolf Lüders, *A Monetary History of Chile 1925–1958*, Ph.D. diss., Univ. of Chicago, 1968; Misión Klein-Saks, *El programa de estabilización de la economía chilena y el trabajo de la Misión Klein-Saks*, 1958; Ministerio de Hacienda, *Cuentas fiscales de Chile: 1925–1957*, 1959; Max Nolff and Felipe Herrera, *La inflación: naturaleza y problems*, 1954; ODEPLAN, *Cuentas nacionales: 1960–1970*, 1971; Enrique Sierra, *Tres ensayos de estabilización en Chile*, 1970.

Sectoral development in industry, agriculture, mining, and banking tax or exchange rate policy receive treatment in: Rafael Agacino, Cristián González, and Jorge Rojas, *Capital transnacional y trabajo. El desarrollo minero en Chile*, 1998; Pedro Aguirre Cerda, *El problema agrario*, 1929; and *El problema industrial*, 1933; Oscar Alvarez Andrews, *Historia del desarrollo industrial de Chile*, 1936; Sergio Aranda and Alberto Martínez, *Industria y agricultura en el desarrollo económico*, 1970; Solon Barraclough, "Reforma agraria: historia y perspective," *Cuadernos de la Realidad Nacional*, No. 7, 1971; Marcello Carmagnani and C. M. Hernández, "Evolución de la industria en Chile: 1860–1940," *Boletín del Centro de Estudios Socioeconómicos 1*, 1967; F. Durán Bernales, *Población, alimentos y reforma agraria*, 1966; Ricardo Lagos, *La industria en Chile: antecedentes estructurales*, 1966; Daniel Martner, *Estudio de política comercial chilena e historia económica nacional*, 2 vols., 1923; Oscar Muñoz G., *Crecimiento industrial de Chile: 1940–1965*, 1968; *Chile y su industrialización*, 1986; and et al., *Proceso a la industrialización chilena*, 1972 (collection of articles considering development under conditions of dependence, and various aspects of industrial development in Chile); *Los inesperados caminos de la modernización económica*, 1995; Aníbal Pinto, *Chile: un caso de desarrollo frustrado*, 2nd ed, 1973; Mariano Puga Vera, *El petróleo chileno*, 1964.

Concern with foreign investment and concentration of wealth and power in Chile are found in: Jorge Ahumada, *En vez de la miseria*, 1958; Genaro Arriagada, *La oligarquía patronal chilena*, 1970; Sergio Bitar, "La inversión extranjera en la industria chilena," *Trimestre Económico 13*, No. 4, Oct.–Dec. 1971; CORFO, *Análisis de las inversiones extranjeras en Chile: 1954–1969*, 1972; and *La inversión extranjera en la industria chilena*, 1970; F. Dahse, *El mapa de la extrema riqueza*, 1979; Hugo Fazio, *Mapa actual de la extrema riqueza en Chile*, 1997; Fernando Galofré, *Entrepreneurial and Governmental Elites in Chilean Development*, Ph.D. diss., Tulane Univ., 1970; Ricardo Lagos, *La concentración del poder económico, su teoría, realidad chilena*, 1961; and "La nueva burguesía chilena," *Revista APSI*, June 1981; Patricio Rozas and Gustavo Marín, *El mapa de 'extrema riqueza' 10 años después*, 1989; Maurice Zeitlin et al., "New Princes for Old? The Large Corporation and the Capitalist Class in Chile," *American Journal of Sociology 80*, July 1974.

CHILEAN AGRICULTURE, RURAL LIFE, AND AGRARIAN REFORM

Many writers have analyzed Chilean politics and society against the backdrop of the land tenure system, *inquilinaje*, deficient agricultural production, and the relationship between rural life and urban power. CIDA, *Chile: Tenencia de la tierra y desarrollo socio-económico del sector agrícola*, 1966, and the annotated bibliography published by the Land Tenure Center at the University of Wisconsin at Madison—*Agrarian Reform in Latin America: An Annotated Bibliography*, 1974—are excellent sources of bibliographical references on agriculture, rural life, and agrarian reform in Chile. Key studies on rural Chile and the formation of the hacienda system include: Rafael Baraona et al., *Valle de Putaendo*, 1960; Luis Correa Vergara, *Agricultura Chilena*, 2 vols., 1939; Ramón Domínguez, *Nuestro sistema de inquilinaje*, 1867; M. Drouilly and Pedro Lucio Cuadra, "Ensayo sobre el estado económico de la agricultura en Chile," *Boletín de la Sociedad Nacional de Agricultura 10, 1878*; Mario Góngora, *Encomenderos y estancieros, 1970*; *Origen de los "inquilinos" de Chile central*, 1960, with Jean Border, *Evolución de la propiedad en el valle del Puange*, 2 vols., 1956; Silvia Hernández, "Transformaciones tecnológicas en la agricultura de Chile central: siglo XIX," *Cuadernos del Centro de Estudios Socio-económicos*, No. 3, 1966; Gonzalo Izquierdo, *Un estudio de las ideologías chilenas: la sociedad de agricultura en el siglo XIX*, 1968; Carlos Keller, *Una revolución en la agricultura*, 1956; George McBride, *Chile: Land and Society*, 1936, Tancredo Pinochet Le-Brun, "Inquilinos en la hacienda de su excelencia," *Antología chilena de la tierra*, Antonio Corvalán, ed., 1970; Moisés Poblete Troncoso, *El problema de la producción agrícola y la política agraria nacional*, 1919; Teodoro Schneider, *La agricultura chilena durante los últimos cincuenta años* (1904). Jaime Valenzuela Márquez, *Bandidaje rural en Chile central, 1850–1900*, 1991, is a revealing study of rural social conditions and banditry. Alberto Cardemil offers a historico-cultural interpretation of the Chilean "cowboy" in *El huaso chileno*, 1999.

Significant contributions include the long list of works published at ICIRA in Santiago under the direction of Solon Barraclough prior to the military coup of 1973. Perhaps foremost on the list is Almino Affonso et al., *Movimiento campesino chileno*, 2 vols. (1970). Among others are: Andrés Pascal, *Relaciones de poder en una localidad rural*; Solon Barraclough, *Notas sobre tenencia de la tierra en América Latina*; Pablo Ramírez, *Cambios en las formas de pago a la mano de obra agrícola*; A. Corvalán et al., *Reforma agraria chilena: seis ensayos de interpretación*; Antonio Corvalán (ed.), *Antología chilena de la tierra*; Alejandro Saavedra, *La cuestión mapuche*; Hugo Zemelman, *El migrante rural*; Brian Loveman, *El campesino chileno le escribe a su excelencia*.

Other important studies include: José Bengoa, *El Campesinado Chileno después de la reforma agraria*, 1983; *El poder y la subordinación*, 1988; José Del Pozo, *Historia del vino chileno*, 1998; Lovell S. Jarvis, *Chilean Agriculture under Military Rule, From Reform to Reaction, 1973–1980*, 1985; Cristóbal Kay, *Comparative Development of the European Manorial System and the Latin American Hacienda System: An Approach to a Theory of Agrarian Change for Chile*, Ph.D. diss., Univ. of Sussex, Eng., 1971; Cristóbal Kay and Patricio Silva, ed. *Development and Social Change in the Chilean Countryside: from the pre-land reform period to the democratic transition*, 1992; Robert R. Kaufman, *The Politics of Land Reform in Chile*, 1972; Brian Loveman, *Struggle in the Countryside: Politics and Rural Labor in Chile 1919–1973*, 1976; William Thiesenhusen, *Chile's Experiments in Agrarian Reform*, 1966; Thomas C. Wright, *Landowners and Reform in Chile: The Sociedad Nacional de Agricultura 1919–40*, 1982.

COPPER

Since 1930 copper has dominated Chile's economy. At the mercy of international economic forces and controlled until 1971 by foreign firms, the copper industry was the source of perpetual political conflict. No other study has done so much to put the Chilean copper industry into an international perspective as Theodore Moran, *Multinational Corporations and the Politics of Dependence*, 1974. Another study, less sympathetic to Chile and more sensitive to the interests of the American firms is Eric Baklanoff, *Expropriation of United States Investments in Cuba, Mexico, and Chile*, 1975. By far the most detailed work relating the Chilean copper industry to American investment is George Mason Ingram IV, *Nationalization of American Companies in South America: Peru, Bolivia, Chile*, 2 vols., Ph.D. diss., Univ. of Michigan, 1973. Ingram's massive study includes an extensive bibliography on foreign investment in Chile, as well as Peru and Bolivia, along with sources on the Chilean copper industry. Both the public sector (CODELCO) and the many private firms in the copper economy maintain elaborate Internet Web sites with relatively up-to-date information, along with news releases on new mining ventures and concessions. Other valuable works on copper in the Chilean economy include: Jorge Alvear Urrutia, *Chile, nuestro cobre: Chuquicamata, El Salvador, Potrerillos, El Teniente, Enami, Mantos Blancos* . . . , 1975; Gregorio Amunátegui, "The Role of Copper in the Chilean Economy," *Latin America and the Caribbean: A Handbook,* Claudio Véliz (ed.) 1968; Jorge Bande and Ricardo Ffrench-Davis, *Copper Policies and the Chilean Economy, 1973–1988,* 1989; "Contribution of Copper to Chilean Economic Development: 1920–1967," *Foreign Investment in the Petroleum and Mineral Industries: Case Studies of Investor-Host Country Relations,* Raymond F. Mikesell et al., 1971; William Culver and Cornel Reinhart, "Capitalist Dreams: Chile's Response to Nineteenth-Century World Copper Competition," *Comparative Studies in Society and History 31:* 722–44; Ricardo Ffrench-Davis and Ernesto Tironi, ed., *El cobre en el desarrollo nacional,* 1974; Janet Finn, *Tracing the Veins, Of Copper and Community from Butte to Chuquicamata,* 1998 (a fascinating comparative study of two communities influenced by Anaconda Copper Company); Joanne Fox Przeworski, *The Decline of the Copper Industry in Chile and Entrance of North American Capital,* Ph.D. diss., Washington University, 1978; A. Fuenzalida, *El trabajo y la vida en el mineral El Teniente,* 1918; Norman Girvan, *Copper in Chile,* 1972; L. Hiriat, *Braden, Historia de una mina,* 1964; Oscar Mac-Clure Hortal and Iván Valenzuela R., *Conflictos en la gran minería del cobre, 1973–1983,* 1985; Markos Mamalakis, "The American Copper Companies and the Chilean Government, 1920–1967: Profile of a Foreign-owned Export Sector," *Foreign Investment in the Petroleum and Mineral Industries: Case Studies of Investor-Host Country Relations,* Raymond Mikesell et al., 1971; Santiago Marín Vicuña, *La industria del cobre en Chile,* 1920; Ricardo Nazer Ahumada, *José Tomás Urmeneta: Un empresario del siglo XIX,* 1994; Eduardo Novoa Monreal, *La nacionalización del cobre: comentarios y documentos,* 1972 (important source for copper policy under the Allende government); C. W. Reynolds, "Chile and Copper," *Essays on the Chilean Economy,* M. Mamalakis and C. W. Reynolds (eds.), 1966; María Rosaria Stabili, "Relaciones de producción capitalista; los empresarios norteamericanos en la minería del cobre de Chile, 1905–1918," *Revista Latinoamericana de Historia Económica y Social,* VI (1985); Paul Sigmund, *Multinationals in Latin America: The Politics of Nationalization,* 1980; Iván Valenzuela, *Panorama de la industria elaboradora del cobre en Chile,* 1989; Mario Vera Valenzuela, *El cobre en el centro de la política,* 1996. P. Vayassière, "La division internationale du travail et la desnationalisation du cuivre Chilien (1880–1920)," *Cahiers du Monde Hispanique et Luso-Brésilien,* No. 20 (1973); Mario Vera Valenzuela, *La política económica de cobre en Chile,* 1961. Two important studies with extensive bibliographies are: Juan Agustín Allende, *State Enterprises and Political Environments: Chile's National Copper Corporation,* 1985; Thomas Miller Klubock, *Contested Communities, Class, Gender, and Politics in Chile's El Teniente Copper Mine, 1904–1951,* 1998. Luis Valenzuela, *Tres estudios sobre el comercio y la fundición de cobre en Chile y en el mercado mundial 1830–1880,* 1995, synthesizes work on the copper industry in the nineteenth century.

REGIONAL AND LOCAL HISTORIES, URBANIZATION

Any study of urbanization in Chile must start with Gabriel Guarda's *Historia urbana del reino de Chile,* 1978. The list of sources, archives, and bibliographical references in this book is monumental. From colonial times the formation and growth of urban centers has inspired local and regional histories. In recent times rapid urbanization has become a most salient feature of Chilean life. Studies that focus on regional development or on Chilean urbanization more generally include: DESAL, *Poblaciones marginales y desarrollo urbano: el caso chileno,* 1965; John Friedman and Thomas Lackington, "La hiperurbanización y el desarrollo nacional en Chile," *Estructura social de Chile,* H. Godoy, ed., 1971; Guillermo Geisse G., *Problemas del desarrollo urbano regional en Chile,* 1968; Gabriel Guarda, "Influencia militar en las ciudades del reino de Chile," *Boletín de la Academia Chilena de la Historia 33*, No. 75, 1966; and "El urbanismo imperial y las primitivas ciudades de Chile," *Finis Terrae* No. 51, 1957 (these two articles describe the early urbanization in colonial Chile); Carlos Hurtado Ruiz-Tagle, *Concentración de población y desarrollo económico*, 1966; Bruce Herrick, *Urban Migration and Economic Development in Chile*, 1965; Eduardo Secchi, *La casa chilena hasta el siglo XIX*, 1952; Astolfo Tapia Moore, *Legislación urbanística de Chile: 1818–1959*, 1961; Tomás Thayer Ojeda, *Las antiguas ciudades chilenas . . .* , 1911; Frederick S. Weaver, Jr., *Regional Patterns of Economic Change in Chile: 1950–1964*, 1968.

Numerous historical descriptions of the evolution of individual cities or towns also exist. For Santiago see: Guillermo Feliú Cruz, *Santiago a comienzos del siglo XIX: crónica de los viajeros*, 1970 (excerpts from numerous travel accounts referring to physical environment, economy, and social life of Santiago in the early 19th century); Joseph Fichandler and Thomas O'Brien, "Santiago, Chile 1541–1581: A Case Study of Urban Stagnation," *The Americas*, 1976; Vicente Grez, *La vida santiaguina*, 1879. On the province of Valparaíso see: Roberto Hernández D., *Valparaíso en 1827*, 1927; Carlos J. Larraín, *Viña del Mar*, 1946; René M. Salinas, "Caracteres generales de la evolución demográfica de un centro urbano chileno: Valparaíso, 1685–1830," *Historia*, No. 10, 1971; *Población de Valparaíso en la segunda mitad del siglo XVIII*, 1970; Benjamín Vicuña Mackenna, *Historia de Valparaíso*, 2 vols., 1936; and *Quintero: su estado actual y su provenir*, 1874.

La Serena, Copiapó, Antofagasta, and other northern urban places are treated in: Domingo Amunátegui Solar, *El cabildo de La Serena: 1678–1800*, 1928; Oscar Bermúdez, *Orígenes históricos de Antofagasta*, 1966; and "Pica en el siglo XVIII; estructura económica y social," *RCGH 3*, 1973; Manuel Concha, *Crónica de la Serena desde su fundación hasta nuestros días: 1549–1870*, 1971; Domingo Contreras Gómez, *La ciudad de Santa María de Los Angeles*, 2 vols., 1972–44; Bernardo Cruz, *San Felipe de Aconcagua*, 2 vols., 1949–50; Eugenio Chouteau, *Informe sobre la provincia de Coquimbo presentado al supremo gobierno*, 1887; Julio Figueroa G., *Historia de San Felipe*, 1902; Martin I. Glassner, "Feeding a Desert City: Antofagasta, Chile," *Economic Geography*, No. 45, 1969; Carlos Keller, "Los orígenes de Quillota," *BACH*, No. 61, 1959; J. Larraín de Castro, "Los orígenes de Zapallar, contribución a la historia de la propiedad territorial," *BACH*, No. 12, 1940; Joaquín L. Morales O., *Historia del Huasco*, 1896; Andrés Sabella, *Semblanza del norte chileno*, 1955; C. M. Sayago, *Historia de Copiapó*, 1854.

Leonardo Mazzei, "Ensayo de un recuento bibliográfico relativo a la zona sur de Chile: Talca-Magallanes: 1812–1912," *HGFC*, provides a comprehensive bibliography of regional studies for the territory from Talca south. Illustrative studies for urban centers and their hinterlands from the Central Valley south include: Armando Braun Menéndez, *Pequeña historia Magallánica*, 2nd ed., 1954; Fernando Campos H., "Concepción y su historia," *BACH*, 1970; Guillermo Cox y Méndez, *Historia de Concepción*, 1822; Pedro Cunill, "Castro: centro urbano de Chiloé insular," *Antropología 2*, Primer semestre, 1964; Gabriel Guarda, *La economía de Chile austral antes de la colonización alemana*, 1973; René León Echaíz, *Historia de Curicó*, 2 vols., 1975; S. Manuel Mesa, *Proyección histórica de la provincia de Linares*, 1965; Isabel P. Montt, *Breve historia de Valdivia*, 1971; Reinaldo Muñoz Olave, *Chillán: sus fundaciones y destrucciones: 1580–1835*, 1921; Carlos Olguín B., *Instituciones políticas y administrativas de Chiloé en el siglo XVIII*, 1971; S. Carlos Oliver, *El libro de oro de Concepción*, 1950; Eduardo Pino Zapata, *Historia de Temuco*, 1969; N. Alberto Recart, *El Laja un río creador*, 1971; John H. Whaley, *Transportation in Chile's Bío Bío Region: 1850–1915*, Ph.D. diss., Indiana Univ., 1974.

EDUCATION

The organization and role of education in Chilean society has received insufficient attention by historical researchers. Regarding the teaching of history and the country's official school texts, an important recent contribution by Rafael Sagredo and Sol Serrano has entered this unexplored terrain: "Un espejo cambiante: La visión de la historia de Chile en los textos escolares," *Boletín de Historia y Geografía 12*, 1996: 217–44. Among the few significant contributions in this area, the following sources are foundations for future research: Oscar Alvarez, "Aspectos sociológicos del problema educacional en Chile," *Revista Mexicana de Sociología 20*, No. 3, 1958; Domingo Amunátegui Solar, *Los primeros años del instituto nacional, 1813–1835*, 1889; *Recuerdos del instituto nacional*, 1941; Miguel Luis Amunátegui, *Estudios sobre instrucción pública*, 3 vols., 1897–98; Manuel J. Barrera, "Trayectoria del movimiento de reforma universitaria en Chile," *Journal of Latin American Studies*, No. 10, 1968; José Joaquín Brunner, *Informe sobre la educación superior en Chile*, 1986; Margaret Campbell, "Education in Chile: 1810–1842," *Journal of Inter-American Studies 1*, July 1959; Fernando Campos Harriet, *Desarrollo educacional: 1810–1960*, 1960; Raúl Cortés Pinto, *Bibliografía anotada de educación superior*, 1967; Ricardo Donoso, *Recopilación de leyes, reglamentos, y decretos relativos a los servicios de enseñanza pública*, 1937; "El Instituto Pedagógico: tres generaciones de maestros," *Journal of Inter-American Studies 6*, Jan. 1964; Kathleen Fischer, *Political Ideology and Educational Reform in Chile, 1964–1976*, 1979; Manuel A. Garretón, "Universidad y política en los procesos de transformación y reversión en Chile, 1967–1977, *Estudios Sociales 26*, No. 4, 1980; Clark C. Gill, *Education and Social Change in Chile*, 1966; Carlos Huneeus M. *La reforma en la Universidad de Chile*, 1973; Iván Jaksić, *Academic Rebels in Chile: The Role of Philosophy in Higher Education and Politics*, 1989; Enrique Kirberg, *Los nuevos profesionales: educación universitaria de trabajadores en Chile: UTE, 1968–1973*, 1981; Amanda Labarca Hubertson, *Historia de la enseñanza en Chile*, 1939; Daniel Levy, "Chilean Universities Under the Junta: Regime and Policy," *Latin American Research Review 21*, 1986; Enrique Molina, *El liceo y la formación de la élite*, 1933; Juan G. Muñoz C. et al., *La Universidad de Santiago de Chile: Sobre sus orígenes y su desarrollo histórico*, 1987; Roberto Munizaga Aguirre, *El estado y la educación*, 1953; Máximo Pacheco Gómez, *La Universidad de Chile*, 1953; Tancredo Pinochet, *Bases para una política educacional: al frente del libro de Amanda Labarca*, 1944; Maximiliano Salas Marchant, *Reflexiones educacionales en torno a nuestra situación social*, 1942; Danilo Salcedo, *La Universidad de Chile y su reforma inconclusa*, 1975; Gabriel Sanhueza, "Panorama de la evolución de las ciencias pedagógicas y la investigación educacional en Chile: 1900–1960," *Anales de la Universidad de Chile 120*, No. 125, 1962; Sol Serrano, *Universidad y nación: Chile en el siglo XIX*, 1994; Sol Serrano and Iván Jaksic, "In the Service of the Nation: The Establishment and Consolidation of the Universidad de Chile, 1842–1879," *HAHR* 70:1, 1990: 139–71. José Toribio Medina, *Historia de la Real Universidad de San Felipe de Chile*, 2 vols., 1928; William Sywak, *Values in Nineteenth Century Chilean Education: The Germanic Reform of Chilean Public Education 1885–1910*, Ph.D. diss., Univ. of California, Los Angeles, 1977; Luis Terán, *Nuestra enseñanza secundaria: los problemas y las soluciones*, 1938; Patricia Weiss Fagen, *Chilean Universities: Problems of Autonomy and Dependence*, 1973; Allen L. Woll, "For God and Country: Historical Textbooks and the Secularization of Chilean Society: 1840–1890," *Journal of Latin American Studies*, No. 7, 1975. Mario Monsalve Bórquez provides a documentary history on primary education in *El Silencio comenzó a reinar, Documento para la historia de la instrucción primaria, 1840–1920*, 1998.

POLITICS — POLITICAL HISTORY, MEMOIRS, AND GENERAL INTERPRETATIONS OF CHILEAN POLITICS IN THE TWENTIETH CENTURY

Chilean politics in the 20th century has attracted considerable attention from Chilean authors and foreign observers alike. Before 1973, scholars routinely depicted Chile as a permanent exception to the common pattern of caudillismo and military government in Latin America. Not surprisingly, much of the literature on Chilean politics focuses upon constitutional history, elections, the party spectrum, and the various presidential administrations. For the

English-language reader, the most important pre-1970 description and analysis of Chilean politics remains Federico Gil, *The Political System of Chile*, 1966. For the period from the 1950s to 1973, see Arturo Valenzuela, *The Breakdown of Democratic Regimes. Chile*, 1978, and Alan Angell, *Chile de Alessandri a Pinochet: En busca de la utopía*, 1993. An insightful interpretive work on Chilean politics and society is Mario Góngora, *Ensayo histórico sobre la noción de estado en Chile en los siglos XIX y XX* (1981). Tomás Moulián, *Democracia y socialismo en Chile* (1983), is an important retrospective analysis and critique of the development of Chilean democracy and the role of the leftist parties and movements through 1973. Moulián calls for a "secularization" of Chilean Marxism. Other general works on Chilean politics, constitutional history, policy dilemmas, and class conflict range from the memoirs of Chilean presidents to careful studies of interest groups, the military or the Chilean legislature. Listed below are a number of books and articles of general interest to students of Chilean politics followed, in turn, by a list of works concerned particularly with elections, the political party system, and individual parties or movements: Weston Agor, *The Chilean Senate: Internal Distribution of Influence*, 1971; Jorge Ahumada, *La crisis integral de Chile*, 1966; Arturo Alessandri, *Recuerdos de gobierno*, 3 vols., 1967; Robert Alexander, *Arturo Alessandri: A Political Biography*, 2 vols., 1977; *The Tragedy of Chile*, 1978; Carlos Andrade Geywitz, *Elementos de derecho constitucional chileno*, 1963; Mario Bernashcina, *Los constituyentes de 1925*, 1945; *Derecho municipal chileno*, 3 vols., 1952; and *Manual de derecho constitucional*, 1955; H. E. Bicheno, "Antiparliamentary Themes in Chilean History: 1920–1970," *Allende's Chile*, Kenneth Medhurst (ed.), 1972; Ricardo Boizard, *Cuatro retratos en profundidad: Ibáñez, Lafferte, Leighton, Walker*, 1950 (brief biographies of leading political figures); Frank Bonilla and Myron Glaser (eds.), *Student Politics in Chile*, 1970; Claude G. Bowers, *Chile Through Embassy Windows: 1939–1953*, 1958; Donald Bray, *Chilean Politics during the Second Ibáñez Government*, 1952–1958, Ph.D. diss., Stanford Univ. 1961; Fernando Campos Harriet, *Historia constitucional de Chile*, 1956; César Caviedes, *The Politics of Chile: A Sociogeographical Assessment*, 1979; Peter Cleaves, *Bureaucratic Politics and Administration in Chile*, 1975; Luis Correa, *El presidente Ibáñez: la política y los políticos*, 1962; Ricardo Cruz-Coke, *Geografía electoral de Chile*, 1952; Francisco Cumplido C., "Constitución política de 1925: hoy crisis de las instituciones políticas chilenas," *Cuadernos de la Realidad Nacional*, No. 7, Sept. 1970; Ricardo Donoso, *Alessandri, agitador y demoledor: cincuenta años de historia política de Chile*, 2 vols., Mexico, 1952–54; and *Desarrollo político y social de Chile*, 1943; Paul Drake, "The Political Responses of the Chilean Upper Class to the Great Depression and the Threat of Socialism: 1931–1933," *The Well Born and the Powerful*, F. C. Jaher (ed.), 1973; and *Socialism and Populism in Chile*, 1932–1952, 1978; Guillermo Edwards Matte, *El Club de la unión en sus ochenta años, 1864–1944*, 1944; Enzo Faletto et al. (eds.), *Génesis histórico del proceso político chileno*, 1971; Herman Finer, *The Chilean Development Corporation*, 1947; Patricio F. García, *Los gremios patronales*, 1973; Jorge González von Marées, *El mal de Chile: sus causas y sus remedios*, 1940 (analysis of Chile's "problem" by Chilean Nazi leader); José G. Guerra, *La constitución de 1925*, 1929; Ernst Halperin, *Nationalism and Communism in Chile*, 1965; Julio Heise González, *Historia constitucional de Chile*, 1954; Eduardo Goddard Labarca, *Chile invadido: reportaje a la intromisión extranjera*, 1968; Elías Lafferte, *Vida de un comunista*, 1957; Norbert Lechner, *La democracia en Chile*, 1970; Francisco José Moreno, *Legitimacy and Stability in Latin America: A Study of Chilean Political Culture*, 1969; Arturo Olavarría B., *Chile entre dos Alessandri*, 2 vols., 1962–65; James Petras, *Politics and Social Forces in Chilean Development*, 1969; Frederick B. Pike, *Chile and the United States: 1880–1962*, 1963; Fernando Pinto, *Crónica política del siglo XX*, 1970; Ernesto Wurth Rojas, *Ibáñez, caudillo enigmático*, 1958; Kalman Silvert, *The Chilean Development Corporation*, Ph.D. diss., Univ. of Pennsylvania, 1948; *Chile: Yesterday and Today*, 1965; *The Conflict Society: Reaction and Revolution in Latin America*, 1961; Barbara Stallings, *Class Conflict and Economic Development in Chile, 1958–1973*, 1978; Osvaldo Sunkel, "Change and Frustration in Chile," *Obstacles to Change in Latin America*, Claudio Véliz (ed.), 1965; Germán Urzúa Valenzuela, *Diccionario político institucional de Chile*, 1984; Arturo Valenzuela, *Political Brokers in Chile: Local Government in a Centralized Polity*, 1977; Jordan Marten Young, *Chilean Parliamentary Government: 1891–1924*, Ph.D. diss., Princeton Univ., 1953; Maurice Zeitlin, "The Social Determinants of Political Democracy in Chile," *Latin America*, J. Petras and M. Zeitlin (eds.), 1968.

POLITICS—ELECTIONS, POLITICAL PARTIES, AND POLITICAL MOVEMENTS

The evolution of Chilean political parties and the electoral system are treated in: Roger Abbot, "The Role of Contemporary Political Parties in Chile," *APSR*, 45, June 1951; Carlos Bascuñán Edwards, *La izquierda sin Allende*, 1990; Atilio Borón, "La evolución del régimen electoral en Chile," *Revista Latinoamericana de Ciencia Política*, Dec. 1972; Bernardino Bravo Lira, *Régimen de gobierno y partidos políticos en Chile 1924–1973*, 1978; Alberto Edwards, *Bosquejo histórico de los partidos políticos chilenos*, 1936; and Eduardo Frei Montalva, *Historia de los partidos políticos chilenos*, 1949; Reinhard Friedmann, *1964–1988, La política chilena de la A a la Z*, 1988; Federico Gil, *Genesis and Modernization of Political Parties in Chile*, 1962; Sergio Guilisasti Tagle, *Partidos políticos chilenos*, 2nd ed., 1964; René León Echaíz, *Evolución histórica de los partidos políticos chilenos*, 2nd ed., 1971; Karen L. Remmer, *Party Competition in Argentina and Chile: Political Recruitment and Public Policy, 1890–1930*, 1984; Timothy Scully, *Rethinking the Center, Party Politics in Nineteenth & Twentieth Century Chile*, 1992; Fernando S. Silva, *Los partidos políticos chilenos*, 1972; Germán Urzúa Valenzuela, *Historia político electoral de Chile*, 1986; *Historia política de Chile y su evolución electoral* (desde 1810 a 1992), 1992. Arturo Valenzuela, "The Scope of the Chilean Party System," *Comparative Politics 4*, January 1972; J. Samuel Valenzuela, *Democratización vía reforma: la expansión del sufragio en Chile*, 1985. A sympathetic interpretation of Carlos Ibáñez role in Chile politics is Ernesto Würth Rojas, *Ibáñez, Caudillo enigmático*, 1958. Brian Loveman and Elizabeth Lira, *Las ardientes cenizas del olvido, Vía chilena de reconciliación política, 1932–1994*, 2000 offers an unconventional political history of the 1932–1994 period, focused on the use of amnesties, pardons, and other modalities of elite bargaining to hold together Chile's vaunted "democracy."

On the Radical party and the Popular Front period, in addition to the excellent study by Drake mentioned above, see: Salvador Allende Gossens, "Pedro Aguirre Cerda," *Arauco*, Jan. 1964; Francisco Barría Soto, *El partido radical: sus historia y sus obras*, 1957; Florencio Durán Bernales, *El partido radical*, 1958; Juan C. Fernández, *Pedro Aguirre Cerda y el frente popular chileno*, 1938; Jaime García Covarrubias, *El partido radical y la clase media, La relación de intereses entre 1888 y 1938*, 1990; Gabriel González Videla, *El partido radical y la evolución social de Chile*, 1962; Luis Palma Zúñiga, *Historia del partido radical*, 1967; and *Pedro Aguirre Cerda: maestro-estadista-gobernante*, 1963; Darío Poblete and Alfredo Bravo, *Historia del partido radical y del frente popular*, 1936; Eudocio Ravines, *The Yenan Way*, 1951 (ex-Comintern agent in Latin America recounts his role in formation of Chilean Popular Front and activities of Chilean Marxists); Peter Snow, *El radicalismo chileno*, 1972; John Reese Stevenson, *The Chilean Popular Front*, 1942; Germán Urzúa V., *La democracia práctica, Los gobiernos radicales*, 1987.

Chilean socialism is discussed in: Agustín Alvarez Villablanca, *Objetivos del socialismo en Chile*, 1946; Jorge Arrate, *La fuerza democrática de la idea socialista*, 3rd ed. 1986; and Paulo Hidalgo, *Pasión y razón del socialismo chileno*, 1989; Fernando Casanueva and Manuel Fernández C., *El partido socialista y la lucha de clases en Chile*, 1973; Carlos Charlín, *Del avión rojo a la república socialista*, 1972 (excellent source of material on late 1920s and early 1930s); Alejandro Chelén Rojas, *Trayectoria del socialismo*, 1967; Salomón Corbalán, *El partido socialista*, 1957; Eduardo Devés and Carlos Díaz, *El pensamiento socialista en Chile, Antología 1893–1933*, 1987; Manuel Dinamarca, *La República Socialista chilena, Orígenes legítimos del Partido socialista*, 1987; Paul Drake, *Socialism and Populism in Chile*, 1978; Julio Faúndez, *Marxism and Democ-*

racy in Chile, From 1932 to the Fall of Allende, 1988; Mirian Hochwald, *Imagery in Politics: A Study of the Ideology of the Chilean Socialist Party,* Ph.D. diss., Univ. of California, Los Angeles, 1971; Julio César Jobet, *El partido socialista de Chile,* 2 vols., 1971; and Alejandro Chelén R., *Pensamiento teórico y político del partido socialista,* 1972; *Socialismo y comunismo,* 1952; and *El socialismo chileno a través de sus congresos,* 1965; Ricardo Núñez, ed., *Socialismo: 10 años de renovación* 2 vols., I, *De la Convergencia a la unidad socialista;* II, *el adiós al marxismo-leninismo,* 1991; Benny Pollack and Herman Rosenkranz, *Revolutionary Social Democracy, The Chilean Socialist Party,* 1986; Jack Ray Thomas, "The Evolution of a Chilean Socialist: Marmaduke Grove," *HAHR* 47, No. 1, 1967; Oscar Waiss, *Presencia del socialismo en Chile,* 1952; Ignacio Walker, *Socialismo y democracia, Chile y Europa en perspectiva comparada,* 1990;

Key works for understanding the origins and growth of the Chilean Communist party and Soviet influence in Chile include: Andrew Barnard, *The Chilean Communist Party, 1922–1947,* Ph.D. diss., University of London, 1978; "Chilean Communists, Radical Presidents and Chilean Relations with the United States, 1940–1947," *Journal of Latin American Studies 13,* November 1981; Carlos Contreras Labarca, *La conspiración de los enemigos del pueblo,* 1940; and *Por la paz, por nuevas victorias del frente popular,* 1939; Carmelo Furci, *The Chilean Communist Party and the Road to Socialism,* 1984; César Godoy Urrutia, *Vida de un agitador,* 1982; Luis Guastavino, *Caen las catedrales,* 1990; Jorge Jiles Pizarro, *Partido comunista de Chile,* 1957; Hernán Ramírez Necochea, *Origen y formación del partido comunista en Chile,* 1965; Augusto Varas, ed., *El Partido comunista en Chile,* 1988; *De la Komintern a la perestroika, América Latina y la URSS,* 1991.

The Conservative and Christian Democratic parties are studied by: Ignacio Arteaga Undurraga, *Reseña histórica de las XVI convenciones del partido conservador,* 1947; Renato Cristi and Carlos Ruiz, *El pensamiento conservador en Chile,* 1992; Patricio Dooner, *Cambios sociales y conflicto político: el conflicto político nacional durante el gobierno de Eduardo Frei (1964–1970),* 1984; Michael Fleet, *The Rise and Fall of Chilean Christian Democracy,* 1985; George Grayson, *El partido demócrata cristiano chileno,* 1968; Bartolomé Palacios and Héctor Rodríguez de la Sotta, *El partido conservador y la democracia cristiana,* 1933; Teresa Pereira, *El Partido conservador, 1930–1965,* 1994; Marcial Sanfuentes C., *El partido conservador,* 1957. Michael Potashnik treats the Chilean Nazi movement in *Nacismo: National Socialism in Chile: 1932–1938,* Ph.D. diss., Univ. of California, Los Angeles, 1974.

New work on women and gender includes Thomas Klubock, *Contested Communities. Class, Gender, and Politics in Chile's El Teniente Copper Mine, 1904–1951,* 1998; Elizabeth Hutchison, *Labors Appropriate to Their Sex: Gender, Labor and Politics in Urban Chile, 1900–1930;* Karin Rosemblatt, *Gendered Compromises: Political Cultures and the State in Chile 1920–1950,* 2000.

POLITICS — CATHOLIC CHURCH

The Catholic Church has played a significant role in recent Chilean history. With leading Church intellectuals and dignitaries associated with the Christian Democratic government and a sweeping anti-Marxist campaign after 1962, Church activity took on an overtly political character that contrasted markedly with its earlier linkage to the Conservative party. A number of studies captured this reformist orientation of the Church; only David Mutchler, *The Church as a Political Factor in Latin America; with Particular Reference to Colombia and Chile,* 1971, details the role of Church policy and programs in the Cold War, the Alliance for Progress, and the domestic anti-Marxist movement in Chile. Brian H. Smith, *The Church and Politics in Chile,* 1982, provides both a history of the Church and Church doctrine in Chile and an analysis of the Church's role in socio-economic and political change.

Other important works on the Catholic Church and reform in Chile include: Isidoro Alonso, Renato Poblete, and Ginés Garrido, *La iglesia en Chile: estructuras eclesiásticas,* 1961;

Fidel Araneda Bravo, *El Arzobispo Errázuriz y la evolución política y social de Chile*, 1956; Virginia Marie Bouvier, *Alliance or Compliance: Implications of the Chilean Church Experience for the Catholic Church in Latin America*, 1983; Michael Dodson, "The Christian Left," *Journal of Inter-American Studies and World Affairs* 21, Feb. 1979; Oscar Domínguez, *El campesinado chileno y la acción católica rural, Fribourg*, FERES, 1961; Patricio Dooner, *Iglesia, reconciliación y democracia*, 1989; Jaime Guzmán, "The Church in Chile and the Political Debate," in Pablo Baraona Urzúa, *Chile, A Critical Debate*, 1972; Jorge Iván Hubner Gallo, *Los Católicos y la política*, 1959; María Antonieta Huerta and Luis Pacheco P., *La iglesia chilena y los cambios sociopolíticos*, 1988; Ricardo Krebs (ed.), *Catolicismo y laicismo: Las bases doctrinarias del conflicto entre la iglesia y el estado en Chile, 1875–1885*, 1981; Henry Landsberger and Fernando Canitrot, *Iglesia, intelectuales y campesinos*, INSORA, 1967 (an excellent study of the role of progressive Catholics in the Chilean rural labor movement); Henry Landsberger (ed.), *The Church and Social Change in Latin America*, 1970; Kenneth Langton and Ronald Rapoport, "Religion and Leftist Mobilization in Chile," *Comparative Political Studies* 9, Oct. 1976; Alejandro Magnet, *El padre Hurtado*, 3rd ed., 1957; J. Lloyd Mecham, *Church and State in Latin America*, 1966; Luis Pacheco P., *El pensamiento sociopolítico de los obispos chilenos 1962–1973, perspectiva histórica*, 1985; Renato Poblete, *La iglesia en Chile*, Fribourg and Bogotá, FERES, 1962; Secretariado General del Episcopado de Chile, *La iglesia y el problema del campesinado chileno*, 1962; Eugenio Yáñez, *La iglesia y el gobierno militar: Itinerario de una dίficil relación, 1973–88*, 1989.

THE MILITARY

Many Chilean sources, including government publications, deal with the history of the armed forces or particular military institutions such as the Escuela Militar. A doctoral dissertation by Tommie Hillmon, Jr., *A History of the Armed Forces of Chile from Independence to 1920*, Syracuse Univ., 1963, provides seventy pages of annotated bibliographical references to primary sources and secondary materials on the Chilean military and diplomatic relations with its neighbors as well as detailed studies of military campaigns in the independence period, Chile's 19th-century wars, and the civil wars of 1851, 1859, and 1891. Frederick Nunn's *Chilean Politics: 1920–1931*, cited earlier, is a key source on the important role of the military in Chilean politics and society. Nunn's selective bibliography is extremely helpful. The same author's *The Military in Chilean History*, 1976, explores the role of the Chilean military from 1810 to the military coup of 1973. On corruption in the armed forces in the early twentieth century, see William Sater and Holger Herwig, *The Grand Illusion: The Prussianization of the Chilean Army*, 1999. For the Army's view, see Estado Mayor del Ejército, *Historia del Ejército de Chile*, multiple volumes, 1985. Other especially useful sources on the Chilean military in politics in the 20th century include: Arturo Ahumada, *El ejército y la revolución del 5 de septiembre 1924: reminiscencias*, 1931; R. Aldunate Phillips, *Ruido de sables*, 1971?; Genaro Arriagada H., *El pensamiento político de los militares* (CISEC), 1981; Pablo Baraona Urzúa et al., *Fuerzas armadas y seguridad nacional*, 1973; General Juan Bennett, *La revolución de 5 septiembre*, 1925; General Jorge Boonen Rivera, *Participación del ejército en el desarrollo y progreso del país*, 1917; Gonzalo García Pino and Juan Esteban Montes Ibáñez, *Subordinación democrática de los militares. Exitos y fracasos en Chile*, 1994; Roy Hansen, *Military Culture and Organizational Decline: A Study of the Chilean Army*, Ph.D. diss., Univ. of California, Los Angeles, 1967; Alain Joxe, *Las fuerzas armadas en el sistema político chileno*, 1970; Alberto Lara, *Los oficiales alemanes en Chile*, 1969; Carlos López V., *Historia de la marina de Chile*, 1929; Carlos Maldonado, *La milicia republicana*, 1988; René Millar C., "Significado y antecedentes del movimiento militar de 1924," *Historia* 2, 1972–73; Carlos Molina Johnson, *Chile: Los militares y la política*, 1989 (a revisionist history by an influential Chilean general);

Lisa North, *Civil-Military Relations in Argentina, Chile and Peru*, 1966; Alberto Polloni Roldán, *Las fuerzas armadas de Chile en la vida nacional*, 1972; Carlos Portales, "Militarization and Political Institutions in Chile," in P. Wallensteen, J. Galtung, and C. Portales, *Global Militarization*, 1985; Dauno Tótoro Taulis, *La cofradía blindada, Chile civil y Chile militar: Trauma y conflicto*, 1998; Verónica Valdivia Ortiz de Zárate, *La milicias republicanas, Los civiles en armas, 1932–1936*, 1992; Augusto Varas (ed.), *Transición a la democracia*, 1984; Augusto Varas et al., *Estado y fuerzas armadas en el proceso político chileno*, 1982; Augusto Varas, *Los militares en el poder*, 1987; Augusto Varas and Felipe Agüero, *El proyecto político militar*, 1984; General Carlos Sáez Morales, *Recuerdos de un soldado*, 3 vols., 1933–34 (good source for Chile's "Socialist Republic"); George Strawbridge, Jr., *Militarism and Nationalism in Chile: 1920–1932*, Ph.D. diss., Univ. of Pennsylvania, 1968; Terrence S. Tarr, *Military Intervention and Civilian Reaction in Chile: 1924–1936*, Ph.D. diss., Univ. of Florida, 1960; Agustín Toro Dávila, *Síntesis histórico-militar de Chile*, 2 vols., 1969.

CHRISTIAN DEMOCRACY

From 1964 to 1970 Christian Democratic ideology and leadership dominated Chilean society. For over three decades Christian Democratic intellectuals had proclaimed their doctrine, criticized Chilean society, and promised an alternative to capitalism and socialism. Key works of the Christian Democratic leaders provide some insight into their goals, values, and hopes for a new "communitarian" society in Chile: Jaime Castillo Velasco, *Los caminos de la revolución*, 1972; and *Las fuentes de la democracia cristiana*, 1963; Jacques Chonchol and Julio Silva Solar, *Hacia un mundo comunitario: condiciones de una política social cristiana*, 1951; Patricio Dooner, *Crónica de una democracia cansada, El partido demócrata cristiano durante el gobierno de Allende*, 1988; Eduardo Frei Montalva, *Chile desconocido*, 1937; *La verdad tiene su hora*, 1955; *El social cristianismo*, 1951; *Pensamiento y acción*, 1958; *La política y el espíritu*, 1940; and *Aún es tiempo*, 1942; and *El Mandato de la historia* (1975); Cristián Gazmuri et al., *Eduardo Frei Montalva (1911–1982)*, 1996; Cristián Gazmuri, Patricia Arancibia, and Alvaro Góngora, *Eduardo Frei Montalva, Una biografía*, 1999; Oscar Larson, *La ANEC y la Democracia Cristiana*, 1967; Julio Silva and Bosco Parra, *Nociones para una política demócrata cristiana*, 1947; William Thayer Arteaga, *Trabajo, empresa, y revolución*, 1968.

CHRISTIAN DEMOCRACY AND THE REVOLUTION IN LIBERTY

Despite the idealism of some Christian Democrats, the hard realities of Chilean politics and the historical legacy of the Chilean social question obstructed implementation of their reformist program. Supported heavily by United States policymakers with loans and "foreign aid," the Christian Democrats found themselves caught between the strong forces of the past and the calls for revolution from the political left. The hard road of political reform—the successes, failures, and the ultimate electoral defeat in 1970—are documented in a large and still growing literature. Key sources include: Alan Angell, "Chile: The Difficulties of Democratic Reform," *International Journal*, No. 24, 1969; and "Christian Democracy in Chile," *Current History*, No. 58, 1970; Ricardo Boizard, *La democracia cristiana en Chile*, 1963; Luis Corvalán L., *Chile hoy: la lucha de los comunistas chilenos en las condiciones del gobierno de Frei*, 1965 (analysis by leader of Chilean Communist party); Thomas Edwards, *Economic Development and Reform in Chile*, 1972; Eduardo Frei M., with R. Tomic, J. Castillo, and G. Arriagada, *Democracia cristiana y Partido comunista*, 1986; Eduardo Frei et al., *Reforma constitucional: 1970*, 1970; Edward de Glab, Jr., *Christian Democracy, Marxism and Revolution in Chile:*

The Election and Overthrow of Allende, Ph.D. diss., Northern Illinois Univ., 1975; Leonard Gross, *The Last Best Hope: Eduardo Frei and Chilean Democracy*, 1967; Norbert Lechner, *La democracia en Chile*, 1970; David Lehman, "Political Incorporation versus Political Stability: The Case of the Chilean Agrarian Reform: 1965–1970," *Journal of Development Studies*, No. 7, July 1971; Sergio Molina, *El proceso de cambio en Chile*, 1972; Arturo Olavarría B., *Chile bajo la democracia cristiana*, 6 vols., 1966–71; James Petras, *Chilean Christian Democracy: Politics and Social Forces*, 1967; Osvaldo Sunkel, "Change and Frustration in Chile," *Obstacles to Change in Latin America*, Claudio Véliz (ed.), 1965; Edward J. Williams, *Latin American Christian Democratic Parties*, 1967; Luis Vitale, *Esencia y apariencia de la democracia cristiana*, 1964; Sergio Vusković, *Problemática demócrata-cristiana, propiedad, revolución, estado*, 1968; Ricardo A. Yocelevzky R., "La Democracia Cristiana chilena, trayectoria de un proyecto," *Revista Mexicana de Sociología 47*, April–June 1985 (offers a historical view of the party and describes the role of the party under the military); and *La democracia cristiana chilena y el gobierno de Eduardo Frei (1964–1970)*, 1987.

UNIDAD POPULAR AND AFTER

Never has more been written about Chile than appeared after 1970 with regard to the Popular Unity coalition and the subsequent military coup. The published literature is truly massive. Moreover, the number of books on non-political topics also mushroomed, creating a veritable wave of Chilean publications. Lee H. Williams, comp., *The Allende Years*, lists almost 3000 Chilean imprints held in selected North American libraries.

Existing materials on the Unidad Popular experience itself represent a mix of ideological and descriptive summaries of the events of the Allende years. A preliminary review of more than thirty of these analyses from differing ideological perspectives can be found in Arturo and J. Samuel Valenzuela, "Visions of Chile," in *Latin American Research Review 10*, Fall 1975.

A Marxist-oriented review of the early literature after the coup is found in Ron Chilcote and Terry Dietz-Fee, "Assessing the Literature since the Coup," *Latin American Perspectives 1*, Summer 1974; a special issue, *Chile: Blood on the Peaceful Road*. Federico Gil, Ricardo Lagos, and Henry Landsberger, *Chile at the Turning Point, Lessons of the Socialist Years, 1970–1973*, 1979, an English translation of a book published in Spanish in 1977, offers a number of valuable assessments by actors in the Popular Unity government, other prominent Chileans, and social scientists of the Allende administration's efforts and dilemmas. Two important books on the role of labor and working-class politics during the Unidad Popular administration are Peter Winn, *Weavers of Revolution*, 1986 and Juan G. Espinosa and Andrew S. Zimbalist, *Economic Democracy, Worker Participation in Chilean Industry, 1970–1973*, 1978.

Stefan de Vylder's *Allende's Chile, The Political Economy of the Rise and Fall of the Unidad Popular*, 1974, is a careful and extremely well-developed analysis of the political, economic, and social context of the Allende experience and the factors leading up to the military coup of 1973. Sergio Bitar's *Chile, Experiment in Democracy*, 1986, is the most balanced retrospective by a minister in the Unidad Popular government. The polemical volumes published by the political party, MAPU, *El primer año del Gobierno Popular* and *El segundo año del Gobierno Popular*, originally issued in March and November, 1972, and reprinted by ISHI in 1977, are vivid reminders of the polarization and maximalist rhetoric that led to the coup in 1973. Arturo Fontaine T. and Miguel González, eds., *Los mil dias de Allende*, 2 vols., 1997, is a very useful retrospective with appended documents, chronology, testimonies from the era, photographs, and a look at the political humor that accompanied the three years that culminated in the 1973 military coup. A highly polemical view of the role of right-wing paramilitary groups during the Popular Unity government by an ex-activist is Manuel Fuentes W., *Memorias secretas de Patria y Libertad y algunas confesiones sobre la Guerra Fría en Chile*, 1999.

For the role of the United States in destabilizing the Allende government and subsequent collaboration with the military government (1973–90) declassified documents from the National Security Archives are invaluable. Key documents (many still heavily censored) are available on-line via the Internet at http://www.seas.gwu.edu/nsarchive/.

An extremely useful edited collection on Chile in the 1960s and early 1970s is Arturo and J. Samuel Valenzuela, *Chile: Politics and Society*, 1976. Walden F. Bello, *The Roots and Dynamics of Revolution and Counterrevolution in Chile*, Ph.D. diss., Princeton Univ., 1975, provides a detailed political-historical analysis in the context of theories on economic development and class conflict. Bello's bibliography includes hundreds of periodical and journal articles on the Unidad Popular years. Paul Sigmund's *The Overthrow of Allende and the Politics of Chile, 1964–1976*, Pittsburgh, 1977, offers an analysis of Chilean politics from the mid-1960s through the Unidad Popular years, with brief treatment of the military regime.

Beyond these basic sources the following selection offers an ideologically diverse treatments of the Unidad Popular years: Salvador Allende, *La lucha por la democracia económica y las libertades de difusión de la Presidencia de la República*, 1972; and *El mensaje del Presidente Allende ante el Congreso pleno*, Messages delivered May 21, 1971, 1972, 1973; Genaro Arriagada H., *De la vía Chilena a la vía insurreccional*, 1974; Pablo Baraona Urzúa, *Chile: A Critical Survey*, 1972; A. Bardón, et al., *Itinerario de una crisis política económica y transición al socialismo*, 1972; Jacques Chonchol, "La reforma agraria en Chile: 1970–1973," *El Trimestre Económico*, No. 53, 1976; Luis Corvalán, *Camino de victoria*, 1971; Régis Debray, *Conversations with Allende*, 1971; Les Evans (ed.), *Disaster in Chile*, 1974 (Trotskyist view of 1970–73); Joan Garcés, *1970: La pugna política por la presidencia de Chile*, 1971; *El estado y los problemas tácticos en el gobierno de Allende*, 1973 (analysis by Allende's political adviser); and (ed.), *Nuestro camino al socialismo—la vía chilena*, 1971 (excerpts from speeches and writings of Salvador Allende); Ricardo Israel, *Politics and Ideology in Allende's Chile*, 1989; Sergio Onofre Jarpa, *Creo en Chile*, 1973 (analysis by right-wing político); Dale C. Johnson (ed.), *The Chilean Road to Socialism*, 1973; Edy Kaufman, *Crisis in Allende's Chile*, 1987; Gonzalo Martner (ed.), *El pensamiento económico del gobierno de Allende*, 1971; Kenneth Medhurst (ed.), *Allende's Chile*, 1972; Hernán Millas and Emilio Filippi, *Chile 1970–1973: crónica de una experiencia*, 1974; Orlando Millas, *Exposición sobre la política económica del gobierno y del estado de la hacienda pública*, Ministerio de Hacienda, Folleto No. 122, 1972; Robert Moss, *Chile's Marxist Experiment*, 1973; Claudio Orrego, *El paro nacional*, 1972; José del Pozo, *Rebeldes, reformistas y revolucionarios. Una historia oral de la izquierda chilena en la época de la Unidad Popular*, 1992; Ian Roxborough, Phillip O'Brien, and Jackie Roddick, *Chile: The State and Revolution* (contains a very helpful "chronology of main events" 1969-September 11, 1973, and Marxist-oriented analysis of the Unidad Popular experience), 1977; Unidad Popular, *Programa básico del gobierno de la Unidad Popular*, 1970; Florencia Varas, *Conversaciones con Viaux*, 1972.

A variety of explanations for the failure of the Unidad Popular administration appear in: Solon Barraclough, "The State of Chilean Agriculture before the Coup," *Land Tenure Center Newsletter*, No. 43, Jan.–March 1974; Sergio Bitar, *Transición, socialismo y democracia: la experiencia Chilena*, 1979; François Borricaud, "Chile: Why Allende Fell," *Dissent*, Summer 1974; René Castillo, "Lessons and Prospects of the Revolution," *World Marxist Review*, No. 17, June 1974; Nathaniel Davis (ex-U.S. Ambassador to Chile), *The Last Two Years of Salvador Allende*, 1985; Pío García (ed.), *Las fuerzas armadas y el golpe de estado en Chile*, 1974; Robert Kaufman, *Transition to Stable Authoritarian-Corporate Regimes: The Chilean Case*. 1976; Brian Loveman, "Allende's Chile: Political Economy of the Peaceful Road to Disaster," *New Scholar*, 1978; Gary MacEoin, *No Peaceful Road: The Chilean Struggle for Dignity*, 1974; North American Congress on Latin America, "Chile: The Story Behind the Coup," *Latin America and Empire Report*, Oct. 1973; Philip O'Brien (ed.), *Allende's Chile*, 1976; Lois Oppenheim, *Politics in Chile: Authoritarianism and the Search for Development*, 2nd ed., 1999; General Carlos Prats González, (ex-Commander-in-Chief), *Memorias*, 1985 (offers special insight into the personalities, issues and daily confrontations that led up to the military coup of 1973); David Plotke, "Coup in Chile," *Socialist Revolution*, No. 3, 1973; Paul N. Rosenstein-Rodan, "Why Allende Failed," *Challenge*, May–June 1974; Guillermo Sunkel, *El Mercurio: 10 años de educación político-ideológica 1969–1979*, 1983; Alan Touraine, *Vida y muerte del Chile popular*, 1974; Armando Uribe, *The Black Book of American Intervention in Chile*, 1975; L. Whitehead, "Why Allende Fell," *World Today*, Nov. 1973.

THE 1973 COUP AND EARLY YEARS OF MILITARY RULE

Official explanations by the Chilean military of the rationale for the *golpe* and information on subsequent policies can be found in: *Chile, 11 de septiembre de 1975*; Chile, Junta de Gobierno, *Declaración de principios del gobierno de Chile*, 1974; *Algunos fundamentos de la intervención militar en Chile*, 2nd ed., 1974; and *Libro blanco del cambio de gobierno en Chile*, 1974; *Constitutional Acts Proclaimed by the Government of Chile, Sept. 11, 1976*; Gerardo Cortés Rencoret, "Introducción a la seguridad nacional," *Cuadernos del instituto de ciencia política*, Feb. 1976; Enrique Ortúzar Escobar, "La nueva institucionalidad chilena," *Cuadernos del Instituto de Ciencia Política*, Jan. 1976; "Primero de Mayo 1976," Speech by Minister Sergio Fernández on Labor Day, 1976 (includes decrees related to labor).

In 1998 Patricia Verdugo published *Interferencia secreta, 11 de Septiembre de 1973*, a brief journalistic account of September 1973 and a transcript of a "lost" recording of the communications among the military commanders during the coup of 1973. The book was accompanied by a CD disk that contained the recorded conversations among General Pinochet and the other military officers who directed the coup. Verdugo's book is a new starting point for understanding September 1973 that brings back the ferocity and desperation of the events of September 11, 1973. General Pinochet's remarks leave no doubt as to both his feelings and his vulgarity. "Todo este montón de *jetones* que hay ahí, el señor Tohá y el otro señor Almeyda, todos estos mugrientos que estaban echando a perder el país, hay que pescarlos presos . . . y el avión que tienes dispuesto tú, arriba y sin ropa, con lo que tienen *p'a* fuera, viejo." ("Grab that whole bunch of idiots over there, Mr Toha, Mr Almeyda that whole dirty rotten bunch that was ruining the country, arrest them! . . . put'em on that plane you got up there, with no luggage, no clothing, just what they're wearing, nothing, just out, buddy.") At another moment, Pinochet instructed his colleagues: "la opinión mía es que esos caballeros se toman y se man . . . se mandan a dejar a cualquier parte. Por último, en el camino, los van tirando abajo." ("My opinion is that we get these gentlemen and we take them anywhere . . . If need be, we just throw them out, in route . . .") So began the military regime that governed Chile until 1990. Shortly after Vedugo's book and CD appeared, Manuel Antonio, Roberto, and Carmen Garretón published *Por la fuerza sin razón*, 1998, a short political, legal, and communicational analysis of the *bandos* (military decrees) issued by the military junta that emphasized the illegal nature of the coup and reprinted many of the *bandos* of the junta and of some regional military commanders. To commemorate the 25th anniversary of the death of Salvador Allende and of the military coup, many new (and not so new) looks at the Popular Unity years and the military regime appeared in late 1998.

CHILE UNDER THE MILITARY, 1973–90

The literature on Chile under the military government tends to be highly partisan—whether the topic is human rights, economic performance, or social change. Two partly journalistic and partly academic overviews of the military regime provide a good starting point: Pamela Constable and Arturo Valenzuela, *Chile under Pinochet, a Nation of Enemies*, 1991; and Mary

Helen Spooner, *Soldiers in a Narrow Land, the Pinochet Regime in Chile*, 1994. Ex-president Patricio Aylwin Azócar's personal account of Chilean politics from the ouster of Allende until 1989 is an extremely valuable insight into the world of Christian Democracy and political opposition during the military dictatorship: *El reencuentro de los demócratas, Del golpe al triunfo del NO*, 1998. On the topic of human rights abuses and resistance under the military regime see José Aldunate, S.J. et al., *Los derechos humanos y la iglesia chilena*, n.d.; Rodrigo Atria et al., *Chile: La memoria prohibida, Las violaciones a los derechos humanos 1973–1983*, 3 vols., 1989; Ascanio Cavallo et al., *La historia oculta del régimen militar, Memoria de una época, 1973–1988*, 2nd ed, 1997 (an impressively documented story of the abuses and human rights violations of the military regime); Mark Ensalaco, *Chile under Pinochet. Recovering the Truth*, 1999; Mónica González and Héctor Contreras, *Los secretos del comando conjunto*, 1991; Pamela Lowden, *Moral Opposition to Authoritarian Rule in Chile 1973–1990*, 1996; Patricio Orellana and Elizabeth Hutchison, *El movimiento de derechos humanos en Chile, 1973–1990*, 1991; Elizabeth Lira and María Isabel Castillo, *Psicología de la amenaza política y del miedo*, 1991; Elizabeth Lira et al., *Reparación, derechos humanos y salud mental*, 1996; Patricia Politzer, *Fear in Chile: Lives under Pinochet*, 1989; Raúl Rettig et al., *Informe de la Comisión Nacional de la Verdad y Reconciliacion*, 1991 (Chilean "truth commission" on human rights violations); Patricia Verdugo, *Los zarpazos del puma*, 1989 (account of the "helicopter of death" in 1973); Hernán Vidal, *Dar la vida por la vida, Agrupación Chilena de Familiares de Detenidos Desaparecidos*, 2nd ed., 1996. On the left and exile: Katherine Hite, *When the Romance Ended: Leaders of the Chilean Left*, 2000; Thomas Wright and Rody Oñate, *Flight from Chile: Voices of Exile*, 1998.

A critical view of the first ten years of military rule is J. Samuel and Arturo Valenzuela (eds.), *Military Rule in Chile, Dictatorship and Oppositions*, 1986. An ongoing assessment of politics, economic policy, and social development in Chile since 1973 (along with other topics) can be found in the articles in the periodical *Colección Estudios CIEPLAN*, 1979–. Alejandro Foxley's *Latin American Experiments in Neo-conservative Economics*, 1983, and *Para una democracia estable, economía y política*, 1985, are important examples of the prolific work of the CIEPLAN academics. Somewhat of a counterpoint is the periodical *Estudios Públicos*, which publishes many articles by the "Chicago Boys" and other conservative economists. Articles in *Chile-America* (Rome) also offer a running commentary from a number of ideological perspectives on Chile since 1973. In addition, a variety of Chilean news and opinion magazines (when they aren't censored or closed) provide analysis and updates. These include *Análisis, Apsi, Cauce, Cosas, Ercilla, Estrategia, Hoy, Panorama, Qué Pasa*. Gary M. Walton (ed.), *The National Economic Policies of Chile*, 1985, provides a synthesis in English of economic policy, predominantly from the viewpoint of conservative economists, but with a minority position on distributive issues. Work on Chilean art and literature after the coup, as well as literature published in exile and in Chile, reflects the tragedy of human suffering and the continuing sharp divisions in Chilean society. Examples of these trends can be found in Fernando Alegría, *Chilean Writers in Exile*, 1982; Poli Délano et al., *Primer coloquio sobre literatura Chilena (de la resistencia y el exilio)*, 1980; and Antonio Skármeta, *Joven narrativa chilena después del golpe*, 1976. From exile the reviews *Literatura chilena en el exilio* and *Araucaria de Chile* were the most well-known forums for Chilean writers, while publications like *La bicicleta* struggled to survive within the country. Three of the most moving testimonial works concerning repression by the junta and conditions in the prisons are Hernán Valdés, *Tejas Verdes*, 1974; Alejandro Witker, *Prisión en Chile*, 1975; and Aníbal Quijada Cerda, *Cerco de Púas*, 1977. Grinor Rojo, *Muerte y resurrección del teatro chileno, 1973–1983*, 1985, documents the evolution of the Chilean theater under the Pinochet regime.

As in the case of the Unidad Popular years, the literature on the military regime is massive and growing. The list here is a selection of *diverse* views on the policies and consequences of the military regime, ranging from investigations of human rights, labor, and role of the Catholic Church after 1973 (see also the earlier section on the Catholic Church) to the environmental and social consequences of the neoliberal economic policies. A starting point for the official military point of view is República de Chile, Presidencia, *Memoria de Gobierno 1973–1990*, 3 vols. (I. Político Institucional; II. Económico Productivo; III. Social), March 1990. A key civilian figure in the military regime provides a very personal account of the effort to design and institutionalize "authoritarian and protected democracy" from 1978 to 1990: Sergio Fernández, *Mi lucha por la democracia*, 2nd ed., 1997. For passionate defenses of the military regime see Luis Heinecke Scott, *Chile, Crónica de un asedio, Una larga amenza que se cumple*, 4 vols., 1992 (a retrospective history of the marxist threat to Chilean society since the early 20th century); Rafael Valdivieso A., *Crónica de un rescate, Chile 1973–1988*, 1988. For a scathing journalistic account of brutality, corruption, and avarice by Pinochet and his government see Hernán Millas, *La familia militar*, 1999. *Años de viento sucio*, 1999, Patricia Lutz's barely novelized denunciation of Pinochet and the dictatorship, is also revealing. (Lutz is the daughter of general Augusto Lutz, who died in the hospital under unusual circumstances after opposing Pinochet's policies.)

The following books, selected from hundreds, treat social, economic and political topics, or offer specialized research on issues of interest since 1973: Americas Watch, *Chile Since the Coup: Ten Years of Repression*, 1983; Alan Angell and Benny Pollack, *The Legacy of Dictatorship: Political, Economic and Social Change in Pinochet's Chile*, 1993; José P. Arellano et al., *Modelo económico chileno: trayectoria de una crítica*, 1982; Genaro Arriagada, *Por la razón o la Fuerza, Chile bajo Pinochet*, 1998 (assessment by an important figure in politics and government in the 1990s); Xabier Arrizabalo M., *Milagro o quimera: la economía chilena durante la dictadura*, 1995; Jere Behrman, *Macroeconomic Policy in a Developing Country: The Chilean Experience*, 1977; Sergio Bitar (comp.), *Chile: liberalismo económico y dictadura política*, 1980; Guillermo Campero, *Los gremios empresariales en el período 1970–1983: Comportamiento sociopolítico y orientaciones ideológicas, 1970–1983*, 1984;——and José A. Valenzuela, *El movimiento sindical en el régimen militar chileno, 1973–1981*, 1984;——and René Cortázar, "Lógicas de acción sindical en Chile," *Colección Estudios CIEPLAN 18* (Dec. 1985); Sergio de Castro, *"El Ladrillo," Bases de la política económica del gobierno militar chileno*, 1992 (history of the University of Chicago-Universidad Católica de Chile connection, the development of neoliberal economics in Chile and the military junta's economic reforms); Marcel Claude, *Una vez más la miseria: es Chile un país sustentable?*, 1997 (an important survey of the environmental consequences of the neoliberal model); Colección Mensaje, *Chile visto por Mensaje. 1971–1981*, 1981 (selection of editorials from influential Catholic review); Joseph Collins and John Lear, *Chile's Free-Market Miracle: A Second Look*, 1995; Raquel Correa, Malú Sierra, and E. Subercaseaux, *Los generales del régimen*, 1983; Paul Drake and Iván Jaksić, *The Struggle for Democracy in Chile, 1982–1994*, 2nd ed., 1995; Manuel Delano and Hugo Traslaviña, *La herencia de los Chicago boys*, 1989; ECLA, *La transformación de la producción en Chile: Cuatro ensayos de interpretación*, 1993; Sebastián Edwards, "Stabilization with Liberalization: An Evaluation of Ten Years of Chile's Experiment with Free Market Policies," *Economic Development and Culture Change*, Jan. 1985; and Alejandra Cox Edwards, *Monetarism and Liberalization, the Chilean Experiment*, 1991; Ricardo Ffrench-Davis, "El experimento monetarista en Chile: una síntesis crítica," *Colección Estudios CIEPLAN*, 9, Dec. 1982; Arturo Fontaine, *Los economistas y el Presidente Pinochet*, 2nd ed., 1988; Patricio Frias, *El movimiento sindical chileno en la lucha por la democracia 1973–1988*, 1989; Manuel Antonio Garretón, *El proceso político chileno*, 1983; *Dictaduras y democratización*, 1984; *The Chilean Political Process*, 1989; Patrick Guillaudat and Pierre Mouterde, *Los movimientos sociales en Chile, 1973–1993*; Arnold Harberger, "The Chilean Economy in the 1970s: Crisis, Stabilization, Liberalization, Reform," in K. Brunner and A. Melzter (eds.), *Economic Policy in a World of Change*, Carnegie Rochester Conference Series, 17, 1982; David E. Hojman (ed.), *Chile After 1973: Elements for the Analysis of Military*

Rule, 1985; Lovell S. Jarvis, *Chilean Agriculture under Military Rule*, 1985; Joaquín Lavín, *Chile, a Quiet Revolution*, 1987; Fred D. Levy et al., *Chile: An Economy in Transition* (World Bank Country Study), 1979; Ricardo Lagos, *Democracia para Chile, proposiciones de un socialista*, 1985; Jonathan Marshall, "Did Milton Friedman Really Ruin Chile?," *Inquiry*, Aug. 1983; Javier Martínez and Alvaro Díaz, *Chile, the Great Transformation*, 1996 (a UNRISD and Brookings Institution synthesis of economic policy and social change from 1970 until the early 1990s); Tomás Moulian, *Democracia y socialismo en Chile*, 1983; G. Munizaga, *El discurso público de Pinochet, 1973–1976*, 1983; Oscar Muñoz (ed.), *Después de las privatizaciones: hacia el estado regulador*, 1993; H. Muñoz and Carlos Portales, *Una amistad esquiva. Las relaciones exteriores del gobierno militar chileno*, 1987; Phil O'Brien and Jackie Roddick, *Chile: The Pinochet Decade*, 1983; James Petras and Fernando Ignacio Leiva, *Democracy and Poverty in Chile, the Limits to Electoral Politics*, 1994; Augusto Pinochet, *Camino Recorrido, Memorias de un Soldado*, 1991 (General Pinochet's memoirs); *Política*, Special Issue, *Chile, 1973–1983, Enfoques para un decenio*, 1983; Jeffrey Puryear, *Thinking Politics: Intellectuals and Democracy in Chile, 1973–1988*, 1994; Rayén Quiroga Martínez, *Chile, globalización e insustentabilidad: una mirada desde la economía ecológica*, 1996; (ed.), *El tigre sin selva: consecuencias ambientales de la transformación económica de Chile, 1974–1993*, 1994; Joseph Ramos, *NeoConservative Economics in the Southern Cone of Latin America, 1973–1983*, 1986; Gonzalo Rojas Sánchez, *Chile escoge la libertad, La presidencia de Augusto Pinochet Ugarte, 11.IX.1973–11.III.1990, I (1973–80)*, 1998 (a virtual panegyric, useful for its documentation, official statements, and decrees of the military regime); Antonio Schneider, "Supply-Side Economics in a Small Economy: The Chilean Case," in Edward Nell (ed.), *Free Market Conservatism, A Critique of Theory and Practice*, 1984; Cathy Schneider, *Shantytown Protest in Pinochet's Chile*, 1995; Eduardo Silva, *The State and Capital in Chile: Business Elites, Technocrats and Market Economies*, 1996; Patricio Silva, *Estado, neoliberalismo y política agraria en Chile 1973–1981*, 1987; Eugenio Tironi, *Los silencios de la revolución*, 1988; Juan Gabriel Valdés, *La escuela de Chicago: Operación Chile*, 1989; Teresa Valdés, *La mujeres y la dictadura militar en Chile*, 1987; María Elena Valenzuela, *La mujer en el Chile militar*, 1987; Augusto Varas, F. Agüero, and F. Bustamante, *Chile, democracia, fuerzas armadas*, 1980; Sylvia Venegas, *Una gota al día . . . un chorro al año: el impacto social de la expansión frutícola*, 1992; Pilar Vergara, *Auge y caída del neoliberalismo en Chile*, 1984 (an excellent analysis of the ideological and policy evolution of the Pinochet government); *Políticas hacia la extrema pobreza en Chile, 1973–1988*, 1990; Gonzalo Vial (ed.), *Análisis crítico del régimen militar*, 1998 (a useful collection of short essays on the 1973 military coup and policies of the military government by prominent academics and politicians from left to right on the political spectrum); J. R. Whelan, *Out of the Ashes: Life, Death, and Transfiguration of Democracy in Chile, 1833–1988*, 1989 (massive anti-Marxist history focusing on the last half of the 20th century); Daniel Wisecarver (ed.), *El modelo económico chileno*, 1992. R. Zahler, "El neoliberalismo en una versión autoritaria" in ILADES: *Del liberalismo al capitalismo autoritario*, 1983; "Recent Southern Cone Liberalization Reforms and Stabilization Policies: The Chilean Case, 1974–1982," *Journal of InterAmerican Studies and World Affairs* 25, Nov. 1983. Kenneth Aman and Cristián Parker (eds.), present a collection of articles that consider "popular culture" from a historical perspective, bringing the topic through resistance to the military government, in *Popular Culture in Chile, Resistance and Survival*, 1991. For insight into General Pinochet's political ideology and motivations, see *Pinochet: Patria y Democracia*, 1983; *The Crucial Day* (translation of *El día decisivo*), 1982.

CHILE AFTER 1990

Research has only barely begun on the post-military regime era and prospects for the future. Useful journalistic and academic first efforts to assess the transition, in addition to some collections of speeches and government documents, include Ascanio Cavallo, *Los hombres de la transición*, 1992; Patricio Aylwin Azócar, *La transición chilena, Discursos escogidos, marzo 1990–1992*; Eduardo Boeninger, *Democracia en Chile. Lecciones para la gobernabilidad*, 1997; Paul Drake and Iván Jaksic, (eds.), *The Struggle for Democracy in Chile*, 2nd ed., 1995; Paul Drake-Iván Jaksic (comp.), *El modelo chileno. Democracia y desarrollo en los noventa*, 1999; Camilo Escalona, *Una transición de dos caras, Crónica, crítica y autocrítica*, 1999, (an angry retrospective on the 1990–99 period by a Socialist congressman); Hugo Fazio R., *El progama abandonado, Balance económico social del gobierno de Aylwin*, 1996; *Mapa actual de la extrema riqueza en Chile*, 1997 (a critical look at the internationalization of the Chilean society and the social, environmental, and political effects of the post-1990 economic policies), *El 'tigre' chileno y la crisis de los 'dragones' asiáticos*, 1998; *La crisis pone en jaque al neoliberalismo*, 1999; Alejandro Foxley, *La economía política de la transición*, 1994; Clarisa Hardy, *La reforma social pendiente*, 1997; David Hojman, *Chile: The Political Economy of Development and Democracy in the 1990s*, 1993; Felipe Larraín B., ed., *Chile hacia el 2000*, 1994; International Labor Organization (OIT), *Chile, Crecimiento, empleo y el desafío de la justicia social*, 1998; Tomás Moulián, *Chile actual, Anatomía de un mito*, 1997 (a best-selling dissection of neoliberalism and the credit card society in the late 1990s); Rafael Otano, *Crónica de la transición*, 1995; Crisóstomo Pizarro et al., *Social and Economic Policies in Chile's Transition to Democracy*, 1996; Francisco Rojas (ed.), *Chile 1998, Entre la II Cumbre y la detención de Pinochet*, 1999; Cristián Toloza and Eugenio Lahera (eds.), *Chile en los noventa*, 1998 (over 700-page policy analysis published by the Research Office of the Presidency); Augusto Varas and Claudio Fuentes, *Defensa nacional, Chile 1990–1994, Modernización y desarrollo*, 1994. An extremely useful collection of articles that surveys social and economic policies and consequences from 1973 until 1996 is René Cortázar and Joaquín Vial, *Construyendo opciones, Propuestas económicas y sociales para el cambio de siglo*, 1998.

Environmental politics have emerged as an important topic since the early 1990s; useful summaries of the issues and perspectives are Pablo San Martín, *Conflictos ambientales en Chile: 1995–96*, 1997; César Padilla Ormeño and Pablo San Martín, *Conflictos ambientales, Una oportunidad para la democracia* (IEP), n.d.; Francisco Sabatini D. and Claudia Sepúlveda L., *Conflictos ambientales, Entre la globalización y la sociedad civil*, 1997; Roberto Morales (comp.), *Ralco: Modernidad o etnocidio en territorio pewenche*, 1998. Changes in gender relations, family, and "private life" are considered in María Elena Valenzuela, S. Venegas, and C. Andrade (eds.), *De mujer sola a jefa de hogar. Género, pobreza y políticas públicas*, 1994, and Teresa Valdés, "Entre la modernización y la equidad: mujeres, mundo privado y familias," in Toloza and Lahera (eds.), *Chile en los noventa*, 1998: 471–519. Pinochet's detention in London in 1998 and the request by a Spanish judge for his extradition to Spain have also generated an incipient literature, both defending and attacking his role after 1973. Among the best-selling defenses of Pinochet was Hermógenes Pérez de Arce, *Europa vs Pinochet, Indebido Proceso*, 1998.

In the late 1990s some Chileans returned to an old literary and political device to comment on current developments—the open letter. Two particularly revealing examples of this genre are Sergio Marras, *Carta apócrifa de Pinochet a un siquiatra chileno*, 1998 (an imaginary letter in answer to Marco Antonio de la Parra's *Carta Abierta a Pinochet*, 1998), and Armando Uribe, *Carta abierta a Patricio Aylwin*, 1998, a bitter assessment of the 1990–94 administration. Political, journalistic, and literary memoirs also add significantly to information on the transition: Andrés Allamand, *La travesía del desierto*, 1999; Edgardo Boeninger, *Democracia en Chile: lecciones para la gobernabilidad*, 1997; Ascanio Cavallo, *La historia oculta de la transición*, 1998; Tomás Moulián, *Conversación interrumpida con Allende*, 1998; Marco Antonio de la Parra, *La mala memoria, Historia personal de Chile contemporáneo*, 1997.

Index